EGYPT and PALESTINE

A Millennium of Association (868-1948)

Published with the assistance of the
Harry S. Truman Research Institute for the Advancement of Peace
at the Hebrew University of Jerusalem

EGYPT and PALESTINE

A Millennium of Association
(868-1948)

edited by
Amnon Cohen and Gabriel Baer

מכון בן צבי

Ben Zvi Institute for the
Study of Jewish Communities
in the East

יד יצחק בן צבי

Yad Izhak Ben Zvi
Institute for the Study of
Eretz Israel

Jerusalem

St. Martin's Press / New York

St. Martin's Press, Inc., 175 Fifth Avenue, New York, N.Y. 10010

Printed in Israel
Phototypesetting: Astronel, Plates: Shani, Printing: Daf-Chen

First published in the United States of America in 1984

ISBN 0-312-23927-0

Library of Congress Cataloging in Publication Data
Main entry under title:

Egypt and Palestine.

Includes bibliographical references and index.
1. Palestine — Relations — Egypt — Addresses, essays, lectures. 2. Egypt — Relations — Palestine — Addresses, essays, lectures. 3. Jews — Egypt — History — Addreses, essays, lectures. 4. Jewish-Arab relations — 1917-1949 — Addresses, essays, lectures. I. Cohen, Amnon, 1936- . II. Baer, Gabriel, 1919-1982. III. Makhon Ben-Zvi le-ḥeḳer ḳehilot Yiśra'el ba-Mizraḥ.
DS119.8.E3E 1984 956 84-16109
ISBN 0-312-23927-0

Table of Contents

Preface

The historical developments that led Egypt and Israel to sign a peace treaty and establish a mutually amicable relationship triggered off different reactions in the two countries. Our own community witnessed a sharp upsurge of interest in the neighboring society and state, once so remote — now suddenly becoming so close. In the wake of our first visit to Egypt, the late Prof. Gabriel Baer and I conceived the idea of looking at the relations between the two countries in a somewhat different perspective, that of their historical links over the last one thousand years.

About fifty scholars participated in a three-day international seminar that was held in Shoresh, outside Jerusalem, between June 15-18, 1981. We never tried to establish any broad rules or reveal a fixed historical pattern applicable to such a vast span of years. Ours was an attempt to look at the relations existing between two regions and their respective communities (the overwhelming Muslim majority, the Jewish and Christian minorities), which were more often than not a part of larger political, administrative and cultural entities. The articles presented in this volume are revised versions of selected papers read and discussed in Shoresh. Financial constraints dictated a volume more modest in size than the one originally planned. However, the choice of topics and perspectives retains the balance that prevailed during the seminar.

In the years that followed the millennium sketched in this book the relationship between Egypt and Palestine has assumed — as we all know — a much more intensive and violent character. Although Egypt underwent certain changes in nomenclature and even in political configuration in the late 1950s, these proved to be marginal and hardly affected the mainstream of the country's history. For Palestine, on the other hand, the new name adopted — Israel — signified a most substantive change in almost every sphere of life. This had an immediate, direct effect on the interaction between the two states. Some of the elements that had existed in the past declined to the point of almost total disappearance (economic exchange, educational activity, or the very presence of certain religio-ethnic groups dealt with in this volume, such as Jews or Greek Catholics in Egypt). Military involvement, an element that had not been missing during earlier periods, became much more dominant after 1948. The boundary between the two countries, drawn in 1906, proved to be less impregnable than it was originally expected to be.

But the last thirty-five years are only of a marginal quantitative relevance to the long history of association between these two neighboring countries. The last five years reintroduced some of the old patterns that seemed to have ceased to exist during the previous three decades, thereby reminding those among us who may have been carried away by the years of intermittent wars, of one historical truth: the multi-faceted association between Egypt and Palestine over the ages. Let us all hope, endeavor and pray that the peaceful, constructive course upon which Egypt and Israel have just embarked will persist for many years to come.

★ ★ ★

I would like to thank all those who helped in the publication of this volume: The Bronfman Memorial Foundation in New York, the Truman Institute of the Hebrew University of Jerusalem and the Center for Integration of the Oriental Jewish Heritage in the Ministry of Education and Culture. Special thanks are due to Prof. Nehemia Levtzion who was extremely helpful in moving this project forward after Prof. Baer's sudden death and during my own absence from Jerusalem. A word of thanks is due to Mrs. G. Milkov who painstakingly edited the manuscript, as well as to Mr. Y. Nadav who checked the Arabic transliteration. Michael Glatzer's supervision of the final stages of this book well deserves our gratitude and appreciation.

It was my privilege to plan both the conference and this volume together with Gabriel Baer. It was with a deep sense of personal loss that I learned of the sudden and premature death of this dear friend, devoted teacher and brilliant scholar. We shall all miss him.

Jerusalem, March 1984 — Amnon Cohen

Introduction

This collection of studies on Egypt and Palestine is divided into three general sections: the pre-Ottoman period, the Ottoman period and the twentieth century. The general outlines of the historical setting and some of the major trends and developments are presented in Prof. Ayalon's introductory paper.

David Ayalon draws a wide and thorough *tableau* of the interrelations within the core of the Muslim world throughout history, focusing on those that evolved between Egypt, Syria and Palestine. In the ongoing contest over Syria, which started from the very early days of the Muslim empire, Egypt stood better chances than Iraq, a process which is both described and analyzed. Syria and Palestine were one of three directions of Egyptian expansion. Between the late ninth and the early sixteenth centuries it constituted the major one, and in most cases the attempts of this expansion were accompanied by the awareness of absolute Egyptian predominance over Syria. The permanent occupation of Syria by Egypt, through competition with the Seljuks, the Byzantines and other Christians, could only be achieved through armies originating from the Mashriq, the East. Turcoman Seljuks and Turkish Mamluks brought this about as part of wider historical developments, one of which was the victory of *Sunna* over the *Shīʿa*. The Seljuks, the Fatimids and the Ayyubids increasingly based their armies on Turkish Mamluks, whose presence in Egypt enabled the Muslim world to drive the Franks out of Syria and Palestine, thereby defending the world of Islam. Then for almost three consecutive centuries Mamluk Egypt ruled over Syria, once more turning it, and most particularly its Southern-Palestinian parts, into a position of inferiority. The destruction of the Syro-Palestinian coast, while preserving the Egyptian one intact, was of far-reaching consequences. The Ottoman conquest in the sixteenth century brought about basic changes in the relations between Egypt and Syria and Palestine. The Mamluks, although uprooted in Syria, were left in Egypt, bleeding their own factions white. But it was not until the late eighteenth century that 'Ali Bey al-Kabīr tried to renew the old pattern and reimpose Egyptian-Mamluk rule over Syria and Palestine. The built-in difficulties for an Egyptian army to rule over Syria and Palestine are well presented with regard to a later episode, that of Abu Dhahab's campaigns. The final phase of Egyptian expansion into Syria, and the historical reason for its success there, are analyzed with regard to Muḥammad 'Ali in the early nineteenth century, then projected within a wider perspective of world history.

* * *

Jere L. Bacharach not only compares the policies of the Tulunids and the Ikhshidids (the first Egyptian rulers since the days of the Ptolemys who effectively controlled Palestine) but focuses on a specific source to illustrate it: coins. For the Tulunids (868-935) Palestine played a minor role, which underwent certain fluctuations, all of which were expressed in the coinage policies: low at the beginning, but increasing in importance towards the end of the ninth century, with the re-establishment of the mint in Ramle. The Ikhshidids (935-969), aware of the vulnerability of their country to an invasion from the north, regarded Palestine as of great security importance to them. This was also reflected in their monetary policies. Palestine played the major role in this context, best expressed by the massive production of silver *dirhams* and even more so of gold *dīnārs* there.

Donald P. Little, after summing-up the relations between Jerusalem and Egypt during the Mamluk period as they emerge from the literary sources, mostly chronicles of the time, focuses on a recently discovered and most important source: a collection of approximately 900 documents in the Islamic Museum of al-Ḥaram al-Sharīf. They seem to represent the remains of papers kept by a Shafi'i judge in late fourteenth century Jerusalem. These documents demonstrate, *inter alia*, the involvement of the Mamluks in the administrative and religious life of Jerusalem, the active participation of individual Mamluk officers in ordinary life, the interaction of the religious systems of Jerusalem and Cairo, and the considerable number of Egyptians who were living in Jerusalem.

Boaz Shoshan, noting that Palestine was not a political but rather a geographical unit during the Mamluk period, addresses himself to the political position of its various districts in relation to Egypt. Safed, Gaza and Jerusalem formed separate administrative units, the officer in charge of the latter being of a lower rank than the others. Frequent replacement of governors by the Mamluk sultans in Cairo, plus the maintenance of an independent military unit in the fortress, were both aimed at preventing the creation of too powerful local elements. Egyptian physical presence in Palestine was limited to times of disorder or to occasional visits to the holy shrines in Jerusalem and Hebron.

A Christian perspective is used by **Andrew S. Ehrenkreutz** in his paper which presents the Fatimids in Palestine as having facilitated, if not invited, the Crusaders there. Fatimid policies towards Christendom were tolerant — if not cooperative — from the early years of their political importance. Having taken over Egypt, they continued to show diplomatic flexibility towards Byzantine Constantinople which they regarded as a potential ally against the common Seljuk enemy. In Palestine they tolerated, and even protected Christian merchants, pilgrims and places of worship. Their concern for it was mainly a strategic one: they regarded it as a buffer-zone against potential invaders from the north. In the last quarter of the eleventh century they hardly exercised effective control over Palestine, and the political vacuum created there when they finally withdrew to Cairo should be viewed as having unwittingly invited the Crusaders.

Another aspect of Muslim-Christian relations is highlighted in **Butrus Abu-Manneh**'s article on the Georgians in Jerusalem under the Mamluks. Having recently discovered 18 edicts and letters exchanged between the Mamluk sultans, the kings of Georgia and the monks in Jerusalem, he describes various favors conferred upon the Georgians in Palestine. What emerges is a growth in the property and number of shrines possessed by the Georgians in Jerusalem, and in rural Palestine too, parts of which were granted to them by the Mamluks. These improvements should be seen in the light of closer commercial ties between the Mamluk Sultans and the Kings of Georgia. All these declined rapidly after the Ottoman occupation.

Another minority group in Jerusalem were the Jews, whose relations with their Egyptian co-religionists under the Fatimids are portrayed by **Mark R. Cohen**. Drawing extensively on *Geniza* documents, he describes the changing center of gravity between Jerusalem and Cairo, as far as Jewish communities were concerned. The tension created by a situation in which Jerusalem, an administrative periphery, enjoyed supreme administrative jurisdiction over Cairo, the center of Muslim imperial power, was a source of much friction and discontent during the late tenth and the eleventh centuries. This tension finally came to an end when the Fatimids introduced the office of *ra'īs al-yahūd* in Cairo, thus relieving the Jewish community there from administrative subordination to the *gaons* of Jerusalem. This rectified state of affairs endured until the Ottoman takeover of both Palestine and Egypt.

★ ★ ★

Michael Winter, drawing mainly on Ottoman official archives, addresses himself to the military connections between Egypt and the Syrian-Palestinian provinces in the early Ottoman period. Military units were occasionally sent to Syria to help in attempts to check the Beduins, or in building fortifications in southern Palestine. On the whole, Egyptian units were stationed no farther north than Safed so that the governors of Egypt would be able to keep a closer eye on their performance. This, in turn, caused some friction between them and their local counterparts.

Uri M. Kupferschmidt collected the biographical data on Palestinian *'ulamā'* from the various available compendia and compared their relations with Egypt to those that existed with other centers in the Empire. Traditional links with Damascus underwent a certain decline during the Ottoman period, and connections with Istanbul for the sake of study or administrative benefits were rather limited. It was to Cairo, and most particularly to al-Azhar, that Palestinian students went from the various urban centers of Palestine. They stayed there for five to ten years, in most cases studying *fiqh* (although also medicine and astronomy), and very seldom settling there after graduation. These findings were true for four centuries of Ottoman rule.

The biographies of three Jerusalem *'ulamā'* who lived in Cairo during the eighteenth century, as described by al-Jabarti, are summed up and analyzed by the late **Gabriel Baer**. They were immigrant notables, members of the al-Ḥusaini family. Considered by their own society to be *ashrāf*, they had many opportunities to establish connections with other towns, Cairo among them. Their specific links were based on education in al-Azhar, the general organization of the *ashrāf*, and economic relations (export of soap from Jerusalem to Cairo). Nevertheless, they had to resort to the patronage of a local dignitary in order to reach a position of prominence and influence.

Another group of notables, the traditional leadership in the mountainous area of Nablus, is scrutinized by **Miriam Hoexter**, who inspects at close range the Egyptian policies towards this part of Palestine in the 1830s. In the process of implementation of traditional politics of notables, favoring some families and hurting others, the Egyptians never totally destroyed their prestige or economic might. On the whole they did tighten the hold of the central government there by this, as well as other means, most specifically conscription and agrarian policies. Here, too, they avoided carrying their policies to their logical conclusion. However, even this decade of Egyptian rule prepared for the eventual centralization imposed by the Ottomans in later years.

The very same decade of Egyptian rule is examined in a wider perspective by **Shimon Shamir**, who suggests that it be regarded as the beginning of modern times in the history of Palestine. The remarkable changes which took place there during the eighteenth century did not reach the level of a comprehensive process of change. The Egyptian rule in Palestine, while still oriented towards the traditional leadership and their clients, introduced changes in many important fields: power structure, administration, intercommunal relations, urban life, international interests and conditions for economic developments. It did, in fact, inaugurate "the opening of Palestine" to modernizing influences.

Relations between Ottoman Egypt and Palestine were not limited to Ottoman and Egyptian officials or to Palestinian notables. Religious minorities were another segment of the population who entertained active links between the two. **Thomas Philipp** interprets the ascendancy of the Greek Catholic community during the eighteenth cenutry as a result of political and economic developments. The changing patterns of international trade shifted the center of gravity from the Syrian inlands to the coast. As a result, Greek Catholics moved to the coastal towns where they enjoyed greater economic advantages, communal local autonomy and related political importance. The semi-autonomous rulers who stood to benefit from their new element were willing to grant them these multi-faceted chances. First in coastal Syria, then, towards the mid-18th century in Egypt, the Greek Catholics consolidated their economic base, and subsequently rose into administrative power. By 1840, when they acquired the status of an autonomous Ottoman *millet*, they had already lost most of their earlier importance.

The history of relations between Jewish communities of Egypt and Palestine did not undergo such sharp turns, as did the Greek Catholics, which is by no way an indication of its volume or intensity. Their relative importance is alluded to by three papers which present different approaches to various aspects of inter-Jewish communal links of the time. **Amnon Cohen**, drawing almost exclusively on the Muslim court archives (*sijill*), portrays a picture of multi-faceted relations between Cairo and Jerusalem. There was some demographic movement, but economics was even more important: soap, highly regarded in Egypt, was exported there by Jews, while spices of various kinds were imported to Palestine via Gaza. Some of these merchants invested in real estate at the other end of this commercial line. Of a wider nature were Jewish visits to Jerusalem either by way of escaping there in order to avoid punishment in Cairo which seemed far away, or in the course of the annual pilgrimage to the Holy Land. These regular visits, although predominantly of a religious character, had an economic dimension of their own, bearing upon life in both communities and consolidating their links.

Joseph R. Hacker arrives at similar conclusions from Jewish sources. The economic dependence of Palestinian Jews on the Cairo community, prevalent in the beginning of Ottoman rule, became much more important (especially for Safed) during the second half of the sixteenth century. Jerusalemites not only benefited by the pilgrims arriving from Egypt as well as by other forms of financial support, but also tended to invest some of their own money there. Some spiritual links prevailed between the two: Egyptian Jewish scholars regarded their stay there as temporary in nature, and many of them actually emigrated to Palestine. Others went in the opposite direction, i.e. to Cairo, both as students and as scholars. Still, the Jews living in Palestine were regarded by their brethren living in Egypt as vicars in the Holy Land whom they expected to protect their interests there.

Minna Rozen identified very similar patterns during the seventeenth century. These were threefold in nature: demographic, economic and spiritual. A two-way movement of pilgrims and immigrants between Jerusalem and Cairo was a regular phenomenon. More important were economic ties: donations to Jerusalem came either directly from Cairo or through Cairo which served as an intermediary for North-African financial support. The former were greatly diminished for some time in the seventeenth century, while the latter actually increased. In the other direction Jerusalemites invested their money in Cairo, and even retained special officials (*fattor*) to take care of their properties there. And there were also the steady flow of legal opinions (*responsa*), the occasional Egyptian-born rabbis who sought career positions in Jerusalem, and others who left Palestine and settled in Egypt.

★ ★ ★

Although formally still part of the Ottoman Empire up to the First World War, Egyptian history entered a new era with the British occupation of 1882. The very same year witnessed the beginning of a new phase in Palestine, also: that of the consecutive waves of Jewish immigration (*'Aliyot*). British military presence in Egypt and the changing demographic traits of Palestine were two new objective elements that moulded the modern history of both countries, as well as the interrelations of their respective societies. The frontier between Egypt and Palestine had to be drawn in a definite manner to be agreed upon by both parties. **J.C. Hurewitz** describes and analyzes the diplomatic background of the demarcation of this border in 1906, which later became the international boundary between Egypt and mandatory Palestine.

'Abbās Ḥilmī, who ruled Egypt when the 1906 Taba incident as well as the demarcation of this line took place, was deposed by the British in 1914. Most of his attention was aimed at an attempt to regain his old time importance in Egypt, and perhaps a permit to return there. **Thomas Mayer** uses Zionist and British archives to describe one episode in Ḥilmī's relentless political activity: his contacts with Dr. Weizmann in an amateurish and fruitless attempt to promote Arab-Jewish understanding in Palestine.

Much more representative of Egyptian society, and indicating its growing awareness of and involvement in what later became known as "The Palestine Problem", were the writings of Rashīd Riḍā in *al-Manar*. **Sylvia G. Haim** presents a detailed content analysis of this journal's evolving position towards Zionism and its Palestinian dimension between 1898-1935. The Zionist Organization was presented to the readers of *al-Manar* as a positive phenomenon, which should serve as a model for Muslims to emulate. After the War Riḍā's references to Jews and Zionism became increasingly less favorable, and the growing political tension in Palestine further contributed towards an increasingly negative Muslim approach to what he describes as their encroachment on Arab acquired rights in Palestine.

From precisely the opposite direction **Jacob M. Landau** sums up and describes the image of Egypt as projected in the works of Egyptian-born Israeli writers one generation later. Two models emerge of the Egypt they remember and convey to their readers: that of a sheltered and alienated Jewish minority hardly aware of, let alone involved in, the life and aspirations of Egyptian society, and that of some writers who knew a much more representative, traditional Muslim Egypt they nostalgically recall.

The most modern link between Egypt and Palestine is that created with the emergence of Zionism, and its relationship with modern Egypt. **James Jankowski** draws mostly on Egyptian journalistic sources in the 1920s and 1930s, that is, when Egyptian public opinion and national movement were moving very slowly from neglect to awareness, and later even to active interest in Zionism in the twenties, exemplified by the attempts of Egyptian politicians to serve as mediators in Palestine, was undergoing a gradual negative change in the thirties. Hostility towards Zionism turned into anti-Jewish propaganda. It emerged in the late thirties and took three forms: verbal warnings, calls for an economic boycott, and finally several attempts of physical violence against the Jewish quarters. Prevalent among marginal political groups of an ultra religious or ultra nationalist shade, these verbal and physical responses to Zionism were conducted against the explicit position of the Egyptian governments.

Robert Tignor addresses himself to the other end of the spectrum, i.e. to the Jewish community in Egypt and its attitudes towards Zionism. Historical lines of cleavage which developed within the two major Jewish communities, those of Cairo and Alexandria, were social, economic and cultural. Hindsight wisdom, describing the warm support of Egyptian Jewry for Zionism, really applies only to a certain, rather limited segment. Although the first Zionist society was founded in Cairo towards the end of the nineteenth century, Zionism was not an important issue among the Jews of Egypt until the late twenties. As a result of political events in the Middle East and most particularly in Egypt, Zionism grew in prominence there. Its protagonists were among the less privileged within the community who combined these sentiments with their opposition to the Jewish establishment. Much like similar cases among the other minority groups, members of the lower class embraced Zionism as a facet of their alienation from their own communal elite.

Gudrun Krämer, drawing on extensive archival material (European, Arab, and Jewish), describes the reasons for the relative weakness of Egyptian

Zionism up to the Second World War: partly external (lack of appropriate propaganda material, small numbers of certificates allocated), but mostly internal (security and material comfort, indifference to things specifically Jewish, a rejection of the explicitly secularist attitudes of the Zionist representatives). Zionists in Egypt were young lower-middle class, although some of the traditional community leaders also supported the movement. After the war, with the growing impact of the Palestine issue on Egyptian politics, and the increasing insecurity among minorities, political rather than cultural Zionism became more important, both as a result of organized attempts from Palestine, and radicalization of Islamic and nationalist groups in Egypt.

Amnon Cohen

DAVID AYALON

Egypt as a Dominant Factor in Syria and Palestine during the Islamic Period

Contents

Introduction

The Hijaz, Egypt and the Fertile Crescent form a central part of the Muslim world. The relations which developed between the various countries of this area and between them and other areas within and without the lands of Islam are of particular significance in the history of that religion.

Under the Umayyads, Syria reached a position of importance and power the like of which it had never previously attained, neither in the pre-Islamic nor in the Islamic periods, and which after that, it was never to reach again. In view of the rapid expansion of the Muslim empire the transfer of its capital from Arabia to a more central place was unavoidable. It was not, however, self-evident that Damascus would become that capital. Had 'Alī defeated Mu'āwiya, he might well have chosen a more eastern capital. Yet under the circumstances Damascus was perceived as having some very important advantages: during the great conquests it had been quite well situated strategically between the eastern and western fronts of Islam; in the struggle against Byzantium, the then major enemy of the Muslims, which had been conducted both on land and at sea, Damascus was again very adequately placed.

Gradually, however, the power of the Muslims and Byzantium became more or less balanced, especially on land, and Muslim expansion slowed down everywhere. This and other internal factors (some of which are well-known), greatly facilitated the transfer of the focus of the empire from Syria to Iraq. Syria lost its temporary focal position, and sooner or later was bound to become a target of conquest and occupation by its neighbors and others, as of old.

Egypt versus Iraq in Relation to Syria

In contrast to the pre-Muslim period, Egypt's chances within the framework of the Muslim empire to occupy Syria were, at least in the long run, superior to those of Iraq. And that is what actually came about. The advantage of Egypt over Iraq as far as concerned the domination of Syria was based on a number of factors which complemented and strengthened each other, and of which the following can serve as examples: (1) Egypt is a far more compact and homogeneous country than Iraq; (2) Egypt gravitated towards Syria more powerfully than towards any other country; Iraq, on the other hand, was drawn in various directions, of which Syria did not have first priority (this is particularly true of southern Iraq); (3) Egypt did not suffer so many nor so excessive afflictions, caused by internal and external factors, as did Iraq; (4) Egypt's geographical position between two major seas gave her a steadily-growing advantage over Iraq.

We shall now deal with the effects of these factors, first on Iraq, then on Egypt, and see how they influenced their respective attitudes towards Syria.

The links connecting southern and northern Iraq were, to make an understatement, not too strong, in spite of the two rivers binding them. This fact is clearly reflected, *inter alia*, in the descriptions of the Muslim geographers, who usually deal with each of them separately, limiting the name of *al-'Irāq* to the south only, and calling the north *al-Jazīra*. Northern Iraq was conquered from northern Syria. Its south was conquered from north-eastern Arabia. During the long period of the Caliphate's decline, when the direct authority of the Caliph was confined, at best, to the south, the links between these two major parts of Iraq were certainly not strengthened. By contrast, the fact that the Byzantine front stretched, unbroken, to the north of both Syria and the Jazīra, and that along that front a whole system of Muslim frontier fortresses *(al-thughūr al-shāmiyya wa'l-thughūr al-jazariyya)* had been gradually built, strengthened the ties between these two regions. These ties lasted, with ups-and-downs (including some very serious breaks), till the end of the reign of the Ayyubids, who had a very strong foothold in the Jazīra and beyond. The existence of these selfsame ties was very important in the struggle against the Crusaders, although, as might be expected and as future events proved, the Jazīra could be only a secondary partner to Egypt in this respect. At the same time it should be pointed out that northern Syria was not the only direction towards which the Jazīra turned.

The history of the relations between northern Iraq and northern Syria is very important indeed, but the really great history of Islam took place in southern Iraq and in the eastern areas mainly conquered from there. It was in southern Iraq that the two main military cities of early Islam, Kūfa and Baṣra, were built, and from both of them were dispatched the Muslim armies that conquered the East. It was the Muslim East, and especially Khurāsān and Transoxania, which became the decisive factor in Islam, militarily, as well as in some other very important fields. The military forces of the east (still mainly Arabs and *not* Iranians, although these Arabs might have already been considerably Iranianized), in cooperation with supporters in Kūfa, brought about the downfall of the Umayyads, the rise of the Abbasids and the transfer of the capital of Islam from Damascus to Baghdad. About sixty years later the Arab element was finally relegated to a secondary place by a combination of mainly Iranian and Turkish forces coming from the East (the victory of al-Ma'mūn over al-Amīn). This chain of formidable events brought about, *inter alia*, the subjugation of metropolitan Iraq by Khurāsān, and was supplemented by the final conquest of Transoxania by the same Khurāsān. The conquest was immediately followed by Muslim raids from Transoxania deep to the east and north-east. Thus the way was paved for the advent from central Asia of the Turkish-Mamlūk military aristocracy which became, from the first half of the ninth century onwards, the major Muslim military power, and without which Islam could not have become a world religion on the present scale and within the present far-flung boundaries. From the East also came the Turkish-Seljuq element, which was to decide, for many generations to come, the issue of the internal religious struggle in Islam, and which, together with the Mamluks, constituted the mainstay of Islam in its war against Byzantium (including the conquest of Anatolia) and West European Christianity. *Ultimately it was first and foremost armies originating from the East and based mainly in Egypt which fought the Christians of Europe and defeated them on Syrian and Egyptian soil.*

In this immense process of the ever growing impact of the East (including the pagan East) *southern Iraq turned to face more and more eastwards*, and, consequently, its involvement in Syria greatly diminished (throughout the very long period dealt with in this article, there were, of course, fluctuations, but these did not much affect the general trend).

The Effect of the Iraqi Marshlands

The process discussed above was not, however, the sole reason for the greatly limited role of Iraq in Syria. There was yet another cause of great moment. The same southern Iraq, from which the mighty East had been conquered, suffered from the disintegration of a very substantial part of its irrigation system, which had collapsed in 629 (viz. a few years before the Muslim conquest), as a result of an unusual rise of the Euphrates and Tigris. The attempt of the Sasanids to curb the flood failed. During the wars between the Muslims and Persians there was no time to deal with this calamity. The area of swamps or marshes, which was created as a result, became a permanent fixture, and played a central role in the history of Iraq under the Abbasids, and far beyond their rule.[1] Until this day these marshes form a very conspicuous part of the Iraqi landscape. Soon after the Muslim occupation, the marshlands became a place of refuge for adventurers, escaped slaves and all kinds of embittered persons. Because of the difficulty in employing the regular army, especially the cavalry, in an area of swamps, canals and thickets, the authorities did not succeed in totally eradicating the unruly and often rebellious element. The great danger implicit in such a situation was the proximity of the area to Baghdad, and the fact that the ships plying between the Indian Ocean and the Persian Gulf and the Muslim capital had either to traverse that area or pass it. They were at the complete mercy of the anti-government elements who found refuge there.[2] (The obvious alternative for the constantly threatened international maritime commerce was the Red Sea and Egypt). The disobedience of the marsh area to the central government reached its peak in the revolt of the Zanj, which lasted for fourteen years (870-883) and which sapped the strength of the Caliphate.[3] The almost total absorption of the Abbasids in that revolt is

1 It is difficult to follow chronologically the changes in size of the marshes of southern Iraq. Although, as a result of human effort, arable lands had surely been reclaimed from them at certain periods, the fact remains that basically the marshlands always remained sufficiently big to constitute a major factor in the history of Muslim Iraq. Swamps created by the overflow of the rivers had existed in that area even before the advent of Islam (see *EI*[2], art. *al-Baṭīḥa* by M. Streck and Saleh el-Ali). But they did not become as permanent as in Islam. There might well have been other causes which prevented the creation of centers of resistance to the authorities in those swamps in the pre-Islamic period, but this is beyond the scope of the present article.

2 Al-Balādhurī gives a very illuminating description of how the plundering of ships in the marshes had begun by begging for tiny things from the crews and passengers and ended with the thorough robbing of their belongings and merchandise. As a result, the cargoes which formerly had to reach Baghdad from Baṣra, ceased completely *(wa-inqaṭa'a 'an Baghdād jamī' mā kāna yuḥmal ilayhā fī 'l-sufun — Futūḥ al-Buldān*, Leiden, 1863-66, p. 375, ll. 9-17). Of considerable help to the marauders was the great difference between the ebb and tide of the Persian Gulf, which affected the water level well into the hinterland. During the ebb the ships would often run aground, and thus fall easy prey to the robbers.

3 In addition to the topographical conditions, a main cause of the amazingly long

well-illustrated by the fact that throughout that long period the main chronicler of the time, al-Ṭabarī, has little to say about what was happening in the lands of Islam outside the area of the revolt. What is particularly significant in the present context, is that the uprising of the Zanj presented the opportunity to the rulers of Egypt to achieve during that selfsame period, and within the general process of the disintegration of the Abbasid empire, their *de facto* independence and to embark on the conquest of Syria. As for Iraq, the rebellion was suppressed, indeed, but the marshes and their problems remained. Even as recently as the twentieth century, the Iraqi marshes played no mean part in the slowing down of the advance of the British army towards Baghdad, in the First World War.

Additional Factors Favoring Egypt

Iraq was subject to attack from external enemies as well as from raids and damage by nomadic tribes, including non-Arab tribes. The deep penetration of the non-Arab tribes into the lands of Islam, centuries after the start of the Muslim expansion, contributed immensely to the preservation and strengthening of that religion, but the same did not apply in other respects. It happened more than once that what proved to be good for the Muslim religion was not always so good for the Muslim, and other populations, as far as concerned their material well-being.

Egypt, as compared to Iraq, was much more compact and homogeneous. From time to time, especially under the Ottomans, antagonisms between Upper and Lower Egypt came to the fore (for this see below); but these cannot be compared to the flimsiness of the ties between the two major parts of Iraq.

Directions of Egyptian Expansion

As for the directions of expansion on land, Egypt had three alternatives: to the south — along the Nile; to the west — to North Africa; and to the north-east — Palestine and Syria.

resistance of the Zanj rebels was that resistance had not been confined to the Zanj who were in southern Iraq at the time of the outbreak of the revolt. Those rebels had a very determined non-Zanj leadership. They were also greatly helped by important neighboring beduin elements. Besides the abundant plunder from the ships, they acquired much booty from their raids on the rich province of al-Ahwāz. The only explanation I can offer for their ability to replace their immense human losses (casualties and prisoners-of-war) is that they continued to import slaves from East Africa. There was no obstacle to bringing these slaves from their countries of origin: the slave-traders had every reason to sustain their means of livelihood and source of riches; and the rebels were in desperate need of fresh manpower. Furthermore, the abolishment of slavery was certainly not the aim of their revolt. The leader of the Zanj had promised them that when they win the war, they will become rich and own slaves (Ṭabarī, III, pp. 1749, 11. 15-16, 1751, 11. 1-3).

Expansion Southwards along the Nile

Immediately after the conquest of Egypt, the Arabs made repeated attempts to advance along the Nile. But these attempts were totally thwarted by the Christian Nubians, as we learn from the unequivocal evidence of the Muslim sources.[4] The Nubian front remained stable for more than six centuries, up to the Mamluk period, with a certain degree of weakening already during the Ayyubid reign. The long stalemate on that front tempts one to ask the following question: What would have happened if the Arabs had succeeded in pushing into the Sudan at the beginning of their expansion, as was their intention? This question is put forward for two reasons: (1) In northern Sudan existing conditions favored the nomadic life, similar to that of the beduins; (2) Arab military manpower was limited. Hence, it can be assumed that the shrinkage of that force, as a result of the very probable absorption of part of it in the Sudan, would have affected the Muslim advance on a much more important front: North Africa.

This is, of course, a hypothetical question. What is not at all hypothetical is that the probable attraction of the nomads to the Sudan was not shared in any way by the rulers of Egypt in medieval times and much beyond that period. The Ayyubids, who had no mean a share in undermining the Nubian power, wanted, at first, to prepare themselves a shelter in Nubia, in the event that their master, the Zankid Nūr al-Dīn, would conquer Egypt. They discarded that idea, because of the poverty of that country, and gave preference, with full justification, to the Yemen as a place of possible retreat. When the Mamluks routed the Nubians, they showed no interest in fully incorporating that country into their realm, and certainly not in advancing beyond it. The Arab nomads, on the other hand, increased their penetration southward, thus accelerating the Arabization and Islamization of northern Sudan. The Egyptian advance to the south took place much later, in the nineteenth century, under completely new circumstances, which will be discussed below.

Expansion Westwards in North Africa

A very different situation prevailed in North Africa. Egypt which served as the basis for the conquest of that area was itself conquered by the Fatimids in the second half of the tenth century. But if we conclude from

4 Our best authority on the Muslim conquests, al-Balādhurī, brings a series of traditions in which it is repeatedly stated that the reason for the Arabs' giving up their advance southwards from Egypt was the determined resistance of the Nubians, who excelled in archery (*Futūḥ al-Buldān, op. cit.*, pp. 236, l. 18 - 240, l. 2. See also al-Mas'ūdī, *Murūj al-Dhahab*, vol. II. pp. 328, l. 8 - 383, l. 4).

these two instances, which are, admittedly, of the highest significance, that there existed constant and very close ties between the land of the Nile and the Maghrib (from Cyrenaica westward), especially as far as territorial expansion is concerned, we would be quite mistaken. The gradual disintegration of the Muslim empire greatly loosened these ties. They were strengthened for some time by the Fatimid conquest, but quite quickly the Fatimids directed their main attention eastwards to Syria and beyond, and gradually turned their back, willingly or otherwise, on the Maghrib. The feeble gropings of Ṣalāḥ al-Dīn, Baybars and Muḥammad 'Alī towards the Maghrib carried little weight.

Expansion North-Eastwards in Palestine and Syria

The direction which attracted Egypt constantly and steadfastly was Syria, and the absence of other permanently strong and compact Muslim states neighboring upon Syria could only encourage Egypt in its desire to dominate that country. From the seventh decade of the ninth century, and up to the second decade of the sixteenth, namely, for six hundred and fifty years, Syria served as the main (and almost exclusive) target of Egyptian expansion. The attempts at expansion in that direction, irrespective of their degrees of success, were almost always accompanied by the awareness of Egyptian absolute preponderance over Syria. Egypt enjoyed throughout the ages, as it enjoys today, an immense geographic advantage over Iraq: its being situated between the Mediterranean and the Red seas. Among other things, this greatly increased its ability and inclination to intervene in Syria (including naval intervention, a fact of the greatest consequence). The present temporary supremacy of the Persian Gulf, because of its oil, should not obscure the basic and permanent realities.

Another unique advantage enjoyed by Egypt was its proximity to the Hijaz, and that country's great dependence on it, economically and otherwise. The fact that the two places holiest to Islam are situated in the Hijaz was most advantageous to Egypt. On the other hand, the occupation of Egypt by a non-Muslim power in the Middle Ages would have deprived both Syria and the Hijaz of their Muslim mainstay, with all the obvious catastrophic results to Islam. We shall return to this central subject.

Egypt also enjoyed a far greater degree of security than Iraq and large parts of Syria. It was not directly affected by the two great nomadic invasions into the Muslim world: The Seljuq-Turcoman and the Mongol. It should be remembered that the Seljuq penetration, though far more moderate than the Mongol, was also accompanied by much damage and devastation.

Egypt, furthermore, did not experience a collapse of its irrigation system as that experienced by southern Iraq at such an early date of its Islamic history. Even at a much later period, when the Egyptian economy greatly deteriorated and its irrigation system suffered heavily as a result of predatory rule, neglect and other causes, Egypt seems to have still been better off than Iraq.

There was one destructive factor which was common to Egypt, to the Fertile Crescent and to the other Arabic-speaking parts of the Muslim world: the beduins. It is difficult, however, to determine on which country or area they inflicted the greatest damage. At the same time, the positive aspects of the beduins, economic and others, should not be overlooked.

Al-Muqaddasī's Evidence on the Capitals of Iraq and Egypt

I do not know whether it is possible to reconstruct the various stages of the rise of Egypt and its capital as compared to the stages of the decline of Iraq and its capital in the first three centuries of Islam, but we do possess unequivocal evidence on this subject for the 4th/10th century. I shall confine myself here to the evidence of one Muslim author, the famous Jerusalem geographer, al-Muqaddasī, who wrote his book in 985-990. I chose him because of his originality and insight, and because of the numerous subjects he discusses which are relevant to my line of argument. Moreover, his evidence is very often that of an eyewitness. Many of his statements are also confirmed, wholly or partly, directly or indirectly, by other sources.

Of Baghdad, whose glory al-Muqaddasī speaks of in the past tense *(kānat jalīla fī 'l-qadīm),*[5] he says that "at present" it is in a state of deterioration and ruin *(tadā'at al-āna ilā 'l-kharāb wa-ikhtallat wa-dhahaba bahā'uhā),*[6] as a result of the decline of the power of the Abbasids.[7] "Every day it goes backwards, and I am afraid that it will end up like Samarra" *(wa-hiya fī kull yawm ilā warā wa-akhshā an ta'ūd ka-sāmarrā).*[8] In a meeting of Baghdadi dignitaries (men of learning and others) which he attended, it was unanimously concluded that Baṣra was, at that time, as big in size as Baghdad, if the ruined parts of Baghdad were excluded *(wa-kuntu bi-majlis jama'a fuqahā' Baghdād wa-mashāyikhahā fa-tadhākarū Baghdād wa'l-Baṣra fa-tafarraqū 'alā annahu idhā jumi'at 'imārāt Baghdād wa-undira kharābuhā lam takun akbar min al-Baṣra).* And this after taking into account that part of Baṣra also lay in ruins *(wa-qad khariba ṭaraf al-Baṣra al-barrī).*[9] Speaking of the towns of the Baghdad area he says that in

5 Al-Muqaddasī, *Aḥsan al-Taqāsīm fī Ma'rifat al-Aqālīm, BGA,* vol. III, Leiden, 1906, p. 36, ll. 7-8.

6 *Ibid.*, p. 36, ll. 8-9.

7 *Ibid.*, p. 120, ll, 5-6.

8 *Ibid.*, p. 120, ll. 10-15.

9 *Ibid.*, pp. 117, l. 20 - 118, l. 2.

Khurāsān there are many villages which are more significant than most of those towns.[10]

By contrast, he declares that the Egyptian capital, Fusṭāṭ (Cairo had been built only shortly before, and he dedicates but a few lines to it)[11] is "the cupola of Islam" *(miṣruhu*[12] *qubbat al-Islām).*[13] "It is like Baghdad in the past, and I know not in Islam a greater or more glorious town [than Fusṭāt]. It supersedes (lit.: abrogates) Baghdad and replaces it. It is the pride of Islam and the commercial center of the human race. It is the treasure house of the Maghrib and the stopping place of the Mashriq... It is the most populated of all the capitals." *(wa-Fusṭāṭ Miṣr al-yawm ka-Baghdād fī 'l-qadīm wa-lā a'lam fī 'l-Islām baladan ajall minhu.... fa-huwa.... nāsikh Baghdād wa-mafkhar al-Islām wa-matjar al-ānām wa-ajall min madīnat al-Salām khizānat al-Maghrib wa-maṭraḥ al-Mashriq... laysa fī 'l-amṣār āhal minhu).*[14] In no other Muslim land are there more ships than on its coast *(wa-laysa fī 'l-Islām... akthar marākib min sāḥilihi).*[15]

And in a very direct connection to the present subject al-Muqaddasī makes the following laconic but most revealing comparison between Egypt and Syria: "Suffice it to say that Syria, in spite of its importance, is only a rural sub-district when compared to Egypt" *(ḥasbuka anna al-Shām 'alā jalālatihā rustāquhu).*[16] According to our author, if the ships arriving in Fusṭāt, had reached his birthplace, Jerusalem, a big town *(balad kabīr),* they could have removed in one voyage the whole town, with its population, trees and stones to another place. And afterwards people would say: "Once upon a time there was a town here" *(kānat hāhunā madīna).*[17]

Al-Muqaddasī's Evidence about the Mashriq versus the Maghrib

So far we have cited al-Muqaddasī's evidence about Egypt vis-à-vis Iraq, plus an illuminating remark of his about Egypt vis-à-vis Syria. But the situation in Egypt and the Fertile Crescent will not be properly understood without reference to other major parts of the Muslim world, which had an

10 *Ibid.*, p. 122, ll. 10-12.

11 *Ibid.*, p. 200, ll. 11-15. See also pp. 55, l. 4, 199, note f.

12 For *miṣr* in the sense of a capital of an important state in al-Muqaddasī's terminology, see *ibid.*, pp. 7, ll. 15-20, 9, note 1.

13 *Ibid.*, p. 193, ll. 5-6.

14 *Ibid.*, pp. 36, ll. 9-10, 197, ll. 10-12. And in the same vein: "It [i.e. Fusṭāṭ] is the most glorious of all the capitals of the Muslims. It is their greatest pride and it is the most populated of all their towns" *(innahu ajall amṣār al-Muslimīn wa-akbar mafākhirihim wa-āhal buldānihim)* (*ibid.*, p. 199, ll. 10-11).

15 *Ibid.*, p. 197, ll. 14-15.

16 *Ibid.*, p. 193, l. 8.

17 *Ibid.*, p. 198, ll. 11-15.

immense impact on the area presently under discussion. I refer to the Maghrib and the Mashriq.

On the subject of the Maghrib (including Spain) our author had the following to say: "It is situated in the corner of Islam, and part of it is cut off beyond the sea. Nobody wants it and nobody goes to it. Nobody asks about it, and nobody speaks favorably of it" *(fī zāwiyat al-Islām mawḍū' wa-ba'ḍuhu khalf al-baḥr maqṭū' wa-lā fīhi rāghib wa-lā lahu dhāhib wa-lā 'anhu sā'il wa-lā yufaḍḍiluhu qā'il).*[18] This is only a part of al-Muqaddasī's unfavorable evaluation of the Maghrib. Especially worthy of attention is the fact that this view was expressed so shortly after the unification of Egypt and the Maghrib, under the sway of a dynasty that conquered the land of the Nile from the Maghrib. It is difficult to imagine more favorable circumstances in which to speak of the Maghrib with greater respect, and to assess the chances of its becoming less remote from the east. Yet even this did not affect al-Muqaddasī's judgment.

For the Mashriq, which, according to his definition, includes Khurāsān and Transoxania, namely, the main part of the Samanid empire, al-Muqaddasī has a very different evaluation. Of the many praises he pours on it only a few will be mentioned. Speaking of its great economic might and its numerous population he adds: "This is the greatest and mightiest fortress of Islam . . . Its army is the best of all armies . . . its people are very courageous... It is the rampart against the *Turk* and the shield against the *Ghuzz*" (*huwa ḥiṣn al-Islām al-a'ẓam . . . junduhu khayr al-junūd wa-qawmuhu ūlū ba's shadīd... huwa sadd al-Turk wa-turs al-Ghuzz).*[19]

The Maghrib cerainly does not deserve such a negative and harsh verdict. It had not been isolated to such a degree, and its contribution to the greatness of Islam was immense. Suffice it to say that without the Maghrib the role of Islam in the Mediterranean, the most important sea of the world at that time, would have been dwarfed. Yet two central things are correctly reflected in al-Muqaddasī's statements:

(1) The overwhelming preponderance of the Mashriq over the Maghrib. Many other important Mashriqīs shared al-Muqaddasī's view, and no adequate retort came from the Maghrib. Al Iṣṭakhrī, for example, says that if the Muslim world is the garment *(thawb)* the Maghrib is its sleeve *(kumm).*[20] Of unusual importance in the context of the subject under discussion is the evaluation of Islam's situation made by the Mamluk Sultan Quṭuz on the eve of the battle of 'Ayn Jālūt. He stated that after the conquest of the Iranian East and Iraq by the Mongols *what was left was only*

18 *Ibid.*, p. 216, ll. 3-5 (for the whole passage see *ibid.* ll. 2-6).

19 *Ibid.*, p. 260, ll. 1-11. Al-Muqaddasī called the Samanid empire *al-Mashriq*, to distinguish it from the whole Muslim East which he called *al-Sharq* (*ibid.*, p. 7, ll. 20-21). This terminology was not adopted in the present paper.

20 Al-Iṣṭakhrī, *BGA*, I, Leiden, 1927, pp. 11, l.20 - 12, l.1.

Egypt and Syria (wa-lam yabqa illā al-Shām wa'l-Diyār al-Miṣriyya).[21] The obvious implication of this statement is that after the loss of the Muslim East the only countries which counted in the yet unconquered lands of Islam, and which could be expected to try and resist the Mongol onslaught, were Egypt and Syria. In this respect the Maghrib (including the weakening Spain) had simply to be ignored. This was not the evaluation of an uncommitted historian, but that of a man who had been charged with staving off what was then believed to be a mortal danger to Islam. The statement of Quṭuz serves as a good indicator of the role of Egypt and Syria in the struggle against Islam's external foes (a subject which is also discussed below). At the same time it leads us to the second point in al-Muqaddasī's evidence.

(2) While speaking so highly of the Samanid army, al-Muqaddasī says nothing comparable about the army of the Fatimid empire, which was then at the peak of its greatness, and towards which he showed a growing sympathy[22] (the Fatimid army was still at that time the one built mainly in the Maghrib).

The Mashriq as the Major Source of Muslim Military Power

This brings us to the very core of Syro-Egyptian relations: the kind of army that is most suitable for the area, from both the internal and external points of view. The answer to this crucial question lies in a military comparison between the Mashriq and the Maghrib. Such a comparison cannot be confined to the already islamized parts of those two regions. The pagan areas stretching immediately beyond each of them must be included. What can be said with absolute certainty about these pagan areas is that there was a profound difference in the level of appreciation of the Muslims for the military ability of the various peoples inhabiting them. They had, for example, a much higher regard for those living to their east, north-east and north, than for those living to their south.[22a] That profound difference

21 Ibn al-Furāt, *Ta'rīkh al-Khulafā' wa'l-Mulūk,* MS. Vatican, ar. 726, vol. VII, fol. 219a.

22 See e.g. al-Muqaddasī, *op. cit.*, p. 193, ll. 9-10.

22a The term *pagan* in this context is, on the whole, correct. An important exception is the Christian Nubians. They are also exceptional in comparison to the pagan peoples of Africa bordering on *Dār al-Islām* in the decisive way they stopped the southern advance of the Muslims for so long, and in the unstinting praise for their valor and military ability (their success was due to the combination of their military qualities, their religious conviction and the topographical advantages which they enjoyed). However, the praise was far less durable and far less frequent and intensive than that heaped by the same sources on the Turks. The blacks occupied a low rung in the socio-military ladder not only because of military considerations, but also because of the existence of a color bias (see my "The Muslim City and the Mamlūk Military Aristocracy" in *Proceedings of the Israeli Academy of Sciences and Humanities*, vol. II (Jerusalem, 1967).

in appreciation dictated the socio-military structure of the Muslim armies for the greater part of Islam's existence, because the elite armies of the major Muslim states were recruited mainly from Islam's north-eastern and northern "Abode of War".[23]

The meaning of this most fundamental fact is as follows: under the existing circumstances and the psychological mood of the time there was no chance that a North African army, recruited from both the Muslim and pagan territories of the region, and based on Egypt, would be able to conquer the whole of Syria and establish a steady rule there, when other external powers, like the Seljuqs on the one hand, and the Christians (Byzantines and West Europeans) on the other, were trying to do the same thing. Such a chance did not exist even when Egypt and the Maghrib were united under the Fatimids, who, in addition to other obstacles, had very difficult access to the real reservoir of military manpower in the north-east (on this see below). By contrast, the same objective, a permanent and stable occupation of Syria by Egypt, through competition with those and other external powers, could be and was carried out, by comparatively small numbers of people who came from the pagan area lying beyond the Mashriq. They achieved this despite the immense distances separating them from their countries of origin, which made their reinforcement and replenishment particularly difficult. Neither were these people in need of a base broader than Egypt, such as that possessed by the Fatimids, in order to carry out that task. The importance of this human element cannot be measured only by its success in occupying Syria permanently, but also by its ability to defend Egypt and, what is far more important, by its ability to stave off mortal dangers to Islam.

In order to properly comprehend the share of the Mashriq in shaping the destiny and the character of Islam both internally and externally, and to understand, in the same context, the process of Egypt's domination of Syria, the following facts should be remembered. In the 4th/10th century the prospects for Islam as a whole, as well as for the Sunna in its struggle against the Shīʿa, did not look at all bright. The frontier holding back the Byzantines, the main adversaries of Islam at that time, crumbled. No Muslim factor was to be seen, even in the distant horizon, which could stop, or even curb, the Byzantine advance. Inside the lands of Islam the Abbasid Caliphs were the captives of a Shīʿite dynasty, the Buwayhids. The Fatimid Shīʿites registered very impressive achievements under the leadership of their Caliphs. In Syria there were very strong Shīʿite elements, not to

23 For the difference between the major fronts bordering the Muslim lands, as a source of military manpower to Islam, see my "Aspects of the Mamlūk Phenomenon", Part A, *Der Islam*, vol. 53 (1976), pp. 197-204. The center of gravity of the recruitment of Mamluks from the northern "Abode of War" moved gradually from east to west (see my "Mamlūkiyyāt", *JSAI*, II (1980), pp. 323-4).

mention other Shīʿite and pro-Shīʿite factors then at work in the Muslim countries.

The gloomy outlook for Islam and the Sunna was thoroughly transformed in the course of the 5th/11th century (by changes on land, if not at sea). The new situation and the decisive developments which it brought about both in western Asia and in Egypt were caused, first and foremost, by two elements which came from the Mashriq, or, more precisely, from the lands of the pagans through the Mashriq: the Turk-Turcoman Seljuqs and the Turkish Mamluks. The fact that the first meeting with Islam of these two elements was through the population of Transoxania and its neighbors, a population which, according to repeated evidence in the contemporary sources, was rich, numerous, imbued with strong Islamic-awareness, and with the spirit of *jihād*,[23a] and was mainly Sunnite-Ḥanafite, had far-reaching consequences. The Turkish-Seljūq armies brought about the victory of the Sunna over the Shīʿa, defeated the Byzantines, occupied Anatolia or most of it, and penetrated deeply into northern Syria. *The strategic position of Islam against Christianity was thus improved, on land, beyond recognition, an improvement which was vital, particularly in view of the impending attack of the Crusaders.* However, the spectacular change just described could by no means be carried out by the free-born Turkish element alone. The Turkish Mamluks, who were imported to the lands of Islam long before the Seljuq penetration, and who had quickly become the dominant military factor in the Muslim east, were incorporated in the Seljuq armies at a very early date, and constituted their elite. According to what I consider to be our best Muslim source on the battle of Manzikert, which opened the gates of Asia Minor to Islam, and led ultimately to the creation of the Ottoman empire, the mainstay of Alp Arslan in that battle were his 4,000 Mamluks *(mamālīk, ghilmān)*, who remained with him throughout, whereas the rest of his army disintegrated (*wa-lākinna iʿtimādahu baʿda Allāh ʿalā ha'ulā' al-arbaʿat ālāf).*[24] The core of the armies of the Seljuqs' successor states also consisted of Mamluks. This is true, of course, of the army of the Zankids, some of whose commanders established the Ayyubid state, which included Egypt and Syria.

23a In addition to Transoxania's being, according al-Muqaddasī, most fertile, thriving and populous, and its people upright and imbued with an unwavering spirit of *jihād*, the Islam of that region was fresh *(al-Islām bihi ṭariyy) (Aḥsan al-Taqāsīm*, p. 261, ll. 5-11 and especially l.8.). The Mamluks arriving in the lands of Islam could not have had a more favorable first encounter with their new religion than the one they had in that region. The combination of Islamic freshness and the unmarred qualities typical of their countries of origin, was one of the basic traits of the Mamluks. This was already stressed so aptly and convincingly by Ibn Khaldūn (see "Mamlūkiyyāt", *JSAI*, II (1980), pp. 345-6).

24 See the account of Ghars al-Niʿma Abū al-Ḥasan Muḥammad, the son and continuator of Hilāl al-Ṣābī in Sibṭ ibn al-Jawzī, *Mir'āt al-Zamān*, Ankara, 1968, pp. 147-152. Compare especially p. 147, ll. 14-18 with pp. 148, ll. 15-18 and 152, ll. 6-9. This account and related ones are discussed in detail in a study dealing mainly with the transition period from Ayyubid to the Mamluk reign, which is in an advanced stage of preparation.

The Drawbacks of the Fatimids

The Fatimids, who preceded the Ayyubids and were supplanted by them, seem to have realized, quite soon after having conquered Egypt from the Maghrib, the superiority of the Muslim eastern armies, and especially their Turkish-Mamluk component. However, they were faced with a problem the like of which no other great Muslim state had ever faced. For no other such state had transferred its center of gravity from one area to another, very different area, after its military and other structures had already reached a quite advanced stage of development. The older patterns and older allegiances and commitments which had crystallized under most dissimilar conditions, could not be brushed aside. This, as well as other most weighty reasons (including the existence of hostile Sunnite states separating Egypt from the distant countries of the pagan Turks), prevented the Fatimids from adequately rebuilding their army to meet the new conditions and, especially, from making that army's Turkish-Mamluk component its uncontested mainstay.[25] No wonder, therefore, that the achievements of the Fatimids against the Byzantines and Crusaders were so much less impressive than those of the Seljuqs against these two adversaries, and those of the Ayyubids and Mamluks against the Crusaders (not to mention the Mamluk achievements against the Mongols), and this in spite of the comparatively strong navy the Fatimids had at a certain period, and which their successors lacked. I have shown elsewhere that the army of the

25 A piece of information of unique significance on the relative importance of the races from which Mamluks were recruited and on the weight of the Mamluk element in comparison with non-Mamluk military bodies is furnished to us in the reign of the Abbasid Caliph al-Muqtafī (530-555/1136-1160). The Seljuq Sultan forbade him to acquire Turkish Mamluks. He therefore built a Mamluk army composed of Armenians and Rūm. I discuss this evidence at great length in my study "From Ayyūbids to Mamlūks". I shall confine myself here to a very brief comment. The prohibition regarding a force of Turkish Mamluks did not cause al-Muqtafī to shift his reliance to a non-Mamluk body as his mainstay. Non-Mamluk soldiers are not even mentioned in this crucial context. Neither the Seljuq Sultan nor the Abbasid Caliph bothered about them. At the same time it is made quite obvious here that within Mamluk military society the most preferable race was the Turks, and it was they whom the Seljuq Sultan feared. If al-Muqtafī had had freedom of choice, he would have certainly recruited Turkish Mamluks, in spite of the fact that from Baghdad it was much easier to acquire *Arman* and *Rūm* than to bring over *Turk* from their much more distant countries of origin. If this was the situation which a Sunnite ruler had to face, how much more so a Fatimid Shī'ite ruler — an avowed enemy of the Seljuqs — whose capital had been about twice as distant from the same countries of origin? It is against this background that we have to understand and explain the prominence of the Armenian Mamluks under the Fatimids. On the other hand, the independence of the Fatimids and their great power and resources enabled them to circumvent, to a certain extent, those enormous obstacles, and bring Turkish Mamluks to Egypt.However, the Turkish Mamluk body in their army was not sufficiently strong to become the uncontestedly dominant force of the realm.

Ayyubids, already in the time of Shīrkūh, Ṣalāḥ al-Dīn's uncle, was mainly Turkish and Turkish-Mamluk (and the most important of the two was Turkish-Mamluk). The Kurdish factor was, with fluctuations, of secondary importance.[26] Additional reading has only served to strengthen that conclusion.[27]

The Combination of Egypt and the Mamluks from the North-East and the North as Vital for the Defence of Syria and Islam

I now reach the focal point of my argumentation. Both Muslims and Franks reached the right conclusion, namely, that Egypt is the pivot of the whole struggle. The Franks came to realize that in order to safeguard their hold on Syria and Palestine, or parts thereof, they must occupy Egypt (or at least key points in it), whereas the Muslims became convinced that only from the Egyptian base would they be able to drive the Franks out of their Syro-Palestinian possessions. But the Muslims did not stop at that. They believed that the loss of Egypt to the Franks meant the end of Islam.

The centrality and cruciality of Egypt was thus beyond doubt. But what had been proved at the same time, no less convincingly, was that the mighty Egyptian base was not sufficient in itself, and that when the Fatimids ruled Egypt they were incapable not only of removing the Franks from Syria and Palestine, but also of preventing them from occupying Egypt (from a certain date onwards).[28] It was also proved unequivocally that the combination of Egypt and the Turkish and Turkish-Mamluk factor, inside and outside Egypt, was capable of doing both, even if after a supreme and protracted effort. It was the selfsame combination which later stopped the advance of the Mongols, an advance unexampled in its strength.

The greatness and might of Egypt were revealed to the Syrian armies commanded by the Kurd Shīrkūh and his nephew Ṣalāḥ al-Dīn upon their arrival to expel the Franks, and, therefore, they decided to stay. Shīrkūh defined Egypt as the major part of the lands of Islam and as the milch cow of their treasury *(hiya muʿẓam dār al-Islām wa-ḥalūbat dār mālihim),*[29] and

26 "Aspects of the Mamlūk Phenomenon", part B: "Ayyūbids, Kurds and Turks", *Der Islam*, vol. 54 (1977), pp. 1-32.

27 The results of such additional reading are presented in a study mentioned in note 24. It was not my intention to enumerate all the drawbacks of the Fatimids in their attempts to conquer Syria, some of which are very well known and often mentioned. I wanted to call attention to one major and decisive drawback, the importance of which was not sufficiently noticed.

28 The Muslims had great admiration for the military might, the art of war and the bravery of their Frankish adversaries during the Crusader period, which resembled their admiration for the military qualities of the Turks. A special chapter is dedicated to the subject in the study mentioned in note 24.

29 Abū Shāma, *Kitāb al-Rawḍatayn,* Būlāq, 1288H, vol. I, p. 172, l.3.

added that if the Syrian army would evacuate it, the Franks would reoccupy it. That is why he [Shīrkūh] decided to take possession of it. Ṣalāḥ al-Dīn said that when God enabled [the Syrian army] to occupy Egypt, he [Ṣalāḥ al-Dīn] knew that God [ultimately] intended the conquest of the Syro-Palestinian coast from the Franks. The Franks, on the other hand, were convinced, according to the Muslim sources, that that would be their end, and that the coastal area *(al-sāḥil)* which they held was on the brink of a tottering precipice *('alā shafā jurfin hārin).*[30]

The Muslims almost achieved their aim of wiping out the Crusaders in Palestine and Syria shortly after the Ayyubids came to power (the battle of Ḥaṭṭīn in 1187 and its sequel), but because of Frankish naval supremacy they ultimately failed (viz. the third Crusade). But the resultant situation only accentuated Egypt's centrality in the struggle. The Franks twice tried to conquer Egypt in the first half of the thirteenth century (1218, 1249). In both cases they had barely set foot on Egyptian soil when panic seized the Muslims, who believed that this was the end of their religion. More specifically, it had been argued that the Franks would conquer from Egypt the Arabian coastal region of the Red Sea as far as Ḥaḍramawt, and would wipe out *('afū āthār)* Mecca, Medina and Syria,[31] which would obviously constitute a mortal danger to Islam. With the hindsight we possess about the decline of the Crusaders and their end, this fear may appear very exaggerated. But at the time of those events, things looked different, and rightly so. First of all, the Crusaders' intention to dominate Egypt was very serious. Secondly, Egypt in Frankish hands would have created a completely new situation with immense possibilities, both economic (the command of the granaries of this country and of the international commercial route from India to the Middle East and Europe) and religious (the absolute domination of Egypt over the holiest places of Islam). It is worthwhile noting in this context that King St. Louis, who headed a huge invading army in 1249, planned a Frankish agricultural settlement in Egypt.[32] To all this should be added the very deep dejection and despair among the Muslims, resulting from the loss of the land of the Nile, which was revealed at the very beginning of each Frankish invasion of Egypt. In these circumstances numerous and great opportunities would have been created for the Franks, and it is hard to believe that they would have let them pass by.

The decisive factor in the total defeat of St. Louis's formidable army, and

30 Ibn Wāṣil, *Mufarrij al-Kurūb,* vol. I. Cairo, 1953, pp. 168-179.

31 Abū Shāma, *Tarājim Rijāl al-Qarnayn al-Sādis wa'l-Sābi' (= Al-Dhayl 'alā 'l-Rawḍatayn),* Cairo, 1947, p. 128, ll. 20-22.

32 As an alternative to the occupation of the whole of Egypt or the whole of the Delta area (including Cairo) the holding of key points by the Franks, especially on the Mediterranean coast of Egypt, might be considered.

in removing the Frankish threat to Egypt for many generations, was the Baḥriyya Mamluk regiment stationed in Cairo, which, a year or two later, established the Mamluk sultanate, one of the greatest and most powerful states that Islam had ever known. Barely ten years after the battle of al-Manṣūra and the toppling of the Ayyubid reign, the same Mamluk regiment faced yet another trial of strength, of unique importance, and from which it emerged, once again, victorious. Once more it was the decisive factor in the victory over the Mongols in 1260 at ʻAyn Jālūt. This was the first time that the Mongols had been stopped, permanently, by an adversary, in any of the directions of their expansion: China; Russia and Eastern Europe; and the lands of Islam. It is true that the case of the Mongols is fundamentally different from that of the Crusaders, for the pagan Mongols were bound, sooner or later, not only to adopt Islam, but also to constitute a major vehicle of its expansion far beyond its existing borders. But when the Mongol advance was at its peak things looked otherwise: the infidels of the West and the infidels of the East were going to finish off Islam by dint of their sweeping advance from two opposite directions, even without the advantage of combined planning and alliance. Thus the Mamluks of Egypt enjoyed almost unparalleled prestige and admiration immediately before and after the establishment of their sultanate. That prestige was augmented by the final expulsion of the Crusaders, and by additional victories over the Mongols, which from a purely military point of view were much greater than the victory of ʻAyn Jālūt. This greatly facilitated the absorption of Syria into the Mamluk sultanate.

Egypt and Syria under the Mamluks

With the establishment of the Mamluk sultanate relations between Egypt and Syria entered an era the like of which had never been matched before nor would be again. It was the end of divided and competing Ayyubid principalities within both countries, of shared rule over Syria with the Franks, and of danger for Egypt. For about 270 years Egyptian rule of Syria was unqualified and uncontested, and this in spite of severe divisions and struggles inside the Mamluk military aristocracy of Egypt and the growing number of insurrections by local elements in Egypt and in Syria. No local factor had the slightest chance of wresting from the Mamluks their hold over Syria and Palestine. But for the external Ottoman factor which defeated the Mamluks and put an end to their sultanate by means of firearms, it is difficult to see what could have shaken Mamluk rule over Syria for many years after 1516, and this notwithstanding the decline of the Mamluk state both militarily and economically. In short, never in its history was Syria ruled by Egypt for so long and with such a degree of thoroughness as under the Mamluks (although, admittedly, that thoroughness was only relative).

As for the relations of Egypt and Syria under the Mamluks, one could briefly summarize them as follows. As a constituent part of the Mamluk sultanate, Syria was very important. Without it that sultanate would not have been the strongest and most important Muslim state during the greater part of the late Middle Ages. Yet, within the framework of that state, Syria was a province much inferior to Egypt. Mamluk aristocracy very often shunned service in Syria. Usually, though not always, such service was considered as exile or banishment.[33] The main body of the Mamluk military society, the Royal Mamluks (i.e. the freedmen of the ruling and the preceding sultans) was stationed in Cairo. Those segments of the Royal Mamluks, who had, for one reason or another, to stay permanently in Syria, soon deteriorated and became military bodies of secondary importance. Stationed in the Syrian towns were the armies of Mamluk Emirs whose socio-military standing was much inferior to that of the Royal Mamluks. Furthermore, these armies always included, side by side with the Mamluks, numerous free-born troops. Moreover, in addition to the armies of the Emirs, there were considerable military bodies in Syria, comprised solely of free-born soldiers.[34]

The physical structure of Syria, so fundamentally different from that of Egypt, was also reflected in the rule of the Mamluks, and was well-exploited by them. Syria was not governed through a single Syrian center, but was divided into seven provinces, each with its own capital (Damascus, Aleppo, Tripoli, Hama, Safed, Gaza and Kerak), each being directly responsible to Cairo. Moreover, most of these capitals had a fortress *(qal'a)*. Each fortress had a governor, appointed by the Mamluk Sultan and subordinate only to him (or in other words: completely independent of the governor of the province). A considerable number of the holders of key military and administrative offices in each of the Syrian provinces was appointed from Cairo. To all this should be added the following major factor. Whereas in the whole of Egypt there existed only one single fortress *(qal'at al-jabal)*, Syria was strewn with numerous fortresses, each of which had to be manned. The inevitable result of this state of affairs was that the relatively sparse layer of second-rate Mamluks stationed in Syria was spread over seven capitals and tens of fortresses, a fact which made it

33 This in addition to the fact that most of the dismissed Mamluk Emirs were sent to various places in Syria and Palestine, the most important place of exile in the Mamluk sultanate being Jerusalem (see my "Discharges from Service, Banishments and Imprisonments in Mamlūk Society", *Israel Oriental Studies,* Tel-Aviv, 1975, pp. 25-50).

34 To avoid any misunderstanding I would like to stress the obvious: compared here is the attitude of the *ruling military society* to Syria with its attitude to Egypt. This might allow Syria latitude in various fields. The greater military role of the local populace of Syria as compared with that of Egypt, is discussed immediately below. This latitude might have its influence on the economic and religious-cultural life in Syria as well. On the whole, however, Egypt's preponderance over Syria was very considerable.

extremely vulnerable to the influence of non-Mamluk elements. Moreover, the units composed of free-born soldiers which were stationed in the Syrian towns and fortresses, carried, from the outset, much more weight vis-à-vis the Syrian Mamluks than did their counterparts vis-à-vis the Egyptian Mamluks. The already strong position of these Syrian units derived additional strength from the fact that most of the great field battles and sieges took place on Syrian soil. This necessitated keeping a strong infantry and siege-experts in Syria, in addition to the cavalry. There was little sense in dragging most of the foot-soldiers from the comparatively distant Egypt. Therefore, the Syrian infantry was much stronger and much more important than its Egyptian counterpart. The share of the urban population in the Syrian infantry was very great, although numerous *fellaḥs* and other people from the countryside served in it too. The existence and the weight of the urban infantry made its mark on the everyday life of the Syrian towns. Also well marked were the infantry's relations with comparable elements in the countryside. On the whole, a substantial part of the Syrian urban population was armed. The overall result was that the social and socio-military gap between the Mamluk aristocracy on the one hand and the other military bodies and the civilian population on the other, was much narrower in the Syrian capitals than it was in Cairo. Consequently, the relations formed in these capitals between the military and the rest of the population, were substantially different from those formed in the Egyptian capital. In Cairo, where practically all the Royal Mamluks were stationed, the chances of successful use of force by the civilian population were nil. In the not too numerous instances where that population resorted to some kind of violence, it rarely exceeded the throwing of stones at the Mamluks. No connection was ever made for the purpose of common action, between the people of Cairo and the nomads and semi-nomads in the capital's vicinity, who repeatedly rebelled against the government.[35]

A case in point of the absolute preponderance of Egypt over Syria is the following. It happened more than once that one or another of the Syrian Mamluks succeeded, mainly through close cooperation with a strong oppositionary Mamluk faction in Cairo, in supplanting the ruling faction in the Egyptian capital. Such a success was never followed up by an attempt to remove the Mamluk capital to Syria. Moreover, no Mamluk revolt in Syria, and there were not a few such revolts, was ever conducted with the intention, or under the slogan, of Syria seceding from Egypt, even temporarily.

The inferiority of the Syro-Palestinian region, and especially of its

35 See also my "The Muslim City", pp. 328-329. A very important military element which existed within the Mamluk sultanate in Syria only, was the Turcomans, whose status and importance in that sultanate were higher than those of other nomads (Kurds and beduins). For the danger posed by the Turcomans to the Mamluk Sultanate see below.

southern parts, in relation to Egypt was accentuated by yet another factor, the importance of which far transcends the limits of our subject, viz. the increasing naval weakness of Islam from the eleventh century onwards. That century witnessed, more or less simultaneously, a very remarkable Muslim military recovery on land, which would have its effect on western Asia and Egypt for many generations to come, and an even more remarkable helplessness at sea, which has been affecting human history to the present day.

The Mamluk military institution, in its various forms, mitigated on land, for a long period, the effects of the steadily growing technological gap between Christian (especially western) Europe and Islam. At sea the Muslims did not have any similar response,[36] with the exception, perhaps, of a very limited one, in respect of area and time, given by the Ottomans at a later period. The manner in which the Muslims decided to solve the problem of their naval weakness in connection with the Crusades, is of unique significance. The Ayyubids, from the last years of Ṣalāḥ al-Dīn's reign onwards, and especially the Mamluks, destroyed most of the Syro-Palestinian (and particularly the Palestinian) ports and their fortifications with the purpose of preventing a resurgence of the Crusades.[37] This was the biggest and most thorough operation of permanent destruction for defence purposes which had ever been carried out in the history of that coast, in the history of Islam, and, to the best of my knowledge, in the history of mankind. By contrast, the Egyptian coastal towns, with the exception of Tinnīs (Damietta was destroyed and rebuilt) were left intact, both because the commerce with Europe was vital to the Mamluks, and because it was possible to send substantial reinforcements quite quickly to any point on Egypt's northern coast, from Cairo, where the pick of the Mamluk army was stationed. The Mamluks' differing treatment of their sultanate's two respective Mediterranean coasts could only increase Syria's inferority to Egypt.

The destruction and devastation of the Syro-Palestinian coast serves as incontestible proof of Islam's admission of European naval preponderance

36 The increasing Muslim naval inferiority was greatly mitigated during the Crusades by the fact that the Crusader states did not have any navies of their own, and were completely dependent in this vital matter on outside Frankish naval power. The Muslims, by contrast, had the strongest extant Muslim navy, based mainly on Egypt, constantly at hand (insofar as it was in an operational condition). See also my "The Mamlūks and Naval Power — A Phase of the Struggle between Islam and Christian Europe", *Proceedings of the Israel Academy of Sciences and Humanities,* vol. I, Jerusalem, 1965, pp. 1-12.

37 During their struggle against the Crusaders, the Muslims destroyed, quite often, some of their own inland fortifications, in order that they would not serve the enemy. This destruction however was neither as systematic nor as comprehensive as the destruction on the coast. In any case, the inland forts were so numerous that the disappearance or decline of a number of them was of no great consequence.

and of its total loss of hope that things in this field would change in its favor in the foreseeable future. In the long run such an admission meant that Islam had lost its chances of world domination for a good number of centuries. For sea-power was the first and most formidable expression of European technological superiority and it was on board ships that Christian Europe carried and made use of that superiority in other spheres, even in the remotest corners of the earth. The map of the globe in modern times: the great empires of the eastern hemisphere and the discovery and settlement of the western hemisphere, were made possible first and foremost by the command of the seas.[38]

In view of the comparatively small size of any army composed of Mamluks, the concentration of the cream of that military aristocracy in Cairo was, in all probability, fully justified. Splitting that body by permanently garrisoning substantial parts of it along the coast and at various points in Syria and Upper Egypt, would have greatly weakened it. Yet that very concentration had its grave drawbacks. One of them was that it made the destruction of the Syro-Palestinian coast, referred to above, even more imperative. Another was that the main enemies of the Mamluk sultanate on land were concentrated in the north. No major battle against such an enemy was ever fought without the Royal Mamluks forming the backbone of the expeditionary force. Now to move a sizeable army with its equipment and baggage from Cairo to Aleppo took up to forty days.[39] Even the quelling of internal insurrections in Syria posed a difficult problem. What greatly aggravated the difficulties in coping with both external and internal enemies was the decline and ultimate crumbling, from approximately the middle of the fourteenth century and onwards, of the superb Mamluk information system, based mainly on the official postal services carried out on horseback or by means of carrier pigeons. In northern Syria a looming danger was gathering momentum. The power of the Turcomans was ominously growing. We have the evidence of a contemporary eyewitness from the reign of Qā'itbāy in the second half of the 9th/15th century that the dominant language from Latakiya to al-Bīra (today's Biredjik on the Euphrates) was not Arabic but Turkish.[40] What made the Turcomans of the Mamluk sultanate so dangerous was the contiguity of their territory to that of the Turcomans beyond the border. It was their fighting the Turcomans that embroiled the Mamluks in war against the Ottomans, and which brought about an end to their rule.

38 See also my "A First Attempt to Evaluate the Mamlūk Military System" (in the series *Mamlūkiyyāt*, part I), *Jerusalem Studies in Arabic and Islam*, vol. II (1980), pp. 334-335.

39 See art. *Ḥarb*, *EI*², vol. III, p. 185, col. b.

40 Abū al-Baqā' Ibn al-Jī'ān, *Al-Qawl al-Mustaẓraf fī Safar Mawlānā al-Malik al-Ashraf* (ed. R.V. Lanzone), Torino, 1878, p. 17.

Egypt and Syria under the Ottomans

The Ottoman conquest created a completely new situation. No longer Syria in relation to Egypt within the framework of a state in which they constituted the two main parts, but these two countries as provinces in an empire with far-flung borders, whose capital was situated a long way away from them both, and whose interests were greatly different. The inclusion of Egypt and Syria in the Ottoman empire constituted part of a revolutionary transformation of the map of the Muslim world. Between August 1514 and January 1517, i.e. in less than two and a half years, the Ottomans conquered the entire Mamluk sultanate, and detached vast areas from the Persian-Shī'ite-Safawid empire which had just come into being. The territories they occupied in this very short space of time greatly exceeded in size all their conquests in Europe for centuries long (this excluding further Ottoman expansion, direct or indirect, in Asia and Africa, resulting from their gains in the middle of the second decade of the sixteenth century). The major cause of their success was that, contrary to their Muslim adversaries, they adopted firearms on a huge scale, and used them in the proper way.

As for the Ottomans' policy towards the Mamluks, it was quickly transformed. Sultan Selīm, who intended at first to liquidate them all physically, changed his mind while still in Egypt, and decided to spare them. His son and successor, Suleymān the Magnificent, incorporated them into the Ottoman army in an orderly manner. There can be no doubt that the major reason for that policy was the shortage of suitable military manpower. The Ottomans faced a very knotty problem, created almost overnight, of the manning of the garrisons in the vast areas just conquered, and of dealing with the old adversaries, the Christian-Europeans in the Mediterranean sea, as well as with new ones: the Safawids in the east, and the Portuguese in the south. The Mamluks constituted the best military element in all the newly-conquered areas. Within the Ottomans' general policy of including local military elements of their provinces in their armed forces, the Mamluks must have received first priority.

From the point of view of the Ottomans, the incorporation of the Mamluks into their army was both wise and essential. But in the process they, and especially Sultan Selīm, made some grave mistakes. The first was their appointment of Mamluk Emirs who collaborated with them as viceroys in Egypt and Syria (Khāyrbek and Jānbirdī al-Ghazālī respectively). Their second mistake was making Jānbirdī al-Ghazālī the viceroy of most of Syria, from the borders of the province of Aleppo to al-'Arīsh (an Ottoman was appointed as viceroy of Aleppo). Thus, almost immediately after the destruction of the Mamluk sultanate, most of its territory was governed by Mamluk Emirs. But this was not all. The Ottomans discarded the time-honored and well-tried governing policy of the Mamluks, namely: the division of Syria into numerous provinces. True, the Ottomans considered Egypt and Syria (and rightly so) as but two provinces of a huge empire, an empire accustomed to much bigger administrative units than those existing in the Mamluk state, and whose center of government (Constantinople) was a long way off from these two provinces. However, in view of the recentness of the Mamluk defeat, it was extremely dangerous to put the greatest part of the defunct sultanate under the rule of the defeated, and destroy so quickly in Syria the structure which had guaranteed its obedience for so long.

From the very beginning Jānbirdī al-Ghazālī did not conceal his extreme Mamluk inclinations. He also made contact with the Safawids of Iran, and as soon as he learned of the death of Sultan Selīm, threw off the Ottoman yoke. At that date a Mamluk revolt, even if Egypt joined it, was bound to fail. Since Egypt kept aloof, it was easily quelled. But even the very cautious Khāyrbek, who outwardly demonstrated excessive loyalty and obedience to the Ottomans, seems to have nourished Mamluk hopes in his heart.[41] This was already indicated in his lifetime, by his building a strong private Mamluk army, but only came fully into the limelight after his death (as far as we can deduce from the account of Ibn Iyās). He very carefully preserved the Mamluk character of the Cairo citadel, the heart of Egypt and the heart of the Mamluk empire. This structure was destroyed immediately after his death. Thenceforward no Mamluk viceroys were appointed in Egypt and Syria. The Mamluks were totally uprooted from Syria, but were left in Egypt.[42]

The Mamluks began their history in Ottoman Egypt at the bottom of the socio-military ladder (they formed the lowest-paid unit in the Egyptian garrison). However, more or less concurrently with the weakening of the Ottomans (although perhaps not in exact parallel with that process), the Mamluks became more powerful. During the course of the eighteenth century the appetite of their leaders to conquer Syria was greatly whetted. The great dream of 'Alī Bey al-Kabīr was to reestablish the Mamluk sultanate. But any Mamlūk attempt to conquer Syria at that time was bound to fail, even if factors confined solely to the Mamluk society are considered (some of which were old, going back to the Mamluk sultanate; others were new).

As already stated, Syria was an inferior province under the Mamluks,

41 After the quelling of Jānbirdī al-Ghazālī's revolt, the trust of the Ottomans in Khāyrbek must have diminshed. Although they did not dismiss him, they withheld the yearly confirmation of his appointment.

42 I discuss the transition from Mamluk to Ottoman rule in detail in a yet unpublished study entitled "Mamluk Military Aristocracy during the First Years of the Ottoman Conquest of Egypt", and briefly in an article in Hebrew entitled "The Mamluk Army at the Beginning of the Ottoman Conquest", and published in *Tarbiz*, Jerusalem, 1952, vol. XXIII (in the section presented to Prof. Gotthold E. Weil on the occasion of his seventieth birthday). pp. 221-226.

where the elite Mamluk units refused to stay for long. It can be said with a great degree of certainty that some 250 years after the eradication of the Mamluks from Syria, the ordinary Egyptian Mamluk did not develop a desire to go to Syria in order to revive the great sultanate of his predecessors. But this was not the only obstacle. Mamluk society in Ottoman Egypt underwent a far-reaching transformation which was not conducive to activity and long stays outside Egypt. This society became a strange and quite unique combination of a one-generation aristocracy, as the Mamluks had always been, and an hereditary aristocracy. It was characterized by a peculiar mixture of Mamluk ties and blood ties. As a result, enmities and hatreds between the competing Mamluk factions lasted for generations and, therefore, became unrivalled in their bitterness. Factional struggles were conducted with the undisguised purpose of literally wiping out the rival faction. And when a faction achieved that aim (as for example the Faqāriyya v. the Qāsimiyya in 1142/1729) it very soon underwent the identical process of internal rifts, with the resultant emergence of new factions, eager to annihilate each other, as in the past. The unprecedented growth of the power of the nomads and semi-nomads affected Mamluk society and curbed its freedom of action in two forms. In northern Egypt each of the rival Mamluk factions of Cairo formed a long-standing alliance with a neighboring confederation of *'urbān* (the Faqāriyya with the Sa'd or Niṣf Sa'd and the Qāsimiyya with the Ḥarām or Niṣf Ḥarām), and from time to time adopted even the name of that confederation. Both the alliance on such a level and the name-adoption were unique to the Egyptian Mamluk society under the Ottomans. I know of no comparable kind of relations between Mamluks and nomads anywhere else or at any other time, in the lands of Islam.[43]

It was also under the Ottomans that the main mitigating factor in central rule in Egypt — the great length of its inhabited area — made itself felt more strongly than even before or after in the Muslim period. In the south, in Upper Egypt, Mamluk exiles and refugees, together with nomads and semi-nomads, created a center of power (around Girga) which competed with the Mamluks of Cairo and fought against them, both defensively and offensively.[44] It happened more than once that the Mamluks and nomads of Upper Egypt occupied Cairo, and those of Cairo found refuge in Upper Egypt. The Cairo center was, of course, by far the stronger of the two, but it was not strong enough to eradicate the southern center. Uprisings and manifestations of opposition in the Ṣa'īd were, of course, known, and sometimes were even quite frequent, but these either subsided or were suppressed. In any case, no comparable center, of a permanent character,

43 See also my "Studies in al-Jabartī: Notes on the Transformation of Mamlūk Society in Egypt under the Ottomans", *JESHO*, III (Leiden, 1960), pp. 148-174, 275-325.

44 This is not to say that the Upper Egypt center was independent of that of Cairo.

existed in Muslim Upper Egypt outside the time of Ottoman rule.[45] True, 'Alī Bey al-Kabīr temporarily neutralized that center, but he was very far from liquidating it. A by no means negligible cause for the difficulties which the invading French army encountered in 1799, during its advance in Upper Egypt, despite its overwhelming superiority to the Mamluks and their allies in weapons and in the art of war, was the fact that the defenders of this area had been accustomed for generations to cope with the attacks of stronger armies from the north. Typical of their tactics was to vanish from the Nile valley and find refuge in well-prepared positions and caves in the neighboring desert and mountains, observing from there the movements of the heavily-equipped enemy, who was much less familiar with the terrain. From these positions the defenders would harass the attackers by hit-and-run raids and inflict on them heavy losses.

In view of this state of affairs in Ottoman Egypt it is possible, I think, to determine what was the main cause (or, more exactly, which was sufficient in itself), to foil, at least ultimately, 'Alī Bey's attempt to conquer Syria in 1771/2. The army of that ruler made a sudden retreat to Egypt, after having conquered southern Syria, including Damascus. A quite common explanation of this retreat is that it had been the result of Ottoman and European pressure. Without expressing any view as to the correctness of this explanation, I would nevertheless like to point out that the great historian of Ottoman Egypt, 'Abd al-Raḥmān al-Jabartī (died 1825) gives a completely different explanation. According to him Muḥammad Abū Dhahab, the commander of the expeditionary force and the Mamluk of 'Alī Bey, gathered together the high-ranking and the senior Mamluks of that ruler (i.e. Abū Dhahab's *khushdāshiyya*) and told them that their master wanted them to spend the rest of their lives in campaigns far away from their

45 The growing might of the nomads and semi-nomads was certainly a major contributor to the creation of the center of power in Upper Egypt under the Ottomans. However, without the Mamluks who joined it, it had no chance of becoming so important or of lasting so long. As already stated (note 33), most of the banished members of the Mamluk aristocracy were sent to various places in Syria. With the loss of Syria, Egypt lost its chief depository for exiles. True, exiles could be, and were, sent to various parts of the Ottoman empire. But this was done in agreement with the Ottoman government, or by its exclusive decision. Most of the exiles did not fall within this category, and had to be sent to places inside Egypt. Within the boundaries of that country the local Mamluk society had a large and growing say in the matter of banishments, as in other matters. Many of the exiles were dispatched to various localities in Lower Egypt. But apparently they had little difficulty in running away from there probably because they had not been well-guarded. (Within the Mamluk sultanate, for example, exiles were ususally shackled when sent to the places of banishment. This does not seem to have been the method ordinarily used inside Ottoman Egypt.) The escape of exiles from northern to southern Egypt is very frequently mentioned. It is often said that they used the way which passes "behind the mountain" *(min warā' al-jabal)*. Members of a defeated faction in the struggle for power in Cairo also found refuge in Upper Egypt. Thus there was no lack of supply of Mamluks to that southern center.

homeland *(al-awṭān)*. He suggested that they return home, to which they all willingly agreed, and consequently the Egyptian army withdrew immediately from Syria.[46] Thus the internal relations in the Mamluk society, as reflected in this evidence and in al-Jabartī's account of 'Alī Bey's reign, as well as the accentuated aversion of the Mamluks to moving outside Egypt's boundaries, were sufficient in themselves to foil 'Alī Bey's ambition of expansion in the direction of Syria. Even if we suppose, for argument's sake alone, that the Egyptian army would have stayed in Syria, it could not have stayed there for long, because 'Alī Bey had no chance of holding under his sway both Upper Egypt and Syria. The great reduction in the numerical strength of the Mamluks in Cairo, as a result of the annexation of Syria or parts of it, would have inevitably led to Upper Egypt's trying to rid itself of the central government's rule. Under such conditions continued occupation of Syrian soil, even without the existence of any local Syrian or external threat to that occupation, would have been sheer madness.

An irrefutable proof for my contention that at that time there was no need for external pressure in order to bring about the withdrawal of an Egyptian army from Syria, is furnished by events which took place a few years later. The same Abū Dhahab, who succeeded his patron as the ruler of Egypt, advanced into Syria once again in 1775, this time with the acquiescence of the Ottoman Sultan. The account of this campaign by the same al-Jabartī is even more illuminating than his account of the earlier one. The officers and soldiers *(al-umarā' wa'l-ajnād)* under Abū Dhahab's command believed that the campaign would be a short one (a belief which could not take root without the help of their commander), and that the return to Egypt *(al-rujū' ilā 'l-awṭān)* would take place soon. After the capture of Acre, preceded by the capture of Jaffa, they expressed their joy at the prospect of their early return home. But in a meeting with Abū Dhahab their hopes were shattered, for he told them that he intended to appoint them to offices and rulerships in Syria and its coastal area *(wa-annahu yurīd taqlīdahum al-manāṣib wa'l-aḥkām bi'l-Diyār al-Shāmiyya wa-Bilād al-Sawāḥil)*. He also ordered them to write home to their families about the prolongation of their stay. This greatly distressed them, and they returned to their tents each pondering his own affairs *(wa-'inda dhālika ightammū... wa-dhahaba kullun ilā mukhayyamihi yufakkir fī amrihi)*. Luckily for them all, Abū Dhahab fell ill and died within three days. As soon as his death became known, the entire army returned to Egypt. (He died on 8th of Rabī' II 1189 and the retreating army arrived in Cairo as early as the 24th of that month.)[47]

46 Al-Jabartī, *'Ajā'ib al-Āthār*, the Būlāg edition, vol. I, p. 365, ll. 12-22.

47 *Ibid.*, p. 414, ll. 1-20. One of the reasons for Abū-Dhahab's concealing his intention of occupying Syria permanently (and, consequently, leaving there a considerable part of his army for a long period), might have been the fact that it was only in Acre that he received news from Istanbul, of the confirmation of his appointment as governor of Egypt and

Egypt and Syria in the Reign of Muḥammad ʿAlī

Whereas under the Ottomans and until the end of the eighteenth century Egypt could at best serve, for its Mamluk garrison, as a very poor basis for expansion beyond its borders, the situation underwent a thorough transformation in the early decades of the nineteenth century. This transformation was due to Muḥammad ʿAlī, who, within the framework of his far-reaching reforms, revolutionized the military society and the army. Such a fundamental revolution had never taken place there or anywhere else in Asia and Africa (from Japan and the Philippines to the western coast of the black continent). It involved the wiping out of the old military structure, together with the socio-military elements which sustained it, and the building, from top to bottom, of a new army based on the European model.

In this context it is worthwhile noting that the armies in the lands of Islam (at least in the more important ones), as gradually built up since Muḥammad ʿAlī onwards, came to be far removed from the military pattern which had developed organically in the course of many centuries within Muslim civilization. The Muslim armies of today, as far as their structure, functioning, equipment, etc. are concerned, have very little, if any, connection with the Muslim armies of the past.[48] This is highly significant, in the light of the central role of the army and military society in Islam throughout its existence. It needed a good number of centuries of repeated and painful military defeats and setbacks delivered by Christian-European adversaries to bring Muslim rulers very slowly and very reluctantly, and against strong internal opposition, to the conclusion that they had to adopt the military system of those adversaries. Once such a conclusion had been reached, and a decision to put it into practice had been carried out, the way was paved for westernization that went considerably beyond the army. The main channel, although by no means the only one, for absorption of western influences in various fields in the independent Muslim states was nevertheless the army.[49]

Syria (*ibid.*, p. 414, ll. 1-3). The return of the Egyptian army, in this campaign, to Cairo from Acre in sixteen days should be considered as rapid. In the Mamluk sultanate it took the army ten to twelve days to cover the distance between Cairo and Gaza, and five to six days from Cairo to Baysān (not including three to five days of rest in Gaza before or after crossing the Sinai desert) (art. *Ḥarb, EI*[2], vol. III, p. 185, col. b). Note that in both campaigns the desire to go home is stressed, and in both cases the same word is used *(al-awṭān).*

48 Pride in the Muslim military past and in the Muslim heritage in general, as well as a Muslim religious atmosphere in the army, which certainly exist (and in some armies very strongly), do not in any way affect this affirmation. Neither does the use of a certain traditional terminology in the Muslim modern armies.

49 At least during the crucial stage of the introduction of the westernized armies, and well beyond that. The story is, of course, different in the countries which had been dominated

What immensely facilitated Muḥammad 'Alī's task in building his modern army was the weakening, indeed the decimation, of the Mamluks prior to his arrival in Egypt, caused by their internecine wars; by their being bled white during the very recent French invasion of Egypt and by the growing difficulty in importing new Mamluks from their countries of origin, in the wake of the Russian advance towards the Caucasus.[50] After eliminating the Mamluks, the natural target for neutralization was the nomads, who would most likely be strengthened as a result of the decline of Mamluk power. In their case denomadization was the solution.[51] Only a person of Muḥammad 'Alī's caliber, resolution and cunning could start such a process which ultimately brought about the elimination of the nomads and semi-nomads as a factor of any consequence in Egypt.[52] In breaking the power of the beduins and in bringing about their almost complete disappearance, Egypt was far ahead of any other Arab country.

by European powers for long periods. But even here the local armies, built by those powers, had far less connection with the past than many other domains which came under European influence.

50 See my "Notes on the Transformation of Mamlūk Society in Egypt, etc." *JESHO*, vol. III (1960), pp. 162-3 in the note.

51 As is well-known, Muḥammad 'Alī built not only a modern army but also a modern navy. When assessing his military successes as well as his ultimate contribution to the financial bankruptcy of Egypt, the combination of the two has to be taken into account. One basic difference between these two main branches of Muḥammad 'Alī's military might should be pointed out. In building his navy he did not have to remove obstacles comparable in their formidability to the Mamluks and the beduins, and this because of the generally low status of the navy and its personnel in Islam. Manning the navy with whomsoever he pleased caused no difficulty to Muḥammad 'Alī from the very beginning. Within a very short period he succeeded in creating a navy which was superior to that of the Ottomans', in spite of the fact that the Ottomans had much greater understanding of the importance of seapower than most other Muslim states. The share of the Egyptian navy in quelling the Greek revolt was very great indeed.

52 In studying the beduins of Egypt, the fact that many of them were semi-nomads long before Muḥammad 'Alī's time should be remembered. As early as the first half of the fourteenth century Ibn Faḍl Allāh al-'Umarī stated that the *'urbān* of Egypt included a strong semi-settled element (*Ta'rīf*, Cairo, 1312/1894, p. 76). This statement is confirmed by the rich and diversified information which the medieval sources furnish about the *'urbān*, and is undoubtedly true for periods earlier than the fourteenth century. The full sedentarization of the beduins from Muḥammad 'Alī onwards was realized directly — by settlement, stimulated by giving them ownership-rights on the land — and indirectly — by way of other agricultural reforms which made the beduins face the alternative of benefiting from such reforms, or being pushed into the desert. Because of their relative paucity of pasture, the Egyptian deserts could not sustain great numbers of nomads, so that the beduins had little choice. In this context it is worthwhile noting that the entire history of the nomads of Egypt is dominated by the abrupt passage from the desert to the sown in that country, which has no real parallel in the other Arab lands. This made it imperative, from the very beginning of the Arab conquest, that the beduins who were not stationed as garrisons in the urban areas would stay mainly inside the cultivated or cultivable land. A kind of *modus vivendi* between them, the villagers and the central government (including the military society, whose members drew much of their means of

Muḥammad 'Alī chose the Egyptian *fellaḥ* to form the backbone of his new army. It was the right choice, for the *fellaḥ* was unencumbered by older military traditions, particularly that of the cult of horsemanship *(furūsiyya)* from which neither the Mamluk nor the beduin could be weaned.[53] The Egyptian army did not need to wait until it was completely transformed nor even until great strides had been taken in its transformation (including the recruitment of the *fellaḥ)* in order to demonstrate its capacity to conquer when fighting rivals of limited military capacity. Shortly after eliminating the Mamluks, Muḥammad 'Alī conquered most of the Arabian Peninsula, albeit with many losses and setbacks, due to the stubborn resistance of the highly motivated Wahhabis.[54] Such wide Egyptian conquests in Arabia had never occurred before Muḥammad 'Alī's reign. A few years later the Sudan was conquered with considerable ease, again for the first time in Egypt's history. But the really great trial of strength awaited the new Egyptian army in Syria and beyond, at a time when its build-up had already reached a very advanced stage. A host of causes made the Egyptian success in this arena possible. Of these only two will be mentioned: (1) The Mamluks, who had already outlived their purpose many generations earlier, were eliminated (1811) fifteen years before the Janissaries (1826). (2) The compact, centralized and comparatively small size of Egypt (particularly its inhabited area, most of which is narrow, and almost all of it is flat — thus easier to control) enabled Muḥammad 'Alī to build an army on new foundations during a much shorter time than the Ottomans needed for the same purpose. By means of his military machine Muḥammad 'Alī not

livelihood, riches and power from agriculture) had to be reached even under a very strong rule. Such an equilibrium was disrupted from time to time by disorders in which the beduins usually registered additional gains. At the same time, however, the proverbial richness of the Egyptian soil encouraged many of the beduins to turn to some kind of land cultivation. When Muḥammad 'Alī and his successors reversed the process of many centuries, of the ever-growing power of the *'urbān*, they found a quite substantial body of beduins, which was already on the way to sedentarization, a fact which certainly facilitated the complete denomadization of the *'urbān*. Distinctive of the history of the beduins of Egypt is that it took place mainly on the arable soil of that country.

53 As is well known Muḥammad 'Alī at first tried to base his modern army on the recruitment of Sudanese slaves, and this was one of the reasons for his conquest of the Sudan. The fact that in the period immediately preceding his reign there was a shortage of white Mamluks and they had to be supplemented by black slaves might have had a certain share in Muḥammad 'Alī's decision to recruit the Sudanese (see "Notes on the Transformation, etc.", *JESHO*, III (1960), pp. 316-317, including W.G. Browne's evidence on p. 317). Muḥammad 'Alī discarded the Sudanese because of their dying in the thousands when brought over to Egypt. His shifting to *fellaḥīn* was a turning point in the history of Egypt, in spite of the fact that he did not let them rise from the ranks.

54 What facilitated the Egyptian army's conquest of the Hijaz was that the Wahhabis were unwelcome newcomers there. One of the greatest handicaps of that army in its advance eastwards into the Wahhabi heartland was that it was dependent, to a great extent, for its means of transportation, on the local beduins.

only succeeded in conquering on this front areas never conquered by any previous Egyptian ruler, but he threatened the very existence of the Ottoman empire.

The main lesson to be learnt from Egypt's unprecedented expansion in three directions in the first half of the nineteenth century is that it demonstrates most vividly and convincingly the huge and widening gap, up to Muḥammad 'Alī's time, between Muslim Art of War and the Art of War as developed in Europe. As far as Egypt is concerned, the military feats of Muḥammad 'Alī had little chance to survive anyway, for they were too big for Egypt's resources. Once the Ottomans were given the breathing space to recover and carry out their military reforms, however inadequately, the chances of any Muslim rival trying to measure swords with them were very meager indeed. Even against superior foes "the sick man of Europe" showed amazing resilience. As late as the First World War, on the eve of his demise, the "sick man" managed to tie down for years a very substantial part of the military might of the British Empire, in Gallipoli, in Iraq, and, finally, on the Egyptian-Syro-Palestinian front.

Appendix to pp. 18-19

Pointing at the flimsiness of the links between northern and southern Iraq does not reflect sufficiently the looseness characterizing that land. Northern Iraq, for example, did not constitute a compact body. In the Muslim period it was not always ruled by a single ruler. From time to time it was split between two or more local rulers. Furthermore, Iraq was sometimes divided between two major Muslim external powers, which frequently fought each other, pushing the frontier back and forth inside that country and causing much havoc as a result. Egypt, by contrast, when it was ruled by an external power, was wholly incorporated within the boundaries of the empire of that power. The wider terms of 'Irāq al-'Arab and 'Irāq al-'Ajam are irrelevant in our context.

Appendix to pp. 20-21

In placing such special emphasis on the safety of commerce via Egypt, as compared with its counterpart via Iraq, there was no intention to belittle other factors. In a bird's eye view like the present paper one has to confine oneself to certain salient aspects. The relative tranquility of Egypt allowed agriculture (based on a very delicate system of irrigation) and industry to benefit from more or less normal conditions over quite long periods. In view of the great interdependence between the two (so much of the Egyptian industry was based on products of the land) they should be considered, to no small extent, as an entity. A systematic study of their combined contribution to the prosperity of Egypt as compared to other Islamic countries is much needed.

As far as international commerce is concerned, it should be remembered that Baghdad remained a focal point of the first magnitude of so many land routes of Islam, a fact which certainly mitigated the effects of its weaker commercial ties through the Persian gulf route. On the other hand, the unavoidable need of moving the capital of the Islamic empire from Baghdad to Samarra (as a result of the creation of the Mamluk regiment of Caliph al-Mu'taṣim), necessitated the expenditure of immense funds and was accompanied by almost half a century long struggle between the old and new capitals (including very heavy fighting). This certainly had its share in the devastation and decline (economic and otherwise) of Iraq, and the weakening of its hold on the provinces. The *de facto* independence of Egypt, which took place during the Samarra period, and its growing intervention in Syria, were greatly helped by these events (in addition to the Zanj rebellion).

THE PRE-OTTOMAN PERIOD

JERE L. BACHARACH

Palestine in the Policies of Tulunid and Ikhshidid Governors of Egypt (A.H. 254-358/868-969 A.D.)*

The concept of "relations between Egypt and Palestine" is misleading for the pre-modern era.[1] Palestine, a region whose boundaries shifted, rarely had independent (or even semi-independent) governors who set policies which had a "foreign" relations dimension. Therefore, this paper has shifted the focus to a study of the actions in Palestine by the leaders of two short-lived dynasties: the Tulunids (A.H. 254-293/868-905 A.D.) and Ikhshidids (323-358/935-969), both of whose base of power was Egypt. As will be indicated below there are a number of reasons why these two dynasties can be compared. What will become evident is that each family took a very different view toward Palestine in terms of their respective "foreign" policies. One dynasty considered Palestine only part of Greater Syria, a policy which was to be followed by the later Mamluk Sultans when they controlled Palestine (1260-1517). The second dynasty considered Palestine very important and established an approach toward the area, which was followed by their immediate successors, the Fatimids.

Both the Tulunids and Ikhshidids were founded by powerful military leaders, sons of Mamluks who were Sunni Muslims. Both Aḥmad ibn Ṭūlūn and Muḥammad ibn Ṭughj al-Ikhshīd spent part of their careers in the Abbasid imperial center at Samarra and in the area of Greater Syria before becoming rulers of Egypt. In a classical Ibn Khaldūn-type case of the disintegration of a dynasty, both Ibn Ṭūlūn and al-Ikhshīd were succeeded by less effective rulers. While both families acted as independent dynasties, they recognized the supremacy of the Sunni Abbasid Caliphate and wished to legitimize their family's rule over Egypt. A minor point of comparison is that both families governed for almost thirty-five years. A surprising observation is that, in controlling Palestine and lands to the

* I wish to thank my colleague, Dauril Alden, as well as those in the University of Washington's History Research Group — particularly Frank F. Conlon and Peter F. Sugar — for their valuable comments.

1 Cf. in this volume: Boaz Shoshan, "On the Relations between Egypt and Palestine: 1382-1517 A.D.," pp. 94-101.

north, these two dynasties incorporated territories which had not been held by rulers or governors of Egypt since the end of the Pharaonic age. But the reasons for controlling Palestine differed radically between the Tulunids and Ikhshidids. In drawing this conclusion, the severe limitations of the data available must be recognized.

Chronicles and other textual sources are limited for both eras. Within the chronicles and biographical dictionaries there are few references to developments in Palestine, and even the data for Egypt are relatively scarce. In many cases scholars can only reconstruct the chronology and must speculate on causes or motivation. Such basic questions as how an individual governor perceived his responsibilities to the Caliph or what identification he made with the territories he ruled cannot be answered from the existing sources.

There were a number of ways a governor could publicly express his claims to power. He could include, in addition to the Caliph's name, his own name in the Friday sermon (*khuṭba*), in the inscribed bands on honorific robes (*ṭirāz*), on monuments such as mosque dedication plaques, in formulae legitimizing the religious courts and on coinage (*sikka*). In theory, all of these were prerogatives of the Caliph; but as his power weakened and local governors such as the Tulunids and Ikhshidids asserted varying degrees of independence, they used these systems of public propaganda for themselves. Therefore, in addition to textual sources, material remains are used as evidence for interpreting policy. Coins, in particular, are a valuable and relatively abundant contemporary source as they were minted during most of the years both families ruled. In addition, a governor was kept informed about his coinage because of the prestige associated with minting Muslim gold (*dīnār*) and silver (*dirham*) coins. Even if a governor could not read the inscriptions, any changes in them were the result of deliberate, political decisions, not the whims of a mint master.

There is still the problem of definitions of territories. For the purposes of this study, Palestine (Filasṭīn) refers to the Umayyad-Abbasid military district (*jund*) with Ramle its capital. Unless otherwise qualified, it includes Jerusalem and Tiberias. In this text Syria is the territory around Damascus, while Aleppo is the district around that city. The lands from Gaza to the Euphrates are referred to as Greater Syria. Finally, al-Thughūr indicates the frontier zone along the Byzantine border in south-eastern Anatolia.

Tulunids

Almost every general survey of medieval Egyptian history stresses that the Tulunids were the first independent or quasi-independent Muslim dynasty governing the Nile Valley. The arrival of Aḥmad b. Ṭūlūn in Fusṭāṭ, the Abbasid capital of Egypt, on 23 Ramaḍān 254/15 September

868, is seen as a significant turning point in Muslim Egyptian history.[2] Here was a family, the Tulunids, ruling the Nile Valley and parts of Syria, whose policies appeared to coincide with the political and strategic priorities of Egypt and not those of Abbasid Iraq.[3] Historical atlases visually reinforced the same sense of a large Tulunid state by shading Egypt, Greater Syria and al-Thughūr the same color.[4] There is no evidence that these generalizations or atlases referred to anything but the territories held by the founder of the dynasty, Aḥmad b. Ṭūlūn. What he actually governed and when are more difficult to determine.

In 254/868 Aḥmad b. Ṭūlūn arrived in Fusṭāṭ, not as governor of Greater Syria and Egypt, but as the legal representative of his step-father, Bāybāk, who was in the Abbasid capital of Samarra.[5] This was not an unusual arrangement, as a number of the previous governors or apangists had individuals acting on their behalf in Fusṭāṭ.[6] In addition, Aḥmad b. Ṭūlūn's legal position was further restricted because he controlled only parts of Egypt. For example, his legal domains did not include Alexandria.[7] While Ibn Ṭūlūn was consolidating his position in Fusṭāṭ, Bāybāk, still in Iraq, was assassinated in Ramaḍān 256/June 870. The new governor Yārjūkh, also located in Samarra, married a daughter to Ibn Ṭūlūn in order to secure some influence over the *de facto* ruler of Egypt. At the same time Ibn Ṭūlūn gained authority over Alexandria and Barqa in addition to the areas of Egypt he had previously governed.[8]

The primary concerns of Ibn Ṭūlūn, during these first years in Egypt, were to consolidate his military and economic positions. While he had control over the *Dār al-'Iyār* (Bureau of Standards) and could issue coin weights with his title on them,[9] he did not have legal jurisdiction over the mint or the *ṭirāz* factories. Furthermore, he was involved in a major power struggle with the locally established family of Ibn Mudabbir, for control of the office of finances, including tax collection, a struggle which Ibn Ṭūlūn

2 "For the first time since Ptolemaic days Egypt had become a sovereign state, and for the first time since Pharaonic days it ruled Syria," from Philip Hitti, *A History of the Arabs* (London, 1958), p. 453. Michael C. Dunn, "The Struggle in 'Abbāsid Egypt" (Ph.D. dissertation, Georgetown University, 1975), p. 103.

3 Ibn Taghrī Birdī, *al-Nujūm al-Zāhira fī Mulūk Miṣr wa'l-Qāhira*, Vol. III (Cairo, 1929), p. 6. Carl Brockelman, *A History of the Islamic Peoples* (New York, 1947), pp. 138-141.

4 Marshall Hodgson, *The Venture of Islam*, Vol. I (Chicago, 1961), p. 311. Jere L. Bacharach, *A Near East Studies Handbook*, 2nd ed. (Seattle, 1976), p. 60. R. Roolvink, *Historical Atlas of the Muslim Peoples* (Amsterdam, 1957), p. 9, is much more accurate in its visual representation of Tulunid holdings.

5 al-Maqrīzī, *al-Mawā'iz wa'l-I'tibār bi-Dhikr al-Khitāt wa'l-Āthār*, Vol. I (Cairo [n.d.], reprint of Bulaq, 1853), p. 314. Ibn Sa'īd, *Kitāb al-Mughrib fī ḥula al-Maghrib* (Cairo, 1954), p. 7.

6 Dunn, *op. cit.* p. 222, for other examples.

7 al-Maqrīzī, *op. cit.* I:314. Ibn Sa'īd, *op. cit.* p. 7.

8 Ibn Sa'īd, *op. cit.* p. 11. al-Kindī, *Kitāb al-Wulāt wa-Kitāb al-Quḍāt* (Beirut, 1908), p. 216.

9 Paul Balog, *Umayyad, 'Abbāsid and Ṭūlūnid Glass Weights* (New York, 1976), p. 264.

won due to his influence at the Abbasid court of Caliph al-Mu'tamid (256/279/870-892), as well as his political activities in Fusṭāṭ.

A more critical development came in 257/871, when the Caliph called upon Aḥmad b. Ṭūlūn to raise an army to put down a revolt led by 'Īsā ibn Shaykh, governor of Palestine. Before Ibn Ṭūlūn could act, Amājūr, governor of Damascus, quelled the revolt and probably put his own appointees in office.[10] Without fighting, Aḥmad b. Ṭūlūn gained control over Egypt's finances and created an army which he could use for his own purposes, but did not control Palestine nor make any major effort to do so.

Yārjūkh, the apangist of Egypt, died in 258/872 and, according to some sources, Caliph al-Mu'tamid's son Ja'far, heir to the Caliphate, became legal governor of all the western provinces or the new apangist.[11] The political picture of Abbasid politics is further clouded by the fact that the Caliph's ambitious brother, al-Muwaffaq, controlled the eastern provinces where he was engaged in suppressing the Zanj revolt. At the same time he saw Aḥmad Ibn Ṭūlūn as a rival in the West who had to be removed.

The rivalry between Aḥmad ibn Ṭūlūn and al-Muwaffaq intensified, when the latter complained to the Caliph that the former had failed to send adequate revenues and gifts to the Abbasid capital. The Caliph was receiving private gifts from Ibn Ṭūlūn. In 263/877 al-Muwaffaq was able to raise a force to remove Ibn Ṭūlūn. It had gone no further than Raqqa before it dispersed and its leader died. These last events took place in Muḥarram 264/September 877 and shortly thereafter Amājūr, governor of Damascus, died.

It is my view that the death of Amājūr marked a major turning point in Aḥmad b. Ṭūlūn's plans. The removal of this powerful figure from the Syrian scene and the collapse of al-Muwaffaq's army permitted Ibn Ṭūlūn to move into the one area where he had a great interest, al-Thughūr or the frontier zone around Tarsus. In Sha'bān 264/April 878, after designating his son al-'Abbās as heir-apparent and naming Aḥmad b. Muḥammad al-Wāsiṭī *wazīr*, Ibn Ṭūlūn marched northwards to Ramle. There he confirmed Muḥammad b. Rāfi', an appointee of Amājūr, as governor. Moving on to Damascus, he confirmed Amājūr's son 'Alī as governor of that city. After encountering some problems in Antioch, he finally reached his goal of Tarsus.[12] Ibn Ṭūlūn made no attempt to establish his own appointees in Greater Syria, maintain military garrisons or lay legal claim to the area. He was merely marching through these lands to reach al-Thughūr. Control of Palestine was not his priority.

Unfortunately for him, his plans had to be changed. Ibn Ṭūlūn had to

10 Ibn al-Athīr, *al-Kāmil fī al-Ta'rīkh*, Vol. III (Beirut, 1965), p. 238. al-Ya'qūbī, *Ta'rīkh al-Ya'qūbī*, Vol. II (Beirut, 1960), pp. 507-508.

11 Ibn Sa'īd, *op. cit.* p. 19. al-Ya'qūbī, *op. cit.* II: 510. Oleg Grabar, *Coinage of the Tulunids* (New York, 1957), p. 30, pp. 42 ff.

12 Ibn Sa'īd, *op. cit.* pp. 115-118. Ibn al-Athīr, *op. cit.* VII:316-317. al-Kindī, *op. cit.* p. 219.

return to Egypt a year later, on receiving word from al-Wāsiṭī that his son al-'Abbās had rebelled. The details of this revolt need not concern us, but Ibn Ṭūlūn and his army returned to Fusṭāṭ in order to re-establish his own rule. I believe it was at this point that Aḥmad b. Ṭūlūn's attitude toward his legal and public position shifted. He expressed this change by the inclusion of the titles *amīr, mawlā amīr al-Mu'minīn* and his name (*ism*) on monuments, the *ṭirāz*, and coinage.

Under the Abbasids new *dīnārs* had been minted on an almost annual basis in Fusṭāṭ. (The mint name was Miṣr.) The gold was acquired from ancient mines in the eastern mountains of Upper Egypt and through trade. There were virtually no silver or copper coins minted at Egypt by the third/ninth century. It is not clear what the local population used for small-scale transactions other than barter.[13] In addition to a series of standard Quranic and pious phrases, the *dīnār*s included the name of the reigning Caliph and, occasionally, the name of the heir-apparent.

During the reign of Caliph al-Mu'tamid, the fields of the coins began to include more information. Many of those minted in the eastern regions of the Abbasid Empire inscribed with al-Mufawwaq's name, indicated his key role as the Caliph's legal representative. Those in the western regions, such as Egypt, included the previously mentioned name of al-Mu'tamid's son Ja'far.[14] From 263 A.H., his title of al-Mufawwad ilā Allāh appeared in place of "Ja'far."[15] Only in 266 A.H. did the governor of Egypt decide to add his name on the Miṣr coinage to those of the Caliph and al-Mufawwad. These issues were minted until Aḥmad b. Ṭūlūn's death in 270/882. This act must be viewed as part of an entire series of actions taken by Aḥmad b. Ṭūlūn during 265-266/877-878, expanding his legal claims and asserting his relative independence in a public manner.

The history of minting in Greater Syria is more difficult to reconstruct, because there are few pre-Tulunid coins with which the new issues can be compared. For example, the Palestine mint at Ramle had been fairly active before 218/833, following which there are virtually no coins until 277/890, when Ibn Ṭūlūn's son Khumārawayh began to mint them.[16] I assume that, in the absence of coins, Egyptian and Iraqi coinage met the monetary needs of the local Palestinian population. The political implications of Ibn Ṭūlūn not minting Filasṭīn issues will be discussed below.

Aḥmad b. Ṭūlūn's other coins were minted at Rāfiqa and Damascus. In

13 Michael Bates, "The Function of Fatimid and Ayyubid Glass Weights," *JESHO*, Vol. XXIV (1980), pp. 63-92. Paul Balog, "Fatimid Glass Jetons: Token Currency or Coin Weights," *JESHO*, Vol. XXIV (1980), pp. 93-109.

14 'Abd al-Raḥmān Fahmī, *Fajr al-Sikka al-'Arabīya* (Cairo, 1965), pp. 646-648.

15 *Ibid.*, p. 648. There is a series of coins with the mint Miṣr and the name Naḥrīr for the years 259 and 261 A.H. Naḥrīr was sent by al-Muwaffaq to spy on Aḥmad ibn Ṭūlūn. *ibid.*, pp. 121-123.

16 Samīr Shamma, *al-Nuqūd al-Islāmīya Allatī Ḍuribat fī Filasṭīn* (Jedda [n.d.]), pp. 94-95.

comparison to the number of Egyptian pieces which have survived, the two provincial mint series produced very few coins and these may, in fact, have had a more symbolic role than a monetary one. Professor Oleg Grabar has pointed out that the coins of Rāfiqa came from the easternmost area — "the Euphrates" — for which Aḥmad b. Ṭūlūn would have had responsibility. The very few Damascus coins may have been issued when Ibn Ṭūlūn gathered the *'ulamā'* in Damascus to reject al-Muwaffaq's claims to control the western regions of the Abbasid Empire; that is, Ṭūlūn-controlled lands.[17]

The last two years of Ibn Ṭūlūn's reign are marked by an intensive power struggle between the governor of Egypt and the Caliph's brother, al-Muwaffaq. In 269/882, after leaving Fusṭāṭ for Tarsus, Ibn Ṭūlūn invited the Caliph to join him, but the Abbasid was only able to reach Raqqa before he was forced to return to Iraq. Also, Lu'lu, Ibn Ṭūlūn's governor over Homs, Qinnasrīn, Aleppo and Diyār Muḍar, switched sides.[18] Al-Muwaffaq began to move against Ibn Ṭūlūn and appointed, on his own and illegally, Isḥāq b. Kundāj as governor of Ibn Ṭūlūn's lands.[19] There was also a clash in Mecca between Tulunid troops and those of al-Muwaffaq. As indicated above, Aḥmad b. Ṭūlūn called a meeting in Damascus of the *'ulamā'*, *fuqahā'* and nobles in order to reject al-Muwaffaq's claim to succession and his granting to Isḥāq b. Kundāj the governorship of Egypt and Greater Syria. Al-Muwaffaq was to be cursed from the *minbār*s of Ibn Ṭūlūn's land. Before the issue was resolved, Aḥmad b. Ṭūlūn died in Dhū'l-Qa'da 270/March 884.

A great deal of space has been devoted to Aḥmad b. Ṭūlūn's career because there is the impression in textbooks and surveys that his rule was a smooth, successful one dating from his arrival in Fusṭāṭ in 254/868. This was not the case, however; it took a number of years and the opportunities afforded by a rebellion in Palestine to consolidate his position. His external or "foreign" policy was focused on the Tarsus region (al-Thughūr) and his legal relations with the Abbasids. He made no move into Palestine until 264/877 and, even then, made no serious attempt to incorporate this territory under his direct control. Whatever benefits the control of Palestine might have brought to an Egyptian ruler, Aḥmad b. Ṭūlūn did not seize the opportunities available to him, nor did he use the medieval forms of public propaganda — in particular, coinage — as a vehicle for asserting his territorial claims to Palestine. There would be a shift in the relative role of Palestine in Egyptian policies under Ibn Ṭūlūn's son and successor, Khumārawayh (270-282/884-896).

17 Grabar, *op. cit.* p. 58.
18 Ibn al-Athīr, *op. cit.* p. 393.
19 *Ibid.*, p. 395. al-Kindī, *op. cit.* p. 226.

The Later Tulunids

Western scholars have traditionally treated Khumārawayh as a buffoon, lacking all skills except an ability to spend money.[20] A reappraisal of his reign is warranted, and the recent *Encyclopaedia of Islam* article by Ubrich Haarmann lays the appropriate groundwork.[21] The present study is concerned only with the role of Palestine in Khumārawayh's policies and career.

Khumārawayh's reign did not commence under auspicious conditions. His brother and preceding Tulunid heir-designate, al-'Abbās, had been murdered under mysterious circumstances. Al-Muwaffaq, who had begun negotiations with Aḥmad b. Ṭūlūn, no longer felt restrained and organized an Abbasid army to invade Tulunid lands. This army included Isḥāq b. Kundāj, al-Muwaffaq's appointee as governor of Egypt and Syria; Aḥmad b. al-Muwaffaq [the future Caliph al-Mu'taḍid (279-289/892-902)] and even some former Tulunid governors who felt the future lay with the Iraqi rulers. The two opposing armies met in southern Palestine at a site called al-Ṭawāḥīn (The Mills) in Shawwāl 271/February-March 885. Both Khumārawayh and al-Muwaffaq fled from the battle, but the Tulunid forces won and pressed their advantage. Khumārawayh was able to recover from his panic and embarrassment and established a respectable military record after this date.

The military campaigns of Khumārawayh in the Euphrates region and his successes in Central Syria led to a peace agreement, in Rajab 272/December 886, between the Tulunids and the factions running the Abbasid court. Khumārawayh and his family were granted control over Egypt and Greater Syria (al-Shāmāt) for thirty years. In exchange, al-Muwaffaq was no longer cursed in the Friday sermon (*khuṭba*) in Tulunid lands. An annual tribute was established, but there is no record from this time indicating how much Khumārawayh had to pay.[22]

Khumārawayh still faced problems, however, in the Syrian regions and even along the Abbasid frontier. After his defeat of another rebel in 275/888, a more successful policy for consolidating Tulunid control over Syrian territories emerged. For example, Rāfiqa which had changed hands a number of times from 270/884 was held continuously by the Tulunids from 275/888 into 279/892. The governor of Tarsus, Yāzamān, who had recognized the Abbasids since 269/883, wrote to Khumārawayh in Jumādā II 277/October 890, recognizing Tulunid overlordship.[23]

Finally, in Rabī' I 280/June 893, the new Caliph, al-Mu'taḍid, and

20 Stanley Lane-Poole, *A History of Egypt in the Middle Ages* (London, 1925), pp. 7-75.
21 U. Haarman, "Khumārawayh," *E.I.*², Vol. V, pp. 49-50.
22 al-Kindī, *op. cit.* p. 239. al-Maqrīzī, *op. cit.* I:321.
23 al-Kindī, *op. cit.* p. 239.

Khumārawayh reached an agreement confirming the earlier arrangement, with slight modifications. Khumārawayh's territory was to extend from the Euphrates to Barqa in North Africa, implying the return of Rāfiqa on the east bank to Abbasid hands. Khumārawayh was to have control over the prayer, *kharāj* taxes and *qāḍī* courts in his lands, in return for which the Tulunids would send an annual tribute of 200,000 *dīnārs* and remit 300,000 for each year it had not been paid.[24] Khumārawayh did not have control over the *ṭirāz* factories of Fusṭāṭ and Alexandria, but he did control the mints.

Khumārawayh introduced a major change in Tulunid minting practices. Virtually every *jund* in Greater Syria had an active mint; that is, coins were issued from Ramle (*filasṭīn*), Damascus, Homs, Aleppo and Antioch.[25] The inscriptions are not particularly illuminating as they include the name of the reigning Caliph (in 279 A.H. there is a series for al-Mu'tamid and then al-Mu'taḍid, both of whom ruled that year), the Tulunid governor and, until 279 A.H., the Abbasid heir-apparent. Compared to the number of coins known from Miṣr, the production of all these Syrian mints was low. Furthermore, the weights of the Greater Syrian *dīnārs* are lower than those of their Egyptian counterparts. Unfortunately, specific gravity tests have not been run on non-Egyptian Tulunid *dīnārs*, but the purity of the non-Miṣr issue probably dropped as much as, if not more, than did those of the Fusṭāṭ gold coins.[26]

The numismatic data permit us to postulate that Khumārawayh asserted a greater degree of control over his Syrian provinces than did his father. Moreover, the coinage may have been issued to demonstrate the administrative concerns of Khumārawayh and not any shift in economic developments or monetary policy. Palestine was only one of a number of *junūd* which Khumārawayh oversaw, and there is no evidence that it was a high priority for him. Thus, the mint activities only demonstrated that the earlier administrative lines for Greater Syria were being reaffirmed.

The politico-military history of the Tulunids, after the murder of Khumārawayh in Dhū'l-Qa'da 282/January 896 in Damascus, is a depressing record of continual power struggles. Neither medieval nor modern authors devote much space to the nine-month reign of Jaysh (282-283/896-897), his brother Hārūn (283-292/896-905) or their uncle, Shaybān (292/905), whose governate lasted two weeks before collapsing before the Abbasid army under Muḥammad ibn Sulaymān. The Qarmatian attacks in Greater Syria during the years 289-291/902-904 received more attention. Very little is recorded of the history of Palestine for these years.

24 al-Kindī, *op. cit.* p. 240. al-Maqrīzī, *op. cit.* I:321.

25 Grabar, *op. cit.* pp. 65, 71-78.

26 Andrew S. Ehrenkreutz, "Monetary History of the Near East in the Middle Ages," *JESHO*, Vol. II (1959), p. 159.

When, in 283/896, Hārūn marched from Syria to seize Fusṭāṭ from his brother, he placed Ṭughj b. Juff in charge of Damascus.[27] Ṭughj's position was reconfirmed later that year when Hārūn sent two officials from Fusṭāṭ to determine the income from Syria.[28] It appears that Ṭughj was able to consolidate his position in Damascus and become the most powerful lieutenant of the later Tulunids. Another sign of the growing weakness of the Tulunid dynasty was Hārūn's agreement with the Caliph in 286/899, by which Hārūn retained control over Egypt and Syria (al-Shām), but gave up the districts of Qinnasrīn and al-'Awāṣim. Hārūn also agreed to pay 400,000 *dīnār*s annually.

The numismatic data for this last decade of Tulunid rule are of limited value. Miṣr was the most active mint, but *dīnār*s were also produced in Damascus and Palestine. There are also issues in gold for the year 285 A.H. from Homs and Aleppo. As during the reign of Khumārawayh, the coinage indicates a recognition of the old *jund* zones, but without any major expansion of the economic or monetary role of the coinage. In terms of military developments, Palestine was not of primary importance to the last Tulunids, even when the Abbasid armies moved toward Egypt in 291/904.

When Aḥmad ibn Ṭūlūn decided to campaign outside the Nile Valley, he set out to control all of Greater Syria. His armies even crossed the Euphrates and he himself put a high priority on the Byzantine frontier (al-Thughūr region). One would have to return to the Pharaonic New Kingdom to find a ruler of Egypt whose armies held such extensive territories in Greater Syria. But Aḥmad ibn Ṭūlūn was a Muslim ruler concerned about the legality of his position and his relations with the Abbasids. He was fortunate that his chief rival, al-Muwaffaq, needed the main Abbasid forces to fight in southern Iraq against the Zanj.

In short, Palestine played a very minor role in the "foreign" policy of Aḥmad ibn Ṭūlūn. His failure to expand the output of Filasṭīn coinage symbolizes his attitude. Even the expansion of Acre as a naval port was not done to enhance the political, military or economic status of Palestine. The naval base was a link in the communication system with Ibn Ṭūlūn's more northern territories, particularly al-Thughūr.

Khumārawayh raised the position of Palestine relative to his father's by re-establishing the mint in Ramle after a lapse of half a century. Palestine, however, was not the only mint opened, and there is no evidence that it was the most important. No other policy followed by Khumārawayh indicated that Palestine was of primary importance to the military or economic needs of the ruler of the Nile Valley. Hārūn followed his father's policies but, either by choice or due to military weakness, permitted his governor in Damascus to become the most powerful figure in that region. Ṭughj, the

27 Ibn Taghrī Birdī, *op. cit.* III:89.
28 *Ibid.*, III:101.

governor, and his family, having lived in Damascus, would have a different perspective on the importance of Central Syria and Palestine. Ṭughj's son Muḥammad was the founder of the Ikhshidid dynasty.

Ikhshidids (323-358/935-969)

On 23 Ramaḍān 323/26 August 935, Muḥammad ibn Ṭughj ibn Juff, the future al-Ikhshīd, entered Fusṭāṭ and set about establishing a dynastic rule: that of the Ikhshidids, which lasted until 358/969. Prior to governing Egypt, al-Ikhshīd had had extensive governmental experience in Syria and briefly in Egypt.[29] He began as a tax supervisor in Syria, went on to become a court official in Fusṭāṭ and, by 306/918, was governor of Amman and involved in protecting the caravan route. By 316/928, al-Ikhshīd had become governor of Palestine and, in 319/931, his career advanced further as he became governor of Damascus. From there he moved on to Egypt as the legal representative of the Caliph al-Rāḍī (322-329/934-940).

Thus, Muḥammad ibn Ṭughj al-Ikhshīd (born in 268/882) had close ties with Greater Syria. He had lived in the area when his father had served the Tulunids and had extensive experience himself in governing in the area. If his "foreign" policy as a ruler of Egypt was to have a strong "Palestinian" component, it was because he understood the regional politics of Palestine and Central Syria. The idea of Palestine as a gateway to Egypt and, thus, an area of prime importance to "Egyptian" rulers was a familiar concept. An unusual military factor al-Ikhshīd faced was that Egypt was threatened by a military force by land from the West: that of the Fatimids, but al-Ikhshīd had a previous experience to draw upon even in this case. He had accompanied the Abbasid forces under Mu'nis in 306/918 to Egypt to prevent a Fatimid military conquest, and one of his earliest responsibilities as governor was to stop a Fatimid invasion in late 324/November 936, which he accomplished.

Although al-Ikhshīd governed Egypt by authority from the Caliph after 323/935, the critical factor in his success was the ability of his army to conquer and control the land. The struggle was a complex one, as it involved subduing numerous factions within Egypt, as well as dealing with the previously mentioned Fatimid invasion from North Africa. After Ikhshidid troops met and defeated the Fatimid army at Alexandria, al-Ikhshīd's rule of Egypt was one of almost unbroken tranquility. Thus, al-Ikhshīd was militarily and politically secure enough to issue coins with his own name on them from at least 324/936 onward.

As demonstrated elsewhere,[30] al-Ikhshīd had *dirhams* issued in his own

29 Jere L. Bacharach, "The Career of Muḥammad b. Ṭughj al-Ikhshīd," *Speculum*, Vol. L (1975), pp. 586-612.

30 Jere L. Bacharach and Samir Shamma, "Les premiers dirhams ikhshidides," *Revue numismatique*, 6e serié, Vol. XVII (1975), pp. 139-144.

name at the mint of Miṣr for 324 A.H.; but then worked out an arrangement with Caliph al-Rāḍī, whereby he dropped his name from the coinage in return for the Caliph's continuing legitimization of al-Ikhshīd's governorship of Egypt. Hence, the coinage issued by Muḥammad b. Ṭughj al-Ikhshīd was "Ikhshidid" in the sense that he controlled the mints, set the monetary policies, and decreed what was inscribed on the coins.

In 329/940, al-Muttaqī (329-333/940-944) became Caliph, and the Ikhshidid coinage included the new Caliph's name in place of al-Rāḍī's. By 330/941, Muḥammad b. Ṭughj had added his own *laqab* ("al-Ikhshīd") to his issues. The decision to inscribe the title "al-Ikhshīd" on the coinage was an imitation of the policies the Hamdanids were following.[31] Additional pieces of evidence for the impact of the Hamdanids on Ikhshidid numismatics will be given below.

Another dimension of Ikhshidid monetary policy was the further development of Palestine as a major mint. Palestine had been an active center for the production of *dīnār*s in the years after the fall of the Tulunids, but al-Ikhshīd expanded the production to include *dirham*s. He opened the mint at Tiberias where *dirham*s were produced on an irregular basis. I would suggest that in the post-Tulunid era silver coinage was the most common coinage produced in Greater Syria, and that al-Ikhshīd's policies linked Palestine monetarily to both the gold-dominated coinage of Egypt and the silver-dominated zone of Central and Northern Syria. Therefore, the economic importance of Palestine was greater for the Ikhshidids than the Tulunids.

However, certain minting policies of al-Ikhshīd may have been related to his military activities — in particular, his campaigns in Palestine and Central Syria. The largest number of Palestinian Ikhshidid *dīnār*s date from the mid-330s/940s, and are possibly connected to the Ikhshidid-Hamdanid wars. Damascus and Homs issues — and they are only *dirham*s — coincide with al-Ikhshid's military activities in Central Syria. The production of silver coins in Tiberias does not follow a pattern which can be related to particular political or military events.

There were no significant differences between the inscriptions on the Egyptian and Palestinian coins, but the Palestinian *dīnār*s tended to show a wider range of weights and less adherence to a norm than those from Egypt. Modern science permits scholars to establish the degree of purity of silver and gold coins without damaging them as historical artifacts. One method for determining the percentage of silver is by neutron activation analysis.[32]

31 Jere L. Bacharach, "Al-Ikhshīd, the Ḥamdānids and the Caliphate," *JAOS*, Vol. 94 (1974), pp. 360-363.

32 The data on Ikhshidid and Hamdanid *dirhams* were produced for the University of Michigan Ph.D. of Ramzi J. Bikhazi by Prof. Adon A. Gordus. Ramzi Jibran Bikhazi, "The Hamdanid Dynasty of Mesopotamia and North Syria . . . " (Ph.D. dissertation, University of Michigan, 1981), I:96-118.

Ikhshidid *dirhams* averaged about 90 percent silver and were not significantly different from other silver coins used in market transactions.

The quality of the *dīnārs* minted in both Egypt and Palestine declined during the early years of al-Ikhshīd's governate. Those which were minted during Muḥammad b. Ṭughj's last years and which included his *laqab* ("al-Ikhshīd") on them were of much higher quality. There is evidence that medieval writers knew that the gold issues of Egypt and Palestine were being debased. Under the heading of the year 331 A.H., the anonymous author of the *Kitāb al-'Uyūn wa'l-Ḥadā'iq fī Akhbār al-Ḥaqā'iq* wrote:

> In the year 331 letters reached Egypt concerning the reform of the coinage. The Barīdī Emirs in Iraq had corrupted it. Al-Muttaqī *dīnārs* were struck in Egypt and obliterated ones in Palestine. Inscriptions could not be made on the Palestine *dinars* because they were so debased. Al-Ikhshīd ordered the striking of Ikhshidid *dīnārs* and their fineness was to be like that of the Hamdanid issues. He seized all who worked in the mint who had profited (*mirfaq*) and the coinage improved.[33]

There is another piece of evidence which indicates that contemporaries knew that the early Ikhshidid pieces minted, with only the name of a Caliph on them, were not of the highest quality. In 363/973, after the Fatimids had consolidated their hold on Egypt, Ya'qūb b. Killis and 'Asluj were placed in charge of the *kharāj*. They refused to accept any *dīnārs* except those of al-Mu'izz. The chroniclers specifically mention the fate of the al-Rāḍī and "white" *dīnārs* of Egypt.[34] The latter was probably a *dīnār* of low gold content and, therefore, a pale color. The former were issues with a gold purity of less than 90 percent. It is also interesting to note that the Fatimid decree did not mention issues with al-Ikhshīd's name or that of his heirs on them, as these *dīnārs* had a fineness very close to that of the Fatimid *dīnārs*.

The purpose of this digression is to demonstrate the important role that monetary developments played in al-Ikhshīd's policies, the position of Filasṭīn as an active mint, and the direct impact that fiscal developments in Hamdanid lands had on Egypt and Palestine. However, the more obvious way to illustrate the centrality of Palestine for al-Ikhshīd is to survey his military activities in that region. These have been discussed elsewhere by others and myself, but a summary of them is appropriate here.[35]

Once established in Fusṭāṭ, al-Ikhshīd appointed his brother governor of Damascus, where his primary responsibility was to defend Ikhshidid lands against military incursions from the East. Muḥammad ibn Ṭughj rarely

33 Anonymous, *Kitāb al-'Uyūn wa'l-Ḥadā'iq fī Akhbār al-Ḥaqā'iq* (Damascus, 1973), IV: 393.

34 al-Maqrīzī, *op. cit.* II:5-6.

35 Bacharach, *Speculum. op. cit.* Bikhazi, *op. cit.* pp. 511-531, 605-621.

marched from Egypt unless Palestine was threatened or invaded. For example, in 327/939, al-Ikhshīd worked out a settlement with the former Iraqi military leader, Ibn Rā'iq, granting him the lands from Tiberias northwards. Al-Ikhshīd kept Central Palestine, with Ramle its administrative center, as his frontier zone. In 325/939, Ibn Rā'iq moved against Ramle and a series of battles took place in which the Ikhshidids lost, but eventually the district around Ramle was established again as Muḥammad ibn Ṭughj's northern boundary.

The governor of Egypt led two minor campaigns into Palestine and Central Syria in the early 330s/940s, but his most important trip took him to Raqqa on the Euphrates where, in Muḥarram 333/September 944, he met Caliph al-Muttaqī and asked him to join the Ikhshidids in Egypt. The Caliph refused, but an agreement was worked out whereby Muḥammad ibn Ṭughj al-Ikhshīd and his descendants were made governors of Egypt (and Syria and the Hijaz) for thirty years. In an exact parallel to the Tulunid case, the Abbasid Caliphate had been willing to grant to a governor and his heirs temporary but legal control over Egypt and Syria.

The final example of the importance of Palestine for al-Ikhshīd is seen in his response to or fear of the growing power of the Hamdanid, Sayf al-Dawla. Al-Ikhshīd raised an army under his two best generals, Kāfūr and Fātik, but they were defeated by the Hamdanids and Sayf al-Dawla took Damascus in Ramaḍān 333/April 945. Al-Ikhshīd offered favorable peace terms which were refused by the Hamdanids. Then the Egyptian governor undermined Sayf al-Dawla's support among his own troops, permitting an Egyptian military victory. But Sayf al-Dawla was still offered generous peace terms, which he finally accepted in Rabīʿ I 334/October 945. Al-Ikhshīd retained complete control over Egypt and Palestine, but agreed to pay an annual fee for holding Damascus. Nothing demonstrates better how important Palestine was in the thinking of al-Ikhshīd than this treaty which, again, was offered by the victor!

Later Ikhshidids

Muḥammad ibn Ṭughj al-Ikhshīd died in Dhū'l-Ḥijja 334/August 946 and was succeeded by his son, Anūjūr (334-394/946-960). The key figure in the Ikhshidid state was not a descendant of Ṭughj, but the African eunuch, Kāfūr (d. 357/968). It is not clear from the textual sources when Kāfūr ruled Ikhshidid lands. Coins are of greater help. The first letter of Kāfūr's name, the Arabic *k*, appears on Ikhshidid issues from 347/957. This can be interpreted as a public symbol of the power he had held behind the scenes from the death of al-Ikhshīd. However, Kāfūr's first job was securing the succession of Anūjūr in Fusṭāṭ.

In mid-335/August 946, Sayf al-Dawla occupied Damascus, probably taking advantage of troubles in Ikhshidid lands. This was in violation of the earlier Hamdanid-Ikhshidid agreement. Anūjūr and Kāfūr, the *de jure* and *de facto* rulers of Ikhshidid Egypt, respectively, raised an army and marched into Palestine. Sayf el-Dawla moved south, but was beaten severely in a battle in Palestine. The Hamdanids tried to raise a new force, but were pushed back and, by the end of 335/June 947, the Ikhshidids occupied Aleppo. But Northern Syria was not an Ikhshidid priority, even for Kāfūr and Anūjūr. The Ikhshidids retreated and Sayf al-Dawla retook Aleppo, which became his capital. Peace negotiations followed. The old agreement was renewed, save for the ending of an Ikhshidid tribute for Damascus.

The northern border of Ikhshidid lands became relatively quiet. Military events in Palestine and Central Syria became important again only at the end of the dynasty. This not to say that Palestine was not important; rather, it is to argue that the border zone was relatively secure. Coin production in Palestine continued on a high level and, in fact, more *dīnārs* exist from the Filasṭīn mint than they do from the Miṣr one for the post-345/956 years. *Dirhams* were also struck in Ramle and it was the most active mint for the production of Ikhshidid silver issues.

The last time Palestine played a critical role in Ikhshidid history was at the very end of the dynasty. After the death of Kāfūr, Aḥmad b. 'Alī b. Ṭughj (357-358/968-969) was made nominal head of the family while the real power rested with his cousin, al-Ḥusayn b. 'Ubaydallāh. The latter served as governor of Palestine. In late 357/November 968 he had to face a military threat from the Qarmatians. Defeated, al-Ḥusayn fled to Fusṭāṭ, where he regrouped his troops. In the meantime, the Qarmatians left Palestine. By Rajab 358/June 969, al-Ḥusayn had retaken Ramle and Damascus, but a new Qarmatian force defeated him. Fortune did not smile on the Ikhshidids, as Egypt had just fallen to the Fatimid armies of Jawhar. This dynasty established itself over the Nile Valley and pressed its politico-military claims in Palestine.

The Ikhshidids followed a consistent policy toward Palestine from the time of Muḥammad ibn Ṭughj's success at establishing himself as governor of Egypt. Based upon his earlier career, he recognized the vulnerability of the Nile Valley to invasion from greater Syria and beyond. Therefore, Palestine — particularly the territories south of Tiberias — became of critical importance to him. Whenever this area was threatened, he would fight. The territories through Damascus served as a buffer zone with which al-Ikhshīd was willing to negotiate, while no serious effort was made to secure control over lands further north, such as Aleppo.

The monetary policies of al-Ikhshīd and his descendants reflected the same priorities as those of his military campaigns. Along with the mint of Miṣr, Filasṭīn played the major monetary role in Ikhshīdid economic policies. The production of *dīnārs* in Palestine and at no other mint in Greater Syria lent even greater prestige to the area of Ramle. Thus, both material and textual evidence demonstrate the importance of Palestine for the Ikhshidids.

Conclusion

The contrast between the significance of Palestine for the Tulunids and the Ikhshidids is obvious. Despite the parallels between the two dynasties in other areas, they did not consider Palestine to have the same priority in their military, political, monetary and economic policies. Aḥmad ibn Ṭūlūn considered al-Thughūr and the Euphrates his territorial boundaries, while his descendants reduced them only under Abbasid pressure. Muḥammad ibn Ṭughj considered Palestine the heart of his Syrian holdings. He and his heirs often governed Damascus and sometimes Aleppo, but these were secondary areas of control compared to Palestine. Perhaps Ibn Ṭūlūn's education in Tarsus, al-Thughūr, and al-Ikhshīd's administrative experience in Greater Syria explain their differences. We will never know why they had their particular goals in Syria but, as a result, Palestine played a very different role in the "foreign" relations of these two Nile Valley-based dynasties.

The Fatimids who succeeded the Ikhshidids may have sought to control all of Greater Syria, but their failures in Northern Syria led them to adopt policies for Palestine similar to those of al-Ikhshīd. The double onslaught of Crusaders and Turks forced the Fatimids back to Egypt. After the Mamluk victory over Il-Khanid's forces in 658/1260, these rulers of Egypt controlled all of Greater Syria. The Mamluks, and not the Ikhshidids, are the best example of a Muslim Egyptian "foreign" policy toward Palestine which parallels that of the Tulunids. But the cases of succeeding Muslim dynasties, whose actions parallel those of the Tulunids and the Ikhshidids, obscure the significance of these dynasties breaking with Egypt's past. They were the first rulers of Egypt since the days of the Pharaohs, who effectively controlled Palestine and other lands in Greater Syria.

ANDREW S. EHRENKREUTZ

The Fatimids in Palestine — the Unwitting Promoters of the Crusades

The nature of this presentation may best be introduced by a reference to the relations between the Byzantines and the Crusaders. As it is well known, in A.D. 1204, the allied forces of the Venetians and the Crusaders sacked Constantinople, inflicting a blow from which the Greek Empire was never to recover. This catastrophe came in the wake of a series of incidents and explosive frictions between the Byzantines and the Crusaders ever since their first contacts on Greek territory. Paradoxically enough, this arrival of the first hosts of the armed "pelegrini Christi" i.e., of the First Crusade, in the waning years of the eleventh century, was to a large extent brought about by the efforts of Byzantine diplomacy seeking military assistance against the Saljuqid foe in Asia Minor.

In a similar way, one can easily establish a connection between the operations of the Crusaders in Syria and the downfall of the Fatimid Caliphate (A.D. 909-1171). What I propose to demonstrate is that the Fatimids themselves were, to a large extent, responsible for generating and tolerating certain specific social and economic trends in Palestine and Egypt, trends that facilitated — and even virtually invited — West European intervention in the form of a Crusade.

Obviously, when in the late spring of 1099 the Crusaders penetrated Palestine — a sensitive area in assuring Egypt's external security — the conflict between the forces of Western Christendom and the Ismā'īlī Fatimid establishment became inevitable. It must be stressed, however, that during most of the eleventh century, Fatimid policy towards the world of Christendom was far from actively antagonistic. Except for the aberrant behavior of Caliph al-Ḥākim (A.D. 996-1021), the Ismā'īlī Caliphate pursued a policy of coexistence with the Greek Empire and maintained a businesslike policy toward the ever-growing numbers of European merchants and pilgrims converging on the Syro-Egyptian coast to visit the Holy Land.

Had the confrontation between the West European invaders and the Fatimids been limited to the issue of the domination over the Holy Land, or to an ideological showdown between the forces of Christendom and of Islam, then the demise of the Fatimids would have merely constituted a transient episode in Syrian-Egyptian history. After all, the downfall of the Fatimids was neither the first nor the last dynastic change in Medieval Egypt. And, as for the Crusader challenge to Muslim domination over the Holy Land, eighty-eight years after its inception the Latin Kingdom of Jerusalem barely survived the onslaught of Ṣalāḥ al-Dīn's armies only to be totally eliminated from the Near Eastern mainland by the end of the thirteenth century by the systematic offensives of the Mamluk Sultans. It is because of the relatively localized nature of military activities and because of the ultimate military triumph of Islam that Muslim chroniclers, unlike their West European counterparts, viewed the subject of the Crusades in a less emotional and glorified perspective, regarding it as one of many episodes in the long story of military and dynastic rivalries involving Palestine.

In my opinion, the direct military confrontation between West European Christians and the Muslims in Egypt and Syria constituted but a spectacular aspect of the more profound conflict which both preceded and transcended the frame of the Crusades and which produced decisive and lasting effects in the relations between Western Europe and the Near East. In this context, Fatimid policy towards the Christians of Europe and towards their presence in Palestine prior to the launching of the First Crusade deserves an interpretational discussion.

★ ★ ★

The rise of the Fatimid Caliphate in the tenth century A.D. coincided with the beginnings of certain new trends in Western Europe, which ultimately contributed to the launching of the First Crusade and the establishment of the Latin Kingdom of Jerusalem. The Fatimid Caliphate was founded in A.D. 909 in North Africa; in A.D. 969 it took over Egypt and by the end of the tenth century its dominions stretched from the coast of the Atlantic Ocean in the West to Southern Syria (including Palestine) in the East. In Western Europe, in A.D. 911, the Abbey of Cluny was founded, to initiate an era of Church reforms which culminated in the revival of the political power of the Holy See. In Germany, during the period of the Saxon Dynasty many new towns sprang up which were at once religious centers and merchant settlements.[1] During the sixty-six years from the accession of Otto the Great to the death of Otto III (A.D. 936-1002), twenty-nine new markets were created by imperial privileges.[2] Commercial demands generated by the proliferation of these markets

1 Latouche, Robert, *The Birth of Western Economy*, New York, 1961, p. 253.
2 *Ibid.*, p. 255.

stimulated expansionist activities of the nascent Italian mercantile republics. Before the end of the tenth century, Venice secured commercial privileges from the Byzantines (March, 992),[3] and the Amalfitans from the Fatimids (A.D. 978).[4] In the military sphere, in A.D. 961 the Byzantines recovered Crete, in A.D. 963 they acquired Cyprus and in A.D. 969 they captured the key North-Syrian town of Antioch. Some daring raids carried out in Southern Syria and Northern Palestine by Byzantine contingents during the rule of Emperor John Tzimiskes (A.D. 969-975) rekindled Christian hopes of retrieving the Holy City of Jerusalem from Muslim domination.

During that period Fatimid propaganda reiterated the obligations and duties of the Ismā'īlī Imāms with respect to the safety of the world of Islam, the *Dār al-Islām*.[5] However, although the duty of the Holy War (the *jihād*) figured high on the list of their ideological priorities,[6] the Fatimid leaders did not object to truce agreements with Constantinople, as in A.D. 957/58,[7] and in 967,[8] nor to diplomatic deals involving the surrender of important territory such as the island of Crete in A.D. 961.[9]

It is quite likely that such a flexible Fatimid policy toward the Byzantines was dictated by the requirements of their eastward drive aiming at the conquest of Egypt, a necessary military objective in their supreme anti-Abbasid strategy. In that pursuit they did not mind availing themselves of the naval support of the Amalfitans.[10] But following the submission of Egypt in A.D. 969, this attitude of restraint and of diplomatic flexibility in respect to the Infidels did not change. Moreover, contrary to their supreme ideological goal of supplanting the Caliphate of the Abbasids, the Fatimids adjusted their policy to conform with the traditional Egyptian "raisons d'état." These involved the establishment of internal stability, external security, and the creation of optimal social and administrative conditions to enhance agricultural, industrial and commercial activities for the people of Egypt. Conscious of the economic dividends yielded by such a "Nilocentric" policy, the Fatimids not only abandoned the implementation of a

3 Schaube, Adolf, *Handelsgeschichte der Romanischen Völker des Mittelmeergebiets bis zum Ende der Kreuzzüge*, München, 1906, p. 18.

4 Citarella, Armand O., 'Patterns in Medieval Trade: The Commerce of Amalfi before the Crusades,' *The Journal of Economic History*, 28, 1968, p. 544.

5 Vatikiotis, Panayiotis J., *The Fatimid Theory of State*, Lahore, 1957, p. 113.

6 *Ibid.*, p. 99; Sivan, Emmanuel, *L'Islam et la Croisade*, Paris, 1968, p. 12-13.

7 Stern, S. M., 'An Embassy of the Byzantine Emperor to the Fāṭimid Caliph al-Mu'izz,' *Byzantion*, 20, 1950, p. 243.

8 Dölger, Franz, *Corpus der griechischen Urkinden des Mittelalters und der neueren Zeit*, Regesten, 1, Teil, Berlin, 1924, no. 708, p. 91.

9 Hamdani, Abbas, 'A Possible Fāṭimid Background to the Battle of Manzikert,' *Ankara Üniv. D.T.C. Falkültesi Tarih Araştırmaları Dergisi*, Cilt VI., Cilt VI., Sayı 10-11 den ayrıbasım, 1968, p. 17.

10 Citarella, Armand O., *art. cit.*, p. 545.

showdown with the Abbasid Caliphate of Baghdad, but became less and less concerned about their fundamental duty to prosecute the *jihād* against those who threatened the security of the *Dār al-Islām*. Typical in this regard was their policy towards the Byzantines best defined in a formula attributed to the great Fatimid statesman and vizir, Ya'qūb ibn Killis, who advised Caliph al-'Azīz to "keep peace with the Byzantines whenever they keep peace with you."[11]

A similar attitude characterized the policies of the Fatimids in the eleventh century in spite of some portentous changes in the power relationship between Western Christendom and Islam. One could hardly expect the Fatimids to be aware of the fact that as a result of the Cluniac remedial influence, the papacy was becoming a real factor in West European politics. Nor could they necessarily be aware of the negotiations between the Byzantine Emperor Constantine X Dukas and Pope Honorius II in A.D. 1063, aiming at the liberation of the Church of the Holy Sepulcher,[12] or of the diplomatic initiatives of Pope Gregory VII in 1074, for the purpose of assisting the Byzantines against the pressure of the Saljuqids in Asia Minor.[13] But the Fatimids were certainly aware of the resurgence of the naval power of the Italians, who resorted to military force in order to enhance their commercial activities in Muslim territories. Likewise, in the Western Mediterranean the naval power of Pisa and Genoa allowed the Christians to pass to the offensive. After driving the Muslims away from Sardinia, the Pisans and Genoese carried out devastating naval raids against Bona (A.D. 1034), Palermo (A.D. 1063), and the former capital of the Fatimids, al-Mahdīya (A.D. 1087). In this last instance, besides carrying home enormous booty, the Christian invaders enforced on the vanquished Zīrīd enemy advantageous commercial concessions for the benefit of Pisan and Genoese merchants, much to the detriment of the indigenous trade community. Even more significant were the military exploits of the Norman leaders of Southern Italy, who, between A.D. 1061 and 1072, had captured all of Sicily. In subsequent years they deployed their expansionist energies in an eastern direction by capturing, in A.D. 1082, the Byzantine fortress of Durazzo on the Dalmatian coast.

By that time the Fatimids were neither interested in nor capable of defending the *Dār al-Islām*, especially against the Italian and Norman attacks in the Western Mediterranean. Besides having lost their sway over their North African provinces the Fatimid regime experienced a prolonged socio-economic crisis in Egypt (A.D. 1054-1074), aggravated by the eruption into Syria of Saljuqid and related Turcoman forces. Consequently, in the last thirty years of the eleventh century the Fatimids concentrated on

11 Ibn Khallikān, *Wafayāt al-A'yān*, Cairo, 1948, vi/31.
12 Dölgers, Franz, *op. cit.*, 2. Teil, 1925, no. 952, p. 15.
13 Setton, Kenneth M., Ed., *A History of the Crusades*, Vol. I, Philadelphia, 1958, p. 223.

protecting Egypt from Turcoman peril. It is for that reason that they dispatched diplomatic missions to the Byzantines to secure their cooperation against the common Saljuqid enemy.[14]

While the Fatimid concern about the presence of the Turcomans in Palestine was quite warranted, their lack of precautionary measures against the growing presence of Italian merchants in the Eastern Mediterranean was bound to bring about — sooner or later — developments similar to those which had already taken place in the West. Although the Fatimids were in an excellent bargaining position because of their control over the rich Egyptian deposits of alum — a mineral in great demand for the nascent Italian textile industry[15] — they nonetheless allowed European merchants to spread their commercial influence in Egypt and Syria. By the second half of the eleventh century the Amalfitans, Genoese and Pisans not only frequented Egyptian and Syrian ports but were allowed to hold annual market days and to build churches and hostels in Jerusalem.[16] "There are few Muslim theologians (*'ulamā'*) (in Jerusalem) but many arrogant Christians. . . Christians and Jews constitute a majority," complained a contemporary geographer, al-Muqaddasī (d. ca. A.D. 990).[17] Indeed, the Fatimids not only tolerated but tried to protect an ever increasing traffic of West European pilgrims to Jerusalem and to other religious sites in Palestine.[18] Obviously, they underestimated the role of these pilgrims as disseminators of divers news about the situation in the Holy Land. Upon their return home, some of them must have told tales of the wealth and the much higher living standards enjoyed by Syrian society. Others who had experienced some adversities, or even been prevented from reaching Jerusalem because of the internal struggles waged by different Saljuqid factions or by Arab Bedouins, lamented the predicament of the Holy City and the plight of Christian minorities in Syria. Some of them, as in the case of Peter the Hermit, propagandized the need of European intervention to liberate the Holy Land from Muslim domination.

This mounting development resulted from a marked difference between the European and Egyptian perception of Palestine. To the Christians, West European and Byzantine alike, the religious aura of Jerusalem meant much more than it did to the ruling regimes of Egypt. The Byzantine emotional attitude towards Jerusalem was demonstrated as early as A.D. 631, when Heraclius had restored the Holy Cross to Jerusalem upon his

14 Hamdani, Abbas, *art. cit.*, p. 29-30.

15 al-Bakrī, *Kitāb al-masālik wa'l-mamālik*, ed. de Slane, Paris, 1913, p. 341; Cahen, Claude, 'Alun avant Phocée,' *Revue d'Histoire Économique et Sociale*, 41, 1963, p. 440.

16 Schaube, Adolf, *op. cit.*, p. 36-37.

17 al-Muqaddasī, *Aḥsan at-Taqāsīm fī Ma'rifat al-Aqālīm*, trad. par André Miquel, Damas, 1963, p. 182.

18 Brundage, James A., *The Crusades, A Documentary Survey*, Milwaukee, 1962, p. 7; Goitein, S. D., *A Mediterranean Society*, Vol. II, Berkeley, 1971, p. 370.

victory over the Sasanids. In the tenth century, the warlike emperors Nicephorus Phokas and John Tzimiskes while waging their wars in Syria, invoked the ideal of the holy war of liberation of Jerusalem. The rise of religious feeling around the end of the first Christian millennium likewise reinforced this interest in the cause of the Holy Cross. In 1095, the attitude of West European Christians was best summed up by Pope Urban II who declared in his historic oration of Clermont: "Jerusalem is the navel of the world. . . This royal city, situated in the middle of the world, is now held captive by His enemies and is made a servant, by those who know not God, for the ceremonies of the heathen. It looks and hopes for freedom; it begs unceasingly that you will come to its aid. It looks for help from you. . ."[19] In contrast, to the Fatimids of Egypt Jerusalem was only one venerable city along with Mecca, Medina, Karbala, and Najaf. However, their concern for Palestine rested not on emotional or religious but on strategic grounds. Palestine constituted a buffer zone interposed between Egypt and potential invaders from Northern Syria and Mesopotamia. Likewise, Palestinian coastal towns played an important part in East Mediterranean maritime trade and the lowlands of Palestine abounded in arable farms and orchards. Jerusalem's venerable status notwithstanding, prior to the Crusades, it had not generated emotional interest among the Fatimids and their contemporaries, comparable to that prevailing in the world of Christendom. One would look in vain for the *Faḍā'il* type of texts, extolling the merits of Jerusalem, prior to the coming of the Crusaders.[20] It was Ramle, not Jerusalem, which served as Fatimid provincial capital of Palestine; and it was in Ramle, Tiberias, and Acre, not in Jerusalem, that Fatimid gold coinage of Palestine happened to be produced.[21] The issue of a *jihād* for Jerusalem's sake could hardly arise before the period of the Crusades, but even during the period of the Crusades, Muslim successors of the Fatimids bargained off the Holy City to the Christians in return for Egypt's security.[22]

In the last quarter of the eleventh century, the Fatimids hardly exercised effective authority over Palestine. After two unsuccessful expeditions (A.D. 1078/9; 1085/6) aimed at the recovery of Jerusalem, they withdrew behind the newly constructed, powerful walls of Cairo. With Fatimid prestige undermined by an internal ideological split caused by the rise and secession of the Nizārīya sect (the "Assassins"), the Ismā'īlī Caliphate appeared to abdicate its responsibility towards Palestine. Syria, including Palestine, was divided up among various Turcoman (mainly Saljuqid) petty

19 Brundage, James A., *op. cit.*, p. 19.

20 Cf. Sivan, Emmanuel, 'The Beginnings of the Faḍā'il al-Quds Literature,' *Israel Oriental Studies*, I, 1971.

21 Cf. Shammā, Samīr, *al-Nuqūd al-Islāmīya Allatī Ḍuribat Fī Filasṭīn*, 1980, p. 143-151.

22 On February 18, A.D. 1229, al-Kāmi, and in the summer of A.D. 1241 al-Sāliḥ Ayyūb.

rulers and local Arab chieftains who asserted their authority over small districts and semi-autonomous towns.[23] The whole area thus stood open to a foreign aggression. That aggression became a reality with the arrival of the "pelegrini Christi", whose determination to liberate the Holy Land proved as decisive as their weaponry in defeating separate Muslim contingents and town garrisons, and in founding the Latin Kingdom of Jerusalem in the political vacuum created by the withdrawal of the Fatimids.

An instrumental part in the rapid expansion of the Christian Kingdom along the coast of Palestine and Syria was played by Italian fleets. After having benefited from attractive trade opportunities extended to them by the Fatimids, the Italians succeeded in exploiting the striking power of the Crusaders to pursue their strategy of establishing commercial hegemony over the outlets of Near Eastern transit routes.[24] This commercial domination gained by the Italians outlived the presence of the Crusaders in Palestine and was decisive in pushing the *Dār al-Islām* along the road of lasting societal and economic decline.

And yet, during the course of the First Crusade, there was a crisis which might have resulted in total failure of that West European adventure. After several months of painful siege operations at the impregnable fortress of Antioch, the forces of the Crusaders reached the brink of exhaustion. It was at that moment, in March of 1098, that the Fatimids appeared on the scene, not as an army bringing relief to the besieged Muslim garrison but as a diplomatic mission proposing a deal to the Crusaders, involving a partition of Syria at the expense of the Saljuqid foe. The failure of the Fatimids to join in a naval or land operation to protect the *Dār al-Islām* made easier the acquisition of the key fortress by the Crusaders. And with the Christian victory at Antioch the road to Palestine lay invitingly open. The Fatimid awakening late in the summer of 1098, came too late to reverse the progress and decisive success of the West European invasion which the Fatimids had earlier unwittingly promoted.

23 Cf. Ashtor, Eliyahu, 'Republiques urbaines dans le Proche Orient à l'époque des Croisades?' *Cahiers de Civilisation Médiévale*, 18, 1975, p. 117-131.

24 For a discussion of the evolution in Italian trade expansion, see Ehrenkreutz, Andrew S., 'Strategic Implications of the Slave Trade between Genoa and Mamlūk Egypt in the Second Half of the 13th Century,' *Islamic Middle East, 700-1900: Studies in Economic and Social History*, Princeton, N.J., 1981, p. 335-345.

DONALD P. LITTLE

Relations between Jerusalem and Egypt during the Mamluk Period according to Literary and Documentary Sources

The period of Mamluk rule in Jerusalem is dark, relatively unknown. Except for one major work, *al-Uns al-Jalīl fī Ta'rīkh al-Quds wa'l-Khalīl*, by Mujīr al-Dīn al- 'Ulaymī (d. 928/1521-22),[1] there is really no literary source in Arabic which records much information on the history of the city under the Mamluks. As is well known, *al-Uns* is unrivalled as a source for the physical character of Jerusalem during the Mamluk period, and from the point of view of Mamluk interest in the city the section describing its monuments is particularly valuable, mentioning as it does no less than twenty-seven religious buildings — *madrasas*, *zāwiyas*, and *turbas* — which were built with funds provided by Mamluk Emirs.[2] Another valuable section in this respect summarizes the history of the Mamluk Sultans.[3] Here Mujīr al-Dīn focuses on those rulers who did something to benefit al-Masjid al-Aqṣā in Jerusalem or Masjid al-Khalīl in Hebron. For these sultans he gives the dates of the reigning Caliph, the date of the Sultan's death, and the good deeds that he performed during his reign for the benefit of one or the other city. Other Sultans he mentions by name only. In this section Mujīr al-Dīn gives what amounts to an outline of the reigns of the Mamluk Sultans of Egypt containing the main features of their reigns but highlighting their activities in Palestine, be they military expeditions or construction projects.

Thus, for the reign of al-Malik al-Ẓāhir Baybars, for example, Mujīr al-Dīn lists in chronological order Baybars' military exploits in Palestine and elsewhere, including the destruction of a church in Nazareth, an attack against Acre, and the conquest of Qaysariyya, Arsūf, Safed, and Jaffa. Then Mujīr al-Dīn reports on Baybars' pilgrimage to Mecca and Medina as well as a visit to Jerusalem itself in 668/1269 and trips into the surrounding countryside. Other conquests are noted, and then a list of the benefits

1 Two volumes (Amman: Maktabat al-Muḥtasib, 1973).
2 *Ibid.*, II, 33-50
3 *Ibid.*, pp. 85-100.

which the Sultan bestowed on the Muslim holy places in and around Jerusalem. These include restoration work in the Ḥaram at al-Aqṣā and al-Ṣakhra and in Hebron at the tomb of Abraham as well as the construction of a *khān* bearing his name outside Jerusalem.[4] Needless to say, the provision of data relating to the Mamluk Sultans' activities in Palestine in such a convenient form is one of the chief merits of Mujīr al-Dīn's book. From these data it can be easily determined that six of the Baḥrī Sultans — Baybars, Qalā'ūn, Kitbughā, Lājīn, al-Nāṣir Muḥammad and Sha'bān — undertook improvements to the buildings of Jerusalem and Hebron and/or for the construction of new edifices. Only one of the Baḥrī Sultans, Baybars, is mentioned as having visited Jerusalem, although several of them — Baybars, Qalāwūn, and Khalīl — are said to have waged military campaigns against the Crusaders in Palestine. The matter of royal visits raises the question of Mujīr al-Dīn's reliability as a source for Mamluk history since we know from other historians that Baybars made three visits to Jeruslem in addition to the one mentioned by Mujīr al-Dīn.[5] Two other Baḥrī Sultans are known to have visited the city without, apparently, the knowledge of Mujīr al-Dīn.[6] Among the Burjī Sultans, five — Barqūq, Barsbāy, Jaqmaq, Īnāl and Khushqadam — are singled out for their beneficence to the two holy cities, which took the form of renovations to existing structures for the most part, but also gifts of ornamental Qur'āns to the shrines and contributions to endowments.[7] Qā'itbāy is not listed among the Burjī benefactors only because his reign is treated in full in the last chapter of the book, wherein his services to Jerusalem are discussed. One of the Burjīs, Jaqmaq, is given credit for wresting holy places from the hands of Christian monks, most notably the tomb of David on Mt. Zion, and for destroying renovations which Christians had made to churches and monasteries, presumably without the permission of Muslim authorities.[8] Three Burjī Sultans, including Qā'itbāy, are mentioned as having visited Jerusalem.[9]

Even though each and every Sultan did not contribute to the welfare of the holy places, Mujīr al-Dīn gives clear evidence that the Mamluk Sultans as a group sent generous support from Egypt to Jerusalem and that this support was sustained from the beginning until the author's own day. It is also evident that Mamluk authority in Jerusalem and Hebron was exercised by an official who often, but not always, combined the functions of viceroy and supervisor of the Ḥaram. During most of the Baḥrī period the

4 *Ibid.*, pp. 86-88.
5 Rashād al-Imām, *Madīnat al-Quds fī'l-'Aṣr al-Wasīṭ, 1253-1516 m.* (Tunis: al-Dār al-Ṭunisiyya li'l-Nashr), p. 62.
6 Qalāwūn and al-Nāṣir Muḥammad. *Ibid.*, pp. 66-68.
7 *Al-Uns*, II, 94-99.
8 *Ibid.*, pp. 97-98.
9 Barqūq, Faraj and Qā'itbāy. *Ibid.*, pp. 95, 164, 314.

official in charge of Jerusalem seems to have borne only the title Nāẓir al-Ḥaramayn al-Sharīfayn, and it was not until the reign of al-Nāṣir Muḥammad that one of these officials, al-Amīr Sanjar al-Jāwlī, was also made viceroy of the two towns (Nāẓir al-Salṭana bi'l-Quds al-Sharīf wa-Balad Sayyidinā al-Khalīl).[10] But this combining of the two offices was not followed by subsequent Sultans until close to the end of the Baḥrī period, in 777/1375-76, at which time it became a practice which lasted until Faraj declared, during a visit in 808/1405, that the two functions should be separated;[11] the principle was reiterated in 843/1439-40 by Sultan Jaqmaq.[12] Nevertheless, in the reign of Barsbāy (825-41/1422-37) and frequently thereafter the same individual, invariably an Emir, served in both capacities with both titles.[13]

From the standpoint of Egyptian-Palestinean relations we would like to know under whose jurisdiction these officials fell. Were they appointed by and subject to the Sultan in Egypt or was some other authority responsible? According to Mujīr al-Dīn, "the viceroys had been appointed by the viceroys of Damascus in the early days, and this remained the practice until around 800/1397-98. Thereafter, the authority came again from the Sultan in Egypt, and he remains in command at the present time."[14] A reference in the annals of Ibn Taghri Bardī for the year 850/1446-47 indicates that the change came somewhat later. He states that during the time that his father was Viceroy of Damascus (813-15/1410-13), he, i.e. the Viceroy of Damascus, appointed the Viceroy of Jerusalem, which also implies that the Sultan made the appointment at a later, unspecified, date.[15] Al-Qalqashandī, who died in 821/1418, includes the governorship (*wilāya*) of Jerusalem among the offices subject to Damascus but states that the appointment of military officials who filled such posts was made by the Sultanate ("fa-fīhā min waẓā'if arbāb al-suyūf 'iddat waẓā'if, wa-tuwallī fīhā al-abwāb al-sulṭāniyya").[16] Al-Qalqashandī goes on to say that this office "in the past had been a small governorship (*wilāya*) filled by a soldier (*jundī*); then, in 777/1375-76, it had become established as a viceroyship (*niyāba*) filled by an Emir of forty, to which by custom supervision of the two shrines was added."[17] From all this evidence it seems safe to conclude that the principal

10 *Ibid.*, pp. 271-72.

11 *Ibid.*, p. 95.

12 *Ibid.*, p. 276.

13 For examples see *ibid.*, pp. 274-78. In addition there is a list of thirty-four persons, apparently Mamluks for the most part, who were appointed to the *niyāba*, "to some of whom was added the *naẓar*, both before and after 800, until around 840 or 850." *Ibid.*, p. 276.

14 *Ibid.*, p. 283.

15 *Al-Nujūm al-Zāhira*, ed. William Popper, VII (Berkeley: University of California Press, 1926), 146.

16 *Ṣubḥ al-A'shā* (Cairo: al-Maṭba'a al-Amīriyya, 1913-19), XII, 104.

17 *Ibid.*, p. 105.

Mamluk officer in Jerusalem was appointed by the Viceroy of Damascus throughout the Baḥrī period and into the Burjī period as late as 815; thereafter the Viceroy of Jerusalem was appointed by the Sultan. In any case, very little information is recorded about this official by Mujīr al-Dīn before the reign of Qā'itbāy, whose reign he records in great detail insofar as Jerusalem is concerned. Before that time we learn only the dates of the Viceroy's service and his building activities in the holy cities.

The remainder of *al-Uns al-Jalīl*, with the exception of the biography of Qā'itbāy that closes the book, is devoted to biographies of the *'ulamā'* who flourished in Jerusalem and Hebron from the time of Ṣalāḥ al-Dīn to Mujīr al-Dīn's own day. Under the rubric " 'ulamā' " these biographies are arranged in sections according to affiliation with a legal school, beginning with the Shāfi'īs because of their dominance in the city since the time of Ṣalāḥ al-Dīn.[18] Whereas the Shāfi'īs had been entrenched in Jerusalem and Hebron since the late twelfth century, the other schools were not given official recognition until considerably later. From Mujīr al-Dīn it is clear that only the Shāfi'īs had judges in Jerusalem from the Ayyubid conquest until 784/1382-83, when a Ḥanafī judge was installed in the city by Barqūq.[19] The Mālikīs and the Ḥanbalīs had to wait until 802/1399-1400 and 804/1401-2 respectively, when Faraj appointed members of these schools to judgeships.[20] Apparently appointment to judgeships in Jerusalem by Sultans had not been a general practice before the year 800/1398-99; previously, Mujīr al-Dīn says, the Shāfi'ī judge in Jerusalem had been appointed by the *qāḍī* of Damascus.[21] Be that as it may, there is ample evidence in the biographical notices that many of the religious figures of Jerusalem, both before and after 800, had some connection with Egypt. For example, of the twenty-three persons mentioned by Mujīr al-Dīn as having held the position of Shaykh al-Madrasa al-Ṣalāḥiyya between 677/1269 and 878/1473-74, no less than eleven are described as having spent time in Egypt for some purpose or other, either as students, like Mujīr al-Dīn himself, or as judges in Shāfi'ī courts, or both.[22] Apart from the judgeships appointed after the year 800, there is little evidence in *al-Uns* that the Mamluk Sultans made any appointments to any religious posts in Jerusalem.[23] With the reign of Qā'itbāy (872-901/1468-96), however, there is a change, as there are several references to appointments to and depositions from the judiciary and other posts.[24]

18 *Al-Uns*, II, 101.
19 *Ibid.*, pp. 119, 219.
20 *Ibid.*, p. 119.
21 *Ibid.*, p. 119.
22 *Ibid.*, pp. 107-15, 337-82.
23 An exception is Khushqadam's appointment of *Qāḍī'l-Quḍāt* Burhān al-Dīn b. Jamā'a and the latter's son, Najm al-Dīn, as *shaykhs* of al-Madrasa al-Ṣalāḥiyya. *Ibid.*, p. 116.
24 For examples see *ibid.*, pp. 288, 290-91, 292, 304.

On the basis of *al-Uns al-Jalīl* alone we would have to conclude that evidence for strong direct links between Egypt and Jerusalem is not readily forthcoming before the time of Qā'itbāy. True, individual Sultans and Emirs did take an active interest in maintaining the shrines of the holy cities and in building new religious structures there; some Sultans, moreover, including Qā'itbāy, are known to have visited Jerusalem, and Mamluk Emirs were certainly in residence there. Moreover, it is clear that there was considerable mobility between Jerusalem and Egypt on the part of the *'ulamā'* of the city. Nevertheless there is little direct evidence for judicial or administrative control of Jerusalem from the Sultanate in Egypt until around 800 when appointment to posts in Jerusalem seems to have been taken over by the Sultan from his representatives in Damascus. Why, Mujīr al-Dīn does not say. Granted, the *qāḍīs* and viceroys of Syria were themselves responsible to the Sultan of Egypt, but the fact remains that there are only scattered references in Mujīr al-Dīn to intervention from Cairo in the affairs of Jerusalem before the reign of Qā'itbāy.

Other literary sources contain only sparse data on Jerusalem under the Mamluks. Reference to fifteenth century chancery manuals indicates that Jerusalem was of little significance in the structure of the Mamluk Empire. In the *Zubdat Kashf al-Mamālik*, by Khalīl ibn Shāhīn al-Ẓāhirī (d. 973/1468), the city is discussed only as a holy city, a place of visitation, along with Mecca and Medina.[25] But in the chapter on the administrative organization of Syria, Jerusalem is not mentioned at all among the eight *mamālik* into which Syria was divided (Damascus, Kerak, Aleppo, Tripoli, Hama, Alexandretta, Safed, and Gaza).[26] In al-Qalqashandī's *Ṣubḥ al-A'shā*, the administration of Jerusalem is discussed in two short paragraphs, one of which is a summary of the other.[27] In both places al-Qalqashandī categorizes Jerusalem as a *niyāba* within the four territories under the jurisdiction of Damascus. Along with Gaza it is a viceroyship located "in the western district";[28] in this district, as we have already seen above, there are a number of military posts appointed by the Sultanate. Besides the viceroyship these posts include governorship of the citadel of Jerusalem and governorship of the city, appointments to which were formerly made by the Viceroy of Damascus, until, that is, 777/1376-77, when Jerusalem was made a viceroyship for an Emir of forty and appointments were made to these two posts by the Viceroy of Jerusalem.[29] Of the non-military officials of Jerusalem, al-Qalqashandī mentions only a Shāfi'ī *qāḍī* and a *muḥtasib* and states that both were deputies (*nā'ibāni*) of their counterparts in Damascus. In fact, he claims, "all offices in Jerusalem are

25 (Paris: al-Maṭba'a al-Jumhūriyya, 1894), pp. 16-25.

26 *Ibid.*, pp. 131-35.

27 IV, 199; XII, 104-5.

28 *Ibid.*, IV, 197.

29 *Ibid.*, p. 199.

deputies of the holders of office in Damascus" ("*wa-ka-dhālika jamī' al-waẓā'if bihā niyābāt 'an arbāb al-waẓā'if bi-Dimashq*").[30] This statement is not necessarily in conflict with Mujīr al-Dīn's claim that after 800 judges were appointed by the Sultan, since they may well have been appointed by him, but they were still subordinate to their counterparts in Damascus. It is also worth noting that al-Qalqashandī's knowledge of Jerusalem was incomplete: there are blank spaces in his text where he obviously intended to give the standard weights and measures used in the city.[31] His inability to obtain this information may well betray a certain lack of knowledge in Egypt, even in the chancery, about the affairs of Jerusalem, which may in turn reflect the lack of close ties between the capital and this provincial town.

This impression is supported by the four Mamluk chronicles of the period that I have consulted: *Ta'rīkh al-Duwal wa'l-Mulūk* by Ibn al-Furāt (d. 845/1441-42);[34] and *al-Nujūm al-Zāhira* by Ibn Taghrī Bardī (d. b. Muḥammad b. Ṣaṣrā (d. after 801/1399);[33] *Kitāb al-Sulūk* by al-Maqrīzī (d. 845/1441-42;[34] and *al-Nujūm al-Zāhira* by Ibn Taghrī Bardī (d. 874/1469-70).[35] As a further limitation I have restricted the years for which I have sought information on Jerusalem in these works to the last decade of the eighth Islamic century, 790-800/1388-98, for reasons of convenience, partly, but also for a more important reason which will emerge later. I am aware, of course, that any findings based on research so limited are subject to revision, but for the time being I can only hope that the chronicles and the years that I have chosen to survey are fairly representative.

From the point of view of time and subject matter it makes sense to begin with Muḥammad b. Ṣaṣrā, since his extant work, ostensibly a chronicle of the reign of Barqūq, was written from the point of view of a contemporary witness of events in Syria during the period 791-98/1389-1397. If Jerusalem was subject to the jurisdiction of Damascus during this period we might expect to find more references to its affairs here than in works of a more general nature written in Egypt. But the fact is that the city is mentioned only once in the long fragment of this work, namely on the occasion of a visit by the Jalāyirid Sultan Aḥmad b. Uways, who stopped there in 796/1393-94 on his way to Cairo from Baghdad via Damascus.[36] Since the

30 *Ibid.*

31 *Ibid.*

32 Three volumes. Ed. by C. Zurayk and N. Izzedin (Beirut: American University Press, 1936-42).

33 Two volumes. Edited and translated by William M. Brinner, *The Chronicle of Damascus, 1389-97* (Berkeley and Los Angeles: University of California Press, 1963).

34 Four volumes. Edited by M. M. Ziada and Sa'īd 'Āshūr (Cairo: Maṭba'at Lajnat al-Ta'līf and Maṭba'at Dār al-Kutub, 1934-73).

35 Five volumes. Edited by William Popper (Berkeley and Los Angeles: University of California Press, 1909-36).

36 *Chronicle*, II, 146; I, 195.

author's informant for this event was the Governor (*wālī*) of Jerusalem, with whom he was apparently acquainted, it seems likely that he had access to information about Jerusalem but chose not to include it within the framework of a history of the reign of Barqūq. It is also telling, I think, that even when Muḥammad b. Ṣaṣrā made a point of listing the Viceroys of Syria for the year 798/1395-96 he saw fit to name those of Damascus, Aleppo, Hama, Homs, Gaza, Tripoli, Safed, and Baalbek, but did not mention the Viceroy of Jerusalem.[37] Whether this is because the author did not know his name, or whether he did and did not think it important enough to record, is a matter for speculation. Nevertheless, its omission strengthens the feeling that Jerusalem did not loom large in the consciousness of historians outside the confines of the city.

A contemporary of Muḥammad ibn Ṣaṣrā's, Ibn al-Furāt, writing from the vantage point of Egypt and within the context of a universal history, saw fit to mention Jerusalem a number of times, twenty-two in fact, in connection with events that transpired between 790-99.[38] In many instances these citations concern persons, Mamluk Emirs usually, who took up residence in Jerusalem, either by their own decision, for pious purposes, or involuntarily, as exiles discharged from active Mamluk service.[39] From the work of David Ayalon and others, we know that Jerusalem was a favorite place of exile throughout the Mamluk period for officers whose offenses were not so heinous as to warrant banishment to a less attractive spot in the Mamluk empire.[40] Other citations refer to appointments to posts in Jeruslem; one of these gives us the name of a Viceroy not provided by Mujir al-Dīn,[41] and others refer to religious posts, such as that of *khaṭīb* of Jerusalem that turn up routinely in obituary notices that cover a person's entire career.[42] Otherwise, there are reports on extraordinary occurrences in the history of the city such as the visit of the Jalāyirid Sultan mentioned by Muḥammad b. Ṣaṣrā,[43] but also on the incidence of high prices paid for wheat in 790, a phenomenon which was observed throughout Syria that year.[44] However, the only event in the entire decade which receives more than Ibn al-Furāt's passing notice was the public denunciation of Islam and the Prophet Muḥammad by four Christian monks (in 795), which resulted, of course, in their execution.[45] In general, however, there is not much to be

37 *Ibid.*, II, 171-72; I, 224-25.
38 See the index, "al-Quds (Bayt al-Maqdis)", *Ta'rīkh*, IX, 583.
39 E. g., *ibid.*, IX, 275, 361, 399, 464.
40 "Discharges from Service, Banishments and Imprisonments in Mamlūk Society", *Israel Oriental Studies*, II (1972), 34.
41 Al-Amīr Qardam al-Ḥasanī, appointed by Barqūq in 796/1393-94; *Ta'rīkh*, IX, 381.
42 *Ibid.*, p. 466.
43 *Ibid.*, p. 403.
44 *Ibid.*, p. 25.
45 *Ibid.*, p. 351.

learned from his history about events in Jerusalem. And there is certainly no more to be found in al-Maqrīzī's *Suluk*, which for these years is based primarily on Ibn al-Furāt's history. In any case, as far as I have been able to determine al-Maqrīzī adds nothing about Jerusalem to Ibn al-Furāt's annals for the years in question. The same is true of Ibn Taghrī Bardī's *Nujūm*. This is to be expected since much, if not most, of this section of the work is derived from al-Maqrīzī's *Sulūk*.

Finally, in order to gain some idea of the quantity and quality of information about Mamluk Jerusalem that might be gained from biographical dictionaries of the era I have used Wiet's resumé of Ibn Taghrī Bardī's *al-Manhal al-Ṣāfī* to examine biographies of notables who flourished in Mamluk territory. Of the 2822 biographies comprising the *Manhal*, only fifty-seven (if Wiet's index is an accurate guide) mention Jerusalem;[46] of these fifty-seven citations, more than half (thirty-two) apply to persons who had no other connection with Jerusalem than the fact that they were sent there as exiles.[47] Twenty references concern persons who were associated at some point in their careers with the religious life of Jerusalem, either as appointed officials in the judiciary or in shrines or as scholars or ascetes.[48] Many, if not most, of these, it should be noted, spent only a limited portion of their lives in the city and served in similar capacities elsewhere in the Mamluk empire; probably, then, they were not chosen for inclusion in the dictionary solely on the basis of their service in Jerusalem. The same is true of the forty-eight individuals bearing the *nisbas* Qudsī or Maqdisī, for whom we can only assume that they may have been born in Jerusalem or lived there for a while; most of these are *'ulamā'*, either Ḥanbalī or Shāfi'ī, who flourished elsewhere in Syria or in Egypt.[49] Three references to al-Quds apply to persons who served in an administrative post in the city.[50] On the basis of this survey it would seem that as little information about Jerusalem was recorded in biographical dictionaries as in chronicles. We are left, then, with the conclusion that apart from *al-Uns al-Jalīl* very little can be learned from Mamluk histories about the life of Jerusalem other than fleeting mention (1) of administrators and religious figures whose career or reputation went beyond the confines of the city and (2) of Mamluks and other officials who were sent to the city in exile. Otherwise, there are only occasional references to events of some magnitude, such as inflation of prices, the visit of a foreign dignitary, or a

46 Index, "Jérusalem", in Gaston Wiet, *Les biographies du Manhal Safi* (Cairo: Imprimerie de l'Institut Français d'Archéologie Orientale, 1932), p. 454.

47 Nos. 363, 370, 382, 465, 527, 579, 590, 610, 618, 684, 723, 733, 751, 759, 803, 952, 972, 992, 1143, 1150, 1160, 1184, 1190, 1197, 1217, 1224, 1226, 1280, 1588, 1884, 2187, 2652.

48 Nos. 38, 150, 232, 282, 322, 434, 589, 630, 1000, 1313, 1480, 1500, 1968, 1985, 2037, 2058, 2174, 2247, 2355, 2375.

49 See index in *ibid.*, "Ḳudsī", p. 458, and "Maḳdisī", p. 460.

50 Nos. 375, 1151, 2702.

sensational incidence of blasphemy culminating in a public execution. From this it seems clear that Mamluk historians had little interest in Jerusalem and very little information about it which they saw fit to include in their writings. This may well mean that for the greater part of the Mamluk period relations between Egypt and Jerusalem did not seem to be of great importance.

That being the case, we are in a better position now to appreciate the value of Mujīr al-Dīn's *al-Uns al-Jalīl*, especially as a record of the beneficent interest of the Mamluks, both Sultans and Emirs, which was expressed primarily in the form of endowments and buildings, many of the latter of which still stand as monuments to their interest. In this concern to collect data about these buildings it is interesting to observe that Mujīr al-Dīn made use both of *waqfiyyāt* and other legal documents as well as inscriptions found on the monuments themselves. These latter, according to van Berchem, he used with considerable care, so that the data that he derived from them and incorporated in his history reflect accurate transcription and interpretation.[51] Also important in this respect is Mujīr al-Dīn's use of documents as sources for his biographies of religious personages, most notably their certifications (*isjālāt*) of legal documents.[52]

Although Mujīr al-Dīn very rarely, if ever, identifies his literary sources,he quite frequently refers to documents that he examined in connection both with buildings and persons and even complains on occasion when he was unable to find such a document.[53] From his references to documents which considerably predate his own lifetime, it is obvious that there must have been an effort to preserve legal records in Jerusalem. Indeed, van Berchem alludes to rumors of the existence of such records in the Jerusalem of his own day but states that he was unable to verify these rumors.[54] Even so, given the poor survival rate of documents of any kind anywhere in Muslim territory prior to the time of the Ottomans, the recent discovery in the Islamic Museum of al-Ḥaram al-Sharīf of a collection of approximately nine hundred documents dating from the Mamluk period is surprising to say the least and constitutes an event of considerable importance for the study of mediaeval Islamic history in general and the history of Jerusalem under the Mamluks in particular.[55]

51 *Matériaux pour un corpus inscriptionum arabicarum*. Deuxième partie, I, *Jérusalem "ville"*, p. 11.

52 *Al-Uns*, II, 119.

53 E.g., *ibid.*, I, 42, 46, 53, 118, 119, 126, 129, 130, 131, 144, 146, 151, 182, 219, 220, 221, 235, 244, 245, 260, 269, 271.

54 *Matériaux*, II, I, pp. 10-11, note 3. See also M. Clermont-Ganneaux, *Archaeological Researches in Palestine during the Years 1873-1874*, I (London: 1899), 237.
I am indebted to Dr. Michael Burgoyne of the British School of Archaeology in Jerusalem for these references.

55 See Linda S. Northrup and Amal A. Abul-Hajj, "A Collection of Mediaeval Arabic Documents in the Islamic Museum at the Ḥaram al-Sharīf", *Arabica*, XXV (1978), 283,

Except for twenty-five Persian documents, and fourteen Arabic documents which seem to be related to them, all the documents deal with transactions concluded in Mamluk Jerusalem or in the surrounding area. The majority of them have dates and were issued in the period between 793 and 797/1390-95, which is, in fact, the reason that I chose to restrict my survey of the Mamluk chronicles to the last decade of the eighth century, so as to be able to compare the documents with the chronicles as sources for this period. A significant number of the documents, I have observed, were authorized by, addressed to, or otherwise mention the name of a Shāfi'ī judge of Jerusalem who, we know from Mujīr al-Dīn, held office during the very years in which they originated. There is no doubt in my mind that these documents, consisting of court records, petitions, estate inventories, contracts, and legal depositions in the main, represent the remains of papers kept by that judge. It is also known that this same man, al-Qāḍī Sharaf al-Dīn 'Īsā b. Jamāl al-Dīn Ghānim al-Anṣārī al-Khazrajī, in addition to his post as Shāfi'ī *qāḍī* held simultaneously the positions of Shaykh Khānqā al-Ṣalāḥiyya as well as Supervisor of the Endowments of al-Māristān al-Ṣalāḥī and other institutions in Jerusalem.[56] Many of the documents which lack dates and do not mention Sharaf al-Dīn's name I believe to be accounts which were kept for him in his capacity of supervisor of *awqāf* of the *khānqā*, hospital, and other institutions. The Persian and related Arabic documents that I have mentioned concern transactions conducted, I think, in Azerbaijan and contiguous areas, in the mid-eighth century for the most part; these documents I believe were brought to Jerusalem by immigrants to the city from the east and deposited with the Shāfi'ī Court in conjunction, perhaps, with a claim or claims registered there. Moreover, there is a considerable number of Arabic documents which predate the period in which Sharaf al-Dīn could have flourished. Many of these were issued by judges who preceded him as Shāfi'ī judge of Jerusalem. Finally, there is a handful of royal decrees relating to the Ḥaram which were issued well after his death. It therefore seems to be probable that the collection as a whole constitutes the remains of a collection, perhaps even an archive, of Shāfi'ī Court records for the city of Jerusalem; if this is correct, then the presence of so many records from the office of one judge would have to be explained as an accident. For present purposes I shall focus on the documents as sources of information on relations between Egypt and Jerusalem under the Mamluks. I must stress however, that my observations at this stage of research are not intended to be definitive; while I have scanned all the documents, I have not studied all of them in equal detail and, indeed, do

and my "The Significance of the Ḥaram Documents for the Study of Mediaeval Islamic History", *Der Islam*, LVII (1980), 189-218. For detailed descriptions of the documents, see my *Catalogue of the Islamic Documents from al-Ḥaram aš-Šarīf in Jerusalem*, in press, *Bibliotheca Islamica*, Beirut.

56 Mujīr al-Dīn, *al-Uns*, II, 127, and Ḥaram documents 25 and 615.

not hope to do so until they are properly published. What I have to say, then, is meant to be tentative and suggestive of the lines further search might take.

The category of documents from the Ḥaram most directly concerned with the topic at hand is that of royal decrees issued by Mamluk Sultans. Seven such decrees which can be positively identified were issued by six Sultans: Baybars (34, dated 664/1266); al-Nāṣir Muḥammad (8, 701/1302); Sha'bān (6, 766/1364); Jaqmaq (308, 844/1441, and 304, 850/1446); Īnāl (309, 861/1457); and Khushqadam (1, 886/1481). All these decrees concern endowments for shrines and probably found their way into the records of Shāfi'ī judges who, like al-Qāḍī Sharaf al-Dīn, must have also been charged with supervising *awqāf* of various kinds. The first two of these decrees, those issued by Baybars and al-Nāṣir Muḥammad, are cast in the standard scroll format for royal Egyptian decrees made familiar by the publications of Hans Ernst[57] and Samuel Stern.[58] The remaining five are very interesting from a diplomatic point of view inasmuch as they are written in a format described by al-Qalqashandī but not recognized as such by Hans Ernst — the *murabba'a*, or square format. Irrespective of format, six and possibly all seven of the decrees concern al-Ḥaram al-Sharīf, and it is interesting that all six of the Sultans who issued these decrees are mentioned by Mujīr al-Dīn as benefactors of the holy city. The two scroll decrees are addressed to Syrian officialdom in general, including, in Baybars' decree, governors, viceroys, superintendents, supervisors, and administrative officers, and, in al-Nāṣir Muḥammad's, all these plus the *umarā'* of Syria. The former constitutes an announcement to these officials that the district (*nāḥiya*) known as al-'Awjā bi'l-Ghawr shall remain an endowment for the exclusive benefit of Jerusalem and that not one *dirham* of its income is to be spent for any other purpose. The second scroll decree, signed by al-Nāṣir Muḥammad when he was seventeen years old and had been reinstated in the Sultanate for the second time, was issued with the advice (*bi'l-ishāra*) of one of the two Mamluk Emirs said to have been the real powers behind the throne. The import of this document is that the Sultanate in Egypt was announcing to the officials of Syria that the *awqāf* established in favor of al-Ḥaramayn al-Sharīfayn were to be honored and revitalized and that specified revenues were to be directed to those responsible for these endowments without delay or hindrance. Unfortunately, it cannot be established with certainty that by "al-Ḥaramayn al-Sharīfayn" this decree has reference to Jerusalem and Hebron rather than Mecca and Medina since the

57 *Die mamlukischen Sultansurkunden des Sinai-Klosters* (Wiesbaden: Otto Harrassowitz, 1960).

58 *Fatimid Decrees* (London: Faber and Faber, 1964); "Two Ayyubid Decrees from Sinai", in *Documents from Islamic Chanceries*, ed. S. Stern (Oxford: Bruno Cassirer, 1965), pp. 9-38; and "Petitions from the Mamluk Period. . . ", *BSOAS*, XXIX (1966), 233-76.

term does refer to both.[59] While it would seem more likely, given the provenance of the documents, that the Palestinian *ḥarams* were meant, it is certainly possible that they were not, since there are documents in the collection dealing with the endowments of the two cities of Arabia. Whatever the case may be, the decree still has relevance for the relations between Egypt and Jerusalem inasmuch as it provides an example of a royal decree to be circulated amongst Syrian officialdom which found its way to Jerusalem. There is no difficulty in determining that all five of the *murabba'āt* have reference to Jerusalem. Three of them (304, 308, and 309) mention al-Masjid al-Aqṣā specifically; another mentions al-Ṣakhra al-Sharīfa (1); and the last (6), al-Ḥaram al Sharīf bi'l-Quds al-Sharīf. Unlike the scroll documents the *murabba'āt* have no addressees: they seem to be directed rather to certain *dīwāns* or ministries such as *Dīwān al-Jaysh* and *Dīwān al-Naẓar 'alā l-Juyūsh al-Manṣūra* for their endorsement and subsequent action. Like the scroll decrees the *murabba'āt* concern the disbursement of *waqf* income in favor of the holy places and their personnel, in order, that is, to insure that the revenue from such endowments would be spent for the purpose for which they were intended. As a group, then, the decrees offer striking evidence of the interest of the Mamluk Sultanate in Cairo over a period of almost two hundred years in insuring financial support for the maintenance of the shrines in Jerusalem and the activities associated with them. Accordingly, they provide impressive support to statements made by Mujīr al-Dīn in his history to the same effect.

At this point mention should be made of another group of Mamluk decrees found in Jerusalem and also referring to holy places, namely the decrees preserved at the Franciscan Monastery, which contain, for the most part, concessions granted by the Sultans to the monks for construction and maintenance projects carried out on their property.[60] The fact that they exist in such relatively large numbers in contrast to the Ḥaram decrees does not mean that the Sultans had a correspondingly greater interest in the Franciscan Monastery than in the Ḥaram but that the monks were more careful to preserve their decrees than were the Muslim officials into whose hands the Ḥaram decrees fell. Unfortunately, in the present context I am unable to give the Franciscan decrees the attention that they undoubtedly deserve for the history of Palestinian-Egyptian relations during the Mamluk period.[61]

Related to the decrees signed by Mamluk Sultans are those issued on the authority of Mamluk Emirs. Of a total of ten, four are written in the form of scroll decrees (2, 4, 12, and 214); four as *murabba'āt* (3, 5, 14, and 303); and

59 Bernard Lewis, "al-Ḥaramayn", *EI*², III, 175-76.

60 Some of these documents have been published by Noberto Rishani, *Documenti e Firmani* (Jerusalem: Franciscan Printing Press, 1931).

61 For discussion of these see Aḥmad Darrāj, *Wathā'iq Dayr Ṣahyūn bi'l-Quds al-Sharīf* (Cairo: Maktabat al-Anjlū al-Miṣriyya, 1968).

two as responses written on petitions (7 and 305). Issued within a period beginning in 776/1375 and ending with 788/1386, all of them constitute appointments to pious offices in and around the Ḥaram. Nine, in fact, are decrees of appointment for one and the same man — al-Shaykh Burhān al-Dīn Ibrāhīm al-Nāṣirī — to posts as reciter of Qur'ān and *ḥadīth* at al-Aqṣā, Qubbat al-Ṣakhra, Bāb al-Silsila, and the Madrasa and Turba known as al-Tāziyya after al-Amīr Tāz who had spent some time before 762/1361 in Jerusalem, after being released from prison in Kerak.[62] Obviously Mamluk Emirs such as those named in the decrees were responsible for managing the endowments for such offices in Jerusalem and in this capacity issued official letters of appointment with the terms, including salary, governing the positions. Burhān al-Dīn must have been an enterprising scholar who was successful in obtaining several such appointments for himself as a means of livelihood. Unfortunately, I have not been able to determine where these particular Emirs came from, whether, that is, they came from Egypt or from Syria. Nevertheless, these decrees demonstrate the involvement of the Mamluks in the religious life of the city at a level below the Sultanate and indicate their interest in keeping the religious institutions alive in accordance with the founders' wishes.

Other than these decrees issued by Mamluk Emirs only scattered documents shed any light on the activities of the Mamluks in Jerusalem, since most are records of transactions involving the common people of the city, who were, of course, civilians. However, there are some routine documents which show that individual Mamluk officers were engaged in the ordinary life of the city and in transactions with its citizens. Of the thirty-nine bills of sale found in the collection, only two involve Mamluks: no. 324 is a deed for a horse (*ikdīsh*) which our *qāḍī* Sharaf al-Dīn bought from al-Amīr Sayf al-Dīn Alṭunbughā al-Zāhirī, and no. 370, dated 712/1312, is a record of land sold in Jerusalem by al-Amīr 'Imād al-Dīn Da'ūd to a resident of the city. One proxy deed (*wakāla*, 490), dated 781/1380, shows an Emir with the rank of *muqaddam alf* in Damascus appointing the same religious functionary whose name we have already mentioned, Burhān al-Dīn al-Nāṣirī, as his agent in Jerusalem for a salary of one *dirham* per day. In a similar document (331), dated 796/1393, an Emir appoints a fellow Emir along with two civilians as executor of his estate, with his wife, absent in Cairo, as his heir. Two court documents establish the fact that Mamluk Emirs came under the jurisdiction of the courts of Jerusalem in cases involving estates, although, as we shall see later, their own estates do not seem to have been subject to the same regulations as those of civilians. In no. 356, dated 797/1395, an Emir appears in al-Qāḍī Sharaf al-Dīn's court in regard to a legacy left to him by his brother, also an Emir and a member of the

62 Ibn Ḥajar al-'Asqalānī, *al-Durar al-Kāmina*, edited by Muḥammad Sayyid Jād al-Haqq (Cairo: Dar al-Kutub al-Ḥadītha, 1967), II, 315. Cf. Mujīr al-Dīn, *al-Uns*, II, 45.

Damascus *ḥalqa*, and in no. 355, dated 795/1393, an Emir from Baalbek appears in the same court to claim a legacy left to him in the estate of a Baalbek merchant and his his wife. That Mamluks had recourse to, or were subject to, civil courts in other matters as well as is proved by a fragmentary document (29), dated 745/1344–45, which contains testimony by an Emir in Gaza regarding the murder of his sister. Still another example of Mamluk involvement in the normal processes of the city is provided by a marriage contract (47), the only one of the nine such contracts in the Ḥaram that involves a Mamluk. Dated 770/1369, this document specifies that al-Amīr Urmanjī, a member of al-Ḥalqa al-Manṣūra, shall pay his bride, who, by the way, he was marrying for the second time, a *ṣadāq* of 100 Egyptian gold *dinars*; a second document, dated 774/1373 and written on the same sheet of parchment, bestows an additional 200-*dinar ṣadāq* on her. The amount of the *ṣadāq* is probably the most interesting aspect of this document from our point of view since it is so large in comparison to the sums mentioned in the other marriage contracts involving civilians. A weaver (610) who married in 793/1391 was able to manage only 6 gold *dinars*, while a woman who married a brick-maker (*labbān*; milk dealer?) in 791/1389 (646) had to be satisfied with only 3 *dinars*. Finally, mention might be made of a *shahāda* (311), dated 745/1344, which shows a Mamluk officer availing himself of a *waqf* for the benefit of a public fountain in Hebron, the poor and sick, and his own progeny. Though no provisions were made for Jerusalem in this endowment, it is worth mentioning as a further example of the Mamluks' interest in maintaining the holy places.

In addition to documents which record the private transactions and activities of the Mamluks, there are a few which yield bits of information on their public actions and duties. Most of these concern viceroys and supervisors. There are three documents, all dated 706/1306-07, which mention al-Amīr Sayf al-Dīn Bulghāq al-Naṣirī al-Manṣūrī with the title Nāẓir Awqāf al-Ḥaramayn al-Sharīfayn bi'l-Shām al-Maḥrūs (75) or Nāẓir al-Ḥaramayn al-Sharīfayn (320 and 332). Although his name is not included in Mujīr al-Dīn's list of the *nuẓẓār* of the Palestine *ḥaramayn*, we know from al-Ṣafadīs's biographical dictionary *A'yān al-'Aṣr* that Bulghāq b. al-Ḥājj Yartamish al-Khwārazmī (d. 709/1309) did indeed serve as "Nāẓir al-Ḥaramayn, al-Quds wa-Balad Sayyidinā al-Khalīl" at "the end of his life."[63] One of the documents (332) contains the certification of a Shāfi'ī judge that Bulghāq had gone to the village of al-Ghāziya, in the district of Sidon, in order to purchase the village's olive crop. Interestingly enough, this village is identified in the document as an endowment for al-Ḥaramayn al-Sharīfayn al-Nabawī, i.e. the Arabian *ḥarams*, and, incidentally, it is the village where, according to al-Ṣafadī, Bulghāq died. A related document (320) has Bulghāq's son, also an Emir (al-Amīr 'Alam al-Dīn Sanjar b.

63 Istanbul Atıf Efendi MS 1809, fol. 131b.

'Abd Allāh al-Sayfī Bulghāq Nāẓir al-Ḥaramayn al-Sharīfayn) selling the olive crop of Bayt Ūnya, in the district of Jerusalem, to men of that village for 5000 *dirhams*. Whether this transaction and the preceding one were in any way connected with Bulghāq's duties as supervisor of endowments or were strictly private transactions cannot be determined from the documents alone. However, the third document (75) leaves no doubt that he was acting in an official capacity when he was present at a session of a court in Hebron to hear a charge of murder. The main interest of this document from our point of view is the very presence of this Mamluk official at the court, with the implication that he was involved in its proceedings. Several other documents show courts and judges acting on the instructions of Mamluk officers.

By far the most interesting of these is the record (335) of a judicial hearing prepared and signed by al-Qāḍī Sharaf al-Dīn al-Shāfi'ī in Dhū'l-Qa'da 795/October 1392. The hearing was convened in connection with charges brought by Shaykh al-Maghāriba, obviously the leader of the Maghribī community, that officials in Jerusalem had been extorting money from the Jews of the city. It is noteworthy that the *shaykh* submitted the charge not to the authorities in Jerusalem but to the Viceroy of Damascus, who, in turn, instructed al-Amīr Sayf al-Dīn Buluwwā, Viceroy and Supervisor of Jerusalem and Hebron, to look into the matter. It was apparently at Buluwwā's order that the hearing was held before the Shāfi'ī *qāḍī*. Two other court records (30 and 642) show the Shāfi'ī Court in Jerusalem responding to instructions of the Viceroy of Jerusalem. The more interesting of these (30), dated 796/1394 and signed by al-Qāḍī Sharaf al-Dīn, concerns a complicated case of assault and murder perpetrated against villagers of al-Quṣūr by villagers of Jericho. When the Quṣūrīs brought charges before the Viceroy of Jerusalem, al-Amīr Shihāb al-Dīn Yaghmūr, and requested his sanction for revenge, he replied that he could not grant this without authorization in the form of a royal decree (*marsūm sharīf*). Thereupon the Quṣūrīs betook themselves to al-Bāb al-Sharīf, which I take to be Cairo, where they did gain authorization and returned to their village. But surprisingly, another case was heard thereafter, this time before the Viceroy's son, al-Amīr Sha'bān, involving two corpses which obviously constituted the Quṣūrīs' retribution. Clearly empowered to act on his father's behalf, Sha'bān instructed the Shāfi'ī Court to send legal witnesses to investigate the attack and to draw up a court record. This document is interesting for its evidence both of the close involvement of the Mamluk viceroy with the Shāfi'ī Court of Jerusalem and of the Viceroy's refusal to act in an alarming situation without instructions from his superiors, presumably in Cairo. Here mention might be made of a document (307) which indicates the possibility of rapid communication between Cairo and the cities of Palestine. This document, dated 706(?)/1306-07(?), seems to be a report (*muṭāla'a*) prepared by an officer in Gaza in response to the request of officials in Jerusalem or elsewhere in Syria for information on the Sultan's movements in Egypt.

There is also evidence in the documents that the courts and judges of Jerusalem were at times subject to the superior courts and superior judges of Cairo. This is at any rate the implication of a court record (31), dated 797/1394, in which it is recorded that al-Qāḍī Sharaf al-Dīn secured the permission of the Shāfi'ī Grand *Qāḍī* in Egypt before he authorized the sale in Jerusalem of slaves whose claim to manumission he (Sharaf al-Dīn) disallowed in court. There is proof, too, of al-Qalqashandī's claim that the offices (*waẓā'if*) of Jerusalem had the status of deputies (*niyābāt*) to those of Damascus. This proof comes in a series of documents (833) of various dates ranging between 664/1266 and 697/1298 in which a Ḥanafī judge in Nablus and two Shāfi'ī judges in Jerusalem are identified as deputies to judges in Damascus.

There are other court records which demonstrate the interaction of the Mamluk administration of Jerusalem with the judiciary of the city, but at this point I shall turn instead to a different type of document which also bears on that relationship as well as on another aspect of relations between Egypt and Jerusalem. I refer to the approximately 450 estate inventories in the Ḥaram collection, the most numerous type of document represented.[64]

Without going into great detail it can be said that the Ḥaram inventories consist of a list of the possessions and the heirs of a person who was either terminally sick or already dead, compiled by legal witnesses with the authorization of a judge. In almost all the inventories from the Ḥaram the court was Shāfi'ī and the judge was usually Sharaf al-Dīn; with only two or three exceptions, all are dated between 793-97/1390-95, the period when he was known to have served as Shāfi'ī judge. But there are two inventories (705 and 738), dated 796/1394, which were drawn up with the authorization of the Ḥanafī *qāḍī*, and three (90, 436, and 438), dated 795 and 796, which were issued jointly by the Ḥanafī and the Shāfi'ī *qāḍīs*. The main purpose of such documents was probably to provide an official list of the property constituting a person's estate so that a distribution could be made after his death in accordance with the detailed and complex rules of the *Sharī'a*. In any case, the main value of these documents is the light they shed on the material possessions of persons present in late fourteenth-century Jerusalem and the social and economic history of the city at that time. But they also have considerable 'fringe benefits', and two of these are relevant in the present context. The first derives from the fact that the documents usually end with an enumeration of the persons who were present at the inventory. While it can be assumed that these always included the two or more witnesses who signed each document with the

64 A sample of one of these documents is being published by Hoda Lotfy, "A Specimen of the *Ḥaram* Estate Inventories from al-Quds in 1393 A.D.", *JESHO*, forthcoming.

authorization of the *qāḍī*, there is frequently mention of other individuals who observed the inventory in an official capacity. As might be expected, representatives of the *Wakīl Bayt al-Māl* (Agent of the Public Treasury) or the *Wakīl* himself were often present since the residue of an estate not exhausted by the distribution of *shar'ī* shares reverted to the Treasury. These representatives were civilians, as was the *Wakīl*. But Mamluk Emirs attended with equal frequency, sometimes in the capacity of *Shādd Bayt al-Māl* (Superintendent of the Public Treasury) and other times as *Shādd al-Mawārīth* (Superintendent of Inheritances). Emirs also attended as representatives of the Viceroy of Jerualem, in which case they were usually referred to as *ṣāḥib*, and on the occasion of at least one inventory (124), dated 795, the Viceroy himself was present. From these references it is evident that the Mamluk officials took an active supervisory interest in finances in conjunction with the courts to the extent that they themselves regularly attended what would seem to be routine enumerations of possessions. As often as not these turned out to be worn-out clothes and a few pots and pans, if the inventories can be trusted; but there were also instances in which substantial wealth was involved in the form of cash, real estate, and jewelry, and it was undoubtedly these estates that the Mamluks were eager not to miss and to keep under surveillance. Although the Mamluks of Jerusalem participated in conducting the inventories and also, at a later stage, in conducting public sales of items from estates, they were not themselves, apparently, subject to the laws which governed these inventories. In any event, in the whole collection there is only one inventory for the estate of a Mamluk (256); there are none for judicial or administrative officials. This probably indicates, unless this omission is an accident, that the estates of such persons were treated in a different manner.[65]

This raises the question as to who was subject to this procedure. If we exclude the ruling élite there are still two possibilities. For a long time I assumed that everyone who died, or who was on the verge of death, would have his assets enumerated. This I hope is the correct assumption since it allows results of greater significance that the alternative hypothesis. Recently I have come to the realization that none of the persons for whom we have an inventory bears the *nisba* al-Maqdisī or al-Qudsī; instead, all

65 The best indication that I have seen of this, even though it is late, comes in a passage in Mujīr al-Dīn, *al-Uns*, II, 325: "In the year [8]84 al-Qāḍī Abū al-Baqā' set out from Cairo for Damascus in order to make an inventory of the estate of Malik al-Umarā' Jānī Bīk Qilqīs, the Viceroy of Damascus." Although it would seem improbable that a special judge from Cairo would be designated to handle the estates of mamluks of lesser rank, this reference does make it clear that high-ranking Emirs were given special treatment toward the end of the Mamluk period. Michael W. Dols' study of the registries of *Dīwān al-Mawārīth al-Ḥashriyya* (Bureau of Escheat Estates) as sources for the mortality rate of Egypt during plague years indicates that mamluks' estates were recorded separately at an earlier period as well. *The Black Death in the Middle East* (Princeton: Princeton University Press, 1977), p. 179.

those for whom a locative *nisba* is specified bear a "foreign" *nisba* such as Dimashqī, Ḥalabiyya, Rūmī, Karakī, Nishābūrī, Maghribī, Ḥijāziyya, Ṣaltī, Bukhārī, and, of course, Miṣrī. This gave rise to the suspicion that perhaps only non-residents of Jerusalem were surveyed. Since, however, some of the persons surveyed owned houses and businesses in the city, this hypothesis is not tenable. But it also occurs to me that the enumerators may have visited only those people in Jerusalem who had, or who were thought to have had, heirs outside the city. Some degree of support for this hypothesis comes from a document (181) containing a list, presumably, of the inventories made during Dhū' l-Ḥijja with the authorization of al-Qāḍī Sharaf al-Dīn; these are designated as "*ḍabt māl al-ghuyyāb wa-gharihim*" (enumeration of the property of those [heirs] who are absent and others [who are present]). In the documents themselves the heirs are almost always specified along with an indication as to whether or not they were present in Jerusalem, and, if not, where they were located. The importance of presence in or absence from the city is further emphasized by a filing notation that was sometimes placed on the verso of the document; this notation included in addition to the person's name and the date of the inventory an abbreviated reference (*ḥ*) for *ḥāḍirīn* and (*gh*) for *ghuyyāb*. Finally, the prevalence of foreign *nisba*s permits the inference that most of those surveyed were not natives of the city but had settled there during his or her lifetime or were visiting the city at the time of death and very likely would have heirs outside Jerusalem. While it is true that a small number lack both a foreign *nisba* and absent heirs, the authorities may have had some reason to suspect the existence of absent heirs. On the other hand, further study may establish that the persons lacking a locative *nisba* were indeed natives of Jerusalem, that the predominance of inventories for non-natives is a fluke, and that inventories were made for all residents of the city of a certain class.

What do the estate inventories tell us about possible connections between Jerusalem and Egypt? The only clear-cut answer is that there was a considerable number of persons — tradesmen, artisans, housewives, and visitors — who had some form of contact with Egypt or an Egyptian. The evidence for this is rather intricate. Of the 423 Ḥaram documents containing estate inventories for the years 793-97, sixty-two contain references which establish a connection between the subject of the inventory and Egypt. These connections are of various types: (i) an Egyptian *nisba*, such as Miṣrī, al-Dimyāṭī, al-Iskandarī, etc., which indicates the possibility of Egyptian origin of the person in question; (ii) a spouse with an Egyptian *nisba*; (iii) heirs located in Egypt. These categories are not mutually exclusive, and there are four examples (148, 217, 399, 670) of persons who fit into all three. There are only three more examples of both spouses bearing Egyptian *nisba*s (277, 468, and 479), which means that only a small percentage of the persons of Egyptian extraction were married to Egyptians.

Obviously, then, most marriages involving an Egyptian were "mixed." Of these, however, at least ten (164, 236, 253, 299, 319, 444, 470, 743, 746, and 760) also mention heirs who were in Egypt at the time that the document was drawn up, including children, spouses, siblings, and more distant heirs. It is, in fact, documents of this type which fit into at least two of the categories that I regard as the best proof of the soundness of the *nisba* as an indicator of the person's birth. Is it possible to give any estimate of how large the "Egyptian" population of the city was? Nothing more than a guess is possible, since we cannot be sure that the inventories were taken for the population at large, besides the fact that we do not have all the inventories for any given year.[66] Nevertheless, it might be instructive to look at the figures for the years in which we have the greatest number of inventories, 795 and 796, for which there are 154 and 115 respectively. For 795 there are twenty-nine inventories for persons with Egyptian connections or about twelve per cent; for 796 we have eighteen "Egyptian" inventories or about sixteen per cent. Thus, on a highly speculative level, we might guess that between twelve and sixteen per cent of the total non-elite population of Jerusalem in these years had fairly close ties to Egypt, if, that is, inventories were made for the total population. If they were not, then we can only guess that these figures give a rough indication of their weight in the "foreign" population of the city. Whatever the case may be and no matter how imprecise our parameters may be, it would seem that considerable numbers of Egyptians or persons with Egyptian family contacts were living in the city toward the end of the fourteenth century if at least forty-seven persons of that nature died in the space of two years.

But I would not like to end on such a speculative note, for the whole purpose of this paper has been to show what can be known about Jerusalem-Egyptian relations under the Mamluks on the basis of literary and documentary sources with some degree of certainty. About the Mamluks themselves we know that they were there either as administrators, exiles, or visitors, that they were active in building, staffing and maintaining the holy places and other religious edifices, that they worked closely with the courts in collecting money for the public treasury and in supervising (Christian) construction, and looking into crime. What is surprising, though, is that we know so little about the Mamluk presence in the city. We have no idea, for example of how many of them were posted in the city at any time or precisely how many administrative offices they filled. From the sources that I have examined we do not even know whether there were any Mamluk troops garrisoned in the city. Although the Ḥaram documents suggest that Mamluks did avail themselves of courts and notaries in some

66 Besides, if these inventories were made in conjunction with *Dīwān al-Mawārīth al-Ḥashriyya*, it is important to remember that its records of deaths were "highly selective"; *ibid.*, p. 207.

cases, they do not seem to have been subject to some of the legal procedures which applied to the civilian population. Nor do the Mamluks loom very large in literary sources. Other than their building activities they receive very little attention from the historians of the period, including Mujīr al-Dīn. Significant in this regard is the statement with which Mujīr al-Dīn prefaces his discussion of the Mamluk *nuwwāb* and *nuẓẓār* of Jeruslem and Hebron:

> I have exhausted neither their names nor their biographies, for that would require length without benefit. This is especially true of the police magistrates (*ḥukkām al-shurṭa*) of the viceroys, and to go to the trouble of mentioning them would be of no great advantage. Instead I mention only notable *nuẓẓār* and *nuwwāb* of some repute, about whom a good or virtuous deed is known.[67]

It emerges later that by *ḥukkām al-shurṭa* Mujīr al-Dīn was referring to an official called *amīr ḥājib*. The presence of such an officer in Jerusalem, he says, "was in accordance with the custom of other towns. He used to give judgment, and matters connected with criminals and similar matters raised before police magistrates were raised before him."[68] But even this office which was filled by a Mamluk Emir was abolished in Jerusalem around 860/1455-56, Mujīr al-Dīn says, and his jurisdiction was transferred to the Viceroy.[69] Besides the Viceroy, the *shādds* of *Bayt al-Māl* and *Dīwān al-Mawārīth*, the *amīr ḥājib*, the *wālī*, the *wālī al-qal'a* and the *wālī al-madīna*, I have found references to only a few other Mamluk officials who served in Jerusalem, namely the *mutawallī al-layl* (night officer), a *dawādār* (secretary), and a *ustādār* (major-domo). There are indications that the Viceroys were reluctant, on occasion at least, to take action without authorization from Cairo, and we have seen that there were apparently means available for rapid communication with the capital. Qā'itbāy seems to have kept his *nuwwāb* and *nuẓẓār* on a short leash and did not hesitate to dismiss them or to recall them to Cairo for consultation if he thought it necessary.[70] In all probability there was a fuller contingent of Mamluk officers posted in Jerusalem than is evident from the sources, but the point is that their presence has to be inferred. Whether the dearth of information on the Mamluks of Jerusalem means that they did not play a strong role in the life of the city or whether the historians were not interested in their activities and the extant documents simply do not reflect them accurately or fully is a matter for conjecture.

Within another segment of society, that of the *'ulamā'*, we must again be

67 *Al-Uns*, p. 269.
68 *Ibid.*, p. 281.
69 *Ibid.*, pp. 281-82.
70 For examples, see *ibid.*, pp. 311, 322, 323.

satisfied with hints insofar as their relations with Egypt are concerned. Certainly there is ample indication of the mobility of the *'ulamā'* in general during the Mamluk period, and we have observed that many of the scholars covered by Mujīr al-Dīn studied or worked in Egypt at some point in their careers. This is a point which is to be covered in other papers. As far as the relationship of the judicial and religious functionaries to the state is concerned, we have seen that this was originally channelled through Damascus but that this jurisdiction was later assumed by Cairo. In *al-Uns al-Jalīl* there are examples, especially in the Burjī period, of direct intervention by the Sultan in Cairo in cases of appointment to and deposition from religious offices in Jerusalem. There is evidence, moreover, both literary and documentary, that judicial and religious offices in Jerusalem were subordinate to those of Damascus for what seems to have been a considerable part of the Mamluk dominion. In Jerusalem itself the courts worked closely with the viceroy, responding to his directives and working in tandem with his representatives in the important matter of estate settlements. On occasion the Jerusalem court would seek the authorization of Cairo before taking action in a case.

Below the level of the administrative, judicial, and intellectual élites, we find some evidence for the possibility of still another channel of communication between Egypt and Jerusalem in the form of residents of the city or visitors to it who maintained ties of kinship with their relatives in Egypt. Just how significant this channel may have been has yet to be determined.

BOAZ SHOSHAN

On The Relations between Egypt and Palestine: 1382-1517 A.D.

A merit of the conference-commissioned paper is the opportunity it presents to raise questions on a pre-determined general subject that would otherwise almost certainly be neglected. Such papers, however, also carry the risk of treating issues of secondary importance. This is exactly the problem one faces when considering relations between Egypt and Palestine during the period of the Circassian Mamluks (1382-1517 A.D.). Since the Circassian regime controlled both Egypt and Palestine (as well as Syria), some sort of relationship must have existed between these two regions and is deserving of historical investigation. Yet even a preliminary attempt to verify the nature of such relations yields insignificant results, a conclusion which in itself may be of some historical importance, but is certainly far from satisfying the researcher. Now that I have disclosed some uneasiness about my topic (which is related, of course, to the period considered in my paper), I will proceed by making two points worth bearing in mind when discussing relations between Egypt and Palestine during the late medieval period.

In the first place, it should be questioned whether one is entitled to refer to Palestine as a viable entity in pre-modern times. The available information suggests that the answer should be in the negative. Palestine under the Mamluks does not appear to have enjoyed the status of a distinctly administrative or political unit, so instead of Palestine one should perhaps refer to a number of "Palestinian" districts.[1] Generally, these were subordinated to Cairo, occasionally to Damascus, but it is important to stress that each had its own independent contacts with the Mamluk centers. These districts are only seldom mentioned by our historical sources as part of a larger entity (namely Palestine, Arabic Filasṭīn) which, however, is not to say that the name Filasṭīn does not occur here and there. Yet the small number of references to Palestine that I have come across while checking Mamluk

1 For these districts see below. I have used the term "district" not as an equivalent to any specific Arabic term but simply in the sense of a major town and its surroundings.

sources are strictly geographical in meaning; in other words, they are devoid of an administrative, let alone political connotation. It is perhaps noteworthy that *'Amal Filasṭīn, Bilād Filasṭīn* and *Arḍ (Arāḍī) Filasṭīn* are, in the chronicles, almost always a scene of flood, plague and famine.[2] As such they have, of course, little to do with our topic. This becomes especially meaningful when one compares the rare use of *Filasṭīn* with the frequent appearance in the sources of both Egypt *(al-Diyār al-Miṣriya)* and Syria *(Bilād al-Shām)* as clearly administrative entities.[3] Moreover, the area between the Euphrates and Gaza is occasionally subsumed under *Bilād al-Shām*, which is to say that districts which would naturally be associated with Palestine (Gaza, in this case) are sometimes mentioned as part of Syria.[4] My first point, then, less a matter of novelty and more for the sake of precision, is that, when discussing relations between Egypt and Palestine in the pre-modern period, we tend to use a term that was rarely employed by the contemporaries of the time.

The second point, based on a cursory glance at some of the relevant material, is that an analysis of the relations between Egypt and Palestine in the Mamluk period cannot be complete unless one takes into consideration the larger political context, that is to say, the Cairo-Damascus axis. The available information leaves no doubt regarding the impact of political developments along this axis on the Palestinian districts. At this stage of research, however, we still lack a detailed study of relations between Mamluk Egypt and Syria.[5] Consequently, any attempt at providing a comprehensive picture of Egyptian-Palestinian relations is premature, and in the present discussion I shall deal primarily with two questions. (1) What was the formal (that is: politically decreed) position of the various Palestinian districts vis-à-vis the Circassian centers of power? (2) Apart from formal subordination, how significant was Egyptian presence in fourteenth and fifteenth-century Palestine and what form did it

2 See, for example, al-Maqrīzī, *Kitāb al-Sulūk li-M'arifat Duwal al-Mulūk* (Cairo, 1936-58, 1970-73), IV, 225, 803, 1233; al-Jawharī, *Nuzhat al-Nufūs wa'l-Abdān fī Tawārīkh al-Zāman* (Cairo, 1970-73), I,474; III,159.

3 The precise meaning of Egypt and Syria in a pre-modern context needs to be studied. The cohesiveness of the two regions, however, is much clearer. Among the numerous examples in our sources we find, for instance, the use of phrases such as "the people of Syria" *(ahl al-Shām), Sulūk*, IV, 1090; "Egypt's currency" *(naqd Miṣr), Sulūk*, IV, 1103; "the Jews of Egypt" *(yahūd Miṣr), Sulūk*, IV, 1236; "the viceroys of Syria" *(nuwwāb al-Shām), ibid.* 1071. In 1399 A.D. the viceroy in Damascus *(nā'ib al-Shām)* was given the command of "all Syrian affairs" *(marsūm sharīf bi-tafwīḍ umūr al-bilād al-Shāmiyya ilayhi)*. See *Sulūk*, III, 983. Egypt's administrative unity was manifested, among others, by the existence of a "chief judge" *(qāḍī al-quḍāt)* whose saying applied in all of Egypt *(Diyār Miṣr)*. See *Sulūk*, III, 1101; IV, 1069, 1150; *Nuzhat*, I,461.

4 See *Sulūk*, IV, 1043, 1047. Palestine is also omitted in references to Egypt and Syria. See, for example, *Sulūk*, IV, 1055, 1066, 1188, 1191.

5 There is a useful introduction to this subject in Ira M. Lapidus, *Muslim Cities in the Later Middle Ages* (Cambridge, Mass., 1967), 1-43.

take? Now these questions can be discussed by looking into various types of historical material such as chronicles, the so-called biographical dictionaries, inscriptions, and perhaps some numismatic data. For the present discussion I have consulted some major chronicles of the Circassian period.[6] Future use of non-narrative sources will probably add to the picture.

Political Subordination

Safed, Gaza and Jerusalem, in descending order of importance, were the main Palestinian towns during the Circassian period. Each of the three, together with its respective surroundings, formed a *niyāba*, which is to say it was the seat of a "viceroy" *(nā'ib al-salṭana)*. But whereas the viceroys of the first two, together with those of some major Egyptian and Syrian towns such as Alexandria, Damascus, Aleppo and Tripoli, formed a privileged group *(a'yān nuwwāb sulṭān Miṣr)*, the Jerusalem *nā'ib*, like the viceroys of Homs, Baalbek, Damietta and a number of Egyptian and Syrian towns, was of a lower rank.[7] That the viceroy of Safed was indeed more esteemed than his peer in Gaza may be gathered from the following account. Commenting on the transfer of one Safedi *nā'ib* to Gaza some time in the early decades of the fifteenth century the contemporary historian stated that the move was "from higher to lower" *(wa-hādha intiqāl min al a'lā ilā'l-adnā)*, not merely in the topographical sense, it seems.[8] That the posts in both Safed and Gaza were, however, superior to that in Jerusalem may have had to do with the longer history of the first two as a *niyāba*.[9]

On a lower level of administrative importance was the town of Ramle

6 I have used the following sources:
Ibn Iyas, *Badā'i' al-Zuhūr fī Waqā'i' al-Duhūr*, 5 vols. (Istanbul and Wiesbaden, 1931-36, 1972-75), henceforth Badā'i'.
Ibn Taghrī Birdī, *al-Nujūm al-Zāhira fī Mulūk Miṣr wa'l-Qāhira,*, ed. William Popper, *University of California Publications in Semitic Philology*, vols. V, VI, VII (Berkeley and Los Angeles, 1915-30), *(Nujūm)*.
Ibn Taghrī Birdī, *Ḥawādith al-Duhūr fī Maḍa'l-Ayyām wa'l-Shuhūr*, ed. William Popper, *University of California Publications in Semitic Philology*, VIII (Berkeley and Los Angeles, 1930-31), *(Ḥawādith)*.
Al-Jawharī, *Nuzhat al-Nufūs wa'l-Abdān fī tawārīkh al-Zamān*, 3 vols. (Cairo, 1970-73), (*Nuzhat*).
Al-Maqrīzī, *Kitāb al-Sulūk li-M'arifat Duwal al-Mulūk*, 4 vols. (Cairo, 1936-58, 1970-73), (*Sulūk*).
Mujīr al-Dīn al-'Ulaymī, *al-Uns al-Jalīl fī Ta'rīkh al-Quds wa'l-Khalīl*, 2 vols. (Najaf, 1968), *(Uns)*.

7 *Ḥawādith*, 282, 505.

8 *Nuzhat*, III, 429.

9 For Safed and Gaza as *niyābāt* as early as the beginning of the fourteenth century see *Sulūk*, II, 36, 39. For Jerusalem as a *niyāba* for the first time in 1394 A.D. see *Sulūk*, III, 813; *Nuzhat*, I, 387.

which was generally ruled by a "provincial governor" *(kāshif)*,[10] but sometimes by the *nā'ib* situated in Jerusalem.[11] All the viceroys and governors in Palestine were, in the Circassian period, appointed by the Sultan in Cairo, but in times of Syrian rebellion appointments were occasionally made in Damascus and Aleppo.[12]

Although they were the prominent figures in each of their respective districts, the *Nuwwāb* and governors were not the only functionaries serving in Palestine under the Mamluks. It has been pointed out that in an attempt to reduce the power of the viceroys and their ability to revolt against the Sultan in Cairo, the fortress in the major town of each *niyāba* was completely independent of the viceroy's rule and was subject to a special officer, the "head of the fortress" *(nā'ib al-qal'a)*.[13] We also find that at the beginning of the fifteenth century, there served in Safed, next to its viceroy, an officer entitled *muqaddam al-bilād al-Ṣafadiyya*,[14] but we lack further details concerning his position. In Gaza there functioned a "chamberlain" *(ḥājib)* next to the viceroy and he also substituted for the latter during his absence *(nā'ib al-ghayba)*.[15] The Jerusalem *nā'ib* was in charge of the Muslim shrines in both Jerusalem and Hebron but he was sometimes assisted in these duties by a special official, the *nāẓir al-Quds wa'l-Khalīl* or *nāẓir al-ḥaramayn* who, unlike the viceroy and the other aforementioned functionaries, did not have to be a Mamluk officer but could be a scholar.[16]

What lent force to Cairo's dominance in its Palestinian *niyābāt* was the Mamluk Sultans' general ability to replace, according to their own desires, the viceroys and governors throughout the Sultanate. That this prerogative

10 *Sulūk*, IV, 40, 87-88, 119, 121, 150, 249, 251, 451. The *kāshif* as a "district governor" or "supervisor" survived down to the early Ottoman period. See Sir Hamilton Gibb and Harold Bowen, *Islamic Society and the West*, vol. I: *Islamic Society in the Eighteenth Century* (London, 1950-1957), pt. I, 260; pt. II, 40; Stanford J. Shaw, *The Financial and Administrative Organization and Development of Ottoman Egypt 1517-1798* (Princeton, 1962), 31; Helen Anne B. Rivlin, *The Agricultural Policy of Muhammad Ali in Egypt* (Cambridge, Mass., 1961), 363.

11 This was the case in 1436 A.D. See *Sulūk*, IV, 975; *Nuzhat*, III, 348.

12 Concerning the Jerusalem viceroy, Professor Donald P. Little in his article included in the present vulume quotes Mujīr al-Dīn's information that starting in 1397-98 A.D. the officials posted in Jerusalem were appointed by the Sultan in Cairo. Then he relies on Ibn Taghrī Birdī and concludes that until 1413 A.D. the *nā'ib* in Jerusalem was appointed in Damascus. However, references in the *Sulūk* contradict Little's conclusion and suggest that starting in 1394 A.D., and except for times of Syrian rebellion, the Jerusalem Viceroy was nominated in Cairo. See *Sulūk*, III, 813, 1038; IV, 88.

13 David Ayalon, "Discharges from service, banishments and imprisonments in Mamluk Society", *Israel Oriental Studies*, II (1972), 47. For Safed see *Sulūk*, IV, 114; *Ḥawādith*, 478; *Nujūm*, VII, 232.

14 *Sulūk*, IV, 398; *Nuzhat*, II, 387.

15 Sulūk, III, 1002, 1150; IV, 364, 959, 975; *Nuzhat*, II, 304; *Ḥawādith*, 24-25.

16 *Sulūk*, IV, 81, 440, 662, 702, 959, 1192; *Nuzhat*, I, 342; III, 132; *Ḥawādith*, 10, 485; *Uns*, II, 94, 96; *Nujūm*, VII, 290.

was indeed frequently exercised in the case of Palestine is clearly demonstrated by the fact that during the first forty years or so of the Circassian regime, over thirty viceroys served in Safed, none for a period exceeding four years and a few were in office for less than a year. The situation in Gaza appears to have been little different in this respect. It should be noted, incidentally, that such a policy of frequent replacements dates back at the latest to the middle of the fourteenth century.[17] Whether or not it continued throughout the fifteenth century is not indicated in our sources.

Be that as it may, the frequent dismissal of Palestinian viceroys could certainly become a double-edged sword. On the one hand, such a policy most likely aimed at the prevention of a long-term association between subjects in the provinces and local governors, an association carrying potential danger for the central government. The policy was not, of course, a Mamluk invention since it was based on fears shared by many premodern (as well as modern) rulers. On the other hand, dependence on short-term services in the provinces had some marked disadvantages in a medieval context, notably the risk of instability and disintegration. What then was the result in the case under consideration? Here we face one difficulty already mentioned, namely, the incomplete picture of the larger political context. One scholar has maintained that "never in her history was Syria so long and firmly dominated by Egypt [as it was in Mamluk days] and rarely have the two regions been so well protected against external forces."[18] This may be a valid assessment of the situation in Syria, yet we are also reminded that the rise of the Circassian Sultans to power signaled the decline of the Mamluk regime. In the last decades of the fourteenth and early decades of the fifteenth centuries, the office of Sultan changed hands several times within a few years and the crises in Cairo had their influence in Syria as well. Only under al-Mu'ayyad Shaykh (1412 A.D.-1421 A.D.) and Barsbāy (1422 A.D.-1438 A.D.) was the imperial fabric restored, but it was dismantled once again in the second half of the fifteenth century, never to be recovered under Mamluk rule.[19]

I have already suggested that the situation in Palestine appears to have been, to a large extent, a reflection of Egyptian control in Syria. What emerges from the many reports about Syrian attempts to challenge the Sultans' authority in their northern domains is that the Palestinian *niyābāt* were frequently drawn into the Egyptian-Syrian struggles, sometimes even contrary to their own desires. Any serious revolt in Damascus or Aleppo was never restricted to the surrounding area and thus seldom left the major Palestinian towns unaffected. The success of the famous rebel, Nurūz, during the first two decades of the fifteenth century in controlling the entire

17 *Sulūk*, III and IV, *passim*.

18 Lapidus, *op. cit.*, 12.

19 *Ibid.* 32-43.

Bilād al-Shām, including Safed and Gaza, and in appointing his own viceroys there, is not the only example of Egypt's shaky rule in both Syria and Palestine.[20] What clearly added to Palestine's precarious position in times of political conflict was its location as a natural battleground for both Egyptian and Syrian armies.[21]

Egyptian Presence in Palestinian Towns

One should start by observing that, except for the act of appointing *nuwwāb*, Egyptian physical presence in Palestine was limited to times of disorder. Such a discovery need not surprise those familiar with the Mamluk political "mentality"; Professor Ayalon has reminded us time and again that the Mamluk military aristocracy virtually despised any region except Egypt, even the regions outside Cairo. If we nonetheless find Circassian Sultans setting foot in certain Palestinian *niyābāt*, almost without exception it is because they were *en route* to resolve problems in Syria. This is best illustrated by the case of both Gaza and Ramle. Serving as the main transit stations between Cairo and Damascus, these towns were visited by Sultans and their troops much more frequently than anywhere else in Palestine.[22] Incidentally, the inhabitants of the two were charged by the Circassian administration with a special tax *(iqāmāt)* in the form of barley and other unspecified items, which were intended for supply to Egyptian troops in transit.[23]

While Safed, apparently, was never visited by a Circassian Sultan, a number of Mamluk rulers made side trips to both Jerusalem and Hebron while returning from military campaigns in Syria. Although these two towns were of little political importance, they had a special attraction due to their religious significance. Thus Sultan al-Mu'ayyad Shaykh was in Jerusalem twice, and on his second visit, in 1417 A.D., he attended the Friday prayer gathering in the Aqṣā mosque, listened to a recital of Bukhārī's *Saḥīḥ*, and also dispensed charity to the local inhabitants.[24] A few years later, al-Ẓāhir was in the Holy City and on that occasion acceded to the people's demand to reduce the taxes imposed by their *nā'ib*.[25] After

20 For the turmoil in Palestinian towns during Nurūz's reign in Syria see *Sulūk*, III, 38, 41, 68, 110-23, 251. Al-Maqrīzī (*Sulūk*, IV, 127-28) stated under the year 812 H./1409-10 A.D., that the only towns under the Sultan's control in all of Syria (sic!) (al-bilād al-Shāmiyya) were Gaza and Safed. However, even these two were not permanently subordinated to Cairo. For revolts there see, for example, *Sulūk*, III, 604, 663, 669-70, 1007, 1044-46; IV, 320.

21 *Sulūk*, III, 1008-10; IV, 41, 151, 199, 320; *Nuzhat*, II, 40.

22 *Sulūk*, III, 690, 695, 760, 813, 825, 1008, 1010, 1016, 1038; IV, 32, 55, 93, 108, 199, 282, 284, 327, 398, 422, 576, 891.

23 *Sulūk*, III, 1159, 1160; IV, 138.

24 *Sulūk*, IV, 284, 421-22. For earlier instances see *ibid.*, 108, 164.

25 *Ibid.*, 584.

the 1420s, however, we seldom find Mamluk Sultans visiting Palestinian towns. Barsbāy's stay in Gaza, in 1433 A.D., on his way to Syria, seems to be an exception.[26] Thereafter, until 1475 A.D., when Qā'itbāy was in Jerusalem and Hebron,[27] no Sultan is reported as having been in the region.

The presence of Egypt's highest political echelon in Palestinian towns was, then, determined by political (mostly military) needs in Syria and marked by its short duration. In contradistinction, the presence of other Egyptian elements in Jerusalem and to some extent also in Hebron, was largely independent of special political circumstances and had to do with the sanctity of the two towns. Of great interest in this regard is the constant (yet little recorded) stream of Muslim (as well as non-Muslim) pilgrims who used to perform a *ziyāra* in both Jerusalem and Hebron.[28] Jerusalem, despite its lack of political importance, was considered a major scholarly center and as such enjoyed some kind of cosmopolitan atmosphere. Thus, in an obituary of the Jerusalem *qāḍī*, Shams al-Dīn al-Dayrī (d. 1424 A.D.), it is stated that he was able to associate himself with many Egyptian and Syrian *'ulamā'* who found Jerusalem to be their haven *(il-anna Bayt al-Maqdis maḥaṭṭ riḥālihim wa-ghāyat maqṣūdihim wa-āmālihim).*[29] Quite a number of scholars and even military officers tended to move to Jerusalem in their old age in order to find there eternal peace.[30]

But Jerusalem during the later Mamluk period emerges not only as a Holy City. The town was very much connected with Mamluk punitive measures. To quote Professor Ayalon, "the overwhelming majority of references to Jerusalem in the Mamluk chronicles (with the obvious exclusion of the chronicle of Mujīr al-Dīn) deal with its function as a place of exile for the members of the [Egyptian] military aristocracy."[31] Now, to realize the significance of this observation it is essential to bear in mind that most Mamluks "were not lucky enough to finish their military career without ever having been dismissed, banished or imprisoned. Most of them were subjected to one or more of these punishments quite often during their career."[32] Noteworthy in this regard is that most of the dismissed officers were not kept in Egypt but rather sent away to the north, and in particular to Jerusalem. The town thus turned into the Mamluks' place of exile *par excellence* and throughout the Mamluk period hundreds if not thousands

26 *Ibid.*, 891; *Nuzhat*, III, 259.

27 *Badā'i'*, III, 108; *Uns*, II, 314-16. The same Sultan was back in Jerusalem and Gaza two years later. See *Uns*, II, 318-19. Mujīr al-Dīn informs about several Sultans sending *Qur'āns*, *kiswas* and money to Jerusalem and Hebron. See *Uns*, II, 96-99.

28 See, for example, *Sulūk*, III, 293; IV, 666, 675, 835; *Badā'i'*, III, 85.

29 *Nuzhat*, III, 61.

30 See, for example, *ibid.* 430; *Sulūk*, III, 889.

31 Ayalon, *op. cit.*, 34 n. 49.

32 *Ibid.*, 33.

of discharged officers settled there, including some ex-prisoners whose sentences had been commuted.[33]

The importance of Jerusalem as a place of banishment far exceeding that of Safed and Gaza,[34] is never explained in our sources. Was it a result of an arbitrary decision on the part of the Egyptian regime? Did it have to do with the desires of the discharged? Be that as it may, the Mamluks' contempt for their provinces explains not only Palestine's role as a region of exile, but also its peripheral status in the Mamluk state.

33 In addition to material provided in Ayalon, "Discharges from service", 34 n. 49 see examples in *Sulūk,* III, 466, 687, 796, 878, 917, 918, 1023, 1087, 1176; IV, 10, 13, 284, 372, 420, 474,475, 520, 533, 580, 602, 641, 670, 775, 783, 906, 976, 1007, 1088, 1157, 1165; *Nujūm,* VII, 215, 219; *Badā'i',* IV, 58, 88, 94, 345, 349.

34 For Safed see *Sulūk,* III, 13-14, 524, 541, 581; IV, 286, 358, 362, 522. For Gaza see *Sulūk,* III, 637.

BUTRUS ABU-MANNEH

The Georgians in Jerusalem in the Mamluk Period*

There is scant recollection of the Georgians in Jerusalem today, yet along with the Greeks, Syrians, Armenians and others, they once enjoyed a substantial presence in the Holy City. They first appeared, it would seem, in the early centuries of the Christian era, soon after their conversion to Orthodox Christianity, approximately at the beginning of the fourth century.[1] For a long time their main residence was the Monastery of the Cross, which had been constructed some two kilometers west of the old city of Jerusalem, on the site where, so it was claimed, the wood of the Holy Cross had been cut.[2]

According to the chronicle of Mujīr al-Dīn, written about the end of the fifteenth century, the monastery was then one of the four most important Christian edifices in Jerusalem. The other three were the Church of the Holy Sepulcher, the Monastery of the "Franks" on Mount Zion[3] and the Armenian Monastery.[4]

In the earliest period of the Mamluk Sultanate, the Georgian presence in Jerusalem already figured considerably in Mamluk-Georgian relations. When the Mongols invaded the Caucasus (in about 1240) the Georgian Kingdom fell under their yoke and paid allegiance to the Il-khans of Persia.[5] Georgian units fought with the Mongols against the Mamluks in

* My thanks are due to Father Christodholos of the Greek Orthodox Patriarchate of Jerusalem for his help in obtaining the source material for this paper.

1 Theodore E. Dowling, "The Georgian Church in Jerusalem" in *Palestine Exploration Fund Quarterly Statement* vol. 43 (1911) pp. 181-187 see p. 181 f.

2 W.M. Thomson, *The Land and the Book* (London 1859) p. 663. This monastery seems to have been founded by King Tatian, in the fifth century, see Dowling, *op. cit.* p. 183f.

3 This belonged to the Franciscans, who returned to Jerusalem in 1330. See S.D. Goitein, "al-Kuds" in *EI²*, V, 333.

4 Mujīr al-Dīn al-'Ulaymī, *al-'Uns al-Jalīl fī Tarīkh al-Quds wa'l-Khalīl* 2 vols. (Cairo 1866), II 401f. He states that there were about 20 Christian shrines in Jerusalem *"min zaman al-Rūm"*.

5 W.E.D. Allen, *A History of the Georgian People* (London 1932) pp. 112f.; see also Ibn Faḍl Allāh al-'Umarī, *al-Ta'rīf bi'l-Muṣṭalaḥ al-Sharīf* (Cairo 1312/1894), pp. 53f.

the battle of 'Ayn Jālūt, in 1260.[6] During the reign of Sultan Baybars (1260-1277), the monks of the Monastery of the Cross were suspected of transmitting information about the Mamluks to the Mongols, information they were said to have heard from Coptic pilgrims in Jerusalem. Baybars executed the spies and ordered that the Monastery be converted into a mosque.[7]

After the death of the Il-khan Ghazan in 1304, however, Mongol control over the Georgian homeland apparently became less effective.[8] A Georgian embassy, accompanied by delegates of the Byzantine Emperor, reached Cairo and opened negotiations with Sultan al-Nāṣir Muḥammad b. Qalā'ūn (1293-4, 1298-1308, 1309-1340) for the restoration of the Monastery to the Georgians.[9] As a Christian nation it was apparently important for them to secure a presence in Jerusalem and to have a place in which their pilgrims could stay while visiting the Holy City.

Negotiations appear to have been protracted but the Sultan finally consented and the Monastery was restored to them[10] (in 1305). This agreement on the Sultan's part formed it seems the core of Mamluk-Georgian relations for the next two centuries.

Ibn Faḍl Allāh al-'Umarī (d. 1349) of Damascus,[11] a high official at the chancery of Sultan al-Nāṣir Muḥammad, recorded that the act "was not done in vain".[12] Maqrīzī added that the letter of the Georgian king contained a promise that "the Georgians will be obedient to the (Mamluk) Sultan and will come to his aid whenever he needs them",[13] with no further elucidation.

These intimations explain little but they clearly indicate that the return of the Monastery of the Cross to the Georgians implied more than the renewal of relations between the two governments. They suggest that an understanding may have been reached that was to Mamluk advantage, although

6 P.M. Holt *et al.* (eds.) *The Cambridge History of Islam*, vol. 1 (Cambridge 1970) p. 212; apparently the Georgians participated in other Il-Khani attacks on Syria in 1281 and 1299-1300 which were led by Ghazan. See T.A. al-Maqrīzī, *Kitāb al-Sulūk* ed. by M.M. Ziyādeh vol. 1 pt. 3 (Cairo 1939) p. 692 and appendix no. 12, I, 1011.

7 Ghazi b. al-Wasiṭi, "al-Radd 'Ala al-Dhimmiyīn" in *JAOS* vol. 21 (1921) pp. 411-12. My thanks are due to Mr. 'Amiqam Elad of Jerusalem for drawing my attention to this treatise.

8 Allen, *op. cit.* p. 120; cf. B. Spuler, *The Muslim World... Part II The Mongol Period*, translated by F.R.C. Bagley (Leiden 1960), p. 38.

9 Maqrīzī, *op. cit.* vol. 2, pt. 1, p. 17 and n. 2 of the editor; see also Ibn Faḍl Allāh al-'Umarī, *op. cit.* p. 54. According to D.M. Lang, "Georgia in the reign of Giorgi the Brilliant (1314-1346)" in *BSOAS*. XVII (1955) pp. 74-91, it was King Wakhtang III of Georgia who sent the embassy. See p. 79.

10 Qalqashandī, *Subḥ al-A'shā*, VIII, 28; Mujīr al-Dīn, *op.cit.* II, 402.

11 On the life of al-'Umarī see K.S. Salibi in *EI*², III, 758-9.

12 *"wa-in lam yu'mal sudan"*, see his al-Ta'rīf p. 54.

13 Maqrīzī, *op. cit.*, vol. 2, pt. 1, p. 17. (*wa-anna al-Kurj takūnu fī ṭā'at al-sulṭan wa-'awnan lahu matā 'iḥtāja 'ilayhim*)

Mamluk sources are silent on the subject. In this paper, with the help of certain new evidence, we shall nevertheless attempt to analyse the attitude of the Mamluks towards the Georgian monastic community in Jerusalem and thus shed light on some aspects of Mamluk-Georgian relations during the Mamluk period.

* * *

Once a place of worship had been expropriated from non-Muslims and turned into a mosque, it was contrary to Islamic tradition to restore it to its original owners or previous function. The agreement made by Sultan al-Nāṣir was interpreted by the *'ulamā'* and other Muslim dignitaries in Jerusalem as such an act, and was apparently implemented against their will. Ibn Faḍl Allāh who visited Jerusalem more than a generation later, recorded the resentment of these *'ulamā'* and dignitaries even so long after the event.[14]

But Mamluk interest took precedence and seems to have dictated a friendly attitude towards Georgia and favorable treatment of the Georgian monks in Jerusalem. This was reflected not only in the restoration of the Monastery of the Cross but in many other benevolent acts conferred upon them throughout the Mamluk period, as this paper will try to show. Such treatment annoyed local *'ulamā'* and other dignitaries and antagonised them towards the Georgian monks and pilgrims, who they would have preferred to see treated strictly in accordance with the *Sharī'a*, which did not always conform with Mamluk interests.

We are apprised of this and many other issues through edicts issued by various Mamluk Sultans to Georgian monks in Jerusalem as well as through letters written by the Sultans in response to correspondence from the Georgian kings.

I have recently discovered eighteen such edicts and letters which were apparently preserved in the Monastery of the Cross for a long time. Three of these documents are letters sent to kings of Georgia by the Mamluk Sultans Jaqmaq (in 844/1444), Īnāl (in 857/1453) and Qānṣūh al Ghawrī (in 910/1504). The other fifteen are edicts handed down to the monks in Jerusalem.[15]

14 See his *Masālik al-Abṣār fī mamālik al-Amṣār* vol. 1 ed. by Ahmad Zakī (Cairo 1924) p. 339; see also Qalqashandī *op. cit.* VIII, 28.

15 Comprising:
1 edict issued by al-Nāṣir Muḥammad himself.
1 edict issued by al-Muẓaffar Ḥājjī.
4 edicts issued by Barsbāy.
2 edicts issued by Jaqmaq.
3 edicts issued by Qā'itbāy.
1 edict issued by Qānṣūh al-Ghawrī.
3 others yet undeciphered.

The first edict, issued by al-Nāṣir Muḥammad, states that Georgian monks came from their country "and complained of interference" by local people and that "they are not being treated according to the noble edicts in their hand". The Sultan ordered "that care should be taken to treat them kindly and to deal with them according to the [Sultan's] noble edicts in their hands without deviation from them...".

But they continued to complain of the local people. Seventeen years after the edict of al-Nāṣir, his son and successor al-Muẓaffar Ḥājjī (1346-1347) issued an edict which was in fact an expanded version of the previous one. He stated that as the Georgians were *dhimmīs*, they were first of all under his *amān*, which meant that according to the *Sharī'a* their personal security and their property were under the Sultan's protection. The edict further stated "that their king had done beforehand (certain) services to our gracious predecessor",[16] whereby hinting at what lay behind his father's benevolent attitude towards them.

Moreover, the text continued "no one of them is accused of disloyalty".[17] Following this the Sultan enjoined the dignitaries of Jerusalem to treat them and their pilgrims properly and to prevent anyone from obstructing their way, harming them or demanding uncustomary payments from them. Care should be taken, he added, to avoid injuring their endowments. In all these matters they should be dealt with according to the noble edicts in their hands. He ended by ordering that under the supervision of the *Qāḍī*, they be permitted to rebuild according to the original structure what time had destroyed of their monastery.

This appears to have been no ordinary edict. The fact that Sultan Ḥājjī gave reasons to justify his policy towards the Georgians, and that he referred twice to *Sharī'a* norms, may have indicated his desire to conciliate the *'ulamā'* and dignitaries of Jerusalem. Whether his successors of the first Mamluk period followed a similar line and took the *'ulamā'* and *Sharī'a* into consideration is not clear. No more edicts of this period have been found. However, it may be no accident that all the other edicts and the three letters belong to the Circassian period of Mamluk history. This may suggest a growing relationship between the two governments at this period and subsequently an increase in the favor conferred on the Georgian monastic community in Jerusalem, as we shall see below.

No edict, among the documents found, belongs to the time of Barqūq

As far as I am aware, nobody else has made use of them as yet. I am presently engaged in preparing them for publication.
For other Mamluk edicts that have been published see H. Ernest, *Die Mamlukischen Sultansurkunden des Sinai-Klosters* (Wiesbaden, 1960); and S.M. Stern, "Petitions from the Mamluk Period" in *BSOAS* vol. 29 (1966) pp. 233-276.

16 *Miman aslafa malikuhum li-salafinā il-karīm khidaman.*

17 *Lam yakun aḥad minhum bi'l-ikhlāṣ muttahaman.*

(784/1382-801/1398), the first Sultan of the Circassian line. Thus we do not know what was his policy as regards the Georgians. However, his period was regarded as one to which later Sultans would refer.

Thus in an edict dated 26 Jumādā al-Ūlā 838/28 December 1434, Sultan Barsbāy (825/1422-842/1438) stated that correspondence had reached him from "the gracious king, the king of the Georgians" asking his "noble bounties to double the care for his people who are residing in Jerusalem". He continued that it had come to his knowledge that it was intended in Jerusalem to increase the tithe on the lands of the Monastery of the Cross and of the village of Dayr Ka'kūl. This, he added, was not customary in the times of Sultan Barqūq, and he enjoined the governor to refrain from this and "to deal with them (the Georgians) according to their old custom [as it was] at the end of Barqūq's reign". This may imply that the Georgians did enjoy certain favors during that Sultan's reign.

Indeed, analysis of the edicts and letters issued by the Sultans of the Circassian period indicates a growth in the property and number of shrines possessed by the Georgians, or under their control. Moreover, other sources show that the Georgian monks and pilgrims apparently enjoyed at that time more privileges and immunities than perhaps *Sharī'a* rules would have allowed.

As far as concerns the first point, it is known that the Monastery of the Cross was returned to the Georgians in 1305; no other place was mentioned as being part of the deal. Whether they possessed other places at that phase, there is no way to ascertain. By the second half of the fifteenth century, however, we learn of many places and shrines owned by them. Thus in a letter to the Georgian court, Sultan Īnāl (857/1453-865/1460) referred to "monasteries, places, endowments and shrines", all in the plural.[18] In an edict issued by Qā'itbāy in 874/1469-70 it is said that "they own monasteries from old times from the [days of] conquest";[19] and at the beginning of the fifteenth century Sultan Qānṣūh al-Ghawrī (906/1500-922/1516) spoke in an edict "of seven monasteries that belong to the Monastery of the Cross"[20]

We find a similar view expressed in the European sources and travel literature. Travelers of the fourteenth and fifteenth centuries were in agreement that the Georgians owned many shrines and that their possessions increased with time, so that by the last several decades of the fifteenth and the early sixteenth century they controlled as many as eleven or twelve shrines.[21] If we compare this with the total number of Christian monu-

18 *Duyūratihim wa-amakinihim wa-awqāfihim wa-ma'ābidihim.*

19 *Wa-lahum adyira bi-aydīhim min taqādīm al-sinīn mina 'l-futūḥ.*

20 *Wa-li-dayr al-Muṣallaba sab'a duyūra.*

21 Gregory Peradze, "An Account of the Georgian Monks and Monasteries in Palestine" in *Georgica* vol. 5 (London, 1937) pp. 181-246, See pp. 192ff. and list in 217ff. See also Dowling, *op. cit.* p. 185.

ments in the city as cited by Mujīr al-Din,[22] we can imagine how great this was in proportion to the other communitites, in spite of their being a small church.

There was, it seems, a direct connection between the number of shrines they possessed and the amount of property they owned. In his edict mentioned above, Sultan Qānṣūh speaks of houses for rent, agricultural lands and even two villages, Jaljaleh and Dayr Mūsā, the income of which was assigned for the expenses of the Georgian shrines and the monks. We know of another village — Dayr Ka'kul and other pieces of land mentioned in the edicts.

There is ample evidence that a considerable part of this property was granted to the Georgians by the Mamluks. Ibn Faḍl Allāh who visited the Monastery of the Cross stated that adjacent to it there was "a village running on it by the decree of the Sultan"[23] *(Qarya tajrī 'alayhi bi-marsūm al-sulṭān)*. In other words, al-Nāṣir Muḥammad did not only restore the Monastery to them but granted them agricultural lands for their up-keep.

Sultan Jaqmaq, in his letter to the Georgian king stated that the monks "still (enjoy) what is running upon them of our noble bounties and still exploit the estates *(iqṭā')* assigned [by him] for the church of Golgotha".

It is likely that other sultans did grant them estates as a token of favor, otherwise it is difficult to explain these relatively large possessions of theirs.[24]

Along with this growth of property and the number of shrines in their possession, the Georgians were also enjoying certain privileges apparently not enjoyed by other non-Muslim communities. Thus, there is some evidence that from the days of al-Nāṣir Muḥammad they held the keys of the Holy Sepulcher Church.[25] The German traveler, M. von Baumgarten, who visited Jerusalem in 1507, observed that their pilgrims were free from those vexatious imposts which others had to pay, and their men and women entered the city in full armor.[26] Other sources added that they used to enter the city on horseback.[27]

Obviously these acts were incompatible with *Sharī'a* provisions concerning non-Muslims. Indeed the whole tableau of the growth of the Georgian presence under Mamluk protection disturbed, as we have seen, the *'ulāmā'* and dignitaries of the city. The question is, what impelled the Mamluks to

22 Mujir al-Dīn, *op. cit.* p. 1 and n. 4.

23 Ibn Faḍl Allāh al-'Umarī, *Masālik al-Abṣār* vol. 1, p. 339.

24 Peradze, *op. cit.* p. 216.

25 Peradze, *op. cit.* p. 189 and Dowling, *op. cit.* p. 185.

26 Quoted in G. Williams, *The Holy City: Historical, Topographical and Antiquarian Notes of Jerusalem,* 2nd ed. (London 1849) p. 552; see also R. Janin, "Les Georgiens à Jérusalem" in *Echos d'Orient* Tome XVI (1913) pp. 32-38 and pp. 211-219. See p. 212.

27 Sh. Khūrī and N. Khūrī, *Khulāsat Tā'rīkh Kanīsat Urshalīm al-Orthodoksiyya* (Jerusalem 1925) p. 97.

follow this line, how did it serve their interest and what were their guiding considerations?

It could be claimed that in the later Mamluk period the Sultans as well as a great number of Mamluks came from the Circassian tribes who dwelled in a region neighboring Georgia. This may have facilitated mutual understanding but this fact alone, though not insignificant, cannot serve as an explanation for the policy or the attitude of the Sultans in the first Mamluk period. There were, indeed, substantial Mamluk interests involved, which go a long way to explain the preferred treatment extended to the Georgians.

As mentioned above we have three letters sent by the Sultans Jaqmaq, Īnāl and Qānṣūh to the Georgian king, from which we can gather certain factors regarding Mamluk policy towards Georgia and its people. It is known that later Mamluk Sultans were in the habit of purchasing new conscripts from among the Circassian tribes, a practice started in fact by Sultan al-Manṣūr Qalā'ūn (1279-1290).[28] For this reason Mamluk merchants apparently needed to pass through Georgia. In consequence, the cooperation of the Georgian authorities would appear to have been necessary in the acquiring of new Mamluks and their transit through Georgia. A concrete example of this may be found in the incident related in Sultan Jaqmaq's letter. He complained to the Georgian king that one of the merchants of Sultanic Mamluks, one Muḥammad b. Muṣṭafā al-Qaramānī,[29] had reported to him that on his way through Georgia the authorities forced him to pay a duty of one thousand *dīnār* without right or reason. Jaqmaq asked the king to return the money to the merchant, saying that if he did not do so himself, the Georgian monks in Jerusalem would be forced to pay. He then admonished the king "to make the paths of travelers and merchants easier, and not to charge them except the customary duties".

This was not the only reason for the Mamluk's favorable treatment of the Georgian monastic community. In the letter of the Georgian king (as related in Sultan Jaqmaq's own letter to him) he referred to a church destroyed in Damascus by orders of the Mamluk emir, Tamr, and asked for care for the Georgians in Jerusalem and for the Christians in the Mamluk Sultanate in general. The king added that he treated benevolently the many Muslims living in his country and that they practised their rites freely, and their mosques and *zāwiyas* were open without interruption. He demanded equal treatment for his countrymen and implicitly also for local Christians. We find a similar argument in a letter sent by Sultan Īnāl to the king, eight years after the letter of Jaqmaq, and in the letter of Sultan Qānṣūh. From Īnāl's letter we understand that the Georgian king stated that many Mus-

28 *The Cambridge History of Islam*, I, 219.

29 For a list of merchants of Sultanic Mamluks see D. Ayalon, "L'esclavage de Mamelouk" in *The Mamluk Military Society* (London 1979), article 1, pp. 1-4.

lims from *al-Shām* and from other places visit his country and stay freely and unharmed. He even sent *sūfī shaykhs* to Cairo to attest before the Sultan the truth of his claims.

The Mamluk Sultans had no choice but to take this argument into consideration. For, having assumed the title of "Servitor of the two noble sanctuaries" *"Khādim al-Ḥaramayn al-Sharīfayn"*, and claimed special status among Muslim rulers by virtue of their control of the Muslim holy places and the routes leading to them, the fate of Muslims in a Christian country must certainly have been of close concern to them.[30] The Georgians, who may have understood this situation, were determind to exploit it for the protection of their own community in Jerusalem and Palestine and for the broadening of its immunities.

In addition to these considerations there may have been yet another factor which will serve to increase our understanding of how the Georgians came to acquire an eminent position among the Christian communities of Jerusalem, especially during the last sixty years of the Mamluk Sultanate.

It appears that after the fall of Constantinople to the Ottomans, the Greek Orthodox monks in Jerusalem were suspected by the Mamluks of an inclination towards the new masters of Byzantium. With the increase of tension between the Mamluks and the Ottomans they (i.e. the Mamluks) threatened to persecute the Greek monks.[31] But the Georgians seemed to have intervened on their behalf and succeeded in having the Greek shrines and monasteries in Jerusalem placed under their protection.[32]

There is some evidence as well that a number of the shrines owned by the Armenians passed into the hands of the Georgians some time in the second half of the fifteenth century, for reasons unknown to us.[33]

However, following the Ottoman occupation of Syria in 1516, the picture seems to have been reversed.[34] Now, the Greeks regained the upper hand and in 1517 the Orthodox Patriarch of Jerusalem apparently obtained a *firmān* according to which the Georgians and other small Orthodox communities fell under his protection.[35]

This marked a watershed for the Georgians in Jerusalem; henceforth they went into a rapid decline. Their monasteries and shrines passed one after the other into the hands of the Greeks, the Armenians, the Franciscans and others.[36] Indeed, for many years now, nothing has remained of them in Jerusalem.

30 On the treatment of the Muslims in Georgia see also Peradze, *op. cit.* p. 233.

31 See Janin, *op. cit.* p. 34.

32 Khūri and Khūri, *op. cit.* p. 104; see also K.I. Qazaqiyya, *Ta'rīkh al-Kanīsa al-Rasuliyya al-Urshalīmiyya* (Cairo 1924) pp. 84f. and p. 89.

33 Peradze, *op. cit.* p. 193.

34 Janin, *op. cit.* p. 35

35 Qazaqiyya, *op. cit.* pp. 90f; Khūri and Khūrī, pp. 110f.

36 Peradze, *op. cit.* p. 210, p. 216; Janin, *op. cit.*, pp. 35ff; Dowling, *op. cit.* p. 185.

APPENDIX

The letter of Sultan Jaqmaq to the Georgian King*

In the name of God the Merciful, the Compassionate

May God prolong the life of His Royal Majesty the King, the gracious, the brave, the bold the holy the spiritual, our reverend father (!) the stronghold of the Christian *umma*, the treasure of the community of the Cross, the pride of the Christian religion, the king of the Georgians and the Jurjans, the friend of kings and Sultans, may (God) preserve his bliss and protect him from misfortunes and guard his realm through him and preserve his friendship.

This correspondence was forwarded to His Majesty to express thanks for his friendship and to fulfill his wish and request from our Royal Highness. It informs him too that his correspondence had arrived at our August Gates. [It was delivered] by his emissaries who are returning with our reply. [It was sent] in answer to what we have forwarded in our letter delivered to him by Najm al-Dīn al-Ẓāhirī, one of the sultanic *mamluk*s. We have studied it and learnt what it contains concerning his claim of devotion to our August Gates, and his showing humility the moment he received our noble letters by kissing the ground again and again and by expressing obedience. [We have learnt also] that the Muslims in his country are treated kindly and allowed to dwell safely out of consideration to us and owing to his care. He informed us too that the Muslims [enjoy freedom] in their mosques and convents and that travelers constantly come and go to [his country] on the best of terms, without [any] injury befalling them and only the customary duty is imposed upon them. So that now, more than four thousand Muslim families from Northern Persia Iraq from among the followers of His Royal Highness Shāh Rūkh have arrived at his country and that His Majesty had received them graciously and allowed them to dwell in his country and treated them with kind attention.

On the other hand he has asked our noble bounties that care be taken in the treatment of Christians and Georgians in the Muslim countries [of the Mamluks] and of their monks, and in issuing orders to allow the trustees of the Church of Mary (Mariam) in Damascus which Emir Ṭamr destroyed to have it restored as it was. We have learnt these [requests] and taken them into consideration. We have given instructions to treat his emissaries well throughout their sojourn at our August Gates.

Concerning the Christians the Georgians and the monks they are treated with kindness and are dwelling safely as suits our noble justice. At the same time they still [enjoy] the customary rewards of our noble bounties [bes-

* Possibly King Alexander the First (1412-1443) the last king of united Georgia (See Allen *op. cit.* pp. 126-7).

My thanks are due to Larry Miller for revising the translation of this letter.

towed] upon them, as well as the exploitation of the lands bestowed [by us] upon the church of Golgotha. However a certain merchant of the sultanic *mamluks* called Muḥammad ibn Muṣṭafā al-Qaramānī appeared before our noble presence and complained of inequity which His Majesty had committed towards him when he passed through his country. [He stated] that His Majesty had wronged him and took from him one thousand *dīnār*s without right or a clear reason. We are utterly astonished that His Majesty would treat merchants and Muslim subjects in such a way although he knows that his Christian subjects and the clerics of their churches are treated, owing to our noble bounties, with benevolence and justice.

We have issued a decree requiring those in charge of Georgian churches and the Golgotha in Jerusalem [to appear before us], in order to impose upon them [the payment] of one thousand *dīnār*s. But when they did appear before our Royal Highness, we treated them with forbearance and granted them a respite until we send back the emissaries of His Majesty and write to him this letter [demanding] that he forward the one thousand *dīnār*s to the merchant. If he recognizes the justice [of our request] and dispatches the money to him, then we shall keep up our usual attention towards His Majesty and increase our just and benevolent treatment of the Christians and monks in our country. Moreover we shall fulfill his request concerning the church of Mary.

But if His Majesty has taken the one thousand *dīnār*s and does not give them back and if he has been remiss in his treatment of Muslims in his country either in terms of justice and benevolence or in [allowing] the public practice of Islam among them, then we shall issue instructions to use the sword of justice and equity to take vengeance upon the Christians and Georgians in the Muslim countries according to what they deserve.

But if His Majesty claims that what the merchant had stated before our noble presence is not at all true and that he did not treat him unjustly and did not take from him one thousand *dīnār*s or not a smaller amount, let His Majesty assemble the clergymen and monks at his place and swear in their presence a most solemn oath in accord with [the requirements] of his religion and belief, that what the merchant had stated is not true wholly nor partly. The copy of this oath carrying the signatures of the clergymen and monks should be forwarded to our August Gates so that our mind will be set at ease and that we may abolish [the fine of thousand *dīnār*s] imposed upon the Christians [as well as the call] to take vengeance upon the Christians and monks.

Let His Majesty study closely everything which we have indicated to him, and let him not depart from its provisions. He should also spread justice among his Muslim subjects and make the routes of travelers and merchants easier to traverse. He should only charge them the customary duties. So that [our] friendship and good will towards him will be preserved and we shall treat his subjects in the Muslim countries kindly.

We have sent back his emissaries [with due] honors and fowarded with them the following twenty pieces of cloth as a favor from us as follows:

four velvet silk robes,
five pieces of silk,
five veils of finest Venetian linen
four kerchiefs of full texture [!] (*manādīl mushba*'),
two under-garments.

His Majesty should accept that and receive it by kissing the ground frequently and doing what we have indicated. He should send back his answer to our August Gates quickly according to his customary zeal.

May God the sublime help us. If God [may He be exalted] wills.

Written at the beginning of Rabī' II of the year 844, according to the noble decree. Praise be to God alone and prayer and peace be upon our Master Muḥammad and upon his family and companions.

God is sufficient unto us; how excellent a Keeper is He.

Mark R. Cohen

Administrative Relations between Palestinian and Egyptian Jewry during the Fatimid Period

The subject of this paper may seem a bit strange at first glance. How can one speak of "administrative relations" in the context of the non-Muslim peoples? As members of a minority group, existing on the fringes of Islamic society and subject to a host of legal disabilities, the non-Muslims were instrinsically excluded from political participation in the Muslim state. The answer, however, is inherent in the question. Political exclusion carried with it as a corollary a large measure of autonomy, which Islam granted the protected non-Muslim communities in the expectation that they would regulate their own religious affairs and see to their communal needs. This dispensation, a legacy of ancient Near Eastern custom, necessarily involved Jewish and Christian religious institutions in a complex political system that incorporated administrative functions normally associated with the state.

In their main contours, the administrative practices of the Jews did not differ markedly from those of the Muslims. For instance, there existed a structure of political relationships between center and periphery similar to the political inter-connections in Islam between centers of imperial authority and their provincial and local dependencies. The parallel is most striking in the case of the institution of the exilarch, or the "head of the diaspora" (*resh galuta* in Aramaic; *ra's al-jālūt* in Arabic). During the early Islamic centuries, this royal Davidic dignitary, whose seat was in Baghdad and whose sovereignty was recognized by the Abbasid Caliph, ruled over the Jewish communities of the Middle Eastern periphery, whether in Iran or in the lands of the Mediterranean, with the full support of the Abbasid Caliph. The pomp and authority of the exilarch impressed Jewish and Muslim observers, alike.[1]

By way of contrast, the other principal institution of central Jewish

1 A sampling of Jewish and Muslim descriptions of the exilarch is conveniently accessible in English translation in Norman A. Stillman, *The Jews of Arab Lands: A History and Source Book* (Philadelphia, 1979), pp. 171-177, 252-254.

authority in the early Islamic period, namely, the *yeshivah*, or Talmudic academy — two in Iraq and one in Palestine — seems more exclusively "spiritual" and ecclesiastical than the exilarchate. However, it must be borne in mind that among the religious minorities of Islam the boundaries between religious and political leadership were somewhat less clearly drawn than they appear to have been, at least in the tenth and eleventh centuries, in the majority society.[2] Hence, even the *yeshivahs*, with their Talmudic conclaves and responsa, were partly political bodies, involved in administrative relations with the Jewish communities of the wider Muslim world.

This point has not always been recognized. As a result, important aspects of Jewish administrative history have been overlooked. The specific topic of administrative relations between Palestinian and Egyptian Jewry, which concerns us here, provides a case in point.[3] Take Jacob Mann's landmark study, *The Jews in Egypt and Palestine under the Fāṭimid Caliphs*,[4] based on the rich deposit of letters and documents preserved in the Cairo Geniza. In these sources, the adjacent lands of Egypt and Palestine are extremely well represented, and it is not surprising that Mann chose Jewish life in Fatimid Egypt and Palestine as an appropriate central theme for his work.

As a pioneer, Mann was necessarily preoccupied with establishing the chronological sequence of events and identifying the major personalities of the period. Only in his short, final chapter did he reflect back on the mass of detail he had uncovered and attempt systematically to describe the administrative institutions of the community and their interrelationships. On the question of administrative relations between the adjacent Jewish communities of Egypt and Palestine, however, Mann resorted to a theory that rested on literary sources outside the Geniza. These were the famous account of the arrival of the first *nagid* in Egypt, preserved in the 17th-century chronicle of Joseph b. Isaac Sambari (and a shorter variant in a responsum of the 16th-century Cairo Chief Rabbi, David ibn Abi Zimrah), and the biography of the "*nagid*" Palṭīel b. Shephaṭyah in the 11th-century *Megillat Aḥima'aẓ*. Adopting a view voiced by several predecessors who had studied these accounts, Mann believed that the center of Jewish communal administration during the entire Fatimid period was located in

2 On the Islamic case, see Roy P. Mottahedeh, *Loyalty and Leadership in an Early Islamic Society* (Princeton, 1980), pp. 135-150.

3 This paper is based principally on Geniza materials that have appeared in print. My own research has been centrally concerned with the Jewish community of Egypt and only peripherally with that of Palestine — specifically, where pertinent evidence has illuminated questions of Egyptian Jewish communal history. When Professor Moshe Gil publishes his corpus of Geniza documents about Palestine and Palestinian Jewry from the Islamic conquest to the first crusade, new data relevant to the topic at hand will doubtless come to light.

4 2 vols. (Oxford, 1920-1922); reprint edition, 2 vols. in one, with Preface and Reader's Guide by S.D. Goitein (New York, 1970). Henceforth: *Jews in Egypt*.

the Egyptian capital, in the office of the *nagid*, a dignitary portrayed in the literary sources in terms reminiscent of the exilarch of Baghdad. Mann argued that, as part of their anti-Abbasid foreign policy, the Fatimids created the institution of the Nagidate shortly after conquering Egypt in 969, in order to divest Egyptian Jewry of loyalty to the Jewish "head of the diaspora" in Baghdad. In Mann's words, the *nagid* (in Arabic: *raīs al-yahūd*, "head of the Jews") became "the leading political position in the community," exercising authority over the Jews in Fatimid Palestine and Syria, as well.[5]

In Mann's construction, therefore, Egypt constituted the center of administrative authority in the Fatimid empire. Fatimid Jewry had its surrogate exilarch in the person of the *nagid*, who, like his Baghdad counterpart, lived near the center of imperial authority. Regarding the *yeshivah* of neighboring Palestine, Mann concluded that it exercised only "spiritual" influence over Egyptian Jewry.[6] Characteristically, his summary discussion of "the academy and those connected with it," which fills the last nine pages of the final chapter of his book, concerns the *internal* organization of the *yeshivah* only. The *yeshivah*'s connection with Jews outside its walls amounted, in Mann's understanding, to the seemingly trivial practice of dispensing honorific titles to benefactors and to scholars.[7]

Since the publication of *The Jews in Egypt and in Palestine*, historians, including Mann himself, have continually added "flesh and blood" to the original "skeleton", as Mann modestly characterized his study. Regarding administrative relations between Palestinian and Egyptian Jewry, a major breakthrough was achieved by S.D. Goitein. Goitein found documents in the Geniza from the early part of the eleventh century proving that, originally, the Fatimid Caliph recognized the *gaon*, or head of the *yeshivah*, of Jerusalem as the chief administrative official of the Jewish community in the empire. One of these documents, a letter from a *gaon* to a Jewish notable in Fusṭāṭ, written after the Caliph al-Ẓāhir's accession to the throne in 1021, requests that confirmation in office be secured on the *gaon*'s behalf from the new Caliph. It states that "three of his (the Caliph's) ancestors have been beneficent to us, and their rescripts are with us, the rescript of his great-grandfather, that of his grandfather, and that of his father."[8] Thus under the first four Fatimid Caliphs of Egypt, al-Mu'izz (d.

5 *Ibid.*, I, 251-257.

6 *Ibid.*, I, 16.

7 *Ibid.*, I, 272-280.

8 S.D. Goitein, "New Sources on the Palestinian Gaonate," in *Salo Wittmayer Baron Jubilee Volume*, ed. Saul Lieberman in association with Arthur Hyman (Jerusalem, 1974), English section, I, 517-523, 531-533 [reprinted in his *Ha-yishuv be-eretz yisrael be-reshit ha-islam uvi-tequfat ha-tzalbanim (Palestinian Jewry in Early Islamic and Crusader Times)*, ed. Joseph Hacker (Jerusalem, 1980), pp. 70-76] (TS 24.43 = Taylor-Schechter Collection, Cambridge University Library, Cambridge, England).

975), his son al-'Azīz (reigned 975-96), the latter's son and successor, al-Ḥākim (996-1021) and al-Ḥākim's son al-Ẓāhir (1021-36), the *gaons* of Palestine solicited and received letters of appointment from the Fatimid ruler confirming them in office.

No Fatimid decree investing a Palestinian *gaon* in office has yet been found, but one of the other documents discovered by Goitein indirectly conveys the contents of such a document. The item in question is a testimony written in Arabic characters and outlining the prerogatives of a Palestinian *gaon*. Doubtless it was meant to be submitted to the Fatimid Caliph in the form of a petition, requesting government approval of the community's candidate for the Gaonate and confirmation of his authority to administer Jewish affairs.[9] Whether the petition was drawn up on the occasion of the designation of a new *gaon*,[10] requesting a rescript transferring to him the prerogatives exercised by his Gaonic predecessor, or on the occasion of the accession of a new Caliph,[11] whereupon to ensure continuity the incumbent *gaon* would have wanted to renew the rescript granted by the previous Caliph, is not important for our purposes. Important is the evidence this document provides regarding the suzerainty of the *gaon* over the Jews living in the Fatimid state.

In form, the petition is a legal affidavit in which the signatories attest to the fitness of the candidate and accept the yoke of his rule. We know from the texts of Islamic diplomas of investiture for Christian and Jewish community heads outside of Egypt that the Islamic ruler required some evidence of communal satisfaction with its candidate prior to issuing a decree of appointment. For instance, in the only extant diploma of investiture for a new *gaon*, dated 1209 in Baghdad, the Caliph notes, before confirming the *gaon*'s jurisdiction and authority: "Since it has come to be known how he is esteemed by the people of his sect and what good qualities he possesses, and since he is worthy of that which he has petitioned by virtue of his good conduct amongst them and his impeccable demeanor . . . ."[12] Similarly, the Fatimid Caliph, upon receipt of communal approval in

9 S.D. Goitein, "The Head of the Palestinian Academy as Head of the Jews in the Fatimid Empire: Arabic Documents on the Palestinian Gaonate" (in Hebrew), *Eretz-Israel* 10 (1971), 100-106 (= *Ha-yishuv*, pp. 52-60); English translation in "New Sources," pp. 523-525; discussion of same by Goitein in *A Mediterranean Society*, 4 vols. (Berkeley and Los Angeles, 1967-1983), II, 16-17, and in his article "The Interplay of Jewish and Islamic Laws" in *Jewish Law in Legal History and the Modern World*, ed. Bernard S. Jackson (Leiden, 1980), pp. 62-64 (Dropsie 354 = Dropsie University Collection, Philadelphia, Pennsylvania).

10 Goitein, "The Head of the Palestinian Academy," p. 101 (= *Ha-yishuv*, p. 54).

11 Goitein, "New Sources," p. 528.

12 Ibn al-Sā'ī, *Al-jāmi' al-mukhtaṣar*, vol. 9, ed. Muṣṭafā Jawād and Father Anastase-Marie (Baghdad, 1934), pp. 266-269; English translation in Stillman, *op. cit.*, pp. 178-179. Phraseology that appears in an Abbasid diploma of investiture for a Nestorian Catholicos, dated 1138, further explicates the administrative reality underlying the

the form of a testimony like the one found by Goitein in the Geniza, would have issued the appropriate letter patent incorporating the prerogatives of Gaonic office.

During the early Fatimid period, therefore, the center of administrative leadership in the Jewish community was located in Jerusalem, not in Cairo. The office of the head of the Jews (or *nagid*) did not come into existence until much later. I am not suggesting, however, that the Fatimids granted central leadership to the Palestinian *gaon* in order to divest their Jewish subjects of loyalty to the exilarch of Abbasid Baghdad, as had been argued by Mann in the case of the Nagidate. In reality, things probably had more to do with the exigencies of Fatimid administration than with the internal political orientation of the Jewish community. Having just established an independent Caliphate in Egypt and in Palestine, the Fatimid ruler needed to begin acting the part of Caliph. An important Caliphal prerogative was the right to invest non-Muslim religious dignitaries with authority over their communities. As the Abbasid Caliph issued diplomas of investiture to Christian and Jewish leaders in his realm, so, too, his rival, the Fatimid Caliph, would have desired to do the same in *his*. Abbasid letters of appointment for Jewish communal heads went to the *gaon*s of the *yeshivah*s and to the exilarch.[13] Their counterpart in the Fatimid empire was the head of the Palestinian *yeshivah* who, since Roman times, had enjoyed considerable prestige and authority in Egypt. He, therefore, was the obvious and natural choice as leader.

selection of Jewish communal heads like the *gaon*: "Your case was brought to the attention of the Commander of the Faithful, to the effect that you are the most exemplary of the people of your creed in conduct, the closest of them to rectitude in both deportment and character, the one of them most fully endowed with those qualities which they agree distinguish you from them . . . ; and further, that you satisfy the conditions recognized among them for [accession to] the catholicate, and that testimony on your behalf confirms you as the epitome of its attributes and characteristics . . . There was in attendance a group of those Christians whose assistance is sought for examining the life history of men like you and for bringing facts to light about men of similar status and position. . . . And they asked that their petition be put into effect concerning you through the approval by which its rules would be established, its promises fulfilled, its foundations consolidated, and its intents strengthened." Translation taken from a new edition and discussion of this important document, by Lawrence I. Conrad, "A Nestorian Diploma of Investiture from the *Tadkira* of Ibn Ḥamdūn: The Text and its Significance," in *Studies in Honour of Iḥsān 'Abbās*, ed. Wadād al-Qāḍī (Beirut, 1980), p. 97.

13 I do not agree with the view that Samuel b. Eli, Baghdad *gaon* from 1164 to 1194, was the first Babylonian *gaon* to receive a letter of appointment from an Abbasid Caliph [see A. Schochat, "Some Topics from the Period of the Gaonim" (in Hebrew), in *Meḥqarim be-toledot 'am yisrael ve-eretz yisrael* (*Studies in the History of the Jewish People and the Land of Israel*), vol. 2, ed. B. Oded *et al.* (Haifa, 1972), pp. 66-67, n. 19; and Salo W. Baron, *A Social and Religious History of the Jews*, 2d ed., vol. 17 (New York and Philadelphia, 1980), p. 148]. When Nathan the Babylonian (tenth century) reports of Sa'adyah Gaon's enemy, Caleb (Khalaf) ibn Sargado, that he "paid 60,000 dirhems of his own in order to

The selection of the head of the Jerusalem *yeshivah* as leader of Fatimid Jewry was necessitated by a further consideration which had little to do with Jewish ties to Baghdad. The principal element in the Islamic grant of autonomy to the non-Muslim religious communities consisted in the prerogative to maintain a system of courts and judges and to exercise internal legal control over most aspects of life.[14] This dispensation flowed naturally from the ancient Near Eastern tradition, which the Muslims inherited, that law is personal rather than territorial and that religio-ethnic groups have the right to be governed by their ancestral laws.[15] Accordingly, the non-Muslim leader recognized by the Islamic state had to possess the qualifications to license judges. Within the borders of the Fatimid empire, it was the Jerusalem *yeshivah* and its head, the *gaon*, that laid exclusive claim to this distinction. Naturally, therefore, the head of the *yeshivah* of Palestine was the logical choice of the Fatimids to receive the Caliph's letter of appointment installing him as administrative chief of the Jews residing in their empire.

In short, the position of the Palestinian *gaon* as head of the Jews in the Fatimid state resulted, in the first instance, from administrative needs of the newly established Fatimid Caliphate, rather than from concern about Jewish loyalties toward Abbasid Baghdad.

The *details* of Jewish administrative authority, on the other hand, were largely determined by Jewish, rather than by Fatimid, interests. Apart from judicial supervision, the Islamic state cared little about the other functions that constituted religious authority among the Christians and Jews. Generally, the Muslims left it to the respective minority communities to define the competency of their leaders. Thus, the petition to the Fatimid Caliph mentioned above lists several other leadership functions of the *gaon*. These include: the expounding of religious law in public lectures;

remove Sa'adyah from his position" [A. Neubauer, ed. *Mediaeval Jewish Chronicles*, vol. 2 (Oxford, 1895), p. 80.] it can only mean that he bribed the Caliph to rescind Sa'adyah's letter of appointment as head of the *yeshivah* of Sura. Possibly the procedure of issuing patents to *gaons* went into abeyance during the period of Babylonian Gaonic decline in the late eleventh and early twelfth centuries, so that it had to be *revived* when Samuel b. Eli assumed office. Samuel's vigorous campaign to restore Babylonian Gaonic hegemony in the Near East, and with it the Gaonate's cherished prerogatives, is well attested.

14 See, regarding the Christian communities, Néophyte Edelby, "L'autonomie législative des chrétiens en terre d'Islam," *Archives d'histoire du droit oriental* (*Bruxelles*) 5 (1950-1951), 307-351, and Baron's seconding of the motion as regards the Jews, in his *Social and Religious History*, vol. 5 (New York, 1957), p. 294. The version of the rights and disabilities of the non-Muslims codified by al-Shāfi'ī in *Kitāb al-umm* [Bulaq, 1903-1904, IV, 118-119; English translation in Bernard Lewis, *From the Prophet Muhammad to the Capture of Constantinople*, vol. 2 (New York, 1974), pp. 219-223] specifically incorporates this prerogative.

15 Goitein, *Mediterranean Society*, I, 66; Gustave E. von Grunebaum, "Eastern Jewry under Islam," *Viator* 2 (1971), 366.

supervision of marriage and divorce; the imposition of the ban of excommunication; and the appointment and dismissal of preachers, cantors, and meat slaughterers. Much if not all of this was probably incorporated into the Fatimid letter of appointment for the *gaon*, if we may extrapolate backward in time from the few extant Mamluk patents defining the powers of the *ra'īs al-yahūd*, who inherited the Palestinian *gaon*'s position as leader of Egyptian and Syro-Palestinian Jewry at the end of the eleventh century.[16]

With the support of the Fatimid government, therefore, the *yeshivah* and Gaonate of Jerusalem enjoyed the status of central ruling authority over the Jews in the Fatimid realm; the Egyptian Jewish community was, so to speak, a province on the administrative periphery of the Palestinian Gaonate. Indeed, much of the Geniza evidence about Jewish life in Egypt during the first century of Fatimid rule, especially as regards the pivotal prerogative of juridical supervision, accords with the assumption of Palestinian sovereignty over Egypt. Local judicial leadership usually rested in the hands of persons bearing the scholarly title of *ḥaver*, that is, "member" of the *yeshivah* of Palestine. Of the nine judges in Fusṭāṭ and Cairo whose careers can be fixed during this period on the basis of dated legal documents, all but two, namely, Shemaryah b. Elḥanan (ca. 980-1010) and his son Elḥanan (d. ca. 1025), bore the title *ḥaver*. They are: Ephraim b. Eli b. Ṭarson, ca. 965-95; Ephraim b. Shemaryah, 1016-47; Shmuel b. Avṭalyon ha-Kohen, 1016-41; Avraham b. Sahlān, 1016-ca. 1032; Sahlān b. Avraham, 1034-49; Natan b. Yeshu'ah ha'Levi, 1040-50; and Eli b. 'Amram 1055-66.[17] Avraham b. Sahlān and his son Sahlān, notables of Babylonian extraction who in succession headed the Babylonian congregation of Fusṭāṭ and held the Babylonian title of leadership, *alluf*, both received second ordinations as *ḥaver* from the Palestinian *yeshivah*.[18] This titulature symbolized their deputization by the chief juridical authority in the empire, the *gaon* of Jerusalem.

If Fatimid recognition of the sovereignty of the Palestinian *gaon* strengthened the hand of the *yeshivah* of Jerusalem vis-à-vis the Egyptian Jewish courts, as it most certainly did, it did not guarantee undivided Egyptian loyalty to the Jerusalem *gaon*. With respect to the larger complex of elements that comprised administrative-religious leadership in the Jewish community, the Palestinian Gaonate had powerful competition. By the tenth century, the Babylonian *yeshivah*s had come to overshadow the

16 Al-Qalqashandī, *Ṣubḥ al-a'shā* (Cairo, 1913-1918), XI, 390-391; English translation in Stillman, *op. cit.*, pp. 269-270. See also C.E. Bosworth, "Christian and Jewish Religious Dignitaries in Mamlūk Egypt and Syria: Qalqashandī's Information on their Hierarchy, Titulature, and Appointment," *International Journal of Middle East Studies* 3 (1972), 210-215.

17 Goitein, *Mediterranean Society*, II, 511-512.

18 Mann, *Jews in Egypt*, I, 96-100.

yeshivah of Jerusalem as regards scholarly stature and religious authority among the Jews of the Islamic world. This was largely a consequence of the migration of Babylonian Jews to the Mediterranean provinces of the Muslim empire in the early Islamic centuries. Egypt, for instance, possessed a considerable population of Babylonian Jews by the tenth century. These *'Irāqiyyūn*, as they were called in Arabic, established separate synagogues following the Babylonian liturgical rite and maintained strong ties with the *yeshivah*s and *gaon*s of their ancestral homeland. As the eleventh century wore on, large numbers of Tunisian Jews settled permanently in Egypt.[19] These Maghrebis hailed from a region that had absorbed large numbers of Jews from Iraq and Iran in the early Islamic period and which had a long-standing *halakhic* orientation toward the Babylonian Gaonate. Even the establishment of independent *yeshivah*s and of indigenous rabbinic scholarship in Qayrawan at the end of the tenth and the beginning of the eleventh centuries did not stem the flow of *halakhic* questions from that city to Baghdad.[20]

In Fusṭāṭ during the early part of the eleventh century, Joseph b. Jacob ibn 'Awkal, a merchant from an Iraqi family that had migrated to Tunisia and later on to Egypt, mediated the flow of North African and Egyptian *halakhic* questions to the Babylonian *gaon*s and the counterflow of Babylonian responsa.[21] His position within the Egyptian Jewish community represents one of the most concrete manifestations of the transplantation of Tunisian Jewry's Babylonian orientation onto Egyptian soil. It also might help explain why, even among the *halakhic* riches of the Cairo Geniza, responsa emanating from the *yeshivah* of neighboring Palestine are scarcely to be found.[22]

Given the acknowledged *halakhic* subordination of the Palestinian Gao-

19 The web of commercial and family connections linking native Egyptian Jewry with the Jews of Tunisia, which, in turn, laid the groundwork for the permanent settlement of so many Maghrebis in Egypt in the eleventh century, constitutes one of the most fascinating demographic revelations to have emerged from the systematic study of the Geniza documents. See Goitein, *Mediterranean Society*, I, *passim*, and elsewhere in Goitein's extensive bibliography [for which refer to *A Bibliography of the Writings of Professor Shelomo Dov Goitein*, compiled by Robert Attal (Jerusalem, 1975) and numerous items published by Goitein since 1975].

20 H.Z. Hirschberg, *Toledot ha-Yehudim be-Afriqa ha-Tzefonit*, vol. 1 (Jerusalem, 1965), pp. 226-230, 236-255; English translation, *A History of the Jews in North Africa*, vol. 1 (Leiden, 1974), pp. 298-304, 311-339.

21 On Joseph b. Jacob ibn 'Awkal see Norman A. Stillman, "The Eleventh Century Merchant House of Ibn 'Awkal (A Geniza Study)," *Journal of the Economic and Social History of the Orient* 16 (1973), 15-88; *idem*, "Joseph Ibn 'Awkal: A Jewish Communal Leader in Eleventh-Century Egypt," in *The Eleventh Century*, ed. Stanley Ferber and Sandro Sticca (Binghamton, New York, 1974), pp. 39-50; S.D. Goitein, *Letters of Medieval Jewish Traders* (Princeton, 1973), pp. 26-28 and *passim* (see index s.v.).

22 On the relative absence of Palestinian Gaonic responsa, in general, and from the Geniza in particular, see Mann, *Jews in Egypt*, I, 151, and Goitein, *Ha-yishuv*, p. 45.

nate to the Gaonate of Babylonia, and the strong pro-Babylonian sympathies of a considerable segment of Egyptian Jewry, it is not surprising to find periodic signs of conflict in Egypt over the administrative hegemony of the Palestinian *yeshivah*. The Geniza documents of the Fatimid period bear witness to a continuing tension generated among Egyptian Jews by conflicting loyalties and by a latent desire to reduce their dependency upon a center of learning and religious authority that had become seriously attenuated.[23]

These tendencies came to the fore, for instance, when Shemaryah b. Elḥanan was active in Jewish life in Fusṭāṭ (ca. 980-1010). Shemaryah, it will be recalled, was one of the "four captives" whom Abraham ibn Daud in his *Sefer ha-Qabbalah* credited with transferring rabbinic authority from the *yeshivah*s of Babylonia to Spain, North Africa, and Egypt.[24] In reality, Shemaryah b. Elḥanan's role in Egyptian Jewish history was considerably more complex than Ibn Daud knew, or at least cared to portray. Shemaryah did not precipitate a break with Babylonia, after the manner of Moses b. Ḥanokh, his co-captive who was ransomed in Spain. On the contrary, Shemaryah was a loyal disciple of the Babylonian *gaon*s Sherira and Hay, and probably had studied under Sherira in Baghdad at the *yeshivah* of Pumbedita. In Egypt, Shemaryah forwarded legal queries from Qayrawan addressed to these *gaon*s, sent them queries of his own, and received lavish praise from them for his superior scholarship.[25]

Shemaryah's Babylonian connections strengthened rather than weakened Egyptian Jewry's bonds with Iraq. However, his presence must have been a source of tension as regards their official administrative subordination to the *yeshivah* of Palestine. This tension seems to have been resolved in Shemaryah's time through some sort of concession on the part of the leadership of the Palestinian *yeshivah*. Apparently with at least the tacit

23 Such tensions over conflicting loyalties had marked the communal landscape even before the time of the Fatimids. During the acrimonious calendar dispute of the year 920-921, which pitted the Palestinian *gaon* Aharon Ben Meir against the Babylonian *yeshivahs* and their defender, Sa'adyah b. Joseph al-Fayyūmī, Egyptian Jewry was torn between allegiance to the opinion of the Palestinian *gaon* and that of their countryman in Babylonia, Sa'adyah [see H.J. Bornstein, "The Controversy between R. Sa'adyah Gaon and Ben Meir" (in Hebrew), in *Nahum Sokolow Anniversary Volume* (Warsaw, 1904), pp. 19-189; and Henry Malter, *Saadiah Gaon: His Life and Works* (1921; reprint edition New York, 1969), pp. 69-88]. While the calendar dispute did not involve the issue of juridical administration, it did concern religious authority, namely, competing Palestinian and Babylonian claims to the important religious prerogative of fixing the annual Jewish holiday cycle. When successfully exercised, this right reinforced a more general claim to political sovereignty over provincial Jewish communities, such as that of Egypt.

24 Abraham ibn Daud, *Sefer ha-Qabbalah*, ed. Gerson D. Cohen (Philadelphia, 1967), pp. 46ff. (Hebrew), 63ff. (English translation).

25 S.D. Goitein, "Shemaryah b. Elḥanan" (in Hebrew), *Tarbiz* 32 (1962-63), 266-272; Shraga Abramson, *Ba-merkazim uva-tefutzot bi-tequfat ha-geonim* (Jerusalem, 1965), pp. 156-173; Goitein, *Mediterranean Society*, indices s.v.

approval of the Jerusalem Gaonate, Shemaryah established, for the first time as far as we know, an academy of Talmudic learning in Fusṭāṭ, a so-called "*midrash*," patterned on the model of the school for students attached to the *yeshivah*s in Baghdad.[26] Officially, as noted above, the prerogative to teach Jewish religious law in the Fatimid empire was reserved for the Palestinian *gaon*. We must therefore surmise that the latter did not object to the establishment of a *midrash* in Fusṭāṭ. At least, no protest against Shemaryah for exercising this privilege is known from the Geniza evidence thus far analyzed. Quite the contrary, it seems that the leadership of the Jerusalem *yeshivah* maintained friendly ties with Shemaryah, through correspondence, personal contacts and by appointing his son, Elḥanan, to the six-man governing board of the *yeshivah*.[27] Nor do we hear any objections to Shemaryah's issuing responsa on his own authority, even though this constituted another infringement upon Gaonic functions.[28] Shemaryah also adopted some of the trappings of Gaonic office, such as the use in his letters of the conventional Gaonic epistolary preface containing greetings from the master of the academy and his pupils.[29] Moreover, his title of *Av beth din* further symbolized a claim to Gaonic authority. The *Av beth din* was head of the rabbinic court of the *yeshivah* and heir apparent to the Gaonate.

While, as it appears, open opposition to Shemaryah b. Elḥanan from the Jerusalemites did not surface during his lifetime,[30] our sources do reveal that his son and successor, Elḥanan, was the object of considerable Palestinian dissatisfaction.[31] The reasons behind Palestinian Gaonic hostility toward Elḥanan b. Shemaryah, which even led to his temporary excommunication and to his expulsion from membership in the Jerusalem

26 *Ibid.*, II, 199, 202; *idem*, "Shemaryah b. Elḥanan," p. 271 (states that the *midrash* probably met in the synagogue) (TS 12.43).

27 An example of the correspondence: Mann, *Jews in Egypt*, II, 23-24 (TS 16.68). Appointment as "sixth" *(shishi)* in the *yeshivah* hierarchy: Abramson, *Ba-merkazim* etc., p. 109 (referring in note 20 to a text published by Simha Assaf, *Teshuvot ha-geonim* [see next note]).

28 Responsa: Simha Assaf, *Teshuvot ha-geonim* (Jerusalem, 1942), pp. 113-116 (TS Loan 17 and 18); Louis Ginzberg, *Ginze Schechter (Genizah Studies in Memory of Doctor Solomon Schechter)*, vol. 2 (1929; reprint edition New York, 1969), pp. 261-265 (TS 20.35).

29 Goitein, "Shemaryah b. Elḥanan," p. 268.

30 Unless we are to take the omission of the Palestinian title of *ḥaver* from documents mentioning Shemaryah by name as a negative echo of Palestinian protest.

31 On Elḥanan b. Shemaryah see, especially, Abramson, *Ba-merkazim* etc., pp. 105-155, 175-179; S.D. Goitein, "Elḥanan b. Shemaryah as a Communal Leader" (in Hebrew), in *Joshua Finkel Festschrift*, ed. Sidney B. Hoenig and Leon D. Stitskin (New York, 1974), Hebrew section, pp. 117-137; and *idem*, *Mediterranean Society*, indices s.v. A recently-completed Hebrew M.A. thesis deals, in part, with the life and career of Elḥanan; Elinoar Bareket, "Elḥanan b. Shemaryah and Sahlan b. Abraham" (M.A. thesis, Tel Aviv University, 1980).

yeshivah, have not been fully explained.[32] We approach an understanding of the *yeshivah*'s opposition if we consider it within the context of administrative relations between the Egyptian and Palestinian communities. Shemaryah's activities in the Egyptian capital had gone unchallenged because he was viewed as an illustrious rabbinic scholar, and not as a competitor for administrative authority. As time passed, however, and the position Shemaryah had held by virtue of his learning and personal stature became more institutionalized in the hands of his son and successor, Elḥanan, the situation, as viewed from Jerusalem, became more threatening. It seems that Gaonic anxieties were well-founded. Everything we know about Elḥanan from the Geniza indicates that he attempted to enlarge his authority by appropriating administrative prerogatives and functions that were confirmed in the Fatimid letter of appointment for the Palestinian *gaon*. Evidently without the permission of the *gaon*, he adopted the practice of delivering public lectures (*peraqim*). He even had a "repeater" broadcast his sermons to the audience, thus taking over another time-honored custom of the *yeshivahs*.[33] He issued bans of excommunication[34] — ordinarily the exclusive province of the *gaon* — and extended his hand into the administratively significant realm of family life.[35] Moreover, he cultivated the loyalty of Jewish congregations in Syria and Palestine (Damascus, Acre), at the very back door of the *yeshivah*, and successfully extracted donations from them for his Fusṭāṭ college.[36] Surely, Elḥanan's incursion

32 Jacob Mann wrote: "The cause of the resentment (i.e. by the Palestinian *gaon* Solomon b. Judah) is only vaguely discernible, but it seems to have had to do with a change in attitude on the part of Elḥanan toward the Palestinian academy"; Mann, *Texts and Studies in Jewish History and Literature*, 2 vols. (1931-1935; reprint edition with Introduction by Gerson D. Cohen, New York, 1972), I, 200. Shraga Abramson wrote: "We do not know what caused it (i.e. Solomon b. Judah's condemnation of Elḥanan). It seems that internal affairs of Fusṭāṭ Jewry were the cause. Apparently, relations between the 'Jerusalemite congregation' of Fusṭāṭ, which was led by Ephraim b. Shemaryah, and the 'Babylonian congregation,' which was led by Elḥanan, became damaged at a certain point, and that is what caused the change in attitude of the Palestinians toward Elḥanan"; *Ba-merkazim*, p. 109. Goitein, focusing on Elḥanan's personality, comes closer to the mark: "Elḥanan was an ambitious man, and, as a critical writer recounts, had his lectures broadcast by a scholar specifically appointed for the task, a custom, we remember, prevailing in the yeshivas"; *Mediterranean Society*, II, 202; and Goitein's remarks elsewhere: "Elḥanan yearned to receive the status of '*Av beth din* of all Israel' held by his father, bu the yeshiva apparently did not agree to this, and relations cooled"; "Elḥanan b. Shemaryah as Communal Leader," p. 119.

33 Abramson, *Ba-merkazim*, p. 111; Goitein, *Mediterranean Society*, II, 202, 213. The important Geniza letter which cites these infringements, Heidelberg 910, is discussed below. For examples of Elḥanan's sermons, see Abramson, *Ba-merkazim*, pp. 142-155.

34 Goitein, "Elḥanan b. Shemaryah as a Communal Leader," pp. 121 (TS 8 J 22, fol. 14).

35 Abramson, *Ba-merkazim*, p. 116; cf. Goitein, "Elḥanan b. Shemaryah as Communal Leader," pp. 124-125 (TS 16.134).

36 Damascus: Mann, *Jews in Egypt*, II, 39-40; cf. I, 38-39; Abramson, *Ba-merkazīm*, pp. 176-178 (TS 18 J 4, fol. 5). Acre: Goitein, "Elḥanan b. Shemaryah as Communal Leader," pp. 133-134 (TS 13 J 35, fol. 2).

into communities beyond the borders of Egypt that stood in close geographical proximity to Jerusalem, and his bid for funds that might otherwise have gone to support the *yeshivah*, posed a serious threat to the authority of the Gaonate. Elḥanan went even further and procured a stipend for his school from the Fatimid Caliph, thereby duplicating an earlier achievement of the Palestinian Gaonate.[37]

In the eyes of the Palestinian *yeshivah*, therefore, Elḥanan's prinicipal transgression was administrative usurpation. It is no wonder that Solomon b. Judah, who was "Third" in the hierarchy of the *yeshivah* while Elḥanan carried on his communal activities in Egypt, and succeeded to the Gaonate at just about the time that Elḥanan disappears from our records, found him so intolerable. We, however, should not make the mistake of thinking that Elḥanan acted in a vacuum. He could not have attained the power he did without the support of at least a segment of his local community. Indeed, the wide range of communal functions that he exercised suggests that Egyptian Jews genuinely desired his leadership.

It is possible that external factors made the community particularly receptive to an expansion of administrative power in the Egyptian capital during the time of Elḥanan b. Shemaryah. These were the years when the Caliph al-Ḥākim's persecution of Christian *dhimmīs* spilled over into the Jewish quarters of Egypt.[38] Many anxious Jews may have begun to question the wisdom of having their leadership located in Jerusalem, so far from the Fatimid court. True, intercession on behalf of the Fatimid Jews had always been relegated to the hands of Cairene Jewish notables, a situation necessitated by the great distances that separated central Jewish administration from the imperial capital. Nonetheless, in a time of trouble, the geographical gap may have loomed ever larger, and a need may have been felt to establish a closer relationship between Jewish and Fatimid central government. Elḥanan b. Shemaryah evidently had some connection with the Fatimid court. His letter mentioning the Fatimid stipend indicates that he had access to the Caliph.[39] The community may very well have desired to capitalize on Elḥanan's relationship with the ruler of Egypt to have his administrative authority expanded.

One of the published Geniza letters about Elḥanan hints that something of this sort was actually contemplated. The document in question is the oft-discussed letter from the Heidelberg papyri collection, first published by A. Kamenetzky in 1908. The missive criticizes Elḥanan for demanding that the Palestinian *gaon* grant him the title of *Av beth din* (held by his

37 Elḥanan's stipend: Mann, *Jews in Egypt*, II, 40; cf. I, 38-39; Abramson, *Ba-merkazim*, pp. 108, 177 (TS 18 J 4, fol. 5). Stipend of Palestinian Gaonate: Mann, *Jews in Egypt*, II, 69-70; cf. I, 71-72 (TS 13 J 26, fol. 16).

38 See *Encyclopaedia of Islam*, 2d edition, s.v. "al-Ḥākim bi-Amr Allāh"; Goitein, *Mediterranean Society*, II, 28-29; Stillman, *The Jews of Arab Lands*, pp. 201-203.

39 Mann, *Jews in Egypt*, II, 40; Abramson, *Ba-merkazim*, p. 177 (TS 18 J 4, fol. 5).

father) and for usurping the Gaonic prerogative to deliver public lectures on Jewish law (*peraqim*).

Much disagreement exists over the provenance of this letter, its destination, and the meaning of several of its passages.[40] Here I would like to discuss a few details whose significance has hitherto gone unnoticed. Paraphrasing an *aggadic* statement, the writer says of Elḥanan:

ואולם ש ר ר ה הוא מבקש והיא בורחת הימנו

"However, he seeks *serarah* ("dominion"), but it escapes him."[41] The *aggadic* statement upon which the letter-writer drew reads (Babylonian Talmud Erubin 13b):

כל המחזר על הגדולה גדולה בורחת ממנו

"Whoever runs after greatness, greatness escapes him." The substitution of the word *serarah* ("dominion") for *gedulah* ("greatness") can be found in the Talmud commentary of Ḥananel b. Ḥushīel, Elḥanan b. Shemaryah's North African contemporary, though the reading *gedulah* is attested in the Munich manuscript of the Babylonian Talmud.[42] As I have shown elsewhere, the rabbinic word *serarah* carried a specific connotation in the Middle Eastern Jewish vocabulary. Related to the Biblical noun *sar*, which Arabic-speaking Jews employed as the equivalent of the Arabic title *ra'īs*, *serarah* conveyed roughly the same range of meanings associated with the Arabic term for leadership, *ri'āsa*.[43] *Ri'āsa*, an extremely flexible component of the medieval Arabic political vocabulary,[44] had a variety of uses among the Jews. For instance, it denoted the leadership of the *yeshivah* (the official Arabic title of whose head was *ra's al-mathība*) or that of the exilarch (*ra's al-jālūt*). More loosely, *ri'āsa* designated, simply, scholarly leadership. As mentioned earlier, however, in Judeo-Arabic society the boundary between scholarly (*halakhic*) and administrative leadership was less rigid than in the world of Islam. The writer of our letter seems, therefore, to be accusing Elḥanan of seeking *serarah/ri'āsa*, that is to say, scholarly *cum* administrative leadership in the community. Far from being satisfied with the title *Av beth din*, second-in-rank to the *gaon*, he says,

40 Heidelberg 910. See Shaul Shaked, *A Tentative Bibliography of Geniza Documents* (Paris, 1964), p. 165, for bibliography up to 1963; Abramson, *Ba-merkazim*, pp. 110-112; Goitein, *Mediterranean Society*, II, 202. I have examined the bromide print of this manuscript in the possession of Professor S.D. Goitein.

41 Lines 12-13 of the letter.

42 R. Ḥananel may have been influenced by a version of this *aggadic* statement found in the late *midrashic* collection, *Tanḥuma*, Leviticus 3 (standard printed edition): "Kol mi sherodef aḥar serarah, serarah boraḥat mimenu; Kol mi sheboreaḥ min haserarah, haserarah rodefet aḥarav" (ed. Buber, Leviticus 4, omits the first half of the saying). Or, R. Ḥananel may have paraphrased the statement in Erubin with the word *serarah*, under the influence of the contemporary connotation of the term discussed below.

43 Mark R. Cohen, *Jewish Self-Government in Medieval Egypt: The Origins of the Office of Head of the Jews, ca. 1065-1126* (Princeton, 1980), pp. 166-168.

44 Mottahedeh, *op. cit.*, pp. 129-157.

Elḥanan really wanted some of the administrative-religious authority held by the *gaon*, himself.[45]

Another overlooked detail of the letter strengthens this hypothesis. I refer to its date of Adar, 1021. In the year 1021, the month of Adar began on February 17 and ended on March 17. On February 13 of that very year (27 Shawwāl) the Caliph al-Ḥākim met his mysterious end (the sources say that he "disappeared" while walking at night in the hills around Cairo).[46] This chronological coincidence is quite suggestive. As stated above, upon the succession of a new Caliph, the Fatimid Jewish community habitually petitioned for a renewal of the government patent appointing its administrative leader. Is it not possible that, at the time of the accession of al-Ḥākim's son and successor al-Ẓāhir, on or about February 13, 1021, Elḥanan b. Shemaryah, with the support of local Jewish backers, contemplated petitioning for his own appointment as chief administrative authority over the Jews? As we have seen, *de facto* Elḥanan already fulfilled many of the administrative-religious functions inscribed into the *gaon*'s Fatimid patent. Moreover, Elḥanan's scholarly credentials for leadership were unchallengeable. The death of the Caliph on Feruary 13, 1021, at which time it became necessary to renew the patent for the *gaon*, would have provided a logical occasion for requesting such an amendment to the existing arrangement.

It is not necessary to view this as an attempt to abolish the Gaonate. Rather, I suggest that Elḥanan planned to become the recognized *ra'īs* of Egyptian Jewry,[47] that is to say, to make the *de facto* state of affairs *de jure*.

45 *Ri'āsa* refers to the office of head of the diaspora (i.e. the exilarchate) in the Arabic original of Nathan the Babylonian's tenth-century account of Jewish life in Baghdad; Israel Friedlander, "The Arabic Original of the Report of R. Nathan Hababli," *Jewish Quarterly Review*, o.s. 17 (1904-1905), 755: "*Fa-aqāmat al-riyasah mu'aṭṭalah mithl g(3) sinnin aw d(4)*" The word was rendered as *serarah* by the medieval Hebrew translator: "Wenisharah haserarah kemo d(4) o h(5) shanim belo rosh" (Neubauer, ed., *Mediaeval Jewish Chronicles*, II, 79); "The leadership (i.e. the office of the head of the diaspora) remained vacant for about 4 or 5 [Arabic original: 3 or 4] years." *Serarah* as a technical term for high office in the Palestinian *yeshivah* occurs in a letter from Solomon b. Judah regarding the anticipated struggle for power in the *yeshivah* hierarchy, that indeed broke out in 1038: "Hu hitḥil lehithalel ki ai[n] kamohu vekhi [rauy] liserarah." Mann, *Jews in Egypt*, II, 159 (TS 13 J 23, fol. 19). It is not clear to whom the description in these lines applies; cf. Mann, *Texts*, I, 326 re: lines 4 ff. in the letter. Cf. also in another letter of Solomon b. Judah's, Mann, *Jews in Egypt*, II, 121, line 34: "Mi hu asher asah serarah al beit Is[rael]" (TS 13 J 11, fol. 9). In a Hebrew letter (ENA 3765, fol. 1 = Elkan Nathan Adler Collection, Jewish Theological Seminary, New York), Daniel b. Azarya employs *serarah* to mean the office of the exilarch; Mann, *Jews in Egypt*, II, 216, no. 22, line 6.

46 See *Encyclopaedia of Islam*, 2d edition, s.v. "al-Ḥākim bi-Amr Allāh," p. 80.

47 In the address of a letter to Shemaryah and to his son Elḥanan, the father is referred to as *ra'īs al-yahūd*, "head of the Jews." It is not impossible that the Fatimid government, recognizing that Shemaryah b. Elḥanan exercised many of the prerogatives of the Palestinian *gaon*, actually granted him some sort of official recognition and title. The title itself, however, was adopted as the chancery designation for the central authority

The Jerusalem *gaon* could have continued to maintain his position as head of the *yeshivah* and perhaps of Jewry in Palestine.[48] One need not even suspect Elḥanan of coveting more of the *gaon*'s prerogatives than he already exercised. On the other hand, the *gaon* and his circle certainly would have considered him a usurper. That, I think, explains their vigorous opposition to Elḥanan, to which the Geniza letters bear such eloquent witness.

Following Elḥanan b. Shemaryah's disappearance from the Geniza documents, *circa* 1025, no new attempts to establish independent administrative leadership in Egypt are heard of until the 1060s, when the court physicians Judah and Mevorakh b. Saadya began to carve out a new basis of central Fatimid-Jewish administration in the office of *ra'īs al-yahūd*. The three intervening decades saw two imposing figures dominate the leadership of Fatimid Jewry: Solomon b. Judah of Fez, Palestinian *gaon* from 1026 to 1051, and the *nasi* Daniel b. 'Azaryah of Baghdad, *gaon* in Jerusalem from 1051 to 1062. The Geniza is particularly rich in documentation for this period, and much has been written on it from a variety of angles. Viewed in the context of administrative relations between Palestinian and Egyptian Jewry, some new aspects of the picture come to light. Briefly: "the period of Solomon b. Judah," as Mann labelled the years between 1026 and 1051, can be seen as a time of reassertion of Palestinian hegemony after the nearly successful attempt to transfer some of the *gaon*'s administrative power to Elḥanan b. Shemaryah in Cairo. The correspondence by and about Solomon b. Judah shows that this *gaon* expended considerable effort to preserve Jerusalem's pre-eminence in Fatimid Jewish affairs. At the same time, the sources contain echoes of rebelliousness in Egypt which suggest that the centrifugal forces that had surfaced during Elḥanan's time continued to make waves in the quarter century following his demise. Only

over Fatimid Jewry only toward the end of the eleventh century. The editor of the letter misinterpreted the Arabic words in the address. The correct reading is: *ilā Abī 'l-Ḥasan Shemaryā ra'īs* [*al-ya*] *hūd wa-li-Elḥanan fatāhu*. See Bernard Chapira, "A Letter from the Gaon R. Ṣemah b. Isaac to R. Elḥanan b. Shemarya" (in Hebrew), *Ginze Kedem* 3 (1925), 3-13. The editor's interpretation of the letter needs revision in the light of the correction made here.

48 Possibly an allusion to renewal of the *gaon*'s appointment is to be found in the enigmatic phrase in the letter: "Shalaḥ mikhtav el morenu geon ẓevi yeḥi la'ad leval yeḥadesh davar 'ad asher yikveno beshem avot." "He wrote to our master the *gaon* of Palestine, may he live forever, warning him *that he would renew nothing* unless he (i.e. the *gaon*) gave him (i.e. Elḥanan) the title of *Av* (i.e. *Av beth din*)." Elḥanan was in a position to block Fatimid renewal of the *gaon*'s patent by thwarting the presentation of the required petition. This, I think is the nature of the threat that Elḥanan held over the *gaon*'s head. Presumably, once granted the title of *Av beth din*, Elḥanan would have permitted the petition for renewal of gaonic authority to go through. However, the letter-writer goes on to warn about Elḥanan's ambition to obtain his own *serarah*. For a different interpretation of the enigmatic phrase, leval yeḥadesh davar, see Abramson, *Bamerkazim*, p. 111.

with the rise to power of Daniel b. 'Azaryah in 1051 were the forces of disintegration for a time reversed.

Like other Palestinian *gaons* before him, Solomon b. Judah's authority as supreme administrative chief of Fatimid Jewry received confirmation in a Fatimid letter of appointment. Though he encountered considerable opposition during his long term of service, by and large he maintained the Gaonic prerogatives incorporated into that patent. In addition, he labored to fulfill his responsibility as head of the Fatimid Jews to maintain a flow of donations for the upkeep of the *yeshivah* and its court of law.

However, both the fiscal strength and the political dominion of the *yeshivah* during the administration of Solomon b. Judah were only with great difficulty preserved. The Fatimid stipend that had once helped assure the *yeshivah*'s financial security was not resumed in the 1020s, after the other deleterious effects of al-Ḥākim's persecution had been effaced.[49] Income from answering legal questions (responsa) could not compensate for this loss, because by the eleventh century, and certainly during the period of Babylonian Gaonic resurgence under the illustrious Sherira and Hay of Pumbedita, Jews rarely turned to the Palestinian *gaon* for responsa.[50] Solomon's constant and plaintive appeal for monetary help from Egyptian Jewry should be understood against this background.

Moreover, the early years of Solomon's tenure in office were devastating, for Palestinian Jewry in general and for the *yeshivah* in particular. I refer to the years of warfare attending the Beduin rebellion against Fatimid sovereignty (1024-1029).[51] The hardships accompanying this era of unrest and insecurity sapped the vitality of the *yeshivah*, and made it difficult for the beleaguered *gaon*, Solomon b. Judah, to assert his supremacy over adjacent Egypt.

Solomon's leadership suffered equally from the Babylonian orientation of part of the Egyptian Jewish population, which, as we have seen, had tended to loosen Egyptian ties to Jerusalem in earlier years. During Solomon's Gaonate in Jerusalem, the Baghdad *gaon* Hay (d. 1038), who was greatly respected by Egyptian Jewry for his Talmudic mastery (and respected by Solomon b. Judah himself, who sent one of his sons to study at Hay's feet), attempted to extend his influence over that country. In a letter

49 In contrast, financial contributions to Christian religious institutions were revived, by the repentant mad Caliph himself, it would seem. For an explanation of this apparent discrimination in favor of the Christians, see my *Jewish Self-Government*, p. 54.

50 See n. 22, above. Significantly, among the various types of financial assistance solicited in the Geniza documents published by Goitein in his recent study of "The Organization of Support of the Scholars and the Poor in Palestine during the Eleventh Century" (in Hebrew), in *Ha-yishuv*, pp. 115-131, donations accompanying legal questions are not mentioned.

51 Mann, *Jews in Egypt*, I, 110, 158-162, II, 120, 179-184; Stillman, *Jews of Arab Lands*, pp. 205-206, and the article by Goitein cited in the footnote there, which has now been reprinted in Goitein, *Ha-yishuv*, pp. 191-192.

to an Egyptian supporter, Solomon b. Judah reacts to news that Hay had requested donations for his *yeshivah*: "They [i.e. the Babylonian leadership] are always sending letters about this, and their sole purpose is to try to extend their borders. If they could cast their net over everyone, it would be with the sole purpose of expanding their income."[52] In the same missive, Solomon refers to people who abandon their loyalties toward the Palestinian *yeshivah* and transfer them to "the *yeshivah* outside" (i.e. "outside" the Land of Israel, namely in Babylonia).[53]

A weakening of the bonds tying Egyptian Jewry to the Jerusalem Gaonate is reflected further in local Egyptian Jewish politics during Solomon b. Judah's reign. Solomon's appointee as chief judge in Fusṭāṭ, the communal leader Ephraim b. Shemaryah of Gaza, Palestine, experienced considerable resistance to his own leadership. Part of this stemmed from Babylonian Jews who had reservations about the jurisdiction of the Palestinian *yeshivah*. A Babylonian cantor and preacher in a small provincial Egyptian community, Abraham b. Aaron al-Baṣrī (of Baṣra in Iraq), challenged Ephraim's authority by "disparaging his honor and the honor of those who appointed him to office, namely, the *gaon*s of Palestine, living and dead."[54] Another document discloses that the Jews of Fusṭāṭ were split into factions over Ephraim b. Shemaryah's appointment.[55] The opposition party also cast blame upon the *gaon* Solomon for having made life difficult for Ephraim's predecessors, notably Elḥanan b. Shemaryah.[56] Doubtless we have here one more manifestation of Egyptian preference for the Babylonian scholarship represented by Elḥanan b. Shemaryah and his father, as well as for the potential administrative independence from Jerusalem which Elḥanan's leadership had symbolized.

During Ephraim's time, he and his superior, Solomon b. Judah, had to deal with yet other threats to Palestinian administrative sovereignty. Several Geniza texts, edited and summarized by Jacob Mann, deal with a Jew in Egypt who spurned his Palestinian title of *ḥaver* after receiving the Babylonian counterpart honorific, *alluf*, from the Baghdad *gaon*.[57] In the world of medieval Islam, titulature had more than merely token value. The

52 Mann, *Jews in Egypt*, II, 126, lines 26-28; cf. I, 115 (TS 13 J 14, fol. 8 [not 18]).

53 *Ibid.*, II, 126, lines 12-13.

54 *Ibid.*, II, 119, lines 7-9; cf. I, 109 (TS 13 J 11, fol. 9).

55 *Ibid.*, II, 120, lines 11-15; cf. I, 110 (TS 13 J 9, fol. 2). Following his accession to power Solomon b. Judah reconfirmed the appointment to office that previous Palestinian *gaons* had accorded Ephraim; see S.D. Goitein, "On the History of Palestinian Gaonate" (in Hebrew), *Shalem* 1 (1974), 16-20 (= *Ha-yishuv*, pp. 83-86) (TS 13 J 7, fol. 25). Local opposition to Ephraim's authority, evidently during Solomon b. Judah's Gaonate, resulted in the designation of a ten-man board of "elders" in Fusṭāṭ to monitor Ephraim's administration; see Goitein, *Ha-yishuv*, pp. 109-111 (TS 13 J 30, fol. 5).

56 Mann, *Jews in Egypt*, II, 121, lines 28 ff. (TS 13 J 9, fol. 2).

57 *Ibid.*, pp. 124-129; cf. I, 114-118. Also II, 347-350.

award and acceptance of an honorific created or cemented a bond of loyalty between the giver and the receiver. Rightly, therefore, in Jerusalem, as well as in the circle of Ephraim b. Shemaryah in Fusṭāṭ, this act was viewed as treacherous. One of Solomon's letters about this affair states that the disloyal *ḥaver* had denigrated the Palestinian *yeshivah* for its alleged low level of rabbinic learning when compared to that of the academy of Babylonia.[58] This criticism, largely valid during this period when Hay Gaon directed the *yeshivah* of Pumbedita, seems to have underlain much of the dissatisfaction in Egypt with subordination to Palestinian Gaonic authority.[59]

This tension certainly played a role in Egyptian support for Nathan b. Abraham, who fomented a schism in the Palestinian *yeshivah* between 1038 and 1042 and established a counter-Gaonate in Ramle. Elsewhere I have discussed the broad and complex political dimensions of this crisis, which involved Jewish communities in Palestine, Syria, Egypt, and North Africa.[60] Nathan's successful political challenge to Solomon b. Judah owed much to the backing he received from influential Jews in Egypt. One reason for Egyptian admiration was doubtless Nathan's rabbinic expertise. Nathan had been a disciple of the Qayrawan *yeshivah*, where, as stated, a strong Babylonian *halakhic* orientation permeated Jewish scholarship. We have noted the corrosive political impact that pro-Babylonian sympathies among Egyptian Jewry had on the administrative authority of Solomon b. Judah. This, too, may have had something to do with the support which a segment of Egyptian Jewry showed for Nathan b. Abraham.

Solomon b. Judah's personal authority, and with it much of the administrative sovereignty of the Palestinian *yeshivah*, was severely curtailed as a result of the conflict with Nathan b. Abraham; and while the aging Solomon continued in office for nine more years after the schism was ended in 1042, he himself admitted that he ruled thereafter in name only.[61] A revival of Palestinian administrative preeminence occurred only after Solomon's death in 1051, upon the accession to Gaonic office of the Babylonian *nasi*, Daniel b. 'Azaryah.

Recent scholarship has disclosed that Daniel arrived in Egypt many

58 *Ibid.*, II, 124, lines 11-12 (TS 13 J 15, fol. 1).

59 Solomon vividly describes the erosion of his *yeshivah*'s authority among Egyptian Jews in a letter addressed to Ephraim b. Shemaryah, edited by Solomon Schechter, *Saadyana* (Cambridge, 1903), pp. 111-113, and correctly reinterpreted by Mann, *Jews in Egypt*, I, 126-128 (TS 20.102).

60 Mark R. Cohen, "New Light on the Conflict over the Palestinian Gaonate, 1038-1042, and on Daniel b. Azarya: A Pair of Letters to the Nagid of Qayrawan," *AJS (Association for Jewish Studies) review* 1 (1976), 1-40.

61 Mann, *Jews in Egypt*, II, 146, line 21; reinterpreted by Goitein, *Mediterranean Society*, II, 14 (cf. Cohen, "New Light," p. 2 n. 1 and p. 8) (TS 12.217). More recently, Goitein has revised the dating of this letter somewhat earlier in Solomon's reign; see *Ha-yishuv*, pp. 81 and 109.

years before 1051, and that by the time of Solomon's death he had achieved enormous prestige among Fatimid Jewry both on account of his aristocratic lineage (as a member of the family of the exilarch) and his rabbinic learning.[62] Among the Egyptian Jews, Daniel had developed a network of supporters long before being installed as administrative chief of Fatimid Jewry, and this doubtless helped propel him to power in 1051. Even Solomon b. Judah seems to have come out in favor of Daniel succeeding him in office,[63] perhaps because he was aware of the Babylonian *nasi*'s widespread support.

The crucial Geniza letter regarding Daniel b. ʻAzaryah's arrival in Egypt, written c. 1039, extols the *nasī* for instituting badly needed legal reforms (*taqqanot*) in the area of family life and related social abuses. In this, Daniel followed the example of the Babylonian *gaons*, including Hay b. Sherira, doubtless his own teacher in Baghdad. Daniel's Babylonian scholarship was clearly one of the factors that led Fatimid Jewry to pass over the heir apparent to the Gaonate of Jerusalem, Joseph ha-Kohen b. Solomon, when Solomon b. Judah died in 1051.

Once established as head of the Fatimid Jewish community, Daniel exploited his rabbinic learning, his political connections with Egypt, and his aristocratic genealogy, to restore the prestige of the Jerusalem *yeshivah* as central administrative authority over the Jews in the Fatimid state. Egyptian Jewry had little difficulty submitting to his jurisdiction. As a scion of the exilarchal house, Daniel merited the loyalty of all Jews in the diaspora. As a Babylonian, Daniel appealed to those in Egypt with pro-Babylonian sympathies. As a graduate of the Babylonia *yeshivah*, he earned the special respect that Egyptian Jews held for those trained in that prestigious academy. Significantly, Daniel b. ʻAzaryah is the only Palestinian *gaon* of the first century of Fatimid rule regarding whom we have conclusive evidence that he regularly issued rabbinic responsa for the community.[64] In addition, the Geniza letters and documents concerning his reign prove that, better than his predecessor, Daniel effectively exercised the wide range of administrative functions that the Fatimid government invested in the Palestinian Gaonate.

Daniel's administration lasted until 1062. He was succeeded by Eliyah ha-Kohen b. Solomon, who, after the death of his brother, Joseph, in 1053, had become Daniel's chief rival. Eventually, however, hostilities had ended, and Eliyah had become Daniel's second-in-command (*Av beth din*) and heir apparent. During the Gaonate of Eliyah ha-Kohen (1062-1083)

62 Cohen, "New Light," pp. 12-13, 20; S.D. Goitein, "New Sources on Daniel b. Azarya, Nasi and Gaon," *Shalem* 2 (1976), pp. 43-63 (= *Ha-yishuv*, pp. 133-149); Cohen, *Jewish Self-Government*, pp. 80-81.

63 Goitein, "New Sources on Daniel b. Azarya," pp. 51-55 (= *Ha-yishuv*, pp. 139-143; relevant line is line 29 of the letter); Cohen, "New Light," p. 9.

64 Cohen, *Jewish Self-Government*, p. 97 and n. 22 there.

and that of his son and successor, Evyatar (1083-ca. 1110), the Palestinian *yeshivah* lost its administrative control to the new Egyptian office of head of the Jews (*ra'īs al-yahūd*), also known as the Nagidate.

In my study of the origins of this important representative of medieval Jewish self-government,[65] I attempted to explain why it emerged in the last third of the eleventh century. I suggested among other things that Daniel b. 'Azaryah's successor in the Jerusalem Gaonate paled so in significance to Daniel that Fatimid Jewry in 1062 suddenly found itself standing on the brink of a spiritual void. This void was filled in Egypt by three immigrant Jewish notables of considerable rabbinic achievement, Judah ha-Kohen "the Rav" b. Joseph, Nahray b. Nissim and Isaac b. Samuel the Spaniard (*ha-sefaradi*), all of whom issued responsa for local Jews. These three scholars had come to reside in Egypt as a result of a major shift of populations in the Fatimid domain that took place in the latter part of the eleventh century. The most important consequence of this demographic change was that former supporters of the Palestinian *yeshivah* were concentrated in the Egyptian capital at a crucial moment in time, when a political and economic crisis in the larger Muslim world, coupled with imperial contraction (especially the loss of Syria-Palestine to the Seljuks between 1071 and 1076), ushered in a trend toward Egyptian centralization. This development had a corresponding pull towards Cairo on the leadership of the minority communities, evidenced in sources regarding the Coptic patriarchate. Responding to these events, as well as to the isolation of the Palestinian *yeshivah* in distant Tyre, which from 1071 to 1089 lay outside Fatimid control, the new constellation of local Jewish leadership in Egypt set about fashioning an alternative form of central administration for Fatimid Jewry, with its seat in Fusṭāṭ-Cairo. Over a period of several decades, a new institution emerged, under the leadership of an official to whom the Fatimids gave the title of *ra'īs al-yahūd*, "head of the Jews." His office evolved slowly and organically out of the traditional structure of Jewish self-government in the Fatimid domain, until by the year 1100 it had absorbed nearly all the significant prerogatives of the Palestinian Gaonate. Thus, the office of head of the Jews replaced the office of head of the *yeshivah* as the chief governing body of Fatimid Jewry.

The Palestinian *gaons* resisted the loss of administrative sovereignty, especially during the reign of Head of the Jews David b. Daniel (1082-1094), the son of Daniel b. 'Azaryah.[66] In the long run, however, the concatenation of external and internal forces summarized above rendered the *yeshivah*'s defense of its prerogatives fruitless. The rise of the office of

65 Cohen, *Jewish Self-Government.*

66 *Ibid.*, chapter 5, and Moshe Gil, "The Scroll of Evyatar as a Source for the History of the Struggles of the Yeshiva of Jerusalem during the Second Half of the Eleventh Century: A New Reading of the Scroll" (in Hebrew), in *Peraqim be-toledot Yerushalayim bi-mei ha-beinayim (Jerusalem in the Middle Ages)*, ed. B.Z. Kedar (Jerusalem, 1979), pp. 39-106.

head of the Jews was, in fact, inevitable. As we have shown, Egyptian Jewry had long experienced dissatisfaction with the rule of Jerusalem. At times, they manifested their unease by taking tentative steps toward independence, notably during the time of Elḥanan b. Shemaryah.[67] True, under Solomon b. Judah, the Palestinian Gaonate had recovered much of its power. Nonetheless, it had continued to suffer intermittent episodes of Egyptian disaffection. During the 1050s, Daniel b. ʻAzaryah, armed with aristocratic lineage and Babylonian learning, had temporarily restored Gaonic prestige among Egyptian Jewry. However, a renewal of Gaonic authority based principally upon respect for the person of the *gaon* could not guarantee a permanent reversal of the long-term trend of Egyptian resistance to the authority of the institution of the Gaonate. After Daniel b. ʻAzaryah's death, therefore, Palestinian leadership lost its sovereignty to Egypt, and to the office of head of the Jews.

The formative period in the life of this new institution lasted from about 1065 to 1126, and was dominated by the House of Mevorakh b. Saʻadyah, a family of scholarly court physicians in Fusṭāṭ.[68] In 1127, following the reign of Mevorakh's son and successor, Moses b. Mevorakh, the title and office of *ra'īs al-yahūd* passed into the hands of the *gaon* Matzliaḥ ha-Kohen b. Solomon, the grandson of the Palestinian *gaon* Eliyah ha-Kohen b. Solomon. The event has usually been seen as the inauguration of the "Gaonate of Fusṭāṭ." In actuality, it was more symptomatic of the shift of central administrative authority from Palestine to Egypt that had taken place under the aegis of the House of Mevorakh b. Saʻadyah and that of their temporary rival, David b. Daniel.

Why Matzliaḥ abandoned the Palestinian academy, which in the second decade of the twelfth century was situated in exile in Damascus under the leadership of Matzliaḥ's father, Solomon ha-Kohen, and moved to Egypt, is not clear. I have suggested that it had something to do with a resurgence of Palestinian Gaonic political activity in Egypt. After the establishment of the office of head of the Jews, the Gaonic ruling family of the deceased Eliyah ha-Kohen realized that in order to revive its administrative authority over Egyptian Jewry it would have to transplant itself onto the very soil in which its withering powers had taken new root. This became possible around 1126. In that year the Fatimid government entered a period of political instability. It is not inconceivable that Moses b. Mevorakh's political demise resulted from court intrigue attending that crisis. Whatever the actual circumstances of his fall from office, however, his replacement by the Palestinian *gaon* Matzliaḥ is plausibly explained by the hypothesis I have proposed.[69]

67 Mentioned briefly in the conclusion to my book, *Jewish Self-Government*, p. 288, and developed more fully in this paper, above.

68 This is the period covered in my above-mentioned book.

69 Cohen, *Jewish Self-Government*, pp. 283-286.

Matzliaḥ became head of the Jews, then, in order to recapture for the Jerusalem Gaonate the powers which it had lost. For the decade that he held office the old regime was nominally restored. Characteristically, however, it did not last. In 1138, Matzliaḥ was succeeded in the headship of the Jews by another Egyptian notable, the scholarly court physician, Abū Manṣūr Samuel b. Ḥananyah. Egyptian Jewry had long ago abandoned its loyalty to the Palestinian Gaonate. Moreover, the balance in administrative relations between Egypt and Palestine had irreversibly shifted. Politically speaking, Egypt was now the center of Jewish administration and Palestine was the periphery.

The shift of central Jewish administrative authority from Palestine to Egypt during the Fatimid period conforms to a general pattern of relationships between centers of political power and peripheral dependencies that can be observed in the Jewish communities of the Islamic world. Centers of Jewish authority strove to locate themselves at the center of Islamic imperial rule. This served a reciprocal purpose. Muslim potentates desired the immediate proximity of non-Muslim religious leaders in order to hold them accountable for possible infringements of the laws regulating non-Muslim relations with their Muslim neighbors. Non-Muslim leaders, for their part, favored direct access to Islamic rulers so that they could influence them, via personal petition and well-placed gifts, in their treatment of the minorities.

The most obvious example of this pattern can be seen in the Abbasid empire, where the exilarchate and the *yeshivah*s, situated in central Babylonia since Parthian and Sasanian times, found themselves conveniently close to the center of Islamic imperial authority beginning with the middle of the eighth century. The triumph of Babylonian Judaism over the greater Islamic Jewish periphery during the early Abbasid period was due in no small measure to the early association between the center of Islamic imperial rule and its Jewish administrative counterpart.

The Palestinian *yeshivah*, likewise dating from pre-Islamic times, experienced a rather different history. Invested since late antiquity with a religious authority in Judaism equivalent to that of the Babylonian *yeshivah*s, the Palestinian academy stood at the outset of Islam as a rival to the Babylonian organs of Jewish spiritual leadership. Unfortunately, however, our sources about the Palestinian *yeshivah* during the early centuries of Islam are scarce, and it is impossible to reach definite conclusions regarding its administrative relationship with neighboring Egyptian Jewry. When the veil over Palestinian and Egyptian Jewish life is lifted at the beginning of the Fatimid period, the Gaonate of Jerusalem indeed appears in the ascendancy. It is not unlikely that this relationship represented a continuation of the state of affairs that had existed under the prior Muslim regimes, and that it went back as far as the Byzantine period.

Nonetheless, under the Fatimids, for the first time in the region, a center of Muslim imperial power was established in Cairo. Thus, the relationship between center and periphery among the Jews was not symmetrical with its Islamic counterpart. The imbalance was bound eventually to create tensions among Egyptian Jewry, who lived at the center while supreme administrative jurisdiction over their community was situated in distant Palestine. This tension was exacerbated, as we have tried to show, by the special preference which a significant segment of Egypt's Jews felt for the spiritual leadership of the Babylonian *gaons*. This tension was finally relieved when, after a century of Fatimid rule, the office of *ra'īs al-yahūd* was established, and the center of Jewish administration was transferred to the center of Fatimid government. Thus the administrative structure of Fatimid Jewry was finally made to conform with the familiar pattern of relations between center and periphery observable in Abbasid Jewry. This state of affairs in Egypt endured until the beginning of the sixteenth century, when the Ottomans reduced Egypt to the status of a province on the periphery of an empire whose center lay elsewhere and accordingly abolished the office of *ra'īs al-yahūd*.

THE OTTOMAN PERIOD

MICHAEL WINTER

Military Connections between Egypt and Syria (including Palestine) in the Early Ottoman Period

The Fatimids' incomplete rule over Syria and Palestine, especially in the twelfth century, and the Crusaders' occupation of the Holy Land obscured for a long period the importance of military connections between Egypt and Syria (including Palestine). It was also forgotten that Egypt was potentially superior to Syria as a military power. Even Ṣalāḥ al-Dīn al-Ayyūbī, who at long last transferred Islam's center of gravity to Egypt, did not fully realize Egypt's predominance.[1] After Ṣalāḥ al-Dīn, the empire consisted of a federation of the Ayyubid princes and it was becoming increasingly clear that the virtual head of the empire was he who ruled Egypt.[2] The conception of an empire solidly based on Egypt was the guiding strategic principle of the Mamluk state. Cairo became the center of that empire and the seat of the Sultan and the symbolically important Caliph. Professor Ayalon has provided abundant evidence to prove that the best-trained and most privileged military units were stationed in Egypt, especially in Cairo, whereas service in the Syrian provinces was considered less prestigious and often was a means to punish or to exile Mamluk Emirs.[3] Politically and strategically Syria and Palestine were relegated to a subordinate and inferior position, that of a bulwark to protect Egypt or to absorb the first thrusts of the Mamluks' main enemies, the Mongols.

With the overthrow of the Mamluk Sultanate by the Ottomans in 1516-17, and the inclusion of Syria, Palestine and Egypt as provinces in the Ottoman Empire, the political, administrative and military situation of the Arab lands was completely transformed. The old Mamluk military structure (though not the Mamluks themselves) ceased to exist. The garrisons of

1 See A.S. Ehrenkreutz, *Saladin* (Albany, N.Y., 1972), especially pp. 187-88.

2 See the article 'Ayyūbids' in *Encyclopaedia of Islam*, second edition, by Cl. Cahen; H.L. Gottschalk, *al-Malik al-Kāmil* (Wiesbaden, 1958); H.A.R. Gibb, 'The Aiyūbids', in K.M. Setton, *A History of the Crusades*, vol. 2 (Philadelphia, 1962), pp. 693-714.

3 D. Ayalon, 'Discharge from service, banishment and imprisonment in Mamluk society', *Israel Oriental Studies* (Tel Aviv, 1972), vol. 2, pp. 46-47.

Syria and Egypt became pawns on the huge Ottoman chessboard, which the central government in Istanbul could move at will and dispatch to faraway fronts. Yet, the territorial armies of Egypt and Syria were becoming increasingly disparate. The military and administrative organization of Syria (including Palestine) resembled in principle the familiar Ottoman structures, the two principal elements in the army being the janissaries and the fief-holder, the 'timariots' *(erbāb-i timar)* and the *zu'amā'*. In Egypt, on the other hand, the *timar* system was never applied. Egypt was garrisoned by Seven Corps: two infantry and five cavalry. The defeated Mamluks were organized as one of the seven corps, which was called *Cherākise Ojaği*, the Circassian Corps.[4]

Some scholars seek an explanation of the Mamluks' disappearance from Syria in the abortive revolt of Jānbardī al-Ghazālī, the Mamluk Emir, who was appointed by the Ottomans as Governor of Damascus. He attempted to exploit the occasion of Sultan Selīm's death (1520) to restore the Mamluk regime in Syria. It is true that Khā'ir Bey, the first Ottoman governor of Egypt, a former Mamluk Emir himself, carefully distanced himself from the Syrian revolt, but many Circassian Mamluks of Egypt tried to join their Syrian comrades. Moreover, after Khā'ir Bey's death in 1522, several serious rebellions against the Ottoman Sultan, Süleyman 'the Magnificent', *Qānūnī* (1520-66), broke out; the most dangerous one was instigated in 1523 by Ahmed Pasha, later called *'al-Khā'in'* 'the traitor', the governor of Egypt.[5] Mamluk elements were also predominant in other rebellions which took place during the sixteenth and early seventeenth centuries. These revolts and their brutal suppression by the Ottoman army did not prevent the re-emergence (rather than the continuation) of Mamluk patterns and traditions of recruitment and organization.[6] The origins of the advent of the Mamluks in Ottoman Egypt should be sought not in their loyalty or quiescence at the beginning of the Ottoman period, but rather in the decline of the Ottoman empire, in the relationships between Egypt and the central Ottoman government and, last but not least, in the economic and social characteristics of Egypt, so different to those of Syria. It should be emphasized that in the sixteenth century we hear almost nothing of the Circassians, and their corps is hardly distinguishable from the other mounted regiments. Only in the seventeenth century does the term *Cherākise beyleri*, Circassian *beys*, become frequent, both in the chronicles and in official usage. It is my belief that the process of the 'Mamlukization' of the

4 See P.M. Holt, *Egypt and the Fertile Crescent, 1516-1922* (Ithaca and London, 1966), p. 44; U. Heyd, *Ottoman Documents on Palestine 1552-1615* (Oxford, 1960), pp. 40-41, 63-64; S.J. Shaw, *The Financial and Administrative Development of Ottoman Egypt* (Princeton, 1962), pp. 189-97.

5 On these events, see Holt, *op. cit.*, pp. 46-51.

6 *Ibid.*, pp. 71-84; 'Abd al-Karīm Rāfiq, *'Thawrāt al-'asākir fī'l-Qāhira...'* in *Abḥāth al-Nadwa al-Dawliyya li-Ta'rīkh al-Qāhira* (Cairo, 1969), vol. 2.

Egyptian army during the Ottoman period, which culminated in the total control of the Seven Corps by the Mamluk *beys* in the eighteenth century, is still obscure, the important studies by Professors Ayalon, Holt and Shaw notwithstanding.[7]

The present paper, on the connections between the Ottoman armies of Egypt and Syria, in which Palestine was included, is based on Ottoman archival materials of the tenth/sixteenth centuries and supplemented by Turkish and Arabic contemporary chronicles.[8] The principal sources are some fifty *firmāns* from the *Mühimme Defteri* in the Archives of the Prime Minister's Office in Istanbul. Six of the documents used for the present article were studied by my late teacher, Uriel Heyd, in his *Ottoman Documents on Palestine, 1552-1615.*[9]

It has been stated that, under the Mamluk Sultans, the army stationed in Egypt was much larger and better trained than that in Syria, and that the reasons for this deliberate discrimination were mainly political. This state of affairs did not change, basically, under the Ottomans, although of course the reasons for the superiority of the Egyptian army in numbers and training were different. Egypt was considered a much more important province, economically and strategically. Besides Egypt's potentiality as a revenue-yielding land to Istanbul, it became in the sixteenth century a huge military, naval and logistic base for operations in the Red Sea, the Yemen and Ḥabesh. The province was also charged with providing for the Holy Cities and guarding the pilgrims' caravan. Syria and certainly Palestine, which, as is well-known, never constituted a separate administrative division, did not possess similar assets. Syria did not need, nor could the province afford to maintain, such a large army.

This is not the place to make calculations as to the complement of the Egyptian and Syrian garrisons, which fluctuated considerably during the sixteenth century. It is obvious from the phrasing of many *firmāns* that Istanbul itself was not certain of the correct numbers of soldiers; this becomes especially true toward the end of the century, when discipline in the Ottoman army was on the decline, and the troops did not always obey orders and go to their destination.[10] Yet the picture which emerges is one of a permanently understaffed Ottoman army in Syria. Its largest single body,

7 D. Ayalon, 'Studies in al-Jabartī', JESHO, III, parts 2 and 3, 1960; P.M. Holt, *Studies in the History of the Near East* (London, 1973), pp. 151-251; S.J. Shaw, *op. cit.*

8 Al-Khallāq, *Tarih Mısır-i Qāhire*, Ms. Istanbul University Library, T.Y. 628; 'Abd al-Karīmb. 'Abd al-Raḥmān, *Tarīh-i Mısır*, Ms. Süleymāniye Library, Istanbul, Haci Mahmud Efendi 4877; Muḥammad ibn Abī'l-Surūr al-Bakrī al-Siddiqī, *al-Tuḥfa al-Bahiyya fī Tamalluk Āl 'Uthmān al-Diyār al-Miṣriyya*, Ms. Vienna, H.O.35.

9 See Heyd, *op. cit.*, pp. 72-74, 123-24.

10 See, for example, *Mühimme Defteri*, Başbakanlık Arşivi, Istanbul (will be referred to henceforth as M.D.), vol. 7, p. 735, no 2015, 11 Rebī' I 976; p. 821, no. 2251, 20 Rebī' I, 976; p. 952, no. 2621, 22 Cumāda II, 976.

the janissaries of Damascus, officially numbered one thousand soldiers, but the actual figure was always lower.[11] The number of all the fief-holders under the command of the governor of Damascus, *Shām beylerbeyi*, was about six hundred. Garrisons in other towns in Syria and Palestine which fell under the jurisdiction of the governor of Damascus were considerably smaller. The combined military forces in Egypt in the sixteenth century must have numbered well over 10,000 men, up to 15,000 soldiers.[12] When Yavuz 'Alī Pasha, the governor of Egypt from 1010/1601 to 1012/1603, went to Istanbul with the *hazīne*, the annual tribute (lit. 'treasury'), he led an Egyptian force of 10,000 soldiers, which enabled him to impose his will on several governors and pashas in Syria and Anatolia.[13] Although the number given by the chroniclers seems exaggerated, there is reason to believe that the appearance of the Egyptians overwhelmed the fewer and the inferior-organized Syrian troops.

The smallness of the Syrian garrisons can be gathered from the *firmān*s ordering the dispatch of troops from Syria and Egypt respectively. The highest number of Syrian troops ordered into combat was in 986/1579, when 500 janissaries and 600 fief-holders (i.e. all the fief-holders of the Damascus Province) were sent to the Persian front. But even this number is misleading, since they were to be replaced by 1,000 to 1,500 Egyptian troops whose arrival the Syrians were ordered to await before marching.[14] The largest number of troops ordered to the Yemen from Syria was 500, whereas the governors of Egypt had to send as many as 1,000 to 3,000 men.[15]

Thus, the Ottoman high command moved troops to the various fronts and from one province to another. For example: when Syrian troops went to the Persian front, Egyptian soldiers were moved into Syria to replace them; when large numbers of Egyptians were sent to the Yemen, the Sultan dispatched soldiers from Istanbul to Egypt.[16] Here the absence of symmetry between the two provinces becomes clear: while it was quite usual to send Egyptian troops to replace or reinforce Syrian troops, the reverse never took place. Syrian soldiers were occasionally sent to Erzerum, Cyprus, or to the Yemen; they were never sent to serve in Egypt, even temporarily.[17] The reasons for this policy are not stated in the documents,

11 Heyd, *op. cit.*, pp. 72-74.

12 *Ibid.*, M.D. vol. 14, p. 216, no. 310, 14 Safer 978.

13 Al-Khallāq, fols. 96b-102b; 'Alī Efendi, *Chronicle of the Pashas of Egypt,* Ms. 1050 in the Muzaffer Ocak collection, University of Ankara, fols. 8a-14b.

14 Heyd, *op. cit.*, pp. 72-74.

15 M.D. vol. 7, p. 250, no.695, 13 Receb 975; pp. 768-69, no. 2099, 24 Rebī' I, 976; p. 769, no. 2100, 24 Rebī' I, 976; p. 860, no. 2356, 4 Cumāda I; vol. 14, p. 120, no, 170, 19 Safer, 978; p. 216, no. 310, 14 Safer, 978.

16 See, for example, M.D. vol. 32, p. 245, no. 455, 20 Şa'bān, 986; vol. 7, p. 769, no. 2100, 24 Rebī' I, 976; vol. 60, p. 254, no. 595, 8 Cumāda I, 994.

17 M.D. vol. 14, p. 912, no. 1348, 17 Ramazān 978. See also Heyd, *op. cit.*, pp. 72-74.

but can be guessed: the Egyptian army was better disciplined than the Syrian, and the deterioration had began much earlier in Syria. It is probable that the decision-makers in Istanbul estimated that Syrian soldiers would not be respected and obeyed in Egypt and that the Syrians would not be accepted by their Egyptian counterparts.

One indication of the decline of the Syrian army was its infiltration by *Awlād 'Arab* (in Turkish *Evlād-i 'Arab*), local Arabic-speaking men. By the military and social standards of the times, only Turkish-speaking recruits, janissaries or Anatolian *(Rūmī) sipahis* were qualified to serve in the army. If regular soldiers (*qullar,* the Sultan's slaves) were not available in sufficient numbers, the central government permitted the local *beylerbeyi* to enlist 'able sons and brothers of regular soldiers' *(yarar qul oghullari, qul qarındashları)*, but by no means Arabs and other non-Turkish elements to whom the official language of the *firmāns* systematically applied the derogatory term *tāt.*[18]

It is true that the same problem, namely, the penetration of *Awlād 'Arab* into the army also took place in Egypt and caused riots within the ranks of the Egyptian Seven Corps (particularly in the janissary regiment),[19] but the troubles in the Syrian army preceded those of Egypt by at least twenty years. *Firmāns* dispatched to the *beylerbeyi* of Damascus ordering him to be personally responsible for only 'sons, brothers and progeny of the Sultan's slaves *(qul ṭā'ifesi)*', and no Arabs and *tāt*, receiving appointments in the army, are dated A.H. 976.[20] We have not come across any *firmān* from the sixteenth century which refers to this problem with regard to Egypt, and when the *firmāns* do refer to the need to enlist outsiders, they merely advise the governor of Egypt to take in 'able young men' (*yarar yiğitler*).[21] A comparison between the phrasing of *firmans* sent to Egypt and Syria at one and the same time demonstrated that the authorities in Istanbul were not worried about the standards of the locally enlisted Egyptian soldiers nearly as much as they were about the Syrians; nor is the term *Awlād 'Arab* ever mentioned with regard to Egypt at that time.[22] The earliest mention in the Arabic and Turkish chronicles of Egypt of *Awlād 'Arab* in the army appears during the term of Üveys Pasha, governor of Egypt from 995/1587 to 999/1591, a quarter of a century later than in Syria.[23]

18 M.D. vol. 7, p. 279, no. 789, 3 Şa'bān 975; p. 735, no. 295, 11 Rebī I, 976; p. 952, no. 2621, 22 Cumāda I, 976.

19 I have discussed this subject at some length in a paper entitled 'Turks, Arabs and Mamluks in the Army of Ottoman Egypt', *WZKM*, vol. 72, pp. 97-122.

20 M.D. vol. 7, p. 952, no. 2621, 22 Cumāda II, 976.

21 See, for example, M.D. vol. 7, p. 768-69, no. 2099, 24 Rebī' I, 976 and vol. 73, p. 277, no. 634, 27 Zilhicce, 1003.

22 Compare, for example, M.D. vol. 7, no 3099 with vol. 7, no. 2621, referred to above.

23 The struggles of the Turkish-speaking *ojaqlis* against the *Awlād 'Arab* continued in the 17th century, and should not occupy us further in this context. See my article referred to in note 19 above.

It is interesting to note that when the infiltration of *Awlād al-'Arab* into the ranks of the Egyptian army finally reached serious dimensions in the early seventeenth century, there were Syrian-born Arabs among them. (The chronicles mention an addition to Egyptian Arabs, natives of Damascus and Aleppo — *Shāmli* and *Ḥalepli*.)[24] The loose discipline in the Syrian army is reflected, for example, in *firmāns* sent in 976/1568-69 to the *beylerbeyi* of Damascus. The preparation of lists of soldiers who actually went to the Yemen was far from reliable, and the soldiers took advantage of the bureaucratic disorder. Of the 500 Syrians ordered to go to the Yemen only 330 arrived in Egypt and even they did not proceed to the Yemen. Janissaries, *sipahi*s and *chavush*s shirked their routine duties in Syria, falsely claiming that they had enlisted to go to the Yemen.[25] In his book, Heyd has included a *firmān* in which fief-holders are accused of bribing their officers, thereby avoiding their duty to go to war.[26]

The Egyptian army maintained contacts with Palestine, although not on a very regular and close basis. In the first place, there was the annual convoy which brought to Istanbul the *hazīne*, the 'Treasury' or the Egyptian annual tribute, across Palestine, Syria and Anatolia. The *hazīne* had of course to be heavily guarded. Whenever possible, it was sent with a military force which was in any case headed north. Thus, in one instance a newly-appointed *beylerbeyi* of Egypt was ordered to send back most of the thousand janissaries who had escorted him on his journey to Cairo; he was permitted to keep 200 or 300 of them in his service if he considered it necessary. The returning soldiers were to take the tribute with them.[27] Likewise, when Yavuz 'Alī Pasha returned to Istanbul at the end of his term of office in Egypt, he was enjoined to bring the treasury with him, since he was leaving with an unusually strong force, as we have already seen.[28] The task to command the convoy of the *hazīne* was one of the most coveted by the Egyptian Emirs, since it gave them access to persons of influence at the Sultan's court. The Emir who brought the tribute of Egypt could hope to secure a desirable appointment for himself or for his friends.[29]

That the passage of the Egyptian convoy through Palestine was not always a smooth undertaking can be learned from another *firmān*. The *qāḍī* of Safed complained to the Porte that some of the slave-merchants, who imported black male and female slaves from Egypt, evaded paying the legal tolls, by obtaining the protection of the Egyptian officers and soldiers who were guarding the *hazīne*. Naturally, the governor of Egypt was ordered to ensure that this practice should cease.[30]

24 Khallāq, fol. 149a.

25 M.D. vol. 7, p. 735, no. 2015, 11 Rebi' I, 976; p. 821, no. 2251, 20 Rebī' I, 976.

26 Heyd, *op. cit.*, pp. 63-64.

27 M.D. vol. 3, p. 204, no. 564, 2 Rebī' I, 967.

28 Al-Khallāq, fols. 97a-97b.

29 See M.D. vol. 30, p. 275, no. 639, 18 Rebī' I, 985; vol. 36, p. 304, no. 803, 9 Rebī' II, 987.

30 M.D. vol. 3, p. 568, no. 1659, 9 Rebī' I, 968; Heyd, *op. cit.*, pp. 123-24.

Occasionally, the Egyptian army was summoned to help quell turbulent bedouins or rebellious Druzes, to man fortresses, or to reinforce or replace Syrian troops.[31]

The salaries of the Egyptian soldiers who were serving in Palestine were paid by the Egyptian treasury. A *beylerbeyi* of Egypt tried to convince the Porte that it would be safer if the Syrian and not the Egyptian treasury paid the salaries, the Emirs' *sālyānes* and the men's *mevājib*, since it was feared that the bedouins might rob the money on the way. In the *firmān*, the governor of Egypt is told to send the money under heavy guard.[32]

The Egyptian soldiers served in Syria and Palestine under their own officers, *agha*s or *bey*s. Egyptian *bey*s were commissioned to act as *serdār*s (commanders-in-chief) charged with guarding the province and maintaining law and order. Egyptian *bey*s were sometimes appointed as *sanjaq beyi*s in Palestine. The *sanjaq*s mentioned in our period are Gaza, Jerusalem and Safed. The Egyptian *bey*s served in Palestine not under the command of the *beylerbeyi* of Damascus, in whose jurisdiction their *sanjaq*s lay, but under the *beylerbeyi* of Egypt, who remained their direct superior officer and commander during their service in Syria. As soon as their term of office in Palestine was over, they were ordered to return to Egypt, to be employed there as the governor deemed fit.[33]

The fact that Egyptians considered their services in Palestine as only temporary and regarded Egypt as their home country is revealed in a *firmān* dated 987. This edict specifies how to handle a treasure of 6,497 *flori*s which had been concealed in a cavity in a wall in the Cairo home of Qā'id Bey, an Egyptian Emir who died during his service as *serdār* of the Egyptian troops charged with guarding Syria.[34] On the other hand, when Dervīsh, an Egyptian Emir is appointed as *sanjaq beyi* of Tripoli, the governor of Egypt is specifically enjoined to give him a few soldiers to help him move his 'house', i.e. his property and belongings, from Egypt to his new post. It is clear that he was being transferred to Syria on a permanent basis.[35] (In principle, of course, no appointments in the Ottoman empire at that time were permanent).

It is especially significant in our context to note that in the sixteenth century Egyptian *bey*s were never appointed as *sanjaq beyi*s for districts lying to the north of Safed, which is to say they served as temporary *sanjaq beyi*s only in Palestine, properly speaking.

The reason why Egyptian soldiers and officers were to serve only in Palestine and not in Syria should be explained first of all by the geographi-

31 See, for example, Heyd, *op. cit.*, p. 103; M.D. vol. 42, no. 647, vol. 50, p. 106, no. 653, 17 Ṣa'bān, 993.

32 M.D. vol. 36, p. 343, no. 900, 9 Rebī' II, 987; vol. 38, p. 154, no. 306, 6 Rebī' II, 987.

33 See, for example, M.D. vol. 36, p. 172, no. 472, 9 Safer 987.

34 M.D. vol. 39, p. 159, no. 348, 25 Zilhicce 987.

35 M.D. vol. 7, p. 498, no. 1437 and no. 1438, 20 Zilkaada 975.

cal facts. It was natural that the proximity of Palestine to Egypt played a central role in the decision to extend the responsibility of the *beylerbeyi* of Egypt to include Palestine when manpower was short, without changing the existing administrative divisions, and without encroaching on the power of the *beylerbeyi* of Damascus. Thus, Yavuz ʻAlī Pasha, the governor of Egypt at the beginning of the seventeenth century, built the fortress of Khān Yūnis, although the area fell outside of his jurisdiction. In addition to the fact of geographical proximity, as Professor Heyd has pointed out, Lebanon, Syria and Transjordan had different topographical and social conditions which required methods of administration different to those of Palestine.[36]

Inevitably, there were instances of friction between the Egyptians and the Syrians and of animosity at the highest level. Muṣṭafā Pasha, the *beylerbeyi* of Damascus, was named *serdār* and given the task of pacifying the Yemen in 975/1567-68. There are indications that his failure to accomplish his task was connected with the hostility between him and Sinān Pasha, the Governor of Egypt. Sinān did not consent to grant Muṣṭafā Pasha the soldiers and the funds he had requested. After eight or nine months of inaction Muṣṭafā was dismissed and Sinān himself was appointed and achieved the pacification of the Yemen.[37] It is significant that Sinān had been Governor of Egypt before he went to the Yemen and that he was re-appointed to the same position upon his return. The Governor of Egypt held the keys to the Yemen and could easily frustrate the preparations of the Governor of Syria. Only Egypt had the resources and the men for the job; at best the Syrian army could provide supplementary forces.

There were quarrels in Palestine on lower and local levels as well, as will be illustrated by the following *firmān* directed to the *beylerbeyi* of Egypt on 9 Rebīʻ II 987:

'It has come to my attention that some *beys* among the Egyptian Emirs who were sent to guard Jerusalem, Gaza and Safed, meddle with [the business of] the *subashis* (police superintendents in the Ottoman feudal system) of the local *beys*. I decree: When this edict reaches you, the above-mentioned *beys* should be warned to refrain from interfering with matters concerned with the yields of the *beys*' *ḥāṣṣ*-lands. They should [merely] supervise the *subashis* and they (the Egyptians) should be occupied with guarding and protecting the kingdom and disciplining the subjects.'[38]

This edict deals with the Egyptian *beys* who temporarily replaced[39] in Palestine Syrian *beys* who had been sent elsewhere. As has already been

36 Heyd, *op. cit.*, pp. 40-41, 185-86; al-Khallāq, fol. 96b.

37 See *Muṣṭafā ʻAlī's Description of Cairo of 1599*, A. Tietze ed. (Vienna, 1975), p. 72; M.D. vol. 7, p. 212, no. 584, 28 Cumāda I, 975; p. 693, no. 1913, 20 Safer 976.

38 M.D. vol. 36, p. 358, no. 929.

39 The term used is *muḥāfaẓada olmak*, Heyd, *op. cit.*, p. 47.

pointed out, it was addressed to the Governor of Egypt, whose orders they had to obey even when they were serving in Palestine. Indeed, in Palestine the regular Syrian *beys* were *hāṣṣ*-holders and did not draw annual salaries *(sālyānes)* as did the *beys* in Lebanon and Egypt.[40] Certainly they had no business to infringe on the absent *beys*' sources of income.

Another conflict which took place in Palestine in the same year is the subject of the following *firmān*:

'To Qānṣah, the *sanjaq beyi* of 'Ajlūn: The *beylerbeyi* of Egypt has sent [me] a letter [complaining that] he learned that you challenged and defied Qā'id, one of the Emirs charged with the defense of Egypt, who has been sent with Egyptian soldiers *(Mıṣır qulı)* to guard Syria, saying to him: "You are not needed to guard Syria. I will do it alone". Now the above-mentioned Qā'id has been sent with My Imperial Edict with the Egyptian soldiers to assist you to guard Syria. I decree: When this *(firmān)* reaches you, you will behave towards him in a friendly manner, and act harmoniously with him in guarding the Province of Syria.'[41]

It is probable that the quarrel referred to in the *firmān* was caused not simply by personal disagreements between the two *beys*, but because Qā'id, whose name we have already come across, had been sent as a *serdār*, commander of an Egyptian task force. His orders were of a general nature, namely to guard the province. As far as we know, the exact geographical boundaries of his activities had not been set. Under these circumstances it was not difficult to clash with a local *sanjaq beyi*.

Simultaneously, Qā'id himself received a *firmān* from Istanbul enjoining him to employ his soldiers in helping Qānṣah against the rebellious Arabs (i.e., bedouins) in the Nablus area, should Qānṣah ask him to do so.[42] It is obvious that the Porte found it necessary to encourage the Egyptian and Syrian *beys* to be more cooperative in fulfilling their common duties in Palestine.

Muṣṭafā 'Ālī, the historian, who describes Cairo as he saw the city in 1599, tells us of long-standing animosity between the Egyptian soldiers and the janissaries of Damascus. An Egyptian soldier is described as bragging that his sole purpose in going to Mecca was not to perform the Pilgrimage, but to fight the janissaries of Damascus.[43] This anecdote is reported, however, in a literary rather than an historical way, and should not be interpreted too seriously. Besides, similar brawls were common among the men of the Egyptian corps themselves.

Finally, conflicts of another nature should be mentioned. As we know from another *firmān* published by Heyd, there were some connections

40 *Ibid.*, p. 41.
41 M.D. vol. 36, p. 369, no. 954, 9 Rebīʿ II, 987.
42 *Ibid.*, p. 370, no. 956, 9 Rebīʿ II, 987.
43 Muṣṭafā 'Alī, pp. 55-56.

between Egypt and Palestine with regard to the maintenance of the *'imāret*, the free kitchen for the poor in Jerusalem. Rice was imported from Egypt for that *'imāret*, while wheat grown on lands which belonged to the *waqf*, and which covered the costs of the Jerusalem institution, was shipped to Egypt.[44]

Yet in Syria there were other *waqf*s which were registered in Egypt, specifically called 'Egyptian *waqf*s', *Miṣriyyūn Evqāfı*. A *firmān* dated 6 Rebī' I 981 reveals the efforts of Syrian officers to control these Egyptian pious foundations. The *firmān* is addressed to the *beylerbeyi* and to the *defterdār* (director of the treasury) of Egypt, with copies to the *beylerbeyi* of Aleppo, where the financial accounts of Syria and Palestine were drawn and kept: 'It has been reported to Me that in some cases where the posts of directors in charge of *waqf*s became vacant, [Syrian] *zu'amā'* took them over, and the *zu'amā'* and timariots *(erbāb-i timar)* seized the posts of directors and trustees of *waqf*s belonging to the administration of Egypt. Now, it is forbidden that *zu'amā'* and timariots act likewise wrongly. I have decreed that when [this *firmān*] arrives, you will dismiss any *za'īm* or *sipahi* who manages as director, supervisor or trustee a *waqf* which belongs to the Egyptian administration. From now on, you shall not permit *zu'amā'* and timariots to administer positions of this kind. You should employ in positions of this kind Egyptian soldiers of integrity and religion *(müstaqīm ve mütedayyin olan Mıṣır qulların istiḥdām idesiz)*. If a diploma *(berat)* [as a director of an Egyptian *waqf*] is obtained by some means, send it [back] to My court and do not let *zu'amā'* and timariots hold positions of this sort in the future.'[45]

Another *firmān* about the same issue was prompted by a letter from Mesīḥ Pasha, governor of Egypt from 982/1575 to 988/1581, and from his *defterdār*. It is directed to the *qāḍīs* in Damascus and Aleppo who are in charge of the Egyptian *waqf*s: 'You have written to Istanbul and [consequently] have been granted a diploma [to supervise these *waqf*s]. This caused [bureaucratic] disorders. From now on do not write to Istanbul, since the books [of the *waqf*s] are in Egypt. Correspond directly with Mesīḥ Pasha in Egypt.' A copy of this *firmān* is sent to the trustees *(nāẓirs)* in Aleppo.[46]

Unfortunately, I do not have further information concerning these 'Egyptian *waqf*s' in Syria. They may be foundations dating from Mamluk times. It is possible that, since it was not practical for Egyptian military personnel to directly manage the *waqf*s (as required in the former of these *firmān*s dating from A.H. 981), it was decided five years later (in A.H. 986, the date of the second *firmān*) that Syrian *qāḍīs* and other administrators

44 Heyd, *op. cit.*, pp. 132-33.
45 M.D. vol. 22, p. 125, no. 254, 6 Rebī' I, 981.
46 M.D. vol. 36, p. 86, no. 252 and 253, 17 Zilhicce, 986.

would perform these duties, but that the accounts and other documents would remain in Egypt.

It cannot be concluded that connections between the armies of Egypt and of Syria at the beginning of the Ottoman rule in the Arab lands were particularly strong or important. It is clear, however, that such connections existed and there is evidence that the presence of the Egyptian army was felt in Palestine more strongly than in Syria proper. The Egyptian military presence in Palestine was only sporadic. As the *firmāns* concerning the Egyptian *waqf*s in Syria seem to indicate, it was not possible for Egyptian military men to engage in administrative work in Syria, which would have required daily contact.

In the middle of the seventeenth century a tractate entitled *Sefer-nāme be-jānib-i Rūm*[47] was written by 'Alī Efendi, an obscure clerk in the military administration of Egypt, with the purpose of defending the Egyptian army against their Istanbul critics. 'Alī Efendi reports all the services rendered by the Egyptian army to the Ottoman Empire from the conquest in 1517 until his day and records in detail all the campaigns in which the Egyptians participated. It is interesting to note that while he lists campaigns in Persia, Hijaz, the Yemen, Crete and other places and the Egyptian escort of the Pilgrimage caravan, their guarding Egypt, fighting bedouins there and collecting taxes, Egyptian services in Syria are never mentioned. It is obvious that the service and operations in Syria did not occupy an important place in the collective memory of the Egyptian army.

47 Ms. no. 1050 in the Muzaffer Ocak collection, University of Ankara. I have prepared an annotated translation of this tractate to be published in *Turcica*.

THOMAS PHILIPP

Jews and Arab Christians Their Changing Positions in Politics and Economy in Eighteenth Century Syria and Egypt

The eighteenth century witnessed a precipitous rise in the affluence and political influence of the Greek Catholic community in all the coastal towns of the Mediterranean, from Alexandria to Beirut. The Greek Catholics were Arabic-speaking Christians who originated from the Syrian commercial centers of Damascus and Aleppo. Along the length of the coast they gained control over customs stations, and at times they came close to monopolizing the functions of scribes, bankers and advisers in the administrations of the various local rulers. They made maritime trade between Egypt and Syria their exclusive domain. The Greek Catholic success is the more remarkable if we consider the fact that the community only began to organize itself at the beginning of the eighteenth century and remained, in the view of the Ottoman government, an illegal group for a further one hundred years.

The rise of the Greek Catholic community occurred frequently at the cost of a diminished position for the Jewish community, which had previously held similar influential positions in commerce, finance, and administration.

Dhimmīs had, of course, played an important role throughout Muslim history though their status within society remained ambivalent. Muslim law had defined the status of the *Dhimmī*, unequivocally, as one inferior to that of Muslims. From building regulations for houses of non-Muslims to their rights in a Muslim court, everything attested to their inferior status. Yet the theory of Muslim law did not necessarily reflect the reality of Muslim society. The actual role and status of the *Dhimmī* in Muslim society was, in addition — and often in contradiction — to the religious law, also determined by such aspects as occupation, wealth, and proximity to the sources of power, i.e., access to the political rulers. The skills of the Jews and Christians as physicians and scribes, and their wealth as merchants and bankers frequently provided them with access to the powerful and the mighty. Muslim rulers, for their part, would often prefer *Dhimmīs* to Muslims as their administrators, bankers, and physicians for the same reasons that they used imported mercenaries in their armies. Lacking a popular local basis of support, these groups were dependent for their welfare upon the good will of the ruler and were therefore more likely to remain loyal. Thus, throughout Muslim history, we see *Dhimmīs* occupying positions of power and status which were quite inappropriate for them in view of the tenets of religious law. Needless to say, the very circumstances of their weakness and lack of popular support which recommended the *Dhimmīs* for employment by the Muslim rulers, also made them extremely vulnerable to the whims of the ruler and to changes in his political fortunes. The *Dhimmīs*' positions as administrators, tax collectors, court physicians, etc. never received institutional sanction, but remained defined by a relation "ad hominem" in which only the good will and the requirements of the individual ruler gave substance to the elevated position of the *Dhimmīs*.

The same ambivalence in the *Dhimmī*'s status and role in society can be observed in the Arab provinces of the Ottoman Empire. In the first two centuries of Ottoman rule and despite their legally inferior position, *Dhimmīs* were able to obtain key positions in the financial affairs of the government. Especially as tax farmers of the custom stations could they play a decisive role in trade, as well as in the financial affairs of the administration. At the same time, they frequently constituted the major suppliers of loans and cash to the *wālīs* and Pashas and could thereby exert powerful influence upon them.

As early as 1575, Rauwolff reported: "There is abundance of Jews through all of Turkey in any Trading Town, but chiefly in Alepo and this Town of Tripoli, where they have built a very large Habitation and a delicate Synagoge. These Jews have the revenues of the Customes of the Grand Signior in their hands . . . ".[1] By 1700, Tripoli had a population of about five hundred Jews, but also "an abundance of Maronites and Greeks."[2] In the 1720s the customs of Tripoli were still in the hands of Jews.[3]

In about 1600, Texeira estimated that there were one thousand Jewish and one thousand five hundred Christian houses in Aleppo, but in contrast to the Christians, "many of them (the Jews) are rich, most Merchants, the rest Brokers, and Handycrafts as Goldsmiths, Lapidaries and the like."[4] In

1 L. Rauwolff, "Travels into the Eastern Countries" in J. Ray (ed.), *A Collection of Curious Travels & Voyages*, London, 1693, p. 31.

2 J. Dandini, *A Voyage to Mount Libanus*. London, 1693, p. 24.

3 In 1730, a certain Abraham de Léon, who had been "douanier" of Tripoli for the preceding four years, had to go into hiding at a time of popular unrest and rebellion against the local Pasha; Correspondence Consulaire, Lemaire to Maurepas, Oct. 1730, Tripoli, in A. Ismail, *Le Liban — Documents Diplomatiques et Consulaires. Les Sources Françaises*. 12 vols. Beirut, 1975, vol. III, p. 331.

4 P. Teixeira, "The Travels of Peter Teixeira from India to Italy by Land" in J. Stevens (ed.), *A New Collection of Voyages and Travels*, London 1711, II, p. 70. He describes the

the middle of the seventeenth century the chief of customs was a Jew who worked hand in glove with the *wālī* of Aleppo to extort maximum custom fees from the French.[5] As late as 1753, the long-time resident of Aleppo, A. Russell, asserts: "From the extensive connection of the Jews with the commercial world, their fasts and festivals occasion an almost universal stagnation of trade. They not only prove an impediment to the departure of the great caravans but retard their march when actually on the road; and even the Bashaws, and other Grandees, are sometimes obliged to postpone the dispatch of their affairs, when it interferes with the Jewish holidays."[6]

At the same time, the French Consul in Cairo writes "Les Fermiers de la douane qui sont deux Juifs pleins d'Esprit et de subtilité sont ses (Ibrāhīm Kākhyā) satellites. Ils ont acquis tant de pouvoir sur luy qu'ils luy font faire le bien et le mal par un simple mot . . . ".[7]

A similar picture can be drawn of the Armenian community. With the destruction of Julfa, Armenians were resettled in Isfahan, but many also emigrated to the Ottoman Empire and went even as far as India and Indonesia to the East, Venice, Livorno, and Amsterdam to the West. By the beginning of the seventeenth century the Armenian family of Khocha Petik controlled the entire silk trade with the English, Dutch, Venetians, and Spanish in Aleppo. Khocha Petik himself was made Customs Director of all Syria.[8]

Trade and management of government revenues, wealth and political influence seem to have gone hand in hand. Though inferior under the religious law, the Jewish and Armenian communities flourished economically and wielded considerable political influence. Especially as tax farmers of custom stations they had ample occasion to enrich themselves. But it would be erroneous to consider the control over these positions as the primary source of the wealth of the Jewish and Armenian *Dhimmīs*. In order to obtain the tax farming rights to any customs station, it was necessary to advance considerable sums to the authorities; in other words, only the rich could hope to become wealthier.

The original wealth of the Armenians and Jews was accumulated in the international trade passing through the Ottoman Empire. The two minorities had, since the Ottoman conquest of Syria, established their role in commerce through the help of so-called ethnic trading networks. In times when international trade was not regulated and secured with the help of

houses and churches of the local Christians as "near one another, small, poor, and of mean structure."

5 B. Sarāh, "Tarjamat al-Sayyid Francis Piquet" *al-Mashriq* XXIII, p. 102.

6 A. Russell, *The Natural History of Aleppo*, 2nd ed. London 1794 II, p. 78.

7 Correspondance consulaire et commerçiale du Caire. Archives Nationales, Paris, B1 330 p. 67.

8 A. K. Sanjian, *The Armenian Communities in Syria Under Ottoman Dominion.* Ch. III, p. 47.

international banking systems, insurance companies, etc., the risks of such trade could be reduced to a reasonable level only on the basis of personal trust. The most reliable relations of this sort were of course family relations. Almost equally reliable, but providing a much wider base for the development of trade, were the relations of an ethnic and/or religious group, which was spread as a minority over a variety of lands, cities and societies. A common cultural or religious background, shared values, and a feeling of loyalty to the group made commercial relationships between members of the same minority especially reliable, and yet could stretch at the same time over great geographical distances. Jews and Armenians were uniquely equipped to build up such ethnic trading networks. Both possessed a strong group loyalty. Recent migration had brought the Jews from Spain to Europe and to every major city in the Ottoman Empire. Armenians, coming from the East, had penetrated the Ottoman Empire and reached the European commercial centers. The close coherence of the group together with the wide geographical distribution of its members ensured the success of the Jewish and Armenian merchants.

In contrast to these communities, the Copts in Egypt and the various native Christian communities in Syria were geographically very confined. Consequently they did not participate in the international trade and never could amass the capital needed to acquire tax farming rights over the customs. The local *Dhimmīs* remained, therefore, less wealthy and less politically influential, though they were far more numerous than the Armenians or Jews.

This situation was to change for the first time in eighteenth-century Syria when a group of native Arab Christians established a new community and began to strive for positions of wealth and influence similar to those of the Jewish and Armenian *Dhimmīs*. In order to understand the reasons for the rise of the Greek Catholic community and the concomitant decline of the Jewish community, it is necessary to first examine some of the major political and economic changes that took place in Syria and Egypt during this period.

The Ottoman conquests of the Arab provinces had brought Syria and Egypt under the direct political control of Istanbul. The central government established its military and administrative domination over the provinces and ensured the annual flow of revenues to the capital. In the present context one cannot discuss the reasons for and the origin of the decay of central power in the Ottoman Empire. Suffice it to say that heavy military defeats in Europe at the beginning of the eighteenth century highlighted the internal weakness of the Empire. The hold of the center over the periphery loosened and resulted in increasing provincial autonomy. The first sign of rising provincial power was the rule of the al-'Aẓm family in Syria. Ẓāhir al-'Umar quickly followed suit and developed local autonomy into almost complete independence from the Ottoman Empire. In Egypt, Ibrāhīm

Kākhyā had reduced the Ottoman Pasha of Egypt to insignificance by mid-century. His successor, 'Alī Bey al-Kabīr, challenged the Ottoman government in military action and even tried to assert his independence formally.

The second major development in the area that concerns us here is of an economic nature. Recently, attempts have been made to name the European economic penetration of the area as the cause for disruption of traditional patterns. These interpretive efforts have concentrated on eighteenth century Egypt, arguing basically that increased trade with Europe during this period led to social change and new forms of intellectual expression.[9] The problem with this argument is that a closer examination of the trade statistics (especially with regard to French trade) do not support the assertion of drastic increase in trade with Europe and, therefore, the assumed integration into the European-dominated world economy with the concomitant changes in the social structure.[10]

European economic penetration had a profound effect on the society in the Middle East and contributed greatly to the departure from traditional patterns and the development of new social, economic and intellectual formations. But I consider it much more justified to look in the direction of Syria if we wish to observe the earliest effects of this impact. During the eighteenth century the economy, political structure, and demographic patterns of Syria underwent profound transformation determined by international economic developments as well as the above-mentioned internal political changes in the Ottoman Empire.

After the Arab lands had become part of the Ottoman Empire in the sixteenth century, a revival of trade and economy took place in Syria. Aleppo became the most important emporium for merchandise from Central Asia, Iran, the Persian Gulf and South Asia. From Aleppo, merchandise was brought either by caravan to Trabezund and shipped from there to Istanbul or, via Alexandretta, to Europe. Merchants from England, Venice, and Holland settled in Aleppo and the city soon became the third or fourth largest in the Ottoman Empire. During the seventeenth century, the English were the most important traders in Aleppo, exchanging mainly their woolen cloth for silk: the silk, one of the major items of trade in Aleppo, was imported from Persia.

Damascus gained its commercial importance from the circumstance that it was the starting point for the annual pilgrim caravan to Mecca. On the return journey, merchandise from South Arabia, East Africa, and India could be imported. Probably because of its specifically religious character, Europeans and minorities played an insignificant role in this trade.

9 See P. Gran, *Islamic Roots of Capitalism*. Austin, 1978.

10 See for instance the trade statistics in P. Masson, *Histoire du Commerce dans le Levant*. Paris 1911, 510, 522.

This economic structure of Syria in which transit trade via Damascus and Aleppo, Alexandretta and Anatolia was the dominant feature, was profoundly changed during the eighteenth century. The silk trade with Aleppo lost its importance for England, not as a result of a diminished demand but because more convenient sources of supply had been developed.[11] Simultaneously, Aleppo lost its main supplier of silk with the disintegration of Safavid Iran.

During the same period we can observe a revival of French trade in the Levant. Originally, this was the result of the reorganization of the Chamber of Commerce of Marseilles by Colbert; but the rapidly increasing demand of France for silk and cotton soon became the determining factor. By the middle of the eighteenth century the French had replaced the British as the most important European commercial power in Aleppo. Earlier, and more important, however, they had developed their trade relations with the Syrian coastal cities from Jaffa to Tripoli. In the hinterland of these port cities the cultivation of silk and cotton increased steadily. The crops could be sold to the French in the coastal towns directly, without making the detour by way of Aleppo. The economic point of gravity moved slowly from the inland to the coastal lands of southwest Syria. International trade lost some of its importance and local cultivation of cash crops became a significant economic factor. At least since the middle of the eighteenth century we can observe the decay of trade in Aleppo[12] and, for partially different reasons, in Damascus.[13]

11 For the development of English trade see R. Davis, *Aleppo and Devonshire Square*. London, 1967.

12 D'Arvieux (quoted in Masson, 374), Consul of Aleppo, estimates French imports from Aleppo in 1680 at less than 1 million livre annually. English exports to Aleppo were estimated as being 6 mill livre worth of merchandise which covered the cost of their silk imports. In other words a total English trade volume of around 12 mill livre. If French and Dutch trade is added, a total trade volume of perhaps 15 mill livre is reached. In 1785, French trade in Aleppo reached its peak at 7.9 mill livre, at which time it represented four-fifths of the total European trade. Paris *Histoire de la Chambre du Commerce de Marseille* V, 415.

Average values of French imports from Aleppo in millions of French livres:
(Source: *ibid.* V 415)

1671-1675	0.982	1736-40	1.666
1686-1700	0.736	1750-54	22.078
1711-1715	0.924	1765-69	2.578
1717-1721	1.179	1773-77	2.293
1724-1728	1.582	1785-89	3.517

The increase after the year 1785 is related to the destruction of the coastal trade at that time. If we add to that the inflation of the livre between 1740-1785 which led to price increases (e.g. silk: 60%; cotton: 250% *op. cit.* p. 583) the actual volume of merchandise increased much less. At the prices of 1740 the 1785 total volume of merchandise would have actually been 5.5 mill livres (imports and exports). A clear decrease in total trading activities during the eighteenth century in Aleppo compared to 1680.

13 al-Shaykh Aḥmad al-Budayrī, *Ḥawādīth Dimashq al-Yaumiyya 1153-1175 (1741-1762),*

Also discernible during the eighteenth century, are migratory movements that reflect the shifts in economy. Maronite peasants from North Lebanon migrated southwards, established new settlements and expanded the silk cultivation. A numerically much smaller migration occurred from Cyprus and the Aegaean to the same area of southwest Syria. It consisted mainly of Greeks who were, however, soon arabized, many becoming Greek Catholics in the process. Finally, from the inland cities of Damascus and Aleppo thousands of people — mainly Christians — moved to the coastal towns and their surroundings, lured by trade and other economic opportunities. The third phenomenon, namely the migration of Arab Christians from the inland cities to the coastal lands, is closely related to the genesis and development of the Greek Catholic community. The schism between the Greek Catholic and the Greek Orthodox in Aleppo and Damascus in the early eighteenth century was not just to create yet another religious minority: it also signified the formation of a new Arabic speaking middle class with its own organizational and ideological framework.

The customary explanation for the emergence of the Greek Catholic community as a separate entity from the Greek Orthodox runs along the following lines: Under the umbrella of the expanding economic and political position of France, the Roman Catholic Church sent missionaries to the Levant whose purpose was the conversion to Catholicism of the local population. Catholic missionary activities and expanding French trade were both expressions of the growing power of Europe vis-à-vis the Ottoman Empire. Local Christians were hired by French merchants as agents, and conversion to Catholicism cemented this relationship. It is further argued that upon becoming Catholics and formal protégés of the French, such Christians gained certain tax and customs advantages and their capital and merchandise could be protected from the capricious demands

Cairo 1959, is concerned throughout his chronicle with increasing prices, especially of food. His complaint however, is much more dramatic than is indicated by the actual prices quoted by him. Considerable oscillation of prices over the twenty-year period is evident, with most food prices increasing by 50-100%. The increase is particularly evident after 1757 (the date of the death of As'ad Pasha). Budayrī maintains that hoarding and inclement weather and not trade were responsible for the increased prices.

Two conditions had to be met to guarantee flourishing trade for Damascus: 1) The pilgrimage route to Mecca had to be safe, although with the growing might of the Wahhabi movement in the second half of the eighteenth century, this was less and less the case. 2) The Pasha of Damascus had to be securely enough established in his position so as to be able to leave Damascus for some four months each year and he also had to be wealthy enough to finance sufficient troops to cover the Pilgrim caravan. After the death of As'ad Pasha, this was rarely the case. Abdul Karim Rafeq, *The Province of Damascus 1723-1785*. Beirut, 1966, 314-317.

See also Mikhāīl al-Dimashqī, *Kitāb Ta'rīkh Ḥawādith Jarat bi'l-Shām wa-sawāḥil barr al-Shām wa'l-Jabal* in *al-Mashriq XV* (1912) who writes of the pilgrimage in 1805 "*al-ḥajj . . . haraban min 'Abd al-Wahhāb alladhī tasallaṭa 'alā'l-Ḥijāz.*"

of the Ottoman authorities. Thus favored, indigenous Christians who had converted to Catholicism expanded in trade and began to constitute a new commercial bourgeoisie working for French interests in the Levant.

This explanation has a certain validity insofar as it assumes a relationship between the build-up of French trade in Syria and Catholic missionary activities on the one hand and the development of the Greek Catholic community on the other. But the assumed causality of the relationship is too simplistic and disregards completely the internal factors that led to the genesis of the Greek Catholic community. Even a cursory glance at the events shows that (a) the open breach with the Orthodox Church began where French trade and diplomatic protection were least — in Damascus; (b) families, like the Mishāqa, Far'ūn, Ṣabbāgh, or dī Ṭirrāzī were probably already engaged in trade before they became Catholic — and certainly long before they enjoyed any kind of French protection: (c) the French conducted intensive trade elsewhere, as, for instance, in Egypt, without causing a Uniate movement to develop among the local Christians.

At the beginning of the eighteenth century we see an Arab Christian community in Aleppo and Damascus which had gained economic prosperity with high-skill crafts, had attained a certain educational level, and was about to seriously enter the world of commerce. This new, well-to-do, and self-assured urban class also began to demand a greater say in its own communal affairs. The issue of local autonomy came into the open over the question of the appointment of the Patriarch in 1724 and caused the split between the local communities and church authorities in Istanbul. Unwilling to accept an outside appointment, the Damascene Christians named their own Patriarch of Antioch, Cyrillus VI. When the Church authorities in Istanbul appointed their own Greek-speaking Patriarch of Antioch, the Damascene Patriarch sought accreditation from the Roman Catholic Church. From then on Orthodoxy was irrevocably identified with centralist interests, while Catholicism came to symbolize local interests. This split also assumed an ethnic coloring in the contrast between a Greek-speaking Orthodox clergy and an Arabic-speaking Catholic clergy and community.[14]

It would, of course, be premature to speak here of a nascent Arab nationalism. But certainly we can observe the growing strength of local groups, who, just because secular ideologies such as nationalism were still irrelevant, clothed their challenge to the central authorities in the traditional garb of dogmatic deviation.

Catholicism had been made "available" by the presence of the missionaries, but the establishment of the Greek Catholic community was not a result of successful missionary activities as regards conversion. The French

14 For a detailed discussion of the formation of the Greek Catholic Uniate community in Damascus see T. Philipp *The Syrians in Egypt* (forthcoming).

had neither promised diplomatic protection nor made Catholicism a condition for trade relations. If the Arab Christians in Aleppo and Damascus nevertheless adopted Catholicism, it was first and foremost a symbolic expression of their demand for local communal autonomy congruent with their recently achieved social and economic status. Local autonomy was the key issue in the genesis of the Greek Catholic community.

The drive toward local autonomy at the time was, not, as we have seen, a phenomenon restricted only to the Christians in Syria. Although the two events do not seem to have been directly related, it is nevertheless indicative of the mood of the time that the election of Cyrillus VI and the appointment of the first Arab Governor, Ismā'īl al-'Aẓm, occurred within a few months of each other.

The economy of Damascus, during the first half of the eighteenth century, benefited to a degree from the general shift of the economic center of gravity toward the Southwest of Syria. But more important, the rule of the 'Aẓm family, in particular that of Sulaymān al-'Aẓm (1734-38, 1741-43), and that of As'ad al-'Aẓm (1743-57), gave effective protection to the annual pilgrimage caravan to Mecca. This resulted in a trade boom in Damascus. The Damascene Christians seem to have participated in the economic prosperity and also enjoyed a new tolerance on the part of the local authorities.[15]

Damascus, the assembly point for the annual pilgrimage from the Ottoman Empire, was too important to the central government for it to permit the city's autonomy to grow unchecked. Besides, "As'ad Pasha was a typical example of a governor interested in furthering his own prestige and fortune within the 'Establishment.' During his rule in Damascus, he did not attempt to exploit military power in order to retain his post in defiance of the Sultan's order."[16] The considerable local authority that the al-'Aẓm governors enjoyed, mixed with their loyalty to the Sultan, meant for the Greek Catholics that they were fairly free to run their own affairs unless the protests of the Greek Orthodox clergy reached Istanbul and were heeded by the central government.[17] The position of the Greek Catholics during this period remained precarious in Damascus but was still more secure than that of their coreligionists in Aleppo, where the economic decline had already begun.

Even at times when the pilgrimage caravans were well protected, the economic position of Damascus remained shaky as long as the government seated there could not establish its control over all of Southwest Syria, with

15 M. Burayk, *Ta'rīkh al-Shām 1720-1782*, Ḥarīṣa 1930, p. 62-65. Also Jesuit reports assert that As'ad al-'Aẓm was favorably disposed toward the Catholics. Aimé-Martin (ed.), *Lettres édifiantes et curieuses*, Paris 1838, vol. I, p. 251.

16 A. K. Rafeq, *The Province of Damascus 1723-1783*, Beirut 1966, 107.

17 See for instance Burayk *op. cit.* p. 12-13.

its silk and cotton production and with its coastal towns the decisive outlets for trade with Europe. For short periods the Damascus governors of the al-'Aẓm family were able to establish control over Sidon, the closest port to Damascus, by having one of their family appointed governor there.[18]

The Druze in Mt. Lebanon had always made the connection with Sidon hazardous and the Shihābi Emirs gained control over Beirut. Further south, Ẓāhir al-'Umar al-Zaydānī was able to carve out a territory of his own in spite of the various military actions the al-'Aẓm governor undertook against him. Ẓāhir's control over the cotton-growing region and the port of Acre barred any attempt by Damascus to expand economic control in this direction.

The coastal lands were the center of the new economic prosperity induced by the French market's demands for raw materials. It was here and not in Damascus (or Aleppo) that in mid-eighteenth century the new tendencies toward local autonomy found their fullest expression — financed largely by the newly arrived at economic wealth of the area. Ẓāhir al-'Umar could establish his quasi-independent rule over Acre and the Galilee and at one point control the coast from Jaffa to Sidon. In the Mt. Lebanon area the Shihābi Emirs ruled virtually independent of any Ottoman interference.

The semi-autonomous rulers of these areas could provide the Greek Catholics with effective protection from Ottoman, i.e., Greek Orthodox harassment. The Greek Orthodox, like the Jews and Armenians, were classed as officially recognized minorities in the Ottoman Empire. They could invoke Ottoman law and the police authorities to proceed against dissent within their own communities. This power of the Church was of course contingent on the ability of the Ottoman government to actually enforce its law in any given province or town. Under these circumstances throughout the eighteenth century the Greek Catholics flocked from the inland urban centers to Mt. Lebanon, the coastal lands and ultimately to Egypt. In Zahle, the first Greek Catholic church was built in 1740. Originally Druze, the settlement became an almost exclusively Greek Catholic town.[19] In or about the year 1750, Jirjis Mishāqa built the first Greek Catholic church in Tyre, where the Greek Catholic immigrants soon formed the major part of the population.[20] A similar development can be

18 1728-1730. Sulaymān al-'Aẓm was governor of Sidon while Ibrāhīm al-'Aẓm held the governorship of Tripoli and his son controlled Latakiya. At the same time Ismā'īl al-'Aẓm ruled as governor of Damascus from 1725 to 1730. This concentration of power in the hands of the al-'Aẓm family lasted however only until 1730, when they were summarily removed from their positions. Rafeq *op. cit.* p. 107. As'ad al-'Aẓm as govenor of Damascus, 1743-1757, tried for many years to have his brother Muṣṭafā appointed governor of Sidon "to tighten the grip on the Druzes." He obtained this appointment only in 1755. *Ibid.* 192.

19 A. Naff, *A Social History of Zahle*. Ann Arbor (unpublished dissertation), 1975.

20 M. Mishāqa, *Muntakhabāt min al-Jawāb*, Beirut, 1955, p. 4.

observed in Acre. Family histories illustrate the same migratory trend. Greek Catholic families rapidly spread out along the coast. They soon built up, on a local level, a well functioning ethnic trading network, and in each place organized their communities. The net of family relations in Syria and Egypt became still more elaborate, through intermarriage among some of the big families. The Greek Catholics also developed an intense loyalty toward their own religious community. Following the "Seilschafts" principle of mountain climbers, any Greek Catholic who had established a base for himself in a new place would invariably draw other Greek Catholics after him and help set them up. Jirjis Mishāqa was the first Greek Catholic to settle in Tyre; others soon followed him and he financed a church for the new community.[21] Ibrāhīm Ṣabbāgh's powerful position in Acre, where he was confidential adviser to Ẓāhir al-'Umar and maintained monopolist control over most of Acre's trade, attracted many Greek Catholics. Acre served as a regular clearing station for Greek Catholics fleeing from repression in the inland, or simply searching for new fortunes. From there they often moved on to Egypt.

Our information on the early immigration of the Greek Catholics to Egypt is very scant. The rather sketchy registers of the Franciscans in Cairo show the first entry for a "Greci Aleppini ma Catholici" in 1698.[22] A marked increase in the number of Greek Catholic baptisms after the mid-century would suggest an increased influx of Greek Catholics. But presumably these registers deal only with people in Cairo and they leave us completely in the dark with regard to the situation in Damietta, the earliest base of the immigrants in Egypt.[23]

In general, it may be said that from the beginning Egypt was an attractive haven for the Greek Catholics. Here the Greek Orthodox presence was weak and the power of the central government was declining. A variety of explanations have been suggested for the economic reasons which brought the Greek Catholics to Egypt. It has been argued that they could obtain documents from the French consuls, certifying as to their Catholicism and by virtue of such documents they, their ships and merchandise were protected from the assaults of the *corsairs*. This supposedly put them in a privileged position in the existing trade between Syria and Egypt, as compared to Muslim or Greek Orthodox traders. However, all our information indicates that there were hardly any Greek Catholics who owned ships and

21 Tyre apparently did not even have a mosque at that time. To avoid embarrassment by building a church in a Muslim town which still had no mosque of its own, Mishāqa also donated money for the construction of a mosque. He made sure, however that credit for its construction went to the governor of Sidon, thereby ingratiating himself with the authorities. Mishāqa, *op. cit.* p. 18.

22 Cairi Veteris Lib. I Mort. et Bapt. 1697-1800.

23 Some fragmentary information can be gleaned from the French consular correspondence.

that in any case most of the coastal shipping was done by French tramps (*cabotage*).[24]

Another reason that is given for the Greek Catholic migration and economic prosperity in Egypt is their supposedly close links with French trade.[25] Though such a link existed in Syria, this was definitely not the case in Egypt. French merchants had been well established in Egypt since the seventeenth century and dealt, like all other European merchants, with the Jews and Muslims of that country.[26] If anything, the Greek Catholic immigrants were considered by the French as potentially dangerous competitors.

The acquisition by the Greek Catholics of an economic base in Egypt was actually a much more mundane process. Trade between Egypt and Syria had, of course, existed before the arrival of the Greek Catholics on the scene. This trade seems to have been firmly in the hands of Syrian Muslims, of whom we find a certain number permanently in Egypt; the reverse cannot be said of Egyptian merchants. Once the Greek Catholics had become the dominant commercial element in the coastal towns of Syria, it seems they also assumed control over the whole Syria-Egypt trade by slowly elbowing their Muslim compatriots out of it. The trade itself changed neither in kind nor, most likely, in volume: hides, rice, sometimes wheat from Egypt in exchange for soap, cloth and wood from Syria. But whereas at the beginning of the century the Syrian merchants in Khān al-Ḥamzāwī — the traditional market for Syrian merchandise in Cairo — had all been Muslims, by its end the market was almost exclusively in the hands of their Christian compatriots.[27] Similar shifts can be observed in Damietta, where, for instance, in 1769 the Greek Catholics were able to dislodge a Muslim merchant from Tripoli, who was eventually sent back to Syria while his property was confiscated.[28] Even under the French occupation there are signs of the hostility between Christian and Muslim merchants from Syria.[29]

24 The only evidence of ships owned by any of the better known merchant families is the case of the Mishāqa family. In 1752 Jirjis Mishāqa *sold* the ship his father, Yūsuf Petrarki, had brought with him from the Greek Islands. Mishāqa *op. cit.* p. 2. When Mikhā'īl al-Jamal was sent back from Acre with presents and messages for 'Alī Bey al-Kabīr, he traveled on a French ship, al-Ṣabbāgh, *M. Ta'rīkh al-Shaykh Ẓāhir al-'Umar al-Zaydānī*, Lebanon 1935, p. 96.

25 J. W. Livingston, "Ali Bey al-Kabir and the Jews," *MES* VII, p. 222, implies that the Jews collaborated with the Venetians, while the Greek Catholics collaborated with the French. Gran, *op. cit.* p. 8-9, note 100, believes that the presence of Greek Catholics in Damietta helped the French there. In fact, the Greek Catholics made every effort to keep the French *out* and to maintain Damietta as their private domain.

26 E.g., the French used Jews as their dragomans. In 1737 the head dragoman was a Jew called Mu'allim Yūsuf; A.N. B1 324:178. In all their business affairs the French dealt with Jewish "douaniers."

27 A. Raymond, *Artisans et Commerçants au Caire*. Damascus, 1973, II, p. 495.

28 A. al-Jabartī, *'Ajā'ib al-Āthār fī'l-Tarājim wa'l-Akhbār*. Cairo A.H. 1297, II, p. 90/91.

29 *Ibid.* III, p. 15.

The Greek Catholics were in control of the trade in Damietta by 1748. It was here that they also made their first important inroad into the trade with Europe — much to the chagrin of the French merchants in Alexandria, Rosetta and Cairo. French ships visited Damietta regularly to pick up cargoes of rice for France or the Syrian coast. Though the rice was paid for in cash, French captains often brought rolls of French cloth to sell on their own account. As Damietta had no official French representation, the French captains could easily disregard the monopoly on French textile imports and their high prices which France tried to maintain in a stagnating market. The captains were willing to sell at a lower price to the Syrians who, in turn, were able to sell French cloth in the markets of Cairo for less than could the French. French consular reports from Cairo are replete with complaints about these captains and the activities of the Greek Catholics. In 1749 almost 12 percent of all French textile imports were sent via Damietta and passed through the hands of the Greek Catholics.[30] In other words, the Greek Catholics had consolidated their economic base in Egypt, competing with the French merchants, and had prospered long before 'Alī Bey al-Kabīr promoted them to the position of tax farmers of Egypt's customs stations. His employment of Greek Catholics in these positions reflected, if anything, his appreciation of their wealth.

Equipped with capital, commercial expertise, and education, the Greek Catholics rose to administrative power in the second half of the eighteenth century. Ibrāhīm al-Ṣabbāgh's role as chief administrator, manager of all export trade, and personal adviser to Ẓāhir al-'Umar is too well known to need retelling here. His sons and relatives held important positions in Acre and other towns of Ẓāhir al-'Umar's realm. He also employed other Greek Catholics, such as Mikhāīl Baḥrī.[31] Jirjis Mishāqa managed the trade for the Mutawalī *shaykhs* in Tyre and the region of Bishāra.[32] He later became head of finances for Emir Bashīr II,[33] whose closest adviser was to be a Greek Catholic from Ḥomṣ, Buṭrus Karāma, a friend and relative of Mikhā'īl al-Baḥrī.[34] The Baḥrī family succeeded for a while in rising in the administration of Damascus under 'Abdallāh Pasha al-'Aẓm and Yūsuf al-Kinj. During the rule of Sulaymān Pasha in Sidon, Ḥanā al-'Awra was

30 A.N. B1 239:5. Since the Chamber of Commerce of Marseille kept watch over unauthorized exports, the French captains usually re-exported French cloth from Livorno.

31 S. Bahri, "Hanna el Bahri" *Le Lien* XXXVII (numéro special), 14.

32 Mishāqa *op. cit.* 2-4.

33 *Ibid.* 30, in 1799.

34 Bahri 14. "die schoensten Haeuser in Deirelkamar waren die der griechischen Katholiken. Waehrend die Drusen verarmten und verbannt worden waren, hatten sich dies Leute kleine Vermoegen erworben . . . was ihnen sowohl durch ihre Ausdauer, Sparsamkeit und Fleiss, als auch durch den Sonnenschein der Gunst des alten Emir Beshir moeglich wurde." E. Wiedemann (ed.), *Die Heutigen Syrier — Geschildert nach den an Ort und Stelle gemachten Aufzeichnungen eines englischen Reisenden 1841.* Tuebingen, 1845, 50.

the head of the Arab scribes there. In Egypt Mikhā'īl Fakhr and Mikhā'īl al-Jamal became *ra'īs al-dawāwīn* and "*douaniers*" for 'Alī Bey al-Kabīr. Later, the Far'ūn family acquired control over all customs stations in Egypt. Though individual tax farmers were repeatedly dismissed, Egypt's customs remained in the hands of the Greek Catholics until the arrival of the French. Under Muḥammad 'Alī, in 1832 Mikhā'īl was put in charge of the administration of Syria and the logistics of the Egyptian occupation army there.[35]

The list of Greek Catholic administrators and officials is long, but the examples mentioned suffice to show that by the second half of the eighteenth century they had acquired a predominant position in Egypt and along the Syrian coast. The quest for security and the attraction of economic opportunities had brought the Greek Catholics in great numbers to these areas during the course of the eighteenth century. A glance at the distribution of minorities at the beginning of the nineteenth century confirms this demographic growth of the previous century.

	Total Population	*Greek Catholics*	*Jews*
Sidon	15,000	4,500	500
Acre	7,500	4,500	appr. 200
Jerusalem	26,000	300 - 500	4-5,000

	Total No. Houses	*Greek Catholics*	*Jews*
Beirut	780	100	50
Haifa	1,000	500	None
Tyre	200	70	None
Tiberias	550	appr. 20	100
Safed	1,250	None	325
Jaffa	1,200	appr. 100	None

In Damietta and Jaffa there were at the time (1815) no Jews, whereas there were several hundred Greek Catholics there and in Alexandria, where the Jewish community had dwindled to 200 persons. In Cairo, there were roughly 3,000 Greek Catholics and an equal number of Jews, though the latter seem to have been reduced to a state of destitution.[36] In Aleppo the total Christian population had dwindled from about 50,000 by 1720, to 26,000 by 1791, while the Jewish population seems to have remained fairly stable, between 3500-4500.[37] In Damascus, the Christian population

35 Bahri *op. cit.* 32-38.

36 All the above data taken from W. Turner, *Journal of a Tour in the Levant*. London 1820, II passim. W. G. Browne, *Travels in Africa, Egypt and Syria From the Year 1792-1798*, London, 1806, speaks of a "few Jews" in Alexandria (p. 8) and with regard to Cairo, he comments, "Jews were once numerous, but are now on the decrease" (p. 76).

37 Aimé-Martin, I, p. 217; B. Qaraleh, *Ahamm Ḥawādith Ḥalab*, Heliopolis, 1933, 63.

dropped from 25,000 in 1730 to about 15,000 in 1790 and 10,000 by 1845.[38]

The exactitude of these data is, of course, debatable as they were not the result of a census but were estimates by more or less well-informed travelers. Nevertheless, the data provide proof of the migration movement of Arab Christians during the eighteenth century from the Syrian inland cities to the coastal area and the establishment of Greek Catholic communities in all the coastal towns. A different conclusion can be drawn from these data with regard to the Jewish population. They were numerous in towns like Tiberias, Safed, and Jerusalem, where for historical reasons the Jewish community had been strong and in the traditional trading centers of Aleppo, Damascus, and Cairo. Unlike the Arab Christians, they would not necessarily have gained new commercial opportunites by moving to the cost and would certainly have lost their place in the traditional commercial links which, though declining, remained in their hands. As late as 1862, it could be stated that "les Juifs sont presque éxclusivement dans les villes de l'interieur telles qu'Alep, Damas, Jérusalem où ils tendent à avoir le monopole de la banque et du commerce."[39]

Part of the reason for the decline of the Jewish community and the rise of the Greek Catholics was the latter's search for political security and their willingness to follow the changing patterns of trade and economy in Syria during the eighteenth century, which caused them to move to the coast. In contrast to the Jews, they had nothing to lose and everything to gain from such a move. The local rulers in these areas needed precisely the skills, capital, and commercial expertise the Greek Catholics were able to offer and thus their rise as administrators and government officials was swift. But this rise was not determined simply by the absence of Jews in those areas where new economic opportunities were in the offing. After all, the Jews constituted a powerful community in Egypt long before the first Greek Catholic set foot there. Ḥaim Farḥī, scion of an important Jewish family in Damascus, held sway over Acre for several decades under the rule of al-Jazzār and, later, Sulaymān Pasha, despite the fact that the Greek Catholic community was numerous there. The Baḥrī family did not succeed in its attempt to challenge Jewish predominance in Damascus.

Clearly, not all rulers appreciated the qualities of the Greek Catholics to the same degree. But for those whose political ambition entailed the assertion of local autonomy and, hence, a challenge to the authority of the central government, as was the case with Ẓāhir al-'Umar, 'Alī Bey al-Kabīr, and Emir Bashīr II, the Greek Catholics were ideally suited for employ-

38 A. Rabbath, *Documents inédits pour servir à l'histoire du christianisme en Orient*, Paris 1905/10, Vol. II, p. 396; C. F. Volney, *Travels Through Syria and Egypt*, London 1787, Vol. II, p. 60; Wiedemann, p. 232.

39 R. Edwards, *La Syrie* 1849-1862, Paris, 1862, p. 14. E. Napier, *Reminiscences of Syria and the Holy Land*, London, 1847, I, p. 140-141, never once mentions Jews when discussing the various religious communities living on the Syrian coast land.

ment. In addition to their skills, capital, and commercial expertise, the Greek Catholics possessed the typical *Dhimmī* "quality" of weakness and lack of power-base, in a heightened and, in the political context, particularly appealing fashion. By constituting themselves into a uniate community, the Greek Catholics had virtually become "outlaws" in the Ottoman Empire. Under the circumstances they were almost forced to identify with the political aims of the autonomy-seeking rulers. In contrast to the wide geographical distribution of the recognized *millets*, the Greek Catholics' geographical distribution and trading network remained regional. They had no interest in influencing matters in Istanbul nor were they able to seek the protection of the central government against local authorities. Their hopes for autonomy as a community were best served by those rulers who aspired to achieve local autonomy for themselves. The basis for the harmonious cooperation between autonomy-seeking rulers and the Greek Catholics was their community of interest. Both were challenging — though in different ways — the authority of the central government.

On the other side of the fence were the officially recognized *millets* whose interests were supra-regional, who had their contacts and representation in Istanbul, and whose strength and security derived ultimately from the authority of the central government.

Conclusion

The Greek Catholics rose to power and prosperity in the particular circumstances that evolved in Syria and Egypt during the eighteenth century. As merchants, they had built up a local ethnic trading network and had exploited the new commercial opportunities that were to be found on the Syrian coast. From there the Greek Catholics expanded their commercial control to Egypt. Politically they were protected by the contemporary trend towards local autonomy, which they themselves helped to promote and strengthen.

But by the time Muḥammad 'Alī's army conquered Syria, the Greek Catholics had long passed the zenith of their power. Conditions in the area were once again undergoing profound change. The trend toward reorganization and centralization of the government administration first in Egypt and later in the Ottoman area continuously reduced the traditional role of the informal but powerful *Dhimmī* adviser and confidant of the ruler. The shifts in trade and economy were, if anything, even more decisive in the loss of power of the *Dhimmī*. Centralization of administration resulted, among other things, in the abolition of tax-farming. Customs were now collected through government employees. Thus, a major traditional source of wealth and economic power of the *Dhimmī* disappeared. The trade between Syria and Egypt came to be insignificant as compared with the trade of each of these countries with Europe. This new trade was in the hands of European merchants and bankers, who also began to serve the financial needs of the various governments. Though rich minority merchants were still in evidence, their wealth could in no way compete with European capital resources. The economic and also the political influence of the *Dhimmīs* therefore diminished accordingly.

The essence of these changes in the nineteenth century not only resulted in the loss of the recently gained predominance of the Greek Catholics in the area, but also prevented the Jews from regaining their previously held positions of economic and political influence.

When, in 1840, the Greek Catholics were finally accorded the long fought for official Ottoman recognition of their status as an autonomous *millet* they had, ironically, already lost most of their economic and political importance in the area.

GABRIEL BAER

Jerusalem Notables in Ottoman Cairo

The Ottoman Middle East of the eighteenth century was an area without territorial or national boundaries. At times when the roads were secure and well-guarded, everyone who so wished and who had the means could move freely from one place to another within the area. The principal purposes of such mobility (in addition, of course, to bedouin transhumance and the *ḥajj*), were the exchange of goods and knowledge. Merchants and *'ulamā' of* the Ottoman Middle East traveled frequently throughout the area and in some cases even left their country or town of origin and settled elsewhere. Some of them rose to prominence in their new places of residence, as was the case, for instance, of various families of Maghribi merchants in Cairo. This paper deals with another group of immigrant notables in eighteenth century Cairo — Jerusalem *'ulamā'*.

To be sure, this group was extremely small. Among the more than two hundred and eighty biographies of *'ulamā'* in Jabartī's chronicle, there were only five whose place of origin was Jerusalem, and two of them should in fact not be included in this group.[1] At least one of the other three, however, played an important political role in Egypt, and the biographies of all three throw light upon the family background, the connections, the motivation and channels of mobility, as well as the manner of absorption and ascent of these immigrant *'ulamā'*.

Perhaps the least prominent and least important of the three was Sayyid Ḥusayn b. Sharaf al-Dīn al-'Asīlī, who was born in Jerusalem in A.H. 1130/1718 A.D.[2] His *sharaf* derived from his mother, Rāḍiya, the daughter

1 See 'Abd al-Raḥmān al-Jabartī, *'Ajā'ib al-Āthār fī'l-Tarājim wa'l-Akhbār*, Cairo-Bulaq, 1297/1880, vol. 1, p. 66 (12-16) and vol. 3, p. 356 (17)-357 (3) [Figures in parentheses represent line numbers]. One was 'Abd al-Raḥīm from the Abī al-Luṭf (Jārallāh) family, who died at the end of the 17th century in Edirne. The other was Muḥammad b. Sīrīn who died in November 1805. Mr. Adel Manna, who drew my attention to this biography, has pointed out to me that Sīrīn was from the Budayrī family. He was taken to Egypt by his father when he was a young boy and later returned to Jerusalem, where he lived most of the time, although he did visit Egypt again.

2 Biography according to Jabartī, *op. cit.* vol. 2, pp. 70-71, and Ḥasan b. 'Abd al-Laṭīf

of Muḥibb al-Dīn b. Karīm al-Dīn al-Ḥusaynī (on whom see further on). Ḥusayn b. Sharaf al-Dīn left Jerusalem for Damascus when he was a young boy and from there, at the age of fifteen, he went to Cairo to join the *Riwāq al-Shawwām* at al-Azhar. After a visit to Hijaz and Turkey he returned to Egypt in A.H. 1172/1758-9 A.D. The circumstances of his return and the functions he subsequently fulfilled in Egypt will be dealt with below. Later, he returned to Istanbul, where he died in A.H. 1195/1781 A.D. His books were dedicated by him as a *waqf* to the *Riwāq al-Shawwām* at al-Azhar.

More important was another scion of the Ḥusaynī family, Sayyid 'Alī b. Mūsā b. Muṣṭafā b. Muḥammad b. Shams al-Dīn b. Muḥibb al-Dīn b. Karīm al-Dīn... al-Ḥusaynī al-Maqdisī, also called al-Karīmī (being a member of the Karīm al-Dīn branch) or Ibn al-Naqīb,[3] because his father occupied the position of *Naqīb al-Ashrāf* in Jerusalem.[4] 'Alī Ibn al-Naqīb was born in Jerusalem about A.H. 1125/1713 A.D. Like his contemporary and cousin, Ḥusayn b. Sharāf al-Dīn, he went to Damascus where he studied with the famous writer and traveler 'Abd al-Ghanī al-Nābulusī. After further studies in Hama and Aleppo he returned to Jerusalem, but while he was in Syria he had been induced to go to Egypt. This he did, together with his family, when his father died (no year being mentioned in the biographies). In Cairo, he studied at al-Azhar and al-Mashhad al-Ḥusaynī, where he achieved fame as a Ḥanafī *faqīh* and as an eloquent writer. Much of his time however was spent in the breeding of horses, in which he was considered a great expert, as well as in hunting and sport such as shooting arrows and throwing spears. After some time he moved to al-Ḥusayniyya quarter where he built a spacious house and a *zāwiya*. In A.H. 1177/1763-4 A.D., for reasons to be dealt with later on, he went to Istanbul, where he taught and where he was married. But intrigues forced him in A.H. 1183/1769 A.D. to return to Cairo, to his house and his position as a teacher at al-Mashhad al-Ḥusaynī. In the same year, however, he fell ill and in Sha'bān (December) he died (according to Jabartī's report, as the result of bloodletting performed by a Jewish physician with an instrument which was said to have been poisoned).

Politically, the most important of the three was 'Alī's brother, Sayyid Badr al-Dīn al-Maqdisī. On his childhood and early manhood we have practically no information. He rose to prominence when his brother died and he succeeded him as teacher at the al-Mashhad al-Ḥusaynī as well as in his elevated social position in the Ḥusayniyya quarter.[5] There, in 1790-1, he

al-Ḥusaynī, *Tarājim Ahl al-Quds fī'l-Qarn al-Thānī 'Ashar*, n.d., photocopy of MS at the Rockefeller Museum, Jerusalem, pp. 111-113.

3 For biographies see Jabartī, *op. cit.* vol. 1, pp. 371-3; Ḥusaynī, *Tarājim, etc.* pp. 137-8; M. Khalīl al-Murādī, *Silk al-Durar fī A'yān al-Qarn al-Thānī 'Ashar*, Bulaq, 1301/1883, vol. 3, p. 246. Jabartī's genealogy extends to Ḥusāyn b. 'Alī b. Abī Ṭālib.

4 The fact that his father, Mūsā, was *naqīb al-ashrāf* is mentioned by Ḥusaynī, *Tarājim*, etc. p. 132 (16).

5 For his biography see Jabartī, *op. cit.*, vol. 1, p. 373 (22)-374 (13).

built a new house, into which he moved, as well as a spacious mosque, which was well endowed with a *waqf* by him. Inside the mosque he built a mausoleum for his deceased brother. His fame derives from the role he played in the first Cairo insurrection against Bonaparte. When the French occupied Egypt, his 'zeal was kindled', as Jabartī says, he assembled his people from Ḥusayniyya and other outskirts of Cairo and fought the *Ifranj*. These events are vividly described by Jabartī in his detailed chronicle of the French occupation of Egypt as follows:[6] "Sayyid Badr al-Maqdisī came accompanied by those mentioned above and those we forgot to mention, such as the scoundrels of al-Ḥusayniyya and the crooks of the outlying quarters, the inhabitants of the 'Uṭūf quarter as well as others distinguished by their roguery and depravity. Al-Maqdisī preceded them, mounted on a well-equipped horse surrounded by these innumerable groups all yelling and clamoring with a great uproar and tumult their voices ringing out, and replying to one another 'May God give victory to the Muslim', as well as repeating the motto 'May God grant victory to Islam'."

When the insurrection was crushed, Sayyid Badr al-Dīn managed to escape to Jerusalem and thus evaded the fate of the five *shaykhs* who were executed as leaders of the revolt.[7] The French pursued him, but to no avail. When they failed to catch him, they took revenge by tearing down his house and mosque and plundering his belongings, "and the mob of the vicinity completed the demolition".[8] After the evacuation of the French, Sayyid Badr al-Dīn al-Maqdisī returned to Cairo, restored his house and mosque, "and now, while this composition is being written, i.e., the year 1120 (1805-6), he lives there and at his place his devotees assemble and visitors alight, may God bless him".[9]

It is remarkable that all the Jerusalemite notables included in Jabartī's biographies (with the insignificant exceptions mentioned above) were members of the Ḥusaynī clan or connected with it and this was, surely, not coincidental. For various reasons, this clan had particular relations with the neighboring countries, especially Egypt. As is well known, the Ḥusaynīs considered themselves as *ashrāf*; moreover, and what is much more significant in our context, the office of *naqīb al-ashrāf* was for centuries vested in members of this clan. According to a family tree of the Ḥusaynīs of Jerusalem published recently, there were at least ten *nuqabā' al-ashrāf* among members of one branch of the family between the end of

6 'Abd al-Raḥmān al-Jabartī, *Tā'rikh Muddat al-Fransīs bi-Miṣr,* Muḥarram-Rajab 1213/15 June-December 1798, edited and translated by S. Moreh, Leiden, 1975, f. 18a (p. 94 of the translation, which is quoted here).

7 Jabartī, *'Ajā'ib, etc.* vol. 3, pp. 27-8; and *Ta'rīkh, etc.* f. 21b (p. 103).

8 Jabartī, *'Ajā'ib, etc.* vol. 1, p. 374 (6).

9 *Ibid.* (12-13). Jabartī has no obituary of Sayyid Badr al-Dīn; he may have lived longer than the historian.

the sixteenth and the middle of the nineteenth century.[10] This does not include members of other branches who occupied this position, such as, for instance, Mūsā b. Muṣṭafā al-Ḥusaynī, the father of 'Alī Ibn al-Naqīb.[11] Thus both 'Alī and his brother Badr al-Dīn had direct connections with a holder of this office, their father. It may be mentioned in this context that Ḥusayn b. Sharaf al-Dīn al-'Asīlī, the third Jerusalemite in Egypt with whom we are dealing, had been the protégé of Sayyid Muḥammad Abī Hādī, a *naqīb al-ashrāf* of Cairo, and later became his assistant, like a *ketḥudā*, as Jabartī says.[12] A *naqīb al-ashrāf* had many opportunities of establishing connections with other Muslim towns and areas. To cite only one example relating to Egyptian connections of the Jerusalemite Ḥusaynīs: when the famous Egyptian *'ālim* Ḥasan al-'Aṭṭār visited Jerusalem some time in the first decade of the nineteenth century, he stayed with the *naqīb al-ashrāf*, who at that time was 'Umar b. 'Abd al-Salām al-Ḥusaynī and he says in the account of his journey: *"wa-laysa thammata dār āhila li'l-wāridīn siwāhā"* (there [in Jerusalem] is no other house [like it] welcoming arriving travelers).[13]

There can be no doubt that such a background facilitated contacts with Egypt and her *'ulamā'*. In some cases such relations were established while the Jerusalemites were still at home. Thus 'Alī Ibn al-Naqīb in his youth received instruction in the Quran from an Egyptian teacher, Shaykh Muṣṭafā al-A'raj.[14] Similarly, Ḥasan b. 'Abd al-Laṭīf al-Ḥusaynī, the author of the biographies of Jerusalemite notables in the eighteenth century, tells us in his autobiography, that when he was young he studied not only with 'Ali b. Mūsā al-Naqīb during one of his visits from Cairo to Jerusalem, but also with various other Egyptian teachers, *"min ahālī Miṣr"*.[15] 'Alī b. Mūsā al-Naqīb himself was induced to go to Egypt *("raghghabahu fī Miṣr")* by the famous scholar and mystic Muṣṭafā al-Bakrī who initiated him into the Khalwatī order. Al-Bakrī spent much of his life in Jerusalem and apparently was in touch with her notables and with the family of the *naqīb al-ashrāf*.[16]

10 Sholomo Ben-Elkana, "Mimtza'īm ḥadashīm le-motza'ah shel mishpaḥat al-Ḥusaynī ha-yerushalmīt" (New findings on the origin of the Jerusalem al-Ḥusaynī family), *Qeshet*, No. 61 (1973-4), p. 127.

11 The family tree published by Ben-Elkana (*Ibid.*, p. 124) is not "almost identical" (*ibid.*, p. 126) with that published by al-Jabartī. They are more or less identical only from 'Alī b. Abī Ṭālib down to the middle of the 8th century A.H. (14th century A.D.). From then onwards Jabartī's genealogy relates to another branch of Jerusalem Ḥusaynīs (*'Ajā'ib*, vol. 1, p. 271 (30)-272 (4)). The veracity of such genealogies is of course a serious problem, but socially and politically they certainly were significant.

12 Jabartī, *op. cit.* vol. 2, p. 71 (12-13). Cf. Ḥusaynī, *Tarājim etc.* pp. 111-2.

13 'Alī Pāshā Mubārak, *al-Khiṭaṭ al-Tawfīqiyya al-Jadīda*, vol. 4, Cairo-Bulaq 1305, p. 39.

14 Jabartī, *op. cit.*, vol. 1, p. 372 (6).

15 Ḥusaynī, *Tarājim, etc.* p. 132.

16 On Muṣṭafā al-Bakrī and his Jerusalem connections see *EI²*, vol. 1, pp. 965-6 (C.

We have just mentioned 'Alī Ibn al-Naqīb's initiation into the Khalwatī *ṣufī* order which certainly facilitated his relations with the Egyptian *'ulamā'*. The Khalwatiyya, as revived by Muṣṭafā al-Bakrī, had become the most prevalent *ṭarīqa* among Egyptian *'ulamā'* and al-Bakrī's principal *khalīfa* for Egypt, Muḥammad b. Sālim al-Ḥifnī, had been Shaykh al-Azhar from 1757 to 1767.[17] Not less important for the Ḥusaynīs' relations with Egypt was the framework of another order, the Wafā'iyya. The Wafā'iyya was an Egyptian derivative of the Shādhiliyya founded by Shams al-Dīn Muḥammad b. Aḥmad Wafā in the first half of the 8th Hijrī century (14th century A.D.) and propagated particularly by his son 'Alī during the second half of that century. Its peculiar feature lay in that it was a *ṭarīqa* confined to *sharīfs*, descendants of 'Alī b. Abī Ṭālib; its members were called *al-Sādāt al-Wafā'iyya* and its head *Shaykh al-Sādāt*, who was one of the two principal dignitaries of Cairo in the eighteenth century. The Wafā'iyya had spread into Syria and Mujīr al-Dīn mentions the existence of a *zāwiya* in Jerusalem belonging to this order at the beginning of the sixteenth century.[18] It would seem that the Ḥusaynīs were closely connected with this order, though the question whether they monopolized it, headed it, or just belonged to it cannot be answered before further research has been carried out. In the published family trees of the Ḥusaynīs, the name Abū al-Wafā', appears from time to time as of the fifteenth century.[19] Moreover, at the beginning of the seventeenth century the *muftī* of Jerusalem was 'Abd al-Qādir b. Karīm al-Dīn al—Wafā'i al-Ḥusaynī, an ancestor of Muḥammad Ṣālih al-Ḥusaynī, the author of the manuscript called *al-Nafḥa al-Ḥabība*;[20] and one of the common ancestors of all three Jerusalem Ḥusaynī notables of Cairo included in Jabartī's biographies was a certain Sayyid Zakī al-Dīn Sālim al-Ḥusaynī *al-Wafā'ī* al-Badrī al-Maqdisī.[21] How this connection facilitated the passage of Ḥusaynīs to Egypt is illustrated by the case of Ḥusayn b. Sharaf al-Dīn al-'Asīlī. When he came to Egypt in A.H. 1172/1758-9 A.D. he joined Shaykh Muḥammad Abī Hādī b. Wafā', the *khalīfa* of the Wafā'iyya order, who educated him

Brockelmann); Jabartī, *op. cit.*, vol. 1, pp. 165-6 (esp. 165 (22)). On 'Alī ibn al-Naqīb's relation with him see *ibid.*, p. 372 (15-17).

17 Cf. F. De Jong, *Ṭuruq and Ṭuruq-linked Institutions in Nineteenth Century Egypt*, Leiden, 1978, pp. 21-2. Among 50 *'ulamā'* in whose biographies Jabartī mentions their *ṣūfī* affiliation, 25 belonged to the Khalwatiyya. See Reuven Paz, "Ha-Misdarīm ha-Ṣūfiyīm be-Mitzrayim ha-'Othmānīt" (Ṣūfī Orders in Ottoman Egypt), unpublished seminar paper, Haifa University, 1975, p. 6.

18 J. Spencer Trimingham, *The Sufi Orders in Islam*, Oxford University Press, 1971, p. 49 and note 6 quoting Mujīr al-Din's *al-Uns al-Jalīl*. See also De Jong, *op. cit.*, p. 76 f. and *passim*.

19 See Ben-Elkana, *op. cit.*, p. 124.

20 Muḥammad Ṣāliḥ b. 'Abd al-Ghanī al-Ḥusaynī, *al-Nafḥa al-Ḥabība fī Ma'rifat al-Awqāt al-Shar'iyya*, MS at the National and Univ. Library, Jerusalem, p. 3.

21 Jabartī,, *op. cit.*, vol. 2, p. 71 (1-2).

and taught him and whose chief assistant and supporter he became.[22] Thus the framework of *ṣufī* orders, in particular such a small one confined to *ashrāf*, seems to have been conducive to mobility from one country to another.

In addition to such relations based on education and the organization of the *ashrāf* and in particular their Wafā'ī order, there may have been economic relations between the Ḥusaynīs and Egypt as well. Recently published documents have shown that an important branch of the economic activity of the Ḥusaynīs was the production of soap. Thus, for instance, 'Umar al-Ḥusaynī established in 1813 a soap mill on a dilapidated property which had been a *waqf* of his great-grandfather, 'Abd al-Laṭīf al-Ḥusaynī. The latter had also established a soap mill on dilapidated *waqf* property.[23] A list dating from the 1750s shows that Sayyid 'Abd al-Laṭīf, *naqīb al-ashrāf* at that time, used to send boxes of soap as gifts abroad (mainly to Istanbul, of course).[24] Probably the Ḥusaynīs also sold soap to Egypt, though on this question further research is necessary. What we do know is that Palestine was the major supplier of soap to eighteenth century Egypt and that among the principal soap merchants in Cairo there were a number of Jerusalemites.[25] Thus we have at least circumstantial evidence of economic relations between the Ḥusaynīs and Egypt, which may be considered as a supplementary explanation of the prominence of Ḥusaynīs among notable Palestinians in Ottoman Egypt.

Nevertheless, these relations could at best serve as a convenient background which facilitated the movement of certain persons from Jerusalem to Cairo. In order to become absorbed into Egyptian society and especially in order to establish a basis for upward mobility in this society, these persons needed an additional factor — patronage. The chroniclers were well aware of this fact and have amply illustrated it in the account of the experience of each of our three Jerusalemites in Cairo. Ḥusayn b. Sharaf al-Dīn returned to Egypt in A.H. 1172/1758-9 A.D. after he had visited Hijaz and Turkey, not alone, but as part of the entourage of a high Ottoman official — *ma'a ba'ḍ umarā' al-dawla*. Then, in Egypt, as we have seen, he became attached to Sayyid Muḥammad Abī Hādī, who was to

22 *Ibid.* (11-13). Ḥusaynī, *Tarājim, etc.* p. 111, erroneously called this dignitary Muḥammad Abū Hānī and considered him to have been the *khalīfa* of the Bakriyya. Unfortunately, this is not the only mistake in this manuscript.

23 See G. Baer, "The Dismemberment of Awqāf in Early 19th Century Jerusalem", *Asian and African Studies*, vol. 13, no. 3, Appendix II.

24 Buṭrus Abu Manneh, "Or ḥadash 'al 'aliyatah shel ha-mishpaḥah ha-Ḥusaynīt bi-Yerushalayim ba-me'ah ha-shmoneh-'esreh" (New Light on the Rise of the Ḥusaynī Family of Jerusalem in the 18th Century), in A. Cohen (ed.), *Jerusalem in the Early Ottoman Period*, Yad Izhak Ben-Zvi, Jerusalem, 1979, p. 329.

25 André Raymond, *Artisans et Commerçants au Caire au XVIIIe siècle*, Damas, 1973-4, vol. 1, p. 190; vol. 2, p. 478.

become the incumbent of the *Khilāfat al-Wafā'iyya* and *Niqābat al-Ashrāf* and through whose patronage Ḥusayn b. Sharaf al-Dīn achieved an influential and prominent position. In this case, however, this was apparently not sufficient for him to establish an independent basis in Egypt and when Abū Hādī died he had to leave Egypt for Istanbul, where his connections seem to have been more auspicious.[26]

'Alī b. Mūsā al-Naqīb needed such patronage on at least two occasions. Murādī tells us that when 'Alī had moved to Egypt after the death of his father he gained the affection of an Egyptian merchant, Aḥmad Çavuş al-Jazā'irī, who furnished him with a dwelling place and thus laid the foundation for his further progress.[27] Later in his chequered life, when at one point he had again become insolvent, he alluded to his plight in a conversation with Muḥammad Bey Abū al-Dhahab, one of the Mamluk grandees of Egypt at that time. Abū al-Dhahab granted him 100,000 *niṣf fiḍḍa,* which was more than enough to solve his financial problems, but he died soon after.[28] The same Abū al-Dhahab made an important additional grant to establish 'Alī's brother, Badr al-Dīn al-Maqdisī, in his place to fulfill his scholarly and social functions. It should be mentioned in this context that Badr al-Dīn had already previously benefitted from the help of his brother, who had established him as a teacher in al-Mashhad al-Ḥusaynī.[29]

After having discussed the background of the movement of the three Jerusalem Ḥusaynīs to Egypt and the forces which assisted them to settle down, we now come, finally, to investigate the means by which two of them, 'Alī and Badr al-Dīn, rose to prominent and influential positions. To judge by the account of the chroniclers, their principal way of ascending to power was lavish spending on people who were destined to become their clients. Even Murādī in his short biography mentions the extraordinary generosity of 'Alī ibn al-Naqīb. Jabartī and Ḥusaynī go into greater detail: any earthly goods which came into his hands were soon given away to whoever asked for them; his house was always open to visitors and many came "to fulfill their hopes"; again, when he returned from Istanbul, he resumed his custom to entertain guests and to distribute favors. According to al-Ḥusaynī, all the gifts he was given by Egypt's grandees were not retained by him but immediately given away again.[30] None of the chroniclers offers an explanation as to his resources to cover these enormous expenditures. Whatever they may have been, clearly they were insufficient.

26 Jabartī, *op. cit.*, vol. 2, p. 71 (10-18).
27 Murādī, *ibid.*
28 Jabartī, *op. cit.*, vol. 1, p. 373 (13-17).
29 *Ibid.* (22-24); Murādī, *ibid.*
30 Jabartī, *op. cit.*, vol. 1, pp. 372 (26-28); 373 (10-11); Ḥusaynī, *Tarājim, etc.* p. 138 (2-5); Murādī, *ibid.*

This follows not only from Ḥusaynī's remark that any time he spent lavishly he put his trust in God the Creator and Provider *(mutawakkilan 'alā al-mawlā al-khallāq al-razzāq)*, but also from the fact that frequently he became insolvent. Thus, in A.H. 1177/1763-4 A.D., his debts became such a burden and his creditors so many that he decided to leave Egypt for Istanbul. Again, after he had returned to Egypt, he became destitute, which was the reason why he asked Muḥammad Abū al-Dhahab to help him out. It is interesting to note that a few years later the *naqīb al-ashrāf* of Jerusalem, Ḥājj 'Abdallāh al-Ḥusaynī, died insolvent, his debts amounting to more than 11,500 *zoloṭa*, while his assets added up to about 7,500 *zoloṭa* only.[31] Apparently some of the Ḥusaynīs, and probably other notables as well, were so much dependent on maintaining their clientele in order to keep up their social position that they saw themselves compelled to spend money well beyond their means.

When Badr al-Dīn al-Maqdisī succeeded his brother he continued his custom of extending patronage in order to bolster his social and political position. In particular he established close ties with the al-Ḥusayniyya quarter and its inhabitants. His noble descent, his learning and his wealth, in addition to his character and his personality, made him the natural chief of this quarter. He cared for all the needs of its inhabitants: he became famous for "*iṭ'ām al-ṭa'ām wa-ikrām al-ḍifān*", i.e. for honoring guests and feeding the poor; he busied himself with their affairs *(al-sa'y fī ḥawā'ij al-nās)*; he judged them and arbitrated their disputes; and he protected them from those who harassed them, "even if they were Emirs and rulers". Thus he became their patron *(ṣāra marja'an wa-malja'an lahum fī umūrihim wa-maqāṣidihim)* and they feared his authority *(yakhshawna jānibahu wa-ṣawlatahu 'alayhim).*[32]

The patron-client relations of Badr al-Dīn al-Maqdisī and the people of the Ḥusayniyya quarter served as the basis on which he built his political position and activity. He was among the few *'ulamā'* of Egypt who became leaders of popular revolt or who fulfilled political functions in general. As we have shown elsewhere, these functions were based, in other cases as well, on similar patron-client relations.[33] But in the context of this paper we must point out that Badr al-Dīn was a unique case — the only non-Egyptian among the *'ulamā'* with political functions listed in the Appendix of our study of patrons and clients in Ottoman Egypt (Shaykh al-'Arīshī, who was

31 Jerusalem *sijill* 276/21 (Muḥarram 1209/August 1794). I am grateful to my student Aryeh Spitzen for this information.

32 Jabartī, *op. cit.*, vol. 1, p. 373 (25-29).

33 G. Baer, "Popular Revolt in Ottoman Cairo", *Der Islam*, Bd. 54, Heft 2 (1977), pp. 213-242; id., "Patrons and Clients in Ottoman Cairo", *Mémorial Ömer Lûtfi Barkan*, Bibliothèque de l'Institut Français d'Études Anatoliennes d'Istanbul, Paris, 1980, pp. 11-18.

born in the fortress of al-'Arīsh, should of course not be counted as a non-Egyptian). This shows that it was not so easy after all for non-Egyptian notables and *'ulamā'*, to achieve a prominent position in Egypt and even less to fulfill political functions. In spite of the manifold relations with Egypt the group of prominent Jerusalem (or "Palestinian", for that matter) notables was extremely small and only one played a political role in Ottoman Egypt.

URI M. KUPFERSCHMIDT

Connections of the Palestinian *'Ulamā'* with Egypt and Other Parts of the Ottoman Empire

Biographical sources on Palestinian *'ulamā'* during the Ottoman era are comparatively scarce and dispersed: the Damascene biographers Ghazzī, Muḥibbī, Murādī and Bayṭār dealt, on the whole, with the region of Palestine in a rather disparate and casual way and their compendia have to be handled with care for a number of reasons.[1] While heavy emphasis is laid on intellectual life and activities, there is little information about secular activities or commercial connections. This is surprising because many of the great *'ulamā'* families were also mercantile families.[2] Furthermore the exact nature and scope of the important and intricate *ṣūfī* networks are more often concealed than elaborated upon. Another source, the Egyptian historian Jabartī, mentions only sporadically personalities of Palestinian origin.[3] Apart from a manuscript by Ḥasan al-Ḥusaynī of Jerusalem, which was written at the request of Murādī, no authentic biographical or historical work has so far come to light, although some of the local Muslim families are known to possess extensive collections of documents.[4] The

1 Najm al-Dīn al-Ghazzī, *al-Kawākib al-Sā'ira bi-A'yān al-Mi'a al-'Āshira*, 3 vols. (Beirut, 1945-59). The appendix volume to this work called *Lutf al-Samar wa-Qatf al-Thamar* which contains additional material was not available to me; Muḥammad al-Muḥibbī, *Khulāṣat al-Athār fī A'yān al-Qarn al-Ḥādī 'Ashar*, 4 vols. (Cairo, A.H. 1284, repr. Beirut, n.d.); Muḥammad Khalīl al-Murādī, *Silk al-Durar fī A'yān al-Qarn al-Thānī 'Ashar*, 4 vols. (Cairo, 1874-83, repr. n.d.); 'Abd al-Razzāq al-Bayṭār, *Ḥilyat al-Bashar fī Ta'rīkh al-Qarn al-Thālith 'Ashar*, 3 vols. (Damascus, 1963). On their historical value and the extent of their accuracy see H. Gibb, "Islamic biographical literature" in B. Lewis and P.M. Holt (eds.), *Historians of the Middle East* (London, 1962), pp. 34-8, and R.W. Bulliet, "A quantitative approach to medieval Muslim biographical dictionaries", *JESHO*, vol. XIII (1970), pp. 195-211.

2 In Hebron, for instance, the Tamīmī family. For an interesting example prior to the Ottoman conquest see the biography of Ibrāhīm al-Muqaddasī al-Miṣrī (d.1517) who lived in Cairo on income from his soap factory in Jerusalem: Ghazzī I, pp. 102-4.

3 'Abd al-Raḥmān al-Jabartī, *'Ajā'ib al-Athār fī al-Tarājim wa'l-Akhbār*, 4 vols. (Cairo-Bulāq, 1880). See also G. Baer, "Jerusalem notables in Ottoman Cairo".

4 Ḥasan ibn 'Abd al-Laṭīf al-Ḥusaynī, *Tarājim Ahl al-Quds fī al-Qarn al-Thānī 'Ashar*. On this manuscript of which the photostat copy in the Jerusalem Rockefeller Museum has

sijills of the *Sharī'a* Courts have proved very useful as a complementary source[5]; some later Palestinian authors have relied heavily upon them. Material on Palestinian *'ulamā'* during the nineteenth and the early part of the twentieth centuries is even more difficult to find than that on the preceding era.[6].

The problem of sources in a way reflects the question to which we should like to address ourselves, namely the place of Palestine in the intellectual Muslim world and its relations with Cairo. Though never intellectually isolated or devoid of Muslim institutions of higher learning, Ottoman Jerusalem — and the region of Palestine in general — was unable to compete with such major centers of learning as Cairo and Damascus, or even with the Holy Cities of the Hijaz and — at a later stage — Istanbul.

It is true that for the entire period under discussion "a full education could be obtained there" (in Jerusalem).[7] Many an *'ālim*, there or elsewhere, was educated by a learned father or uncle, thus perpetuating a family tradition. Many generations had their own outstanding teachers. While studying abroad was highly valued by the notable families of Jerusalem — and only slightly less so in the smaller towns of Palestine — it should be emphasized that probably only a minority of their sons actually went abroad. Biographical sources that deal with famous *'ulamā'* — many of whom indeed studied in Cairo, Damascus or elsewhere — should not mislead us on this point. However, Murādī mentions that a certain prominent *'ālim* "studied the (religious) sciences in the town of Jerusalem and did

been used see also: B. Abu Manneh, "Or ḥadash 'al 'aliyatah shel ha-mishpaḥah ha-Ḥusaynīt bi-Yerushalayim ba-me'ah ha-shmoneh-'esreh" in A. Cohen (ed.), *Peraqīm be-Toldot Yerushalayim be-Reshīt ha-Tequfah ha-'Uthmanīt* (Jerusalem, 1978), and K.K. Barbir, "Scholarship and opportunity in eighteenth century Jerusalem: Ḥasan al-Qudsī's notables", paper presented to the Third International Conference on the History of Bilad al-Sham, Amman, April 1980. A comparison between the works of Murādī and Ḥusaynī clearly indicates that the former had more sources at his disposal. Other notables besides al-Ḥusaynī may have been requested to supply material. For a preliminary description of a family archive see D.P. Little and A.Ü. Turgay, "Documents from the Ottoman Period in the Khalidi Library in Jerusalem", *WI*, vol. 20 (1980), pp. 44-72.

5 The Nablus *Sharī'a* Court *sijill* was used by Iḥsān al-Nimr, *Ta'rīkh Jabal Nābulus wa'l-Balqā'*, 4 vols. (Nablus, 1975). My colleague 'Ādel Mannā' has based his contribution on Arab personalities in Y. Shavit, Y. Goldstein and H. Be'er (eds.), *Leqsiqon ha-Ishīm shel Eretz-Yisrael 1799-1948* (Tel Aviv, 1983) on the Jerusalem and Nablus *sijills* as well as on a number of modern biographical compendia. I would like to thank him for most generously putting some of his material at my disposal as well as for discussing with me some of the ideas expressed in this paper.

6 al-Nimr, *passim*; Aḥmad Sāmiḥ al-Khālidī, *Ahl al-'Ilm bayn Miṣr wa-Filasṭīn* (Jerusalem, n.d.); a general 20th century collection of biographies is *al-Shakhṣiyyāt al-Filasṭīniyya ḥattā 'Ām 1948* (Jerusalem, 1979) which is a reprint of *Man Huwa fī Filasṭīn* (1948).

7 H.A.R. Gibb and H. Bowen, *Islamic Society and the West* (London, 1957), vol. 1, part 1, p. 155n.

not (have to) undergo the grief of absence away from home" (*wa-qara'a al-'ulūm bi-baldat al-Quds wa-lam yadhuq kurbat al-ghurba*).[8]

It would seem that very few well-known Palestinian *'ulamā'* who were not Jerusalemites received their higher religious education in that city.[9] During the first half of the seventeenth century Jerusalem even seems to have been temporarily eclipsed as a center of learning by Khayr al-Dīn al-Ayyūbī al-'Ulaymī al-Farūqī (1586-1671) in Ramle who attracted many students and scholars to that town. He was undoubtedly one of the country's most famous scholars throughout the entire Ottoman period.[10]

Since medieval times many of Jerusalem's Muslim families came from or left for other towns. As a matter of fact, some of her major *'ulamā'* families such as the 'Alamīs and the Abū Sa'ūds came from abroad.[11] This phenomenon, however, has not yet received the systematic study it deserves.

Individual *'ulamā'* of non-Palestinian origin — apart from those who were appointed to state offices — generally came to Jerusalem to pay a *ziyāra*, not to pursue a full education.[12] Among them were many *ṣūfīs*, often of Maghribī origin. Only rarely did these *'ulamā'* and *ṣūfīs* settle permanently in Jerusalem or elsewhere in the country. Among those who stayed only one Egyptian deserves mention, 'Alī al-Khalfāwī, an Azharite originally from Suez who after long wanderings throughout the Middle East settled in Jerusalem in 1768/9 and taught there.[13] More often a visitor would temporarily teach local *'ulamā'* and students, pass on his knowledge

8 Aḥmad al-Muwaqqit who served as Ḥanafī *muftī* of Jerusalem (d.1758), Murādī I, p. 175.

9 For a few cases see: Ṣāliḥ b. 'Alī al-Ṣafadī (d.1667/8), a *ṣūfī* who went on to study in Cairo, Muḥibbī I, pp. 297-8; 'Abd al-Mannān al-Khammāsh (d.1715), Murādī III, p. 139; 'Abd al-Fattāḥ al-Tamīmī (d.1726), *ibid.*, pp. 41-2 and Nimr II, pp. 56-7; 'Āmir al-Shāfi'ī (d.1727/8) (from the village Nu'ayr) who apparently settled in Jerusalem, Murādī II, p. 229 and Ḥusaynī, p. 138 — the three latter ones from the Nablus area; see also Sulaymān Abū Ghazāla from Nablus (b.1890), *al-Shakhṣiyyat al-Filasṭīniyya*, p. 6.

10 Khayr al-Dīn's biography is in Muḥibbī II, pp. 134-9. See also I. 'Abbas, "Ḥair ad-Dīn ar-Ramlī's *Fatāwā*: a new light on life in Palestine in the eleventh/seventeenth century", in U. Haarman and P. Bachman (eds.), *Die islamische Welt zwischen Mittelalter und Neuzeit* (Beirut, 1979), pp. 1-19. Among Khayr-al-Dīn's students were Ibrāhīm al-Janīnī al-'Azūqa from Jenin (d.1696/7), Nimr II, p. 60; 'Umar al-Mashriqī from Gaza (d.1677), Muḥibbī, III, pp. 212-4. See also Muḥammad b. Tāj al-Dīn (d.1685) who first completed his studies in Cairo and then for ten years continued to take lessons from his relative Khayr al-Dīn, Muḥibbī III, pp. 411-2.

11 The 'Alamīs apparently came from North Africa, the Abū Sa'ūds from Damascus.

12 Among the numerous examples see for instance: 'Abd al-Ghanī al-Nābulusī (d.1731), Murādī III, pp. 30-8, or his *Kitāb al-Ḥaḍra al-Anīsiyya fī al-Riḥla al-Qudsiyya* (Cairo, 1902); or Muṣṭafā al-Ṣadīqī al-Dimashqī al-Bakrī (d.1749), Murādī IV, pp. 190-200.

13 On Khalfāwī see Ḥusaynī, pp. 140-1. Others were 'Abd al-'Azīz al-Tamīmī from Basra (?) who settled in Safed (d.1607), Muḥibbī II, p. 464; 'Īsā b. Ibrāhīm al-Kūrānī (d.1706/7) who settled in Jerusalem, Ḥusaynī, pp. 78-89; 'Abd al-Qādir al-Ṣadīqī al-Baghdādī, a *ṣūfī* who settled in Jerusalem (d.1735/6), Murādī III, pp. 61-9 and Ḥusaynī, pp. 13-29; Muḥammad al-Baylūnī al-Ḥalabī who became Ḥanafī *muftī* in Jerusalem (d.1737/8),

about a certain religious work, or initiate new members to his *ṣūfī* order, and then move on. Among these were also several Egyptians.[14]

For an aspiring *'ālim* from Palestine who "sought knowledge" (*ṭalaba al-'ilm*) abroad there were two obvious alternatives: Cairo and Damascus, both formidable centers of learning, both former seats of government and more or less equidistant from the center of Palestine.[15]

We have insufficient data from which to draw definite conclusions on the orientation of Palestinian *'ulamā'* towards either center and have no guarantee that the biographies studied reflect the full picture. Frequently an *'ālim*'s education is not specified at all, although such an omission is more common in the case of *ṣūfī shaykhs* than with regard to *'ulamā'* who obtained high positions or intellectual fame. With all these shortcomings in mind, we have nevertheless attempted to draw up a comparative table which — we hope — will serve to indicate certain basic trends (see appendix).[16]

★ ★ ★

When we take a closer look at the intellectual connections of Palestinian *'ulamā'* with Damascus, our sources seem to indicate a certain decline during the Ottoman period — a decline which does not necessarily parallel the overall connections of the region as a whole to Damascus as an important Ottoman provincial capital. With the improvement of transport

Murādī IV, pp. 123-4; Muḥammad al-Tāfilātī al-Maghribī who after a life full of adventure became *muftī* of Jerusalem (d.1777), Murādī IV, pp. 102-8 and Ḥusaynī, pp. 89-101; 'Alī al-Yashruṭī al-Ṭarshīḥī, the founder of the well-known Acre *ṣūfī* order who — according to his biography — was heading from North Africa to Jerusalem (d.1899), Bayṭār II, pp. 1065-7.

14 Here we should mention the Egyptian Manṣūr al-Suṭūḥī al-Maḥallī (d.1656) who taught many Jerusalemites but was disliked because of his haughtiness and left for Damascus, Muḥibbī IV, pp. 423-6 — Cf. him mentioned as teacher, *ibid.*, p.264, vol. II, pp. 156-7, and vol. III, pp. 414-5; a certain Zayn al-Dīn al-Miṣrī was invited by Khayr al-Dīn and stayed for two years in Ramle, Muḥibbī IV, p. 332; two Maghribīs taught on their way through Ramle as well, *ibid.*, vol. III, pp. 411-2; Ustādh al-Mazṭarī al-Maghribī initiated Aḥmad b. Ṣalāḥ al-Dīn al-'Alamī (d.1699) into the Shādhiliyya order, Murādī I, p. 116 and Ḥusaynī, pp. 76-8, as well as 'Abd al-Ghafūr al-Jawharī in Nablus (d.1680/1), Murādī III, pp. 29-30 and Nimr II, p. 55; 'Uqdī al-Baṣīr al-Miṣrī taught Muṣṭafā al-Tamīmī (d.1769/70) in Nablus, Murādī IV, p. 184.

15 Compilations of travel times between Egypt and Greater Syria are rare and inadequate. We suppose that from Jerusalem to Damascus 7-10 days were needed, from Jerusalem to Cairo 10-14 days. Cf. O.Sprenger, *Die Post- und Reiserouten des Orients* (Leipzig, 1864), pp. 100-3; J.Sauvaget, *La Poste aux Chevaux dans l'Empire des Mamelouks* (Paris, 1941), p. 76; S.Avitzur, *Ḥayyey Yom-Yom be-Eretz-Yisrael ba-Me'ah ha-Yud-Ṭeṭ* (Tel Aviv, 1972), pp. 300-1. Modern transport very much shortened travel time in the 19th century.

16 Not all *Naqībs* of the *Ashrāf* were *'ulamā'*; however, where data on their education was lacking they have been included.

and the nineteenth century *tanẓīmāt*, Istanbul began to overshadow Damascus.

The habit of holding a commemorative prayer at the Umayyad Mosque for deceased *'ulamā'* of fame, including Palestinians, as described by Ghazzī and Muḥibbī, is no longer mentioned by the later biographers.[17] We do not know whether this practice fell into disuse or whether there was a parallel practice in Cairo.

That there were extensive relations between Palestinian and Syrian *'ulamā'* is also clear from the fact that Palestinians occasionally taught in Damascus, delivered a sermon at the Umayyad Mosque or simply visited.[18] We have already drawn attention to the fact that Murādī asked Ḥasan al-Ḥusaynī to collect biographies of Jerusalem notables. Murādī himself tells us how Ḥusayn al-Khālidī, a Jerusalem *Sharī'a* Court official who had been falsely accused of irregularities and had been arrested and brought to Damascus, was freed by his plea.[19] There were similar interactions with other cities as well, but with regard to Damascus it is the *ṣūfī* bonds which most draw our attention. *Ṣūfī shaykhs* from notable Jerusalem families such as the 'Alamīs and the Dajānīs, as well as others from Safed, Nablus and Acre were in close contact with their counterparts in Damascus.[20] It is our tentative conclusion that Damascus in this respect exerted a relatively greater attraction than Cairo.[21]

17 On *ṣalāts* held for Palestinian *'ulamā'* who did not live in Damascus, see for instance: Ghazzī I, p. 18, p. 56, p. 136, p. 232, vol. II, p. 12, p. 62, p. 72, p. 178, p. 219; Muḥibbī I, p. 177, vol. IV, p. 273. These include *'ulamā'* from Jerusalem, Nablus, Safed, Hebron and Gaza. It is not excluded that particularly Ghazzī used these *ṣalāts* as a criterion for inclusion in his lexicon.

18 See for instance: Muḥammad al-'Ajīmī (Jerusalem) (d.±1531/2), Ghazzī II, pp. 11-2; Ibrāhīm Jamā'a (Jerusalem) (d.1542), Ghazzī II, p. 76; Muḥammad Nāṣir al-Dīn (Jerusalem) (gave *khuṭba* in 1540), Ghazzī II, p. 72; Yaḥyā b. Muḥammad al-Ṣafadī (d.1577), Ghazzī III, p. 219; 'Abd al-Karīm al-Ja'barī (Hebron) (to Damascus in 1525/6), Ghazzī I, p. 255; Maḥmūd al-Tamīmī (Hebron) (in Damascus ± 1539/40), Ghazzī II, p. 249; Muḥammad al-'Ajamī (Jerusalem) (d.1645/6), Muḥibbī III, p. 412-4; 'Abd al-Raḥīm Abū Luṭf (Jerusalem) (d.1692), Murādī III, p. 25 and Jabartī I, p. 66; 'Abd al-Laṭīf b. 'Abd al-Qādir al-Ḥusaynī (Jerusalem) (d.1694/5), Ḥusaynī, pp. 116-8; 'Abd al-Ḥalīm al-Shuyūkī (Nablus) (d.1771/2), Murādī II, pp. 254-8; Muḥammad al-Rayyis al-Ghazzī (Gaza) (d.1717/8), Murādī IV, p. 59.

19 Murādī II, pp. 72-5.

20 'Abd al-Ṣamad al-'Alamī (d.1622/3), Muḥibbī II, p. 421; Muḥammad al-'Alamī (d.1628/9), Muḥibbī IV, pp. 78-9; Aḥmad al-'Alamī (d.1645 in Damascus), Muḥibbī I, pp. 219-20; Aḥmad al-Dajānī (d.1562), Ghazzī III, pp. 120-1; Ṣāliḥ al-'Alamī (d.1594), Muḥibbī II, p. 239; 'Abd al-Qādir al-Ṣafadī (d.1519), Ghazzī I, pp. 242-6; Aḥmad b. Asad al-Ṣafadī (d.1601/2), Muḥibbī I, p. 177; Yaḥyā al-Dajānī (d.1720/1), Murādī IV, p. 228 and Ḥusaynī pp. 70-5; Raḍwān al-Rāwī al-Nābulusī (Nablus) (d.1744/5), Murādī II, pp. 115/6. See also Sa'īd al-Khālidī al-Dimashqī al-Yashruṭī (d.1877), Bayṭār II, pp. 669-73, and, of course, 'Abd al-Ghanī al-Nābulusī's biography.

21 While the Khalwatiyya and Shādhiliyya orders were most popular among Palestinian *'ulamā'*, and oriented towards Damascus, the Rifā'iyya order is less often mentioned.On

Of those who actually received a higher education in Damascus we should, first of all, pay attention to a comparatively large group of Ḥanbalī *'ulamā'*, mainly from Nablus and surroundings.[22] Their orientation towards Damascus, however, did not mean that Damascus had a monopoly on Ḥanbalī learning. The alternative center in Cairo where the *madhhab* had never been represented very strongly, was, however, further in decline.[23]

Another group of scholars who studied in Damascus comprises some scions of great *'ulamā'* families from Jerusalem and Nablus. It is interesting to note that while the Nablus *'ulamā'* community maintained a continuing relationship with Damascus — probably due to the above mentioned Ḥanbalī link as well as to earlier waves of emigration — there seems to have been no sequel to the connection on the part of the Abū Luṭfs (Jārallāhs) and Dajānīs from Jerusalem after the seventeenth century.[24] Some of these Jerusalemites came to Damascus in order to supplement the earlier education they had received at al-Azhar in Cairo.[25] The fact that the same families later sent their sons to Cairo only — and in a sporadic case to Istanbul — seems to indicate that Damascus had lost some of its allure as a center of learning. Only in the twentieth century, more particularly after 1919, did Damascus regain some of its former attraction, but by then secular rather than religious subjects were studied.

A third category of students and *'ulamā'* who gravitated towards Damascus were inhabitants of Safed.[26] Here the explanation is easily found in the geographical proximity of the two towns. Nevertheless, our sources seem to

this order see for instance: 'Abd al-Qādir Ibn al-Ghusayn from Gaza (d. 1677), Muḥibbī II, 437; he was initiated into this order by Muḥammad al-'Alamī. For a Rifā'iyya connection with Egypt see al-Khalfāwī's biography, Ḥusaynī, pp. 140-1.

22 Ḥasan al-'Ajamī from Jerusalem (d. 1519 in Damascus), Ghazzī I, p. 176; Aḥmad b. 'Abd al-Raḥmān al-Shuyūkī (Nablus) (d. 1532), Ghazzī II, p. 99; Muṣṭafā b. 'Abd al-Ḥaqq al-Ḥanbalī (Nablus) (d. 1740/1), Murādī IV, pp. 184-5; Muḥammad al-Safarīnī (Nablus) (d. 1775), Murādī IV, pp. 31-2 and Nimr II, pp. 59-60; Ismā'īl al-Jarā'ī (Nablus) (d. 1787/8), Nimr II p. 60; Muḥammad b. Hāshim al-Ja'farī (Nablus) (d. 1813/4), Nimr II, p. 60; 'Abdallāh Ṣūfān al-Qadūmī (Nablus) (d. 1912/3), Nimr IV, pp. 122/3; Mūsā Sūfān al-Qadūmī (Nablus) (d. 1918), *Leqsiqon*, p. 427.

23 Muḥammad al-Qudsī al-Khurayshī (d. 1592), Muḥibbī III, p. 340; Yasīn al-Ḥanbalī (Nablus) (d. ±1649), Muḥibbī IV, pp. 392-3; Mar'ī al-Karmī (Tulkarm) (d. 1623), Muḥibbī IV, pp. 358-61; his nephew Aḥmad al-Karmī (d. 1680), Muḥibbī I, p. 367; Yūsuf al-Ṭulkarmī — grandson of Mar'ī — (d. 1667), Muḥibbī IV, pp. 508-9. Cf. J. Voll, "the non-Wahhabi Hanbalis of Eighteenth Century Syria", *Der Islam*, vol. 49 (1972), p. 289.

24 Muḥammad b. Yūsuf Abū Luṭf (Jerusalem) (d. 1619), Muḥibbī IV, pp. 272-3; 'Abd al-Ghaffār al-'Ajamī (Jerusalem) (d. 1647/8), Muḥibbī II, p. 433; 'Umar b. Yūsuf al-Nimr (Nablus) (2nd half 17th C.), Nimr II, p. 56; 'Umar al-Jawharī (Nablus) (d. 1768), Murādī III, p. 183; Aḥmad al-Baqārī (Nablus) (d. 1780/1), Murādī I, pp. 191-2.

25 'Alī Abū Luṭf (Jerusalem) (d. 1527), Ghazzī II, pp. 191-3; 'Umar Abū Luṭf (Jerusalem) (d. 1594/5), Muḥibbī III, pp. 220/1; Muḥammad al-Da'ūdī (Jerusalem) (d. 1598 in Damascus), Muḥibbī IV, pp. 145-52; Ḥasan al-Ṣafadī (d. ±1583), Ghazzī III, p. 140.

26 Yaḥyā ibn Ḥāmid (Safed) (d. 1577), Ghazzī III, p. 219; Ḥasan al-Ṣafadī, see note 25.

indicate that most of the nineteenth century *muftīs* serving in such north-Palestinian towns as Safed, Nazareth, Tiberias and Acre were educated at al-Azhar.[27]

Some Palestinian *'ulamā'*, not all of them educated in Damascus and not all of them Ḥanbalīs (many of whom traditionally settled in the Ṣāliḥiyya Quarter) acquired permanent teaching positions in Damascus.[28] While it is not clear to what extent *ṣūfī* connections were involved, it may be inferred from the biography of Muḥammad al-'Alamī (d. 1609/10), an *'ālim* and *ṣūfī* trained at al-Azhar, that a sort of Jerusalemite community existed in Damascus (*al-Maqādisa al-muqīmīn bi-Dimashq*).[29] The sixteenth century witnessed about a dozen of our biographees settling permanently in Damascus but in the following centuries only a very few were to do so.[30]

★ ★ ★

Cairo, and in particularly al-Azhar, throughout the ages attracted a constant stream of students from abroad.Those from Jerusalem and other towns in the region of Palestine were naturally absorbed at the *Riwāq al-Shawwām*. If that institution's records were ever to become accessible to scholarly research they would undoubtedly help us to reconstruct a fuller picture of Palestinian-Egyptian intellectual relations. Rarely do we find *'ulamā'* who studied outside the framework of al-Azhar, e.g. the Sayyidnā Ḥusayn or Sulṭān Ḥasan Mosques.[31]

Palestinian students generally came from the established *'ulamā'* families residing in the main towns. Certain families perpetuated a tradition of sending their sons to al-Azhar. The Abū Luṭf (Jārallāh) family in Jerusa-

27 See al-Khālidī, p. 37 (Aḥmad al-Fahūm); p. 38 (Muḥammad al-Ṭabarī, Muḥammad al-Naḥawī, 'Abdallāh al-Fahūm); p. 39 (As'ad al-Shuqayrī, Amīn al-Fahūm, 'Abd al-Laṭīf al-Fahūm, Yūsuf al-Fahūm, 'Umar al-Fahūm); p. 40 ('Abd al-Salām al-Ṭabarī, Shaykh Salīm, 'Abdallāh al-Jazzār, Ibrāhīm al-Jazzār, 'Alī Mīrī).

28 Ḥasan al-'Ajamī (d. 1519), Ghazzī I, pp. 176; 'Alī Abū Luṭf (d. 1527), Ghazzī II, pp. 191-3; Muḥammad al-Da'ūdī (d. 1598), Muḥibbī IV, pp. 145-52; Muḥammad ibn Khaṣīb (d. 1599), Muḥibbī IV, pp. 154-8; Aḥmad al-Shuyūkī (Nablus) (d. 1575), Ghazzī I, p. 136; 'Alī al-Jubrī (Nablus) (d. 1530), Ghazzī II, pp. 200-1; Aḥmad al-Shuyūkī (Nablus) (d. 1532), Ghazzī II, p. 99; 'Alī al-Tamīmī (Hebron) (in Damascus around 1540), Ghazzī II, p. 249. An interesting earlier case was Muḥammad al-Ghazzī (d. 1522) who acted as Mālikī *qāḍī* in Damascus but was apparently dismissed by the conquering Ottomans and returned to Gaza, Ghazzī I, p. 56.

29 Muḥibbī IV, pp. 43-4.

30 Ibrāhīm al-Janīnī al-'Azūqa (d. 1696-7), Nimr II, p. 60; Aḥmad al-Ṣafadī al-Dimashqī (d. 1689), Muḥibbī I, pp. 356-9; Nūr al-Dīn al-Asadī al-Ṣafadī (d. 1696 in Damascus), Murādī IV, p. 227; Aḥmad b. Muḥammad b. Ṭāhā al-Dimashqī (d. 1766/7), Murādī I, p. 169; Muṣṭafā b. 'Abd al-Ḥaqq al-Ḥanbalī (d. 1740), Murādī IV, pp. 184-5; Ismā'īl al-Jarā'ī (d. 1787-8), Nimr II, p. 60.

31 'Alī b. Mūsā al-Ḥusaynī (d. ± 1767), Murādī III, p. 246 and Ḥusaynī, pp. 137-8 and Jabartī I, pp. 371-3 (Sayyidnā Ḥusayn).

lem, of which at least ten Cairo-educated members figure in our sources, is a good example. There are also other names such as the Ibn Jamā'as, 'Alamīs, Dajānīs of Jerusalem, the Akhramīs and Khammāshs of Nablus, the Tāj al-Dīn al-Farūqīs of Ramle, and the Timurtāshīs of Gaza.

The most striking common denominator of the *'ulamā'* who studied in Cairo is the high office in the religious hierarchy which they attained afterwards. Even if we take into account that our sources are biased towards high office and fame, we should note the fact that over sixty percent of these Azharites later became *muftīs* in their towns of origin and that many others became teachers at the most prestigious *madrasas* or otherwise outstanding *faqīhs*. It may therefore be said that an Azhar education often safeguarded a family's hold on a high *'ulamā'* office.

The biographies often contain abundant details about teachers, as well as disciplines and religious works studied. These disciplines often determined one's career.[32] Among the disciplines studied we find all the classic subjects such as *tafsīr, qirā'āt, ḥadīth*, grammar etc., but *fiqh* — contrary to the other subjects always studied under a *shaykh* in one's own *madhhab* — figures prominently in almost any biography. Most of the Palestinians, as might be expected by the spread of the *madhāhib* in the country, studied Shāfi'ī *fiqh*, many others Ḥanafī *fiqh*, and only a few Ḥanbalī or Mālikī *fiqh*. Occasionally we also come across less common disciplines studied, such as astronomy or medicine.[33]

Students often remained in Cairo for a number of years: periods varying from 10 to 15 years were certainly no exception.[34] Since many of these students were still teenagers when they first enrolled at al-Azhar it was not uncommon for them to go together with somewhat older brothers or cousins.[35] After completing their studies most of them returned to their hometowns, but some *'ulamā'* accepted religous positions in Egypt.[36] It is

32 This also included works by Palestinians; whoever memorized the 15th century *Ṣafwat al-Zayd* by Shihāb al-Dīn al-Ramlī (a Shāfi'ī *fiqh* book) was — according to Jerusalem's *'ulamā'* — predestined to become a *qāḍī*: Muḥammad ibn Khaṣīb (later Shāfi'ī *qāḍī* in Damascus) (d.1599), Muḥibbī IV, pp. 154-8.

33 Muḥammad al-Ghazzī from Gaza (d.1714/5), for instance, studied medicine for 11 years and became an outstanding Palestinian physician, Murādī IV, pp. 108-9.

34 'Alī b. Ḥabīballāh Abū Luṭf (d.1731/2) for 15 years, Murādī III, p. 209 and Ḥusaynī, p. 139; 'Abd al-Raḥmān Abū Luṭf (b. 1717/8) for 10 years, Ḥusaynī, pp. 53-6; Muḥammad al-Ghazzī for 11 years, see note 33. Some *'ulamā'* spent two or more terms of study in Cairo, for instance: Muḥammad al-Timurtāshī al-Ghazzī (d.1596), 4x, Muḥibbī IV, pp. 18-20; 'Abd al-Ghaffār al-'Ajamī al-Qudsī (d.1648), 2x, Muḥibbī II, p. 433; Muḥammad al-Surūrī (d.1678), 2x, Muḥibbī III, pp. 414-5.

35 'Arfa al-Dajānī (d.1594/5), Muḥibbī III, p. 110; Muḥammad b. Muḥammad al-'Asīlī (d.1676), Muḥibbī IV, p. 202; Khayr al-Dīn al-Ramlī (d.1671), Muḥibbī II, pp. 134-9; Muṣṭafā al-'Alamī (d.1757/8), Murādī IV, p. 218.

36 Muḥammad al-Ṣafadī (d.± 1583) (*wā'iẓ* at al-Azhar), Ghazzī III, pp. 80-1; Muḥammad al-Mashraqī (d.1572/3) (teacher), Ghazzī III, pp. 26-7; 'Alī b. Mūsā al-Ḥusaynī (d.± 1767) (teacher at Sayyidnā Ḥusayn), Murādī III, p. 246, Ḥusaynī, pp. 137-8 and Jabartī I, pp. 371-3 — he was succeeded by his brother Badr al-Dīn.

interesting to note that the Ḥanbalī background of several of these did not hinder their careers: it might be that the small number of Ḥanbalī *'ulamā'* in Egypt even enhanced their chances. One of these, Yūsuf al-Barqāwī from Nablus (d.1896/7) even became the *shaykh* of the *Riwāq al-Shawwām* at al-Azhar.[37]

It would be interesting to know to what extent these Palestinian students and *'ulamā'* were integrated into the Cairene intellectual community. The opinion that "These foreigners rarely assimilated the manner and dress of the Egyptians. . ." might have applied to people from areas more remote than Palestine rather than to the Palestinians themselves.[38] On the whole they seem to have adapted themselves quite easily. Nevertheless we rarely hear about an *'ālim* who married an Egyptian wife — even if we take into account that our sources are rather reticent on this point. Muṣṭafā al-'Alamī (d.1664/5) who did marry an Egyptian and who was said to have adopted the Egyptian colloquial Arabic (*lughat ahl Miṣr*) as his daily tongue and continued to use it even after his return to Jerusalem, where he acted as a public notary and *nā'ib*, was an exception rather than the rule.[39]

While relatively few Palestinian *'ulamā'* settled permanently in Egypt there can be no doubt that connections between *'ulamā'* in the two countries were firm and frequent. This also included the sending of *ijāza*s — a custom known in other parts of the Middle East as well.[40] We may also suppose that a "position to collect *awqāf* income" (*waẓīfat jibāyat awqāf*), as in the case of 'Uthmān al-'Alamī (d. 1754/5) (probably with regard to the Jerusalem *Ḥaram*'s endowments) entailed more than just frequent trips to Egypt.[41] On the whole it would seem that the Egyptian occupation of 1831-1840, as well as the improvement in communications and security, strengthened these relations, from the first half of the nineteeenth century onwards.[41a]

* * *

37 Yūsuf al-Barqāwī (d.1896/7), Nimr IV, p. 122; Mar'ī al-Karmī (d.1624), Qur'ān reader and teacher at al-Azhar, then *shaykh* at the Sulṭān Ḥasan Mosque, Muḥibbī IV, pp. 358-61; Aḥmad al-Karmī (d. 1680), Muḥibbī I, p. 367.

38 J. Heyworth-Dunne, *An Introduction to the History of Education in Modern Egypt* (London, 1939; repr. 1968), p. 35.

39 Muḥibbī IV, p. 385.

40 On *'ulamā'* who settled see: Muḥammad al-Ṣafadī (d.± 1583), Ghazzī III, pp. 80-1; Muḥammad al-Ghazzī al-Mashraqī (d.1572-3), Ghazzī III, pp. 26-7; Mar'ī al-Karmī (d.1624), Muḥibbī IV, pp. 358-61; Aḥmad al-Karmī (d.1680), Muḥibbī I, p. 367; 'Alī b. Mūsā al-Ḥusaynī and his brother Badr al-Dīn, see note 36; Ḥusayn al-Thawrī al-'Asīlī (d.1780/1) Jabartī II, pp. 70-1 and Ḥusaynī, pp. 11-3. On *ijāzas* see: Muḥammad b. Mūsā al-'Asīlī (d.1621/2), Muḥibbī IV, p. 234; Badr al-Dīn b. Jamā'a (d.1773), Murādī II, pp. 2-4.

41 Murādī III, p. 166.

41[a] See Aḥmad al-Tamīmī (Hebron), Ṭāhir al-Ḥusaynī and 'Umar al-Ḥusaynī (both Jerusalem) in *Leqsiqon*. cf. A. Mannā' "Cultural Relations between Egyptian and Jerusalem *'ulamā'* in the early nineteenth century," *AAS*, vol. 17 (1983), pp. 139-52.

We do not know how many *'ulamā'* and *ṣūfīs* — or Muslims in general — from the area of Palestine made the arduous pilgrimage to Mecca. Judging by our sources which occasionally mention the relevant dates and other details the number of *ḥājj*s was probably not very large.[42] Many a pilgrim made the trip at a more advanced age and died in Mecca or on the way back, a death upon which traditionally a special blessing rests.[43] However, the Holy Cities of the Hijaz cannot be said to have exerted a special attraction as a center of learning for Palestinians. Few studied or taught there.[44]

★ ★ ★

As one might expect, connections with Istanbul gradually increased over the centuries of Ottoman domination. In contrast to Damascus and Cairo, Istanbul had barely maintained any historical ties with the towns of Palestine prior to the sixteenth century due in part to the long traveling time which separated Turkey from Palestine. Whether over land or by sea from Jaffa the trip entailed considerable hardship, borne out by the comparatively large number of biographees who met a tragic death on their way to or from Istanbul.[45]

A journey to Istanbul in most cases had a material rather than an intellectual purpose: while aspiring *'ulamā'* "sought (religious) knowledge"

42 See for instance: 'Abd al-Ṣamad al-'Alamī (d.1622/3), Muḥibbī II, p. 421; Muḥammad al-'Asīlī (d.1676) who went three times, Muḥibbī IV, p. 202; Khalīl al-Shahwānī (d.1740), Ḥusaynī, pp. 68-70 and Murādī II, pp. 104-5; Ḥasan b. Salīm al-Dajānī (Jaffa) (d.1870s) together with his father, Bayṭār I, pp. 521-5; as well as the following notes.

43 'Arfa al-Dajānī (d.1594/5), Muḥibbī III, p. 110; Muḥammad al-Ghazzī al-Dimashqī (d.1522), Ghazzī I, p. 56; Muḥammad b. Jamā'a al-Kinānī (d.± 1700), Muḥibbī IV, p. 94 and Ḥusaynī, pp. 56-60; Najm al-Dīn b. Khayr al-Dīn al-Ramlī (d.1780/1), Ḥusaynī, pp. 102-3; 'Abd al-Nabī al-Nābulusī (d.1741/2), Murādī III, pp. 140-2; Ḥusayn b. Salīm al-Dajānī (Jaffa) (d.1858), Bayṭār I, pp. 537-44.

44 'Alī b. Muḥammad Abū Luṭf (d.1526), Ghazzī II, pp. 191-3; Aḥmad b. Muḥammad al-Shuyūkī (d.1532), Ghazzī II, p. 99; Muḥammad b. 'Umar al-'Alamī (d.1628/9), Muḥibbī IV, pp. 78-9; Ṭāhā b. Ṣāliḥ al-Dīrī (d.1661), Muḥibbī II, pp. 260-1; 'Abd al-Raḥīm Abū Luṭf (d.1692), Murādī III, pp. 2-5 and Jabartī I, p. 66; Aḥmad al-Ṣafadī al-Dimashqī (d.1689), Muḥibbī I, pp. 356-9; Yūsuf al-Ghazzī al-Muqrī (d.1774/5), several times, Murādī IV, pp. 238-9; 'Abd al-Ghanī al-Labadī (d.1899/1900), taught there, Nimr IV, p. 122; 'Abdallāh Ṣūfān al-Qadūmī (d.1912/3), Nimr IV, pp. 122-3.

45 Ibrāhīm b. Walī al-Amīr (d.1552/3), Ghazzī II, p. 81; Muḥammad b. 'Abd al-Ḥaqq Abū Luṭf (d.1661), Muḥibbī III, p. 482; Abū al-Luṭf b. Abū al-Luṭf (d.1661), Muḥibbī I, p. 145; Ḥibatallāh ibn al-'Ajamī (d.1666), Muḥibbī IV, p. 460; 'Abd al-Raḥīm Abū Luṭf (d.1692), Murādī III, pp. 2-5 and Jabartī I, p. 66; Ḥasan b. Awlād Qāḍī al-Ṣalt (d.1777/8), Ḥusaynī, pp. 115-6; Shihāb al-Dīn (al-Khālidī ?) (d.1721/2); Ḥusayni, pp. 113-4; Abū Bakr b. Aḥmad al-'Alamī (d.1731/2), Murādī I, p. 49; Jārallāh ibn Abū Luṭf (d.1731/2), Murādī II, pp. 6-7 and Ḥusaynī, pp. 44-9; 'Alī b. Muḥammad b. Jārallāh (d.1755/6), Ḥusaynī, pp. 49-52; 'Abd al-Raḥīm b. Sharf al-Dīn (al-Imām ?) (d. 1770/1), Ḥusaynī, pp. 114-5; Muḥammad Abū al-Sa'ūd (d.1813), *Leqsiqon*.

(*ṭalaba al-'ilm*), it was generally "(public) office" (*ṭalaba al-waẓīfa*) which they sought in Istanbul.[46] Numerous are the cases in which our biographees obtained a Ḥanafī or Shāfi'ī *muftī*-ship, a *qāḍī*-ship, a prestigious teaching post such as at the Shāfi'ite *Madrasa al-Ṣalāḥiyya* or the Ḥanafite *Madrasa al-'Uthmāniyya* in Jerusalem, or a position as *Naqīb al-Ashrāf*.[47] We do not know whether presence in person was absolutely required, or how easily the favor of obtaining a high position could be arranged by mail: Muḥammad b. Tāj al-Dīn al-Ramlī (d. 1685), for instance, received a Ḥanafī *muftī*-ship on the basis of a written recommendation by his famous uncle Khayr al-Dīn.[48] The Ḥusaynī family in Jerusalem, and probably other families as well, had their own agents in Istanbul to look after their interests.[49]

In the same way *'ulamā'* sometimes personally approached the Ottoman authorities in Istanbul in order to solve disputes about religious positions and rights.[50] Istanbul also seems to have on occasion attracted persons who had run into financial trouble.[51] However, not always was such a trip crowned with success, it seems: Muḥammad al-Kurdī (d. 1761/2), an *'ālim* and poet, for example, apparently returned empty-handed to Jerusalem.[52]

It is interesting to note here that while all those who — according to our

46 For the term *li-ṭalab waẓīfa* see, for instance; 'Alī al-'Afīfī al-Kinānī (d.1766/7), Ḥusaynī, pp. 60-4.

47 Muḥammad al-'Ajīmī (d.± 1531), Ghazzī II, pp. 11-2; Muḥammad ibn Khaṣīb (d.1599) (*Jawziyya* and *'Umariyya* teaching posts in Damascus), Muḥibbī IV, pp. 154-8; Sharf al-Dīn al-'Asīlī (d. ?) (*qāḍī*-ships in Shabshīr and Minya, Egypt), Muḥibbī II, pp. 225-6; Jārallāh ibn Abū Luṭf (d.1619) (Ḥanafī *muftī* and *'Uthmāniyya* teaching post, Jerusalem), Muḥibbī I, pp. 481-2; Muḥammad b. Abū Luṭf (d.1624) (*'Uthmāniyya* teaching post), Muḥibbī III, p. 482; Muḥammad al-'Ajamī (d.1645/6) (*qāḍī*-ships in Tripoli, Bosna, Sofia), Muḥibbī III, pp. 412-4; 'Abd al-Ghaffār al-'Ajamī (d.1647) (Ḥanafī *muftī* and *'Uthmāniyya* teaching post), Muḥibbī II, p. 433; 'Alī b. Jārallāh Abū Luṭf (d.1659/60) (Ḥanafī *muftī*, Jerusalem), Muḥibbī III, pp. 151-2; Ḥibatallāh b. 'Abd al-Ghaffār al-'Ajamī (d.1666) (Ḥanafī *muftī*, Jerusalem), Muḥibbī IV, p. 460; Aḥmad al-Ṣafadī al-Dimashqī (d.1689) (*'Umariyya* teaching post, Damascus), Muḥibbī I, pp. 356-9; Muḥammad b. 'Abd al-Raḥīm Abū Luṭf (d.1728/9) (Ḥanafī *muftī*-ship), Murādī IV, p. 52 and p. 58; 'Alī al-'Afīfī al-Kinānī (d.1766/7), Ḥusaynī, pp. 60-4; 'Abd al-Raḥīm b. Sharf al-Dīn (d.1770/1), Ḥusaynī, pp. 114-5; 'Abd al-Laṭīf al-Ḥusaynī (d.1775), Murādī III, pp. 124-6 and Ḥusaynī pp. 121-30; Muḥammad Sāliḥ al-Imām (d.1828) (Shāfi'ī *muftī* in Jerusalem and Jaffa, *Leqsiqon*; Wajīh al-Kaylānī (d.1828) (began as clerk at the *Shaykh al-Islām*'s office, later Philippines, see above), Nimr IV, pp. 123-4.

48 Muḥibbī III, pp. 411-2.

49 Cf. Abu Manneh, p. 330.

50 Abū al-Luṭf b. Abū al-Luṭf (d.1661) in dispute on Shāfi'ī *muftī*-ship of Jerusalem, Muḥibbī I, p. 145; 'Uthmān b. 'Alī al-'Alamī (d.1754/5) in dispute on *imām*-ship of Noble Rock, Murādī III, p. 166.

51 'Alī b. Muḥammad b. Jārallāh (d.1755/6) could not make a living any more on a teaching post at the *Madrasa al-Ṣalāḥiyya* (due to the decline of Shāfi'ī learning ?), Ḥusaynī, pp. 49-52. Cf. Baer, in this volume.

52 Murādī IV, pp. 81-5.

sources — traveled to Istanbul to obtain jobs before the nineteenth century were Jerusalemites, we find after that date *'ulamā'* from other Palestinian towns as well. This indicates some degree of proceeding Ottomanization.[53] Several examples of Palestinian *'ulamā'* who attained important rank or honor in nineteenth century Istanbul, further attest to the intensification of contact between the two countries: Mūsā al-Khālidī, who served as *qāḍī 'askar* of Anatolia during the reign of Sultan Maḥmūd II, was instrumental in procuring an honorable invitation for the aged *'ālim* Muḥammad Abū al-Sa'ūd to come from their common hometown, Jerusalem, to Istanbul.[53a] Aḥmad al-Tamīmī from Hebron, who served as *muftī* in Cairo, was invited by Sultan 'Abd al-Majīd to attend the circumcision ceremonies of his sons in Istanbul. He seized the opportunity to procure the *muftī*-ship of Hebron for his nephew Khalīl who accompanied him on this trip.[54] Wajīh al-Kaylānī from Nablus first worked at the *Shaykh al-Islām*'s office, then taught the sons of Sultan Muḥammad Rashīd Arabic and was finally asked by the Ottoman authorities (at the request of the U.S.A.) to accept a leading position in the Philippine Muslim community.[55]

However, only a few went to study in Istanbul: distance as well as language probably formed serious impediments. It is impossible to give an exact answer to the question why Muḥammad al-Surūrī (d. 1678/9) — an outstanding *'ālim* from Jerusalem who had also studied in Cairo — became temporarily "possessed by *jinns*" while complementing his studies in Istanbul, but this fact might have had something to do with the unfamiliar environment.[56] On the other hand, 'Alī Abū Luṭf from Jerusalem (d. 1731/2 ?) and Aḥmad al-Timurtāshī from Gaza both married Turkish women in Istanbul, and the former taught there for some time.[57] 'Alī Abū Luṭf was a Shāfi'ī by *madhhab* and studied Bukhārī's collection of traditions at the Aya Sofia Mosque; one may thus wonder why he chose predominantly Ḥanafite Istanbul as a place to study. The fact that somewhat later Muḥammad Ṣāliḥ al-Imām, another Shāfi'ī and a member of an equally outstanding Jerusalem *'ulamā'* family, also pursued his studies (for seven years) in Istanbul, points to the importance of presence in the Ottoman capital rather than to its qualities as a Shāfi'ī center of learning. Two other members of the Abū Luṭf family, indeed, studied Ḥanafī law in

53 Munīb Hāshim al-Ja'farī (b.1855/6) (Nablus), Nimr IV, pp. 124-6; Yūsuf al-Nabhānī (b.± 1849), Bayṭār III, pp. 1612-6; Khalīl al-Tamīmī al-Dārī (d.1900) (Hebron), Bayṭār I, pp. 594-7.

53[a] See *Leqsiqon*.

54 Khalīl al-Tamīmī, see note 53.

55 Wajīh al-Kaylānī (d.1916), Nimr IV, pp. 123-4.

56 Muḥibbī III, pp. 414-5.

57 Murādī III, p. 209; cf. Ḥusaynī, p. 139.

Istanbul.[58] The *Qāḍīs*' College in Istanbul which opened its gates in 1855/6 counted eight Palestinians among its 986 graduates.[59]

At least one of the graduates of the *Qāḍīs*' College, Khalīl Jawād al-Khālidī, who later became President of the Palestinian *Sharī'a* Court of Appeal, had previously studied at al-Azhar.[60] A combined Cairene-Istanbulite education was apparently not uncommon: we find this pattern as early as the seventeenth and eighteenth centuries in the biographies of Muḥammad al-Surūrī (d. 1678/9), 'Abd al-Raḥīm Abū Luṭf (d. 1692) and 'Alī b. Ḥabīballāh Abū Luṭf (d. 1731/2).[61] Some well known Palestinian intellectuals in the first half of the twentieth century also fall into this category: Sulaymān Tājī al-Farūqī of Ramle, who studied law at Istanbul University after an Azhar education;[62] Muṣṭafā al-Khabarī of Ramle, who went on from al-Azhar to the Istanbul Teachers' College;[63] 'Abd al-Raḥmān al-Dajānī of Jaffa who studied at al-Azhar and then at the *Dār al-Funūn* in Istanbul.[64] Mention could also be made of Muḥammad Riḍā al-Dajānī, of the same family, who embarked on a career at the Ottoman War Office and in the army following his studies at al-Azhar.[65] 'Abdallāh al-Qīshāwī of Gaza, another Azharite, also completed his law studies in Istanbul.[66]

These last examples show that al-Azhar, even at a time when Istanbul had evolved into a more effective and vigorous capital of the Ottoman Empire and when a process of secularization had set in, had still not lost its attraction as an intellectual center in the eyes of the population of Palestine.

58 Muḥammad Ṣāliḥ al-Imam, see *Leqsiqon*; 'Abd al-Raḥīm Abū Luṭf (d.1692), Murādī III, pp. 2-5 and Jabartī I, p. 66; Jārallāh ibn Abū Luṭf (d.1731-2), Murādī II, pp. 6-7 and Ḥusaynī, pp. 44-9.

59 'Il *Timiyye Sālnāmesi* (Istanbul, 1334 Mal./1918). These were: Aḥmad Khammāsh (Nablus), p. 701; 'Abd al-Muṭallib (Jerusalem), p. 701; 'Abd al-Majīd (Nablus), p. 709; 'Abd al-Qādir (Jerusalem), p. 709; Khalīl Jawād (al-Khālidī) (Jerusalem), p. 715; Ḥasan Ef. (Ramle), p. 723; Yūnis al-Khaṭīb (Haifa), p. 724; Mutī' Ef. (Nablus), p. 724. See also: U. M. Kupferschmidt, "A note on the Muslim religious hierarchy towards the end of the Ottoman period", in D. Kushner (ed.), *The Legacy of Ottoman Palestine* (forthcoming). See further: Yūsuf Ṣidqī Tahbūb (b.1875) (Hebron) passed the *qāḍī*'s examination in Istanbul, *al-Shakhṣiyyāt al-Filasṭīniyya*, p. 83.

60 al-Khālidī, p. 39.

61 Muḥibbī III, pp. 414-5; Murādī III, pp. 2-5 and Jabartī I, p. 66; Murādī III, p. 209 and Ḥusaynī, p. 139.

62 *al-Shakhṣiyyāt al-Filasṭīniyya*, p. 21.

63 *ibid.*, pp. 49-50.

64 *ibid.*, p. 54.

65 *ibid.*, p. 57.

66 *ibid.*, pp. 121-2.

APPENDIX

Full Biographies

Place of Origin

	Total	Jerusalem	Nablus	Tulkarm	Jenin	Safed	Acre	Ramle	Hebron	Jaffa	Gaza	Nazareth
16th century	46	22	5			8		2	5		4	
educated in Cairo	14	9	1			2					2	
educated in Damascus[1]	10	5	2			2					2	
moved permanently to Cairo	2					1					1	
moved permanently to Damascus	12	6	3						2		1	
connections with Istanbul	3	3										
connections with the Hijaz	4	2	1								1	
17th century	71	42	9	3	1	6	1	3			6	
educated in Cairo	28	11	2	3	1	4		3			4	
educated in Damascus[2]	6	2	1			3						
moved permanently to Cairo	2			2								
moved permanently to Damascus	3				1	2						
connections with Istanbul	11	10				1[3]						
connections with the Hijaz	7	6				1						
18th century	74	43	22				2		2		5	
educated in Cairo	24	12	7						2		3	
educated in Damascus	5		5									
moved permanently to Cairo	3	3										
moved permanently to Damascus	3	1	2									
connections with Istanbul	14	14										
connections with the Hijaz	4	2	1								1	
19th and 20th centuries	49	16	14				2	2	3	7	4	1
educated in Cairo	30	7	7				2	2	2	7	2	1
educated in Damascus	3		3									
moved permanently to Cairo	2		1						1			
moved permanently to Damascus												
connections with Istanbul	16	4	3				1	2	3	2	1	
connections with the Hijaz	4		2							2		

[1] four of these also studied in Cairo
[2] one of these also studied in Cairo
[3] from Damascus where he had settled

MIRIAM HOEXTER

Egyptian Involvement in the Politics of Notables in Palestine: Ibrāhīm Pasha in Jabal Nablus

Throughout most of the Ottoman period Jabal Nablus was able to preserve a large measure of local autonomy. The joint resistance of its inhabitants to the imposition of a governor of foreign origin was the main political expression of the region's solidarity, and its indigenous governor became the symbol of the region's jealously guarded autonomy. Thus, the Ottomans had usually to content themselves with indirect rule, i.e. with the appointment of one of the notables of Jabal Nablus to the post of *mutasallim* on their behalf. The capital of the entire region was the town of Nablus. Even when the area was split into two *mutasallimiyya*s — one with its center at Nablus, the other at Jenin — it was Nablus which dominated the politics of the area.[1]

The *mutasallim* of Nablus thus acted as the principal intermediary between the government and the population of Jabal Nablus. Being a useful intermediary meant serving both the local population and the government. To the local population the *mutasallim* had to appear as protecting its interests vis-à-vis the government. To the central authorities he had to appear as ready to cooperate with them and capable of enforcing their policy and orders on the local population.[2] In order to fulfil this task successfully the candidate for the *mutasallimiyya* had, thus, to be recognized as a leader by the local population. This implied the possession of a power base within society, usually involving patron-client relations with part of the area's inhabitants. It also implied residence in or near the town of Nablus from which the entire region was governed.

The post of *mutasallim* at Nablus had never become an inheritable right within one notable family. Since this was the position most coveted by the

1 For more details see M. Hoexter, "The Role of the Qays and Yaman Factions in Local Political Divisions: Jabal Nāblus compared with the Judean Hills in the first half of the Nineteenth Century", *Asian and African Studies,* vol. 9, no. 3 (1973), p. 251.

2 On the role of notables as intermediaries see A. Hourani "Ottoman Reform and the Politics of Notables" in W.R. Polk and R.L. Chambers (eds.), *Beginnings of Modernization in the Middle East — the Nineteenth Century* (Chicago and London, 1968), p. 46.

notables it became the object of constant competition among them. As the influence of one notable family did not usually extend over the entire area of Jabal Nablus, each of the competing families engaged in drawing other elements of the population into its orbit, thus creating a party or a coalition of forces centered around it. In Jabal Nablus this process usually produced two principal rival coalitions, each based on common interest. However, since the interest of the various elements in the coalition could, and in many cases did change, these coalitions were of a rather impermanent and unstable nature.[3]

The central government had a vested interest in the existence of several rival coalitions, since one strong coalition, uniting the entire region, could endanger its hold over the area. The government tended to support one notable family at a time. At the same time, however, it usually made efforts not to antagonize the other notable families, so as not to destroy the delicate balance of power between the notables and their coalitions. Thus, if need arose, the central authorities could easily shift their support from one notable family to another and still hold sway over the region.[4] The competition between the notables and the maneuvers of the government between them and their coalitions is what is implied here when we refer to the "politics of notables".

Although there had always existed in Jabal Nablus local leaders of various kinds, e.g. *'ulamā', shaykh*s of *nāḥiya*s (administrative units into which the *mutasallimiyya* was divided) etc., only a small number of families was strong enough to compete for the post of *mutasallim* of Nablus. In the period immediately preceding the Egyptian invasion there were four such families — the Ṭūqāns, the Nimrs, the 'Abd al-Hādīs and the Qāsims. Although the four families differed from each other in origin, they all resided in or near Nablus, and had strong ties in parts of the rural area of which they were the *multazim*s, timariots or holders of *malikâne*; each could raise a military power to defend the family's interests; each had its allies in the area and its contacts in the appropriate government circles.[5] When the Egyptians conquered Palestine it was, therefore, these families with whom they had to deal.

3 For the unstable nature of these coalitions in Jabal Nablus see Hoexter, *op. cit.*, pp. 251-284.

4 On the coalitions and the government see Hourani, *op. cit.*, pp. 46,49.

5 For the situation in Nablus on the eve of the Egyptian invasion see Hoexter, *op. cit.*, pp. 251-264. See also M. Abir, "Local Leadership and Early Reforms in Palestine, 1800-1834" in M. Ma'oz (ed.), *Studies on Palestine during the Ottoman Period* (Jerusalem, 1975), pp. 284-310 *passim*. The Jarrārs do not figure on this list, since their base was in the Jenin area. Although, before the Egyptian occupation, they were sometimes granted the post of the Nablus *mutasallim*, this was no more than a temporary measure. The Jarrārs did not move to Nablus and, during the period immediately preceding the Egyptian occupation, they did not play an independent role in the politics of the entire area. They were, however, valuable allies to the principal notables of Jabal Nablus.

This article is divided into two main sections. In the first section we shall describe the principal changes in the positions of *mutasallim* and *shaykhs* of *nāḥiyas* during the Egyptian occupation. We shall go on to describe in detail the relationship between the four principal notable families and the Egyptian authorities. The second section will be devoted to an evaluation of the Egyptian policy in Jabal Nablus. After summing up this policy, as it emerges from the description in the first section, we shall try to determine whether this picture conveys the long term aims of the Egyptians or whether it should be viewed as a temporary measure only.

On November 20, 1831, shortly after Ibrāhīm's invasion of Palestine, but before the fall of Acre (May 27, 1832), four of Jabal Nablus' notables presented themselves at the Egyptian camp declaring their allegiance to the Egyptians. They were Ḥusayn 'Abd al-Hādī, Qāsim al-Aḥmad (the head of the Qāsim family) and his son and 'Abdallāh al-Jarrār. In return for their loyalty to the Egyptians they asked that they be confirmed in the posts they held under the Ottomans. Their request was granted, and on November 21, 1831, the following appointments were made:

Muḥammad al-Qāsim — *mutasallim* of Nablus
Ḥusayn 'Abd al-Hādī — *mutasallim* of Jenin

The *nāḥiyas* were distributed as follows:

Muḥammad al-Qāsim — al-Mashārīq
Yūsuf al-Qāsim — Jammā'īn
Maḥmūd 'Abd al-Hādī — Sha'rāwiyyāt
'Abdallāh al-Jarrār — Mashārīq al-Jarrār
Yūsuf and 'Abd al-Wahhāb al-Jayūsī — Banī Ṣa'b[6]

Between October 1833 and April 1834, the *mutasallimiyya* of Nablus was transferred to the 'Abd al-Hādīs. On October 8, 1833, Muḥammad al-Qāsim was appointed to the *mutasallimiyya* of Jerusalem and left a deputy *(wakīl)* on his behalf at Nablus.[7] Then, on April 21, 1834, Sulaymān 'Abd

6 The above description is a composite of two documents: Asad J. Rustum, *al-Maḥfūẓāt al-Malikiyya al-Miṣriyya*, 4 vols. (Beirut, 1940-3) (Rustum, *Maḥfūẓāt* in later references), vol. I, pp. 128-129. doc. 342, 14 and 15, Jumādā'l-Ūlā, 1247 [20 and 21.11.1831]; Asad Rustum, *Al-Uṣūl al-'Arabiyya li-Ta'rīkh Sūriya fī 'Ahd Muḥammad 'Alī*, 5 vols. (Beirut, 1930-4) (Rustum, *Uṣūl* in later references), vol. I, pp. 75-76, doc. 28, same date. According to the first, which gives more details, the Mashārīq went to the Jarrārs. According to the second they went to Muḥammad al-Qāsim together with the Nablus *mutasallimiyya* and the distribution of the rest of the *nāḥiyas* is not mentioned. The solution of this riddle is probably as mentioned above, since there actually existed two *nāḥiyas* by this name: al-Mashārīq (divided at the start of the 19th century into two *nāḥiyas* — Jūrat 'Amra and al-Baytāwī) and Mashārīq al-Jarrār (also known as *nāḥiyat* al-Ḥāritha). The *nāḥiya* appearing in the first document as al-Sha'rāwiyya should most probably read: al-Sha'rāwiyyāt, including both western and eastern Sha'rāwiyya. As to the division into *nāḥiyas* see Hoexter, *op. cit.*, p. 252.

7 Rustum, *Uṣūl*, vol. II, pp. 82-84, doc. 118, 23 Jumādā'l-Ūlā, 1249 [8.10.1833]; *Ibid.*, pp. 95-97, doc. 125, 29 Jumādā'l-Ākhira, 1249 [13.11.1833].

al-Hādī succeeded to the post of *mutasallim* at Nablus.[8]

Some time between December 1833 and April 1834, Ḥusayn 'Abd al-Hādī — Sulaymān's father — was appointed *mudīr* (governor) of the *eyalet* (province) of Sidon, a position he held until his death in summer 1837.[9] In May 1834, some of the *shaykh*s of the mountainous regions of Jerusalem, Nablus and Hebron revolted against the Egyptians. In July 1834, upon the arrival of reinforcements of troops from Egypt, Ibrāhīm succeeded in crushing the revolt. During the revolt Sulaymān 'Abd al-Hādī and his uncle Maḥmūd served as Ḥusayn 'Abd al-Hādī's deputies at Acre.[10] After Ḥusayn's death, his brother Maḥmūd succeeded to his post as governor of the Sidon province,[11] which most likely he held until the Egyptian withdrawal from Syria and Palestine. Sulaymān was appointed deputy to the *mudīr* of Sidon province. He was, however, allowed to leave at Nablus a deputy in his stead. To this post he appointed Shaykh Ṭāhir al-Mūsā al-'Arābī, probably one of the family's clients.[12]

There is little we can learn from the sources about changes in the distribution of the remaining positions in the area. When Ḥusayn 'Abd al-Hādī was appointed governor of Sidon, the *mutasallimiyya* of Jenin went to his son Sulaymān.[13] We do not know, however, whether the dismissal of the Qāsims from the Nablus *mutasallimiyya* and the promotion of Sulaymān and Maḥmūd 'Abd al-Hādī entailed changes in the posts of *shaykh*s in the *nāḥiya*s of Mashārīq and the Sha'rāwiyyāt. A major change evidently occurred as a result of the 1834 revolt. When Ibrāhīm entered Nablus with his army, the Qāsims, who led the revolt, fled from the area and Ibrāhīm appointed others to their posts.[14] The Qāsims' base was the Jammā'īn *nāḥiya*, where their rivals were the Rayyān family, who did not take part in the revolt. This family apparently replaced the Qāsims in the

8 *Ibid.*, pp. 104-105, doc. 131, 11 Dhū'l-Ḥijja, 1249 [21.4.1834]. See also note 65 below.

9 The *eyalet* of Sidon is sometimes also called *eyalet* of Acre. Ḥusayn 'Abd al-Hādī is first addressed as *mudīr* of the *eyalet* in Rustum, *Maḥfūẓāt*, vol. II, p. 389, doc. 3393, beginning of Dhū'l-Ḥijja, 1249 [11-20.4.1834]. On his appointment see below. According to a document dated 10 Rabī' al-Awwal, 1250 [17.7.1834], *Ibid.*, pp. 425-426, doc. 3564, Ḥusayn 'Abd al-Hādī was confirmed as *mutasallim* of Nablus. As three days later, in Rustum, *Uṣūl*, vol. II, pp. 121-123, doc. 138, he appears as *mudīr* of the *eyalet* of Sidon, we presume that the former is a mistake and should read Sulaymān 'Abd al-Hādī.

10 For Sulaymān see e.g. Rustum, *Maḥfūẓāt*, vol. II, pp. 419-420, doc. 3535, 27 Ṣafar, 1250 [5.7.1834]; Rustum, *Uṣūl*, vol. II, pp. 121-123, doc. 138, 13 Rabī' al-Awwal, 1250 [20.7.1834]. For Maḥmūd, see *Ibid.*, pp. 123-124, doc. 139, 28 Rabī' al-Awwal, 1250 [4.8.1834].

11 We do not have the date of his appointment to this post. He is addressed as such in Rustum, *Maḥfūẓat*, vol. IV, pp. 269-272, doc. 6100, 4 Ramaḍān, 1255 [11.11.1839].

12 Rustum, *Uṣūl*, vol. III-IV, pp. 231-232, doc. 467, beginning of Jumādā'l-Ūlā, 1254 [23.7.-1.8.1838]; Iḥsān al-Nimr, *Ta'rīkh Jabal Nāblus wa'l-Balqā'*, vol. I, 2nd edition (Nablus, 1975) (Nimr in later references), pp. 335-336.

13 *Ibid.*, p. 324.

14 Rustum, *Uṣūl* p. 118, doc. 136, 9 Rabī' al-Awwal, 1250 [16.7.1834].

nāḥiya.[15] As 'Abdallāh al-Jarrār also took part in the revolt, and consequently was put to death by Ibrāhīm, his *nāḥiya* was also given to others.

Relations Between the Egyptians and the Four Notable Families

The 'Abd al-Hādīs

The family's traditional base was at 'Arāba, in the *nāḥiya* of Eastern Sha'rāwiyya, south of Jenin. Until the beginning of the nineteenth century the 'Abd al-Hādīs were a family of village *shaykhs*. Sulaymān Pasha al-'Ādil, the *wālī* of Sidon between 1804-1818, raised the family's standing, and during his rule they became one of the powerful and respected families of the entire Jabal Nablus area. In the course of this process, the 'Abd al-Hādīs established themselves in the town of Nablus, where they bought a mansion, albeit preserving close ties with their original *nāḥiya.*[16]

When the four Nablus notables first declared their allegiance to the Egyptians, the latter asked for one of the four to remain in their camp "for the purpose of [fulfilling] necessary services". It was Ḥusayn 'Abd al-Hādī who remained with the Egyptian army.[17]

During the following two years he served the Egyptians in several ways. He reported to them on events in Jabal Nablus, such as the receipt of letters from the Ottomans by the notables of the area, ordering them to obey the Ottoman *wālī* and trying to dissuade them from siding with the Egyptians.[18] On several occasions his opinion was sought on the affairs of Palestine: how to deal with some of the local leaders; the way various parts of Palestine were administered by the Ottomans; the collection of taxes, etc.[19] He was also asked to help in the recruitment of the labor force necessary for the construction of the fortifications at Acre.[20] On two occasions Ḥusayn 'Abd al-Hādī provided armed forces, probably from among his family's clients in Jabal Nablus, to assist the Egyptians in their military endeavors.[21]

15 Nimr, pp. 322,355.

16 For more details see Hoexter, *op. cit.*, pp. 263-265.

17 Rustum, *Maḥfuẓāt*, vol. I, pp. 128-129, doc. 342, 14 and 15 Jumādā'l-Ūlā, 1247 [20 and 21. 11.1831]; *Ibid.*, pp. 130-131, doc. 350, 19 Jumādā'l-Ākhira, 1247 [25.11.1831]; *Ibid.*, p. 132, doc. 355, 20 Jumādā'l-Ākhira, 1247 [26.11.1831].

18 *Ibid.*, p. 171, doc. 442, 13 Sha'bān, 1247 [17.1.1832]; See also *Ibid.*, p. 132, doc. 355, 20 Jumādā'l-Ākhira, 1247 [26.11.1831]; *Ibid.*, pp. 140-141, doc. 384, 13 Rajab, 1247 [18.12.1831].

19 *Ibid.*, pp. 130-131, doc. 350, 19 Jumādā'l-Ākhira, 1247 [25.11.1831]; *Ibid.*, pp. 189-190, doc. 499, 3 Ramaḍān 1247 [5.2.1832]; *Ibid*, vol. II, pp. 34-35, doc. 1290, 2 Ṣafar, 1248 [1.7.1832]; *Ibid.*, p. 166, doc. 2184, 16 Jumādā'l-Ākhira, 1248 [10.11.1832].

20 *Ibid.*, p. 51, doc. 1411, 23 Ṣafar, 1248 [22.7.1832].

21 *Ibid.*, vol. I, pp. 282-283, doc. 820, 28 Dhū'l-Qa'da, 1247 [29.4.1832]; *Ibid.*, p. 220, doc. 597, 27 Ramaḍān, 1247 [29.2.1832].

It seems, however, that until July 1833, Ḥusayn 'Abd al-Hādī was considered as being on "probation". Although he was commended for his loyalty and assistance to the Egyptians and Muḥammad 'Alī personally expressed his gratitude to him for his various services,[22] he was still no more than a local notable collaborating with the Egyptians and competing for their favors.

On July 27, 1833, Muḥammad 'Alī accepted Ibrāhīm's recommendation to decorate Ḥusayn 'Abd al-Hādī and grant him an annual allowance.[23] Only at this point did he finally acquire official recognition and a position on the Egyptian senior staff. He was sent on several inspection tours to Jerusalem to look into the state of the churches and synagogues and investigate a petition of the staff of one of the mosques.[24] Some time between December 1833 and April 1834 he was promoted to the very important position of *mudīr* of the *eyalet* of Sidon, whose jurisdiction extended over the whole of Palestine.[25]

It was apparently thanks to the influence Ḥusayn 'Abd al-Hādī acquired in Egyptian government circles that his brother Maḥmūd was promoted to the post of *mutasallim* of Jaffa in August 1832, and that the Nablus *mutasallimiyya* was given to his son Sulaymān in April 1834.[26]

Following the 1834 revolt Sulaymān was ordered to collect all the arms in the area and seize those persons who had fled to avoid conscription. Apparently he did not fulfil Ibrāhīm's orders with the zeal expected of him. This behavior enraged Ibrāhīm, who, after making some moderate complaints, resorted to outright threats. In a letter to Sulaymān he explained that the latter was wrong if he thought that since he was Ḥusayn's son he could disobey Ibrāhīm, because "when it comes to *raison d'état (maṣlaḥa)* we do not know either Ḥusayn or his son". Ibrāhīm went on to tell Sulaymān that his favorable disposition towards Ḥusayn rested solely on his faithfulness, so far, to the Egyptians, and that he, Sulaymān, could bring about the rupture of the friendly relations with Ḥusayn and the entire family.[27]

When Ḥusayn 'Abd al-Hādī died, during the summer of 1837, Sulaymān wrote to Ibrāhīm asking for an investigation into the cause of his father's

22 *Ibid.*, p. 231, doc. 649, 14 Shawwāl, 1247 [17.3.1832]; *Ibid.*, vol. II, p. 166, doc. 2184, 16 Jumādā'l-Ākhira, 1248 [10.11.1832].

23 *Ibid.*, p. 345, doc. 3130, 9 Rabī' al-Awwal, 1249 [27.7.1833].

24 *Ibid.*, p. 355, doc. 3186, 27 Rabī' al-Thānī, 1249 [13.9.1833]; *Ibid.*, p. 376, doc. 3315, 21 Rajab, 1249 [4.12.1833].

25 See note no. 9

26 On Maḥmūd's appointment to Jaffa see Rustum, *Uṣūl*, vol. II, pp. 34-35, doc. 87, 23 Rabī' al-Awwal, 1248 [20.8.1832]. On the process whereby Sulaymān was appointed *mutasallim* of Nablus see pp. 202-203.

27 *Ibid.*, pp. 132-133, doc. 146, 12 Jumādā'l-Ūlā, 1250 [16.9.1834]. For further examples see *ibid.*, pp. 131-133; 136-138, several documents, all under the same number: 146, dated between 5 Jumādā'l-Ūlā and 19 Jumādā'l-Ākhira, 1250 [9.10.-23.10.1834].

death, evidently suspecting that his father had died of unnatural causes (according to Nimr, by poisoning). Ibrāhīm, however, did not grant his request "since it is known that such things are decided by God and we all have the same destiny". Therefore, he continued, "you should banish all thought of an investigation".[28]

Ḥusayn's death did not bring about a change in the Egyptian policy towards the 'Abd al-Hādī family. Ḥusayn's brother, Maḥmūd, succeeded him as *mudīr* of the *eyalet* of Sidon. Ḥusayn's three young sons were granted an annual allowance.[29] Sulaymān was appointed deputy to the *mudīr* of the *eyalet* of Sidon, preserving at the same time his post as *mutasallim* of Nablus, where he nominated a deputy on his behalf. According to Nimr, Ibrāhīm's intention was to keep Sulaymān away from Nablus.[30] Whatever Ibrāhīm's plans might have been, no further changes occurred in the appointments to the Nablus *mutasallimiyya* during the Egyptian rule. Neither did Sulaymān change his ways. He continued disobeying Ibrāhim's orders, and on two occasions, his behavior earned him most acrimonious letters from Ibrāhīm, cursing him, threatening to have him killed and imputing that since Ḥusayn's death his services had not been worth a penny.[31] Sulaymān's halfheartedness towards the Egyptians was further expressed by the fact that neither he nor his deputy at Nablus made any move to prevent Aḥmad Aǧā al-Nimr from declaring the return of Ottoman rule to the area in April, 1840.[32] At the same time, however, Sulaymān provided the Egyptians with armed forces from Nablus, probably from among his family's clients, to assist them in quelling the revolt in Lebanon and probably also in the Ḥawrān.[33]

The Ṭūqāns

The Ṭūqāns' base was in the town of Nablus. From 1180 (1766-7) onwards members of the family served on many occasions as *mutasallims* of Nablus. In the course of their ascendance, they acquired several *muqāṭa'as* in Jabal Nablus. However, in their efforts to extend their influence to the rural districts, they alienated many of the leading families of the area.[34]

Shortly before the Egyptian invasion, Muṣṭafā Bey Ṭūqān served as *mutasallim* of Nablus and As'ad Bey Ṭūqān was *mutasallim* of a new

28 Nimr, p. 335; Rustum, *Uṣūl*, vol. III-IV, p. 72, doc. 222, 17 Rajab, 1253 [17.10.1837].

29 *Ibid.*, pp. 68-70, docs. 218, 219, 25 Jumādā'l-Ūlā, 1253 [27.8.1837]; 5 Sha'bān, 1253 [4.11.1837]; Nimrr, p. 335.

30 *Ibid.*, pp. 335-336.

31 Rustum, *Uṣūl*, vol. III-IV, pp. 231-232, doc. 467, beginning of Jumādā'l-Ūlā, 1254 [23.7.-1.8.1838]; *Ibid.*, p. 245, doc. 478, 25 Jumādā'l-Ūlā, 1255 [6.8.1839].

32 Nimr, pp. 336, 337. For details see p. 201 below.

33 Rustum, *Maḥfūẓāt*, vol. IV, p. 239, doc. 6058, 22 Rajab, 1255 [1.10.1839]; *Ibid.*, pp. 372-373, doc. 6324, 17 Rabī' al-Thānī, 1256 [18.6.1840]; *Ibid.* pp. 396-397, doc. 6355, 27 Rabī' al-Thānī, 1256 [28.6.1840]; *Ibid.*, p. 414, doc. 6384, 10 Jumādā'l-Ūlā, 1256 [10.7.1840].

34 For details see Hoexter, *op. cit.*, pp. 255-260; 262-264.

mutasallimiyya of the Maghārīb, which apparently 'Abdallāh Pasha created especially in order to appease him.[35] However, by the end of 1246 — beginning of 1247 (c. June, 1831) relations between the Pasha and As'ad Bey deteriorated and As'ad revolted against the authority. Muṣṭafā Bey was ordered to seize As'ad, and, when he refused, was dismissed from his position. As a result first 'Abdallāh al-Jarrār and then Muḥammad al-Qāsim were appointed to the Nablus *mutasallimiyya*. As'ad escaped from the Nablus area.[36]

By the time the four Nablus notables appeared at the Egyptian camp near Acre, As'ad Bey, who had made his way to the south of Palestine, had already made contact with the Egyptians. Apparently he offered them his allegiance and was asked to proceed to Egypt. While in Egypt As'ad informed the authorities of the decision taken by Muṣṭafā Bey Ṭūqān and one of 'Abdallāh Pasha's army commanders, who were both in Acre, to ask the Egyptians for safe-conduct, which meant that they too were prepared to shift their loyalty to the Egyptians. Muḥammad 'Alī reacted favorably to these overtures. He sent a letter of encouragement to Muṣṭafā Bey, letters of safe-conduct to As'ad Bey to be transmitted to Muṣṭafā and the said officer and a letter to Ibrāhīm, asking him to contact both the latter and hand them the necessary guarantees "in order to win them over to the Egyptian side". Ibrāhīm, however, was unable to execute these orders "because of the state of siege at Acre".[37]

The initiative taken by the four Nablus notables was not altogether disconnected from As'ad's endeavors. During their meetings with the Egyptians, they complained about As'ad Bey and his activities. He was, so they told the Egyptians, hated by the people of Jabal Nablus and had therefore fled to al-Salṭ. Recently he had departed for Egypt, and from al-'Arīsh had sent letters to Nablus spreading rumors that he was requested to proceed to Egypt and that Muḥammad 'Alī had appointed Raḍwān Bey Ṭūqān (As'ad's paternal uncle) to the Nablus *mutasallimiyya*, thus causing perturbation among the people of Jabal Nablus. It was in order to put a stop to these rumors that the four notables asked for official letters of appointment signed by the Egyptians.[38]

Matters between the two parties came to a head during the following month and were brought to the Egyptian authorities for their decision. This time Ḥusayn 'Abd al-Hādī and Muḥammad al-Qāsim presented concrete evidence attesting to the unrest As'ad Bey and his party were instigating in Jabal Nablus. After investigation of the matter, As'ad was rebuked and a

35 Nimr, p. 310.

36 *Ibid.*, pp. 314-316.

37 Rustum, *Maḥfuẓāt*, vol. I, p. 131, doc. 352, 19 Jumādā'l-Ākhira, 1247 [25.11.1831]; *Ibid.*, doc. 353, same date; *Ibid.*, p. 136, doc. 367, 3 Rajab, 1247 [8.12.1831].

38 *Ibid.*, pp. 128-129, doc. 342, 14 and 15 Jumādā'l-Ākhira, 1247 [20 and 21. 11. 1831].

ṣulḥa arranged between him and Ḥusayn 'Abd al-Hādī, through the good offices of Bashīr al-Shihābī.[39]

Although Ḥusayn 'Abd al-Hādī and his party certainly gained a few points over the Ṭūqāns, the contest between the two parties was still not finally decided. As'ad continued meddling in the affairs of Jabal Nablus and Ḥusayn 'Abd al-Hādī and his friends were clearly pressing the Egyptians for a final solution. Thus, a month later (January 1832) it was decided to offer As'ad the *mutasallimiyya* of Beirut in order to have peace restored to Jabal Nablus. As'ad, however, declined the offer.[40]

At this point the situation in Jabal Nablus became aggravated. Ibrāhīm was still unable to conquer Acre. The Ottomans tried to persuade the Nablus notables to side with the Sultan against Muḥammad 'Alī and attempts were under way to bring about the attachment of the Nablus *mutasallimiyya* to al-Shām, where the Ottomans were still masters.[41] As'ad probably had a hand in these maneuvers. A final decision in favor of one of the two parties in Nablus had thus become inevitable. Muḥammad 'Alī decided against the Ṭūqāns, and As'ad was sent to Egypt.[42] Thus ended the first major contest between the Nablus notables for the support of the Egyptian authorities.

The Egyptians, however, made a point of not alienating the Ṭūqāns altogether. In autumn 1832, Muṣṭafā Bey Ṭūqān visited Egypt. On this occasion the Egyptian authorities in Syria wrote to Egypt referring to Muṣṭafā Bey as "the *mutasallim* of Nablus" (which he had never been under the Egyptian rule) and asking that he be received with the honors appropriate to his position.[43] This policy was adopted by the authorities in Egypt, who, apparently, were favorably impressed by Muṣṭafā, and upon his return from Egypt, in March 1833, Muḥammad 'Alī ordered that he be granted a special allowance.[44]

As'ad and Muṣṭafā both died during the period of Egyptian rule,[45] and Sulaymān Bey Ṭūqān apparently succeeded them as head of the family. He is mentioned as taking part in the events concerning the announcement of the return of Ottoman rule to Palestine in April 1840, siding with the people of Nablus against the Ottoman party headed by the Nimrs.[46]

39 *Ibid.* pp. 142-145, doc. 384, 13 Rajab, 1247 [18.12.1831].

40 *Ibid.*, pp. 177-178, doc. 462, 20 Sha'bān, 1247 [24.1.1832].

41 *Ibid.*, pp. 187-188, doc. 495, 2 Ramaḍān, 1247 [4.2.1832].

42 *Ibid.*, p. 201, doc. 543, 15 Ramaḍān, 1247 [17.2.1832].

43 *Ibid.*, vol. II, p. 110, doc. 1820, 19 Rabī' al-Thānī, 1248 [15.9.1832].

44 *Ibid.*, p. 289, doc. 2818, 19 Dhū'l-Qa'da, 1248 [30.3.1833].

45 Nimr, p. 340, Note 2 to document dated 10 Ṣafar 1256 [13.4.1840] mentions that both died prior to the date of the document.

46 Rustum, *Uṣūl*, vol. V, pp. 60-61, doc. 508, 15 Ṣafar, 1256 [18.4.1840]. This was probably more of an anti-Nimr than an anti-Ottoman act. In any case this episode did not prevent the Ottomans, upon their return to Palestine, from appointing Sulaymān to the *mutasalli-*

The Nimrs

The Nimrs were one of the most powerful families of Jabal Nablus in the eighteenth century. But as of the 1770's their power was on the wane. They were first stripped of one of their two traditional power bases — the *mutasallimiyya* of Nablus. Their second power base — the *sipahi alay* of Nablus which the family commanded began to totter in the 1820's, when the Ottomans embarked on its reorganization and the gradual abolishment of the *timar* system. At the time of the Egyptian invasion, however, Aḥmad Ağā al-Nimr held the position of head of the Nablus *alay*, and the family retained a position of influence in the town. It still had its loyal retinue of *sipahis*, as well as supporters in Nablus and the rural area, where the family held a number of *iltizāms* and *timars*. On several occasions, before the Egyptian invasion, members of the Nimr family fulfilled the function of deputy to the Nablus *mutasallimiyya*.[47]

When the Egyptians were besieging Acre, Aḥmad Ağā al-Nimr, the head of the family, just as the other notables of Jabal Nablus, took the trouble to visit the Egyptian camp to pay his respects. As with the rest of the notables, he, too, was apparently granted a favorable reception.[48] A little later, probably because of its association with the Ṭūqāns, the family suffered a temporary eclipse. According to Iḥsān al-Nimr, Ibrāhīm abolished the Nablus *alay* and stripped the Nimrs of their rank and *timars*. Aḥmad Ağā himself escaped death at the hands of the Egyptians only by the skin of his teeth, when the Nablus *shaykhs* accused him of being 'Abdallāh Pasha's man and Ibrāhīm's enemy.[49]

Aḥmad Ağā's relations with Ibrāhīm improved as a result of the 1834 revolt. The Nimrs did not take part in the revolt, and, according to Nimr, even used their influence to try and dissuade the various *shaykhs* from embarking on this adventure. When Ibrāhīm finally approached Nablus with his army, the people feared lest Ibrāhīm would destroy the town and asked Aḥmad Ağā to try and appease him. He succeeded in this mission, and, while in Nablus, Ibrāhīm stayed at one of the Nimrs' mansions. According to Iḥsān al-Nimr, Aḥmad Ağā never concealed from Ibrāhīm his basic loyalty to the Ottoman Sultan. He succeeded, however, in gaining Ibrāhīm's respect. During Ibrāhīm's stay at Nablus, he reinstated Aḥmad Ağā with "his rank, his *timars* and his *alay*" and appointed him deputy to the Nablus *mutasallim*. Moreover, 'Abd al-Fattāḥ al-Nimr, Aḥmad Ağā's eldest son, was enrolled in the Egyptian army.[50]

miyya of Nablus. The Nimrs, however, bore him a grudge for this act — Nimr. p. 341, note 1, pp. 344-345.

47 For details see Hoexter, *op. cit.*, pp. 254, 260-264.

48 Rustum, *Maḥfūẓāt*, vol. I, p. 143, doc. 384, 13 Rajab, 1247 [18.12.1831].

49 Nimr, pp. 352, 327, 333-334.

50 *Ibid.*, pp. 325-329; 333-334; Rustum, *Maḥfūẓāt*, vol. II, p. 398, doc. 3435, 9 Muḥarram, 1250 [18.5.1834]. The dating of the document must be an error, since Ibrāhīm entered

Iḥsān al-Nimr provides us with two versions concerning this event. In his book he relates that it was Aḥmad Ağā who presented his son to Ibrāhīm, so that he be the first of the local soldiers to enrol in the Egyptian army. Aḥmad's son was cherished by Ibrāhīm, who eventually granted him the rank of *miralay* and would consult him on the affairs of his native area.[51] To Asad Rustum, the author of the *Maḥfuẓāt* and the *Uṣūl*, Iḥsān al-Nimr described 'Abd al-Fattāḥ as a hostage in the hands of Ibrāhīm, guaranteeing his father's good behavior. His fate was, therefore, a cause of constant concern and anxiety to his family.[52]

Although they vary, the two versions are not necessarily mutually exclusive. The enrolment of a Nimr in the Egyptian army certainly pleased Ibrāhīm. It could serve as an example for other notables and for the people of the area in general, and could thus be a contributing factor in the smooth execution of his policy of drafting the local population into the Egyptian army. By the same token, such a gesture on the part of Aḥmad Ağā could certainly serve to encourage Ibrāhīm's good will towards the family, and possibly also enhance its standing, in the event that Egyptian rule proved to be permanent. All this, however, does not exclude the possibility of Ibrāhīm using 'Abd al-Fattāḥ as a guarantee for his family's submissiveness to the Egyptians, especially since the family overtly supported the Ottomans.

Ibrāhīm's version of the event, although it dates from a later period, when Aḥmad Ağā was about to be arrested, tends to support Iḥsān al-Nimr's first account, i.e. that it was on Aḥmad Ağā's own initiative that his son joined the Egyptian army. Explaining to his father his relations with the Nimrs, Ibrāhīm states that Aḥmad Ağā's son was enrolled in the Egyptian army "willingly or unwillingly, because of the status his father enjoys among the people (of Jabal Nablus)."[53] When Ahmad Ağā caused trouble to the Egyptians, Ibrāhīm did not even propose to exploit the son's presence in the army in order to put pressure on the father.

On July 27, 1839, about a month after the Ottoman defeat by the Egyptian army at Nessib, the five Great Powers entered the arena. In a joint note to the Ottomans, they enjoined them to suspend any further negotiations with Muḥammad 'Alī and let the Powers settle the matter. Negotiations between the Powers dragged on for about a year, one of the principal bones of contention being the government in Syria and Palestine. Finally,

Nablus only in the middle of July, 1834. See p. 204 below. Nimr's account of Ibrāhīm's returning to Aḥmad Ağā his rank and his *alay* seems highly improbable, since from *Ibid.*, vol. IV, p. 325, doc. 6284, 6 Rabī' al-Awwal, 1256 [8.5.1840] we learn that it was the Ottomans who reinstated Aḥmad Ağā as *miralay* and Ibrāhīm considered this very dangerous.

51 Nimr, p. 333.

52 Rustum, *Uṣul*, vol. II. p. 169.

53 Rustum, *Maḥfūẓāt*, vol. IV, p. 326, doc. 6284, 27 Ṣafar, 1256 [30.4.1840].

the London Convention was signed on July 15, 1840, without France's adherence. As a result of this Convention, and after an armed intervention by the Powers, the Egyptians withdrew from the area. On November 4, 1840, Acre fell, and on February 18, 1841, the Egyptians finally left Gaza, their last stronghold in Palestine, and returned to Egypt.[54]

While the negotiations between the Powers were dragging on, the Ottomans made preparations for the restoration of their rule in Palestine. In this context a messenger was sent to Aḥmad Ağā al-Nimr, at the beginning of April, 1840, carrying a *firmān* from the Sultan, appointing Aḥmad Ağā *miralay* of the *sipahi*s of the four *sancak*s of Jerusalem, Gaza, Nablus and Jenin. Aḥmad Ağā immediately summoned the *sipahi*s of Nablus, together with all the notables of the town to his house, and had the messenger read them the *firmān*. Further, he wrote to the Egyptian authorities requesting that arrangements be made to ensure him the honor due to his rank. He also started training the *sipahi*s, distributed weapons among them, had armed men accompany him whenever he left his house, and in several ways behaved as if he were the local ruler. According to one report Aḥmad Ağā even declared to the *sipahi*s that within forty-one days they would be freed from the *mutasallim*'s rule and placed under his.

Information about these events reached the Egyptians from various quarters, including some of the Nablus dignitaries, who first tried to persuade Aḥmad Ağā to cease his activities. On his refusal, they sent a petition to Ibrāhīm, describing the events and declaring that, since Aḥmad Ağā's doings were in clear violation of orders, and they were afraid of Ibrāhīm's reprisals, they wanted to assure him that nobody in and around Nablus agreed with all this and even the *sipahi*s only obeyed Aḥmad Ağā under force. All the identifiable signatories of the petition were *'ulamā'*, with one notorious exception — Sulaymān Ṭūqān.[55]

Ibrāhīm suggested to his father that Aḥmad Ağā be disposed of quietly. Muḥammad 'Alī, however, decided that he be arrested and sent to Egypt for questioning. He was finally sent to the Sudan, where he stayed until 1257 (1841-2). After the final settlement between the Sultan and Muḥammad 'Alī, Aḥmad Ağā returned to Nablus.[56] We do not know whether any steps were taken against his son, 'Abd al-Fattāḥ, or any other member of the family. In any case, 'Abd al-Fattāḥ survived his father's ordeal and so apparently did all the other members of the family.[57]

54 M.S. Anderson, *The Eastern Question, 1774-1923* (London, 1968), pp. 88-109.

55 Nimr, pp. 336-341; Rustum, *Uṣūl*, vol. V, pp. 60-61, doc. 508, 15 Ṣafar, 1256[18.4.1840]; Rustum, *Maḥfūẓāt*, vol. IV, pp. 325-330, doc. 6284, several reports on these events, dated Ṣafar and beginning of Rabī' al-Awwal, 1256[April — beginning of May, 1840]; *Ibid.*, pp. 330-331, doc. 6286, 10 Rabī' al-Awwal, 1256 [12.5.1840].

56 *Ibid.*, p. 333, doc. 6292, 18 Rabī' al-Awwal, 1256 [20.5.1840]; *Ibid.*, p. 379, doc. 6336, 15 Rabī' al-Thānī, 1256 [16.6.1840]; *Ibid.*, p. 393, doc. 6351, 27 Rabī' al-Thanī, 1256 [28.6.1840]; Nimr, pp. 341-342.

57 Nimr does not mention any retaliation against other members of the family. On the

The Qāsims

On the eve of the Egyptian occupation of Palestine, the Qāsims were in much the same position as the 'Abd al-Hādīs. They, too, were in the process of rising from the position of mere local *shaykhs*, whose stronghold was in the *nāḥiya* of Jammā'īn, in the south-western section of the Nablus *mutasallimiyya*, to that of possible contenders for the position of *mutasallim*. Like the 'Abd al-Hādīs, while maintaining close ties with their *nāḥiya* of origin, the Qāsims moved to the vicinity of the town of Nablus. They built a castle at their new residence — the village of Bayt Wuzin, a few miles west of Nablus.[58]

Shortly before the Egyptian invasion Muḥammad al-Qāsim, son of Qāsim al-Aḥmad, was appointed to the *mutasallimiyya* of Nablus.[59] Both Qāsim al-Aḥmad, the head of the family, and his son were among the notables who went to Acre to declare their allegiance to the Egyptians. Consequently, Muḥammad al-Qāsim was confirmed in his office at Nablus, including the Mashārīq, while his brother Yūsuf was appointed to the *nāḥiya* of Jammā'īn.

Muḥammad al-Qāsim joined the 'Abd al-Hādīs in the campaign against As'ad Bey Ṭūqān.[60] As Ḥusayn 'Abd al-Hādī was gaining influence in the Egyptian councils, the alliance with the Qāsims was useless to him. It was the Qāsims' position at Nablus which he especially coveted. The Qāsims, so it seems, remained loyal to the Egyptians, and there were no particular complaints or grievances against them. They were, therefore, not simply pushed aside. The 'Abd al-Hādīs went about achieving their aim — the *mutasallimiyya* of Nablus — in a more sophisticated way, using a series of diplomatic maneuvers.

When the *mutasallim* of Jerusalem displeased the Egyptian authorities a consultation took place, at the beginning of February, 1832, between Yūḥannā Baḥrī — one of the senior Egyptian officials — the Emir Bashīr and Ḥusayn 'Abd al-Hādī as to the best way to handle the situation. Baḥrī's suggestion was that the *mutasallimiyya* should go to Qōja Aḥmad Ağā, an Egyptian officer. Bashīr, however, with the support of Ḥusayn 'Abd al-Hādī, argued that since Qōja Aḥmad Ağā was a foreigner in the country and since it would take him twenty to thirty days to reach Jerusalem, he should be seconded by Qāsim al-Aḥmad. The final decision was to recommend that Qāsim al-Aḥmad be appointed *mutasallim* of Jerusalem, while Qōja Aḥmad Ağā be charged with defense duties only.[61] It took more than seven months for this recommendation to materialize. Finally, on Sep-

activities of 'Abd al-Fattāḥ after the Ottoman restoration see *Ibid.*, p. 341, note 1; p. 346 ff.

58 For details see Hoexter, *op. cit.*, pp. 263-265.

59 Nimr, p. 316; Rustum, *Uṣūl*, vol. I, pp. 46-47, doc. 14, 25 Rabī' al-Thānī, 1247 [3.10.1831].

60 See pp. 197-198 above.

61 Rustum, *Maḥfūẓāt*, vol. I, pp. 189-190, doc. 499, 3 Ramaḍān, 1247 [5.2.1832].

tember 22, 1832, Qāsim al-Aḥmad was appointed *mutasallim* of Jerusalem.[62]

What at first glance appeared as a chivalrous gesture on the part of Ḥusayn 'Abd al-Hādī was to prove the first step towards the dispossession of the Qāsims from their position at Nablus. The second step had to wait until Ḥusayn 'Abd al-Hādī became officially integrated into the Egyptian senior staff. On October 8, 1833, Qāsim al-Aḥmad was dismissed from his position in Jerusalem "because of old age" and his son, Muḥammad al-Qāsim, was appointed in his stead. Muḥammad al-Qāsim was, however, allowed to nominate his deputy at the Nablus *mutasallimiyya.*[63]

Four months later, on February 8, 1834, Muḥammad al-Qāsim went on *ḥajj* to the holy places. He was, therefore, dismissed and his brother, Yūsuf, was appointed *mutasallim* of Jerusalem in his stead.[64] About two months later, on April 21, 1834, when Ḥusayn 'Abd al-Hādī was finally *mudīr* of the *eyalet* of Sidon, he could bring his plan to a happy conclusion. Sulaymān, his son, was appointed *mutasallim* of Nablus.[65]

The Qāsims, however, did not wait for Ḥusayn 'Abd al-Hādī's final blow. They clearly read the writing on the wall. The transfer of a Nablus *mutasallim* to Jerusalem could only mean one thing: that he was losing official support and that his position in Jabal Nablus was about to be shifted to somebody else. Iḥsān al-Nimr tells us that, when the Qāsims went on *ḥajj*, they were accompanied by some of the other *shaykh*s of the area, who were all enraged by the 'Abd al-Hādīs' blunders. At Mecca they made a joint decision to rise against the Egyptians. When they returned to Nablus, the Qāsims convened a meeting of the *shaykh*s at their mansion at Bayt Wuzin to plan the revolt.[66]

What in the Jerusalem and Hebron areas is described as a revolt against the Egyptian intention to strip the area of its weapons and have its people drafted into the Egyptian army, took on different or additional coloring in Jabal Nablus. The 'Abd al-Hādīs' direct assault on the Qāsims' position in Jabal Nablus certainly played a major role in provoking the revolt, and it was no wonder that Qāsim al-Aḥmad assumed the role of leader of the

62 Rustum, *Uṣūl*, vol. II, pp. 42-43, doc. 93, 26 Rabī' al-Thānī, 1248 [22.9.1832].

63 *Ibid.*, pp. 82-84, doc. 118, 23 Jumādā'l-Ūlā, 1249 [8.10.1833]; *Ibid.*, pp. 95-97, doc. 125, 29 Jumādā'l-Ākhira, 1249 [13.11.1833].

64 *Ibid.*, pp. 101-102, doc. 129, 28 Ramaḍān, 1249 [8.2.1834].

65 *Ibid.*, pp. 104-105, doc. 131, 11 Dhū'l-Ḥijja, 1249 [21.4.1834]. See also *Ibid.*, pp. 43-44, doc. 94, 26 Rabī' al-Thānī, 1248 [22.9.1832]. Both are documents of appointment of Sulaymān 'Abd al-Hādī to the *mutasallimiyya* of Nablus, but with a very considerable difference in their dates. The date given by Rustum for the second document is clearly a mistake, since the document explicitly states that Sulaymān is appointed to Nablus since Muḥammad al-Qāsim is now *mutasallim* of Jerusalem, and the latter's transfer to Jerusalem occurred only on 8.10.1833. On the way the Qāsims were stripped of the Nablus *mutasallimiyya*, see also Nimr, pp. 323-324.

66 *Ibid.*, pp. 325, 332-333.

entire uprising. The revolt started in May, 1834. On July 16, Ibrāhīm entered the town of Nablus. The Qāsims, who succeeded in escaping to the east, were finally caught towards the end of August, 1834. Qāsim al-Aḥmad and his sons Muḥammad and Yūsuf, as well as the rest of the leaders of the revolt, were put to death.[67]

Although the actual leaders of the revolt could obviously not be spared, Ibrāhīm had no intention to ruin the Qāsim family's future. Aḥmad al-Qāsim's three younger sons — Maḥmūd, 'Uthmān and Aḥmad — were sent to Egypt. There they received their education in military schools and later were appointed to positions in the army and navy. When they returned to Nablus they were respected by the people, who referred to them as "the State's orphans".[68]

Moreover, the possessions of the three deceased members of the family were not confiscated by the Egyptians. On the contrary, orders were given that their legacies be put on record in the *sijill* and distributed to their heirs, according to the *Sharī'a* rules of inheritance. After investigation, part of Muḥammad al-Qāsim's legacy was to be sold and his debts to the treasury and to private people returned, as required by the *Sharī'a*. The legacies of Qāsim and Yūsuf al-Aḥmad were to be left intact.[69]

Evaluation of the Egyptian Policy

During the entire period of their rule in Syria and Palestine, the Egyptians never introduced direct rule to Jabal Nablus. This meant that they had to rely on a local notable family to govern the area on their behalf. The first and major contest for this position was between the Ṭūqāns and the 'Abd al-Hādīs. The Ṭūqāns had previous experience as *mutasallims* of Nablus, which was certainly valuable to the Egyptians. Moreover, when the Egyptians entered Palestine, the Ṭūqāns were at odds with the Ottoman authorities. They could, thus, be relied on as potential allies of the Egyptians. The choice, however, fell on the 'Abd al-Hādīs. The 'Abd al-Hādīs did not have previous experience as *mutasallims*. Their status as an ascending family, but one still not promoted to the post of *mutasallim*, was, in a way, an advantage to the Egyptians. It meant that if the Egyptians promoted them to this much coveted position, the family's gratefulness could engender both greater dependence on the Egyptians and a more deeply

67 For a short account of the revolt in Jabal Nablus see *Ibid.*, pp. 325-333. See also e.g. Rustum, *Maḥfūẓāt*, vol. II, p. 404, doc. 3468; p. 411, doc. 3503; pp. 415-416, doc. 3520; p. 422, doc. 3546; p. 424, doc. 3555; p. 425, docs. 3560, 3562; p. 428, doc. 3573; pp. 435-436, doc. 3613; p. 443, doc. 3645.

68 Nimr, p. 332.

69 Rustum, *Uṣūl*, vol. II, pp. 165-166, doc. 161, 13 Dhū'l-Ḥijja, 1250 [12.4.1835]; 28 Dhū'l-Ḥijja, 1250 [27.4.1835]. See also *Ibid.*, pp. 134-135, doc. 146, 27 Jumādā'l-Ūlā, 1250 [1.10.1834].

rooted loyalty to their benefactors. Indeed, although the family held the post of *mutasallim* of Nablus several times after the Ottoman restoration, the 'Abd al-Hādīs were known as "the Egyptian party" long after the Egyptians withdrew from Palestine.[70]

Some additional factors apparently decided the contest against the Ṭūqāns. During the period immediately preceding the Egyptian occupation, the Ṭūqāns seriously alienated some of the influencial *nāḥiya shaykh*s. Essentially, this was why the Jarrārs and the Qāsims joined the 'Abd al-Hādīs in the campaign they were conducting at the Egyptian headquarters against the Ṭūqāns, and why the latter did not manage to ally to their cause notables wielding comparable influence in Jabal Nablus.

Although the four notables who went to Acre to meet the Egyptians did not explicitly make their allegiance to the Egyptians conditional upon the Egyptian confirmation of the *status quo* in Jabal Nablus, this condition was certainly more than implied. A decision by the Egyptians in favor of the Ṭūqāns would have meant a radical change in the *status quo* in the area, and consequently the alienation of the above notables, who controlled an important part of Jabal Nablus. At the time of the contest between the Ṭūqāns and the 'Abd al-Hādīs' party, the Egyptians were still not masters of Syria and Palestine. Alienating the four notables, under these conditions, would most probably bring about their active support of the Ottomans in the war against the Egyptians.

Weighing the situation on the political scales, there was little the Egyptians stood to gain by supporting the Ṭūqāns, whose case was, therefore, rather weak. Their opponents had much more to offer the Egyptians, and consequently won the contest.

After two years of work for the Egyptians, Ḥusayn 'Abd al-Hādī was finally integrated into their senior staff. This meant that the Egyptians had decided to put their stakes on Ḥusayn 'Abd al-Hādī and his family. The fate of the Nablus *mutasallimiyya* and the Qāsims' position was thus sealed. Since the Qāsims did not resign themselves to the political realities, they were made to do so by force. The 1834 revolt finally established the 'Abd al-Hādīs' precedence in Jabal Nablus and, in fact, in the whole of Palestine, for the entire period of the Egyptian rule.

The Egyptian attitude towards the other notable families of Jabal Nablus can be summed up as follows: These families suffered harsh treatment at the hands of the Egyptians only when considerations of *raison d'état* made this imperative, viz. the killing of the leaders of the 1834 revolt; the banishment of As'ad Bey Ṭūqān and Aḥmad Aǧā al-Nimr. Even in these instances, however, the Egyptians made it a point not to totally destroy family prestige nor bring about economic ruin. Thus, Muṣṭafā Bey Ṭūqān

70 M. Ma'oz, *Ottoman reform in Syria and Palestine 1840-1861* (Oxford, 1968), p. 116; J. Finn, *Stirring Times* (London, 1878), vol. II, p. 431.

was honored while visiting Egypt and received a special allowance when he returned to Nablus. The Qāsims' inheritance reverted to their heirs. The enlistment of the Qasims' sons and of 'Abd al-Fattāḥ Nimr into the Egyptian army should also be viewed in the same light. Contrary to the policy pursued by the Egyptians in regard to the rest of the local inhabitants, the scions of the above notable families were not drafted into the army and assigned to one of the Egyptian battalions as simple soldiers. They were either given officer grades forthwith (Nimr) or were educated to become officers (the Qāsims). In both cases the purpose was certainly not only to preserve the standing of the families, but to do so in such a way as to kindle in their scions the spark of gratitude and hence, loyalty, to their benefactors, and possibly also to incorporate them into the Egyptian governing system. That the Egyptians actually succeeded in this policy was proved when, despite the reversals these families suffered during the Egyptian rule, they were able to play their former roles in the politics of Jabal Nablus, when the Ottomans returned to the area.[71] This policy certainly also served as a hint to the 'Abd al-Hādīs that they should not entertain any wrong ideas about the Egyptian dependence on the family. The Egyptians left all the options open. Their policy in Jabal Nablus had, thus, all the characteristics of the wise politics traditional to notables.

Ruling Nablus by means of "politics of notables" was, however, not the Egyptian initial plan. In a letter Ibrāhīm wrote to his father on January 23, 1832, about two months after the confirmation of the Nablus notables in their former positions, he expressed his opinion as to the policy to be followed in regard to appointments to Nablus, Jerusalem and Jenin: "Unless we appoint to the three areas strong *mutasallims* of our own, the affairs of those places will not be run according to our wishes. Therefore, we found it appropriate to appoint Qōja Aḥmad Ağā, *ra'īs al-banādiqiyya*, as *mutasallim* at Nablus, provided that he be accompanied by his cavalry. It has also been decided in our council that people suitable for the post of *mutasallim*, who had been asked for previously, be sent to us". Further on in the same letter Ibrāhīm urged his father to have Qōja Aḥmad Ağā sent to him as soon as possible.[72] Although this officer eventually arrived in Palestine, neither he nor any other Egyptian officer ever assumed the post of *mutasallim* of Nablus during the entire period of Egyptian rule. The question must, therefore, be asked whether the Egyptians abandoned the idea of direct rule in Nablus altogether. The other possibility is that the politics of notables was pursued as a temporary measure, while the necessary preparations were made for the eventual replacement of the notables by Egyptian officers or bureaucrats. Of necessity, the nature of such measures would be to tighten the hold of the central govenment over the

71 Ma'oz, *op. cit.*, pp. 115-118; Hoexter, *op. cit.*, pp. 266-274.

72 Rustum, *Maḥfūẓāt*, vol. I, p. 176, doc. 459, 19 Sha'bān, 1247 [23.1.1832].

area and at the same time weaken the traditional power bases of the notables.

Measures of this kind were taken by the Egyptians in two fields: conscription and the agrarian regime.

Conscription

Once the Egyptians completed the conquest of Syria and Palestine the idea of recruiting the indigenous population, in order to replenish the ranks of the army after the losses suffered during the war, was brought up.[73]

The drafting operation was, however, put off for one year and a special committee was set up to study the subject.[74]

Not until April 1834 did Ibrāhīm finally embark on recruitment in Palestine. He personally came to Jerusalem and held meetings on the subject with notables from Nablus, Jerusalem and Hebron. The meetings did not, however, produce any results. *Shaykh*s refrained from sending their sons to the army and argued that they were unable to provide the quotas of recruits requested by the authorities. The Egyptians ran into still more difficulties trying to collect arms from the villagers.[75]

As Ibrāhīm predicted, these measures could be imposed only by use of force. Soon the 1834 revolt broke out in the mountains of Jerusalem, Hebron and Nablus. The display of Egyptian force certainly contributed to the relatively smooth implementation of the drafting policy. When the revolt was put down, Ibrāhīm succeeded in drafting Nablusis into the army and collecting at least some of the weapons from the area.[76]

The Agrarian Regime

The way the Egyptians handled the agrarian regime in Syria and Palestine still awaits thorough research. We shall limit ourselves here to some principal guidelines which could be gathered from our sources and which are relevant to the subject under discussion.

In accordance with Muḥammad 'Alī's orders all matters concerning the agrarian regime — *iltizām, timar, zeamet, malikâne* — were to be referred

73 *Ibid.*, vol. II, p. 80, doc. 1616, 24 Rabī' al-Awwal, 1248 [21.8.1832]; *Ibid.*, p. 84, doc. 1645, 28 Rabī' al-Awwal, 1248 [25.8.1832]; *Ibid.*, p. 89, docs. 1679, 1680, 3 Rabī' al-Awwal, 1248 [30.8.1832]; *Ibid.*, p. 102, docs. 1762, 1766, 14 Rabī' al-Thānī, 1248 [10.9.1832].

74 *Ibid.*, p. 95, doc. 1720, 9 Rabī' al-Thānī, 1248 [5.9.1832]; *Ibid.*, p. 110, doc. 1821, 19 Rabī' al-Thānī, 1248 [15.9.1832]; *Ibid.*, p. 114, doc. 1852, 23 Rabī' al-Thānī, 1248 [19.9.1832].

75 *Ibid.*, p. 391, doc. 3403, 9 Dhū'l-Ḥijja, 1249 [19.4.1834]; *Ibid.*, p. 397, doc. 3433, 11 Muḥarram, 1250 [19.5.1834].

76 See e.g. *Ibid.*, p. 456, doc. 3708, 22 Jumādā'l-Ūlā, 1250 [26.9.1834]; *Ibid.*, pp. 460–461, doc. 3731, 29 Jumādā'l-Ūlā, 1250 [3.10.1834]; *Ibid.*, pp. 484–485, doc. 3844, 9 Sha'bān, 1250 [11.12.1834]; See also p. 195 above.

for decision to him and later to the *ḥukmdār*. The *qāḍīs* were explicitly ordered to refrain from dealing with such matters without first receiving the approval of the Egyptian authorities.[77]

At the same time, efforts were made to put the books in order, so as to get a clearer picture of the actual situation both as regards the holders of various rights to land taxes and the sums due from them. Clerks were sent to Syria from Egypt for this explicit purpose and Muḥammad 'Alī pressed them hard to present annual balance sheets, without delay.[78]

Furthermore, Muḥammad 'Alī laid down two principal rules which were to govern agrarian relations. Under the first, existing *muqāṭa'as*, *timars*, *zeamets* and *malikânes* were to remain in the hands of their local holders. Upon their request, rights were to be transferred to the heirs of deceased holders.[79] Vacant *(maḥlūl)* estates of all kinds, whose holders died without heirs, or whose heirs did not ask for the rights to be transferred to them, reverted to the treasury. This was actually decided by the Ottomans shortly before the Egyptian conquest of Syria and Palestine.[80]

The second rule laid down that *timars*, *zeamets* and *muqāṭa'as,* which were run by the government under the former *wālīs*, were now to be administered by the Egyptian authorities in exchange for a fixed sum *(badal mu'ayyan)*, which apparently was always low. People who resided elsewhere or were otherwise incapable of running their estates *(muqāṭa'āt* and even *mumtalakāt)* were also to leave them to government control on the same conditions.[81] This also applied to holders of *timars* and *zeamets*, as

77 *Ibid.*, p. 392, doc. 3406, 13 Dhū'l-Ḥijja, 1249 [23.4.1834]; *Ibid.*, p. 395, doc. 3421, beginning of Muḥarram 1250 [10-19.5.1834]; *Ibid.*, p. 390, doc. 3396, 2 Dhū'l-Ḥijja, 1249 [12.4.1834]; *Ibid.*, p. 401, doc. 3447, 18 Muḥarram, 1250 [27.5.1834].

78 E.g. *Ibid.*, p. 251, doc. 2629, 19 Ramaḍān, 1248 [9.2.1833]; *Ibid.*, vol. IV, pp. 65-70, beginning of Rabī' al-Awwal, 1255 [15-24.5.1839].

79 *Ibid.*, Vol. II, p. 363, doc. 3233, 28 Jumādā'l-Ūlā, 1249 [13.10.1833]; *Ibid.*, p. 392, doc. 3406, 13 Dhū'l-Ḥijja, 1249 [23.4.1834]; *Ibid.*, vol. III, p. 253, doc. 5060, 5 Jumādā'l-Ākhira, 1253 [6.9.1837]; *Ibid*, p. 254, doc. 5064, Jumādā'l-Akhira, 1253 [September, 1837]. There are many specific examples of this rule actually being carried out. The terminology used in the documents makes it difficult to determine which kind of rights are meant. *Iqṭā'* probably means *timar* or *zeamet*. Since *muqāṭa'a* sometimes appears alongside *timar* and *zeamet*, we believe it means *iltizām* (probably inheritable or for a long duration). When this term appears on its own, it could, however, also mean *timar* or *zeamet*.

80 Rustum, *Uṣūl*, vol. I, pp. 36-37, doc. 9, 17 Rabī' al-Awwal, 1247 [26.8.1831]. In the 1820's an investigation of the situation of the *timars* took place in Nablus. As a result vacant *timars* were distributed as *iltizāms* (probably inheritable ones) to various notable families. Nimr calls the rights they obtained *zeamet iltizāmiyya* or *iqṭā' iltizāmī* — Nimr, vol. II (Nablus, 1961), pp. 223, 249-250. On p. 261, Nimr claims that Ibrāhīm abolished the *iqṭā'* (=*timar*) system and turned its holders into *multazims*. In the *Uṣūl* and the *Maḥfūẓāt* we did not find information which could substantiate this claim.

81 Rustum, *Maḥfūẓāt*, vol. III, p. 80, doc. 4397, 19 Ramaḍān, 1251 [8.1.1836]; *Ibid.*, p. 159, doc. 4740, beginning of Rajab, 1252 [12-21.10.1836]; *Ibid.*, p. 256, doc. 5074, 8 Jumādā'l-Ākhira, 1253 [8.9.1837]; *Ibid.*, pp. 299-300, doc. 5194, 9 Ramaḍān, 1253 [7.12.1837]; *Ibid.*, p. 303, doc. 5214, 20 Ramaḍān, 1253 [18.12.1837].

well as to *iltizāms* of some dignitaries *(arbāb al-'alāqa)* who resided in Istanbul. Their estates were run by the Egyptian authorities, and the sums due to them (their *badal*) were sent to Istanbul.[82]

These two rules did not introduce any radical change in the agrarian regime. In April-May 1836, some of the senior officials on the Egyptian staff, including Ḥusayn 'Abd al-Hādī, suggested the replacement of the tithe, which, according to local custom, was levied in many different ways, by a fixed sum to be levied from each *feddan*. Although Muḥammad 'Alī was certainly not happy with the existing situation in Syria and Palestine, Ottoman orders or pressure made him abide by the traditional rules governing the agrarian regime. He, thus, rejected the proposed radical change "because this would raise idle talk in high political circles, and there is no way of persuading the world of its merits". He concluded, therefore, it was wisest to content themselves with levying the tithe in the same way as before.[83]

As we have already seen, to tread in the steps of former *wālīs* was Muḥammad 'Alī's directive in all matters concerning the agrarian regime. We believe, however, that this directive should not be taken literally. Muḥammad 'Alī evidently took care not to get into conflict with the Ottoman authorities. He, therefore, declined offers to abolish publicly the traditional rules governing agrarian relations. This should not, however, be understood as wholesale rejection of improvement and reform. It actually meant that reforms were allowed, provided they were handled carefully and could be officially justified as being in line with custom established by former *wālīs*.

The second rule discussed above is a case in point. From Muḥammad 'Alī's reply to the suggestion, which probably led to the establishment of this procedure, it is clear that the motive behind the rule was not the preservation of former practices but rather the anticipated profit to the treasury derived from government control of estates.[84] The distinction between estates formerly run by their holders and those run by the *wālīs*, besides giving the rule a legitimization based on precedent, also points to the Egyptian intention to handle the matter carefully, so as not to antagonize the population and cause trouble in the area and, potentially, also conflict with the Ottomans.

82 *Ibid.*, p. 272, doc. 5101, beginning of Rajab, 1253 [1-10.10.1837]; *Ibid.*, p. 261, doc. 5091, 27 Jumādā'l-Ākhira, 1253 [28.9.1837]; *Ibid.*, p. 482, doc. 5710, 20 Dhū'l-Ḥijja, 1254 [6.3.1839]. On one occasion, apparently before the rule was laid down, several persons and officers came to Syria and Muḥammad 'Alī ordered that they should be given the necessary assistance in order to enable them to collect the tithe from their *timars* — *Ibid.*, vol. II, p. 353, doc. 3179, 25 Rabī' al-Thānī, 1249 [11.9.1833].

83 *Ibid.*, vol. III, p. 105, doc. 4510, 23 Dhū'l-Ḥijja, 1252 [10.4.1836]; *Ibid.*, pp. 115-116, doc. 4554, 13 Muḥarram, 1252 [30.4.1836]; *Ibid.*, pp. 120-121, doc. 4573, 28 Muḥarram 1252 [15.5.1836].

84 *Ibid.*, p. 80, doc. 4397, 19 Ramaḍān, 1251 [8.1.1836].

Because of his delicate position, and probably also due to different geographical conditions, Muḥammad 'Alī could not simply confiscate lands or abolish the *iltizām* system in Syria and Palestine, as he had done in Egypt. We believe, however, that the rules he laid down, although dictating a slower and gradual process, had in fact the same general purpose, i.e. to bring as much land as possible under government control. With this goal in mind the Egyptians sometimes even purchased *muqāṭa'as*.[85] On occasion, the need for government approval of all transfers of rights was used by the central authorities as a means to extract land from private control. This was apparently the case as regards part of Ḥusayn 'Abd al-Hādī's possessions. After his death his three young sons were granted an annual allocation *(ma'āsh)* by the Egyptians. Although this was made to appear as an act of benevolence on the part of the authorities towards the orphans of a loyal servant,[86] a close look reveals that the sum granted to the orphans was in fact "the substitute for income from a number of villages (listed in the document) formerly in their hands",[87] in other words no more than what, according to the rule laid down by the Egyptians themselves, was rightfully theirs. Bending the first of the above two rules was apparently not a rare phenomenon.[88]

The estates which reverted to the government were administered by the Egyptians in various ways, and perhaps the most common was the farming out of the collection of taxes. These *iltizāms* did not, however, establish inheritable rights, since they were explicitly handed out for one year only.[89]

In Aleppo an attempt was made, in January 1838, to introduce the very radical change Muḥammad 'Alī had rejected some two years earlier. An order was issued to levy the taxes at a fixed amount according to the *feddan* and the crop. At the same time another order was issued to abolish the *iltizām* system and replace the *multazims* by tax collectors.[90] We do not know whether a similar attempt was made anywhere else in Syria or

85 E.g. *Ibid.*, vol. IV, p. 325, doc. 6281, 5 Rabī' al-Awwal, 1256 [7.5.1840]; *Ibid.*, p. 334, doc. 6299, 25 Rabī' al-Awwal, 1256 [27.5.1840].

86 See Nimr, vol. I, p. 335.

87 Rustum, *Uṣūl*, vol. III-IV, pp. 68-70, docs. 218, 219, 25 Jumādā'l-Ūlā, 1253 [27.8.1837], 5 Sha'bān, 1253 [4.11.1837].

88 We, of course, know only of cases in which the deprived persons complained. See e.g. Rustum, *Maḥfūẓāt*, vol. III, p. 165, doc. 4767, 23 Rajab, 1252 [26.10.1836]; *Ibid.*, p. 174, doc. 4798, 12 Sha'bān, 1252 [22.11.1836]; *Ibid.*, p. 349, doc. 5328, 7 Dhū'l-Ḥijja, 1253 [4.3.1838]; *Ibid.*, p. 358, doc. 5348, 19 Dhū'l-Ḥijja, 1253 [16.3.1838].

89 For *iltizām* documents see: Rustum, *Uṣūl*, vol. I, pp. 121-123, doc. 55, 14 Dhū'l-Qa'da, 1247 [15.4.1832]; *Ibid.*, vol. II, pp. 24-25, doc. 80, 1 Rabī' al-Awwal, 1248 [29.7.1832] etc. On government-controlled lands handed out as *iltizām* see Rustum, *Maḥfūẓāt*, vol. III, p. 256, doc. 5074, 8 Jumādā'l-Ākhira, 1253 [8.9.1837]; *Ibid.*, p. 261, doc. 5091, 27 Jumādā'l-Ākhira, 1253 [28.9.1837].

90 Rustum, *Uṣūl*, vol. III-IV, pp. 76-78, doc. 228, 25 Shawwāl, 1253 [22.1.1838]; *Ibid.*, pp. 78-79, doc. 229, same date.

Palestine. A more detailed research could, pehaps, clarify how far these measures were successfully implemented in the Aleppo area.

In many areas in Syria and Palestine, including Jabal Nablus, the *mutasallim* was still responsible for the collection of taxes.[91]

The moderate, gradual measures taken by the Egyptians did not solve the problem of very considerable tax arrears in Syria and Palestine. When, towards the end of his rule in the area, Muḥammad 'Alī ran into serious financial difficulties, he ordered Ibrāhīm to make extensive use of the army to levy the arrears from various parts of the country. Apparently these efforts did not bring in enough money to solve the financial problem.[92] At about the same time, when relations with Istabul were strained, Muḥammad 'Alī also ordered Ibrāhīm to digress from the first of the two rules he laid down and postpone the transfer of *zeamet*s which became vacant upon the death of their holders to their heirs. The *zeamet*s which became vacant upon Ḥusayn 'Abd al-Hādī's death came under this order.[93]

Although the Egyptians did not unravel the tangle of agrarian relations in Syria and Palestine, they put in motion two important processes. First, as a result of bureaucratic improvements, the government secured better and more accurate information, and therefore a tighter control over the distribution of rights to taxes in the entire area. Inheritable rights to taxes were not handed out automatically. They were checked and sometimes extracted from their lawful heirs. Second, the area administered by the central government grew during the Egyptian period, and the authorities took care not to grant inheritable rights on these lands. The combination of the two processes was certainly a step towards bureaucratization of the agrarian regime.

Conclusion

The drafting of the local population into the army, the seizure of the villagers' weapons and the changes introduced in the agrarian regime were meant to serve specific Egyptian purposes: replenishment of the ranks of the army, minimization of the possibility of revolt and enlargement of the state portion of land taxes. The same measures also served to undermine

91 See e.g. *Ibid.*, vol. II, pp. 43-44, doc. 94 — this is Sulaymān 'Abd al-Hādī's document of appointment to the Nablus *mutasallimiyya* (as to its date see note 65 above); *Ibid.*, vol. III-IV, pp. 234-235, doc. 471, 9 Dhū'l-Qa'da, 1254 [24.1.1839] etc.

92 See e.g. Rustum, *Maḥfūẓāt*, vol. IV, p. 206, doc. 6001, 19 Jumādā'l-Ākhira, 1255 [30.8.1839]; *Ibid.*, pp. 214-215, doc. 6018, 29 Jumādā'l-Ākhira, 1255 [9.9.1839]; *Ibid.*, p. 318, doc. 6253, 15 Ṣafar, 1256 [18.4.1840]; *Ibid.*, pp. 332-333, doc. 6291, 18 Rabī' al-Awwal, 1256 [20.5.1840]; *Ibid.*, p. 339, doc. 6302, 27 Rabī' al-Awwal, 1256 [29.5.1840]; See also Y. Hofman, "Muḥammad 'Alī in Syria" (in Hebrew), unpublished Ph.D. thesis, The Hebrew University, Jerusalem, 1963, pp. 185-187.

93 Rustum, *Maḥfūẓāt*, vol. IV, p. 415, doc. 6388, 18 Jumādā'l-Ūlā, 1256 [18.7.1840].

the very bases of power and authority of the notables. Local recruitment to the army and the stripping of villagers of their weapons deprived the notables of their military support. The steps taken towards bureaucratization of tax-collection, which put in question the traditional and quasi-automatic right of the notables to transfer their own rights to the collection of taxes to their sons, were of such a nature as to weaken their personal economic security and, more important, undermine the very basis of their notable status — the traditional patron-client relations with their followers. The Nablus *mutasallim* — Sulaymān 'Abd al-Hādī — abolished, or rather was ordered to abolish, several taxes levied from the population by former *mutasallims*. These were taxes which were not destined for the treasury but for the *mutasallim* himself and some of the Nablus notables. Precedent was no sacred rule in this case. It could be, and actually was overruled by a much better, and indeed, sacred, principle. These levies were abolished on the ground of being undesirable innovations (*bida'*),[94] which they in fact were. The motive behind this measure was, however, not any sudden display of righteousness on the part of either Sulaymān 'Abd al-Hādī or his Egyptian masters. It was, so we believe, another step towards the weakening of the local notables and the undermining of the dependence of the local inhabitants on their good will.

It is reasonable to assume that the Egyptians regarded these measures as important steps towards the eventual replacement of the politics of notables by direct rule by Egyptian officials — a goal which, we believe, they never really abandoned.

The Egyptians, however, never attained this goal. Several reasons can be suggested to explain this lack of success. First, the Egyptians actually governed Syria and Palestine for less then ten years, by all standards a short period for the introduction and implementation of radical changes. Second, the geographical, ecological and religious diversity of Syria and Palestine and the long and deeply-rooted tradition of local autonomy, mainly in its mountainous regions, assuredly made the imposition of direct and uniform rule in the area much more difficult than in Egypt. It certainly implied that such an attempt would meet with resistance by the local inhabitants and notables, resistance which would have to be put down by force. Third, during the major part of the Egyptian rule in Syria and Palestine, the Egyptians were either actively engaged in war with the Ottomans or preparing for a possible eruption of such war. They were, thus, not free to confine the use of their strong army for internal purposes only. Fourth, Muḥammad 'Alī's status in Syria and Palestine was still that of an ordinary *wālī* on behalf of the Ottomans. Because of the involvement of the Great Powers in the conflict between Muḥammad 'Alī and the

94 Rustum, *Uṣūl*, vol. III-IV, pp. 23-24, doc. 182, end of Ramaḍān, 1251 [10-19.1.1836]. See also *Ibid.*, vol. II, pp. 148-149, doc. 151, end of Sha'bān, 1250 [22-31.12.1834].

Sublime Porte, Muḥammad ʻAlī was not free to change this status. Diplomatic considerations cerainly deterred him from taking steps which could jeopardize his delicate position.

When the Ottomans returned to the area, their principal aims were to tighten central control over the provinces and to reform their administration. For these purposes they took much the same measures as the Egyptians: local recruitment into their army, doing away with residues of the *timar* system and the inheritable *iltizāms*, etc. In the mountainous regions of Syria and Palestine, however, direct rule had to be imposed by the use of force. In Jabal Nablus this was finally accomplished in 1858, when the Ottomans succeeded in appointing an officer of their own to the post of *mutaṣarrif*.[95] Politics of notables from this period onwards assumed a different and much more peaceful nature, and did not endanger Ottoman direct rule in Jabal Nablus.

To a large extent the Ottomans, thus, followed in the steps of Muḥammad ʻAlī and brought to conclusion processes set in motion during the period of his rule in Syria and Palestine. It would, perhaps, not be an exaggeration to say that, just as the short period of French rule in Egypt facilitated Muḥammad ʻAlī's rise to power in Egypt, so did Muḥammad ʻAlī's equally short rule in Syria and Palestine pave the way for the imposition of direct Ottoman rule in the area in general and in Jabal Nablus in particular.

95 Maʻoz, *op. cit.*, pp. 115-118. On the struggle in Jabal Nablus see also Hoexter, *op. cit.*, pp. 266-274.

SHIMON SHAMIR

Egyptian Rule (1832-1840) and the Beginning of the Modern Period in the History of Palestine

"The division of history into periods is not a fact," wrote E. H. Carr, "but a necessary hypothesis or tool of thought, valid in so far as it is illuminating, and dependent for its validity on interpretation."[1] The periodization of any historical field thus continuously evolves with the progress of research and the crystallization of new interpretative frameworks. A case in point is the definition of the beginning of Modern Times in the history of the Middle East, which is constantly modified in consonance with attempts to refine our understanding of the nature and processes of change in this region. The subject has undoubtedly become one of the major issues in contemporary Middle Eastern historical writings.

Conversely, perhaps one of the salient indications that the historical study of Palestine in recent centuries is still in its initial stages lies in the lack of methodical divisions into historically significant time units, and the erratic way in which the question of periodization is treated in the existing literature on the subject. There is a tendency in studies on Palestine to regard "the beginning of the nineteenth century" as the opening of the new period[2] — taking no heed of Marc Bloch's caveat that "no law of history enjoins that only those years whose dates end with the figure '01' coincide with the critical points of human evolution."[3] Some historians prefer to consider Napoleon's invasion as the beginning of a new era, disregarding the fact that it hardly had any effect on the country;[4] others take the death of al-Jazzār as the turning point, even though for almost three full decades,

1 E. H. Carr, *What is History?* (London, 1964), p. 60.

2 See the section "*Ha-Yishuv ha-Yehudi 'al Saf Tequfa Ḥadasha: Ha-Me'a ha-Tesha' 'Esreh*" in I. Ben-Zvi, *Eretz Yisra'el bi-Mei ha-Shilton ha-'Otmani* (Jerusalem, 1955); Y. Ben-Arieh, *'Ir bi-Re'i Tequfa: Yerushalayim ba-Me'a ha-Tesha' 'Esreh* (Jerusalem, 1977).

3 Marc Bloch, *The Historian's Craft* (New York, 1953), p. 182.

4 See J. W. Parkes, *A History of Palestine from 135 A.D. to Modern Times* (New York, 1949).

the two subsequent *wālīs* (Sulaymān and 'Abdallāh), on the whole, followed Jazzār's path.[5]

The reasons for the relatively less advanced state of the study of Palestine are too obvious to need more than brief mention. Pre-World War I Palestine was a provincial region which, apart from its religious importance, did not hold much attraction for Middle East historians, most of whom (as many historians of other regions) directed their attention to metropolitan power centers, elites, political leaderships and diplomatic affairs. Palestine lacked not only an important government seat, but also the dynamic social forces, significant economic assets or creative intellectual centers that could stimulate the researcher's curiosity.

In addition, the definition of Palestine in the Ottoman period is quite problematic. Not constituting a single administrative political unit with particular well-defined social or cultural characteristics, "Palestine" as a framework for methodical historical study is less meaningful than most Ottoman provinces — at least as far as its Arabic-speaking, predominantly Muslim population is concerned. To the extent that the concept did determine the contours of historical writings, it was usually due to the writers' subjective perceptions that were rooted more in earlier (or later) periods than in the realities of the Ottoman era itself.

Moreover, in Palestine the fragmented nature of Ottoman society manifested itself in a particularly far-reaching way, facilitating the parallel existence in the same land of numerous communities that had very few points of mutual contact. From this evolved a number of self-contained "communal" Palestinian histories, each with its own rhythm and basic patterns, which impeded the development of an integrated historical narrative and interpretation.

Despite all these limitations, a geographically defined Ottoman Palestine would nonetheless seem to be a legitimate unit for historical research and analysis. A geographical sector can serve historical studies, to cite Carr once again, at least as a "valid and fruitful hypothesis," and should not be dismissed from the outset. Nor should its provincial marginality be equated with historical insignificance. What was done by Le Roy Ladruie on Languedoc and by Pierre Goubert on the Beauvaisis[6] could be done on rural Palestine with no less import. One does not necessarily have to subscribe to the tenets of the *Annales* school and "total history" to appreciate the relevance of the peripheries to overall historical insight. Much could also be gained from a comparative study of a number of provincial regions which would bring out the differences in the rhythm and

5 See the 10 vols. *Ha-Historiya shel Eretz Yisra'el* edited by Y.Shavit, where vol. 7 establishes the period 1516-1804 as one unit.

6 Emmanuel Le Roy Ladruie, *Les Paysans du Languedoc* (Paris, 1966); Pierre Goubert, *Beauvais et le Beauvaisis de 1600 à 1730* (Paris, 1960).

the inner dynamics of change in each, and subsequently — the differences in their respective periodizations.

How then can the beginnings of the modern period in the history of Palestine be determined? Surely, concepts of "westernization" and "modernization," long regarded as effective tools for explaining historical change and identifying the shift to Modern Times, can no longer be considered adequately reliable criteria. The model of linear progress from tradition to modernity, always triggered and directed by the influence of the West, as suggested by social scientists and orientalists, is now increasingly challenged in the light of findings that are incompatible with the tradition-modernity dichotomy and the notion of universal convergence towards an essentially Western type of modernity. On the other hand, the alternative theory which stresses the role of indigenous forces seems to have overstated its case, not to mention the fact that, as Kenneth Cuno has pointed out, it sometimes creates an "internal-external dichotomy [which] is as false as the traditional-modern."[7]

Thus, in the absence of generally accepted criteria for modernity, it might suffice to use a list of characteristic developments that can be clearly observed in a region like the Eastern Mediterranean and that by broad consensus are considered related to the evolution of modernity. These characteristic features are suggested here (in telegraphic brevity) as empirical guidelines and no attempt is made to establish causal or sequential relationships between them, or to fit them into any particular over-all theory. Naturally, developments relevant only to metropolitan centers and not to provincial peripheries are excluded from our discussion. Palestine — unlike the capitals of Egypt, the Ottoman Empire or Iran — did not have a central government that could restructure itself and the state; it had no legislating institutions that could introduce legal reforms, no military commands seeking new technologies and capabilities, no central treasury interested in rationalizing the financial and fiscal systems, no ruling elites capable of guiding a multi-faceted process of transformation, and no major intellectual centers able to absorb or develop new ideas and conceptualize change.

Nevertheless, there remain many processes of change that *are* relevant to the provinces. Many of these fall into the general category of the decline of long-established social organizations. In urban society this applies to such institutions as the guilds of artisans and merchants, and in the rural areas to feudal and tax-farming agrarian relationships in all their aspects — financial, military, political and social. In these conditions, the beginning of

7 Kenneth M. Cuno, "The Origins of Private Ownership of Land in Egypt: A Reappraisal", *IJMES* XII (1980), p. 270 n. 4. Cf. the discussion of the same problem in the context of India, in Milton Singer, *When a Great Tradition Modernizes: An Anthropological Approach to Indian Civilization* (London, 1972), pp. 383ff.

systematic land registration usually emerges. These developments are accompanied by the rise of differentiated bureaucracies in the towns, including the establishment of rudimentary forms of representative councils. The latter are usually associated with the urban elite which gains strength at the expense of the rural notables. Local governments become more active and effective. The scope of the *Sharī'a* institutions narrows while the secular legal systems expand. The traditionally superior status of Muslims is challenged by the improved legal and economic status of the *dhimmīs*. The population grows, particularly in the towns, which enjoy better health conditions and attract migrants from the countryside and foreigners from the West. A new middle class begins to emerge in which non-Muslims occupy a salient place. Europeans exercise a considerable level of influence in a number of areas — political, economic and cultural. With the introduction of modern facilities and buildings, the general appearance of towns changes, while ways of life in them and modes of consumption are partially westernized. New schools, modelled on European principles, are established and modern communications media develop — spreading new ideas and values, many of them essentially secular. A cultural awakening is apparent that borrows from the West but also draw on classical sources. Mechanical types of transport, by land and sea, are put into operation. Internal security improves, and the nomads are held in check or even settled. Attempts are made to advance and expand agriculture and to mechanize production in all its forms. Agriculture is commercialized, and shifts from subsistence farming to export-oriented cash crops. Monetary activities in economic life increase, and the nucleus of a new local capitalism emerges. Trade develops in new directions, using new methods. The import of foreign goods grows, gradually undermining local crafts. Foreign capital flows into the country and the economy in general is integrated into the financial and commercial network of industrial Europe.[8]

Now, there can be little doubt that *some* of these processes manifested themselves in Palestine before the nineteenth century, particularly in the second half of the eighteenth. Increasing demand in Europe — generated by the realities of the Industrial Revolution — for agricultural products, such as cotton and grains, had a remarkable impact on Palestine which grew both. It brought about a rise in agricultural products, particularly of cotton, which was sold for cash to European (mostly French) merchants. This trade — as shown by Amnon Cohen[9] — had become the economic base of Ṭāhir and Jazzār, enabling them to maintain regular forces and

8 For a shorter, but essentially similar list of characteristics of the process in the Middle East, see Charles Issawi, *The Economic History of the Middle East, 1800-1914* (Chicago, 1965), pp. 3-13.

9 Amnon Cohen, *Palestine in the 18th Century: Patterns of Government and Administration* (Jerusalem, 1973), pp. 7-77, 119-178.

improve security conditions throughout the Galilee, to develop the towns of Tiberias and Acre and construct fortifications, markets and other public facilities in them, to increase the population by bringing in Jews from Izmir and Greek-Orthodox Christians from Cyprus (respectively), and to repair harbor facilities and encourage shipping — primarily in Acre. Signs of this prosperity were also apparent in adjacent *sanjaq*s such as Lajjūn and 'Ajlūn, and in the coastal towns. Consumption of imported goods, particularly firearms, also rose somewhat. Finally, the concentration of power in the hands of Ṭāhir and Jazzār, followed later by the *wālī*s Sulaymān and 'Abdallāh, began to erode the power of the feudal *shaykh*s.[10]

Thus the remarkable changes of the eighteenth century, as pointed out by Albert Hourani with regard to the Fertile Crescent[11] and Peter Gran with regard to Egypt,[12] took place, in part, in Palestine as well. And yet, it is hard to see these changes as adding up to the beginning of a new era in Palestine. Important as those developments may have been, they did not reach the level of a comprehensive, sustained process of change. They remained dependent on the whims and wishes of essentially traditional local rulers who were also the main beneficiaries of the new situation (thanks mostly to the diminishing power and effectivity of the central government). Their interests were limited to imposing their rule over the region and tapping its financial resources through monopolistic control of trade and taxation. Hence, developments in those years did not bring about any enduring structural changes in the country's economy, society or cultural life. While they undoubtedly justify a reevaluation of the concept "decline," which is so often applied to the eighteenth century, they certainly do not warrant the application of the concept "revival" to the period.

The next period deserving examination as a possible turning point in the history of the country is the decade of Egyptian rule in Palestine, 1832-1840. Referring to that period in the history of Lebanon, William Polk wrote:

> . . .the decade which the Egyptian invasion began can now be seen to have cut across the spectrum of Middle Eastern history like a band. The old ways of life were profoundly altered. The balance of power and expectations in which the Druze, Christians and Muslims; the townsmen, villagers, and bedouins; and the amirs, shaikhs, and peasants had lived was shattered. The relationship of the government to the governed, the market to the producer, the foreigner to the

10 Mordechai Abir, "Local Leadership and Early Reforms in Palestine, 1800-1834," in Moshe Ma'oz, *Studies on Palestine during the Ottoman Period* (Jerusalem, 1975), p. 301.

11 Albert Hourani, "The Fertile Crescent in the Eighteenth Century," in his *A Vision of History* (Beirut, 1961), pp. 35-70.

12 Peter Gran, *Islamic Roots of Capitalism, Egypt 1760-1840* (Austin, 1979), pp. 3-34.

> native were all radically changed. This turbulent decade began the modern period.[13]

The following pages will attempt to examine the extent to which this evaluation is applicable to Palestine as well.

* * *

Muḥammad 'Alī's regime did not affect guilds and *ṭuruq* in Palestinian towns, just as it hardly affected their better organized and much more significant counterparts in Egypt.[14] Of much greater importance was its impact on the feudal structure in Jabal Nablus and the Judean hills. While it is true, as indicated above, that some action to subdue the feudal *shaykh*s had already been taken by Jazzār, Sulaymān and 'Abdallah,[15] the efforts of the Egyptian authorities were of an entirely different order. The three Pashas of the pre-Egyptian period had acted as local power centers, benefiting from the weakness of the central government, and seeking to entrench themselves in the government of the province. Thus their operations against the feudal *shaykh*s were motivated by the ambition to consolidate their own control in the region. Even when they took steps that happened to coincide with the Sultan's reform schemes (the recruitment for the *niẓām* and the abolition of *timārs*), the inner logic of their actions remained embedded in local power politics.[16] Ibrāhīm Pasha, on the other hand, tried systematically to integrate the *shaykh*s into a centralized administrative system. Although his *modus operandi* was gradual and prudent and he found himself compelled to work through the existing notable family system, he was in fact undermining the foundations of the feudal structure and bureaucratizing the functions of the feudal *shaykh*s. The Egyptians sought to neutralize the military capability of the notables and to tighten slowly their bureaucratic control over the *muqāṭa'a-iltizām* system.[17]

When Egyptian rule was terminated, implementation of these policies was still in its initial stage, but the Ottomans' *tanẓīmāt* policies can be seen

13 William R. Polk, *The Opening of South Lebanon, 1788-1840* (Cambridge, Mass., 1963), p. xix.

14 See Gabriel Baer, *Egyptian Guilds in Modern Times* (Jerusalem, 1964).

15 Some attempts to introduce changes in the feudal system of Jabal Nablus had already been made in the 1820s, but without significant consequences. See Miriam Hoexter, "The Role of the Qays and Yaman Factions in Local Political Divisions," *AAS* IX (1973), pp. 261-262.

16 Iḥsān al-Nimr, *Ta'rīkh Jabal Nablus wa'l-Balqā'* Vol. I (Damascus, 1938), pp. 155-245. See Abir, *op. cit.*, pp. 284-302.

17 Nimr I, pp. 246-266; Asad J. Rustum (ed.), *Al-Maḥfūẓāt al-Malikiyya al-Miṣriyya* (Beirut, 1940-43), Vol. 1, p. 176 and many others; see Miriam Hoexter's article in this volume; Muḥammad Kurd 'Alī, *Al-Ḥukūma al-Miṣriyya fī 'l-Shām* (Cairo, A.H. 1343), text of a lecture delivered in 1925, copy at Dār al-Kutub collection in Cairo.

as a continuation of those of Muḥmmad 'Alī. True, their 1839 decree abolishing the *iltizām* was never fully executed, but the system was increasingly brought under the control of the provincial *majlis* and administration. By the end of the 1850s the *timārs* had been completely liquidated and the power of the *shaykhs* neutralized. This was achieved by applying the same methods of curbing their powers, recruiting their followers into the army, destroying their fortresses and exploiting their perpetual rivalries. Summing up the consequences of Egyptian rule in Jabal Nablus, Iḥsān al-Nimr wrote: "After that [the suppression of the feudal *shaykhs*' revolt in the Jabal], its internal unity was broken up and it was given to a devastating civil war which brought about the loss of its power and prestige; and thus the Ottoman State gradually gained control over the country's government."[18] It should however be noted that this was not accompanied by the comprehensive regularization of the land system that the Egyptians evidently had in mind. Throughout the nineteenth century little progress was achieved in registering private ownership of land, and the *mushā'* system remained predominant in the country.[19]

There can be little doubt that Egyptian rule in Syria and Palestine represented the first attempt to introduce concepts characteristic of the period of reforms into the administration: there was an attempt to separate civilian and military authorities, to set up a stable regional sub-division with administrative and financial hierarchies controlled by a provincial government, to recruit local people to the provincial apparatus, and to supervise the integrity and efficiency of the administration's functionaries. In practice, the operation of the Egyptian administration and its hierarchies of *mutasallims* and *mubāshirs* was a far cry from the system as planned; and Ibrāhīm himself was the loudest critic of its deficiencies, but the basic pattern was set.[20] With restoration of Ottoman rule in 1840, the *tanẓīmāt* policy-makers actually followed the same principles — as could be seen in their efforts to strengthen the administrative apparatus of the *sanjaq* of Jerusalem and establish better differentiated and structured bureaucratic hierarchies throughout the province. This trend was intensified by the 1864 Vilayet Law.

Egyptian rule signified, above all, the first application to Palestine of the concept of territorial *state*, a concept that emerged under Muḥammad 'Alī before appearing in the Sultan's *devlet-i 'aliye*. Directly or indirectly, this concept was inherent in most policies applied by the Egyptians in the

18 Nimr I, p. 259. See Moshe Ma'oz, *Ottoman Reform in Syria and Palestine, 1840-1861* (London, 1968), pp. 14-17, 75-78; Hoexter, *Qays-Yaman*, pp. 266-274, 308-309.

19 Gabriel Baer, "The Impact of Economic Change on Traditional Society in Nineteenth Century Palestine," in Ma'oz, *Studies*, p. 495.

20 Yitzhak Hofman, "*Po'alo shel Muḥammad 'Ali be-Suriya*," Ph.D. dissertation (Hebrew University of Jerusalem, 1963), pp. 21-63; Sulaymān Abū 'Izz al-Dīn, *Ibrāhīm Bāshā fī Sūriyā* (Beirut, 1929), pp. 131-140.

Syrian provinces: general conscription into the state's army, imposition of a universal poll-tax (*ferde*), the introduction of a secular legislature and restriction of the powers of the *Sharīʿa* judges, making them dependent on state salaries.[21] Each of these policies materialised in response to a particular political or administrative problem which the Egyptian authorities had to meet with an immediate reaction, but the totality of solutions to these problems fell into a clear pattern and manifested the "statist" principles which later guided the *tanẓīmāt*.

The same is true of the *majlis*es established by the Egyptians in towns that had over 2,000 inhabitants. Although the *majlis al-shūrā*, as it was termed, seemed quite similar to the traditional *dīwān* that had long existed in every province, it in fact embodied a new concept of civic participation in that its basic composition included non-Muslims and it was given a broad range of judicial, administrative, economic and municipal responsibilities.[22] The performance of the *majlis*es left much to be desired but, once again, they represented an innovation that was later implemented more extensively in the *tanẓīmāt*'s *majlis idāre* and *majlis 'umūmī* (both of which existed in Jerusalem).

The *majlis* became the focal point of the activities of a rising urban elite, the *a'yān*, whose influence in the towns and control of lands in the countryside was gradually increasing. This development, however, could not fully evolve before the *tanẓīmāt* period, for the centralization policies of the Egyptians usually sought to weaken rather than strengthen local forces. In Jerusalem the *a'yān* elite initially consisted of the holders of traditional Islamic offices who belonged to the notable families (some of them having rural backgrounds), and later, toward the last quarter of the century, also of the high officials of the province, who were increasingly recruited from the same families.[23]

Christians and Jews were included in the Ottoman *majlis idāre* as they had been in the Egyptian *majlis*. This represented what was probably the most revolutionary aspect of Egyptian rule in Palestine: the granting of new rights to the *dhimmī*s. Having promised the European that he would treat the Christians and Jews in Palestine and Syria fairly, Muḥammad 'Alī imposed policies in these lands that considerably narrowed the gap

21 Hofman, pp. 122-123.

22 M. Sabry, *L'Empire Egyptien sous Mohamed-Ali et la Question d'Orient, 1811-1849* (Paris, 1930), pp. 345-349. Hofman regarded these *majlis*es as "The most important innovation introduced by them to the administration of Syria," *op. cit.*, p. 63.

23 B. Abu Manneh "The Rise of the Sanjak of Jerusalem in the Late Nineteenth Century," in G. Ben-Dor (ed.), *The Palestinians and the Middle East Conflict* (Ramat Gan, 1978), p. 26; H. Gerber, "The Ottoman Administration of the Sanjak of Jerusalem, 1890-1908," *AAS* XII (1978), pp. 33-76; on the main *a'yān* families of Jerusalem and their economic basis, see Gabriel Baer, "Jerusalem's Families of Notables and the Waqf in the Early Nineteenth Century," Paper delivered at a conference on *The Legacy of Ottoman Palestine* (Haifa University, 1979).

between Muslims and non-Muslims. The latter were allowed not only to repair damaged churches and synagogues but also to build some new ones (in 1837 the Jews built the Ashkenazi "Menaḥem Tziyon" synagogue as the first structure in the "Ḥurva" complex). Non-Muslims were protected from long-practiced extortions, and exempted from the traditional levies on pilgrims. More equitable treatment of non-Muslims was also important for activating members of communities that were a relatively significant proportion of the country's population, and for incorporating them into the new system then evolving. Thus, in addition to being given representation in the *majlises*, the Christians were also admitted into the provincial administration.[24]

The Ottomans, who owed the restoration of their sovereignty in Syria and Palestine to the European powers, continued the same policy. Traditional discriminatory practices were eliminated in 1840, and in 1855 the deeply symbolic *jizya* tax was abolished (to be replaced by the *badal*). In 1841, an office of *Ḥakhām Bashi* was constituted in Jerusalem, and in the following years a number of patriarchates were instituted in the city (see below). Benefiting from the new political protection and the economic opportunities, the position of the non-Muslims continued to improve. Nevertheless, neither Ibrāhīm's rule nor the post-Egyptian Ottoman government generated processes of genuine social integration, for the Muslim population reacted with antagonism — particularly toward the Christians — to the loss of its traditional status, and society was therefore further polarized.

The scene of these developments in Palestine was, of course, the mixed towns which began to grow under the Egyptian administration. The growth was essentially slight and did not occur in all towns, but in Palestinian terms it was quite significant. The most conspicuous increase took place in Jerusalem, due primarily to the growth of the Jewish community, which in the last three years of Egyptian rule doubled its size (with the arrival of immigrants from Europe and North Africa, and of refugees from the earthquake in Safed). There was also some increase of the population in the costal towns of Gaza, Jaffa and Haifa — at the expense of Acre, where the population actually started to decline. However, the rapid acceleration of the growth rate in major towns, particularly Jerusalem and Jaffa, took place only in the last quarter of the century, as the influence of immigration from abroad was felt and medical services improved.[25] (Medical services were instituted under Ibrāhīm with the first clinics and quarantine facili-

24 See, for example, the decrees in Asad Rustum, *Al-Uṣūl al-'Arabiyya li-Ta'rīkh Sūriya fī 'Ahd Muḥammad 'Alī* (Beirut, 1930-34), Vol. II, pp. 4-5; Vol. III, pp. 24-26. Also S. N. Spyridon, *Annals of Palestine, 1821-1840* (reprint, Jerusalem, 1979), pp. 76-79.

25 Yehoshua Ben-Arieh, "The Population of the Large Towns in Palestine during the First Eighty Years of the Nineteenth Century, According to Western Sources," in Ma'oz, *Studies*, pp. 49-69.

ties, but the first hospitals were established only in the 1850s and 1860s.) Hence, it would be premature to talk of the emergence of a new urban middle class before the turn of the century.

The outstanding consequence of the Egyptian period was the opening of the country to Europeans who, for better or worse, became the catalysts of modernization. The country's exposure to scientific exploration (by such scholars as Tobler, Robinson, Schubert, Curzon, and in the Jewish community — Schwartz and Mendel) was perhaps less significant for local society than for the Europeans — just as the compilation of the *Description de l'Egypte* under Bonaparte's rule was predominantly a European event — but the flow of foreign travelers, pilgrims, missionaries, merchants, consular envoys and immigrants, was an entirely different matter.

The improvement of security conditions under Ibrāhīm, the development of the means of communication to and from Palestine, the cancellation of levies on travelers, and the improved treatment of non-Muslims in general, sharply increased the number of visitors to the country. The number of pilgrims in the 1830s was estimated at about 5 to 10 thousand annually but in some years it was as high as 20 thousand (Russians constituting a growing component of these pilgrims). This flow of visitors encouraged the development of facilities to accommodate them, facilities that gradually began to serve the local inhabitants as well, mainly in Jerusalem but later in Jaffa and other places.

A contemporary witness, describing the situation in Acre, wrote: ". . . during the Government of Djezzar and Abdallah Pachas, a Christian could not appear in the streets without great danger. In 1838 a Christian, wearing the costume of his country, might go where he would, not only in perfect safety but even without being noticed as he passed."[26]

Of particular importance was the beginning of missionary activities. Under the Egyptian administration, for the first time, Protestant missionaries began to operate openly (mostly among the Jews). The missionaries of the London Jews Society thus started to provide medical and some educational services in Jerusalem. In 1841-2, Protestant activities in Palestine culminated in the establishment, through joint British and Prussian efforts, of an Anglican Bishopric in Jerusalem.[27]

Relations of the Jewish community with Western Europe became closer. Sir Moses Montefiore's second visit to Palestine in 1839 is rightly regarded as the inception of his extensive endeavors to better the living conditions of the Jews. In the 1830s, for the first time, Jewish immigration to Palestine included a Western-educated, affluent component. These were immigrants from Holland and Germany, the founders of the "Kolel Hod," who formed a new elite in the Jerusalem community and made a considerable contribu-

26 John Bowring, *Report on the Commercial Statistics of Syria* (London, 1840), p. 105.
27 Abdul Latif Tibaqi, *British Interests in Palestine, 1800-1901* (London, 1961).

tion towards the development of educational, medical and welfare activities.[28]

Politically, the most important development was the opening of Jerusalem to European consulates. Sporadic attempts to establish consular posts in Palestine had been made before Ibrāhīm (since the seventeenth century — by the French, British and others, located mostly in the towns of the coastal plain, and designed to deal with trade activities only), but the beginning of regular, extensive consular operations, and the emergence of Jerusalem as the focal point of Euopean diplomatic activities, has to be dated from Ibrāhīm's period on. The British, initiators of the process, opened their consulate in Jerusalem in 1838. Other consulates were opened subsequently (Prussia — 1842, France and Sardinia — 1843, the U.S. — 1844, Austria — 1849, Russia — 1858), but many of the initial steps in this direction can be traced back to the Egyptian period.[29]

The consuls rapidly became a principal factor in the life of the country, precipitating processes of change. They were deeply involved not only in local urban politics but sometimes even in factional warfare in the villages.[30] Their main "constituencies" were the local communities of their own nationals, communities that were constantly growing as a result of immigration from Europe and generous policies with respect to granting citizenship. Benefiting from expanding Capitulations privileges, they were free to engage in a wide range of activities. No less important was the fact that the consuls also exerted their influence to broaden the scope of the activities of local non-Muslims by providing benevolent "protection" — actually designed for political purposes — to local congregations (the British and the Prussians — to Protestants and Jews; the French — to Catholics; the Russians — to Greek-Orthodox; the Austrians — to Jews).

Thus the consular system was an umbrella covering activities such as the founding of hospitals, schools and philanthropic institutions; the construction of housing projects and businesses; the publishing of books and newspapers; and the purchase of land. The establishment of the German Templar colonies and the Zionist settlements of the first two *'aliya*s would have been inconceivable without the protection of the European consular system.[31] From the point of view of the local Muslim majority, these were all mixed blessings, but the degree to which they transformed the country was decisive. More extensive changes took place, of course, only in the later

28 Mordechai Eliav, *Ahavat Tziyon ve-Anshei Hod* (Tel Aviv, 1970).

29 Albert M. Hyamson, *The British Consulate in Jerusalem, 1838-1914* (London, 1939), Vol. I, p. XXXV. See a collection of articles on the opening of consulates in Jerusalem in *Cathedra* no. 5.

30 Hoexter, *Qays-Yaman*, p. 306.

31 I. Friedman, "The Regime of Capitulations and Its Influence upon the Attitude of the Ottoman Empire towards the Jewish Community in Palestine. . ." Paper delivered at a Conference on *The Legacy of Ottoman Palestine* (Haifa University, 1979), p. 8.

part of the nineteenth century, but they had their roots in the initial steps taken under Egyptian rule.

There can be no doubt that the Egyptian occupation signifies a turning point in the history of Palestine also by virtue of the fact that pursuant to it the country became involved in the international politics of the modern era. The weakness of the Ottomans, whose hold over Palestine was at least temporarily shaken by the Egyptians, invited the extension of European rivalries to the Holy Land. Muḥammad 'Alī's venture increased the importance in European diplomacy of all of "Asiatic Turkey" and made Palestine one of the focal points of the Eastern Question. As Vereté puts it, "talks, sermons, plans, proposals... for the future of Palestine as a separate, semi-independent entity whether wholly, mainly or partly Jewish or Christian — all these were rife in several European countries during 1839-1941. . ."[32] Hence the rush to establish a "presence" in the Holy Land through forming religious and secular institutions, by extending protection to local communities, by more widespread use of Capitulations privileges, and later through active involvement in railway schemes (most of which did not materialize) and economic investments (which did increase toward the end of the century). Thus, in the wake of the Egyptian occupation, the great powers' interest in Palestine escalated not merely because of the country's importance *per se* but because involvement in its affairs had far-reaching implications with regard to the position those powers held in the Ottoman Empire as a whole (as the instigation of the Crimean War clearly demonstrated).

It was in the 1830s that Palmerston crystallized the British policy of preserving the integrity of the Ottoman Empire, a policy that was immediately applied to Palestine in the endeavor to check the attempts of other powers to gain a foothold there. (The economic dimension of Britain's policy was manifested in the 1838 trade agreement, but initially this had only limited relevance to Palestine.) Muḥammad 'Alī's hegemony in the Eastern Mediterranean and alarming implications for the "lifeline" to India, for it signified that a local government backed by a European power could gain control of both the Egyptian passage and the Fertile Crescent route to the East. This encouraged British entrepreneurs to develop the trade route connecting the Persian Gulf with the Mediterranean coast, which, of course, included Palestine (the Chesney Mission, 1834-36). The opening of the Suez Canal and increasing British control thereof reduced interest in the alternative route, but as Palestine was also close to the Canal, strategic interest in it, which had emerged in the 1830s, continued to grow throughout the late Ottoman period. On another plane, the opening of Palestine in the 1830s also inspired growing interest among British intellectuals and

32 M. Vereté, "A Plan for the Internationalization of Jerusalem, 1840-1841," *AAS* XII (1978), p. 22.

statesmen in the vision of the rebirth there of Jewish nationhood, a vision to which Palmerston himself evidently adhered.

French political ambitions in Palestine also reemerged and intensified during the time of Muḥammad 'Alī, with whom the French were closely associated. It was the international crisis generated by Muḥammad 'Alī's conquest which, to use Temperley's expression, "turned French attention to Palestine."[33] The region encompassed by France's long-standing interest was usually described by the broad term "Levant," which stressed Syria and Lebanon, but it was often indicated that this concept included Palestine as well. One manifestation of this position was Guizot's proposal in 1840 for the internationalization of Palestine or Jerusalem (which, as could only be expected, was firmly rejected by Palmerston). France's growing interest in Palestine was often channeled through the Latin Church in Jerusalem and its influential position in the holy places there (it was therefore supported by other Catholic European states). One of the most consistent demands made by the French was the re-confirmation of the 1740 Capitulations which recognized their privileges in Jerusalem and its surroundings. In 1847 they reinstated the Latin Patriarch of Jerusalem in the city, less than three years after the Greek-Orthodox had reinstated their Patriarch of Jerusalem — two acts that well reflected the international political struggles which had evolved in Palestine since the Egyptian period.[34]

The general interest of the Russians in the region increased as a result of their 1833 military and political maneuvers, designed to counter Ibrāhīm's Syrian expedition. Their actual involvement in the affairs of Palestine began mainly in the wake of the Egyptian occupation and it continued to be nourished by a combination of religious messianism and strategic ambitions. Russian interference in the affairs of the Greek-Orthodox Patriarchate and community in Palestine intensified the rivalry between Arabs and Greeks, which later played such an important role in the development of nationalist awareness among Palestinian Arabs.[35]

Even German interest in this part of the world, which culminated towards the end of the century is a dominant position at the Porte, can be traced back to the period of Egyptian rule, when von Moltke, then military envoy to Istanbul, published a plan to turn Palestine into a buffer state, "preferably under German control."[36] In the years immediately following the Egyptian period, the activities of Prussia in Jerusalem were second only to those of Britian.

33 Harold Temperley, *England and the Near East: The Crimea* (London, 1936), p. 284.

34 R. Simon, "*Ha-Ma'avak 'al ha-Meqomot ha-Qedoshim la-Natzrut be-Eretz Yisrael ba-Tequfa ha-'Othmanit, 1516-1853*," *Cathedra* no. 17 (1980), pp. 107-126.

35 Derek Hopwood, *The Russian Presence in Syria and Palestine, 1843-1914* (London, 1964).

36 Listed in Mordechai Eliav, "German Interests and the Jewish Community in Nineteenth Century Palestine," in Ma'oz, *Studies*, p. 426.

The European presence in Jerusalem, allowed to grow under Ibrāhīm, brought about renewed construction of public buildings, a sphere that had been dormant since the days of Sulaymān the Magnificent. Not much was actually built in the 1830s but directly following that period, in the 1840's and 1850s, new structures began to rise in the Old City. The development of the new city did not begin until 1856, but it was clearly dominated by the minority foreign elements encouraged by the Egyptian rule.[37] Modern public utilities were subsequently introduced at the end of the century. The same rhythm of development was apparent in the field of communications and transportation. A telegraphic service was first set up in Jerusalem in 1865. Major roads were constructed from the late 1860s on, and the Jaffa-Jerusalem railway was inaugurated in 1892. It was already in the Egyptian period that European steamships began to call at Palestinian ports, thus broadening contacts with the West, with all that this entailed.[38]

It was also under Egyptian rule that the first printing press — a Hebrew press moved from Safed (1837) — began to operate. It was soon followed by presses operated by the Latin, Armenian and Greek-Orthodox churches. Local newspapers, however, did not appear until the last third of the century.

The development of new schools that reflected certain Western concepts and teachings, followed the same pattern apparent in a number of other fields: First, the basic conditions for this innovation were created in the Egyptian period, when the forerunners also emerged (the small American school in Jerusalem); significant new institutions than began to appear in the 1840s and 1850s (the Lämel school, Bishop Gobat's schools); and finally there was accelerated proliferation toward the end of the century (Alliance Israelite Schools, Russian Teachers' seminary, the Protestant Diocesan schools, etc.). It was during this last period, mainly in the years of Abdulhamid II, that the first *tanẓīmāt* schools, wherein the curricula also contained some modern concepts, made their appearance in Palestine.[39]

Even at that late phase, such new education on the whole remained confined to elements in the minority communities and affected only a small segment of the native population. The dissemination of new ideas and concepts was also very slow, hardly perceptible in the mainstream of local society during the nineteenth century (those reported had primarily reformist-Islamic orientation).[40] This also applies to more general changes

37 Ben Arien, *'Ir*, Vol. I, pp. 57-58, 133.

38 Shmuel Avitzur, "The Influence of Western Technology on the Economy of Palestine during the Nineteenth Century," in Ma'oz, *Studies*, pp. 485-494.

39 N. Verney and G. Dambmann, *Les Puissances étrangères dans le Levant* (Paris, 1900), pp. 31-135; Bowring, pp. 105-107; Tibawi, p. 158; Jacob M. Landau, "The Educational Impact of Western Culture on Traditional Society in Nineteenth Century Palestine," in Ma'oz, *Studies*, pp. 499-506.

40 Shimon Shamir, "The Impact of Western Ideas on Traditional Society in Ottoman Palestine," in Ma'oz, *Studies*, pp. 507-516.

in the way of life.

Egyptian rule brought with it some developments in the economic field, but they were quite modest in nature and far less significant than those that were taking place in Syria proper. There had been, as we know from Bowring's reports, "a progressive revival of trade," but as far as Palestine was concerned, this meant mostly local-regional trade such as the export of olive oil from Nablus and Safed to Damascus and soap to Egypt.[41] Not much foreign trade was conducted through Palestinian harbors, but Bowring's figures for trade through Syrian ports, particularly Beirut, also included exports from Palestine and some imports to the country.[42] Although data for the period till the last quarter of the century hardly exist, it seems that the foreign trade of Palestine continued to grow slowly in the decade following the Egyptian rule.

Increased importing of European goods threatened local handicrafts in Palestine as well, but since the level of the country's urban and rural industries was quite low to start with, this did not have a disastrous impact on the economy. These industries catered to the habits and tastes of local society and since the overwhelming majority of it preserved its way of life, the demand for local products was not seriously affected. Some industries, notably that of soap, actually increased. In some places industries survived by shifting to English-made cotton yarn, thus narrowing the gap between local and European mechanized production. A considerable segment of local handicrafts was geared to the production of religious articles for Christian pilgrims, production that was also unaffected by European imports.[43]

In agriculture, the export of industrial crops (mostly cotton) that had flourished in the periods of Ṭāhir and Jazzār but declined before the Egyptian occupation, rose again under Egyptian rule. The cotton produced in the Nablus area was particularly acclaimed, being regarded as superior to that of northern Syria.[44] However, Ibrāhīm Pasha's projects to improve agricultural production (in Palestine — mainly in the Ramle and Jezreel plains)[45] did not have significant impact on the country. In addition, many of the economic benefits of the Egyptian administration were nullified by the effect of constantly rising prices.

Although some agricultural experimentations carried out by foreigners (mostly in the Jerusalem region) could be indirectly related to the Egyptian period, the country's agriculture was not seriously affected. The rapid development of cotton crops in Egypt (and America) effectively put an end

41 Bowring, pp. 16, 19, 29-30, 36, 94, 119, 124, 135.
42 *Ibid.*, pp. 19, 54, 119.
43 Baer, *Economic Change*, pp. 495-496; Avitzur, pp. 486-490.
44 Bowring, pp. 9-14, 122, 133.
45 Sabry, pp. 355, 357, 367.

to cotton production in Palestine. The large-scale growth of export-oriented cash crops (such as citrus and vineyards) took place long after the end of Egyptian rule. Similarly, modern machinery was not introduced before the Templar and Zionist colonies were established in the 1870s and 1880s, respectively. The emergence of the first capitalistic entrepreneurs in Palestine (mostly non-Muslims of European or local origins) is related to those late developments and should also be dated in the last quarter of the century.[46]

A major contribution of Ibrāhīm's administration that had positive economic effects on both trade and agriculture was the improvement of internal security and firmer control of Beduins: "il imprima fortement," reported Boislecomte, "le terreur de son nom a celles de ces tribus qui venait dans le pays."[47] This was temporarily offset by the wave of rebellions in Palestine, but after the restoration of Ottoman authority the trend continued and was fully realized toward the end of the century.

★ ★ ★

What then are the conclusions that can be drawn for periodization of the country's Modern History? The changes that had taken place in Palestine in the 6 to 8 decades before the appearance of the Egyptian expedition apparently cannot be regarded as marking a major historical cleavage. What affected Palestine at that period did not amount to more than some faint echoes of the Industrial Revolution in Europe and some more strongly reverberating consequences of the decline of the central government's effective control. They did not bring about any enduring structural changes in the country, nor did they alter the essential features of the realities of the pre-*tanẓīmāt* Ottoman period (which in turn perpetuated many of the features of even earlier periods). Above all, those developments did not generate in the local population a noticeable sense of great upheaval or radical change in the "natural" order of things.

Not so the Egyptian administration, which left a much more significant and lasting impact on the country. This impact was made in spite of the obvious limitations of that administration: it was of relatively short duration, further curtailed by disruptive rebellions and wars; it suffered chronic shortages of financial and manpower resources; and it was more interested in the regions *north* of Palestine. Moreover, it was guided by an external government which even in its own country suffered from inexperience and

46 Nahum Gross, "*Temurot Kalkaliyot be-Eretz Yisrael*," *Cathedra* no. 2 (1976), pp. 111-125.

47 Quoted in Sabry, p. 340. Bowring, pp. 104, 134. For the terror struck by Ibrāhīm's measures throughout the country see Iskandar Abkāriyūs, *Al-Manāqib al-Ibrāhīmiyya wa'l-Ma'āthir al Khadīwiyya* (Cairo, A.H. 1299), pp. 107-119, copy at Dār al-Kutub collection in Cairo.

was not always successful in efforts to transform existing systems. As shown above, Ibrāhīm's rule introduced, or initiated, important changes in the country's power structure, administrative system, relations between Muslims and non-Muslims, urban life, place in international relations, level of security, and the conditions for economic development. These activities provoked a state of turmoil that thoroughly shook the local population. When a Muslim climbed the minaret of the Nablus mosque to denounce Ibrāhīm as a *gavur* and rally the populace to the rebels' side, [48] he was in part following the long-standing practice of using Islam for legitimizing conflicts, but at the same time he was also expressing the Muslims' shocked and angry reaction to innovations that were undermining the traditional order.

Little did the populace know that the transformation attempted by Ibrāhīm was still much more attuned to their traditions and needs than those that would follow later on. Despite the many elements of Egyptian policy that were deeply resented, basically it was still oriented towards the mainstream of the local population — trying to incorporate the feudal *shaykh*s into the new system, to promote the participation of urban notables in the city councils, to defend the villages and increase their production. It was still a policy that focused on the main Aleppo-Damascus-Jerusalem hinterland rather than on the Beirut-Jaffa coast facing Europe. Ibrahim was interested in cooperation with the Europeans, not in the hegemony of foreigners in the economic and socio-political life of the country. No wonder the European consuls in Syria tried to undermine his work in spite of the great advantage that he presented to them[49] (and no wonder a leading Syrian historian like Muḥammad Kurd 'Alī modified the negative impressions left by this rule, and concluded that "the merits of Muḥammad 'Alī's government in Syria surpassed its misdeeds"[50]).

The *tanẓimāt* reformers of the 1840s to 1860s proceeded with roughly the same policies — not necessarily as a direct continuation of Egyptian activities but as a result of the application of essentially similar considerations. However, the continuation of the process of change in those decades clearly exposed the weaknesses of the Muslim-oriented reform policies of the regional governments, as against the non-Muslim oriented, European guided modernizing schemes which loomed much larger in small Palestine than in Egypt, Syria and Turkey.

When the pace of change accelerated in the last quarter of the century, it was noticeable mostly in this latter sector, which by then consisted of German Templars; "New Yishuv" Jews; Greek, Armenian and other non-Muslim Levantines; and European agencies of all kinds. It was this sector

48 Sabry, p. 370.
49 *Ibid.*, pp. 383-392.
50 Kurd 'Alī, *op. cit.*

that introduced new farming technologies, capitalistic enterprise in agricultural marketing, new trading and financing methods, modern public utilities, urban growth, the first beginnings of industrialization, and a new middle class with a different style of life. This sector maintained a parallel, self-contained system of educational, health, welfare, judicial, banking, postal and other services that existed autonomously. It was based on the Capitulations network, consular protection, immigration from abroad, and the dynamism of European capitalism; and was often inspired by a sense of mission generated by various religious and secular ideologies.

This is not to say that the former sector remained stagnant, as various indications attest to the fact that the country's Muslim-Arab majority was significantly involved in the process of change. Certainly in the towns many components of this society, particularly members of its elite, were adapting themselves to the new needs. Moreover, even in the villages, as one study has pointed out, there is reason to believe that the fellahs showed a greater "capability to respond to the new incentives" than is generally assumed.[51] But it is this sector above all that has been so inadequately studied until now, and only after further research on such subjects as the Jerusalem *'ulamā'*, the family system, local artisanship and trade, the Ottoman bureaucracy, Muslim schools, agrarian relations, rural society etc., will we be able to establish the nature, extent and rhythm of change in this society during the nineteenth century.

Whatever such research reveals, it will not change the most conspicuous feature of the emergence of Modern Times in Palestine, namely, the dominance of the European-based sector in that process. It was precisely this aspect of the process that Egyptian rule in Palestine unintentionally set in motion. In the final analysis, that period's most crucial and lasting consequence was what may be termed "the opening of Palestine," in other words, exposing the country to Europe's modernizing influences and subjecting it to various kinds of Western pressures. It thus may very well be that Polk's thesis on the role of the Egyptian period in initiating modernity in south Lebanon is applicable to Palestine as well, if only we view it in the terms in which eventually Polk himself puts it: "In some ways, then, the Egyptian invasion is comparable to the expeditions of Napoleon to Egypt and Perry to Japan, for it opened the area to foreign, modernizing and disrupting influence on a scale not known before."[52]

This conclusion brings us quite near the view that has long biased studies of the modern history of the Middle East. Revision of that slant, however, should not be allowed to develop into a new bias hindering scholars from drawing the kind of conclusions which, in the particular case of Palestine, the evidence so obviously indicates.

51 Gross, *op. cit.*
52 Polk, p. xix.

AMNON COHEN

Sixteenth Century Egypt and Palestine: The Jewish Connection As reflected in the *Sijill* of Jerusalem

The occupation of Palestine by the Ottoman army and its incorporation into the still expanding Empire meant, *inter alia*, the severing of its formal dependence on Cairo. Palestine became oriented towards the north rather than the south, while Egypt was reduced to an administrative rank similar to that of any other province.

In practical terms this did not amount to any major shift in the ongoing relations between Palestine and Egypt. Although coming as it did in the wake of the discovery of the maritime route around the Horn of Africa to the East, the conquest of the Arabic-speaking provinces did not witness any immediate decline in mercantile shipping through the Red Sea to Egypt proceeding — partially at least — to Palestine. Prof. Inalcık has already shown how, contrary to the prevailing view, an active spice-trade was streaming across the Mediterranean during the first half of the sixteenth century. We have tried to further elaborate this concept as far as concerns the second half of that century: various commodities (e.g. coffee beans, indigo) were reaching Egypt via Jedda from the East and thence proceeding to Jerusalem, as late as 1590[1]. The *Taḥrīr* registers very clearly attest to the fact that there was a steady traffic in spices during the entire sixteenth century, from Egypt to Gaza by way of "the road to Egypt", where a special toll was collected (*'Adet-i bac-i rah-i Misr*).[2] One may even go a step further and suggest that although politically cut off from Egypt, economic relations between Palestine and Egypt actually benefited from the replacement of the declining Mamluk rule by the new, dynamic Ottoman master.

Religious affairs was yet another field where the new political reality had

1 H. Inalcık, "The heyday and decline of the Ottoman Empire" in *The Cambridge History of Islam* (Cambridge, 1970) Vol. I, p. 332; A. Cohen, "Local trade, international trade and government involvement in Jerusalem during the early Ottoman period" in *Asian and African Studies*, Vol. 12, No. 1, p. 11.

2 A. Cohen and B. Lewis, *Population and revenue in the towns of Palestine in the sixteenth century* (Princeton, 1978), p. 55.

no negative effect. The disintegration and fall of the Mamluk state did not undermine the most conspicuous marks of tradition and culture constructed by the Sultans in earlier centuries: the pious foundations (*waqf*). Many of these had been established in and for Jerusalem and Hebron, but since the Mamluk Sultans ruled from Cairo, formal and practical links of mutual benefit were created between the two countries. The *waqf*s of *al-Ḥaramayn al-Sharīfayn* in Jerusalem and Hebron received regular Ottoman financial support from Cairo. The free-kitchen (*Simāṭ*) in the Machpela Cave, for example, was annually provided with the sum of 10,000 *akçe*. Still, after the year 1553-4[3] this entry never reappeared in the *Taḥrīr* registers: the official annual contribution had ceased for an unspecified reason. Here, too, the religious court archives (*sijill*) come to our help and shed some light on the issue. An order sent from Istanbul to Jerusalem in mid-May, 1558, copied in one of these volumes, tells us that the abovementioned sum, which until then had been used to buy wheat for the free-kitchen, was discontinued. It was replaced by the allocation of the revenue of Sawāfīr Sharqī, a village in the district (*Sanjaq*) of Gaza.[4] Though the reason for this change is indicated as being an attempt to bring about the development of the aforementioned village, it should also be viewed in the context of a certain loosening of relations between the two countries. This should not be interpreted as an indication of an overall phenomenon: two separate *firmān*s, dated several years earlier (1555, 1556), very clearly point to the annual visits made by government or religious dignitaries from Jerusalem to Cairo in order to collect the various contributions to the pious foundations of the Temple Mount and the Machpela Cave. On the other hand, special, additional gifts (mats, small carpets) were being sent from Cairo to the most prominent mosques in Palestine.[5] Religious offerings, both regular and sporadic, were usually sent in one direction: to the Holy Shrines in Jerusalem and Hebron. Palestinian support, on the other hand, was requested and given to Cairo in other contexts; for example, towards the end of 1568, when preparations were being made in Cairo for the war in Yemen, a large consignment of over 500 water-bags (*qirab*) was sent there from Jerusalem and Hebron *via* Gaza.[6]

Religious, political or administrative relations, referred to so far had one common feature: they were conducted by official functionaries of the Ottoman state or its religion, Islam. There was, however, an elaborate network of links between the two countries carried out on an individual or communal basis. This was true for the various elements of the population: Muslims, Christians and Jews. The following description is confined to the

3 Cohen and Lewis, *op. cit.*, p. 114.
4 Vol. 32, p. 178.
5 Vol. 32, pp. 20, 68.
6 Vol. 47, p. 150.

latter and reference will be made to the possible relations between the Jewish communities of both countries, or rather between Cairo and Jerusalem.

Jews from Cairo bought landed property in Jerusalem, and Jews from Jerusalem did likewise in Cairo. No element of tax-evasion or avoidance of administrative difficulties is implied, circumstances in both provinces being basically the same. Since no apparent economic or political advantages were in the offing, such transactions should be viewed as an indication of demographic fluctuations. It is somewhat difficult to draw general conclusions as to the possible direction these demographic changes took, since our sources are confined to only a few examples of transactions of this kind. Generally speaking, however, it seems that more Jews were coming from Egypt to Jerusalem to settle or at least to buy landed property there.

As early as mid-June 1534, a Jewish spice-dealer from Jerusalem bought in Cairo an expensive house, from a local Jew, and when the wife of the latter objected to this transaction, it was confirmed and re-confirmed by the *qāḍīs* of the four different rites in Jerusalem, and carried through.[7] Several years later, on September 19, 1537, another Jewish spice-dealer, fearing his approaching death, declared his various belongings at the Muslim religious court in Jerusalem. After the marriage of his daughter in Cairo, the head of the family moved to Jerusalem , where he settled and resumed his commercial activities. He purchased a shop in Jerusalem but still retained his former one in Cairo as well as additional property there.[8] A third example[9] is that of another Jew from Cairo who purchased an impressive building in Jerusalem. The transaction was concluded on March 15, 1554, whereupon Isḥāq, son of Menaḥem Qaṭan of Jerusalem, sold it to a Cairene Jew for a third Jewish party, Ṣadaqa son of Menaḥem, who had remained in Cairo. A fourth case dates back to the very end of the century: several Jews from Cairo together purchased a building in the "Jewish Quarter" in Jerusalem from one who had converted to Islam and preferred to move elsewhere.[10]

All of the above-mentioned transactions should be viewed within a somewhat larger context: that of multi-faceted economic links between the two Jewish communities. The international trade between Cairo and Jerusalem described above was by no means exclusively Muslim. In 1549, for example, a Jew from Jerusalem bought from a Muslim merchant in Cairo a consignment of indigo and ginger, most probably imported from the Far East.[11] There are other indications of Jewish active participation in the

7 Vol. 17, p. 108.
8 Vol. 6, p. 661.
9 Vol. 28, p. 222.
10 Vol. 82, p. 37.
11 Vol. 23, p. 575.

international and inter-provincial spice trade of Palestine and Egypt; we may note here that two out of the four real estate transactions described above were carried out by spice-dealers from Jerusalem: not only could they afford these transactions, they had an ongoing trade between the two towns and thus could move from one place to the other more easily. But while spices were imported into Palestine *via* Egypt, another commodity was exported in the opposite direction: soap.

Olive oil was used for the manufacture of soap in various towns of Palestine, both for local consumption and for export. Several soap factories were in operation in Jerusalem during the sixteenth century, but particularly from the mid-century. Some of the product was sent to Damascus but the major customer was Cairo. The *taḥrīr* register of the year 1553-4 quotes an annual tax levied on the export of about 700 "loads" (*ḥiml*). The *sijill* register puts a "load" of Jerusalem soap at 614 *raṭl*. If we take a *raṭl* to be about three kilograms, then we reach the impressive figure of some 1000 tons of soap.[12] The same entry appears in the *taḥrīr* of 1562-3.[13] This fixed sum, underwritten by the lessor of the income of this specific tax on soap means that in practice a higher sum was levied there and then, probably because of the much larger quantities actually transported. There is no way to speculate on the percentage of this trade sent by Jewish merchants. Still, there is no doubt that they played a considerable role: in 1554, a load of soap bought by a Jew in Cairo was attested at court; in 1572, a prominent Jewish silversmith from Jerusalem had a large consignment of soap especially prepared in a local soap-factory ("cooked" is the term used). This, he then sent to Cairo with a Muslim merchant, who sold the four "loads" (approximately six tons) and returned with the impressive sum of 120 gold coins (*Sulṭānī dhahab*).[14] In mid-June, 1579, a deal concluded earlier was formally confirmed by the Ḥanafite judge of Jerusalem. An affluent Jew from Cairo gave a Muslim merchant in Jerusalem the impressive sum of 800 gold coins for a joint enterprise: the Jerusalemite would buy 42 *qinṭār* of local olive oil and have soap produced from it. When ready, the entire consignment would be sent to the Egyptian counterpart in a safe way and accompanied by reliable people.[15] About the same time another commercial transaction of a similar kind was concluded in Jerusalem: 200 gold

12 W. Hinz, in his *Islamische Masse und Gewichte* (Leiden, 1955), p. 14, puts the *ḥiml* at approximately 250 kg. Had this been valid for our case, then the above figure should be reduced to only 175 tons. The *sijill*, however, is very specific (Vol. 28, p. 473) on the above 614 *raṭl*. Hinz (*op. cit.* p. 29) puts the Palestine *raṭl* at 2.3-2.9 kg., or the Syrian *qinṭār*, which equals 100 *raṭl*s, at 185-228 kg. (p. 26), which might bring the total down to about 800 tons.

13 Cohen and Lewis, *op. cit.* pp. 63, 96.

14 Vol. 28, p. 473; Vol. 55, p. 343.

15 Vol. 58, p. 415.

coins were handed over by an Egyptian Jew to a Jerusalem Jew, who took it upon himself to supply him with soap in return.[16]

Moreover, Jewish involvement in the active soap trade between the two countries was established on a formal, even official level: the special toll on the export of soap "loads" (*resm-i aḥmāl-i ṣābūn*) was supposed to be collected before the merchandise left Jerusalem, since, among other reasons, it was intended that this revenue be used for the upkeep of the *waqf*s of the Temple Mount and Hebron. When, in the early 'eighties, a group of Muslim merchants was blamed for not having complied with this regulation, their explanation was that for many years they had been paying the toll to Da'ūd, a Jewish high official in Cairo (*al-'āmil bi-bāb al-Naṣr*), upon entering the town.[17]

There was brisk traffic in merchants and merchandise of a general nature between the two towns. Some of it was but part of an even larger pattern of commerce between Cairo and Damascus, which extended as far as Istanbul. Towards the end of 1583, a Jerusalem Muslim sued a Cairene Jew who had hired him to deliver a letter from Cairo to another prominent Jew ("Yūsuf Bey") in Istanbul and to bring back an answer.[18] More frequent, though, were shorter trips, between Jerusalem and Cairo, when Jewish merchants either sent their goods with Muslim mule-drivers or hired Muslim attendants to escort them and take charge of their baggage (*'akkāma*).[19]

Some of the Jewish passengers on the route from Cairo were not as innocent as they may have looked: they were moving, or rather fleeing to Jerusalem in an attempt to avoid legal prosecution in Cairo. Early in 1581, a special messenger arrived in Jerusalem bearing an order from the governor of Cairo for the arrest of two Jews, previously of Cairo, who had become residents of the "Jewish Quarter".[20] Unlike this case, where the accused were positively identified and located in Jerusalem, were two other instances dealing with somewhat less solid, but prominent Jews. In the case of the first, in August 1541, an order was sent from Damascus to Jerusalem to arrest a fugitive from Cairo, Ya'qūb, a Jewish assistant to the Jewish money-changer of the governor of Egypt. It was suggested that he had come to Jerusalem after having stolen 300 gold coins from the revenues of Egypt. Forty years later, another Jewish high-ranking official, the former "treasurer" (*'āmil*) of Būlāq in Cairo, named Yāsīf, was declared a fugitive and a letter was sent to Jerusalem for his arrest "plus the many coins and existing things" he had brought there.[21] These repeated events indicate that

16 Vol. 58, pp. 410, 414.
17 Vol. 62, p. 53.
18 Vol. 62, p. 325.
19 Vol. 40, p. 388; Vol. 43, p. 370; Vol. 58, p. 55.
20 Vol. 59, p. 269.
21 Vol. 9, p. 47; Vol. 60, p. 40.

Jerusalem was remote enough to be regarded as a potential hiding-place for fugitives from Cairo. In the opposite direction, too, both the distance and the concept were identical: when the Jewish community of Jerusalem forced its former *Shaykh*, Ya'qūb Fallāq, to emigrate to a remote place, he swore a solemn oath neither to stay in Jerusalem nor to go to Gaza, but to leave for Cairo and live (*tawaṭṭun*) there.[22]

A number of the financial and commercial transactions described above were conducted and concluded in Jerusalem by Jewish pilgrims. The combination of trade and religion, or more specifically trade and pilgrimage, had always been a well-established pattern in the Muslim Middle East. But while Mecca could offer its Muslim pilgrims a large variety of goods brought from remote countries, Jerusalem presented its Jewish pilgrims with mostly local products. Another difference was that while the *Ḥajj* to Mecca was limited to one period only, every year, Jewish pilgrimage to Jerusalem was not officially restricted to any specific time. Practically speaking, however, it was mostly conducted in the spring, to coincide with the Passover Festival. Weather conditions then became clement, the "official" *ziyāra* pilgrimage to the neighboring village of Nabī Samwīl — the burial place of the prophet Samuel — also took place at that time, and the Passover itself, one of the most venerated holidays, had always been regarded as a most appropriate occasion to visit Jerusalem. To quote just one clear example from the *sijill*: the two impressive soap purchasing transactions mentioned above, that were made in mid-1579, were actually concluded during the Passover pilgrimage. One could have reached this conclusion by merely looking at the dates these cases were brought before the *qāḍī*. But in one of them the synchronized aspects were most explicitly stated: the deal was reached and the money in question was given "on Tuesday of the week of Passover as is well known by both of them".[23]

Links between Egyptian Jews and Jerusalem were, as one may have rightly concluded by now, also religious. The inclusion of the Arabic-speaking countries in the body-politic of the Ottoman empire meant, *inter alia*, the imposition of law and order. The generally improved atmosphere facilitated not only trade but also pilgrimage conditions. Jerusalem, an age-long target for pilgrims of all three monotheistic religions, came to be visited frequently by Jews. A *firmān* dated May 15, 1564, and dealing with certain difficulties encountered by these Jewish pilgrims refers to "the Jews of Cairo and of Damascus and of Safed".[24] Though this does not necessarily reflect the order of numerical importance, it should be viewed as an indication of the relative importance of Jewish Egyptian pilgrimage.

Fifteen years later, in a series of court orders[25] issued on June 21, 1579, a

22 Vol. 25, p. 198.
23 *Fī nahār al-thulathā' min jum'at 'īd al-faṭīr al-ma'lūm 'indahuma* (Vol. 58, p. 410).
24 Vol. 45, p. 244.
25 Vol. 58, pp. 444, 533, 536.

reported episode of interest sheds light on some unusual aspects of this pilgrimage. At the beginning of March, 1579 — i.e. some time before Passover — a group of pilgrims from Cairo arrived in Jerusalem. It was headed by 'Aṭiyya (i.e. Nathan) ibn Shmū'il ibn Shams al-Kohān (i.e. Ha-Cohen). The latter served as the official money-changer and treasurer of the governor of Egypt (*Ṣayrafī fī 'l-diwān al-'ālī* or *al-'āmil bi'l-diyār al-Miṣriyya*) and had visited Jerusalem on earlier occasions. In April 1576, for example, he donated olive oil for the illumination of the Machpela Cave in Hebron and in the following months he further commuted between the two countries.[26] These visits, though motivated primarily by Egyptian-Jewish considerations, also had some dimensions of great importance to the Jewish community in Jerusalem. When Nathan ibn Samuel Ha-Cohen arrived there in early March 1579, he brought with him a *fīrmān* issued in Istanbul upon an earlier request from the Jews of Jerusalem.[27] This *fīrmān* was an attempt to redress some of the wrong-doings to which the latter community had been exposed, and was of no direct concern to the Jews of Cairo. But they brought with them another *fīrmān*, which was very pertinent to their pilgrimage: it granted them explicit permission to visit the Holy Places in Jerusalem and Hebron and forbade any attempt to harass them or prevent them from so doing. The very fact that such a document had to be presented is a clear indication that on earlier occasions pilgrims from Egypt had encountered difficulties on entering Jerusalem. One version of the event suggests that this time an attempt was made to also prevent their visiting the town.

Eventually, the group was allowed into the town. A short time later, at the approach of the Passover festival, Nathan returned to Egypt, from where he once again brought to Jerusalem "a large group" of pilgrims. This time, also, an attempt was made to prevent their entry and they had to present their authorization. On this occasion another argument was used against them: they were not genuine pilgrims, but people trying to run away from the infected, diseased Cairo. Furthermore, their very presence in Jerusalem seems to have been an issue of public concern among the Muslims. Not so much because of the alleged raging plague in Cairo but for two other reasons: their arrogant behavior and the rise in the cost of food their presence was instrumental in bringing about. The local Muslim population demanded that an end be made to the prolonged stay of these pilgrims; they were given a ten-day ultimatum, and then another. Only towards the end of June, "when a plague and disease" broke out in Jerusalem, did they depart in haste.

26 Vol. 56, p. 585. His father, Shmu'il Ha-Cohen, had been head of the Jewish community (*Tchelebi*) in Cairo during the late 'sixties and early 'seventies (Sh. Rosanes, *History of the Jews in the Ottoman Empire*, in Hebrew, Tel Aviv, 1930, vol. 2, p. 224; vol. 3, p. 315).

27 Vol. 58, p. 299.

The *sijill* describing the entire episode in no way spares the Jews: they are repeatedly referred to in most derogatory terms, which is very unusual, almost exceptional in this context. It must be a reflection of a deep feeling and a wide reaction not only to one incident at court, but prevalent in the town at large. This episode could not be unique, since it contains clear indications of earlier obstacles put in the way of the Egyptian pilgrims. The question is, why should such a pilgrimage be of importance to anyone other than the pilgrims themselves? It seems that on other occasions, too, these groups had some special feature: on the binding of each volume of the *sijill* there are notes scribbled by the *qāḍīs*, very often important dates to be remembered. Usually these are dates of arrival and departure of governors, judges, etc. The volume dealing with the year 964 A.H., includes the following entry: "The arrival of the Jews from Cairo on 7 Jumādā'l-ūlā, 964 (March 8, 1557)".[28] The fact that the judge recalled this event which was of no intrinsic importance to the town or its population is an indication that this was regarded as an event of some special significance. The reference made twenty-two years later to the tricky Jews who pretend to come on pilgrimage while actually they are fleeing the plague could be of a certain validity, but only to a limited extent. After all, once they had presented their permission to enter, not a word was said as to this alleged threatening and contagious danger. Then there is the economic argument: rising prices as a result of an abruptly increased demand and hence a scarcity in certain commodities, which the local population would like to halt. The complaints against the protracted stay of the Egyptian pilgrims were made by the local inhabitants rather than the authorities, which is itself revealing: a sensitive nerve must have been touched somewhere. Could it be that it was the "arrogance" of the Jews, continually arriving in relatively large numbers, that may have been the real cause of concern? The reasons for the emergence of such friction were specified in detail: "Their lengthy stay, their riding of horses, their changing of clothing, their letting the Muslims walk in front of them, their taking of Muslim girls in captivity and employing them as servants, their assuming power over the poor and their excessive bargaining in prices and the protracted period of their pilgrimage".[29]

The time was one of decline in the Jewish community of Jerusalem: it was decreasing numerically at a very considerable rate, as we have shown elsewhere.[30] These years of depression, coupled with increased harassment by the local authorities, could not but have a negative effect on the morale of those who stayed and most probably kept a lower public profile. For reasons unknown, the annual visit of Egyptian Jews at the beginning of spring seems to have been the diametrical opposite: they came in large

28 Vol. 33, p. 547.
29 Vol. 58, p. 444.
30 R. Mantran (ed.), *Mémorial Ömer Lutfi Barkan* (Paris, 1980), p. 59.

numbers, spent a substantial amount of money and did not heed the customary discriminatory regulations.

The arrival of Egyptian Jews in Jerusalem shortly after the Ottoman occupation and the important role they played in the local community is a well-acknowledged fact. Prominent names like Castro or Shullal known from Jewish sources, occur quite often in the *sijill*, and well deserve a separate discussion. Of equal importance, and perhaps more so, are more diverse dimensions which emerge from the multitudinous volumes of the *sijill*: an ongoing process of strengthening relations between the two communities — demographic, economic, religious and political. These links were of a mutual nature, but there was at least one facet where no reciprocity was envisaged: the sanctity of Jerusalem. The Jews who went there did so for their own reasons and needs. Their visits, however, turned out to be of value to the others. Jewish pilgrimages from Egypt to Jerusalem became an important element in the life of that city, every spring. They left a very noticeable mark on the economy and society and quite often antagonized the local Muslim population. But for the dwindling Jewish local community they served as a positive example and as a much needed source of support. Though difficult to measure, it appears that the above-mentioned activity, multi-faceted as it was, became both a manifestation of and a cause for increasing ties between Cairo and Jerusalem. From the Jewish vantage-point (and perhaps even in a wider perspective) the severance of the formal ties between Palestine and Mamluk Egypt resulted in renewed, more active and dynamic interdependence between them.

JOSEPH R. HACKER

Spiritual and Material Links between Egyptian and Palestinian Jewry in the Sixteenth Century

Throughout the late Middle Ages the Jewish communities in Palestine were strongly supported by other Middle Eastern Jewish communities. At various periods of Mamluk rule, the majority of Palestinian Jewry was of oriental origin, i.e., it included emigrants and pilgrims from Egypt, Syria, Persia, Yemen and North Africa, as well as a local element. Only as of the late fifteenth century did European Jews form the major segment of the Jewish population, as a result of the extensive migrations of Jews from Christian Europe and the western zone of the Mediterranean to the eastern, including Palestine.[1] Nevertheless, Palestinian Jewry's ties with Egyptian Jewry, and its dependence on the latter's goodwill were eventually strengthened. Beset by a lack of resources and difficulty in making a livelihood, the growing Jewish population in Palestine became more dependent on their brethren abroad, especially in Egypt, in the first decades of the sixteenth century.[2]

★ ★ ★

The mass emigration of the last decade of the fifteenth century and the first half of the sixteenth brought a considerable influx of Jews into Egypt,

1 On these migrations see J. Hacker, "The Connections of Spanish Jewry with Eretz-Israel between 1391 and 1492" (in Hebrew), *Shalem* (Studies in the History of the Jews in Eretz-Israel), Vol. 1 (1974), pp. 105-154. There, on pp. 128, 132 sources that deal with Oriental Jewry and its migration are cited; *id.*, "Some letters on the Expulsion of the Jews from Spain and Sicily", (in Hebrew) in *Studies in the History of Jewish Society..., Presented to Professor Jacob Katz* (ed. E. Etkes; Y. Salmon), Jerusalem 1980, pp. 64-97.

2 See for example R. Gottheil; W.H. Worrell, *Fragments from the Cairo Genizah in the Freer Collection*, New York 1927, pp. 246-265, and the corrections by S. Asaf, in *Zion* (Measef), Vol. 2 (1932), pp. 120-122; A. Yaari, *Letters from Eretz-Israel* (in Hebrew), Tel-Aviv 1943, no. 25; and other sources on the influence of Isaac Ha-Kohen Sholal on Palestinian Jewry. On the help of the community of Cairo to the community of Safed, see Eliyahu Capsali, *Seder Eliyahu Zuta*, Vol. 1, Jerusalem 1975, pp. 349-350.

too.[3] Some of them found it necessary to explain and rationalize their stay in Egypt, for according to the *Halacha* (Jewish Law) permanent settlement of Jews in Egypt was a controversial and thorny issue[4]. According to some of the sages it was forbidden, even in the Middle Ages, since it violated the command of the Bible: "Thou shalt no more return by this way" (Deut. 17, 16). Nonetheless, Maimonides lived in Egypt after he stayed with his family in Palestine, and an important community flourished there for many centuries. R. David ibn Zimra, who served as Chief Rabbi of Egyptian Jewry (c. 1516-c.1558), expresses this ambivalent attitude: "It is the intention of all of us to return and to dwell in the Land of Israel. It is only on this basis that we permit ourselves to dwell in Egypt; for otherwise we would be violating the command in the Torah.... We are not in Egypt to settle permanently but only to dwell here temporarily and as soon as we are able we shall go to the Land of Israel".[5]

Small wonder then that this attitude, which prevailed among Jewish scholars and sages, together with their yearning to live and settle in the Land of Israel — the Holy Land, led to a continuous migration of scholars from Egypt to Palestine. Nevertheless, according to David ibn Zimra: "...Most scholars and rabbis who come to Egypt [do not settle, they] are just en route to Palestine and that is why they do not interfere with local customs...".[6]

A close examination of the biographies of the celebrated scholars of Egyptian Jewry in the sixteenth century validates this observation. Since the time of the so called Eliah of Ferrara,[7] who emigrated to Palestine in 1437 after serving as rabbi in Cairo, and until the beginning of the seventeenth century, almost all the celebrated scholars in Egypt made pilgrimages, emigrated, or at least attempted to emigrate to Palestine. These scholars include: R. Isaac Sholal and his academy, R. Jacob Mitreil, R. Joseph Saragossa, R. Jacob Berab, R. Abraham Zacuto, the family of Moses of Trani and Joseph of Trani, members of the Castellazzo family, R.

3 See for example E. Strauss (Ashtor), *The History of the Jews in Egypt and Syria under the Mamlūk Rule* (in Hebrew) Vol. 2, Jerusalem 1951, pp. 401 sqq.; M. Littman, "The Connections between Egypt and Crete in the 16th and 17th centuries" (in Hebrew), *Sinai*, Vol. 88 (1981), p. 48, n. 3.

4 There is a considerable amount of rabbinic literature concerning this issue. One of the latest discussions is the article: "Israel and Egypt in Halachic Sources" (in Hebrew), written by Rabbi Judah Gershoni, *Ha-Tzofeh* (daily), 21.9.79; He devoted two chapters of his book: *Kol Zofaich* (in Hebrew), Jerusalem 1980, pp. 439-468 to this topic. Of the former discussions see for example Jacob Sapir, *Even Sapir*, part 1, Lyck 1766, pp. 30b-37b; M. Kasher (ed.), *Torah Shlema* (in Hebrew), Jerusalem 1951, Vol. 14, pp. 279-284, and the sources there.

5 *Responsa*, Vol. IV, no. 73. See I.M. Goldman, *The Life and Times of Rabbi David Ibn Abi Zimra*, New York 1970, p. 13.

6 *Responsa*, Vol. III, no. 94.

7 On him see A. Yaari, *op.cit.* ed. J. R. Hacker, (n. 2), no. 18.

Isaac Luria Ashkenazi (Ha-Ari), R. Bezalel Ashkenazi, R. Jacob Castro and even R. Meir Gavison, R. Haim Kafussi and others. There is no need to emphasize that these central figures and other scholars who preached affection for Palestine and fulfilled their religious duty, deeply influenced their flock. Furthermore, as a result of these migrations strong ties were created between the Egyptian and the Palestinian communities, due to family connections. In the Cairo Genizah we find the correspondence of some of these scholars and their families or friends in Egypt or Palestine, as well as other family correspondence, such as letters in Yiddish of an Ashkenazi widow to her son in Egypt (1566-7).[8]

This attitude of the Jewish scholars and sages in Egypt towards Palestine in the sixteenth century was by no means uniform. As a result of the migration of Sephardi and North African Jews to Egypt in the last decades of the fifteenth and throughout the sixteenth centuries, an important center of learning was established in Cairo.[9] For the first time in the late Middle Ages, scholars and students of various fields in Judaism went to Egypt to study.[10] Well known Spanish scholars and some Ashkenazis taught in the academies of the Jews in Cairo and Alexandria.[11] Economic problems in Palestine (especially in Jerusalem and the southern part of the land, in the first decades of the sixteenth century, and Safed too at the end of the century), and the fame of these scholars and academies, combined to create a different pattern: a migratory trend among scholars and youngsters yearning for better conditions of study under the supervision and guidance of these scholars. We find a figure of the stature of R. Jacob Berab, one of the most celebrated Spanish-Jewish scholars of the first half of the sixteenth century, moving with his family and students back and forth from Jerusalem to Cairo and Safed, leaving his son behind in Cairo;[12] likewise persons such as David ibn Zimra (Jerusalem-Cairo-Jerusalem-Safed),[13]

8 A new edition of the known material and new letters of this later correspondence will be published by H. Turnianski, in *Shalem*, Vol. 4 (1984), in print.

9 See note 3.

10 See for example David ibn Zimra, *Responsa*, Vol. IV, no. 94; Moses ibn Al-Ashkar, *Responsa*, no. 31 and many other sources.

11 A study of the cultural activities of Egyptian Jewry in the 15th-16th centuries is still a desideratum.
See lately: D. Tamar, "The Early Activity of R. Isaac Luria (Ha-Ari) in Egypt" (in Hebrew), *Zion*, Vol. 44 (1979), pp. 229-240 (esp. pp. 232-239); I.M. Goldman, *op. cit.* (note 5); M. Littman, *Egyptian Jewry in the XVI and XVII Centuries* (According to the Responsa of Contemporary Rabbis), Ph. D. Thesis (in Hebrew), Bar-Ilan University, Ramat Gan 1978, p. 169. (This study lacks historical perspective and is based only on a limited section of sources.)

12 See: H.Z. Dimitrovsky, "Rabbi Yaakov Berab's Academy" (in Hebrew), *Sefunot*, Vol. 7 (1963), pp. 41-102.

13 See notes 5 and 11 above.

Moses al-Ashkar, the Trani family,[14] R. Asher Lemlyn Ashkenazi,[15] R. Menahem De Lonzano and many others. Even members of the mystic circle of Isaac Luria of Safed, which disintegrated after his sudden death in the 'seventies, found their way to Egypt. These included Joseph ibn Tabul, Haim Vital, Joshua Ben Nun and others.[16]

This mutual trend and appreciation found its expression in the Responsa of the scholars. Questions and responses were sent from sage to sage, from one country to the other, on the basis of personal acquaintance and mutual esteem. From the vast literature of the scholars of Palestine and Egypt it is evident that while in the first half of the sixteenth century (especially c. 1500-c. 1530) the Egyptian center was as important as the Palestinian, from the 'forties on, the center of Safed overshadowed that of Egypt as well as that of Jerusalem. This fact is properly stated by Moses of Trani of Safed who exclaims: "...We know that they [the scholars of Egypt — J.H.] are versed in the law... and know the intricacies of the calendar. In spite of that, they behave deferentially towards us and show us honor. Because we are in Palestine, they frequently consult us on legal matters on which they themselves disagree or which are problematic for them. Because they are unable to assert their authority over their community we assist them in this and render the decision".[17]

In the 'twenties, R. Abraham Ha-Levi wrote to the scholars in Cairo with great humility: "If I have erred, instruct me and I shall be silent. For you are scholars and sages well suited to teach and render judgment." He continues, referring to the controversy among the scholars of Jerusalem: "Your decisions are authoritative and therefore you must not abdicate your responsibilities in teaching and passing judgment."[18]

However, in the 'thirties and 'forties the Palestinian scholars in Safed and Jerusalem began to assert their supremacy, which by the 'fifties was undisputed. The main reason for this supremacy was the growth, success and originality of the academies of Safed in the field of law and codification on the one hand, and the emergence and immense influence of mystical brotherhoods *(havurot)* on the other. Last but not least, the very fact that these scholars remained in the Holy Land suffering unfavorable economic

14 See H. Bentov, "Autobiographical and Historical Register of Rabbi Josef Trani" (in Hebrew), *Shalem*, Vol. 1 (1974), pp. 195-228 (esp. pp. 206, 218-219).

15 See E. Kupfer, "The Visions of R. Asher ben Meir the so called Lemlyn Roitlingen" (in Hebrew), *Kobez AL-YAD* (Minora Manuscripta Hebraica), New Series, Vol. 8 (18), Jerusalem 1976, pp. 385-423.

16 G. Scholem, *"Shtar Ha-Hitkashrut Shel Talmidei Ha-Ari"*, *Zion*, Vol. 5 (1940), pp. 133-160; M. Benayahu, "Rabbi Haim Vital in Jerusalem", *Sinai*, Vol. 30 (1952), pp. 65-75; *id.*, "Rabbi Ḥiya Rofe and his book 'Maase Ḥiya' ", *Areshet*, Vol. 2 (1960), pp. 109-129.

17 Moses of Trani, *Responsa*, Venice 1630, Vol. II, no. 206.

18 *Kerem Ḥemed*, Vol. IX (1856), pp. 141, 148.

conditions, especially in Jerusalem, and that they devoted themselves to study and to living an exemplary life, lent them an aura of sanctity.[19]

This image and influence was further nurtured by the claim of the scholars of Safed that they were the only ordained *(semuchim)* sages, following the act of ordination initiated by R. Jacob Berab in 1538. This action was the sheer result of the increased number of scholars in Safed on the one hand, and their strong messianic impetus on the other.[20] We do not know to what extent this claim was accepted by Jewish scholars in the diaspora, and in Egypt in particular.[21] But it is evident that since then in only a very few cases were inquiries on the part of sixteenth century Safed scholars addressed to their counterparts in Egypt on questions of *Halacha*, even in instances of dispute amongst them. Rather, we have numerous questions on the subject of proper conduct, according to the *Halacha*, in practical matters, as well as theological matters, directed by scholars in Egypt to the scholars of Safed and Jerusalem. These questions shed light on the vivid and vigorous life of the Jews in Egypt in that period. Various questions deal with disputes and factions within the Egyptian Rabbinical authorities and lay leadership, such as the well known quarrel between *Musta'rib*s and *Maghribi*s in Cairo in 1527;[22] the quarrel of Rabbi Jacob Tibbon and the *Mu'allim* Solomon Al-Ashkar in 1561;[23] or several disputes between Egyptian scholars, i.e. the disputes between Haim Kafussi, Abraham Monson and Solomon Gavison.[24]

In sum, strong spiritual ties prevailed between Egyptian and Palestinian Jewry, based on personal acquaitance and family ties, and sustained by an admiration for the exemplary life of the Palestinian sages and their intellectual acumen.

Whereas at the beginning of the sixteenth century the dependence of Palestinian Jewry on Egypt was both spiritual and economic in nature, in the latter half of the century, especially in Safed, this dependence was primarily economic.

19 See D. Tamar, *Studies in the History of the Jewish People in Eretz Israel and in Italy* (in Hebrew), Jerusalem 1970, pp. 69-86, 95-100; R.J.Z. Werblowski, *Joseph Karo, Lawyer and Mystic*, London 1962; M. Benayahu, "A Document from the First Generation of the Spanish Exiled" (in Hebrew), *S. Assaf Memorial Volume*, Jerusalem 1953, pp. 109-125; *id.*, "The Revival of Ordination in Safed" (in Hebrew), *I. F. Baer Jubilee Volume*, Jerusalem 1960, pp. 248-269.

20 J. Katz, "The Controversy on the Semikha (Ordination) between Rabbi Jacob Berab and Rabbi Levi ben-Habib" (in Hebrew), *Zion*, Vol. 16 (1951), pp. 28-45.

21 In contrast to M. Benayahu, in *I. F. Baer Jubilee Volume, op. cit.*, note 19.

22 H. Z. Hirschberg, "The Agreement between the Mustate'ribs and the Maghribis in Cairo 1527", *S.W. Baron Jubilee Volume*, Jerusalem 1975, pp. 577-590.

23 A. Scheiber and M. Benayahu, "A Communication of the Rabbis of Egypt to Rabbi David ibn Zimra" (in Hebrew), *Sefunot*, Vol. 6 (1962), pp. 127-134.

24 Yom-Tov Zahalon, Responsa, Venice 1694, no. 129. See M. Benayahu, "Rabbi Ḥiya Rofe" etc., *op. cit.*, in note 16.

It goes without saying that on the level of popular religion the Jews of Egypt regarded their Palestinian brethren as their vicars in the Holy Land: they were beseeched to pray for their welfare, to light candles and oil lamps in the holy places, and to tend the graves of their loved ones.

★ ★ ★

At the material level, however, the patterns of relationship between the Jews of Egypt and Palestine in the sixteenth century differed considerably. While Egyptian Jews continued to visit Palestine as pilgrims, few came on business trips.[25] Pilgrimages, especially to Jerusalem were made frequently, and particularly just prior to Passover. On such occasions, money was sent by the Egyptian communities or by individuals in fulfillment of their pledge to support the poor of Jerusalem and other cities, to purchase oil for the lamps of synagogues and holy places, and to finance the academies of Jerusalem and Safed.[26] Jewish merchants arriving at the ports in Egypt were asked to contribute half a *Meidi* per *Balla* to the poor of Jerusalem.[27] These and other contributions and gifts were sent to Palestine regularly to support and strengthen the Jewish communities that were unable to maintain themselves.

In contrast, Palestinian Jews traveled to Egypt mainly for business purposes. The journey between the two countries was considered to be short and safe,[28] and caravans frequently traversed the route. Messengers were sent from Palestine to the Egyptian communities in times of stress or economic decline.[29] In view of the economic plight of the Jews of Palestine, Egyptian Jews settling there would invest their capital in Egypt and use the income therefrom to support themselves. Others were helped by funds or public aid. Egypt's economic activity, especially commerce, and its proxim-

25 David ibn Zimra, *Responsa*, Vol. I, no. 398.

26 See for example *Responsa Tashbez* (Salomon ben Zemah Duran), Vol. 3, no. 201; *The Itineraries of R. Moses Basola to Palestine (1522)* (in Hebrew), ed. I. Ben Zvi, Jerusalem 1939, pp. 62, 83.
On these topics see: A. Yaari, *Letters from Eretz-Israel* (n. 2 above); *id., Travele in Eretz-Israel*, Tel-Aviv 1946; *id., Emissaries of Eretz-Israel*, Jerusalem 1951, s.v. indexes; I. Szepanski, *Eretz-Israel in the Responsa Literature*, Vol. 1-3, Jerusalem 1967-1979, s.v. indexes; A. Shohat et al., "The Synagogue on the Tomb of the Prophet Samuel" (in Hebrew), *Bulletin of the Jewish Palestine Exploration Society*, Vol. 6 (1939), pp. 81-86; 141-144; *ibid.*, vol. 10 (1943), pp. 12-17; A. Cohen, *Ottoman Documents on the Jewish Community of Jerusalem in the 16th Century*, Jerusalem 1976; S. Assaf, *Texts and Studies in Jewish History* (in Hebrew), Jerusalem 1946, s.v. index.

27 *Responsa* of David ibn Zimra, No. 2248 (in the Warsaw edition).

28 *Ibid.*, vol. III, No. 408.

29 See for example: A. Yaari, *Emissaries of Eretz-Israel* (see n. 26), index; A. Marx, "Zwei Briefe Berühmter Gelehrter aus dem 16. Jahrhundert", *Jacob Freimann Jubilee Volume*, Berlin 1937, pp. 167-170; Yom-Tov Zahalon, *Responsa*, No. 129.

ity to Palestine, were important assets. In consequence it became the favored place for financial investment, especially for Jews in Jerusalem who preferred to keep their means of livelihood beyond the reach of local officials. Several documents from the beginning to the end of the century attest that Palestinian Jews continuously went to Egypt to earn their living. Others maintained regular commercial correspondence with Egypt, some of which is preserved in the Cairo Genizah and in scattered manuscripts.[30]

In addition to this general overview of Palestinian dependence on the Egyptian communities, as well as on other Jewish communities of the Ottoman Empire and Italy, the sources allow us to make distinctions of time and place regarding mutual relations between the Jews of both lands.

While the dependence of the Palestinian communities on Egyptian Jewry was immense in the first decades of the sixteenth century, as a result of Mamluk rule in Palestine, following the establishment of Ottoman rule this dependence dwindled until it ceased. Between c. 1500-1516, and as late as 1524, R. Isaac Sholal — the so-called *Nagid* or leader of the Jews in the Mamluk state — was the main supporter of the Jews of Palestine. He granted exemption of taxes to scholars in Jerusalem and to some in Safed, paid for the maintenance of the academies in Jerusalem, and financially supported scholars and communities. Those dissatisfied with his attitude or with reservations about local leaders would try their best to influence his decisions. Nevertheless, and inclusive of Jerusalem, where his influence was enormous, even the community statutes were formulated by him and his court in Egypt, and only later confirmed and endorsed by the local scholars and lay leadership.[31] Later on, under Ottoman rule, some of the statutes were rectified and even annuled for a certain period,[32] but the impact of most was strong and they were adhered to until the nineteenth century. During the late Mamluk rule there was also a *Vice-Nagid*, probably the *Nagid's* substitute in Jerusalem,[33] who maintained great influence in the community.

30 See recently A. Cohen, *The Jewish Community of Jerusalem in the 16th Century*, (in Hebrew) Jerusalem 1982. Data on this aspect is to be found in the archival sources, as well as in the responsa literature and the letters found in the Genizah, on fiscal transactions and commerce, between Palestinian and Egyptian Jews. See for example the published letters of David ibn Zimra and R. Isaac Luria (Ha-Ari) — additional letters of these celebrities are available in manuscripts.

31 See notes 2; 19 above. The full range of his activities and his influence still needs research. See the latest article: I. Robinson, "Messianic Prayer Vigils in Jerusalem in the Early Sixteenth Century", *JQR*, LXXI (1981), pp. 32-42. Cf. the thorough and richly documented description of E. Strauss (Ashtor), (n. 3 above), vol. 2, pp. 84-87, 237-250, 488 sqq.

32 See J. Hacker, "The Djizya Payments of the Jewish Population in Palestine in the 16th Century — A Legal and Historical Inquiry" (in Hebrew), *Shalem*, vol. 4 (1984), in print.

33 See J. Hacker, "The Nagidate in North-Africa at the End of the Fifteenth Century" (in Hebrew), *Zion*, vol. 45 (1980), pp. 127-128.

After the termination of the office of *Negidut*, men of influence and wealth who had connections with the Ottoman authorities, such as Abraham Castro,[34] also wielded great influence over Palestinian Jewry, but this was a long way from and less important than the Egyptian *Negidim*. Since the center of the Ottoman administration in the area moved to Damascus, there was little further need (or use) for intervention on behalf of the Jews of Palestine in Cairo. Palestinian Jewry (especially in Safed) strengthened its connections with the important Jewish community of Damascus and its notables,[35] and when intervention at the central government level was needed the Jews of Constantinople took over the role formerly played by Egyptian Jewry.

The process of these changes was quite different in Jerusalem, Hebron and Gaza on the one hand, and Safed and the Galilee on the other. Jerusalem and other southern communities remained far more under the influence of Egyptian Jewry than did the northern communities. The list of rabbis in Jerusalem in the sixteenth century provides us with clear evidence of this impact. Figures such as R. David ibn Zimra, R. Bezalel Ashkenazi and others served as rabbis in Jerusalem, but in Safed the case was quite different. Here there were close connections with Damascene Jewry; Rabbis and students from Safed stayed in Damascus and vice versa.[36]

There is no doubt that the predominant Egyptian influence in Jerusalem and the dependence of that community on Egyptian Jewry were a consequence of Jerusalem's weak economy. In comparison the large Safed Jewish community, then at its peak, its fame spreading throughout the Jewish world, felt strong enough to intervene in disputes within the Egyptian Jewish community. Its sudden collapse in the last decade of the century brought about radical change and Safed's relations with Egypt became similar to those of Jerusalem.

It is quite evident that there was a similarity in the patterns of relation-

34 On this personality see lately H. Gerber, "An Unknown Turkish Document on Abraham Di Castro" (in Hebrew), *Zion*, vol. 45 (1980), pp. 158-163; A. Cohen, "Were the Walls of Jerusalem Built by Abraham Castro?" (in Hebrew), *Zion*, vol. 47 (1982), pp. 405-417; E. Shochetman, "Additional Information on the Life of R. Abraham Castro" (in Hebrew), *Zion*, vol. 48 (1983), pp. 387-405.

35 These connections, economic and cultural, are richly documented in various Hebrew sources of the period, from the very beginning to the end of the 16th century. See J. Hacker, "On the Intellectual Character and Self-Perception of Spanish Jewry in late Fifteenth Century" (in Hebrew), *Sefunot*, new series, vol. 2 (17) (1983), pp. 39-47, 69-70; A. Cohen, "Damascus and Jerusalem" (in Hebrew), *ibid*, pp. 97-104; H. Z. Dimitrovsky, "Rabbi Yaacov Berab's" etc., op. cit., in no. 12; A. David, "Further Data on the Pogrom of 1517 Against the Jews of Safed" (in Hebrew), *Cathedra*, no. 8 (1978), pp. 190-194.

36 Close ties between the rabbis and intellectuals, as well as students of religious studies, in these centers, prevailed already in the 15th century.

ship between Egyptian Jewry and Palestinian Jewry in the sixteenth and seventeenth centuries, and even throughout the entire period of the Middle Ages and up to the eighteenth century. This was due to factors basic to life in the area and to prevailing attitudes within Jewish society and the latter's place within the non-Jewish society.

The differences over the centuries, it seems, lay mainly in the interplay of the basic forces determining the attitudes, but the forces and the attitudes themselves did not alter radically, and sometimes not at all, from one century to the next. In short, no long-lasting changes really took place — in the size of population, the attitude toward domicile in Palestine and Egypt, the occupations of Jews, their legal status, etc. — at the end of the Middle Ages or in the sixteenth and seventeenth centuries, nor was there any basic shift in the life styles of these communities.

★ ★ ★

The major trends in attitude in these centuries could be summarized as follows:

1. Unlike the Muslims, the Jews of the Middle East under Ottoman rule (as well as Jews in other countries and the Christians) considered Palestine as the Holy Land and as a special and unique entity. They ignored the question of whether the Muslim authorities regarded Palestine as a special entity and whether it had a different policy towards that entity.

   Jews abroad regarded the Palestinian communities primarily as their vicars and protectors of their interests in the Holy Land. This point of view was of course acceptable to Palestinian Jewry who took advantage of it and demanded diplomatic help and economic support, in the name of this ideology. No Jewish community in Europe or in the East, and no Jewish scholar or leader, ever challenged this attitude in the Middle Ages or in the sixteenth and seventeenth centuries.

2. Egyptian Jewry was particularly touchy in its attitude toward the Palestinian Jews, since according to their own ideology, which was accepted at least in scholarly and rabbinical circles, their very stay in Egypt was not proper or was at least subject to debate according to the *Halacha*. This stand nurtured and influenced their attitude towards the Jews of Palestine, who unlike themselves were in line with religious obligations and led an exemplary life.

3. These and other reasons determined the fact that in contrast to the situation within Muslim society, Palestine in the sixteenth century

> was not just a province of Cairo or Damascus in the eyes of Jewish intellectuals, but a center of authority handing down decisions and ideology which had a profound influence on Egyptian Jewry.

The fact that many European (Spanish, Portuguese, German) and Oriental (and North-African) Jewish scholars settled on the eve of the century and later in Palestine, marked the authority of the Palestinian scholars who combined fame, with an aura of sanctity together with an inherited reputation of their former authoritative standing. Egyptian Jewry had its own scholars and intellectuals but it never attained such standing in the sixteenth century, although some of its members were highly regarded on a personal basis.

Personal acquaintance and family ties between Egyptian and Palestinian Jews, especially in scholarly circles, were of major importance in determining the relationship between both these societies.

In contrast to relations at the spiritual and intellectual levels, the dependence of the Palestinian communities on those of Egypt was immense, and in the long run was decisive in determining their dependence on Egyptian Jewry and its leadership in various spheres of life.

MINNA ROZEN

The Relations between Egyptian Jewry and the Jewish Community of Jerusalem in the Seventeenth Century

During the Mamluk period close links were maintained between the Jewish community of Jerusalem and Egyptian Jewry. This linkage was mainly based on the authority of the leader of Egyptian Jewry, in Hebrew, the *Nagid*, over all the Jews of the Mamluk state. It was the *Nagid* who appointed the leaders of the Jewish Communities in the Middle East, the *Shuyūh al-Yahūd.*[1]

The *Nagid* wielded great economic power and was the main source of support of the scholars of the Jewish communities in Palestine; thus Egyptian Jewry brought much influence to bear on the cultural elite of Jewish society.[2]

When the area was conquered in 1516 by the Ottomans, the two communities remained under one rule, but the authority of the *Nagid* over the Jews of Palestine came to an end and, finally, the *Nagid* ceased also to be the leader of Egyptian Jewry.[3].

1 On the *Nagid* of Egyptian Jewry: E. Strauss (Ashtor), *History of the Jews in Egypt and Syria under the Rule of the Mamluks* (in Hebrew), Jerusalem 1951, Vol. 2, pp. 500-509; M. Rozen, "The Position of the Musta'rabs and the Intercommunal Relationships in Eretz Israel from the End of the Fifteenth to the End of the Seventeenth Century" (in Hebrew), *Cathedra* 17 (October 1980), p. 75, No. 9; Rabbi 'Ovadiah of Bertinoro's Letter (1488) in A. Ya'ari, *Letters from Eretz Israel* (in Hebrew), Ramat Gan 1971, p. 122.

2 R. Gottheil & W. H. Worrel (eds.), *Fragments from the Cairo Geniza in the Freer Collection*, New York, 1927, pp. 246-258. See criticism in: S. Assaf (in Hebrew), *Zion* (collection), 1926, pp. 120-122; M. Benayahu, "A Document from the First Generation of the Expulsion from Spain in Safed" (in Hebrew), *Assaf Book*, Jerusalem 1952, pp. 109-125; M. Rozen, *op. cit.*, p. 91; Rabbi Israel of Perugia's Letter (in Hebrew), A. Ya'ari, *op. cit.*, pp. 171; 178.

3 H. Gerber, "An Ottoman Document on Abraham di Castro — Leader of Egyptian Jewry in the 16th Century" (in Hebrew), *Zion* 45 (1980), pp. 158-163; A. David, "On the End of the 'Negidut' in Egypt and the Life of Abraham di Castro" (in Hebrew), *Tarbiz* 41 (1972), pp. 333-334. On Abraham di Castro see also A. Cohen, "Were the Walls of Jerusalem Built by Abraham Castro?" (in Hebrew), *Zion* 47 (1982), pp. 407-418; E. Shochetman, "Additional Information on the Life of R. Abraham Castro" (in Hebrew), *Zion* 48 (1983), pp. 387-405.

The connection between the two communities developed in new directions and in this paper the nature and substance of these connections during the seventeenth century will be described and analysed.

A. Caravans and Pilgrimage

A two-way population movement marked the relationships between the two communities and was the basis of many of the forms and directions in which these relationships and connections developed.

Throughout the generations Jerusalem had remained an object of pilgrimage for the Jews, especially those living in the Middle East for whom access was not difficult.[4] The main Jewish pilgrimage to Jerusalem accompanied the annual caravan from Egypt every Passover.[5]

This caravan, which was described by A. Cohen according to the sixteenth century *sijill* documents,[6] is mentioned in Hebrew letters from Jerusalem, most of them written by the Community's leaders. Its main function was the religious fulfillment of the biblical commandment obligating all male Jews to visit Jerusalem three times a year, including Passover. The popularity of that festival as a time of pilgrimage was no doubt connected with the climate, at that time of the year most conducive to travel. Christians, and probably Muslims too, would join the caravan, taking the opportunity to go to Jerusalem for their own religious purposes, or other reasons.[7]

During the seventeenth century and most likely before that, too, the caravan had a variety of purposes. We have no direct evidence that it was used for trade in the seventeenth century but since other caravans coming from

4 Pilgrimage to Jerusalem in the 17th century: Rabbi Abraham ben Mordekhai Halevi, *Ginat Veradim Responsa* (in Hebrew), Istanbul, 1716, Vol. I, *Oraḥ Ḥayim*, No. 1, 2, p. 1b; Rabbi Moshe ibn Ḥabib, *Kol Gadol Responsa* (in Hebrew), Jerusalem 1970, No. 1, p. 1a; Rabbi Ya'akov Ḥagiz, *Halakhot Ketanot Responsa* (in Hebrew), Jerusalem 1974, part I, No. 4, p. 1a,; Rabbi Ḥisdayi HaCohen Pirḥyia, *Torat Ḥesed Responsa* (in Hebrew), Salonica 1733, No. 1, p. 1a; Rabbi Yoshiyahu Pinto, *Nivḥar Mikesef Responsa* (in Hebrew), Aleppo, 1869, No. 8, p. 9a; Rabbi Shelomo Ben Binyamin Halevi, *Lev Shelomo Responsa* (in Hebrew), Salonica 1808, No. 60, p. 77b; Rabbi Natan Gota & Rabbi Yehuda Ḥavilio, *Responsa* (in Hebrew), Oxford Ms. No. 845 in Neubauer Catalog, microfilm in the National Library in Jerusalem 21606, p. 271a; *Letters carried by Jerusalem Emissaries in the 17th Century* (in Hebrew), Ms. 8°61 in the National Library in Jerusalem (below Jerusalem Ms.), Letter No. 106, p. 142, to a rich Jew in Persia who visited Jerusalem some months before the letter was written; Letter No. 136, p. 160, probably to the same person; E. Roger, *La Terre Sainte*, Paris, 1664, pp. 367-369.

5 Jerusalem Ms. 8°61, Letter No. 21, pp. 65-6; 42, p. 87; 107, p. 143.

6 A. Cohen, "Sixteenth Century Egypt and Palestine: The Jewish Connection", (in this volume).

7 Jerusalem Ms., letter No. 21, pp. 65-66.

Egypt to Jerusalem brought all sorts of commodities, we see no reason to believe that the spring caravan played no commercial role.[8]

An important function of the caravan, from the point of view of the Jews, was the opportunity to transfer money from Egypt to Jerusalem. In several letters sent by the heads of the Jewish community in Jerusalem, there is mention of the fact that financial aid from Egyptian Jewry arrived annually by way of that caravan earmarked for impoverished scholars and the poor in general.[9] The regularity of this aid was sometimes the basis for loans made by the leaders of the community of Jerusalem from rich Muslims of the town, in order to help the poor. If the caravan arrived without the money, the leaders of the Jewish community would write urgent letters to the leaders of the communities in Egypt to ensure its transfer along with the next caravan.[10].

The same caravan and presumably others, too, had also another purpose. Jerusalem was considered the ideal place to be buried. According to the Jewish tradition he who was buried in the Valley of Yehoshafat would not suffer the agonies of transferal beneath the earth to the place of the last Judgement, and would be among the first to be resurrected.[11]

Jews of sufficient means did not hesitate to instruct their heirs to transfer their remains for burial on the Mount of Olives, facing the Valley of Yehoshafat, no matter what distance was involved. For example, a rich Jewish merchant of the Marranos, established in Amsterdam under the name of Senior Manuel Piamential, and known among the Jews as Iẓhak ibn Yakar, wrote a will in the year 1611 in which he requested that if possible his remains should be transferred for burial in Jerusalem.[12] It was only natural that among Jews living so much closer to Jerusalem, the phenomenon of transferal of remains for reinternment in Jerusalem was much more widespread. The spring caravan as well as others were widely used for this purpose a fact which is mentioned both in the *responsa* literature and correspondence.[13]

8 Francesco da Serino, *Croniche o. Annali di Terra Santa*, ed. Teodoro Cavallon, Firenze, 1939, Parte II, Lib. II, Cap. 29 (anno 1638), p. 295.

9 Jerusalem Ms., Letters No. 21, p. 65; 42, p. 87; 107, p. 143.

10 Jerusalem Ms., Letters No. 42, p. 87; 107, p. 143; 111, p. 145; 117, p. 150.

11 On the value of burial in the Valley of Yehoshafat and Mount of Olives, see: Rabbi Shelomo ben Ẓema Duran's *Responsa* (in Hebrew), Lemberg 1891, Part 3, No. 288, p. 42 a-b; Rabbi Natan Shapira, *Tuv Haareẓ* (in Hebrew), Jerusalem 1891, p. 15a; 31b; Rabbi Moshe Ḥagiz, *Sefat Emet* (in Hebrew), Wilna 1876, pp. 24-28. On Jews coming to die in Jerusalem in that period, see: M. Rozen, The Jewish Community in Jerusalem from the End of the 16th Century to the End of the 17th Century (in Hebrew), Ph.D. Thesis, Tel Aviv University 1976, p. 16. No. 1.

12 Rabbi Abraham Halevi, *'Ein Mishpat Responsa* (in Hebrew), Salonica 1802, *Ḥoshen Mishpat*, No. 45, pp. 66a. On that subject also G. Sandys, *A Relation of a Journey Begun A.D. 1610*, London, 1615, p. 148.

13 Rabbi David ibn Zimra's *Responsa* (in Hebrew), New York 1967, Part II, No. 611, p. 40a; No. 741, p. 25a; Jerusalem Ms., Letter No. 118, p. 151.

The importance of the Egyptian caravan in the life of the town, clearly understood from the *sijill* documents of the sixteenth century, is as clearly expressed in the letters of the community leaders. One such letter describes an incident very similar to one described by the *sijill* documents of 1579 ,with slight variations.[14] Since this particular letter is undated it is hard to state with certainty that we are dealing with the same incident, or with another which occurred in the seventeenth century. We have reason to believe that in fact the latter is the case.[15] The leaders of the Jerusalem community complain in this letter that, on the arrival of the spring caravan at the gates of Jerusalem, the *Sanjaq-Bey* collected from the pilgrims the *ghafar*, the tax collected from all non-Muslims at the gates of the city, and did so very violently. He afterwards drove them from the town, since the *Qadi* and Muslim dignitaries had claimed that the Jews were running from the plague in Egypt, and spreading it in Jerusalem.[16] The fact that Egyptian Jews used to flee from plague-stricken Egypt to Jerusalem and vice-versa was well known.[17] On this occasion, however, the leaders accused the *Sanjaq-Bey*, that his sole intent was to acquire money, for he had allowed the Christians, who arrived on the same caravan, to enter the city. They also said that the Jewish pilgrimage to Jerusalem created a very unfavorable attitude towards them and that the *Sanjaq-Bey* had threatened to drive out all Jews over the age of ten. In order to obviate that threat, they had had to pay him a great deal of money. The general discontent of the Muslim population with the Jewish pilgrimage from Egypt takes second place in this document, the main complaint being that the *Sanjaq-Bey* exploits the said Muslim discontent, in order to make money.

The accusation that Egyptian Jews arriving in Jerusalem were carriers of plagues, appears in another letter in which the leaders of the Jerusalem Community beseeched Egyptian Jews not to transport with them remains for reinterment until such time as the plague was over, for the Muslim dignitaries in Jerusalem were accusing them of spreading the plague by this practice.[18]

14 A. Cohen, "Sixteenth Century Egypt and Palestine etc.", *op. cit.*

15 The letter was written in a certain poetical form in which each paragraph started with certain words and ended with certain words. This poetical frame was taken from a letter written by the famous Rabbi and poet, Rabbi Israel Najara, at the end of the 16th century on behalf of the Community of Safed to the Community of Istanbul. The letter was published in his book *Maimai Israel* (Waters of Israel), which appeared in Venice in 1601. The book was very popular and the poetical structure of the letter from the Jerusalem Community was no doubt an imitation of it, which would put the date as later than 1601.

16 Jerusalem Ms., Letter No. 21, p. 65. On that subject see also A. Cohen, *Ottoman documents on the Jewish Community of Jerusalem in the Sixteenth Century* (in Hebrew), Jerusalem 1976, pp. 40-41.

17 Rabbi Mordekhai Halevi, *Darkhei No'am Responsa* (in Hebrew), Venice 1697, *Even Ha'ezer*, No. 4, p. 59b.

18 Jerusalem Ms., Letter No. 118, p. 150-151.

Besides the pilgrimage to Jerusalem itself there was another one that was very popular among Egyptian Jews. This was the *ziyāra* to the grave of the prophet Samuel — Nabī Samwil — which took place on the 28th day of the Hebrew month of Iyar.[19] Jewish pilgrims who came to Jerusalem for Passover usually stayed on until the following month in order to make that *ziyāra* which was not only a religious event but had great social importance; it was a form of entertainment, an occasion to meet with Jews from other parts of the world, and to meet people outside the family circle.

The popularity of the *ziyāra* among the Egyptian Jews is well illustrated by the fact that it was the *Chelebi* — the chief treasurer of Egypt, Shemuel (Samuel) Cohen — who in the year 1591-2 collected money to give to the *Sanjaq-Bey*, the *Qadi* and *Subashi* of Jerusalem in order to buy permission to enter the place, which had been closed to Jews for some time.[20]

B. Economic Ties Between Egyptian and Jerusalem Jewry

1. Financial Assistance

Over and above the financial aid regularly received in Jerusalem with the spring caravan, the community would send emissaries to Egypt, and other places, to collect money, whenever it found itself in trouble.[21] Egyptian Jews would bequeath their inheritance to the community of Jerusalem, usually by creating trusts, the proceeds of which were dedicated to the needs of the community. Especially renowned was the financial help Jerusalem Jewry received from the Jewish treasurers in Egypt.

At the beginning of the seventeenth century, the position of the Jewish treasurers in Egypt declined, a fact connected no doubt with the first signs of deterioration in Alexandria's status as the main port of transport of the Far East spices, since by that time a great part of this trade went around the Cape of Good Hope.[22] In consequence the treasurers' help to the Jerusalem

19 On that pilgrimage see M. Rozen, *op. cit.*, pp. 260-262; Z. Vilnai, *Holy Tombstones in Eretz Israel* (in Hebrew), Jerusalem, 1951, pp. 153-161; I. Ben Ẓevi, "A Jewish Settlement by the Tomb of the Prophet Samuel" (in Hebrew), *Yedi'ot Baḥakirat Eretz Israel Ve'atikot-eha, Selected Papers from Volumes 1-15*, Jerusalem, 1965, Vol. II, pp. 250-256; A. Shoḥat, "On the History of the Synagogue on the Prophet Samuel's Grave" (in Hebrew), *ibid.* pp. 243-244; I. M. Toledano, "Nabi Samuel or the Grave of the Prophet Samuel" (in Hebrew), *Hadevir* 3 (Jerusalem) 1921, No. 10-2 pp. 29-31.

20 "The Travels of Shemuel Ben David the Karaite of Jerusalem" (in Hebrew), A. Ya'ari, *Travels in Eretz Israel*, Ramat Gan, 1976, p. 246.

21 Jerusalem Ms., Letters No. 29, pp. 71-72; 56, p. 100; 80, p. 102; 102, p. 139; 108, pp. 143-144; 111, pp. 145-146; 117, p. 150; 124, pp. 156-157. On other emissaries in Egypt in the 17th century see: A. Ya'ari, *Eretz Israel Emissaries* (in Hebrew), Jerusalem 1951, pp. 285-286.

22 In 1612, W. Lithgow wrote that Alexandria's trade had deteriorated because spices, formerly brought there via the Red Sea and bought by the Venetians, had begun to be

community was greatly diminished for some time, at the beginning of the century. Rabbi Yom Tov Ẓahalon, the well-known Rabbi of Safed, who died around 1618-1620, received a question from Jerusalem which also serves to illustrate the situation. The question concerned the method by which the money coming to Jerusalem from the Diaspora should be distributed. The man sending the question wrote that "in the first days" the Jewish treasurers in Egypt along with rich Jews from other places had generously helped the scholars of Jerusalem, but now that their own position was not good, there was no money coming to the Jerusalem scholars.[23]

A similar picture is drawn in a letter given to the Safed emissaries Rabbi Yeḥiel Ashkenazi and Rabbi Shelomo ibn Ẓur who went to Algiers in the year 1604. The letter was addressed to the rich Algerian Jew, Shemuel Kanshino, in Oran. The senders apologized that they had to bother Kanshino and explained that there were no more Jewish treasurers and men of influence in Egypt, and that they were the main supporters of the Community.[24] There may have been a deterioration in the help coming from Egypt at the beginning of the century but the description is certainly exaggerated.

We know that during the whole period, Jews continued to serve as treasurers in Egypt.[25] From the letters concerning the spring caravan it seems that a certain amount of help continued to arrive regularly, even during difficult times. Towards the middle of the seventeenth century a considerable amount of assistance was once again forthcoming from the Egyptian treasurers. The main figure who stood at the center was the *Chelebi*, the "master". The *Chelebi* was a Jewish businessman whom the appointed governor of Egypt would bring with him from Istanbul, or choose from among the Jews of Egypt, to manage his business and serve as Chief Treasurer. The *Chelebi* leased in fact the taxes of Egypt; at the same time he was the secular leader of Egyptian Jewry. In many ways he inherited the position of the *Nagid*. His political status was very sensitive and on many occasion *Chelebi*s paid with their lives for the high rank they achieved, especially if they failed to pay the governer the sum they had promised.[26] In a letter written by the leaders of Jerusalem, a certain person

transferred through the Cape of Good Hope on Portuguese, English and Dutch Ships (W. Lithgow, *The Total Discourse of the Rare Adventures and Painful Peregrinations of Long Nineteen Years Travels from Scotland to the Most Famous Kingdoms in Europe, Asia and Africa*, Glasgow, MCMVI, p. 285-286).

23 Rabbi Yom Tov Ẓahalon's *New Responsa* (in Hebrew), Jerusalem, 1980, No. 88b, p. 173.

24 S. Assaf. "Letters from Safed" (in Hebrew), *Koveẓ 'Al-Yad*, 13 (1940), p. 142; A. Ya'ari, *op. cit.* no. 21, pp. 245-246.

25 A. Rozanes, *History of the Jews in Turkey and the Eastern Lands* (in Hebrew), Vol. III, Sophia 1938, pp. 315-316; Rabbi Yoseph Sambari, *Divrei Yoseph*, Alliance Ms. H130a, Ph.Ed. Jerusalem, 1981, p. 180.

26 A. Rozanes, *op. cit.*, pp. 315-318; Rabbi Yoseph Sambari, *op. cit.*, pp. 182-184.

was asked to go as an emissary to Egypt because he had already been there once and had met with success. The leaders of the community, which was under great stress, had heard that a new *Chelebi* had been appointed who was known for his generosity, and, more important, he was on very friendly terms with the addressee of the letter. The leaders hoped therefore that the new *Chelebi* would increase his aid to the community.[27]

A similar situation was created in 1664, when the leaders asked Shabbetai Ẓevi to go to Egypt to meet Rephael Yoseph *Chelebi*, with whom he was on friendly terms, to raise money for the community of Jerusalem. The end of that mission is very well known. Shabbetai Ẓevi, who was suffering from a severe depression, went to Gaza to consult Natan ben Elisha Ḥayim, who told him that he was not sick at all, on the contrary, he was the Messiah. The money he collected never reached the leaders of the Jerusalem community, who hurried to excommunicate Shabbetai Ẓevi and have him driven out of Jerusalem.[28]

2. Egypt – an Investment Base for Jerusalem Jewry

The Ottoman administration in seventeenth century Jerusalem used the *Dhimmīs* in the town as a sponge through which money from Christian Europe was absorbed into their own pockets.[29] Consequently, Jews who came to live in Jerusalem preferred to invest their money outside the town and derive a regular income from such investments. Likewise, Jews who founded trusts dedicated to the Jerusalem Community preferred to leave the capital outside Jerusalem. Egypt was among the main places where trusts dedicated for Jerusalem were kept, and where Jews from Jerusalem invested their money.[30] The reasons for Egypt's popularity as a place of investment were its relative proximity, the regular caravan connection, and its intense economic activity, a great part of which was in Jewish hands. It was very convenient for a Jew living in Jerusalem to deposit his money with a merchant who would use it for business purposes, retaining for himself a certain portion of the profit.[31] During the second half of the seventeenth century a new group of economic entrepreneurs took their place beside the Jewish treasurers. Most of these entrepreneurs were Jews from Livorno who came to trade in Alexandria and Cairo under the French flag and took advantage of the privileges which the French government succeeded in

27 Jerusalem Ms., Letter No. 29, p. 71-72.

28 G. Scholem, *Shabbetai Ẓevi and the Shabbetaian Movement During His Lifetime* (in Hebrew), Tel Aviv 1974, Vol. I, pp. 143-144. On Rephael Yoseph Chelebi's help to Jewish scholars in Ereẓ-Israel see Rabbi Yoseph Sambari, *op. cit.*, p. 183.

29 See for example M. Rozen, ed. *Ḥurvot Yerushalem* (in Hebrew), Tel Aviv 1981, pp. 23-67.

30 Rabbi Ya'akov Castro, *Ohalei Ya'akov Responsa* (in Hebrew), Livorno, 1783, No. 1, p.la; Rabbi Mordekhai Halevi, *Darkhei No'am Responsa, Ḥoshen Mishpat*, No. 25, p. 260a.

31 Ginat Veradim Responsa, Even Ha'ezer No. 4,9, p. 29a.

achieving for its traders.[32] This group rendered to Jerusalem Jewry the services formerly accorded them by the treasurers.

Information regarding Egypt as a basis for investments of Jerusalem Jews can be gathered, in particular, from the disputes over inheritances and the collection of money belonging to Jews from Jerusalem. An interesting example is the affair concerning Rabbi Shabbetai Bar,[33] the Ashkenazi Rabbi and emissary of the Ashkenazi community in Jerusalem in the second half of the seventeenth century. Rabbi Shabbetai Bar had a sum of money invested in the business of a well-known firm of merchants, that of Iẓhak Azubib and Shemuel Ben Shelomo Franco, in Egypt. While on a mission to Italy (1674), he passed through Egypt and wanted to take 3000 *Maidis* from the partners. They told him that since he was going to Venice they would arrange through a business acquaintance, a certain Shemuel Ben David Franco (probably a cousin of Shemuel Ben Shelomo Franco) who had a *fattore* (agent) in Venice named Aharon Burgus, for the latter to pay him the money in Venice; this would be convenient for both sides and much safer for Shabbetai Bar. Shabbetai Bar agreed. He took a bill of exchange from the partners and continued to Venice. However, before he was able to collect the money, he died. Bar's widow engaged another emissary of the community, this time the Sephardic Rabbi Abraham Karigal,[34] to collect the money (in 1675). Aharon Burgus claimed that the property of Shemuel Ben David Franco in his hands was insufficient to cover the debt and so refused to pay it. Abraham Karigal returned to Egypt and claimed the money again from the partners. The Rabbi of Cairo assembled a court of law before which the partners appeared. Azubib brought a letter written in Italian from Aharon Burgus, in which he took it upon himself to pay the money after he had sold a delivery of ostrich feathers that Franco had sent him. The Rabbis of Cairo and Alexandria ruled that Burgus must pay the money even though the money he received from the ostrich feathers was less than the debt. But, of course, the dispute did not end at that point and the widow had a protracted stuggle over the money.[35]

The Jewish community in Jerusalem often retained special officials in Egypt to take care of the trust dedicated to the community and the community's property there, who saw to it that income from the trust was forwarded to Jerusalem. At the end of the seventeenth century the leaders of the Jerusalem community appointed an official who would reside in Egypt and take care of the community's property there and would receive

32 Chambre de commerce de Marseille, J. 1584, *De par le Roi* 4.8.1688. The "strangers" mentioned in that order were mostly Jews and Armenians.

33 On him, see A. Ya'ari, *op. cit.*, (no. 21) pp. 292-293.

34 On that emissary see: A. Ya'ari, *ibid.*, p. 293; A. L. Frumkin & A. Rivlin, *History of the Scholars of Jerusalem* (in Hebrew), Jerusalem 1928, Part II, pp. 76-77.

35 "*Darkhei No'am Responsa, Ḥoshen Mishpat* No. 45-53.

wages "like a *fattore*." The *fattore* was an agent of sorts who undertook business affairs on behalf of distant merchants in accordance with the written orders that were sent to him, or with an agreement on the nature of the acts he was authorized to carry out. The wages of the *fattore* as was common in the merchants' law at that time, were two percent of the value of the transaction and nine percent if the deal included obtaining credit or insurance.[36] The above-mentioned *fattore* received a contract for three years. Within that period the leaders of Jerusalem heard that "their man" had other business affairs in Egypt which made it necessary for him to leave that country altogether. Concerned about what would happen to the community's property, they tried to force him to return to Jerusalem. The man refused, saying he was afraid to return during such hard times, when many Jews were leaving Jerusalem. He was sure that the creditors of the community would arrest him saying he had possession of the community's money, and, to sum it up, his wife did not want to go back to Jerusalem at all . . .[37]

3. Egypt as a Transit Station for Money Sent from Europe and North Africa to Jerusalem

Egypt was a transit station for money transferred from Europe and North Africa to Jerusalem. Almost all the emissaries from Jerusalem to North Africa went and returned via Egypt. North African Jews sometimes sent money to Jerusalem on their own initiative, mostly by way of merchant caravans. From Egypt, the money was forwarded to Jerusalem.[38] Not only Jews would send money to Jerusalem through Egypt but also Christians. For example, monks from the Franciscan Order transferred, in 1638, via Egypt, a large sum of money to Jerusalem. The money was sent from Spain to Italy, and from Messina in Sicily to Alexandria. The monk who made the transfer arranged with a Jew from Egypt, one Ya'akov Binyamin who was with him on the same caravan to Jerusalem and who had with him a quantity of boxed merchandise, for him to take the money packed as merchandise. Thus the money was safely brought to the Franciscan convent of San Salvador in Jerusalem.[39]

The transfer of money sent to Jews in Jerusalem through Egypt increased, especially in the second half of the seventeenth century. Rabbi Shemuel Abuhab, the Rabbi of Venice, wrote to Rabbi Abraham Yarak in Casale Monferrato, in the autumn of 1670, a letter containing information

36 On the *fattore* and the *fattoria*: M. Rozen, "The Fattoria — a Chapter in the History of Mediterranean Commerce in the 16th and the 17th Centuries" (in Hebrew), *Miqqedem Umiyyam, Studies in the Jewry of Islamic Countries*, Haifa, 1981, pp. 1091-132.

37 Rabbi Yoseph Halevi Nazir, *Mate Yoseph Responsa* (in Hebrew), Part II, Istanbul, 1757, *Yore De'ah*, No. 4, pp. 23b — 24a.

38 Jerusalem Ms., Letters No. 59, p. 102; 60, p. 103.

39 Francesco da Serino, *ibid.*

on the ways to go to the Holy Land and to send money there. "The special ways to go by sea are two; through this town of Venice or through Livorno on boats going to the region of Jaffa, Acre and Sidon, or to the town of Egypt (meaning Cairo via Alexandria), and that last one of Egypt is the more commonly used, and especially from the town of Livorno from which the boats always come and go, and in a lot of them is to be found the company of Jews coming and going".[40] It seems that Abuhab definitely preferred to send money through Alexandria. In another letter, this time to the leaders of the Jerusalem community, written in the summer 1652, he wrote that he had sent money which came from Frankfurt to Jerusalem through the wealthy doctor Rephael Moreno in Alexandria.[41] At the same time, the revenue from the money belonging to the widow Sarah Vega, which was deposited with the Livorno merchant, Yehoshu'a de Palacios, was sent through his agents in Egypt, Shemuel Bokara and Emanuel de Palacios, along with money and letters to the leader of the Jerusalem community, Abraham ibn Dana.[42]

C. *The Jewish Connection and Jerusalem Muslim Dignitaries.*

The connections between the Jerusalem community and Egyptian Jewry were used to gain influence among the Muslim dignitaries of Jerusalem on whose good will they sometimes depended. Included in one of the letters sent by the leaders of the Jerusalem community to Egypt, is a request to an influential Jew in Egypt to help a Jerusalem Muslim dignitary, who sent one of his servants to Egypt to collect his *'ulūfa*.[43] It seems that the servant's master anticipated trouble in the collection of the money and thus turned to the Jewish community in Jerusalem for help. The leaders of the Jerusalem community explained to the Egyptian Jew that the servant's master helped the community whenever he could and for this reason he should help the servant.[44]

40 M. Benayahu, "The Letters of Rabbi Shemuel Abuhab and Rabbi Moshe Zacut and their Circle in Eretz-Israel Matters" (in Hebrew), *Yerushalayim — Review for Eretz Israel Research*, Vol. 2/5.

41 *Ibid.*, No. 7, p. 164.

42 *Ibid.*, No. 19, p. 167.

43 The *'ulūfa* was the revenue of certain state property in Egypt, allocated to certain people in the empire in place of a salary (see for example: Rabbi Eliahu Kapsali, *Seder Eliahu Zuta* [in Hebrew], ed. A. Shmuelevitz, M. Benayahu, and S. Simonsohn, Vol. I. Jerusalem 1976, pp. 125, 136.

44 Jerusalem Ms., Letter No. 226, p. 275.

D. *The Connections Between Scholars of Jerusalem and Egypt in the Seventeenth Century*

There was constant movement of scholars between the two places throughout the century. Egyptian-born scholars, or those who had lived there a long time, would come to Jerusalem to serve as Rabbis in the later years of their lives. Likewise, there were scholars from all parts of the world who came to Jerusalem, lived there a few years and then tired and despairing of the hardship of life in that city, would depart for Egypt.

The following are some examples of this reciprocity:

Rabbi Israel Binyamin, Chief Rabbi of the Sephardi community of Jerusalem, between 1635-1668, had formerly been an important Rabbi in Egypt.[45] His friend, Rabbi Shemuel ibn Sid who had studied with him in Egypt and became a Rabbi of some importance there, came to Jerusalem and served as a Judge in Israel Binyamin's court.[46] Rabbi Mordekhai Halevi, the Rabbi of Rashīd for forty years, came, late in his life, to Jerusalem (1684) and died there.[47]

And in the other direction: Rabbi David Konforti, the author of "Kore Hadorot", the important bibliographical work of the seventeenth century, had come to live in Jerusalem and stayed there, at least until 1655, but then returned to Egypt where he served as a Rabbi and a judge from 1671.[48] The son of Rabbi Israel Binyamin, Baruch Binyamin, returned to Egypt, where he died in 1668.[49] Rabbi Zeraḥiah Gota of Istanbul lived for some time in Jerusalem and then went to Egypt. He died in 1648 and his remains were reinterred in Jerusalem in 1650.[50] Rabbi Yehudah Ḥavilio, the son of the emissary of the Jerusalem community, Rabbi David Ḥavilio, moved to Alexandria, in the wake of a dispute with the leaders of Jerusalem, where he served as Rabbi of the community. Towards the end of his life he returned to Hebron where, in 1697, he became Chief Rabbi.[51] Rabbi Mordekhai Halevi Nazir who was born and reared in Jerusalem and Hebron, served in the last years of his life, as Chief Rabbi of Cairo,[52] where he died in 1713.

45 For detailed bibliography, see M. Rozen, *Ḥurvot Yerushalem*, *op. cit.*, p. 138, No. 631.

46 *Ibid.*, p. 95, No. 96.

47 Frumkin — Rivlin, *op. cit.*, Part II, pp. 96-98; Rabbi Ḥaim Yoseph David Azulai (Ḥida), *Shem Hagdolim* (in Hebrew), in his name.

48 Frumkin — Rivlin, *op. cit.*, Part II, pp. 48-50.

49 Jerusalem Ms. 8°1500, Rabbi Moshe Ibn Habīb *Sermons* (in Hebrew), Sermon I on section *Tazri'a*, p. 109a; Frumkin — Rivlin, *op. cit.*, p. 29.

50 *Ibid.*, p. 31.

51 On his quarrel with the community of Jerusalem over the money his father collected as an emissary: *Ibid.*, p. 69-71; Rabbi Ḥayim Benvenisti, *B'ai Ḥayai Responsa* (in Hebrew), Part I, Salonica, 1791, No. 30-31, pp. 25a-26a.

52 Frumkin — Rivlin, *op. cit.*, pp. 98-99; Rabbi Yoseph Halevi Nazir, *Mate Yoseph Responsa* (in Hebrew), Part I, Istanbul, 1717-1726. Introduction of his son-in-law Rabbi Yehoshu'a Zain, *Shem Hagdolim* (Name of the Great Ones), in his name.

Much evidence exists regarding the exchange of legal opinions between Rabbis of Jerusalem and Egypt during this period. This subject is worthy of separate and thorough research. In the present paper we will merely attempt to sketch a rough outline of that phenomenon. The usual instance of an exchange of legal opinions between Jerusalem and Egypt was when one of the litigants was from Jerusalem and the other from the Egyptian community. Another type of case was that concerning family law in which the Hebrew law is very strict, and, unless they felt very sure of themselves, Rabbis were not always willing to adjudicate. Jerusalem Rabbis would seek legal opinions when they encountered difficulty in exercising their authority over their communities or their opponents and felt in need of support. Those cases where one party was in Egypt and the other in Jerusalem were mostly disputes over money invested in Egypt, one example of which has already been cited.[53]

The cases concerning family law are numerous and varied. The exchange of legal opinions in these matters is particularly voluminous at the time of the Beit Ya'akov Vega School (1658-1689) whose scholars had, it seems very good connections with Egyptian Jewry.[54] To give an example: the scholars of that school were consulted in 1686, regarding permission to remarry after desertion (*hatarat 'aguna*) for the wife of 'Ovadiah Alfandari from Safed who had disappeared somewhere in the Maghrib and had been seen, when on his way there, in Alexandria.[55] Rabbi Moshe ibn Ḥabīb[56] of the same school gave his opinion in the matter of granting permission to remarry to an Egyptian women whose husband had drowned on his way to Rashīd.[57] The question had been sent to Rabbi Moshe Galante,[58] the head of the school, but he died (1689) before he had handed down his opinion and thus it was that Rabbi Moshe ibn Ḥabīb responded. Rabbi Yehudah Ḥavilio of Alexandria requested the opinion of the court of that school in the matter of Rabbi David Kolon Ashkenazi, whose wife had not borne him sons and who therefore wanted permission to take a second wife despite the rule among the Ashkenazi community which forbade marriage to more than one woman.[59]

53 For more examples: Jerusalem Ms., letters 92, p. 131; 93, pp. 131-2; *Darkhei No'am, Ḥoshen Mishpat*, No. 22, p. 210a; No. 6, p. 187a.

54 On that school and scholars: M. Benayahu, "On the History of Jerusalem Schools in the 17th Century" (in Hebrew), *HUCA* 21, (1948), pp. 1-28; S. Z. Havlin, "On the History of Jerusalem Schools and Scholars at the End of the 17th Century and Beginning of the 18th Century" (in Hebrew), *Shalem* 2 (1971), pp. 113-192.

55 *Ginat Veradim Responsa*, Vol. II, *Even Ha'ezer* No. 3,8, p. 33b Ovadiah Alphandari might have been the last wool manufacturer in Safed: S. Aviẓur, "Safed — Center of Wool Manufacturing in the 16th Century" (in Hebrew), *Sefunot* 6 (1962), p. 69.

56 On him, see S. Ẓ. Havlin, *op. cit.* pp. 89-91, 136-7, no. 79.

57 *Ginat Veradim Responsa*, Vol. II, *Even Ha'ezer*, No. 3,7, p. 31b.

58 Frumkin — Rivlin, *op. cit.*, pp. 56-61.

59 *Ginat Veradim Responsa*, Vol. II, *Even Ha'ezer*, No. 1,9, p. 6b.

Not always did the Rabbis of Egypt accept the authority of those in Jerusalem. For example, the Rabbis of Egypt banned the book of Rabbi Ḥizkiyah da Silva *Pri Ḥadash* (1692), saying he showed disrespect towards the great Rabbi, Yoseph Karo, whose authority had been accepted throughout the Jewish world.[60] Of special historical interest are those cases where Rabbis of Jerusalem enlisted something akin to moral assistance in the exercise of their authority, by asking their colleagues for their legal opinions. These cases draw light on some of the conflicts in Jewish society at the beginning of the modern era. The responsum sent by Rabbi Ya'akov Castro, who was a Rabbi in Cairo and Alexandria at the end of the sixteenth century and the beginning of the seventeenth, to a Rabbi in Jerusalem named Ḥananyah Elyakum, was definitely intended to strengthen the rule of the community over a rebellious member. Castro wrote at the beginning of his responsum: "because of our many sins the people of Jerusalem are ruled by the hardships they suffer each day . .. from the tormenting Gentiles, also some evil-doing Jews who have gone astray, therefore we decided to declare the right way which Israel should follow according to the law".[61] Rabbi Meir Gabizon who lived in Alexandria and Cairo in the first half of the seventeenth century[62] was asked by scholars from Jerusalem to give his opinion in problems concerning their status in the Jerusalem community. It is obvious from the nature of the question that the scholars sought his aid. They complained that the managers of the *Talmūd Tōra* affairs in Jerusalem were doing business with its property. Some of the scholars disapproved of this, and claimed that it did not reflect well on them. Another question illustrated some aspects of the endless disputes between scholars and ordinary members of the community who tried to force the former to pay taxes like every other member of the community.[63]

A legal opinion requested of Rabbi Moshe Yehudah 'Abbas of Rashīd in the middle of the seventeenth century by an unknown Rabbi from Jerusalem, clearly indicates how much the petitioner needed 'Abbas' help. It is not clear where the incident occurred but it is obvious it did not take place in

60 On Ḥizkiyah da Silva and the whole affair see: S. Z. Havlin, *op. cit.*, pp. 140-151.

61 *Ohalei Ya'akov Responsa* No. 77, pp. 121a [Ya'akov Castro died some time before 1614, see Moscow Ms. Ginzburg 914, *Shemuel Ibn Sid, Sefer Ner Adonai* (in Hebrew), p. 52a. According to David Konforti, *Kore Hadorot* (in Hebrew), Berlin, 1846, p. 41b, he died in 1610. See on him also: Rozanes, *op. cit.* pp. 322-323]. The "Torments" mentioned were probably connected with Abu Syfin's rule in Jerusalem (1586-1588).

62 On him see. *Shem Hagdolim* in his name; Rozanes, *op. cit.*, p. 329.

63 Rabbi Meir Gabizon's *Responsa* (in Hebrew), Jerusalem Ms. 8°127, No. 11, p. 27b. On that dispute see also: M. Benayahu, "The Tax Concession Enjoyed by the Scholars of Safed" (in Hebrew), *Sefunot* 7 (1963), pp. 103-118; Rabbi Abraham Ankawa, *Kerem Ḥemer* (in Hebrew), Livorno, 1871, pp. 22b-24b; Rabbi Shemuel Di Avila, *Keter Torah*, Istanbul, 1725, in the introduction; E. Rivlin, *A Selection from Rephael Mordekhai Malki's Commentary on the Pentateuch* (in Hebrew), vol. I, Jerusalem, 1923, pp. 46-50.

Palestine. The question draws light on the status of scholars from Jerusalem in certain communities of Western Europe. The writer of the question was a Rabbi from Jerusalem who had been sent for an unknown purpose as an emissary to a community whose identity is not revealed. The members of the unnamed community did not receive him with the hospitality anticipated. During his stay there he had received a letter from yet another place which contained information that someone had insulted him there. The emissary had placed a ban on the offender, as was common in Jewish society in the East in such cases. The leaders of the community in which he was staying thereupon turned him over to the local authorities saying that in their community only the secular leadership had the right of excommunication. The incident may have happened in Livorno in which the rule of the secular leadership was absolute.[64] As a consequence the emissary spent three days and nights in jail, no one had visited him or brought him food. The humiliated emissary sought moral support and found it in Rabbi Moshe Yehudah 'Abbas of Rashīd who wrote angrily that he had never heard of such a disgrace and bad manners, and justified the emissary.[65]

In the last decade of the seventeenth century Egyptian Jewry became involved in an affair which in itself combined all the expressions of relationship between the Jerusalem and Egyptian communities. We refer to the dispute between the Ashkenazi and Sephardi communities in Jerusalem over the right of the Sephardi community to send emissaries to the Ashkenazi communities in Europe. The leader of the Ashkenazi community at that time was Rabbi Moshe ben Ya'akov Hacohen.[66] He was on friendly terms with Rabbi Mordekhai Halevi of Cairo who came to Jerusalem in the later part of his life. While Hacohen was staying in Venice collecting money for the community, he did a lot to enable the publishing of Halevi's Responsa (1688). On his way back (1690), he found that the money he brought was not enough to pay the Ashkenazi community's debts. With the help of friends in Italy and Egypt, he reached, in 1691, a compromise solution with the creditors who agreed to forgo the interest, and one-third of the debt, on condition that the Ashkenazi community would pay the balance within three years. The leaders of the Sephardi community declared that they would continue to send emissaries to the Ashkenazi communities in Europe, which endangered the whole compromise based as it was on the prospect of the money coming from these countries.

64 S. Toaf, "The Dispute between Rabbi Ya'akov Sasportas and the Heads of Livorno's Community over the Right of Judgement in the year 1681" (in Hebrew), *Sefunot* 9 (1965), pp. 169-191; Y. Tishbi, "The Letters of Rabbi Ya'acov Sasportas against the Heads of the Livorno Community in the year 1681" (in Hebrew), *Kovez̧ 'Al Yad*, 14 (Jerusalem 1946), p. 145.

65 Rabbi Moshe Yehudah 'Abbas' *Responsa* (in Hebrew), Oxford Ms. 823 in Neubauer Catalog, National Library, Jerusalem, Microfilm No. 21584, Part II, p. 40a.

66 On Hacohen and his mission see: A. Ya'ari, *op. cit.*, pp. 313-320; Frumkin — Rivlin, *op. cit.*, pp. 108-112.

Moshe Hacohen requested the help of Rabbi Abraham Halevi, the son of his friend Mordekhai Halevi. Abraham Halevi, who was then one of the Rabbis of Cairo, justified the Ashkenazi community's demand that the money collected in Ashkenazi communities in Europe belong to the Ashkenazi community and help write off the debt.[67] In 1693, the Rabbis of Cairo wrote to Venice that they objected to the emissaries from Hebron and Safed taking the money of the Ashkenazi community in Jerusalem, which was collected in the Diaspora, because this prevented them from paying off their own debt. The debt prevented Rabbi Moshe Hacohen from returning to Jerusalem and endangered the existence of the Ashkenazi community.[68]

Conclusion

The special status of Jerusalem in the Jewish world, the special status of *dhimmīs* in Jerusalem, as well as Egypt's economic importance brought about the close connections between the Jews of Jerusalem and Egypt. These connections started long before the period discussed and continued after its end. They were based on the two-way movement of pilgrims and immigrants, and on cultural and economic connections at the core of which was the assistance rendered by Egyptian Jewry to the Jerusalem community, and Egypt as an investment base for Jerusalem Jewry and a transfer point for money originating in North Africa and Europe and destined for Jerusalem.

67 *Ginat Veradim Responsa*, Vol. I, *Yore De'ah* No. 3,9.

68 I. Sonne, "More on the Attitude of the Committees and Communities in Poland towards Eretz Israel" (in Hebrew), *Zion*, 1 (1936), pp. 252-255. On the Ashkenazi community's struggle one may also learn from their attempt to sell the community's property in Egypt at the same period. Rabbi Efraim Hacohen, *Sha'ar Efraim Responsa* (in Hebrew), Zulzbach. 1688, No. 66.

THE TWENTIETH CENTURY

J.C. HUREWITZ

Egypt's Eastern Boundary: The Diplomatic Background of the 1906 Demarcation[1]

I

The shaping of Egypt's eastern boundary took place in stages. The Suez — Rafah line, intended as a privileged or unchanging provincial boundary, was roughly drawn in 1841 on a poor map without on-site reference but with the guarantee of the major European powers. In 1866, for a tributary consideration, Ismā'īl Pasha, the governor of Egypt, was authorized on a suzerain-vassal basis without European involvement to enlarge his territorial jurisdiction beyond the privileged line. Thus Egypt came to administer the entire Sinai peninsula plus al-'Aqaba and the gulf and Red Sea coast as far south as al-Wajh. The Sublime Porte, in 1892, tried to take back what it had given twenty-six years earlier and only half succeeded. It reassigned the al-'Aqaba — al-Wajh coastal strip to the vilāyet of the Hijaz: but, frustrated by Britain, then the occupying power in Egypt, it reluctantly reaffirmed the status quo of an Egyptian-administered Sinai peninsula still lacking a marked eastern boundary. Finally, in 1906, a mixed Ottoman-Egyptian boundary commission carefully drew the agreed Rafah — Taba line. To each stage in the phased creation of Egypt's fixed eastern frontier

1 Articles by Uriel Heyd ["Ha-Mashber shel Mifratz-Eilat bi-Shnat 1906" in Ha-Ḥevra la-Ḥaqīrat Eretz-Yisrael ve-'Atiqoteha, ha-Kinūs ha-Artzī ha-Shmōna-'Asar li-Yedī'at ha-Aretz, *Eilat* (Jerusalem, 1963, pp. 194-206] and Gabriel Warburg ["The Sinai Peninsula Borders, 1906-47," *Journal of Contemporary History*, vol. 14 (1979), pp. 677-92] and discussions with Ambassador Shabtai Rosenne inspired my interest in the making of Egypt's international boundary in the Sinai peninsula. In the preparation of the present paper, I have accepted as demonstrated the direct evidence assembled and analyzed by Heyd and Warburg and used to good effect the documents in Great Britain, *Parliamentary Papers*, "Correspondence Respecting the Turco-Egyptian Frontier in the Sinai Peninsula", Egypt no. 2 (1906), Cd. 3006. Particularly helpful in Cd. 3006 is the report of May 21, 1906 by the Earl of Cromer, His Majesty's Agent and Consul General in Cairo, to Sir Edward Grey, Secretary of State for Foreign Affairs in the then new Liberal Government. I have not had the benefit of checking the published extracts of Cromer's detailed report against the omissions. In the present paper I have focused on the evolving diplomatic strategies and policies of the British and Ottoman governments and their interplay as they bore upon the issues affecting the delimitation of the Sinai boundary

the United Kingdom made a significant yet behind-the-scenes contribution.

Britain's interest in Egypt, between 1840 and 1906, remained constant: the safeguard of an unfolding major imperial artery, connecting the metropole and India and becoming the imperial lifeline after the completion of the Suez Canal in 1869. In seeking to protect this interest, Whitehall pursued variable diplomatic strategies that were articulated to the evolving realities. In 1840, the strategy called for the internationalization of the Egyptian question — Egypt's threat to the survival of the Ottoman state — by making the European Concert of major powers jointly responsible for upholding the sovereignty of the Ottoman Empire and slowing down its territorial attrition. Four decades later the Egyptian question had developed into a British-French contest for the possession of the patch of real estate at the strategic heart of the Eastern Hemisphere, where a man-made waterway divided two continents and connected two seas. The Egyptian question, by then, turned on the avoidance of war in Europe.

Foreign Minister Viscount Palmerston inaugurated the strategy in 1840-41 when he inspired the collective European intervention and substantially wrote the terms of subordinating Egypt, once again, to the Sublime Porte. Following the occupation of Egypt in 1882, Britain discovered that its freedom of action was hampered by international obligations to the Concert. For example, as occupying power it could not abolish the capitulations or take over full control of Egypt's foreign debt, to say nothing of annexing the country outright. While prolonging the military occupation, and therefore the political and legal ambiguities of the British presence, Whitehall nevertheless created a system of indirect rule that enabled it to exercise de facto sovereignty. Britain continued formally to recognize the legal sovereignty of the Sublime Porte over Egypt but suspended its exercise for the duration of the military occupation.

The Sublime Porte, on its side, from 1831 had sought, as a primary interest, to regain undisputed possession of Egypt and to bridle its governor. The Ottoman Government therefore welcomed Palmerston's initiatives in 1840-41 and the alliance with Britain that the European intervention ushered in. Long-lived even in the nineteenth century, the alliance started to unravel after the British occupation of Cyprus in 1878. Friendship and confidence speedily changed into hostility and suspicion, once Britain occupied Egypt in 1882. In the later years the Sublime Porte, striving to reassert Ottoman sovereignty, evoked a wide range of stratagems to induce Britian to end the occupation. Still, the Sublime Porte's political and diplomatic failure produced a durable cartographic consequence — an eastern boundary that lasted until 1967 and was restored in April 1982.

Let us examine the British and Ottoman strategies and their interplay at somewhat closer range.

II

The first European intervention in the Ottoman-Egyptian dispute occurred in 1833, when Russia, by European default, went to the aid of Sultan Mahmud II (1808-39) and saved the Ottoman dynasty from almost certain overthrow by his insurgent vassal, Muḥammad 'Alī Pasha of Egypt. Tsar Nicholas I exacted a price for the rescue — the preferential defensive alliance of Hünkâr Iskelesi, under which the Sultan secretly agreed, in the event of an international crisis, to close the straits to all foreign naval vessels. Foreign Secretary Palmerston looked askance at the deal, fearing that it would subordinate the Ottoman Empire to Russia. Moreover, in the regional conflict France was underwriting Muḥammad 'Alī. Deep suspicion of the designs of Russia on the straits and of France on Egypt, indoctrinated Palmerston in Eastern affairs in the 1830s. In the lingering eastern Mediterranean crisis, he perceived in the threat to the Ottoman dynasty a threat also to British interests. With the appearance of the steam vessel, the British government at last discovered what the East India Company had begun to grasp more than a half-century earlier — that through the Ottoman realm passed developing primary imperial arteries that linked Britain to India. As Palmerston analyzed the problem, Russia and France had to be kept apart, for if they ever joined hands, Britain would suffer along with the Ottoman Empire.

The Empire, early in the summer of 1839, appeared to be heading toward disaster. Mahmud II died on July 1, without learning the full extent of the massive defeat his troops had suffered in the renewed fighting with the Egyptian army. A week later the Ottoman naval commander surrendered the Sultan's entire fleet to Muḥammad 'Alī. By the month's end the fear spread that the new Sultan, sixteen-year-old Abdülmecid, might simply capitulate to the Egyptian Pasha. As early as June 1839, in a letter to Viscount Beauvale, the British ambassador at Vienna, Palmerston had observed[2]

> that there can be no end to the danger with which these [eastern Mediterranean] affairs menace the peace of Europe, until Mehemet Ali shall have restored Syria to the direct authority of the Sultan; shall have retired into Egypt; and shall have interposed the Desert between his troops and authorities and the troops and authorities of the Sultan. But Mehemet Ali could not be expected to consent to this, unless some equivalent advantage were granted him; and this equivalent advantage might be hereditary succession in his family to the Pashalic of Egypt. . . .

2 From the text in J. C. Hurewitz, *The Middle East and North Africa in World Politics* (New Haven: Yale University Press, 1975), vol. 1, pp. 267-68.

Since Palmerston preferred a weak Ottoman Empire to a strong Egypt astride the unfolding British imperial communications, he responded favorably to tsarist initiatives for a rapprochement over the Eastern Question, which was negotiated at the end of 1839. Tsar Nicholas agreed not to seek renewal of the treaty of Hünkâr Iskelesi. Palmerston in return accepted the Russian condition that the powers should act in concert on the Ottoman-Egyptian crisis. The rapprochement led in mid-1840 to the multilateral convention concluded by Austria, Prussia, and the Ottoman Empire with Britain and Russia, providing for the collective European intervention into the Ottoman-Egyptian dispute. The ultimatum that the Concert delivered to Muḥammad 'Alī to withdraw from Syria clearly derived from the guidelines that Palmerston had framed a year earlier. Note also that the separate act, attached to the convention, which contained the terms of the ultimatum did not mention the Sinai peninsula by name and attached it to "the southern part of Syria," which, as described, closely resembled the contours of post-1922 Palestine;[3]

> This line, beginning at Cape Ras-el-Nakhora, on the coast of the Mediterranean, shall extend direct from thence as far as the mouth of the river Seisaban, at the northern extremity of the lake of Tiberias; it shall pass along the Western shore of that Lake, it shall follow the right bank of the river Jordan, and the western shore of the Dead Sea; from thence it shall extend straight to the Red Sea, which it shall strike at the northern point of the gulf of Akaba, and from thence it shall follow the western shore of the Gulf of Akaba, and the eastern shore of the Gulf of Suez, as far as Suez.

Southern Syria, as thus described, Muḥammad 'Alī was to administer during his lifetime "with the title of Pasha of Acre" but could not pass it on to his heirs.

In the intervention of 1840, France refused to join the European Concert and continued instead to uphold Muḥammad 'Alī. Once the Egyptian troops were cleared out of the Asian Arab provinces of the Ottoman Empire and Muḥammad 'Alī sued for peace, the problem became one of inventing a formula that would safeguard the Ottoman dynasty, while enabling France and its protégé to save face. In three months of negotiations the European powers, including France, mediated between the padishah and the Pasha, generally modifying in Muḥammad 'Alī's favor the terms under which he and his heirs were to govern Egypt. Attached to the *firmān* of June 1, 1841, was a map describing the boundaries of the hereditary *pashalik* of Egypt. A copy of the map along with the text of the *firmān* was sent to London, where it appears to have been lost in the

3 From the text, *ibid.*, p. 273.

archives. Recently a map of somewhat later date, which appears to be a true copy of the original, was discovered in the Public Records Office in London.[4] In that generally indistinct map, the eastern boundary of the dynastic, or privileged, *pashalik* was indicated by a line running from Suez to a point on the Mediterranean between Rafah and Khan Yunis. This line was one of the few drawn with a firm and dark stroke, leaving no doubt in the viewer's mind that it was designed to hem in Muḥammad 'Alī and his successors. It was the kind of border that might well have been suggested first by Palmerston in London and then approved in Istanbul. Be that as it may, only the northwest corner of Sinai was thus attached permanently to Egypt. The arrangement, guaranteed by the Concert, cut Muḥammad 'Alī and his dynastic heirs to provincial size. He was given, it is true, a greater measure of domestic autonomy than other provincial governers in the Empire; but like them he was bound by the international obligations of the Sublime Porte. Moreover, the 1841 settlement, in effect, converted the Ottoman Empire into a quasi ward of the European Concert.

After the settlement of 1841, Egypt became a center of mounting British-French rivalry. Starting in the mid-1840s, French engineers and financiers and the French public grew progressively enthusiastic about the construction of a canal for international shipping between the Mediterranean and the Red seas. Palmerston viewed the proposed venture with alarm. He realized that any such waterway would create in Europe strategic problems at least as great as those of the Turkish straits. He therefore vigorously opposed the French plans for building the canal, favoring instead a trans-Egyptian railroad from Alexandria to Suez via Cairo. A railroad, he contended, would be a domestic enterprise, located wholly within the province and would therefore escape the international entanglements of a canal that could, on completion, not fail to form an essential part of a major world sea lane. The British-sponsored railroad, in fact, went into operation by 1858. Meanwhile, despite Britain's inflexible opposition, Ferdinand de Lesseps succeeded in creating a Suez Canal Company, overcame all obstacles by persistence and faith and in 1869 presided over the canal's opening.

What about the Sublime Porte and its relationship to Egypt? The whole idea of a privileged *pashalik* or province was intended to satisfy both the padishah and the pasha: the Sultan would benefit from the knowledge that the governing viceroy would no longer in moments of ambition move across the designated borders; by the same token, Muḥammad 'Alī and his heirs were given the status of a dynasty and were assured title to the provincial governorship. They achieved this secure dynastic self-

4 Gideon Biger, "The First Map of Modern Egypt: Mohammed Ali's Firman and the Map of 1841," *Middle Eastern Studies*, vol. 14 (1978), pp. 323-25; the map is reproduced on p. 324.

government, as it turned out, precisely at a time when the Sublime Porte, in its reforming zeal was moving away from a system of provincial autonomy to another closely regulated and managed from Istanbul by especially trained bureaucrats. But the new style of provincial administration took a quarter-century to put into shape, emerging as the *vilâyet* regime in a *firmān* issued by Sultan Abdülaziz in 1864. Under this regime, the *vālīs* were rotated by the Sublime Porte, as a rule every three years, at times more often; rarely did a *vālī* remain longer at a single post. In this setting, a dynastic provincial governorship was indeed privileged.

If so, it might be asked, why was Ismā'īl allowed to spill over the 1841 frontier in 1866 and buy for himself and his dynastic line the unique title of Khedive when most of the Empire was administered under the *vilâyet* system? Here again we must speculate, for if there is any evidence, it has not come to my attention. According to conventional wisdom, Ismā'īl was an ambitious and profligate governor, encouraged by greedy European bankers to borrow huge sums of money at exorbitant rates of interest and discount. With these sums, he strived for economic expansion at home in his province and enhanced status abroad in the Ottoman Empire and the world community. The doubling of his tribute did enable him to buy new privileges in Istanbul. But it took two to strike such a bargain. Why did the Sultan and his advisers agree to the increase of Khedive Ismā'īl's domestic and external powers and to the territorial enlargement of his administration? Ismā'īl's encompassment of the entire Sinai peninsula may probably best be explained by its thin population, its substantially desert soil, and its lack at the time of coveted or easily retrievable natural resources. The authors of the *vilâyet* regime probably had difficulty in setting up an administration for the peninsula, either on its own or by attaching it to an adjacent *vilâyet* in Asia. Proximity and experience therefore might well commend its attachment to Egypt. Ismā'īl's acquisition of the 'Aqaba-Wajh coastal strip could also be rationalized on the basis that what the Sultan gave he might later take back, and if he so required, with the help of the European Concert, since the major powers had guaranteed the 1841 settlement. Presumably, the Sultan and his advisers may have thought, the Sublime Porte could do the same with Sinai. Indeed, as we know, they later tried, and failed.

There is no need in this paper to rehearse the details of Disraeli's purchase of the Khedive's shares of the canal company, representing forty-four percent of the total, the inability of the British Government, as the largest single shareholder, thereafter to acquire a commanding voice in the company's policies, the creation of the Egyptian Public Debt commission and with it the British-French Dual control over the finances in Egypt. All these issues have been subjected to minute investigation. For our present purposes, the essential point was the recognition in Europe at the start of the 1880s, that the competition over primacy in Egypt favored

France, if the prevailing criteria among the imperial powers were taken into account. European diplomats and politicians were prone to agree with those Frenchmen who argued that the digging of the Suez Canal on French initiative and largely with French capital justified France's claim to include Egypt within the French sphere of influence. The claim was reinforced by the loans of French banks to the Khedive, the prominent French role in the Egyptian Public Debt Commission, and the substantial cultural influence that came with the Egyptian elite's adoption of French as their chosen European language.

By contrast, Britain's interest in Egypt was overwhelmingly strategic and, in Whitehall's view, transcended that of France. But that interest, by the early 1880s, was placed in double jeopardy, for Britain could not influence the policy of the canal company or of the government through whose property the canal ran. Hence, if the United Kingdom were to protect its stake at the man-made juncture of the British imperial lifeline, it had no choice but to seize Egypt. At least, so it must have appeared to the policy-makers in London. Not that such a decision came easily. This was amply attested in October 1879 by Foreign Secretary Lord Salisbury who instructed Her Majesty's new Agent and Consul General in Cairo that:[5]

> The leading aim of our policy in Egypt is the maintenance of the neutrality of that country, that is to say, the maintenance of such a state of things that no great Power shall be more powerful there than England.
>
> This purpose might, of course, be secured by the predominance of England itself, or even by the establishment of the Queen's authority in the country. Circumstances may be conceived in which this would be the only way of attaining the object; but it would not be the best method. It would not in the present state of affairs confer any other advantages than opportunities of employing English people and introducing English capital; and these would be outweighed by the responsibilities, military and financial, it would entail. The only justification of such a policy would consist in its being the only available mode of assuring the neutrality of Egypt towards us.

British-French rivalry over Egypt manifestly intensified after the opening of the Suez Canal. Once the shortest route to India became an uninterrupted sea lane in 1869, England could no longer protect its vital strategic interest simply by prolonging the intimate alliance with the Sublime Porte. France was accumulating, on the European imperial scale, credits toward

5 From the text in Hurewitz, *The Middle East and North Africa in World Politics*, vol. 1, p. 420.

the eventual addition of Egypt to the expanding French Empire. If France ever installed itself as overlord in Egypt, it would control both company and government policy on the canal, hardening into permanence Britain's vulnerability in the eastern Mediterranean. This anxiety in 1878 largely accounted for the occupation of Cyprus. Britain's takeover of the island, imposed on a reluctant Sublime Porte, marked the abandonment of the earlier strategy of upholding Ottoman territorial integrity. It also paved the way for the occupation of Egypt four years later.

III

There is no need, in the present exercise, for extended treatment of the 'Urābī-led nationalist struggle after September 1881 to strip Tawfīq of his Khedival powers, the British-French démarche to restore those powers in the opening weeks of 1882, the insistence of the remaining members of the Concert on the preservation of the status quo in Egypt under the Sultanic *firmāns* and the European multilateral arrangements, the British and French acquiescence in the wishes of the other European powers, the growing defiance of the nationalists in the spring of 1882, and the inconclusive British-Ottoman negotiations. When all these developments are taken into account, however, it is clear that the occupation did not result from a carefully laid plan. Instead, Britain blundered into Egypt in the summer of 1882, in violation of the multilateral agreements and became hostage to the rest of the Concert, particularly France and Russia. Foreign Secretary Lord Granville explained to the concerned powers in January 1883, that Britain had intervened to put down a military insurrection and to restore peace and order. Granville went on to state that, although "for the present a British force remains in Egypt for the preservation of public tranquillity," the British government was nevertheless "desirous of withdrawing it as soon as the state of the country, and the organization of proper means for the maintenance of the Khedive's authority, will admit of it."[6]

Despite the ambivalence over the occupation, which as it turned out was not replaced until December 1914, when Egypt was declared a protectorate, Britain took decisive measures to protect its interest in the defense of the canal. About this, Whitehall left no doubt in the negotiation of the Suez Canal convention, which the maritime powers and the Sublime Porte initialed in 1888 but did not ratify until 1905. In the end, the signatories approved the contention by England of an exclusive right to protect the canal for the duration of its presence in Egypt.

Meanwhile, prompted by France and Russia, the Sublime Porte continued pressing Britain to withdraw its troops from Egypt. To the Ottoman demands, the Liberal Government of William Gladstone (1880-85) gave

6 From the text, *ibid.* p. 447.

evasive replies, repeating again and again that the British military presence was only temporary. To calm Ottoman anxieties and European jealousies while safeguarding British interests, Lord Salisbury's Conservative Government sent Sir Henry Drummond Wolff to Istanbul in 1885, to negotiate a settlement. Foreign Minister in his own government, Salisbury instructed Wolff to accept the principle of evacuation but without binding Britain "to a fixed date" or to "the formal consent of the Powers to anything we do" and to acquire "a treaty right to occupy Alexandria when we pleased." Salisbury was even prepared, he informed the British ambassador at Vienna, "to get Turkish soldiers — they need not be in any very great numbers — sent to Egypt, both for the obvious convenience of using soldiers who will stand the heat better than ours, and who are of the same religion as the natives — but also and still more for a political reason.... It seems to us that small bodies of Turkish troops, sent there to stay as long as the English, and go when they go, will regularise our position."[7]

The negotiators of the 1885 convention, Wolff and Gazi Ahmed Muhtar Pasha, were named High Commissioners to study the situation in Egypt. Their report led to resumed negotiations to frame a more explicit agreement that would reaffirm Ottoman sovereignty and meet the demands of France and Russia for a full British withdrawal, without compromising basic British interests. Whitehall promptly ratified the 1887 instrument. But the Sublime Porte did not, primarily because of the inflexible opposition of France and Russia to the ambiguity of article 5 regarding the exact date of the proposed British troop evacuation and the right of British military re-entry in the event of a crisis.

Thereafter, British-Ottoman relations became openly hostile. The Sublime Porte kept Muhtar Pasha as High Commissioner in Cairo to oversee Ottoman rights and claims; but Sir Evelyn Baring (later the Earl of Cromer), Her Majesty's Agent and Consul General, refused to accept Muhtar's credentials and dealt with the Porte through the Khedive, the British Embassy in Istanbul, or the Foreign Office in London. The first opportunity for the Porte to attempt to assert its sovereign powers in Egypt and to change the provincial quasiinternational boundaries came in 1892, on the death of Khedive Tawfīq. By then the British occupation was nearly a decade old and seemed to be solidifying. In the draft *firmān* of investiture, Sultan Abdülhamid II inserted a clause removing from Egyptian jurisdiction the 'Aqaba-Wajh littoral strip and the Sinai peninsula beyond the 1841 boundary. When Britain contested the proposed action, the Porte maintained that both areas lay outside the privileged demarcation line.

On prior occasions, as has been noted, the 1841 enabling *firmān* had been modified by the mutual consent of the padishah and the pasha without the

7 Lady Gwendolyn Cecil, *Life of Robert, Marquis of Salisbury*, vol. 2 (London: Hodder and Stoughton, 1921), pp. 235-36.

Concert's taking any position on the amendments: in 1866 when the Khedive was allowed to change the principle of dynastic succession from seniority to primogeniture; and in 1867 when he adopted the title of Khedive for himself and his heirs and was permitted to conclude nonpolitical agreements with foreign powers. In June 1879, Sultan Abdülhamid II enlarged his own powers under the enabling *firmān* by exercising the right to depose the Khedive, following the joint protest of Britain and France over Ismā'īl's effort to eliminate the Dual Control. The other major powers remained silent. In 1892, Sultan Abdülhamid was not proposing to amend the 1841 instrument but to put it into literal effect.

More than three months elapsed, however, between the death of Tawfīq early in January 1892 and the appearance of the *firmān* investing 'Abbās Ḥilmī II as Khedive in the *Journal Officiel* on April 14, the date on which it went into effect. In the interval the draft *firmān* had been amended because of the adamant opposition of the British Agent and Consul General to the removal of any part of the Sinai peninsula from the Egyptian administration. As a concession to Ottoman sensibilities, Sir Evelyn Baring consented to the transfer from the Egyptian sphere to the *vilâyet* of the Hijaz of the police posts at al-'Aqaba, al-Muwaylih, Duba, and al-Wajh which had been assigned to Ismā'īl a quarter-century earlier to enable the Khedivate to expedite the overland movement of its *maḥmal* in the annual pilgrimage to Mecca. The Grand Vezir Ahmed Cevad Pasha, in a telegram to the Khedive 'Abbās Ḥilmī II on April 8, 1892, confirmed the transfer of the 'Aqaba-Wajh strip from Egypt to the *vilâyet* of Hijaz, but "as regards the Peninsula of Tor-Sinai, the *status quo* is maintained, and it will be administered by the Khedivate in the same manner as it was administered in the time of your grandfather, Ismail Pasha, and of your father, Mehémet Tewfik Pasha."[8]

Baring did not stop there. On April 13, he exchanged notes with Tigrane Pasha, the Khedive's Armenian Foreign Secretary. Tigrane assured Baring that the Grand Vezir, in the name of Sultan Abdülhamid II, had entrusted to 'Abbās Ḥilmī II "as to his predecessors the administration of the Peninsula of Mount Sinai." In reply, Baring called Tigrane's attention to the fact "that no alteration can be made in the Firmans regulating the relations between the Sublime Porte and Egypt without the consent of Her Britannic Majesty's Government." This explained why Baring "was instructed to invite your Excellency's attention to the insertion in the present Firman of a definition of boundaries which differed from that contained in the firman issued to His Highness the late Khedive [Tawfīq], and which, if read by itself, appeared to imply that the Sinai peninsula — that is to say, the territory bounded to the east by a line running in a south-easterly direction from a point a short distance to the east of El-Arish

8 From the text of the English translation in Cd. 3006, p. 4.

to the head of the Gulf of Akaba — is to continue to be administered by Egypt. The fort of Akaba, which lies to the east of the line in question, will thus form part of the Vilayet of the Hedjaz." Baring also pointed out in the same note that the British government had notified the Porte several weeks earlier of its willingness to agree to such a deal. He concluded, under instructions from London, with a statement that[9]

> Her Britannic Majesty's Government consent to the definition of boundaries contained in the present Firman, as supplemented, amended, and explained by the telegram of the 8th instant from his Highness the Grand Vizier, which they consider as annexed to and as forming part of the Firman, and that they entertain no objection to the offical promulgation of the Firman, with the addition of the above-mentioned explanatory telegram.

The 1892 episode removed some of the ambiguities about the exercise of de facto sovereignty in Egypt. But it created new ambiguities about the exact location of the eastern boundary of the Sinai peninsula, since Baring's definition — "a line running in a south-easterly direction from a point a short distance to the east of El-Arish to the head of the Gulf of Aqaba" — was far too vague. How far east of al-'Arīsh did the boundary start, and how far west of the fort of al-'Aqaba did it end? Entering into the diplomatic calculus were the subtle realities in the trilateral relations between the padishah, the Khedive, and the British Agent and Consul General. This much could be said with certitude. Britain was determined to remain in Egypt to safeguard its lifeline of Empire; but having entered the Ottoman province under a legal cloud, it seemed unable to remove one ambiguity without creating another. The Sublime Porte, for its part, was no less determined to cling to its claims to Egypt by attempting to reassert its sovereign rights. It won half a victory in regaining administrative control over the Hijazi coast. It had not yet abandoned hope of making the victory complete, as the episode of 1906 demonstrated.

IV

The Sublime Porte by 1905 had completed the Hijaz Railroad as far as Ma'an and was proceeding to implement the plans for the construction of the next section as far as al-'Aqaba. The Ottoman Government sought unchallenged title to the districts through which the railroad was to pass with as much depth as possible west of the projected line for its uncontested operation. The expressed Ottoman concerns about the possible British-Egyptian interference with the projected building of the Hijaz Railroad

9 From texts, *ibid.*, p. 5.

may have been real. But the reality grew out of the perceptions of the responsible Ottoman officials not out of any evident British or Egyptian plans to interfere with the ongoing railroad construction. Any mention, on the other hand, of tampering with the unmarked eastern frontier of Egypt as "defined" by Baring in 1892 caused palpitations in Whitehall and sent its seasoned Agent and Consul General in Cairo scurrying into a flurry of activity. The Mediterranean coast excepted, the Sinai peninsula had not discovered the telegraph, and the overland transmission of messages between Cairo and the Gulf of al-'Aqaba area took four days by camel. Yet British intelligence was sufficiently sensitized to keep the Agent and Consul General informed on the minutest change of Ottoman provincial plans and transient military population in and around al-'Aqaba.

In mid-January 1906 sparks began to fly at the head of the gulf. Ottoman and British military officers were trading charges of cross-boundary encroachment. Both sides resorted to military posturing at the Mediterranean and the gulf extremeties of the contested zone along the unmarked line that was supposed to separate Egypt from the adjacent Ottoman Asian provinces: the independent *sancak* of Jerusalem and the *vilâyet* of Hijaz. On or about January 15, on instructions from Cromer, a minuscule Egyptian desert police force of some twenty-five men, under the command of W. E. Jennings Bramly, the recently appointed Inspector of the Sinai peninsula with headquarters at Nakhl, and Sa'id Bey Rif 'at, his Egyptian deputy, arrived at the top of the Gulf of 'Aqaba aboard a coastguard patrol boat, the *Nūr al-Baḥr*, with instructions to observe and report on Ottoman military actions. The only such actions they could report were those taken against themselves. The Ottoman troops, under the command of Infantry Brigadier Rüshdi Pasha with headquarters at the fort of al-'Aqaba, by threat of forcible resistance prevented the Egyptian patrol unit from landing at Um Rashrash (present-day Eilat) or at Taba, the adjacent coastal settlement to the southwest. Bramly, Rif'at and company therefore set up camp on the nearby island of Fara'un further south, and from there refused to budge despite recurrent orders from Rüshdi Pasha to vacate the premises.

When this token show of force failed to yield the expected results, the Agent and Consul General, with the approval of Foreign Secretary Sir Edward Grey, on February 14 instructed Captain Phipps Hornby, the Commander of HMS *Diana*, a destroyer kept on alert at Suez, to proceed to Fara'un. Upon the anchorage of the *Diana* off 'Aqaba, Rüshdi Pasha ordered his troops (an estimated three-four thousand officers and men) to their battle stations. But an exchange of fire was averted by Hornby's engaging in direct exchanges with Rüshdi. The *Diana* lingered for three months in the Gulf waters until the diplomatic crisis had passed and, in the belief of Cromer, discouraged the Ottomans from thickening their "encroachment" on the contested zone. Meanwhile, at the end of April the British agency at Cairo learned of the Ottoman military takeover of Rafah and the removal of two marble pillars which had "for many years" signified the boundary between Egypt and Ottoman Asia. After consulting the Foreign Secretary and the British Naval Commander in the Mediterranean, Cromer instructed Captain Waymouth of HMS *Minverva* to go to Rafah with an Egyptian official. When Waymouth and his Egyptian aide debarked, they encountered "a detachment of Turkish soldiers... [advancing] towards the shore on the Egyptian side of the boundary in skirmishing order, and the Turkish Commandant openly stated that he had orders to fire if any troops had been landed from the cruiser. He refused to recognize Captain Waymouth in any official capacity, and regarded him merely as a visitor."[10] Despite the minatory welcome, the British naval officer was able to observe and report that the Ottoman soldiers had replaced eleven Egyptian telegraph poles west of Rafah with their own.

Clearly, neither side could do much physical damage with the lilliputian forces that confronted each other at the water's edge, at both ends of the contested zone. Little wonder that no diplomatic progress was made through the end of April. The British moves were largely orchestrated in Cairo. There, the Sublime Porte put to work its still unaccredited High Commissioner, Ahmed Muhtar Pasha, who had originally gained prominence as a hero of the Russian-Ottoman war of 1877-78 for which he was decorated with the title of Gazi. The continued presence in Egypt of High Commissioner Muhtar Pasha was the Sublime Porte's way of signaling Britain that the Ottoman claims to the occupied province had not been given up. Although Muhtar Pasha reported on developments in Cairo, Cromer refused "to recognize . . . [his] pretention to act in this capacity," while at the same time, the Agent and Consul General "in personal relations with his Excellency, treated him with the respect due to a distinguished Turkish General."[11] In this connection, Cromer held in his grip, discreetly yet firmly, the Khedive and his ministers. Thus, in the 1906 boundary crisis, Cromer would not allow Muhtar Pasha to confer with the Khedive except in the presence of the Egyptian cabinet chief and his foreign minister.

Beyond the British Agency's control, however, were the Egyptian nationalists who by 1906 were becoming more assertive and who publicly supported the Porte in its boundary quarrel with Britain. This did not reflect the nationalists' endorsement of Pan-Islamic doctrines, as Cromer reported to London, but their protest against the British occupation. The potential threat to the occupying power doubtless entered into the British diplomatic assessment in the early spring of 1906.

At the start of the crisis, three months earlier, the Khedive had suggested to the Sublime Porte — on British prompting — the appointment of a joint

10 *Ibid.*, 27.
11 *Ibid.*, p. 25.

Egyptian-Ottoman boundary commission to reach agreement on a dividing line between Sinai and Ottoman Asia. The Grand Vezir Mehmet Ferid Pasha dismissed the suggestion out of hand. He contended that 'Aqaba and its environs, Taba included, fell within the Porte's jurisdiction and demanded that Egypt should stop erecting posts in the contested area on pain of forcible expulsion. The Grand Vezir insisted on the immediate withdrawal of the *Nūr al-Baḥr* and the Egyptian detachment from Fara'un island. At the end of January the Foreign Office, on advice from the Agency in Cairo, instructed Ambassador Nicholas O'Conor at Istanbul to protest to the Sublime Porte about its rejection of the proposal for a joint boundary commission and its failure to take into account the 1892 understanding and warned that any threat forcibly to interfere with Egypt's effort to implement in good faith the 1892 understanding would be met with British counterforce. In mid-February the Foreign Office called in Kostaki Müsürüs Pasha, the Ottoman Ambassador in London, to complain about the aggressive stance of the Porte in the Gulf of 'Aqaba, stating that the Ottoman troops would have to withdraw from Taba to ensure a peaceful settlement of the dispute.

And so it went in circles, from Cairo to London to Istanbul and back again without forward movement until early in May, when the British government began deliberately to publicize its accelerated military measures: the reinforcement of the army of occupation and the orders to Admiral Lord Charles Beresford, the commander of the British Mediterranean fleet, to move to the Piraeus. At the same time Ambassador O'Conor presented to the Sublime Porte a peremptory note that, unless it agreed within ten days to take part in a mixed commission to demarcate the disputed boundary, Britain would impose its will by force of arms. Moreover, pending the conclusion of the proposed boundary agreement, all Ottoman military units would have to withdraw from Taba and from their position on the Mediterranean coast west of Rafah. The Sublime Porte, in the end, complied with the British demands. But before doing so, it requested Britain's formal acknowledgement of Ottoman suzerainty over Egypt. The Foreign Office readily complied, subject however to Britain's continued exercise of full freedom of action for the duration of the occupation, or as Cromer paraphrased it, "His Majesty's Government had never failed to recognize the suzerainty of His Imperial Majesty, but. . . if it were found that this suzerainty were incompatible with the right of His Majesty's Government to interfere in Egyptian affairs and with the British occupation, the British position in Egypt would be upheld by the whole force of the Empire."[12]

The Ottoman-British crisis had the practical effect of producing for the first time an agreed demarcation of British Egypt's eastern boundary or

12 *Ibid.*, p. 29.

administrative separating line, as it was called, as a verbal sop to the Sublime Porte. The terms were embodied in a British-Egyptian Agreement with the Porte signed on October 1, 1906. It was a de facto, not a de jure, arrangement, as it had to be, since the British presence in Egypt was that of a military occupation in which Whitehall exercised de facto sovereignty only, without formally repudiating the legal sovereignty of the Ottoman government. Moreover, despite the ambiguities which persisted well beyond the expiry of the Ottoman Empire the administrative separating line of 1906 became the international boundary between Egypt and mandated Palestine.

THOMAS MAYER

Dreamers and Opportunists: 'Abbās Ḥilmī's Peace Initiative in Palestine, 1930-1931

At the end of October 1930, 'Ovadia Camhy, a Jewish journalist residing in Paris, sent a dramatic letter to Chaim Weizmann, President of the Zionist Executive. In his letter Camhy disclosed that he had been approached by a member of the Conseil Central Islamique with a proposal to arrange a meeting between the chairman of the Council, the former Egyptian Khedive, 'Abbās Ḥilmī and a Zionist representative to discuss Jewish-Arab rapprochement.[1] Camhy did not explain why the former Khedive had chosen him to convey this attractive offer to Weizmann, nor why 'Abbās Ḥilmī had suddenly become interested in arbitration between Jews and Arabs in Palestine. To understand 'Abbās Ḥilmī's peace initiative one should look first at the careers of both the ex-Khedive and 'Ovadia Camhy.

A. *'Abbās Ḥilmī in International Politics.*

'Abbās Ḥilmī's career could not be described as either quiet or stable. Between 1892-1914, he ruled Egypt as its third Khedive. In this office he played a part in the rise of both the national movement in Egypt[2] and the Pan-Arab movement in the Arab provinces of the Ottoman Empire.[3] These

1 'Ovadia Camhy (Paris) to Weizmann (London), 30 Oct., 1930, *Weizmann Archives* (Rehovot). In his memoirs, "An attempt at Agreement between Jews and Arabs", *Hed ha-Mizrah*, 1950, No. 25, p. 11, Camhy gives a different date for this letter.

2 Earl of Cromer, *Abbas II* (London, 1915); Arthur Goldshmidt Jr., "The Egyptian Nationalist Party, 1892-1919", in P.M.Holt (ed.), *Political and Social Change in Modern Egypt* (London, 1968), pp. 308-333; Awrāq Muḥammad Farīd, *Mudhakkirātī Ba'da al-Hijra (1904-1919)* (Cairo, 1978), pp. 51-58 (1-4); *al-Misri* (Cairo), 10,14,17,13 May 1951; File 4/4-47, *'Abbās Ḥilmī Papers* (Durham) contain numerous letters by Muṣṭafā Kāmil to the Khedive.

3 Farīd, *op. cit.* pp. 99-100, 116-117 (43, 54-55); Sylvia Haim, *Arab Nationalism* (Los Angeles, 1976), pp. 28-29; Elie Kedourie, *Arabic Political Memoirs* (London, 1974), pp. 107-123, and his, *In the Anglo-Arab Labyrinth* (Cambridge, 1976), pp. 6-13. In a conver-

activities enraged both the British and the Turkish Governments. During the summer of 1914, while the Khedive was on vacation in Turkey, British officials contemplated his deposition, and the Turkish Government, fearing that he would become "the possible leader of an Arab movement",[4] supported an attempt by 'Abd al-'Azīz Shāwīsh's radical Egyptian nationalist group to assassinate him.

The Khedive survived the attempt on his life but was to lose his throne after Turkey's entry into the First World War. The British Government, happy to rid themselves of a local ruler who had proved to be a stubborn rival to their aspirations of absolute rule in Egypt, took full advantage of 'Abbās Ḥilmī's association with enemy agents in belligerent Turkey. The government declared a Protectorate over Egypt, announced 'Abbās Ḥilmī's deposition, and appointed his cousin, Ḥusayn Kemal as Egypt's new nominal ruler with the title of Sultan.[5]

This unilateral act on the part of the British affected 'Abbās Ḥilmī greatly. From then on, the former Khedive went to great lengths to regain his influence in Egypt and the Arab East. First from Vienna, where he arrived in December 1914, and then from Switzerland, where he settled in June 1915, 'Abbās Ḥilmī launched a series of talks with German, British, Turkish, Egyptian, and Arab parties, aiming to improve his position. During 1915-1917, 'Abbās Ḥilmī negotiated and obtained from the German Government huge sums of money, much of which were spent on a futile attempt to bribe the French press to espouse the cause of the Central Powers.[6]

Simultaneously, the former Khedive negotiated the terms of his abdication with British officials. He told British officials that he was a genuine ally mistakenly labelled an enemy. To prove his good faith, 'Abbās Ḥilmī agreed to accept Sultan Ḥusayn Kamil's appointment as a *fait accompli* if his extensive property in Egypt were protected and the right of succession of his two sons recognized. In addition, 'Abbās Ḥilmī requested a new role

sation with J.R. Hamilton in 1945, Prince Muḥammad 'Alī recalled that his brother, 'Abbās Ḥilmī, had presided, prior to 1914, over a 'League' which had been designed to secure from the Turkish Government a greater degree of autonomy (Hamilton's report to London, 4 July 1945, FO 371/45239/E5427). It may be that this was the Society of the Arab League, the foundation of which Amīn Sa'īd, *al-Thawra al-'Arabiyya al-Kubrā* (Cairo, n.d.), Vol. I, pp. 49-50, attributed to Rashīd Riḍā.

4 Cheetham (Cairo) to London, 25 Aug., 1914, FO 141/648/232/pt.I/144; John W. Field (FO), Memorandum on the deposition on Khedive 'Abbās Ḥilmī and the liquidation of his property in Egypt, FO 407/198, No. 20, pp. 20-21; Ronald Storrs, *Orientations* (London, 1937), pp. 144-145; *al-Misri*, 5,10 July 1951.

5 Field's Memorandum, pp. 21-24; Lord Lloyd, *Egypt Since Cromer* (London, 1933), Vol. I, pp. 201, 376-378; Aḥmad Shafīq, *Ḥawliyāt Miṣr al-Siyāsiyya* (Cairo, 1926), Vol. I, pp. 58-64.

6 Detailed accounts of these contacts ('the Bolo Scandal'), and their failure, in FO 141/648/232/pt.I/76,151, FO 141/451/4958, FO 141/817/3864; Fillipo Cavallini, *Il Processo Cavallini* (Milano, n.d.), pp. 25-39.

for himself. Having somehow learnt of the British-Sharīfian talks on an Arab rebellion against the Turks, the former Khedive maintained that he had "great influence" in Syria and Arabia, and that if the intended uprising were successful he would expect Britain to compensate him for the loss of Egypt.[7]

'Abbās Ḥilmī failed to persuade British officialdom that he was a better candidate than Sharīf Ḥusayn of Mecca for leadership of the Arab revolt. This, however, did not put an end to his activities. While negotiating new terms for his abdication with British officials, he supported and financed Egyptian nationalist groups which opposed British occupation of Egypt.[8] In addition, the former Khedive also held talks with Turkish and German officials. In late June 1917, Constantinople, apparently following German advice, offered 'Abbās Ḥilmī a viceroyalty over an autonomous province of Syria to counterbalance the newly created Kingdom of Arabia.[9] When he still hesitated, the former Khedive was further promised his lost throne in Egypt, a generous salary, and his personal safety guaranteed by the German and Austrian Governments.[10] When the Turkish Government also agreed to pay the major part of his debts in Switzerland (£50,000), 'Abbās Ḥilmī returned to Constantinople.

The end of the war found 'Abbās Ḥilmī in Turkey still awaiting the promised viceroyalty. Meanwhile, his cooperation with Britain's enemies during the war substantially damaged his economic and legal position in Egypt. In November 1918, the former Khedive's estates in Egypt were transferred to the supervision of the Public Custodian of Enemy Property who began selling them.[11] In April 1920, the British Government approved the right of succession of Prince Fārūq, son of the new Egyptian Sultan, Aḥmad Fu'ād,[12] and in March 1922, the Government reiterated their approval after Fu'ād, following the British unilateral declaration of Egyptian independence, declared himself King and issued an order establishing the line of succession from father to son.[13]

7 FO to High Commissioner for Egypt, 4 Jan., 1916; Consul's Report (Berne) to London, 17 Dec., 1915, FO 141/648/232/54,55. For 'Abbās Ḥilmī's apparent expectations see also 'Prine Ḥabīb Lutfalla's "Resumé du Programme Separation Arabo-Turquo" (London, 8 Nov., 1915), and his letter of 2 Apr., 1917 (Madrid) which were sent to British officials (FO 141/471/1731/2,9).

8 For his contacts with various Egyptian groups during the War, consult, *'AHP* (Durham), Files 38, 89, 93, 202-203.

9 FO to High Commissioner for Egypt, 12 July, 1917, FO 141/648/232/124. For German pressure on 'Abbās to return to Constantinople, see *'AHP*, File 289/68-76.

10 FO to High Commissioner for Egypt, 12 Oct., 1917, "B" Branch, Eastern Mediterranean Special Intelligence Bureau (Cairo), 9 Oct., 1917, FO 141/648/232/146.

11 Field's Memorandum, pp. 27-34.

12 Shafīq, *op. cit.* Vol. I. pp. 685-686.

13 Sirdar Iqbal Ali Shah, *Fuad, King of Egypt* (London, 1936), p. 179; *The Times* (London), 17 Apr., 1922.

'Abbās Ḥilmī never acquiesced in these obstructions in his economic and legal position in Egypt. Time and again he attempted by various means to bring about their annulment. In 1920 he promised British policy-makers that if he were returned to power he would promote the Anglo-Egyptian alliance which had been contemplated in Lord Milner's agreement.[14]. Simultaneously, the former Khedive, who had moved back to Switzerland in 1921, directed a massive campaign intended primarily to restore himself to power in Egypt. He was reported to have given funds to such Egyptian newspapers as *al-Waṭan* and *al-Liwā'* to promote his cause, smuggled arms and saboteurs into Egypt, and established close relations with radical Egyptian groups in Europe such as 'Abd al-Ḥamīd Sa'īd's League of the Oppressed Nations of the East, which operated from Italy. In addition, 'Abbās Ḥilmī continually approached various political leaders in Egypt in his ceaseless efforts to draw them to his side.[15]

While concentrating his efforts upon regaining power in Egypt, 'Abbās Ḥilmī also helped create other options. In 1921, he was said to have offered to mediate between the French Government and Sharīf Ḥusayn of Mecca over the latter's bid for Syria. These contacts soon led to rumors that 'Abbās Ḥilmī had become the French choice for the throne of Syria.[16] Significantly, he also became the choice of the League of the Oppressed Nations of the East for this throne,[17] and since the Lausanne Conference in November 1922, also the candidate of the Syro-Palestinian delegation for this position.[18] Since the leaders of both organizations were financially supported by the former Khedive,[19] it is likely that he had a hand in their decision to advocate his candidacy for the Syrian throne. It is not surprising therefore that as late as 1928, Shakīb Arslān, Secretary of the Syro-Palestinian delegation, considered 'Abbās Ḥilmī's candidacy for the Syrian throne as "a practical possibility".[20]

14 High Commissioner (Constantinople) to Cairo, 19 Sep., 1920, FO 141/648/232/194.

15 Detailed accounts of these activities in FO 141/650/232/235-289; *'AHP*, File 120.

16 Director, Special Section, Public Security Department's Reports, 6 Aug., 9 Sep., 1932, FO 141/650/232/240,269.

17 Same's report, 19 Dec., 1921, FO 141/650/232/278.

18 Same's reports, 30 Nov., 1922, 2 Jan., 1923, FO 141/650/232/342a, 352.

19 For the former Khedive's contacts with Sa'īd's group, see: FO 141/650/232/239,262,264. Aḥmad al-Sharbasī, *Amīr al-Bayān Shakīb Arslān* (Cairo, 1963), Vol. II, p. 592, cites Shakīb Arslān's letter admitting a monthly salary of 30 Pounds. The evidence in *'AHP*, File 118 suggests that Arslān received a far higher salary for a rather long period.

20 Mahmud Azmi, "The last of the Khedives and the Syrian Throne", *The Arabic World* (London), Vol. I, No. 1, 6 June, 1933, p. 6. In a letter to 'Abbās Ḥilmī as late as 4 Nov., 1929, Shakīb Arslān explained the circumstances that compelled his colleague, Iḥsān al-Jabrī, to deny that the Syro-Palestinian delegation supported the ex-Khedive's bid for the Syrian throne, and further assured 'Abbās that he was "a king among the Muslim Kings, and a Muslim King by right" (*'AHP*, File 118/265-262).

'Abbās Ḥilmī, however, was evidently not the kind of man to confine himself to a single choice. Indeed, in 1921, the former Khedive evinced some interest in the throne of Albania,[21] while in 1924 he was alleged to have come to "an arrangement with Shaykh Aḥmad al-Sanūsī that the latter would become a Caliph and 'Abbās, through the Shaykh's support, King of Tripolitania".[22] In addition, the former Khedive financed and chaired a number of Pan-Islamic and Pan-Arab societies in Europe, such as the Supreme Oriental Revolutionary Council,[23] and the Alliance Musulmane Internationale.[24] By means of these societies, 'Abbās Ḥilmī aspired to promote his image as a Muslim leader and to revive his influence in the Arab East.

Such extensive activity required huge sums of money as did 'Abbās Ḥilmī's large entourage and grandiose life-style. Although he was a very rich man with large properties abroad, including a bank in Turkey,[25] the former Khedive suffered nonetheless from the confiscation of his large estates in Egypt. Since his deposition 'Abbās Ḥilmī had been negotiating the financial terms of his abdication, including compensation for the liquidation of his Egyptian estates. When the British Government seemed reluctant to respond to his financial claims, 'Abbās Ḥilmī brought legal proceedings against them in various courts.[26]

Until October 1930, 'Abbās Ḥilmī could not claim great success for his efforts to improve his economic and political position in the Arab East. The main obstacle to the advancement of his plans in the East continued to be the British Government. In spite of an extensive propaganda campaign portraying him as a friend of Britain, British officials remained suspicious of 'Abbās Ḥilmī's intentions. Therefore, 'Abbās Ḥilmī may have hoped that mediating between Jews and Arabs in Palestine would prove his friendship to Britain and place himself in an influential position in the East. In October 1930, the task of reconciling the Zionists with the Palestinian Arabs would not have seemed impossible to anyone such as 'Abbās Ḥilmī

21 Public Security Dept.'s report, 20 Sep. 1921, FO 141/650/232/248.

22 N.M. Henderson (Constantinople) to A.K. Clark-Kerr (Cairo), 28 June, 1924, FO 141/547/472/322. British officials were inclined to dismiss these allegations made by the Italian representative in Turkey. However, during 1924, Shakīb Arslān persistently asked 'Abbās to cooperate with Aḥmad al-Sanūsī (See, for example, *'AHP*, File 118/96-103, 119-122, 139), and it is not impossible that some sort of cooperation was at last concluded.

23 Public Security's Report, 16 Jan., 1923, FO 141/650/232/357,358; *'AHP*, File 120/170.

24 For 'Abbās Ḥilmī's support for this and other Societies, consult: *'AHP*, Files 36,37,89/124-130.

25 *Oriente Moderno* (Rome), Vol. V, 1925, pp. 246-247; *'AHP*, File 179/18-49. Status of the Bank is in *'AHP*, the Pamphlets' section.

26 For details of the various legal proceedings. consult FO 141/548,549/472; *'AHP*, Files 215,217,224,231,241,243,251; Ardern Hulme Beaman, *The Dethronement of the Khedive* (London, 1929), pp. 80-109, 180-186.

who was not overly well-informed about the Palestinian conflict. In fact, at this time the former Khedive must have been quite sceptical about the veracity of rumors of monstrous Zionist economic and political capabilities.[27] For there was nothing in the state of the Zionist movement in 1930 to indicate that it really had the power alleged by the Protocols of the Elders of Zion. As early as April 1930, following the examination of the International Commission of Enquiry of the Wailing Wall disturbances, a well known advocate of the Palestinian Arab cause, Shakīb Arslān, informed 'Abbās Ḥilmī that the Zionist cause had suffered a severe setback.[28] And by October 1930, when the British Government published the White Paper restricting Jewish immigration into Palestine, many must have thought that the Zionist movement had come to the end of the road. Now that the Zionist vision of free Jewish immigration into Palestine seemed shattered, would it not be easy to make peace between the few Jews already in Palestine and the local Arab residents there? And would not Britain be grateful to the peacemaker? Such considerations might have entered the former Khedive's mind when he sanctioned the meeting with 'Ovadia Camhy. But even if he had had no expectations before the meeting with Camhy, 'Abbās Ḥilmī must have grown rather optimistic after learning that Camhy was so enthusiastic over the prospects of the ex-Khedive's meeting with Weizmann.

B. *The Weizmann-'Abbās Ḥilmī Meeting and its Aftermath.*

In a report to Weizmann on one of his meetings with 'Abbās Ḥilmī 'Ovadia Camhy cites the former Khedive's praise of Camhy as the initiator of their peace-making project.[29] Camhy may be correct on this particular point, though it is clear that strict truthfulness is not characteristic of his reports in general. His numerous letters to Weizmann contain evidence suggesting the existence of a strong personal interest in the forthcoming peace project. A former editor of *Menorah*, a small and unprofitable Parisian journal, Camhy ran into severe financial difficulties after the Zionist Executive in London decided to stop subsidizing this publication in November 1929,[30] and he soon lost his job. For a while he worked as the Paris correspondent of a Hebrew daily in Palestine, *Do'ar ha-Yōm*, while

27 An undated Arabic translation by Anṭūn Yamīn al-Khūrī of a 1920 French edition of the Protocols of the Elders of Zion is in *'AHP*, the Pamphlets' section. This section also contains Marsden's English translation of the Protocols which was published in 1931.

28 Shakīb Arslān (Geneve) to 'Abbās Ḥilmī, 25 Apr., 1930, *'AHP*, File 118/276.

29 'Ovadia Camhy (Algiers) to Weizmann (London), 4 March, 1931, *WA*.

30 Weizmann (London) to Leo Motzkin (Paris), 24 Sep., 1929; same to 'Ovadia Camhy (Paris), 25 Sep., 1929, in Barnet Litvinoff (Gen. ed.), *The Letters and Papers of Chaim Weizmann* (Jerusalem, 1978), Vol. XIV, Series A. July 1929-October 1930, pp. 49, 106.

participating in casual attempts to offer Zionist loans in exchange for the silence of Palestinian Arab leaders.[31] However, the income from these occupations must have been disappointingly small since, in his flood of letters to Weizmann, Camhy constantly asked for money. Therefore Camhy might have valued the contacts with ʻAbbās Ḥilmī, a well-known millionaire, not only for their expected advantages to the Zionist cause, but also for their possible benefit to himself. Indeed, as we shall soon see, Camhy, by way of these negotiations, contemplated a permanent role for himself in the peace project. This ambition evidently blurred Camhy's judgment to such an extent that he saw sincere intentions and good faith in what was an ambivalent and cynical approach. He substituted dreams and personal expectations for reality.

Camhy's enthusiastic report to Weizmann elicited a positive reply, and on November 15, 1930, ʻAbbās Ḥilmī met the Zionist leader in Paris. According to Camhy's account, the only known report of the meeting, the two leaders agreed on the need and merit of Arab-Jewish cooperation. ʻAbbās Ḥilmī offered his good offices to enlist the help of Ḥusayn's sons Fayṣal, King of Iraq, and ʻAbdallāh, Emir of Trans-Jordan. Weizmann, for his part, recalled his meeting and agreement with Fayṣal in 1918, and offered to invest one million pounds in the building of the Iraqi railway line to Haifa if, in return, the Zionists were given Wādī Zarqā' in Trans-Jordan. Weizmann evidently believed that the Hāshemite brothers were in accord and working in unison and that ʻAbdallāh would not object to giving away part of his land for the prosperity of Fayṣal's dominion. We do not know what ʻAbbās Ḥilmī's immediate reaction to this fancy was, but we learn from Camhy's report that the two leaders agreed to meet again twenty days later after Weizmann's return from London.[32]

Unable to attend the next meeting, and clearly not considering the contacts with ʻAbbās Ḥilmī to be very important, Weizmann nonetheless deputed Harry Sacher, a British member of the Zionist Executive, who was then in France, to see the former Khedive. Sacher was not greatly impressed by ʻAbbās Ḥilmī, nor did he find any cause for optimism in his attitude towards an Arab-Jewish rapprochment: ʻAbbās Ḥilmī was "emphatic" that nothing could be done to enhance an entente with the Arabs without the agreement of the Palestinian Arabs. The former Khedive expressed optimism only concerning Weizmann's projected land transaction in which he was more than ready to participate, considering it "quite easy" to achieve on "a joint Arab-Jewish basis". He did not explain how this project could be so easily achieved when any Arab-Jewish rapproch-

31 See, for example, Itammar Ben-Avi (Paris) to Weizmann (London), 17 June 1930, and Weizmann to Ben-Avi, 10 Oct., 1930, *WA* for details of a £300 loan to Rāghib al-Nashāshībī.

32 *Hed ha-Mizrah*, 1950, No. 26, p. 8.

ment depended on the Palestinian Arabs, but Sacher did not take the trouble to enquire. A lawyer by profession, Sacher may have become suspicious of the difference between 'Abbās Ḥilmī's attitude to making peace and doing business. Consequently, Sacher sent a negative report to Weizmann, pointing out 'Abbās Ḥilmī's meager influence in the East.[33]

Sacher's negative report might have ended Zionist contacts with the ex-Khedive had not the initiative been continuously pressed by two persons: 'Ovadia Camhy and Maḥmūd 'Azmī, private secretary of 'Abbās Ḥilmī.[34]

C. *Camhy and 'Azmī's 'Grand Design'.*

Shortly after Weizmann's meeting with 'Abbās Ḥilmī, Camhy sent to the Zionist leader a long and optimistic report in which he set forth some ideas for a Jewish-Arab rapprochement. The ideas were collated in a composition entitled *Confédération Arabe* and sub-titled *Création d'une Revue Littéraire Judeo-Arabe.* The composition, which ran to some five pages, conveyed in detail Camhy's belief that the Arabs would agree to recognize the principle of a Jewish National Home in Palestine within the framework of an Arab Confederation. Camhy considered that within such a confederation an exchange of nationals such as that between Turkey and Greece would be possible. The confederation was to be established in stages. Palestine and Egypt or Palestine and Mesopotamia first, then the Hijaz, Yemen, and so on. Camhy anticipated that if this program were realised, no fewer than 14 million Jews could live in the land between Palestine and Mesopotamia. Camhy further asserted that the Palestinian Arabs, far from being hostile to the Jews, shared similar interests. Their fear of the Jews emanated solely from the growing differentiation between the Palestinian classes and the adverse effect of the Colonial Office. An urgent need had arisen to explain to Arab readers the true nature of Zionism. Camhy proposed the founding of an Arabic journal in which personalities from the Jewish and Muslim world would advocate Jewish-Muslim rapprochement. The publication was to be supervised by a committee of eminent Jews and Muslims and was to run from Paris, where Camhy himself lived.[35]

How did a Jewish journalist residing in France become an advocate of Arab confederation? During the early 1930's, the idea that the Palestine conflict could and should be settled through the creation of an Arab Confederation gained popularity in certain Zionist circles in Palestine.[36]

33 Harry Sacher to Weizmann (London), 29 Dec., 1930, *WA*.

34 For detailed accounts of Maḥmūd 'Azmī's position, consult: *'AHP*, File 121, especially from p. 129 onwards.

35 Camhy (Paris) to Weizmann (London), 2 Dec., 1930, *WA*.

36 For general accounts on this interest consult: Susan Lee Hattis, *The bi-national idea in Palestine during mandatory times* (Haifa, 1970). Aaron Kedar, "Brit Shalom", *The*

But Camhy's views were not affected only by the Zionist literature concerning this confederation. In his memoirs, Camhy also mentions two persons whose staunch belief in this idea encouraged his own support for Arab confederation. They were 'Abd al-Raḥmān al-Tājī, a member of the Supreme Islamic Council in Palestine, who had been Camhy's host in Vichy during the summer of 1930,[37] and Maḥmūd 'Azmī.

Camhy does not elaborate on the period he spent as Tājī's guest in Vichy but the name of Maḥmūd 'Azmī recurs time and again in his memoirs and reports to Weizmann. Since Camhy included Egypt in the projected Arab confederation, an idea advocated by few people other than Maḥmūd 'Azmī, it should prove worthwhile examining 'Azmī's career more closely.

An Egyptian by birth, 'Azmī spent a considerable part of his life abroad. He first left Egypt in 1908 to study law in Paris. He returned to Egypt in 1912, but left again in 1914 following allegations that his Russian wife was involved in unlawful activities. He returned to Egypt at the end of the War and took part in the creation of the short-lived Democratic Party.[38] He earned his living as a journalist and was the editor of, and a reporter for, several newspapers. As a reporter for *al-Siyāsa*, 'Azmī had the opportunity of meeting the former Khedive during the Lausanne Conference.[39] Exactly what transpired between the two is not entirely clear, but from then on, 'Azmī's activities in Egypt were of such a nature that he was placed on police lists of suspected agents of 'Abbās Ḥilmī.[40] In late 1929, the contacts between the two men became official. 'Azmī began working as the former Khedive's secretary after once more leaving Egypt following the Government's restrictions on his journalistic activity and his failure to publish a new Egyptian newspaper.[41] 'Azmī's frequent visits abroad; his numerous encounters with Arab nationalists in Palestine, Syria, and Europe and his contacts with a person such as 'Abbās Ḥilmī, whose political aspirations extended to most of the Arab East, must also have affected his own political outlook. From being a keen advocate of Pharaonism during the early 1920's, 'Azmī became an Arab nationalist preaching Egypt's participation

Jerusalem Quarterly, 1981, No. 18, pp. 55-85.

37 In his memoirs in *Hed ha-Mizrah*, 1950, No. 26, p. 8, Camhy mistakenly gives his name as 'Abd al-Ḥaq al-Tājī, and asserts that he was a member of the Higher Arab Committee. For the correct name and the trip to Vichy, see Itammar Ben-Avi to Weizmann, 17 June, 1930, *WA*.

38 Maḥmūd 'Azmī, *Khabāyā Siyāsiyya* (Cairo, 1950?), pp. 36-41. I am grateful to Dr. Israel Gershoni for drawing my attention to this source.

39 'Azmī, *Khabāyā*, pp. 61-63; *The Arabic World*, 17 June, 1933, p. 8.

40 *'AHP*, File 120/71-73, 214, for lists of suspects.

41 For 'Azmī's difficulties in Egypt see: 'Abd alla al-Bishrī's reports 18 Feb., 1929, 25 Oct., 1929, *'AHP*, File 92/358-362, 397. 'Azmī, *Khabāyā*, p. 126 claimed that the Khedive gave him a monthly salary of EGP 100, which, with expenses, totaled around EGP 150. When he resigned in Dec., 1932 from his Khedivial services his basic salary amounted to ENP 80. See: *'AHP*, File 121/439-444.

in an Arab confederation.[42] Thus, in sending 'his' ideas to Weizmann, Camhy was in fact echoing 'Azmī's views on Arab confederation.

Moreover, the resemblance between Camhy's and 'Azmī's views not only extended to the broad issue of Arab confederation but also to the specific idea of a Jewish-Arab journal. 'Azmī, as we learn from Camhy's reports and memoirs, keenly advocated the creation of an Arabic journal which would call for Jewish-Arab rapprochement. 'Azmī told Camhy that he had been sent by 'Abbās Ḥilmī on a special mission to Palestine to determine if the time were ripe for a Jewish-Arab entente. 'Azmī claimed that it was very ripe indeed. He disclosed to Camhy that editors of the Palestinian Arab press supported his plan to publish a large Arabic newspaper which would advocate a bi-national Palestine within an Arab confederation consisting of Iraq, Trans-Jordan, Palestine, and Egypt.[43]

The possibility of finding a rewarding journalistic position within a newly-created periodical clearly fired the imagination of both 'Azmī and Camhy. The two journalists spared no effort to attract Weizmann's support for this project. Together they composed a list of eminent Jewish and Arab personalities who could be expected to participate. Einstein and Freud were to be included on the Jewish side of the editoral committee, with Aḥmad Luṭfī al-Sayyid, former Egyptian Minister of Education, Dr. Ṭāha Ḥusayn, a famous Egyptian author, Shaykh Muṣṭafā al-Marāghī, former *Shaykh* of al-Azhar, Sayyid 'Abd al-Ḥamīd al Bakrī, head of the Bakariyya Order in Egypt, Aḥmad Shawqī, an illustrious Egyptian poet, 'Alī 'Abd al-Rāziq, a former Egyptian judge, and two Iraqi poets, Risāfī and Zahāwī were to comprise the 'Arab' side.[44]

Neither Camhy nor 'Azmī gave much thought to the possibility that their Jewish or Egyptian and Iraqi candidates might reject the invitations to head such a journal. But even Weizmann, who, if we are to trust Camhy's evidence,[45] doubted the wisdom of approaching Einstein before obtaining the approval of the Egyptian and Iraqi candidates, was impressed by the glowing optimism of Camhy's and 'Azmī's reports. The Egyptian's promising account of his fact-finding mission to Palestine so aroused Weizmann's hopes for a Jewish-Arab entente in Palestine that the Zionist leader requested 'Azmī to join him during his forthcoming trip to Palestine where he expected to discuss the prospects of peace with Arab leaders. In addition, he commissioned Camhy to request the former Khedive's help in arranging meetings between Weizmann and other Arab personalities.[46]

Camhy, however, was not satisfied with the limited political role assigned to the former Khedive and went to London to convince Weiz-

42 Israel Gershoni, *Mitzrayim bein Yiḥūd le-Aḥdūt* (Tel-Aviv, 1980), pp. 159-161.
43 Camhy to Weizmann, 13 Dec., 1930, *WA*; *Hed ha-Mizrah*, 1950, No. 26, p. 8.
44 Camhy to Weizmann, 7 Feb., 1931, *WA*; *Hed ha-Mizrah*, 1950, No. 27, p. 10, No. 28, p. 6.
45 *Hed ha-Mizrah*, 1950, No. 28, p. 6; Cf. Weizmann to Camhy, 9 Feb., 1931, *WA*.
46 *Hed ha-Mizrah*, 1950, No. 27, p. 10.

mann. Accordıng to Camhy, Weizmann expressed sympathy with both projects of Arab Confederation and the Jewish-Arab journal, and agreed to a greater involvement of the former Khedive in the peace project. He asked Camhy to enlist 'Abbās Ḥilmī's support for a round table conference in London of Jews and Arabs. He further asked Camhy to request from 'Abbās Ḥilmī a letter of introduction to the Emir 'Abdallāh whom Weizmann intended to see during his forthcoming visit to Palestine.[47]

Having obtained Weizmann's support, Camhy went to Algiers where he held three meetings with 'Abbās Ḥilmī. In sharp contrast to the sceptical and suspicious Sacher, Camhy found the former Khedive to be a great asset and most cooperative. 'Abbās Ḥilmī, Camhy reported, disliked Sacher's behavior during their meeting and considered Camhy to be the best deputy to Weizmann. 'Abbās Ḥilmī also told Camhy that he had asked King Ḥusayn and his two sons King Fayṣal and Emir 'Abdallāh, to discuss Jewish-Arab relations, and that following this request a meeting had been held in Amman. The ex-Khedive further disclosed that the Emir 'Abdallāh agreed to transfer the Wādī Zarqā' land to Zionist hands in return for one million pounds. However, since 'Abdallāh could not be associated directly in dealings with Zionists, he wished that the transfer of this land should be made through the former Khedive who would receive the money.[48]

The very fact that had aroused Sacher's suspicions — 'Abbās Ḥilmī's eagerness to obtain control of the big land transaction — fired Camhy's enthusiasm. So pleased was he with 'Abbās Ḥilmī's expressed support for Arab-Jewish entente that he paid little attention to the fact that the former Khedive (aside from involvement in the land transaction), never proposed any formula for the advancement of the entente. Camhy is suspiciously silent about 'Abbās Ḥilmī's reaction to Weizmann's alleged request to enlist his support for the round table conference in London. Could Camhy have forgotten to ask for the ex-Khedive's help on this important issue? Or perhaps Weizmann never asked for the former Khedive's assistance in this respect.

Be that as it may, 'Abbās Ḥilmī did send, through Camhy, Weizmann's requested letter of introduction to the Emir 'Abdallāh. Significantly, the letter lacked any reference to the land concession which 'Abbās Ḥilmī had claimed to have obtained for the Zionists. 'Abbās Ḥilmī preferred to praise Weizmann's abilities in an area in which the Emir 'Abdallāh was known to have an interest, i.e. the former Khedive asked 'Abdallāh to welcome Weizmann because of his expected assistance in realising "the beloved Arab Unity" (*al-waḥda al-'arabiyya al-maḥbūba*).[49]

47 *Ibid.*

48 *Ibid.*; Camhy to Weizmann, 4 March 1931, *WA*.

49 'Abbās Ḥilmī's letter dated 27 Feb., 1931, in *WA*.

D. *The Moment of Truth*

In spite of 'Abbās Ḥilmī's letter of recommendation, Weizmann could not meet 'Abdallāh. 'Azmī, who had joined Weizmann on his trip to Palestine, blamed British officials for this failure. In the presence of 'Abbās Ḥilmī, 'Azmī told Camhy that British officials in Palestine prevented the meeting by warning both Arab and Zionist leaders to cancel it.[50] Camhy uncritically accepted 'Azmī's version as did those who believed that Britain had a fundamental interest in preventing peace in Palestine.[51]

Yet of all the sins that British policy-makers have been accused of committing in Palestine, this particular one is surely fanciful. To see the Palestinian conflict as a result of an alleged British policy of 'divide and rule' is to ignore the conflicting national claims to Palestine on the part of Jews and Arabs. Weizmann himself had the opportunity of experiencing the strength of these claims upon his arrival in Palestine, when all his efforts at meeting Palestinian Arab leaders to discuss peace in the land failed. The Higher Arab Committee not only refused to meet Weizmann, but also issued a public proclamation warning the Arabs against any negotiations with the Zionist leader.[52]

Weizmann took lightly the Higher Arab Committee's rejection of his offer. Under the influence of the optimistic reports of 'Azmī and Camhy, he was convinced that in Palestine there was "a considerable number" of Arabs who held moderate views and were ready "to come to some arrangement" provided "all fears about the desire of Zionists to dominate them were dispelled".[53] High Commissioner Chancellor's adamant insistence that there were no signs of such moderate sentiments among the Palestinian Arab population[54] did little to change Weizmann's views. He believed that the hostility of the Palestinian Arab leadership to the Zionist cause could be checked by British action and by way of pressure on the part of those Arab leaders outside Palestine who were "favorably disposed towards the

50 *Hed ha-Mizrah*, 1950, No. 28, pp. 6-7.

51 See, for example, Aaron Cohen, *Israel and the Arab World* (New York, 1970), pp. 192-195.

52 Chancellor (Jerusalem) to London, 3 March, 28 March, 1933, CO 733/203/9/87139/12,13a; *al-Ḥayāt* (Jerusalem), 26 March, 1931, published the Higher Arab Committee's warning dated 24 March. See also Colonel Kisch's explanation to Rabbi Blau in Minutes of meeting of the executive of the Jewish Agency for Palestine with representatives of *Merkaz Agudat Israel*, Jerusalem, 13 March, 1931, in *Minutes of meetings of the Executive of the Jewish Agency for Palestine, 1930-1931*, Vol. 18.

53 Weizmann's account in the 163rd meeting of the Zionist Executive, 12 Apr., 1931, in *Minutes of the Zionist Executive* (London), 1931, Vol. 17 (Copy: Z4/302/20, *Central Zionist Archives*).

54 Chancellor's report of a meeting with Weizmann, 20 March, 1931, CO 733/203/9/87139/13a.

Jews",[55] and who recognized "freely" the tie between the Jewish people and Palestine.[56]

Weizmann's belief that Arabs outside Palestine could moderate the Palestinian Arab stance led him to seek 'Abdallāh's intervention in the conflict. Since he doubted Chancellor's will and ability to improve Arab-Jewish relations, Weizmann did not trouble to consult the High Commissioner about the advisability of meeting 'Abdallāh, and requested an audience with 'Abdallāh through 'Azmī.[57]

It is unlikely that British officials had any part in 'Abdallāh's decision to cancel the audience with Weizmann. The Emir's telegram informing Weizmann that 'Abdallāh would not be able to see him reached the Zionist leader on the very same day that his advisor, Colonel Kisch, officially communicated the news of the expected meeting to Chancellor's private secretary.[58] Chancellor's own report of the episode confirms this fact, for he claimed to have learnt of Weizmann's intended meeting with 'Abdallāh only after the Emir had informed him that he had decided to postpone it, and asked the High Commissioner's help in persuading Weizmann to abandon the project.[59]

'Abdallāh, it seems, took the public warning of the Higher Arab Committee far more seriously than Weizmann. Eager to lead the 'beloved Arab Unity' mentioned in the reference to 'Abbās Ḥilmī, 'Abdallāh had a great interest in answering the Palestinian Arab call to boycott Weizmann. After all, it was through Palestinian Arab, not Zionist support that 'Abdallāh intended to advance his bid for Arab leadership. For this reason, 'Abbās Ḥilmī's letter of introduction might even have had an adverse effect on the Emir. Moreover, it is not entirely clear whether 'Abbās Ḥilmī himself had a real interest in Weizmann's meeting with 'Abdallāh, since such a meeting might have exposed his attempt to make a personal profit from the land concession project. It is not impossible that far from encouraging the audience, 'Azmī, the ex-Khedive's agent took steps to foil it. 'Azmī's excellent contacts with the editors of the Palestinian Arab press might throw some light on the source of the leak of Weizmann's secret trip to Amman, a leak which might have forced 'Abdallāh to cancel the meeting.

'Abbās Ḥilmī's activities after the collapse of the peace initiative do not support Camhy's claim that the ex-Khedive was utterly disappointed at

55 Weizmann's report to the Zionist Executive, *Minutes of the Zionist Executive*, 12 Apr., 1931, Vol. 17.

56 Kisch's explanation to Rabbi Blau, 13 March, 1931, in *Minutes of the Jewish Agency*, Vol. 18.

57 Weizmann to 'Abdallāh; Kisch to 'Azmī, 22 March, 1931, S25/1717, *CZA*.

58 Fu'ād, First Chamberlain (Amman) to Weizmann (Jerusalem), 24 March 1931, *WA*, (Copy: S25/1717, *CZA*); Kisch to L.A.G. Cust (Government Office, Jerusalem), 24 March, 1931, S25/1717, *CZA*.

59 Chancellor to London, 24 March, 1931, CO 733/203/9/87139/13a.

Weizmann's failure to meet 'Abdallāh. 'Abbās Ḥilmī never attempted to renew his initiative, nor did he ever enter into further negotiations with Zionist representatives. In the months following Weizmann's visit in Palestine, 'Abbās Ḥilmī was busy concluding an agreement with the Egyptian government settling his financial claims.[60] Then, new prospects in the East claimed his attention. Shortly afterwards he received an invitation from the *Muftī* of Jerusalem to participate in the General Islamic Conference to be held in that city in December 1931.[61] Obviously, the former Khedive, with his intentions of advancing his claims to the Caliphate at this conference,[62] could no longer be associated with the Zionists, who were condemned as enemies of Islam by the Palestinian Arab leadership.

'Abbās Ḥilmī's failure to realise his dream of the Caliphate at the Jerusalem Conference, and the subsequent failure of his bid for the throne of Syria and Palestine in December 1931,[63] may have discouraged him from further active intervention in Palestinian affairs. He continued his annual visits to Palestine and Trans-Jordan, and even considered the possibility of acquiring land in Jericho.[64] But he preferred to leave to his advisers the task of persuading the British Government to grant him a mediatory role in the Palestine conflict.[65]

Perhaps the only victim of this peace initiative was Weizmann. The Zionist leader never suspected double-dealing on the part of 'Abbās Ḥilmī, 'Azmī, 'Abdallāh or any other Arab or Egyptian leader who had promised him to work for the advancement of peace between Jews and Arabs. Influenced by these promises, Weizmann naively continued to believe that the intervention of Arab and Egyptian leaders in the conflict could promote peace in Palestine. As late as 1939, after the collapse of the London Conference, when it had become clear that the Egyptian and Arab leaders fully supported the Palestinian Arab stance in the conflict, Weizmann refused to abandon this view. One wonders whether Weizmann would have insisted on outside Arab and Egyptian intervention in the Palestinian conflict had he been aware of the massive pressure that Arab and Egyptian

60 Text of the agreement and details of the negotiations in *'AHP*, File 123/2-20, 39-42; Ismā'īl Ṣidqī, *Mudhakkirātī* (Cairo, 1950), pp. 53-56.

61 The invitation dated 10 Oct., 1931, in *'AHP*, File 125/14-15.

62 Consult my "Egypt and the General Islamic Conference at Jerusalem", in *Middle Eastern Studies* Vol. 18, 1982, pp. 311-322.

63 For details of this episode, see: *The Arabic World*, 17 June, 1933, pp. 8-10; 'Azmī, *Khabāyā*, 97-98; *'AHP*, File 123/96-119.

64 See, for example, the various reports of the Egyptian Consuls in Jerusalem, 17 Jan., 1933, 2 March 1935, 8 Jan., 1936, File 01618, *Israel State Archives*; Cavendish-Bentinck's report, 6 Nov., 1937, FO 371/20902/J4373.

65 Hopkin, M.P. to Eden, 23 July, 1937, FO 371/20902/J3558; Campbell's minute, 28 Sep., 1937, FO 371/20902/J4176.

leaders were exerting at that very moment on the British Government to give in to the Palestinian Arab demands to turn Palestine into an independent Arab state.[66]

66 For an account of Weizmann's views that year and the reaction of the Egyptian and Arab leaders consult my *Egypt and the Palestine Question*, 1936-1945 Berlin, 1983, pp. 135-137.

SYLVIA G. HAIM

The Palestine Problem in *al-Manār*

Al-Manār is a treasury of information and a guide to all questions of vital interest to Muslims. Founded in Egypt in 1898 and published regularly — except for a short period during World War I when it was irregular, due to the paper shortage — it only ceased publication with its owner's death in 1935. A life-span of thirty-seven years under the editorship of one man is a long period. Its pages constitute practically the only systematic body of writing attempting to harmonize modern thought with Islamic tradition over such a long period. Considering the character and sympathies of Muḥammad Rashīd Riḍā, it is interesting to follow him in his reportage of a movement and a party which has materialized into a modern state. His religious interests and sympathies are never in doubt. The zeal with which he pursued single-handed every argument, every discovery, every remark and every criticism in order to make the most of it for the Muslims and the Arabs, is a matter for admiration. This is one reason why it is interesting to follow the way in which Zionist ideals and actions struck a zealous Muslim over his long career. Though there were, before the First World War, occasional comments in the Arabic press outside Palestine, particularly in *al-Ahrām* and *al-Muqaṭṭam*, the Islamic view on Zionism was hardly ever articulated as early as in *al-Manār*.

Rashīd Riḍā went through a variety of political stands and he is aware of having been accused of receiving money to induce in him a change of views. But his sincerity about what he considered to be the welfare of Islam is undoubted. Examining his various political stands, it is obvious that whatever he espoused at the time — and some of his positions have been contradictory — can be explained by his message which he never failed to repeat: Islam must be made supreme and stay supreme. He always pursued what he considered to be in the best interest of Islam. The development of his own thought in a Pan-Arab direction, due largely to his disaffection from the Committee of Union and Progress and the Young Turks rather than disloyalty to Ottoman rule, reflects his strong attachment to Islam. Just before the outbreak of war in 1914, he became fully persuaded that the

Young Turks, whom he considered atheistic, were fully in control of the Ottoman Empire and were the enemies of both Islam and the Arabs. Therefore, he began to look in other directions for ways to safeguard Muslim and Arab interests which he, in any case, considered identical. When Sharīf Ḥusayn declared his rebellion against the Ottoman Government, Rashīd Riḍā became his fervent supporter for a time. He was, however, increasingly disappointed in the Sharifian movement and came to the conclusion, by the end of the war, that Ḥusayn and his sons were tools in the hands of the British. He then trasnferred his allegiance to ʻAbd al-Azīz b. Saʻūd and engaged in intemperate and vociferous attacks on Ḥusayn, his family and his followers.

★ ★ ★

Given this background, it is interesting to follow him in his assessment of Zionism, a movement he mentioned for the first time in *al-Manār* in April 1899.[1] Given the diligence with which he watched international events, it would be surprising if he had not directed his attention to Jews and Zionism.

His reference to Jews in the early issue of his journal[2] is not concerned with Zionism, but is a question of vital interest to him and to so many Muslims and Arabs. How can a nation whose existence is threatened by stronger nations, preserve its religion, language and culture? How did the Jews preserve Hebrew in spite of their dispersion and the oppression they have suffered? Here Rashīd Riḍā presents the question which so perplexes him. Why has Arabic lost its grip in spite of the growth and the strength of its rulers? His answer is clear, although one may remark that his observations are not exactly correct, but this would be beside the point. He states that young Jews, from Russia to Argentina, talk Hebrew although they excel in the languages of the people among whom they live. Scholars in Egypt, Syria, Iraq, North Africa and even in the Hijaz and Yemen, are satisfied that Arabic should be confined to mere bookish and out of the way erudition. Admiration for Jews and a desire to emulate them are themes which he takes up in further articles.

★ ★ ★

The Dreyfus Affair was at its height at the time. How, then, did RashīdRiḍā report it? He wrote that Bonaparte came to the throne as the champion of universal freedom and republican ideals, but was quick to trample on these constitutional ideals as soon as he was crowned.[3] During the Dreyfus

1 Vol. I, no. 6.
2 Vol. I, no. 2. (1898)
3 *Ibid.*

Affair and the Zola case, he continues, the Jews have been humiliated and persecuted in France. This cannot be attributed to religious fanaticism for the French are far removed from a religious creed. It is due rather to racial prejudice and to the envy whipped up by a number of journalists who hate the Jews and envy them their wealth. Had these ugly affairs taken place in the East, these same newspapers would have shouted for the heavens to fall over the East and would have attacked the Orientals with pens more dangerous than poisoned darts. Had they been writing about countries as weak as the Jews are in France, they would have screamed for unconditional freedom and universal justice for the whole of mankind. Rashīd Riḍā finds it strange that the disease of the French press should seep into some Egyptian papers who scorch the Jews with tongues of fire and blame them for their great skill in matters of livelihood and profit. He is direct: general freedom is not to be restricted to one group; true civilization and true justice demand perfect equality among all men. Legitimate work and gain are social qualities; let men work and make a profit through all legal means. He who objects is in truth objecting to the principle of universal freedom. This is why, Rashīd Riḍā continues, you will not find a sensible Frenchman who would approve of past or present oppression of Jews in France. He is forthright in his hope that writers will not introduce a new element of strife and conflict into the Oriental social order for 'We are at the moment more in need of the elements of unity than of disunity. Let our Oriental brothers, particularly the Muslims among them, benefit from what we teach about other nations.'

Given this broad outlook concerning Jews, how did Rashīd Riḍā view Zionism? In his first mention of the movement,[4] he reproduces an article from *al-Muqtaṭaf*, vol. XXII no. 4, and comments on it. *Al-Muqtaṭaf* published an article from a correspondent in Frankfurt who, after giving a précis of the aims of Zionism, asks whether the Arabic press of Egypt and of Syria are aware of these aims, i.e. to create, with the permission of the Ottoman authorities and the guarantee and protection of the European powers, a home for oppressed and poor Jews who would cultivate the land and industrialize it. The correspondent asks the paper's opinion regarding the feasibilty of this project, and whether the press have given it much attention. *Al-Muqtaṭaf*'s answer is interesting. The Arabic press have not paid any attention to the Zionist project. The Jews who have come to Palestine are skilled in crafts and trade and have been successful. Should their numbers increase, they could easily control all means of trade and industry. But *al-Muqtaṭaf* does not believe that they will become agriculturalists. Money can buy anything; if the Jews are so determined, they could buy all the land they want for their poor brethren who would find plenty of room on this rich soil able to support many times the number of its

4 Vol. I, no. 6 (April 1899).

inhabitants. What is feasible however, is far removed from what actually happens, it adds; wealthy Jews do not find it necessary to transport poor Jews to Palestine and this transfer is none too easy. Few philanthropists like Baron Hirsch exist. It is more difficult to buy land in Palestine and to transfer Jews there than to transfer them to Argentina. *Al-Muqtaṭaf* is therefore doubtful about the success of the Zionist idea and presumes that it would be easier to improve the condition of the Jews in Russia, Bulgaria or Rumania, especially since the Ottoman Government is unwilling to accept European conditions of protection and guarantees. Rashīd Riḍā saw a moral in this. The oppressed of the whole world choose to come to the Ottoman land because they find there the freedom and the justice absent from other parts of the world. He hopes that his countrymen will see how Jews, in spite of their dispersion, cooperate with one another and will also be inspired with the desire to improve their condition by emulating the Jews in knowledge and industry.

He follows this up with an article on the 'Jewish Zionist Organization,' which he entitles 'A Nation's Life After Death'.[5] During some festive celebrations he happened to talk to Riyāḍ Pasha, for many years minister under the khedives Tawfīq, Ismā'īl and 'Abbās, about the state of the Muslims and what they need in the way of reform. When the question of money, the foundation of all reform, came up, Jews were of course mentioned as well as the Zionist Organization, with its desire to restore power and rule to the Jews. The minister mentioned that he had come across a book by a European author inimical to Jews. The author had written it in order to calumniate and humiliate them, but the book glorifies and extols them in fact. The book, the title of which is not mentioned, claimed that the Jews were in control of all interests in the whole of France. He, Riyāḍ Pasha, tried to persuade some Egyptians to translate it into Arabic 'not in order to hurt the Jews but in order to instruct the Muslims'. The Muslims are deaf to all preaching and so long as they remain in their present state they will be incapable of taking heed. Had the Muslims been heeding news of other nations properly, they would have stopped showing contempt for the Jews for their weakness and would have rather feared that one day they too would become equally weak. What have we got to place us above them, continues Rashīd Riḍā, except that some of our lands are still under princes from among us, whereas they are denied authority? We should ask whether these princes of ours in those remnants of countries are conducting themselves according to the righteous and just ways of our ancestors, or whether they are behaving like those tyrannical and cruel followers who have lost most of the Muslim kingdoms. Now only a few are still left us and our vanity has blinded us to the tyranny that the foreigners exercise over us through those princes.

5 Vol. IV, no. 21 (January 1902).

Let us, he continues, observe the road that the Jews are taking now. Is it the way of their ancestors whose vanity in their descent from the prophets and in their vainglorious name as the *Chosen People*, made them rely on the blessings of their Torah in order to gain control over the nations and victory over their adversaries through no effort on their part? Or is it another way, that which God imposes on his creatures: the preservation of their language and national unity despite their dispersion, as well as the acquisition of the sciences of the age and its useful arts? They have excelled in amassing fortunes which are the foundation of power and independence in this age. The latter way is followed by the Jews today. Their power is growing and their lost greatness returning; they only need a kingdom of their own in order to become the greatest nation on the face of the earth, an aim they are pursuing in the normal way. A single Jew is now more respected than an Oriental king. Any European country can now threaten, in word and deed, the most powerful Oriental Sultan and force him to humble himself. When France tried to humiliate one Jew — Dreyfus — all hell was let loose against her and civil war was on the point of engulfing her.

Jews have many organizations; nations can prosper only through such organizations. The Zionist Organization, which came to his notice five years previously, is a political organization which aims to control the Holy Land in order to rebuild the Jewish kingdom and to make it the seat of authority. This Organization first appeared as a charitable society the aim of which was to transport poor emigrant and exiled Jews to Palestine in order to develop it and live in it under the protection of the Sultan. The Organization has now abandoned its secrecy and even sent Mr. Israel Zangwill to Constantinople to 'negotiate the purchase of Jerusalem'. It is said, so Rashīd Riḍā writes, that Zangwill met with the Sultan's interest and sympathy. Rashīd Riḍā translates part of Zangwill's address to the Organization on his return to London.

Zangwill is quoted to have said that Jews in great numbers will return to their ancient kingdom and will number two million in the year 2,000. The Jews will turn the land into a paradise endowed with a perfect model of government. The people of Israel would thus become a beacon unto the nations on Mount Zion. Every village and town contributed to the $1,000,000 collected to date in order to purchase the land. Zangwill castigated the rich who are too busy with their own interests to pay attention to the Zionist movement. Rashīd Riḍā's comments are interesting. Zangwill, he says, no doubt exaggerated in his denunciation of the rich in order to press the poor to keep on giving. Who could deny the generosity of Baron Hirsch whose every gesture brings that day closer? Rashīd Riḍā draws a moral. Poor Jews have collected $1,000,000 and will continue to give. They have also spread education among themselves. Will the Muslims in Egypt who are as numerous as the Jews of the whole world ever gather enough enthusiasm to collect such a sum in order to found a college which Egypt needs so badly?

He goes on to mention that the Zionist Organization proclaimed its political aims in the Hebrew-French newspaper of its Alexandria branch; he also gives the text of the opening address at their public meeting. He is perplexed. How is he to bring awareness to his people? He claims to have been the first to mention that this is a political and not a purely charitable organization. He had mentioned earlier two lessons to be learned from it, and he now wants to add a third. Stressing once more the state of the Jews: their dispersion, lowliness, weakness, ne contrasts this to their cooperation and mutual assistance. They are in the process of recovering their past glory and restoring their kingdom. He then asks: Will you accept that the papers of the whole world report how the poor of the weakest nation, those people rejected by all governments, know enough about economic development to enable them to gain possession of your land, to colonize it, to make its inhabitants wage-earners and to turn its wealthy ones into poor men? Consider this, he urges, and reflect whether it is right or wrong, true or false.

Rashīd Riḍā then embarks on a diatribe of Muslim rulers. What is the use of talking and of giving advice? People do not listen. They have been made oblivious by their princes. Muslim rulers have not prevented the destruction wrought on the Muslims. His aim is not to incite people to revolt against their princes as this would only enable the foreigners to destroy the Muslims, but he wishes to teach them not to rely on their princes but to strive for useful sciences, large fortunes and good education. Only thus would the nation be able to assist its good princes. They would through their good deeds force the bad prince to reduce the harm he does, until such time when they have become a real nation with its own public opinion.

★ ★ ★

What observations are we, the present-day readers of Rashīd Riḍā, to make of his articles and remarks? We may take it for granted that Rashīd Riḍā reflected many opinions current at the time. This need not imply plagiarism. To say that he reflected a mode does not mean he did it insincerely. To say that he may have lacked originality does not mean that the subject of philo- or antisemitism is a subject which can command any originality. The views and judgments given are indeed of a very limited nature. But we may, however, note the absence of Rashīd Riḍā's usual vehemence in connection with anything he considers a threat to the Arabs or the Muslims. Several explanations may be offered. In spite of his repeated warnings, he was perhaps confident that the Zionist Organization could not be such a threat as it had to rely on the goodwill of the Sultan, without whose permission little could be effected. Seemingly untainted with European type antisemitism, he could not withhold his admiration for a downtrodden people who, through education, cooperation and personal effort, strive to rise again. Their effort not only gains his sympathy but presents him with a model and an example which he urges the Muslims to emulate.

★ ★ ★

Rashīd Riḍā's views are however not devoid of contradictions. He describes what he considers to be Jewish characteristics: communal solidarity, racial identification, exploitation of other nations and their resources. Had they not believed their religion to be particular to themselves and that it should not be propagated, they would have also tried to convert the whole world in the same way as they convert all resources to their own advantage. [At times one wonders what text he used for these purple passages.] All these features would have been praiseworthy had they not been pursued to extremes. That is why Jews have been persecuted everywhere, and only the Muslims offer them a refuge. Witness how all those Jews expelled from various countries have rarely found a refuge elsewhere than in the Ottoman Empire or even Palestine itself where they hope to restore their kingdom and gain independence.[6]

It is to be observed that the pursuit by the Zionist movement of a national home for the Jews, guaranteed by public law, was naturally understood by him to mean that the Jews aimed to gain independence in Palestine. Except as the attempt to establish lordship over territory, politics would have been meaningless to him. He respected the Zionist movement to the extent that he believed it to be seeking just this; power and independence were for him the indispensable hall-mark of great nations. The subject is not mentioned for a number of years. In December 1919,[7] he comments on a Quranic verse (Qur'ān IV:53), *am lahum naṣīb min al-mulk*, and embarks on a diatribe against the Jews as jealous, envious, possessive, vain and conceited about their ancestry. When an Arab prophet appeared, they found it unbearable to be in a kingdom where they would have to obey. Should they succeed in restoring their rule over Jerusalem and their environs, they will expel the Muslims and the Christians and deny them a share in the land and its produce. They had already attempted this. The Jewish carpenter will work in Jerusalem for a lower wage than the Muslim or the Christian: their charitable organizations help them to do so. There is no doubt that they are trying to take over the land and deny others all means of livelihood. This they do without having their own rule — what would it be like if they had it?

Will their kingdom be restored (*hal ya'ūdu lahum al-mulk kamā yab-*

6 Vol. VI, no. 5 (May 1903).
7 Vol. XIII, no. 11.

ghūna)? The verse neither denies nor does it confirm this, but only reveals their character and shows how they would behave if it were to come about. A kingdom must have a large population and they are dispersed among the nations. They are also greatly attached to their property in various countries. Most of them are incapable of fighting or working the land. They however believe with great religious zeal (*ya'taqidūna i'tiqādan diniyyan*) that they will restore their kingdom in the Holy Land and have accumulated a lot of wealth for this purpose. The Ottomans must therefore make it difficult for them to gain ownership and must restrict large immigration. The Jews suffer the delusive vanity that God is concerned only with their interest. They have the whole world in their hands and will allow no one to acquire even as much as the stone of a date. Their envy of the Arabs because of what God has given them in the way of wisdom, the Book and kingship, is great. The Qur'ān, he continues, ascribes envy only to the Jews. In his interpretation of *Sūrat al-baqara* II/109 'Many of the people of the scripture long to make you disbelievers after your belief, through envy on their own account, after the truth hath become manifest unto them' etc., he concentrates on envy. The Jews find it unbearable that the Arabs have gained authority over them. The Christians who had their own large kingdom did not show envy when Islam appeared, nor did the pagans among the Arabs. When they saw the truth of the Prophecy, they adopted Islam. As for the Jews, even if they saw this truth, they refused to convert. Envy prevented the leaders from converting and the masses followed their example.

★ ★ ★

Respectful of divine revelation as he is, Rashīd Riḍā seems bothered by the fact that the Jews believe in the restoration of their kingdom with such religious zeal. On the one hand he cannot dismiss the revelation, but on the other he cannot admit Jewish claims. He has therefore to diminish the Jews by appealing to the unfavorable and hostile picture which the Qurān gives of them. The stereotype which emerges in his exposition of the Quranic text is therefore somewhat different from that of a people whose endeavor is to be admired and emulated. As in all stereotypes, any single Jew seems to represent Jews the world over. It is also assumed that the natural thing is for all Jews to be wanting the furtherance of Zionist aims. It is thus that in the same number in which he complains about the greater freedom that the Copts enjoy over the Muslims in Egypt he has an article about the Jews in the Ottoman state.[8] He warns against their prominence in the Committee for Union and Progress, for their ambitions in Jerusalem and Palestine are well known. Some independent members of parliament have objected to the sale of the best military site in Constantinople to a foreign company

8 Vol. XIV, no. 2 (March 1911).

well below its real value, thanks to Jewish intrigue. He does not wish to investigate the guilty party, however, but is keen to warn.

★ ★ ★

Palestine and Syria — as known to Rashīd Riḍā and his contemporaries — are one and the same: ancient Israel had occupied both lands. Moses led his people to the Promised Land which was distinct from the Hijaz which belonged to the Arabs. Rashīd Riḍā argues as follows. The promise to give the Land to Abraham's descendants came before the mention of Ishmael's birth in Genesis which indicates that it is the Arabs who were meant by the Covenant. This is a fact, since the whole land is Arab now. After Isaac's birth, the Torah does not mention a promise of a land or country to Abraham. There is however a mention of an eternal promise to Abraham and his seed. This promise is made with regard to Isaac; but what kind of a promise is it? It is a promise of prophecy. It is not an eternal promise for Isaac and his descendants and it was broken 2,000 years ago. The seal of the prophets was in fact a son of Ishmael, Muḥammad, an Arab. The promise of possessing the Land was not meant to last till eternity; the Jews lost it long before the Arabs conquered it and assimilated all its inhabitants. It is therefore correct to say that the Israelites have a share in the Land but not that they have an exclusive right to it, nor that they are more worthy of it than their Arab cousins. Everything indicates, he concludes, that the promise was made to Abraham and his descendants, that is both Jews and Arabs.[9]

As it is said in *Sūrat Banī Isrā'īl*, he writes, the Jews became twice corrupt on earth before Islam. They were twice conquered and destroyed. For extra punishment they were attacked by the Romans and by the Muslims; they were thus torn asunder and dispersed. Some verses indicate that their kingdom will never be restored. It is only through their conversion to Islam and their union with their Arab cousins that they will own this as well as other lands. The prospect is however remote because the Jews have become extremely traditional and petrified in their religious and ancestral identification. Our age is one of racial solidarity among nations, he continues. Many Muslims are in fact breaking their religious bonds and replacing them with the linguistic one although they may not have a language worthy of mention. The Jews want to restore their kingdom through a new formation and on a new foundation. However, the strong Christian nations are opposing them. The Arabs are the masters of all the land and will never leave it as booty to the Jews, irrespective of their intrigues.[10]

Cooperation with the Arabs in development will however be the means,

9 Vol. XVII, no. 2 (December 1913).
10 *Ibid.*

the only means, to yield results; the land can accommodate many more times its present inhabitants.

A partial answer to the kind of cooperation recommended may be found in an article published in March 1914.[11] He expresses amazement that the Jews of Europe should wish to build a new country in the Holy Land in order to house the poor Jews of the world. He expresses disbelief that a society founded by one man could achieve its aim to build such a country on a stretch of land ruled over by one of the strongest nations. Nations live and die through energy or lack of it, through learning or ignorance, through grand or weak aims. There is perhaps a lack of will to retain the Land. But the Jews must know that the Great Powers will never allow them to own the seat of prophecy and the birthplace of Judaism and Christianity. Should Turkish rule disappear, the country will no doubt become independent, but under the protection of the Powers. He sees two alternatives for Arab leaders.

1. To come to some agreement with the Zionists in order to harmonize the interests of both parties if possible, and it would be possible if they would approach it in the right way and try to get to the bottom of it. [What this correct way is, he leaves unexplained.]
2. Unite all their energies in order to fight the Zionists in every conceivable way. They could form societies and companies and ultimately armed bands, as some leaders advised at the very beginning. This would be like cautery, but as the proverb goes, cautery is the remedy of last resort.

The recurrent theme 'that anyone with a heart and a head should learn from the Jews' is repeated in April 1914, in which he copies a long article from *al-Hilāl* setting out the history and aims of the Zionist movement.[12] One can learn from the Jews how nations revive after their death and become proud after being humbled. The reportage of Zionist and other activities and writings concerned with Palestine and the future of the Arabs is of course very full and it would be pointless to give references be they to speeches of Zionist leaders or declarations of Arab societies.

Rashīd Riḍā indulged a lot in his own brand of biblical exegesis. He perhaps hoped to appeal to Christians as well as to those Muslims who had come under the influence of European Christianity. He disapproves of the Jews whom Moses took out of Egypt, because they wanted to have the Promised Land without exerting themselves, which is why the Almighty forbade it to them for forty years. God, however, fulfilled his promise to Abraham to give the Land to his descendants. He gave it to Isaac's sons but took it away from them because of their corruption. He then gave it to Ishmael's God-fearing sons, then removed their authority over it because

11 Vol. XVII, no. 4.
12 Vol. XVII, no. 5.

of their self-inflicted injuries. The English, great adepts at sowing dissension, have come to control and to divide the two groups.[13]

The theme that the Torah prophesied the coming of Muḥammad and of Islam is taken up again, in August 1925.[14] Rashīd Riḍā has not only to accept, but to affirm that the Torah is correct and that the prophecy contained in the Torah is proof that Muḥammad is the Seal of the Prophets. What he is saying in effect is that Muḥammad is the Messiah predicted in the Torah. This argument, contained in a long article, is very involved and shows the influence of Christian apologetic literature which he adapts for his own use. He also uses the method of *gimatriyah* to reinforce his case. He quotes New Testament texts which Christian commentators apply to Jesus, in order to apply them to Muḥammad's preaching.

★ ★ ★

A few new themes become clearer in the post-War period and are to be contrasted to his earlier more favorable views:

1. Jews envy the Muslims and hate Muḥammad because he is the Seal of the Prophets and they refuse to recognize him.
2. Jewish success in Europe is recent and is due to the change from a religious to a secular rule within which the Jews not only excel but remain unbeatable.
3. Only Muslims have treated the Jews well whereas all other nations persecuted them.
4. Britain plays a villainous role by reanimating enmity between Jews and Arabs.[15]

Rashīd Riḍā has no doubt that it is Britain which, for ulterior motives, pursued Zionism as a political movement.[16] Britain and the Jews are plotting against each other in order for each to attain his own goal. He has no doubt that the trouble to come will be the worst and most difficult the world has ever seen.

Reporting the troubles of 1928 in connection with the Western Wall,[17] he denounces the wiliness of the British in setting one people against the other in order to satisfy their own ambitions. But the Jews are even more wily he says. They mean to rebuild their temple; Britain knows it and that the site is occupied by the Dome of the Rock. But does Britain know that the Muslims also have signs of prophecy and a prophetic message relevant to that problem? The Muslim prophecies are clearer than the Jewish ones. In

13 Vol. XXV, no. 5 (July 1924).
14 Vol. XXVI, no. 4.
15 Vol. XXV, no. 8 (November 1924).
16 Vol. XXIX, no. 2 + no. 5 (April and June 1927).
17 Vol. XXIX, no. 6 (October 1928).

1929, Rashīd Riḍā gives a survey of the disturbances in Palestine.[18] Some passages in these two articles are worthy of the *Protocols of the Elders of Zion*, and there is always the question of whether he adapted them from some such book. That he might sometimes do that is irrelevant. The main point is that he presents these views as immutably true.

His arguments, having become standardized by the time the troubles in Palestine were becoming acute, run as follows:

1. The character of the Jews.
2. The Jews were given revelations and prophecies, but their corruption caused them to lose their kingdom and their rule.
3. Jewish tribes broke their treaty with Muḥammad more than once. He therefore had to fight them and to expel them. But the Arabs have always been friendly towards them and saved them many times. Through the ages, Jews have lived well under Arab and Muslim rule, enjoying the same rights as Muslims and studying side by side with the Muslims in Baghdad and Spain.
4. The Jews were instrumental in spreading to Europe the sciences they learned in Spain. This was their revenge over the Catholic Church; it was the revenge they took for themselves and their teachers, the Arabs. They spread freedom of thought and partiality to science, both of which became the foe of the Church and brought down its domination.
5. It is undoubted that the Freemasonry which has undermined the religious thrones of Europe, Turkey and Russia is part of a Jewish plot and the Jews are the supreme power in it. The name *Freemasonry* means the founding of the religious Jewish state in the cradle of that state founded by David and completed by Solomon, the Builder of the Jewish Temple.
6. The Jews organized finance, the pillar of modern Western civilization and they wield the greatest influence in all capitalist states. They are able to hide their true self behind their wealth as they have hidden their communal identity in political Freemasonry.
7. Only the Jesuits have been able to assess the danger of Jewish cunning and the real aim of Freemasonry. Just as they fought the Catholic Church in the Middle Ages, the Jews are now undermining the Orthodox Church through their influence over Russian atheists. Likewise, they want to destroy the *Sharī'a* in Turkey, through their influence over Turkish atheists, in order to defeat the Caliphate. They still expect God to establish a religio-civil rule in Palestine over which their Messiah will preside. The tenets of the three religions differ on the question of the Messiah; the Christians and the Muslims are agreed that the Jews are heretics.
8. Most Jews are tired of waiting for the Messiah in whom they do not believe. They have therefore founded the Zionist movement in order to achieve their ideal through financial and psychological powers.

18 Vol. XXX, no. 5 + no. 6 (November and December 1929).

9. It was only with the arrival of the Muslims to Jerusalem that the Jews were again permitted to pray at the Wall and that limited numbers were allowed to reside within the walls of the city.
10. Rashīd Riḍā writes that he got in touch with the Zionist agent in Egypt — it is not clear whether this was before 1914 — in order to learn the real position and to explain the objections of the Arabs who might resort to the formation of beduin armed bands. If the Jews want to live in peace and to flourish in the Arab countries including Palestine, then they had better come to an agreement with the Arab leaders. This apparently pleased the agent who reported it to his Organization. It had quite an effect at the Basel Congress, and the dangers that the beduin tribes would present were discussed. Rashīd Riḍā adds that he discussed the matter with Dr. Weizmann after the War. He also discussed the application of the Balfour declaration with other members of the Organization both in Cairo and Jerusalem. Weizmann was kept informed and agreed that it was feasible for Jews to cooperate with their Arab cousins. He adds that the dialogue stopped because the Jews were relying on British strength in order to restore their kingdom.
11. As a people, Jews are the greatest in learning, endeavor, economy, unity, cooperation and mutual assistance, decisiveness, determination, charitable organizations; cunning, guile, patience, steadfastness, ability to bear misfortune. They are never discouraged from pursuing their ideal. During all the centuries of their lowliness, they have never abandoned their hope, so how can they abandon it now that they are the keepers of the shrine of the supreme idol, money? They have used it to enslave the great nations; great is their influence in the press and powerful their propaganda.

One may well ask what action could be taken against such a powerful people, and how effective it would be. Rashīd Riḍā has the answer. The Jews lack military ability and have no skill in agriculture. They rely on English protection and they exploit the Arabs by using them as paid laborers after having stripped them of their land. But the warlike Arabs are stronger than they are. Their vanity and animosity have united the Arabs, both at home and abroad, in their defense of the Arabs of Palestine. The whole Muslim world has joined in support and Britain will remain helpless in spite of her oppression in Palestine.
12. The Jews have also made a tactical mistake. Had they proceeded slowly in their immigration and purchase of land, the Zionist danger would have been very great.

The British, too, display contradictory features, but on the whole, so Rashīd Riḍā says, they are still wiser and kinder than others. That is why it is possible to win their people's support against their government. The Jews have done this more successfully than the Arabs. They have more cash, but the Arabs have more natural resources because they own large tracts of land. By the late 1920s Rashīd Riḍā elaborates these principal points endlessly.

★ ★ ★

On a more practical level. He was asked whether a Muslim is permitted to sell land to the Jews. In a two-page *fatwa*,[19] he writes that according to Islam, the British and the Zionist Jews in Palestine belong to *Dār al-ḥarb* because they have attacked and conquered a land within *Dār al-Islām*. They have assumed all powers, and plan to divest the people of their land in order to have possession as well as exercise authority. Anyone who helps them gain possession of the land, whether officially through a sale, or unofficially by inducing others to sell, is a traitor to his nation and his community; he is the enemy of God, His Prophet and the Muslims, and is a supporter of the enemy both in his ownership and authority, *milk wa-mulk*. He is no different from one who wages physical and financial war against the Muslims. In fact the harm done by this method of conquest is 'worse than all that has preceded it in the way of military and religious conquests.' Those people who sell or help to sell lands must be boycotted, he tells the *YMMA*.[20] They are traitors: all business with them, social contact, marriage, conversation, and even salutation must be stopped.[21]

★ ★ ★

Consulting *al-Manār* from beginning to end, one is impressed by the variety of topics it discussed. It was not only a forum in which ideas covering every aspect of social and political life of Islam were discussed, but also a beacon to its readers and a mirror held up to Muslim opinion and attitudes. *Al-Manār* is one of the few sources to call upon in order to try and understand the manner in which the conflict in Palestine affected the people outside Palestine itself, in Egypt and elsewhere. Since the Arab Rebellion of 1936 in Palestine, attitudes have become increasingly polarized and have culminated in the current intransigence. The question, academic though it is, is whether the influence of *al-Manār* would have been on the side of moderation or otherwise. In fact the most intransigent currents in Arab politics took over and the question which is bound to crop up while reading Rashīd Riḍā from beginning to end is the following: Was the development of the conflict in the direction it took, inevitable? If so,

19 Vol. XXXIII, no. 4 (June 1933).

20 Vol. XXXIV, no. 8 (March 1935).

21 I am indebted to Dr. Uri M. Kupferschmidt for drawing my attention to the fact that this *fatwa* was used by the *Muftī* of Jerusalem in order to denounce the sale of land to the Jews.

was it inevitable because of Islam and its attitude to Jews, or did it happen as a result of the play of external factors, the strategy of the leaders of the Palestine Arabs, or in response to an intransigent Zionist or Jewish attitude? It is difficult to see what position *al-Manār* would have taken, had it continued until 1948. Would Rashīd Riḍā have counselled moderation? He continually repeated that cooperation was possible and although he prided himself on being the first to see the political ambitions of the Zionist movement, he, unlike European antisemites, nowhere hints that there is no place for the Jews. Or would he perhaps have been so sure of success that he too would have gone headlong into the fight?

JAMES JANKOWSKI

Zionism and the Jews in Egyptian Nationalist Opinion, 1920-1939

Although significant Egyptian involvement in the Arab-Jewish rivalry in Palestine dates only from the later 1930's, Egyptians were not totally unaware of or unconcerned with Zionism prior to that time. Egyptian opinion occasionally expressed an interest in both Zionism as a national movement and in the Jewish people amongst whom it was developing even before the active involvement of the Egyptian public and government in the Palestine question. That interest became much more extensive towards the end of the interwar period, when developments in Europe and Palestine greatly increased the intensity of the conflict between Jewish and Arab nationalism and also generated an Egyptian political involvement in the issue.

The attitudes of articulate Egyptians towards Zionism and Jews during the 1920's and 1930's are the subject of this paper. Obviously, not all Egyptian opinion for the two decades under consideration has been examined and is discussed in what follows. The major sources of data are the Egyptian press, particularly journals associated with Egyptian nationalist groups and political or religious organizations of the interwar period, supplemented by material from British reports pertaining to Egypt. Although the data base is thus selective and less than a quantitative examination of Egyptian positions vis-à-vis Zionism and Jews, nonetheless the paper will provide some indication of widely-articulated opinions concerning Zionism and Jews within Egypt as well as of the direction of movement of Egyptian views over the course of the period.

★ ★ ★

Perhaps the most essential feature of Egyptian opinion concerning Zionism through most of the interwar period was the infrequency with which Zionism drew the attention of articulate Egyptians. Well into the 1930's, Egyptian publicists concerned themselves with Zionism only occasionally. The well-developed Egyptian daily press covered major developments occurring within Zionism such as its annual or bi-annual Congresses, but, other than at moments of crisis in the Palestine Mandate, it gave Zionism no more attention than that accorded other nationalist movements which had their base outside the Middle East. Of the two most prominent Egyptian weeklies of the later 1920's, the Wafdist *al-Balāgh al-Usbūʿī* and the Liberal *al-Siyāsa al-Usbūʿiyya*, the former appears to have published only two articles on Zionism *per se* (one by a French author, the other by a Syrian) in the three-and-a-half years of its existence, while the latter, in spite of its steady interest in both the political affairs of Palestine and Egyptian relations with the Fertile Crescent, contained only a handful of articles on Zionism and/or the Jewish people in the first three years of its publication.[1] Zionism was thus a subject of only tangential interest to articulate Egyptians through much of the interwar period.

Egyptian attitudes toward Zionism in the 1920's in particular demonstrated a considerable openness of mind about the subject. Analyses of events in the Zionist world or in the Palestine Mandate were often dispassionate in tone as well as neutral in content, sometimes seeing both moderation and virtue in specific Zionist positions, and correspondingly sometimes being critical of Palestinian Arab nationalist positions on the same issue.[2] Statements by Zionist leaders or individuals sympathetic to the movement appeared occasionally in the Egyptian press; an exposition on Zionism by Abba Hillel Silver in *al-Siyāsa ul-Usbūʿiyya* in February 1929, statements by several Jewish groups or individuals in *al-Muqaṭṭam* during the violence in Palestine later in that year.[3] Editorial commentary in the Egyptian daily press during the disturbances of 1929 was careful to distinguish between the Jewish people as a whole and Zionism as a movement adhered to by only some Jews.[4] (The same distinction was frequently not made, however, by organizations strongly supportive of the Palestinian Arabs: the manifestoes of these groups tended to blame the problems in the mandate solely on "the Jews," making no "Zionist" distinction.)[5] On the whole, the coverage of the 1929 violence in Palestine on the part of Egypt's establishment press drew the praise of the British for its restraint and avoidance of "provocative comment."[6]

1 See *al-Balāgh al-Usbūʿī*, no. 148 (15 Jan. 1930), 7; *ibid.*, no. 173 (9 July 1930), 6; *al-Siyāsa al-Usbūʿiyya*, no. 81 (24 Sept. 1927), 24; *ibid.*, no. 124 (21 July 1928), 19-20; *ibid.*, no. 125 (28 July 1928), 4, *ibid.*, no. 153 (9 Feb. 1929), 10.

2 For examples from 1929, see *al-Muqaṭṭam*, 24 Sept. 1929, 1; *al-Siyāsa*, 1 Sept. 1929, 1; *ibid.*, 8 Sept. 1929, 1.

3 *al-Siyāsa al-Usbūʿiyya*, no. 153 (9 Feb. 1929), 10; *al-Muqaṭṭam*, 29 Aug. 1929, 7; *ibid.*, 3 Sept. 1929, 5; 22 20 Sept. 1929, 3; *ibid.*, 21 Sept. 1929, 7.

4 See *Ibid.*, 4 Sept. 1929, 1; *al-Siyāsa*, 1 Sept. 1929, 1; *al-Balāgh*, 2 Sept. 1929, 2.

5 Based on public statements by these movements as reported in *ibid.*, 2 Sept. 1929, 1-2; *ibid.*, 4 Sept. 1929, 1; *al-Ahrām*, 30 Aug. 1929, 5; Aḥmad Shafīq, *Mudhakkirāt fī Niṣf Qarn* (three vol.; Cairo, 1934-1937), III, 329.

6 Dispatch from Mr. R. H. Hoare to Mr. A. Henderson, 31 Aug. 1929; FO 371/13753.

In the intermittent substantive comments upon Zionism made in Egypt prior to the later 1930's, occasional admiration for both the goals and the achievements of Zionism can be found. The scholar Aḥmad Zakī (later an opponent of Zionism, but through much of the 1920's cordial towards it), is reported at one point to have declared that "the victory of the Zionist ideal is also the victory of my ideal."[7] In an article on the Zionist Congress of 1927, the journalist Muḥammad 'Abdallāh 'Inān both expressed his admiration for Zionist dedication and predicted that the realization of Zionist aspirations was inevitable if Zionists continued to maintain the same degree of commitment as they had demonstrated in the past.[8] Even a veteran opponent of Zionism such as Muḥammad Rashīd Riḍā (Syrian-born, but long resident in Egypt and of great influence in Egyptian conservative circles) voiced a mixture of opposition and admiration for Zionism in a speech before the Young Men's Muslim Association in 1934: at the same time as warning of the Zionist threat to an Arab-Muslim Palestine and predicting an eventual clash of arms there, he also praised Zionists for their organizing abilities and their hard work, and called on his audience to "imitate" Zionism by replacing ineffectual speechmaking about Palestine with tangible, practical efforts to assist the Arabs of Palestine.[9]

Both the marginality of Zionism to much of Egyptian opinion and the detachment of most Egyptians from the Palestine question *per se* for most of the interwar period had important practical consequences for the tenor of Egyptian politics. Internally, many Egyptian political leaders in effect sheltered Zionism from criticism and attack by those elements hostile to it. Prior to the later 1930's, successive Egyptian ministries took measures to inhibit the expression of extreme or inflammatory anti-Zionist opinion (e.g., the repeated suppression of journals edited by Palestinian Arab nationalists in Egypt)[10] and to prevent the physical manifestation of anti-Zionist sentiments (such as the arrest of Palestinian Arabs in Egypt intent on demonstrating against Lord Balfour on his visit to Egypt in 1925, or the special security procedures taken in Jewish districts of Cairo during the 1929 violence in the Mandate).[11] Even in the later 1930's, when Egyptian sympathy with the Palestinian Arab cause grew rapidly, Egyptian ministries paralleled their assumption of an increasing political role in the question with similar restrictions on Palestinian Arab activism or agitation

7 Quoted in Aharon Cohen, *Israel and the Arab World* (New York, 1970), 245.
8 *al-Siyāsa al-Usbū'iyya*, no. 81 (24 Sept. 1927), 24.
9 As reported in *Majallat al-Shubbān al-Muslimīn*, VI, no. 3 (Dec. 1934), 173-177.
10 See the several instances cited in the career of Muḥammad 'Alī al-Ṭāhir, the leading Palestinian Arab propagandist in interwar Egypt: B. Nuwayhid al-Hut and Khayriyya Qāsimiyya, "Faqīrān Filasṭīniyyān Kabīrān: 'Abd al-Ḥamīd Shūmān wa-Muḥammad 'Alī al-Ṭāhir," *Shu'ūn Filasṭīniyya*, no. 39 (Nov. 1974), 143-163, and also Ṭāriq al-Bishrī, *al-Ḥaraka al-Siyāsiyya fī Miṣr, 1945-1952* (Cairo, 1972), 238.
11 The former is cited in *ibid.*, 241; for the latter, see FO 371/13753.

inside Egypt,[12] with controls on the expression of militant opinion in the Egyptian press,[13] and with generally effective security measures aimed at preventing Egyptian demonstrations hostile to Jews when these began to develop by 1938 and 1939.[14]

This protection of Zionism from extreme criticism within Egypt was accompanied by externally-directed efforts on the part of Egyptian political leaders to interpose themselves as mediators between the Zionist and Palestinian Arab national movements contesting for Palestine. Published Zionist sources and an incomplete sample of British archival sources indicate repeated attempts by Egyptian politicians to mediate in the Palestine problem in the interwar years. In the 1920's and early 1930's it was apparently only non-governmental notables who were involved in such attempts.[15] But in the later 1930's, as both the gravity of the problem and the depth of Egyptian concern over Palestine increased, it was the leaders of the Egyptian state — Regent Prince Muḥammad 'Alī in 1936, 1937, and 1938; Prime Minister Muṣṭafā al-Naḥḥās during his tenure in office in 1936 and 1937 and his successor Muḥammad Maḥmūd in 1938 and 1939 — who offered their services as intermediaries in the Palestine question. These efforts at mediation took official form at the St. James Conference of 1939, where Egypt's representative 'Alī Māhir played a leading role in attempting to reconcile the Zionist and Palestinian Arab positions and to arrive at negotiated settlement for the future of the Mandate.[16]

* * *

Increasingly as the interwar period progressed and as Egyptian involvement in the Palestine question developed, attitudes of openness towards Zionism gave way to more negative impressions of modern Jewish nationalism. Towards the end of this period in particular many variants of Egyptian opinion were expressing a definite hostility both to Zionism and to the implications of the emergence of a Jewish national home in Palestine.

One aspect of Zionism which drew Egyptian commentary was its perceived relationship to religion. Viewed solely in political terms, committed Egyptian liberal nationalists tended to see Zionism as a primarily religious

12 For examples, see FO 371/20110; FO 371/20817; FO 372/21877.

13 FO 371/20035; FO 371/20110; FO 372/21877.

14 FO 371/21875; FO 371/21876; FO 371/21877; FO 371/21883; FO 371/21966.

15 For discussions of these efforts at mediation of the 1920's and early 1930's, see Cohen, *op. cit.*, 192-194, 245-246, 299-300; Frederick Kisch, *Palestine Diary* (London, 1938), 67, 109-110, 118-119, 167, 391-392; Neil Caplan, *Palestine Jewry and the Arab Question, 1917-1925* (London, 1978), 122-123.

16 The efforts at mediation of the later 1930's are discussed in James Jankowski, "The Government of Egypt and the Palestine Question, 1936-1939," *Middle Eastern Studies*, XVII (1981), 427-453.

nationalism based on the bond of religion: as such, Zionism was regarded as both anachronistic and retrogressive in its assumption that the religious bond could or should be the basis of nationality in the modern world.[17] Publicists opposed to Zionism often questioned whether a nation could be based on the bond of religion. Thus by 1929 the historian Aḥmad Zakī was asserting that the Jews had never been a "nationality" in the past and could not become one;[18] in 1938, Muḥibb al-Dīn al-Khaṭīb of *al-Fatḥ* (Syrian by origin, but an influential religious spokesman in interwar Egypt) evaluated the Zionist assumption of an identity between Jewish communities in different lands as "ignorant";[19] while in the same year the historian Dr. Ḥasan Ibrāhīm Ḥasan was questioning whether the Jewish people had ever possessed Palestine as a national homeland and asserting that "Judaism is a name for the religion, not for the nation" [*al-Yahūdiyya ism li'l-dīn, la li'l-waṭan*].[20] Perhaps the most prevalent concomitant of the viewpoint which saw Zionism as primarily religiously-based was the position that it therefore was an impractical and utopian venture. An article in *al-Balāgh* in 1929 expressed this attitude well when it analysed how Zionism had languished through the 1920's, drawing relatively little Jewish immigration to Palestine, and when it concluded by evaluating Zionism's prospects for the future as "an impossible dream."[21] Even with the rapid growth of both Zionism and the Jewish community in Palestine in the 1930's, this was an opinion which continued to be voiced by Egyptian publicists.[22]

For spokesmen of a Muslim religious orientation in interwar Egypt, it was the implications of Zionism for Islam which were most important. Although the perceived religious threat represented by Zionism was not always placed on an exclusively Muslim basis (leading religious publicists such as Muḥammad Rashīd Riḍā and Yaḥyā Aḥmad al-Dardīrī sometimes noted that Zionism was a potential danger for the status of both the Muslim and the Christian religious sites in Palestine and thus that the Palestine issue was "an Islamic and Christian religious question"), [23] nonetheless it was the potential of the rise of Zionism for specifically Muslim interests which most concerned religiously-inclined publicists. Any Muslim-Jewish tension "invariably takes on a religious colour," in the words of the Rector

17 See the editorials in *al-Siyāsa*, 31 Aug. 1929, 1; *ibid.*, 4 Sept. 1929, 1; *al-Balāgh*, 9 Sept. 1929, 2.

18 See the discussion in Anwar al-Jindī, *Aḥmad Zakī* (Cairo, 1964), 140-143.

19 *al-Fatḥ*, no. 606 (17 Rabīʿ al-Thānī 1357), 3-4.

20 *al-Risāla*, no. 276 (17 Oct. 1938), 1693.

21 *al-Balāgh*, 16 Sept. 1929, 2.

22 For examples, see *al-Risāla*, no. 156 (29 June 1936), 1047-1049; *ibid.*, no. 209 (5 July 1937), 1086-1088; *al-Fatḥ*, no. 604 (3 Rabīʿ al-Thānī 1357), 3-4.

23 Quotation from *Majallat al-Shubbān al-Muslimīn*, IX, no. 2 (Nov. 1937), 83; see also *ibid.*, VI, no. 3 (Dec. 1934), 177; *ibid.*, VII, no. 10 (July 1936), 584; *Jarīdat al-Ikhwān al-Muslimīn*, IV, no. 6 (19 May 1936), 19-20.

of al-Azhar, Shaykh Muḥammad Muṣṭafā al-Marāghī, in a private memorandum to the British during the violence of 1929 in Palestine. Noting the Muslim veneration for the al-Aqṣā Mosque and the struggle which had occurred at Medina between the Jews and the Prophet Muḥammad, Marāghī emphasized that "the Moslem always believes that quarrels between Moslems and Jews have to do with religion. . ."[24]

Since the early 1920's the Palestinian Arab leadership had made a point of appealing for external support on the basis of the purported Zionist threat to Muslim holy places in Palestine, especially al-Masjid al-Aqṣā in Jerusalem.[25] The theme of a threat to al-Aqṣā eventually had a considerable impact on Egyptian Muslims, particularly after the communal tension of the later 1920's in the Mandate, sparked by rival claims to the al-Aqṣā-Western Wall area, gave a surface verisimilitude to the claim. Aḥmad Zakī is a convenient bellwether: however sympathetic he may have been to Zionism in the earlier 1920's, by the end of the decade he was warning Egyptians that "al-Masjid al-Aqṣā calls for help" and presenting the historical brief in defense of the Muslim position before the Wailing Wall Commission of the League of Nations that was sent to investigate the disturbances.[26] At the Jerusalem Islamic Congress in Jerusalem in December 1931, the Egyptian delegate 'Abd al-Ḥamīd Sā'id of the Young Men's Muslim Association (YMMA) devoted his opening speech to the alleged Zionist desire to expel Muslims from their position in the Mosque and its environs, and he concluded by calling on his fellow delegates to stand and take an oath to defend the Mosque from attempts at altering the *status quo*.[27] By the later 1930's, the theme of a threat to Muslim religious sites in Jerusalem found an echo in newspaper editorials warning of al-Aqṣā being "transformed into a Jewish temple" and in pamphlets alleging British-Jewish collusion aimed at dispossessing Muslims from their religious sites in Palestine.[28] The analogy later to become so popular between the Crusades and Zionism had made its appearance by the end of the interwar years. In 1937, Muḥammad Tawfīq Diyāb explicitly compared the two phenomena and rated Zionism as the more ominous in nature since, whereas the Crusaders had confined their ambitions to the Holy Land [sic],

24 Marāghī as cited in a dispatch from Percy Loraine to Arthur Henderson, 14 Sept. 1929; FO 371/13753.

25 Y. Porath, *The Emergence of the Palestinian National Movement, 1918-1929* (London, 1974), 263-264; Y. Porath, *The Palestinian Arab National Movement, 1929-1939; From Riots to Rebellion* (London, 1977), 275; Rudolph Peters, *Islam and Colonialism: The Doctrine of Jihad in Modern History* (The Hague, 1979), 100-101.

26 Quotation from al-Jindī, *op. cit.*, 247.

27 *al-Balāgh*, 8 Dec. 1931, 1.

28 Quotation from *al-Jihād*, 19 May 1936, 1; see also *ibid.*, 28 May 1936, 1, 7; FO 371/21877, FO 371/21883.

Zionism wished to "spread into all the Arab lands" in order to accommodate the new waves of Jewish immigration from Europe.[29]

The perceived religious threat posed by Zionism led religiously-inclined Egyptians to place opposition to Zionism on a religious basis. A consistent theme of the statements on the Palestine issue emanating from spokesmen for the Young Men's Muslim Association and the Muslim Brotherhood in the later 1930's was the Muslim religious obligation to oppose Zionism. Since the Islamic holy places in Palestine were the sacred trust of the Muslim community as a whole, it was the religious duty of Muslims everywhere to oppose the Zionist movement which threatened the status of these sites.[30]

The logical conclusion of these analyses portraying the Arab-Jewish clash in Palestine in primarily-religious terms was the call for *jihād*. Already in the later 1930's the summons to *jihād* for the sake of Palestine had been made by Muslim religious publicists in Egypt. Yaḥyā Aḥmad al-Dardīrī of the YMMA wrote two major articles on the theme of *jihād* and Palestine, in 1936-1937; the first lamenting the modern Muslim neglect of this pillar of the faith and implying the necessity of its resurrection regarding Palestine; the second directly applying the concept of *jihād* to the current situation in Palestine and stating that "struggle for the sake of what is holy in religion is incumbent on every Muslim."[31] Pamphlets calling for *jihād* in Palestine were issued by pro-Palestinian committees and groups in Egypt, calling Egyptian Muslims to their "sacred and holy obligation" of *jihād* on behalf of Palestine.[32] According to information reaching the British, the official Egyptian religious establishment of al-Azhar was inclining towards a summons to *jihād* by the fall of 1938, until the intervention of the Rector of al-Azhar, Shaykh al-Marāghī, succeeded in watering down their official declaration on Palestine of August 1938 to a generalized call to Muslim leaders to concern themselves with Palestine.[33] It was not until the 1940's that *jihād* for the sake of Palestine received quasi-official sanction in the Azharite declaration of April 1948, which declared that "opposition to Zionism and the Zionists, by self and wealth, is a religious duty."[34]

* * *

29 *al-Jihād*, 13 July 1937, 1.

30 See *Majallat al-Shubbān al-Muslimīn*, I, no. 2 (Nov. 1929), 148-150; *ibid.*, I, no. 10 (July 1930), 733; *Jarīdat al-Ikhwān al-Muslimīn*, IV, no. 6 (19 May 1936), 19-20; *ibid.*, IV, no. 21 (1 Sept. 1936), 16.

31 *Majallat al-Shubbān al-Muslimīn*, VII, no. 10 (July 1936), 577-584, and *ibid.*, IX, no. 2 (Nov. 1937), 81-87 (quotation from 83).

32 Dispatch from Sir Miles Lampson, 29 Oct. 1938, FO 371/21883; see also Peters, *op. cit.*, 102-103.

33 Discussed in *ibid.*, 102, and *Oriente Moderno*, XVIII (1938), 520-521.

34 Quoted from *al-Siyāsa*, 1 May 1948, 2.

The tendency to see Zionism in predominantly religious terms was by no means the only perspective of Jewish nationalism found in interwar Egypt. Critiques of Zionism of a quite secular nature were also voiced. One such was the interpretation which viewed it as little more than an instrument of western imperialism. As early as 1930, Muḥammad Ḥusayn Haykal was minimizing the depth of the Arab-Jewish clash in the Mandate and asserting that "there is no doubt that it would be possible for Arabs and Jews to reach an agreement on the issues of their conflict, were it not for the finger of imperialism interfering between them."[35] The motive usually perceived as underlying this western manipulation of Zionism was that imperialism, specifically Great Britain, found Zionism a useful tool in its policy of divide-and-rule in the Arab world. Various Egyptian commentators saw the Peel Commission Report of 1937 and its recommendation of the partition of Palestine as being a clever British scheme by which to preserve its position both in the Mandate and the region: as Aḥmad Ḥusayn of Young Egypt put it at the time, the Jewish state proposed by Peel would be "a British thorn stuck into the side of the Arab lands."[36] By 1939, the editor of *al-Siyāsa al-Usbū'iyya* was writing of the "British-Arab triangle" represented by the three areas of the Saudi kingdom, Transjordan, and the Jewish *Yishuv* in Palestine, i.e., three areas indirectly dominated by Great Britain and used by it to maintain its position of regional ascendancy.[37]

A perception of Zionism which seems to have grown appreciably in Egypt over the interwar period related to the movement's presumed expansionist proclivities. The passage of Arab-owned lands into Jewish hands was noted in Egyptian commentary on the situation in Palestine, and was sometimes accompanied by appeals for other Arabs to buy land in Palestine in order to preserve the country's Arab character.[38] But it was political and/or military expansion by Zionism which was more often noted by Egyptian observers. By the later 1930's, the combination of the possibility of the creation of a sovereign Jewish state and the Zionist desire for massive Jewish immigration from Europe led various Egyptian observers to the conclusion that a Jewish state would almost inevitably be compelled to undertake forcible expansion into the areas of Palestine which were still predominantly Arab.[39] With these warnings of expansion came predictions of the ouster of the Arab community from Palestine. As early as 1929, *al-Ahrām* raised the specter of the "expulsion" of the Arabs of Palestine

35 *al-Siyāsa al-Usbū'iyya*, no. 234 (30 Aug. 1930), 3.

36 *al-Thughr*, 12 July 1937; 2; for similar analyses, see *al-Jihād*, 11 July 1937, 1; *Majallat al-Rābiṭa al-'Arabiyya*, no. 61 (4 Aug. 1937), 16.

37 *al-Siyāsa al-Usbū'iyya*, n.s., no. 131 (29 July 1939), 3.

38 A good example is *al-Risāla*, no. 23 (11 Dec. 1933), 3-4.

39 For such predictions made at the time of the Peel Commission Report in 1933, see *al-Jihād*, 11 July 1937, 1; *al-Ahrām*, 14 July 1937, 1, 15.

from the country as the Jewish National Home developed into a Jewish state.[40] These apprehensions of Arab displacement were voiced with more frequency and urgency in the 1930's, with the analogy of the Arab expulsion from Spain sometimes being invoked.[41]

Nor did Egyptian publicists restrict their predictions of the probability of Zionist "expansion" to the Palestine Mandate. Various writers expressed the opinion that the imperatives of absorbing large scale Jewish immigration would lead a Jewish state in Palestine towards expansion into areas beyond Palestine west of the Jordan River. Mandatory Transjordan, Syria and Lebanon were the regions most often mentioned as potentially threatened by future Zionist expansion, but even Iraq and the Hijaz were sometimes cited as potentially in "danger" as well.[42] Most significant in this respect were references to a Jewish state desiring eventual expansion into Egyptian territory. This possibility was being voiced not only in the Egyptian press by the later 1930's: in a conversation with the British Ambassador in July 1937, even Prime Minister Muṣṭafā al-Naḥḥās echoed a growing Egyptian apprehension when he asked "who could say the voracious Jews would not claim Sinai next?"[43] By the end of the interwar period, the catch-phrase warning of "a Jewish state stretching from the Nile to the Euphrates" was to be found in the Egyptian press.[44]

With these more negative images of the potential of Zionism taking hold in Egypt by the 1930's, Egyptians came to see a variety of threats posed by Jewish nationalism and the *Yishuv* in Palestine. In general terms, Zionism was sometimes portrayed as having "a revolutionary, destructive spirit"; Zionism was seen as sharing many of the revolutionary notions characteristic of the *milieu* of its emergence in nineteenth-century Europe; its implantation in Palestine now threatened to spread these ideas in the Middle East.[45] With Zionism often seen as expansionist, it was necessarily viewed as a

40 *al-Ahrām*, 25 Aug. 1929, 3.

41 For warnings of Arab displacement dating from the 1930's, see *al-Siyāsa*, 20 Dec. 1931; 5; *al-Jihād*, 19 May 1936, 1; *al-Muqaṭṭam*, 15 July 1937, 1, 4; *al-Risāla*, no. 164 (23 Aug. 1936), 1363-1365; *ibid.*, no. 213 (2 Aug. 1937), 1247-1249; *ibid.*, no. 215 (16 Aug. 1937), 1321-1323.

42 For general or specific predictions of such Zionist expansion, see *al-Siyāsa*, 27 May 1936, 4; *al-Jihād*, 13 July 1937, 1; *Jarīdat al-Ikhwān al-Muslimīn*, IV, n. 18 (11 Aug. 1936), 1-3; *al-Risāla*, no. 213 (2 Aug. 1937), 1266-1267; *Majallat al-Rābiṭa al-'Arabiyya*, no. 98 (4 May 1938), 10.

43 From a conversation between Naḥḥās and the British Ambassador of July 1937 as reported in a telegram from Sir Miles Lampson, 25 July 1937, FO 371/20810. For a public expression of a similar fear of Zionist expansion into Egypt by a prominent journalist, see *al-Siyāsa al-Usbū'iyya*, n.s., no. 28 (24 July 1937), 10.

44 *al-Risāla*, no. 213 (2 Aug. 1937), 1267.

45 *al-Risāla*, no. 213 (2 Aug. 1937), 1247-1249; *Jarīdat al-Ikhwān al-Muslimīn*, V, no. 44 (13 May 1938), 6-8; *Majallat al-Rābiṭa al-'Arabiyya*, no. 64 (25 Aug. 1937), 7.

threat to Arab Muslim regions and to "the East" as a whole.[46] A quite frequently expressed attitude by the later 1930's was that the emergence of a Jewish state in Palestine had adverse implications for regional Arab cooperation or unity. As Ibrāhīm 'Abd al-Qādir al-Māzinī stated in 1936, the existence of a non-Arab state in Palestine would be the "greatest barrier" to developing Arab hopes for unity since "there is no way to realize that (unity) as long as a foreign people intrudes between Egypt, Syria, Iraq and the Peninsula. That is so obvious that it does not need explication."[47]

Most important were the threats to Egypt itself posed by Zionism. In political terms, Egypt's security position in the eastern Mediterranean would necessarily be influenced by the creation of a Jewish state in Palestine. Such a state could possibly pose a security threat itself in the future; alternatively, its very alienness from Egypt would make it less desirable as a neighbor than a fellow-Arab state linked to Egypt by language and culture.[48] Quite widespread in Egypt by the 1930's were sentiments that Zionism and the Jewish state at which it aimed represented an economic danger to Egypt. The advanced, industrialized economy of such a state would undoubtedly mean stiff competition for Egyptian industry in the "eastern" export markets to which Egyptians were looking at the time, or might even be a possible competitor with domestic Egyptian industry and commerce, to the point where "dominance over the economic affairs of Egypt would be in Tel Aviv."[49] Zionism and a Jewish state could mean social difficulties for Egypt as well: generally, a social danger in that such a state would be a base for the spread of alien western customs;[50] more specifically, a social irritant in regard to the Jews of Egypt, either in the sense that their loyalties might be drawn to the new Jewish state, or that the backlash against Zionism and Jews which was developing in Egypt by the end of the 1930's could threaten Egypt's social peace.[51] What is worth noting is the range of possible threats to Egypt perceived as being affected by Zionism and the Palestine question: by the end of the interwar period,

46 For general expressions of this, see *al-Siyāsa*, 27 May 1937, 4; *al-Jihād*, 10 July 1937, 1; *Jarīdat al-Ikhwān al-Muslimīn*, IV, no. 18 (11 Aug. 1936), 1-3; *al-Risāla*, no. 213 (2 Aug. 1937), 1266-1267.

47 *al-Shabāb*, no. 31 (16 Sept. 1936), 7-8. See also *al-Siyāsa al-Usbū'iyya*, n. s., no. 27 (17 July 1937), 3; *ibid.*, no. 28 (24 July 1937), 10; *al-Jihād*, 14 July 1937, 1; *al-Thughr*, 12 July 1937, 2.

48 *al-Shabāb*, no. 31 (16 Sept. 1936), 7-8; *al-Jihād*, 14 July 1937, 1; *al-Siyāsa al-Usbū'iyya*, n.s., no. 27 (17 July 1937), 3.

49 For variants on the economic threat to Egypt posed by a Jewish state, see *ibid.*; *Jarīdat al-Ikhwān al-Muslimīn*, IV, no. 18 (11 Aug. 1937), 1-3; *al-Jihād*, 13 July 1937, 1; *ibid.*, 14 July 1937, 1; *Jarīdat Miṣr al-Fatāt*, 23 May 1938, 7; *al-Balāgh*, 10 Oct. 1938, 1 (quotation from the last).

50 *Majallat al-Rābiṭa al-'Arabiyya*, no. 61 (4 Aug. 1937), 16-17.

51 See Naḥḥās's conversation with Lampson of July 1937 (FO 371/20810) as well as *al-Balāgh*, 10 Oct. 1938, 1, for expressions of this.

Egypt's political, economic and social development were all seen by some Egyptians to be influenced negatively by Zionism and the growth of the Jewish community in Palestine.

★ ★ ★

A concomitant of the apprehension about Zionism which developed in Egypt over the interwar period was the expression of negative views concerning the Jewish people as a whole. The expression of anti-Jewish sentiment or stereotypes was generally alien to Egyptian nationalist opinion in the 1920's. In the wake of the Egyptian Revolution of 1919, Egyptian nationalist leaders attempted to maintain the tradition of inter-confessional cooperation for national goals which had developed during that struggle.[52] To Aḥmad Ḥāfiẓ 'Awḍ of the Wafd in 1924, there was "no difference between Muslim, Christian and Israelite" in Egypt; all were members of the Egyptian nation.[53] Similarly, in 1929 Muḥammad Ḥusayn Haykal proclaimed that "Egypt does not know sectarianism" such as had manifested itself recently in Palestine: rather, the Christian and Jewish population of Egypt was, along with its Muslim majority, an indivisible part of "the Egyptian bloc" [*al-kutla al-miṣriyya*], and "it is not possible for Egypt to make any kind of division between the various elements within it which comprise the Egyptian bloc. . . ."[54]

With growing Egyptian involvement in the Palestine question in the 1930's, this tolerance of Jews began to give way to negative portrayals of the Jews. For conservative Egyptian Muslim publicists, these negative images seem to have had their basis in traditional Muslim views of the Jews resulting from their early clash with the Prophet Muḥammad. To Muṣṭafā Ṣādiq al-Rāfi'ī, the Jews were both a people singled out for God's punishment because of their "vices" and a group which harbored feelings of malice, rancor, and the desire for exploitation towards others, while to Aḥmad Ḥasan al-Zayyāt "the curse of God" still followed the Jews and condemned them to perpetual rootlessness and restlessness.[55] Especially widespread were characterizations of the Jewish people as the inveterate opponent of Islam and Muslims: even a liberal like Haykal tended to view the Jewish people through the filter of hostility imposed by their portrayal in early Muslim sources, speaking of their relentless "hatred" for Muḥam-

52 The political dimensions of this are discussed, with specific reference to Egypt's Copts, in Leland Bowie, "The Copts, the Wafd and Religious Issues in Egyptian Politics," *Muslim World*, LXVII (1977), 106-126.

53 *Kawkib al-Sharq*, 21 Sept. 1924, 1, as quoted in Fārūq Abū Zayd, *Azmat al-Fikr al-Qawmī fī 'l-Siḥāfa al-Miṣriyya* (Cairo, 1976), 71-72.

54 *al-Siyāsa*, 1 Sept. 1929, 1.

55 For the former's views on the Jews in 1936, see *al-Risāla*, no. 154 (15 June 1936), 961-963. Zayyāt's opinion is from *ibid.*, no. 265 (1 Aug. 1938), 1241-1242.

mad,[56] while more conservative spokesmen developed at length the themes of Jewish opposition to Islam and the Prophet at Medina, of Jewish plots to kill Muḥammad, and of how all of Muslim history had witnessed a continual "struggle between us and them."[57]

Not all pejorative characterizations of the Jewish people which were appearing in Egypt by the 1930's had their primary inspiration in traditional Muslim images of the Jews. More recent anti-Jewish perspectives could also be found in the Egyptian press. Contemporary European stereotypes about the Jews were particularly prominent in the propaganda of the Young Egypt movement in the later 1930's. By 1939, Aḥmad Ḥusayn of Young Egypt was invoking anti-Jewish stereotypes echoing those found in contemporary European anti-Semitism. Thus Jews were "the secret of this decline and decay which afflicts the whole Islamic world";[58] the Jewish character was marked by traits of "cowardice," of "obscenity," and of "destructiveness";[59] and *in toto* Jews were "the secret of this religious and moral decay, up to the point where it has become correct to say 'search for the Jew behind every depravity.'"[60] Decay, cowardice, obscenity, destructiveness, depravity — certainly the imagery parallels that which was employed at the same time by European opponents of the Jewish people.

Perhaps the most prevalent set of negative images concerning Jews which gained currency in Egypt by the end of the interwar period were those concerning the perceived connection of the Jews with finance and of the alleged domination of Jews over both international and regional economies. Allusions to Jewish financial connections and manipulation were a common theme in the writings of Egyptians committed to support of the Arab position in Palestine. The financial position of Jews in the modern Middle East was the subject of repeated attacks in the Arab nationalist journal *al-Rābiṭa al-'Arabiyya*; exposés on "the Jews in Iraq and how they monopolize economic facilities," on the Jewish position of economic affluence in Egypt and on how Jews "dominate commerce and the economy" in contemporary Egypt, or on how European Jewish bankers had been "responsible for Egypt's financial disaster" in the nineteenth century.[61] While *al-Rābiṭa al-'Arabiyya* was a journal most of whose contributors were non-Egyptian Arabs living in Egypt and thus is not fully representative of native Egyptian opinion, similar attitudes could be found

56 Muḥammad Ḥusayn Haykal, *The Life of Muhammad* (n.p., 1976), 312-315.
57 For examples, see *Majallat al-Shubbān al-Muslimīn*, VI, no. 3 (Dec. 1934), 167-173; *Jarīdat al-Ikhwān al-Muslimīn*, V, no. 22 (5 Nov. 1937), 4-5 from which the phrase in quotations is taken; *al-Risāla*, no. 276 (17 Oct. 1938), 1693-1695.
58 *Jarīdat Miṣr al-Fatāt*, 15 July 1939, 1.
59 *Ibid.*, 27 July 1939, 1.
60 *Ibid.*
61 The articles appear in *Majallat al-Rābiṭa al-'Arabiyya*, no. 52 (2 June 1937), 24-26; *ibid.*, no. 100 (18 May 1938), 28-29; *ibid.*, no. 102 (1 June 1938), 23-24.

in those segments of Egyptian society sympathetic to Arab issues.[62] By 1938 and 1939, parallel accusations of Jewish financial domination over Egypt, of "how the Jews have come to dominate the arteries of life in Egypt and how they manipulate them to serve their own ends and goals," were becoming commonplace in the propaganada of a movement like Young Egypt.[63]

As the preceding quotation indicates, the ultimate conclusion of these negative analyses of the Jewish role in the international, the regional, or the local economy was the separateness and the alienness of Jews from the various national communities amongst whom they lived. The economic affluence of Jews was not all that mattered in the framework of these analyses: what was fully as important was that Jews used their success and position to "serve their own ends and goals." That "the interests of the Jews have outweighed the interests of Egypt" was also the point of other articles.[64] As one author summarized it, "the Jew is a Jew before anything else."[65] The implications of this attitude were considerable: the perception of the un-national nature of Jewish communities in Egypt and other eastern countries underlay the suggestions for the economic isolation of Jews and even for the expulsion of Jews which we shall examine shortly.

Given both these perceptions of an ingrained Jewish inclination towards the manipulation of others and the world climate of the 1930's with its grotesque imagery of worldwide Jewish plots, it is hardly surprising that conspiracy theories concerning Jews were being voiced in Egypt by the last years of the interwar period. Articles in the journal of the Muslim Brotherhood in the later 1930's attributed various conspiracies both medieval and modern to Jews; plots against Muḥammad and Islam, plans for Jewish world domination dating back to the Middle Ages, but also involvement in the modern Communist movement which in reality was nothing more than "a Jewish plot to ruin the world."[66] It was the polemicists of Young Egypt who developed the most elaborate conspiracy theories. As Young Egypt presented things by 1939, Jews were planning several schemes to promote their aim of regional political and economic domination: secret plans to dominate Egypt economically; another conspiracy aimed at controlling the press in Egypt in order to prevent the expression of views hostile to Zionism

62 For examples, see *al-Risāla*, no. 154 (15 June 1936), 962; *ibid.*, no. 265 (1 Aug. 1938), 1242; *ibid.*, no. 276 (17 Oct. 1938), 1693.

63 See *Jarīdat Miṣr al-Fatāt*, 6 Oct. 1938, 7; *ibid.*, 10 July 1939, 9 (from which the quotation is taken); *ibid.*, 29 July 1939, 3,5.

64 *Majallat al-Rābiṭa al-'Arabiyya*, no. 104 (15 June 1938), 26-27.

65 *Ibid.*, no. 109 (20 July 1938), 21.

66 *Jarīdat al-Ikhwān al Muslimīn*, V, no. 22 (5 Nov. 1937), 4-5; *ibid.*, no. 34 (25 Feb. 1938), 13; *ibid.*, no. 35 (4 March 1938), 14-15, from which the quotation is taken.

or Jews; not least a plot recently revealed in secret Jewish publications which aimed at Jewish domination of the Arab world.[67]

It is important to note that the preceding anti-Jewish propaganda which was surfacing in Egypt by the later 1930's was found only in certain segments of Egyptian public opinion, and that it was opposed in other, at the time more influential, circles. Conservative Muslim publicists influenced by traditional Muslim images of the Jews; Egyptians of the new generation both more vehemently nationalist than their elders and more inclined towards Arabo-Islamic rather than narrow Egyptian concepts of nationalism; and writers drawn from the non-Egyptian Arab population resident in Egypt — these were the main circles in which anti-Jewish stereotypes and sentiments manifested themselves.

Egypt's dominant political establishment, however, regardless of the apprehension about Zionism which it manifested, seems to have maintained throughout the interwar period the liberal attitude towards Jews and their participation in the Egyptian national "bloc" which had been characteristic of their outlook in the 1920's. The contrast between the two attitudes can be seen clearly from a consideration of the position of major newspapers in October 1938, at the time when the "World Parliamentary Congress of Arab and Muslim Countries for the Defense of Palestine" met in Cairo. That assembly had been preceded by rising anti-Jewish sentiment within Egypt such as some of the articles discussed in the preceding paragraphs, and the Congress itself was the occasion for calls for Palestine to be declared to be a Muslim religious issue by some of the delegates in attendance. What is noteworthy is the resistance of Egypt's leading newspapers to a predominantly religious interpretation of the struggle in Palestine. *Al-Balāgh* stated flatly that "the issue of Palestine is not a religious question" and that "the Congress should not arouse religious sentiments concerning it."[68] *Al-Muqaṭṭam* attempted to reassure eastern Jews that rising Arab Muslim concern over Palestine would not affect the position of Jews in eastern countries.[69] *Al-Ahrām*, while less sanguine about that sentiment and apprehensive that "the struggle in Palestine is beginning to agitate the power of Islamic-Arabic racialism in the lands of the east," nonetheless regretted this trend.[70] Nor was criticism of anti-Jewish agitation restricted to the establishment press: even a journal such as *al-Siyāsa al-Usbū'iyya*, by the late 1930's a staunch supporter of the Arab cause in Palestine, still made a point of defending Egyptian Jewry and its general solidarity with non-Jewish Egyptian opinion about Palestine.[71] Thus, while

67 See successively *Jarīdat Miṣr al-Fatāt*, 10 July 1939, 9; *ibid.*, 29 July 1939, 3, 5; *ibid.*, 7 Aug. 1939, 2.

68 *al-Balāgh*, 10 Oct. 1938, 1.

69 *al-Muqaṭṭam*, 6 Oct. 1938, 1.

70 *al-Ahrām*, 18 Oct. 1938, 1.

71 *al-Siyāsa al-Usbū'iyya*, n.s., no. 95 (5 Nov. 1938), 3-4.

more committed and/or more extremist elements in Egypt were led by their anti-Zionism towards attitudes of anti-Jewishness, sentiments of this type were by no means general in Egyptian opinion.

★ ★ ★

Even with this qualification, the definitely anti-Zionist and in part anti-Jewish sentiment visible in Egypt by the later 1930's was beginning to have ominous implications for the physical position of Jews within Egypt. Through most of the interwar period there appears to have been little or no anti-Jewish agitation or activity occurring in Egypt. As late as June 1936, a British report was still estimating that, just as there was as yet no significant Egyptian concern with the Palestine issue within Egypt, "neither is there any real anti-Jewish feeling" in the country.[72] It was precisely from this point, however, in the context of the lengthy Arab Revolt in the Mandate, that the physical position of Jews in Egypt began to be threatened.

There were three different forms of pressure directed against Jews which began to appear in Egypt by the later 1930's. In a logical sense the first of these was verbal warnings or threats of the possibility of future anti-Jewish activity occurring in Egypt as a result of the growth of popular concern over the Palestine issue. With the outbreak of the Arab general strike in Palestine in the spring of 1936, à leading Egyptian newspaper warned Egyptian Jews of the possibility of anti-Jewish sentiment and action as a by-product of the situation in Palestine, and counselled Jews that "it is better for them if they do not stir up in the East feelings like those which are directed against them in the West."[73] By 1938-1939, warnings of the dire implications of the Palestine problem for Jews in Egypt and other Arab-Muslim lands were appearing more frequently. They came particularly from individuals and organizations committed in support of the Palestinian Arab cause; an open letter from Muḥammad ʻAlī ʻAlluba warning the Jews of Egypt not to support Zionism, a youth conference proclaiming that "there is no excuse" for the Jews living in eastern countries for not joining their compatriots in opposition to Zionism, a student assembly similarly calling on Egyptian Jews to disassociate themselves from Zionism and to support the Arab national cause in Palestine.[74] Some of these warnings raised the prospect of eventual Jewish expulsion from Arab or Muslim lands as a result of the sentiment being aroused by the Palestine issue: the journal of Young Egypt was warning of this possibility by late 1938, and a

72 Telegram from Mr. Kelly, 22 June 1936; FO 371/20035.

73 *al-Siyāsa*, 29 May 1936, 4; cf. *al-Balāgh*, 9 June 1936, 9.

74 *al-Fatḥ*, 609 (9 Jumāda al-Ulā 1357), 16-17; *Majallat al-Rābiṭa al-'Arabiyya*, no. 98 (4 May 1938), 10; *ibid.*, no. 12S (9 Nov. 1938), 47-48, and *al-Fatḥ*, no. 627 (18 Ramaḍān 1357), 16-17.

(presumably non-Egyptian) writer in the Arabist *al-Rābiṭa al-'Arabiyya* explicitly called for Eastern nations to imitate European ones and to expel their Jewish minorities.[75]

The second form of anti-Jewish activity visible in Egypt by the last years of the interwar period was economic; the call for the economic boycott of Jews and the attempt to organize such boycotts. Since the early 1930's the Palestinian Arab leadership had appealed to fellow Arabs for economic action against Jews in order to pressure eastern Jews away from support for Zionism.[76] In the later 1930's various Egyptian groups supporting the Palestinian Arab cause picked up on this idea and attempted to implement it. The Muslim Brotherhood seems to have been the first organization in Egypt to call for the boycott of local Jewish merchants: it did so in 1936, in order to prevent the shipment of goods from Egypt to Palestine while the Palestinian Arabs were undertaking their general strike.[77] The same youth conference which in April 1938 had warned eastern Jews against supporting Zionism also proposed the "boycott of Egyptian Jews connected with the Jews in Palestine."[78] A Committee for the Boycott of Jews in Egypt was distributing propaganda at al-Azhar in mid-1938, and calls for economic pressure and boycott of local Jews appeared in the literature of the Brotherhood and Young Egypt in 1938 as well as surfacing among student groups at the Egyptian University.[79] By 1939, Young Egypt in particular was making the organization of an anti-Jewish boyott the centerpiece of its political activity. The party gave the bulk of its attention in the summer of 1939 to such a boycott, organizing a committee for the Boycott of Jewish Commerce, establishing local boycott committees in the provinces, gathering statistics on the extent of Jewish commercial activities in various localities, and publishing three lists of Jewish merchants who should be boycotted.[80]

The third form of pressure which began to be directed against Jews in Egypt in the later 1930's was physical violence. As early as June 1936, Prime Minister Naḥḥās was warning the British privately of a "possible

75 *Jarīdat Miṣr al-Fatāt*, 1 Sept. 1938, 1; *Majallat al-Rābiṭa al-'Arabiyya*, no. 118 (21 Sept. 1938), 31-33.

76 See the appeal of the Arab Executive to the Arab nation as published in *Majallat al-Rābiṭa al-Sharqiyya*, III, no. 7 (April 1931), 30-32; see also Porath, *The Palestinian Arab National Movement* 34.

77 *Jarīdat al-Ikhwān al-Muslimīn*, IV, no. 6 (19 May 1936), 19-20; *ibid.*, no. 7 (26 May 1936), 15-16.

78 *Majallat al-Rābiṭa al-'Arabiyya*, no. 98 (4 May 1938), 10.

79 Sir Miles Lampson to Viscount Halifax, 17 May 1938 (FO 371/21877); *Majallat al-Rābiṭa al-'Arabiyya*, no. 100 (18 May 1938), 43-44; *Jarīdat al-Ikhwān al-Muslimīn* 13 May 1938), 12; *Jarīdat Miṣr al-Fatāt*, 6 Oct. 1938, 7; dispatch from Sir Miles Lampson, 29 Oct. 1938 (FO 371/21883).

80 *Jarīdat Miṣr al-Fatāt*, 8 July 1939, 3; *ibid.*, 17 July 1939, 6-7; *ibid.*, 20 July 1939, 2; *ibid.*, 22 July 1939, 5; *ibid.*, 24 Aug. 1939, 12; *ibid.*, 26 Aug. 1939, 12; *ibid.*, 31 Aug. 1939, 11.

anti-Jewish outbreak" within Egypt due to rising public concern over the Palestine question.[81] While anti-Jewish violence does not seem to have occurred at that time, it did begin to develop by 1938-1939 when the prolongation and intensification of the Arab Revolt produced a sufficient level of commitment and yet frustration in more volatile elements of Egyptian opinion. An Azharite demonstration concerning Palestine in April 1938 moved to the Jewish quarter of Cairo where the demonstrators shouted anti-Jewish slogans; in the following month another demonstration by Azharites again proceeded to the Jewish quarter and resulted in clashes with the police and the arrest of several demonstrators.[82] By 1939, Young Egypt's intense anti-Jewish boycott campaign was producing anti-Jewish violence: in Asyut, inflammatory pamphlets advocating the boycott and also a cache of explosives were discovered by the police in July 1939, and members of Young Egypt were arrested in al-Maḥalla al-Kubra in the same month on suspicion of placing a bomb in the Jewish district.[83] While these incidents of 1938-1939 were isolated and apparently did not result in actual physical injury to Egyptian Jews, nonetheless they were a portent of the kind of violence which was directed against Jews in Egypt when the Palestine issue reached its climax in the 1940's.

The anti-Jewish sentiment and activity appearing in Egypt by 1938 seriously concerned both the Egyptian Jewish community and the Egyptian government. In the spring of 1938, Egyptian Jewish leaders privately counselled the British that Egyptian popular involvement in the Palestine problem was, in the words of Sir Victor Hariri, "endangering [the] good relations which have always existed between [the] Jewish colony and the people of Egypt."[84] The same apprehension was voiced by the Egyptian government. Prime Minister Muḥammad Maḥmūd approached the British repeatedly in 1938 to inform them of the "extremely difficult position" in which religiously-couched and thus implicitly anti-Jewish agitation over Palestine was placing his government or to warn them that Egyptian concern over Palestine was taking on "an increasingly religious aspect."[85]

81 Telegram from Mr. Kelly, 22 June 1936 (FO 371/20035). It was this conversation which occasioned Kelly's evaluation that as yet there was not "any real anti-Jewish feeling" in Egypt. For Lampson's reversal of this opinion by August 1936, see Sir Miles Lampson to Mr. Eden, 12 Aug. 1936 (FO 371/20023).

82 *Majallat al-Rābiṭa al-'Arabiyya*, no. 100 (18 May 1938), 43-44; telegram from Sir Miles Lampson, 28 April 1938 (FO 371/21875); letter from Lampson to Viscount Halifax, 17 May 1938 (FO 371/21877).

83 *Jarīdat Miṣr al-Fatāt*, 22 July 1939, 8; *ibid.*, 24 July 1939, 5; *ibid.*, Aug. 7, 1939, 5.

84 Quoted from Lampson's summary of his conversation with Hariri in a telegram of 16 June 1938 (FO 371/21877). For other expressions of concern by Egyptian Jews, see FO 371/21876; FO 371 21884.

85 See respectively telegram from Sir Miles Lampson, 8 June 1938 (FO 371/21877); telegram from Mr. Bateman, 7 Sept. 1938 (FO 371/21880); cf. Maḥmūd's conversation with Colonial Secretary Malcolm MacDonald in July 1938 (FO 371/21879).

This disquiet over the implications of the Palestine issue for Egyptian domestic stability and tranquility was one of the factors causing the ministry of Muḥammad Maḥmūd to involve itself in a major way in diplomatic activities concerning Palestine from mid-1938 onwards. In fine, the intensification of the Palestine question and the hostility towards first Zionism and later Jews which it generated were beginning to have destabilizing results within Egypt itself by the later 1930's, a factor which helped to prod the Egyptian government into significant involvement in the problem.

ROBERT L. TIGNOR

Egyptian Jewry, Communal Tension, and Zionism

Reflecting back on his experiences in Egypt, an influential member of the Egyptian Jewish community, Maurice Mizraḥi, claimed that during World War I and afterward Egyptian Jews were warm advocates of the Balfour Declaration and its promise of a Jewish homeland in Palestine. They saw no contradiction in working for this goal and at the same time supporting the aims of Egyptian nationalism. Mizraḥi goes on to contend that the deep divisions that eventually appeared between Jews and Muslims in Egypt stemmed from the fateful events in Palestine in the late 1930s and 1940s and from the xenophobia that crept into Egyptian nationalism after its earlier secular orientation began to diminish.[1]

Yet in interviews I conducted in the 1970s with members of that same Jewish community, now living dispersed in various parts of the world, the consensus was that most Egyptian Jews were apathetic to the appeals of Zionism. Some people very soon realized that Zionism was likely to produce dire consequences for the Jews of Egypt.[2]

Both of these views conceal much of the reality of Egyptian Jewish life in the twentieth century, particularly the deep-seated cleavages which periodically threatened to erupt at various moments. Twentieth century Egyptian Jewry experienced a level of tension which it had not known in the previous century. The oligarchic control of the community was challenged by an alliance of middling and lower middling elements, sometimes in league with the rabbinical religious establishment. Many of the Jewish youth felt themselves alienated from the rest of the community, and the intellectuals; fascinated with the ideas of socialism, anti-imperialism, nationalism and Zionism, they were especially critical of the community's conservative leaders. Although it might seem logical to assume that the communal tension stemmed largely from the impact of Zionism and the dilemmas of

1 Maurice Mizraḥi, *L'Égypte et ses Juifs; Le Temps Revolu* (Geneva, 1978), *passim*.

2 I carried out interviews in London, Paris, New York, Dallas, Geneva, Lausanne, and Cairo between 1974 and 1979.

loyalty it caused for Egyptian Jews, in truth Zionism was only one of many discordant notes that beset Egyptian Jewry in the twentieth century. Indeed for most of the period — up until 1948 and even 1956 — it was not the most troubling issue. But what it did was to exacerbate already existing conflicts, for the varied and discordant responses to Zionism followed along already existing communal lines of cleavage.

That the community was deeply and profoundly fragmented at the outset of the twentieth cenutry was inevitable given the rapidity of social change which Egypt and Egyptian Jewry experienced in the nineteenth century. Egypt's small, residentially-confined, and self-contained pre-1800 Jewish community was transformed almost out of all recognition as the country was steadily integrated into the world economy in the nineteenth century. To begin with demographics, the Jewish population grew at a break-neck pace in the last half of the century, especially by virtue of the influx of new immigrants. These people came from all over the Mediterranean basin (Turkey, Greater Syria, and Italy) and brought with them different cultural and social traditions. The causes for the influx are clear. Enjoying an economic boom, Egypt elaborated political institutions (British overrule and the Mixed Tribunals in particular) which offered protection to groups fleeing persecution or anxious to respond to new economic opportunities.

Although the 1882 census did not break down its figures by nationality, the number of foreigners living in Egypt at the time was 90,886. By 1897 this figure had risen to 109,725, of whom 25,300 were Jews. Data extracted from the twentieth century censuses and displayed in the table below provide further insight into the development of the community. The period of maximum growth was between 1897 and 1917, when the Jewish population more than doubled. It then stabilized at around 60,000 to 65,000 and remained at that level until 1956.

The fact that there had been an earlier, pre-1800 Jewish community, provided a modicum of cohesion and stability. It endowed Egyptian Jewry with historical traditions and claims to permanent settlement in Egypt. Some of the leading Egyptian-Jewish families, notably the Qattawis and the Menasches, traced their origins in Egypt back for many centuries.[3] Also, the Jews living in Egypt had created institutions of communal governance, which though they altered over time, dated at least from the Fatimid period. In the eleventh century the Jewish community in Cairo had established the office of *Nagīd*, sometimes called *Ra'īs al-Yahūd* (head of the Jews).[4] Unlike some of the other foreign or minority immigrant communities who came to prominence in nineteenth and twentieth century Egypt but had few or no pre-existing communal traditions and families to coalesce around (Greeks, Armenians, British, French, Belgians, and to a much lesser extent Syrians), the Egyptian Jews had a solidity stemming from long-standing residence.

TABLE I
Statistical Profile of the Jewish Population in Egypt

1	2	3	4	5	6	7*	8
Year	Population	Percent in Cairo	Percent in Alexandria	Literacy per 1000 excluding 5 and under	Local Subjects	British, French, and Italian citizens	Percent 7÷6+7
1907	38,635	52.5	37.5	438			
1917	59,581	49.0	41.7	438	24,980	17,056	40.1
1927	63,953	53.3	38.8	726	32,320	18,922	36.9
1937	62,953	55.6	39.2	754	40,300	15,343	27.6
1947	65,639	63.8	32.2	823	50,831	8,820	14.8

* These figures certainly contain many errors since in 1956 most Egyptian Jews found themselves without Egyptian nationality and had to be treated as stateless persons. The censuses apparently merely indicated what the individuals themselves reported as their nationality. It would also appear that in some households children were counted and in others they were not. The totals do not add up to the total Jewish population living in Egypt.

Another basis of traditional unity was residential proximity. Egyptian Jews were pre-eminently urban dwellers. In 1907, nine out of every ten Jews lived in Cairo and Alexandria. This proportion had increased to nine and one-half by 1947, with Cairo surpassing Alexandria as the primary city of Egyptian Jewry. By 1947, 63.8 percent of all of the Jews of Egypt resided in Cairo — a figure that was nearly double the Jewish population of Alexandria (32.2 percent of the total).

Within these two cities Jews tended to cluster in a few districts. In Cairo, the main population centers were Jamāliya where the old Jewish quarters were located, Wayli, Muski, Azbakiya, and Darb al-Aḥmar. In Alexandria, they were Jumruk, which contained the old Jewish quarter, Manshiyya, 'Aṭṭārin, and Muḥarram Bey. Although there was no dramatic shift in residential patterns over time (these same quarters continued to have the largest population concentrations), there was some dispersion as Jews

3 See Kurt Grunwald, "On Cairo's Lombard Street," *Traditions: Zeitschrift für Firmen-Geschichte und Unternehmer-Biographie*, Vol. 17, No. 1, January and February, 1972, pp. 8-22. On the Menasche family one should consult Ilyās Zakhkhura, *Mir'at al-'Aṣr fī Ta'rīkh wa-Rusūm Akābir Rijāl Miṣr*, Cairo 1897, pp. 152-154 and a very detailed document tracing the family history in Egypt to the beginning of the nineteenth century, found in C. F. Ryder, Department of Public Security to Chancery, April 11, 1920, Public Record Office, Foreign Office (hereafter PRO FO) 141/655 f 11469.

4 On the origins of this office see Mark R. Cohen, *Jewish Self-Government in Medieval Egypt: the Origins of the Office of Head of the Jews, ca. 1065-1126* (Princeton, 1980).

began to intermingle and to settle in areas where previously they had not resided.

These important sources of unity were not powerful enough to preserve communal cohesion, however, once Egypt had been drawn into the expanding world economy. European expansion into the Middle East in the nineteenth century offered new and exciting opportunities for minority and marginal communities living in the area. Members of these minorities served as political collaborators and economic intermediaries.

The Jewish communities of the Middle East were well placed in this respect. As a minority within the Ottoman Empire, they were subject to numerous disabilities and at the same time encouraged to engage in occupations not accorded high status in the Muslim world. They specialized as merchants, financiers, and middlemen. Their communities stressed the education of their children, especially boys, and placed a high regard on literacy. Thus, when the European economic expansion began to be felt, Middle Eastern Jews emerged naturally as economic collaborators.

Moreover, Middle Eastern Jews were viewed by European Jews as a kin group and were assisted not only by European Jewish merchants and financiers, but also by European Jewish cultural and educational associations. Amongst the Egyptian Jews the first decisive joining of interests came in 1840 when two influential European Jewish leaders, Moses Montefiore and Adolfe Cremieux, visited Egypt in the wake of anti-Jewish agitation in Damascus. As a result of their visit several Europeanized Jewish schools were established there. Although these schools did not endure (in part because of an unwillingness on the part of Egyptian Jews to embrace the westernization effort at this time), the moment symbolized a linking of these two communities.[5] That European Jewry, wealthier and better educated than its non-European counterparts, energetically promoted westernization is evident from the creation in France in 1860 of the *Alliance Israélite Universelle*. One of its numerous activities was to raise funds to create Jewish schools overseas. *Alliance* schools were established in Egypt in the 1890s and the following decade, but because Egyptian Jewry had by this time become wealthy and powerful enough to sustain its own religious schools, these soon passed out of existence.[6]

The Jews had other attractions as European intermediaries. They practiced a religion which was followed in the metropole, albeit by a minority. Unlike the Greeks (at least until the Balfour Declaration of 1917), they had no single homeland to be a focus of their political attention and an eventual area of domicile. Also, in contrast to the Greeks, they seem not to have

5 H. Graetz, *History of the Jews* (Philadelphia, 1895), Vol. 5, pp. 632ff and Bension Taragon, *Les Communautés Israélites d'Alexandrie* (Alexandria, 1932), pp. 85ff.

6 N. Leven, *Cinquante Ans d'Histoire: L'Alliance Israélite Universelle, 1860–1910* (Paris, 1911), Vol. 1, p. 67.

vigorously held on to their own language. Although Hebrew was taught in the Jewish schools in Egypt, Jewish families did not insist, with determination akin to that of Greek parents, that their sons and daughters be fluent in Hebrew. Until the Zionist experiment began to take root in Palestine, Hebrew was largely a formal language of religion.[7] Given their commercial capabilities, their traditional vulnerability as a minority group within the Muslim world, the emphasis they placed on education, the rapidity with which their schools adapted to providing training in western languages, and their capacity for geographical mobility, either in response to new economic opportunities or as a consequence of persecution, it is not surprising that Jews of Egypt were quick to come forward as financial and commercial intermediaries for expanding European capitalism.

This development proved profoundly fragmenting. As trusted intermediaries of European capitalism, wealthy Egyptian Jews were eminently successful in acquiring foreign national status. Amongst the wealthy, different national orientations existed. The Menasches were barons of the Austro-Hungarian Empire. The Levi and Aghion families had Italian citizenship while members of the Harari and Rolo families had knighthoods conferred on them by the British.[8] Indeed, the quest for foreign nationality extended well beyond the wealthy bourgeoisie. Half of the Jews in Egypt in 1897 possessed foreign citizenship.[9] Perhaps sensing the changing balance of powers in the Middle East, the number of families who claimed British, French, and Italian citizenship dropped steadily in the twentieth century and markedly after 1937 (see Table). By the same token those who regarded themselves as Egyptian nationals rose dramatically, although, as the events of 1956 were to demonstrate, the Egyptian government was not willing to treat many of these individuals as Egyptian citizens. The largest group of foreign citizens among the Jews were those with French citizenship. Yet the number of French citizens fell from 7891 in 1917 to 3368 in 1947. These different national statuses not only divided the rich from one another but more importantly the rich were differentiated from those — usually the poor — who had little access to foreign national status.

Another palpable cleavage existed between older and newer families. Although considerable efforts were made by the established groups to assimilate each succeeding wave of newcomers (and apparently this prob-

7 On language see J. M. Landau, "Language Problems of the Jews in Egypt," *Orientalia Hispanica*, Vol. 1, 1970, pp. 439-443 and also "Riv ha-leshonot ba-ḥinnukh ha-yehudi be-Mitzraim ha-ḥadashah," Bar-Ilan, *Annual of Bar-Ilan University* (Jerusalem, 1967), pp. 220-229.

8 L. A. Balboni, *Gli Italiani nello Civilta Egiziana del Secolo XIX* (Alexandria, 1906), Vol. 3, pp. 400ff.

9 Jacob M. Landau, *Jews in Nineteenth-Century Egypt* (New York, 1969), p. 21. David Setton, *Kehilot Yehude Sefarad ve-ha-Mizrah ba-Olam be-Yamenu* (Jerusalem, 1974), pp. 80-87.

lem was not so severe as it was within the Greek community in Egypt[10]), fissures formed along these lines. In the present state of our knowledge, lacking detailed family histories, it is not possible to document the working out of this tension.

Education and language proved equally divisive. In the first half of the nineteenth century most Egyptian Jewish families sent their children to Jewish schools where they learned Hebrew and Arabic. By the twentieth century Jews were presented with a bewildering array of educational opportunities. The wealthy sent their sons and daughters to the elite, non-Jewish Western private schools established in Egypt. Those possessing French nationality enrolled their children in one of the prestigious French lycées of Cairo or Alexandria. The British nationals invariably sent their children to the elite British private school, Victoria College, located in Alexandria. In these unabashedly Western schools children were not taught in Arabic or Hebrew; they grew away from their traditional grounding in Arabic and Hebrew culture.

As for the middling and lower elements they preferred not to send their children to the Egyptian government schools but to the host of private Jewish schools sponsored but not patronized by wealthy Jewish families. The names of these schools identified their main benefactors: Moise Qattawi, Marie Suares, Jabes, and so forth.[11] Children were taught European languages there, but they also learned Hebrew. In the 1920s, 1930s, and 1940s, under the mounting pressures of Egyptian nationalism, they were also instructed in Arabic.

This discussion of education, language, and foreign nationality provides evidence for an increasingly fundamental cleavage within Egyptian Jewry — that between rich and poor. To be sure, in pre-modern times distinctions between rich and poor existed. But in earlier periods the religious, cultural, and social bonds which held Jews together as a minority group were far more powerful than economic differences. All Jews had lived together in the same quarter. They were all subject to Jewish communal governance. Nor were the wealthy usually able to display their wealth, for they did not dress as lavishly as wealthy Muslim citizens. It was common for even the most successful Jewish merchants in the nineteenth century to dress in shabby clothes if they were going to venture out of the Jewish quarter.[12]

The Western intrusion altered much of this. Large socio-economic fissures were opened up within the community. While the poor lived much as they had before, impoverished and in dirty and overcrowded areas, the

10 On Greek family antagonisms see Strati Tsirka, *O Kavafis Ke H Epochi Tou* (Athens, 1958). But a critique of this perspective can be found in Robert Liddell, *Cavafy: A Critical Biography* (London, 1974).

11 *Annuaire des Juifs d'Egypte et du Proche Orient* (Cairo, 1942), p. 177 and 209.

12 Edward William Lane, *An Account of the Manners and Customs of the Modern Egyptians*, p. 558.

rich, with their foreign national status and their protection by the Capitulations and the Mixed Tribunals, gradually moved out of the Jewish quarters. They built sumptuous homes in the new wealthy residential areas of Cairo and Alexandria.[13] In the new quarters of Garden City, Zamālek, Heliopolis, and Ma'ādi in Cairo and the *Quartier Grec* and Ramle in Alexandria, wealthy Jews began to associate with the wealthy of other foreign communities. They fashioned ties of friendship, based on common cultural, political, and economic interests, and though they never completely severed their links with their own ethnic communities, these bonds were much less compelling. The wealthy of Egypt, drawn from many different ethnic and religious communities, were beginning to create a sense of class solidarity. Their political and economic interests were diverging from the poorer members of their communities. Moreover, as this wealth had come primarily from close association with the Western world, their cultural and social orientations were toward the West. They identified with the West, travelled extensively in Europe, valued a knowledge of English and French, and sent their children to elite Western schools in Egypt and overseas. A powerful Western assimilationist impulse distinguished them from the poorer foreign and minority elements in Egypt.

Many of these tensions within the Jewish community were clearly revealed in communal governance. In keeping with traditional Islamic practices the Jews of Egypt were allowed to organize their own internal governing institutions. In the nineteenth century two loci of power emerged and became focal points for communal tension in the following century. The first was the religious hierarchy, at the head of which were the Grand Rabbis of Cairo and Alexandria. Both officials were chosen by the community itself and confirmed in office by the Egyptian government. As guardians of the religious tradition, they were regarded as leaders of the Jewish community in temporal as well as spiritual matters, even though most of them had come to Egypt from the outside and did not understand the country well at first.[14].

The second pole was the emergent wealthy Jewish businessmen, who increasingly dominated local conciliar bodies.[15] Alexandria and Cairo Jewry were governed by a communal council, known as *Majlis al-Ṭā'ifa* or *al-Majlis al-Millī*. To be eligible to vote for the officials of the council, a person had to pay the communal tax, known as *al-Arīkha*, for at least three years in succession. Although the tax was relatively small (rising from LE 1

13 See the description of the Qattawi mansion in Sydney Montagu Samuel, *Jewish Life in the East* (London, 1881), p. 10.

14 It was, for instance, customary for the Grand Rabbi of Alexandria to come from Italy. Setton, *Kehilot*, pp. 80-87.

15 On the rise of the bourgeois elements in communal governance within the Ottoman empire generally, one should consult Roderic Davison, *Reform in the Ottoman Empire 1856-1876* (Princeton, 1963), pp. 114ff.

to LE 25 depending upon a person's income), few people paid it and thus few voted in the elections. Inevitably the *majlis*es were dominated by the wealthy.[16]

The first *majlis* were organized in Alexandria in 1840. Its membership list indicates the prominence of the Jewish bourgeoisie; Tilche, Ismalun, Suares, Bardo, Piha, Sachs, Castro, and Salama were all persons from wealthy families.[17] The Cairo council came into being later, but it, too, was dominated by the wealthy. *Majlis*es selected a President from among their members, and he then became titular secular head of the Jewish community. Almost all of these individuals over a span of one hundred years represented the financial and merchant bourgeoisie. In Cairo, leadership was provided by the Qattawi family — a money-lending family who played a large role in Egyptian commercial and industrial affairs. Moses Qattawi was head of Cairo's Jews in the second half of the nineteenth century. He was followed by Yusuf Aslan Qattawi, who led the community until his death in 1942 and who was succeeded by his son, René Qattawi. In Alexandria there was a dispute over leadership between the Menasche and Rolo families.[18].

The Westernized Jewish bourgeoisie helped to solidify its control over communal governance by generous financial support for the community's important voluntary associations. They founded schools and patronized hospitals and benevolent societies. Any attack on their political predominance was seen as jeopardizing the life of the community.

Although there were many cleavages in the Egyptian Jewish community — education, nationality, language, and even religion (Ashkenazi vs. Sephardi) — the main line of tension was between an emergent *haute bourgeois* element and the rest of the people, however differentiated they might be. By the twentieth century Egyptian Jewry, as an internal semi-autonomous community, was dominated by a plutocracy. Its leaders were drawn from financial, mercantile, and industrial families of great wealth. These individuals controlled the communal governing institutions and were the patrons of educational and public health services for which the community was justly well known. They had acquired this predominace from the middle of the nineteenth century, but whereas oligarchical rule had then been appreciated, opposition began to surface in the next century. This *haute bourgeois* element had distanced itself from the rest of the community. Its members no longer resided in the old communal quarters, did not send their children to the religious schools, and socialized and formed bonds of mutual interest with the wealthy of other minority groups

16 Only 1382 *Arīkhists* were eligible to vote in the Cairo communal elections in 1926 and only 47 persons appeared for the meeting of the General Assembly in that year. *L'Aurore*, June 18, 1926.

17 Taragon, *Les Communautés Israélites d'Alexandrie*, p. 31.

18 *Ibid.*, p. 42.

resident in Egypt. Thus, not surprisingly the varied and discordant responses to Zionism tended to crystallize along this primary line of cleavage.

Zionism

Into this world of flux, movement, and visions entered the Zionist ideology. Although Zionist ideals made slow progress at first, they could not be avoided by the 1930s and 1940s. In some ways Zionism was a new and distinct issue which divided the Egyptian Jewish community in novel ways. But, in fact, Zionism tended to follow the already existent or emerging lines of communal cleavage.

The first Zionist society was founded in Cairo in 1897 by Joseph Marcou Baruch, a native of Constantinople, who had moved to Egypt in 1896. His Bar Kochba society started with seven members; by 1901 it had three hundred and by 1921 there were five Zionist societies in Cairo and one each in Alexandria, Manṣūra, Ṭanṭa, and Port Sa'īd.[19]

Although Egyptian Zionism started slowly, it soon had a devoted and hard working core of supporters. Egyptian Zionist sympathizers espoused many different, sometimes conflicting points of view. There were cultural Zionists, political Zionists, practical Zionists, and Revisionists just as there were in Europe and Palestine at this time. A few of the Egyptian Zionist supporters actually emigrated to Palestine in the 1920s and 1930s, but most Egyptian advocates of Zionism were content to remain in Egypt and to lend whatever financial and moral support they could to strengthen the Jewish community in Palestine. For a long time Zionist ideals were kept alive by a small band of Jewish intellectuals, lawyers, and other well educated persons who played a major role in founding Jewish newspapers and informing the community about Zionist developments.

Even before World War I Egyptian Zionists were issuing a publication (*La Renaissance Juive*), and after the war several additional newspapers came into existence. *Israel* was founded in 1920 and was edited by Albert Mosseri of the famous Mosseri banking family. Like other Jewish organs founded in Egypt it reported news about the Jewish community in Egypt and championed Zionist causes. Two other Egyptian Jewish and Zionist papers came into existence a little later. *L'Aurore* was edited by Jacques Maleḥ, and *al-Shams*, published in Arabic, was founded in 1934 by Sa'd Ya'qūb Malaki, a former director of one of the Jewish communal schools. Articulating Revisionist Zionist policies, *al-Shams* argued for the need of Egyptian Jewry to be an integral part of Egyptian Arab society rather than

19 "Zionism in Egypt," *Encyclopedia of Zionism and Israel*, ed. by Raphael Patai (New York, 1971), Vol. 1, pp. 278-280.

a European enclave. It also followed events in Palestine and favored an independent Jewish-Arab state there.[20]

In the early 1920s Zionism was not an important issue among the Jews of Egypt, and it is probably fair to say that most Egyptian Jews had no opinion about this predominantly European movement. To be sure, Egyptian Jews, like Jews all over the world, held special religious feelings for the land of Israel as the religious homeland and routinely prayed for Israel ending some of their prayers with the expression, "next year in Jerusalem." But most did not know much about Palestine and Zionism.[21]

Three developments forced Egyptian Jews to come to grips with Zionism by the outbreak of World War II. The first was the Wailing Wall incident of 1929 when Muslims and Jews clashed. The repercussions of this event spread throughout the Arab world, and were clearly heard in Egypt.[22] They served to draw the Egyptian Muslim population closer to its Arab Muslim brothers in Palestine and to frighten Egyptian Jews.

The 1930s saw the rise of virulent anti-Jewish forces in Germany and alarmed the Egyptian Jewish community. Some Egyptian Jews were won to the Zionist cause by these events, not necessarily in anticipation of migration to Palestine but for the purpose of creating a haven there where the persecuted European Jews might find safety. A good case in point was Leon Castro, a lawyer and an editor in the 1920s of the influential Wafdist paper, *la Liberté* which was a powerful advocate of secular Egyptian nationalism. In the late 1920s, Castro broke with the Wafd, resigned his position as editor of *la Liberté*, and became an ardent Zionist. By the mid-1930s, he had concluded that Hitler's rise was a threat to world Jewry, and he was devoting all of his energies to Zionist activities.[23]

The editor of the pro-Zionist Egyptian newspaper, *L'Aurore*, Jacques Maleḥ, also assumed responsibility for awakening opinion to the impending tragedy in Europe. *L'Aurore's* reporting and editorials became so irritating to the Germany Embassy in Cairo that Maleḥ was called into the British Embassy and warned about the possibility of provoking religious strife in Egypt.[24]

The third development was renewed communal violence in Palestine between 1936 and 1939. As Jews and Muslims lined up against each other, the Egyptian concern with events in Palestine was once again manifested.

20 On the Jewish press of Egypt one should consult Sihām 'Abd al-Rāziq 'Ashrī Nussar, *Siḥāfat al-Yahūd al-'Arabiyya fī Miṣr*, Master's Thesis, Cairo Universtiy, 1978.

21 Interview with Joseph Mallez in Paris, June 27, 1978.

22 James Jankowski, "Egyptian Responses to the Palestine Problem in the Inter-war Period," *International Journal of Middle Eastern Studies*, Vol. 12 No. 1, August, 1980, pp. 1-38.

23 No. 149, French Minister in Egypt to Laval, May 3, 1935, French Embassy Archives (hereafter FEA), Box 152.

24 Keown-Boyd to Minister of the Interior, April 2, 1933, PRO FO 141/699.

On this occasion, however, the constellation of political forces in Egypt had altered. The depression witnessed the emergence of extremist non-parliamentary, non-secular political formations like the Muslim Brotherhood and Young Egypt. These groups exploited events in Palestine and stressed the religious dimension of political ideologies. A spate of articles appeared in the Egyptian press, perhaps none so anti-Jewish as those that were published in an Islamic journal, *al-Rābiṭa al-'Arabiyya*, in 1938. These branded the Jews as opponents of Egyptian nationalism and crass exploiters of the Egyptian population. One suggested that at heart all Jews were Zionists and enemies of Islam, no matter what statements they might choose to make.[25]

By the outbreak of the War, Zionism had become a salient political issue in Egypt — a concern to Egyptian Jewry as well as the rest of the Egyptian population. The background had been prepared for the events which were to occur at the conclusion of World War II.

As Zionism grew in prominence, its impact on Egyptian Jewry followed pre-existing cleavage lines. The most pertinent breaking points were rich *vs* poor, old *vs* young, Westernized *vs* non-Westernized, highly educated *vs* poorly educated, European-language speaking *vs* Arabic speaking and autocratically and aristocratically inclined *vs* those of democratic inclination.

That wealthy Egyptian Jews were not overt advocates of Zionism, although they may have been quiet admirers and even financial supporters, seems clear from a number of sources. In 1925, when Jacques Elie de Menasche became President of the Zionist committee in Alexandria, the pro-Zionist newspaper, *L'Aurore*, admitted that "the Zionist idea had evolved slowly into the upper strata of society. Democratically rooted at first, it has little by little ascended into the rich classes of the Jewish community."[26] Yusuf Aslan Qattawi, the most revered Jewish leader in Egypt, head of the Egyptian Jewish community in Cairo, and a former minister in the Egyptian government, told the British Embassy in 1933 that he avoided going to Palestine and did not want to get mixed up with Zionism.[27] To be sure there were wealthy converts to the Zionist cause, but on several occasions French diplomatic agents in touch with Egyptian Jewry commented on the distance the wealthy sought to keep between themselves and Zionist activities. In 1946, the French Ambassador, Lescuyer, noted that Cairo was "the center of gravity of the Jewish world in the Middle East. [The Jews] have been established for a long time in the country and refuse to link their fate with that of the Zionist movement."[28]

25 See *al-Rābiṭa al-'Arabiyya*, No. 98, May 4, 1938, pp. 14-15, No. 100. May 18, 1938, pp. 28-29, and No. 104, June 19, 1938, pp. 26-27.

26 *L'Aurore*, March 27, 1925.

27 W. A. Smart to Young, January 17, 1933, PRO FO 141/759.

28 Tel., Lescuyer to Minister of Foreign Affairs, April 30, 1946, FEA, Box 152.

Then again after the tragic events of 1948, the French Consul in Alexandria commented on the division there between the young, not rich, pro-Zionist group and the old and rich Jewish families "who fear the disastrous consequences for their established situation of a too visible Zionism even if this movement enjoys their sympathy and their financial aid."[29]

If the rich either concealed their Zionist sympathies or were opposed, the lower strata were not. In so far as we can tell, their leanings were toward Zionism, democracy, and anti-imperialism — a development perhaps most clearly revealed in the founding of the Egyptian Jewish newspaper, *al-Shams*. Although it probably did not have a wide circulation and was edited by members of the Egyptian Jewish intelligentsia, one senses from its articles and editorials a concerted effort to be in touch with and to reflect the currents of thought and action at work among the lower strata of the Jewish community. Significantly it was issued in Arabic. It urged Jewish youths in Egypt to wean themselves from their European orientation and to learn Arabic and Hebrew. Alive to the currents of Egyptian nationalism and anti-European senitments, the paper asserted that there was no shame in speaking Arabic in the home. The journal endeavored to counter that century-long tendency in Egypt which had persuaded Egyptian Jews to stress European values and European training. The editors of the paper were acutely aware that as European influence in the area receded and Egyptian nationalist impulses advanced those groups who had embraced European ways would be in grave jeopardy.

Al-Shams also advocated a democratization of communal government and saw this reform as a mechanism for breaking the predominant position of the rich elite. This position was in keeping with efforts to restore the Egyptian identity of the community. The super-rich families who ran the councils of Alexandria and Cairo were almost exclusively western-looking personages; those who had lost their fluency in Arabic, sent their children to elite European schools in Egypt or overseas, and possessed foreign nationality status. Only by breaking the control that this clique held over Jewish life could these proponents of communal reform hope to change the orientations of their community.

The paper also championed the interests of Jewish youths in Egypt. Under the aegis of Dr. Alfred Yalluz, *al-Shams* helped to organize a youth society (*Jam'iyat al-Shubbān al-Yahūd al-Miṣriyyin*), hoping that the young would be a force for communal reform.[30]

These programs would seem natural responses to changing Egyptian realities. Yet *al-Shams* also supported the Zionist movement, at least until just before the creation of the State of Israel when overt support of Zionism was certain to lead to seizure of the newspaper and expulsion or incarcera-

29 Tel. No. 1173, Filliol to Minister of Foreign Affairs, October 8, 1949. FEA, Box 152.
30 *al-Shams*, July 12, 1935 and September 26, 1935.

tion of its editors. Although the paper did not make a formal statement in support of Zionism, its sentiments were clearly manifested. But its Zionist vision was different from that of some groups. *Al-Shams* spoke out in favor of a secular and independent state in which Muslim and Jew would cooperate.[31] Whenever events occurred in Palestine that seemed to belie this hoped-for cooperation, the editors of *al-Shams* attributed the breakdown in amity to British imperialism or the machinations of local right-wing fascist groups.[32]

The paper's support of Zionism seems curious on one level, for the editors were much in advance in realizing the needs of the Jews to become more Egyptian, less European. Why then would they associate themselves so openly with a movement which seemed to jeopardize their message? Part of the explanation lies in their hope for inter-communal comity and their faith in a secular independent Palestinian state. But part of the explanation stems from the fact that they were reflecting the ideas and aspirations of certain segments of Egyptian Jewry. The paper spoke for the young, the not so well educated, the democratically and even socialistically inclined, and the poor (or at least the not-so-rich). Within these strata of Egyptian Jewry Zionism had salience. The middling and lower socio-economic groups had not joined Zionist organizations in large numbers and probably had only vague ideas concerning the meaning of Zionism. But vague Zionism — a kind of cultural Zionism and identification with Eretz Israel — represented a statement of ideals distinct from the Europeanism of the Jewish bourgeoisie. It was also a natural response to the rise of a brand of Egyptian nationalism infused with religious appeals. Moreover, these strata within Egyptian Jewry were the very ones for whom religion had always been significant, who had always espoused a real, albeit undefined hope to return to Palestine, who had always sent their children to the communal schools and who were more likely to speak Arabic and to know and value Hebrew.

Tensions over Zionism became focused on communal governance. The lower strata had grown restless with elite rule. While they depended upon the patronage of the rich for communal institutions, they worried about their European leanings. The lower strata organized slates of candidates and ran them against the elite for election to the *majlis*es. In Alexandria they forged an alliance with the Grand Rabbis who used these disputes as an opportunity to reacquire power lost to the rising bourgeoisie in an earlier period. Invariably Zionist issues intruded.

A first occasion when Zionism became involved in governance disputes occurred in 1924, when Ḥaim Naḥum was selected as the Grand Rabbi of Cairo. His selection engendered controversy, largely because elements

31 *al-Shams*, January 25, 1935.
32 *al-Shams*, December 2, 1947.

within the community believed that the Grand Rabbi's influence could be used against the powers of the rich. His opponents believed Naḥum to be the candidate of the rich — the choice of Moses Qattawi and M. S. Abravanel, director of the Singer Sewing Company in Egypt.[33] He was also opposed by rising Zionist groups in Egypt, at least in the early stages of his nomination, because of his close affiliation with Young Turk groups in Istanbul and his presumed coolness toward Zionist causes. After long negotiations Naḥum was eventually accepted by all. He was to prove an influential figure in Egypt, well-connected with the Egyptian ruling elite, notably the royal family. But the earlier fear of his reservations about Zionism proved well-founded. He maintained a studied distance from Zionist activities, and during particularly tense periods he spoke against the movement.

More divisive communal disputes occurred in Alexandria where European influence was especially prevalent among the wealthy. In 1936, Grand Rabbi David Prato ran afoul of the ruling bourgeois group. Alarmed by Prato's democratic inclinations and his ill-concealed Zionism, the ruling clique forced Prato's resignation after a prolonged and bitter dispute.[34] His replacement, Moses Ventura, proved to be an equally ardent Zionist. He, too, drew support from groups beneath the *haute bourgeoisie*.

In 1947, tensions culminated in an open breach. By this time the Egyptian political scene had changed dramatically. The Israeli state was on the verge of becoming a reality, and Egypt was preparing for war. Severe inter-communal violence had erupted on November 2, 1945, the anniversary of the Balfour Declaration. Jewish business firms were being harassed by the government which had passed a new company law in 1947 compelling companies to employ a high proportion of Egyptian employees and workers.[35] By 1947, the Jewish elite of Alexandria was pressing the Grand Rabbi to issue a statement similar to that promulgated by Ḥaim Naḥum, Grand Rabbi in Cairo, distancing himself and his community from Zionist aspirations.[36] But Ventura was not willing to do so. All of the divisive issues were openly debated: education; Jewishness *vs* Europeanness; democratic governance; and Zionism. Eventually Ventura agreed to resign, but not before he and his supporters had forced most of the members of the Alexandria *majlis* to resign as well and seek re-election.[37]

33 See *L'Aurore* and *Israel*, June & July, 1924 and *L'Aurore*, January 2, January 16, and January 30, 1925.

34 *al-Shams*, October 8, 1936 and December 20, 1936.

35 See the files of the Egyptian Ministry of Commerce and Industry, Department of Companies, Boxes 3, 4, and 75 in the Egyptian National Archives at the Citadel in Cairo.

36 No. 499, Filliol to Arvengas, December 23, 1947, FEA, Box 152.

37 No. 52, Filliol to Minister of Foreign Affairs, January 30, 1948, FEA Box 152 and *al-Shams*, April 9, 1948 when Robert Rolo, Rene Ismalun, and Alfred Tilche resigned from the *majlis*. Rolo had been knighted by the British, and Ismalun and Tilche both held French Legions of Honor.

In Cairo the alliance between the rich and the Grand Rabbi proved more durable. Communal discontent surfaced in 1942 when the death of Yusuf Aslan Qattawi brought communal governance to the attention of Cairo's Jews. Arguments were made to democratize communal elections and to select councilors who were not mere European agents, but who knew Egypt. *La Tribune Juive* pleaded with the community to choose as President of the Council an Egyptian "by birth, education, and nationality," and insisted that the appointee know Arabic.[38] It also warned that councilors did not need to represent "le grand commerce ou la haute finance."[39] But once this crisis had been surmounted, tensions remained beneath the surface.

The remainder of this story is by now well-known. In 1948, with Egypt and Israel at war as many as six hundred Egyptian Jews, suspected of being Zionist supporters, were interned.[40] Toward the end of that year numerous attacks upon Jewish businesses, synagogues, and residential areas made clear how precarious the position of the community was. Although some Egyptian Jews emigrated at this time, most stayed. The Egyptian government endeavored to make amends. But only an uneasy truce existed, broken finally and decisively by the 1956 war. The Israeli invasion of Sinai spelled doom for Egyptian Jewry.

We do not have detailed information on where the Jews of Egypt went after they left the country. What seems to have happened is that persons with foreign national status and foreign connections emigrated to Europe and North America. The rest, most of whom were stateless or were treated as stateless because of their inability to prove their Egyptian nationality, emigrated to Israel. If, in fact, this describes the population movements, then the pre-existing attitudes towards Zionism persisted in the break-up of the Egyptian Jewish community. The bourgeois, European-looking elite migrated to Europe; the poorer, less well educated, more religious elements made their way to Israel.

The argument put forth here is that the incorporation of Egypt into the world economic order in the nineteenth century brought social and even class divisions to Egypt, even fracturing the solidarity of the minority groups residing in Egypt. The wealthy, increasingly drawn toward Europe, were isolated from the rest of the community. Eventually, especially as Egyptian nationalism developed, the middling and lower elements, guided by intellectuals, began to organize opposition to oligarchic rule.

The evidence for many of these assertions is far from conclusive. The lower Jewish strata did not have many forums through which to articulate their opinions. A few Jewish newspapers espousing these views is far from a persuasive case. Yet one is more confident in making these claims because

38 *La Tribune Juive*, No. 303, July 15, 1942.

39 *La Tribune Juive*, No. 301, June 17, 1942.

40 No. 328, E. A. Chapman Andrews to Foreign Office, June 22, 1948, PRO FO 371/69259.

of the fact that the same class and communal tensions were at work in other minority communities in Egypt. Within the Greek community oligarchical control was also challenged by an alliance of middling and lower elements, who drew inspiration from leftist, democratic, and nationalist ideals. Amongst the Copts it was the Patriarch — after World War II — who sought to mobilize people against the privileged position of the wealthy.

What these disputes highlight is the fragmentation of minority and foreign communities along socio-economic or even class lines. A European-looking *haute bourgeoisie* emerged and in its turn spawned lower middle class and in some cases working class opposition. In the case of the Jewish community the ideological differences had a religious component. In addition to espousing democracy and socialism, the lower strata embraced Zionism. Although Zionism was a European ideology, in Egypt it became a rallying point of the less-Europeanized groups. Zionism reflected the greater religiosity of the lower strata, their alienation from the elite, and perhaps also a source of hope and refuge as their continued existence in Egypt became more problematical.

GUDRUN KRÄMER

Zionism in Egypt, 1917-1948

Throughout the Islamic era, the Jewish communities in Egypt and Palestine had maintained various religious, social and economic ties. To them was added, at the turn of the twentieth century, a new and very complex factor — Zionism, which for the first time combined the more traditional religio-cultural aspects of Jewish solidarity with clear political notions of Jewish national unity. Zionism had been brought to Egypt at an early date, in 1897, but up to World War I, remained limited in scope and impact to lower and lower-middle class immigrants of Ashkenazi or oriental origin, while the 'Sephardi' majority and its aristocratic leadership showed themselves indifferent, if not openly hostile to the Jewish national movement. Conditions only improved during World War I.[1] Between 1915 and 1918, more than 11,000 Ashkenazi Jews expelled from Palestine by the Turkish governor found refuge in Cairo and Alexandria, where they greatly impressed the local Jewish population with their educational and cultural activities.[2] Vladimir Jabotinsky's attempt to recruit soldiers for a Zion Mule Corps met with some success early in 1915,[3] and when in 1917 calls went out to organize urgent relief for the hard-pressed *yishūv* they

1 For the period up to 1917 see Jacob M. Landau: *Jews in Nineteenth Century Egypt*. London 1969, 115-124 and Tzvi Yehūda: "Ha-Irgūnīm ha-Tziyoniyim be-Mitzrayim (1904-1917)", in *Shevet ve-'Am*. 2nd series, part 3, ch. 8; a source not used by Landau and Yehūda is Haim Gitelman: "Le Sionisme en Egypte", in *Israël* 8.12.1933-15.7.1936.

The post-1917 period was first covered by Aḥmad Muḥammad Ghunaym and Aḥmad Abū Kaff: *al-Yahūd wa'l-Ḥaraka al-Ṣahyūniyya fī Miṣr*, 1897-1947. Cairo 1969 (strongly anti-Zionist, no sources given) and Bat Ye'or: "Zionism in Islamic Lands: The case of Egypt", in: *Wiener Library Bulletin*, vol. XXX, n.s. nos. 43/44 (1977), 16-29 (biassed, newspaper material only).

2 Comité d'assistance aux Réfugiés Israélites de Syrie et Palestine: Rapport général sur la période entière 19 Décembre 1914-15 Juillet 1920. Alexandria 1921 and AIU I.C.I. Sionisme 1915 *passim*.

3 CZA Z3/620 Copenhagen Bureau 30.7.1915 and Bension Taragan: *Les Communautés Israélites d'Alexandrie* . . . Alexandria 1932, 120-122.

were answered in Egypt by a Cairo-based Special Relief Fund of Zionist inspiration and a rival, non-Zionist, Alexandria Jewish Relief Fund.[4]

So the ground was prepared, and a wider public was informed about Zionist aspirations in November 1917, when the Balfour Declaration was issued. At the demand of Chaim Weizmann, a first mass meeting, which was attended by over three thousand community members, was organized in Cairo on October 18, and "enthusiastically" welcomed the forthcoming Declaration as did a similar meeting in Alexandria on November 11, which attracted seven to eight thousand members of the local community.[5] The scenes of enthusiasm repeated themselves in 1918, when the newly formed Jewish Legion and the Zionist Commission headed by Chaim Weizmann passed through Egypt to be cheered by crowds of thousands in the streets of Cairo and Alexandria.[6]

The mass participation of the Jewish public in national meetings augured well for the Zionist movement in 1917-18. After all previous experiments to centralize the movement had failed, the *Comité d'Action* in Copenhagen made a fresh effort in June 1917, and created a new *Fédération des Sionistes d'Egypte*. Its committee included a number of (mostly Ashkenazi) lawyers, doctors and businessmen and was headed by Jack N. Mosseri (1884-1934), a member of one of the richest and most influential Sephardi families, which for over forty years had provided the vice-presidents of the Cairo Community, and one of the very few elite members to sympathize with the aims of political Zionism.[7] It was hoped, therefore, that as a man of means, prestige and connections he would be able to make Zionism more acceptable to his circle of friends and relatives, who, at that time, still dominated the local Jewish communities.

In January 1918, the first issue of *La Revue Sioniste* (1918-1924) as the official organ of the Zionist Federation, was distributed in 1,500 copies,[8] and in 1920, was followed by an independent Zionist paper, *Israël*, edited by Albert D. Mosseri (1868-1933), a physician, cousin to Jack Mosseri and an early convert to Zionism. Of the three original sections in French, Hebrew and Arabic only the French was continued after his death by his Palestinian-born wife, Mazal Mathilda (*née* Mani), until 1939 when she returned to Palestine.[9] In August 1918, a group of Alexandrian nota-

4 RS 4.1.1918 and FO 141/734 f. 4843, 1917-18 *passim*, FO 141/802, 803 and 805 f. 4759, 1917-19 *passim*. For the Alexandria Committee FO 141/802 f. 4759, 5.9.1917 and FO 141/734 f. 4843, 30.8.1917.

5 CZA F21/2 of 21.10.1917 (Weizmann demand); FO 141/802 f. 4759 Mosseri to Weizmann 30.10.1917 (Cairo) and CZA F21/2 of 15.12.1917 (Alexandria meeting).

6 *ib.*, 21.3.1918 and RS 15.3. and 5.4.1918.

7 Obituaries for Mosseri in JC 11.5.1934, *Israël* 15.6.1934 and EG 3.5.1934; for the Federation CZA F21/2 of 8.6. and 7.11.1917.

8 RS 4.1.1918 and CZA F21/2 of 6.1.1918.

9 OH IV, II M.M. Mosseri 12.8.1964 and *Israël* 3. and 24.3.1933.

bles sympathetic to the Zionist movement — Felix de Menasce, Joseph Elie de Picciotto, Alfred N. Cohen, Léon Nacmias and others — founded a "Pro-Palestina Committee", which declared its aims to be "purely humanitarian", i.e. non-political and non-Zionist, but which cooperated with the Zionist Organization of Alexandria. Together with the *Bnai Brith* lodges, it helped to finance an "Information Office of the Zionist Organization of Alexandria", which assisted some 12,000 European Jews to settle in Palestine during the years 1920 and 1927.[10] Public meetings again took place in May 1920 to celebrate — with "délire d'enthousiasme" — the decision of the San Remo Conference to recognize the British Mandate over Palestine. A joint delegation of notables representing the Cairo and Alexandria communities called on the British High Commissioner, Sir Reginald Wingate, to express their warmest thanks and congratulations on that occasion.[11] At the same time, the first Zionists were elected to the community council of Alexandria, and the small Ashkenazi community of Cairo, which even formed a special "Commission for Zionist Affairs".[12] The British Residency, to whom, in August 1917, the Zionist Federation had offered any help it might be able to give,[13] did little to restrict Zionist activity in Egypt. However, it did control the spread of news regarding Palestine, both anti-Zionist and pro-Zionist if liable to "harm Arab susceptibilities".[14]

Yet the favorable conditions existing under benevolent British surveillance were not in themselves sufficient to keep the Zionist Federation alive. Due to inter-personal tension, Jack Mosseri had resigned from the Federation and the *Revue Sioniste* as early as April 1918.[15] The Federation lost control over its two main sections in Cairo and Alexandria, where the Zionist Organizations and various other Zionist groupings continued to work independently and without much coordination. A number of reshuffles within the leadership of the Cairo branch, torn by internal dissension, proved insufficient to halt the process of disintegration, and conditions in Alexandria were no better.[16] The *Revue Sioniste*, which had had four hundred subscribers in 1918, but was suspended several times, ceased to exist in 1924.[17]

10 Comité "Pro-Palestina" d'Alexandrie: Rapport sur sa gestion du 13 Aout 1918 au 30 Novembre 1927. Alexandria 1928; Taragan, *op. cit.* 126-129.

11 FO 141/802 f. 4759 Allenby to Curzon 10.5.1920 or RS 1.5.1920.

12 CZA F21/3 of 20.5.1920, Gitelman *op. cit.*, 2.4.1936 and *L'Aurore* 20.1.1925.

13 FO 141/803 f. 4759 Mosseri to Wingate 24.8.1917.

14 *ib.*, FO to Wingate 3.11.1918 and Wingate to FO 2.12.1917; also FO 371/4995 Syme: Press reports 29.4. and 14.5.1920.

15 CZA F21/2 of 20. and 24.4.1918 as well as *Israël* 15.6.1934.

16 *Aperçu du Travail Sioniste au Caire pendant les années 1920-21-22-23.* Cairo Nov. 1924 *passim* or CZA Z4/32291 Grünhut 14.1.1927; for Alexandria CZA KKL5/438 Union Sioniste d'Alexandrie 27.1.1925.

17 *Aperçu* 8, 33ff and 40, also *L'Aurore* 28.3.1924.

Activities centered mainly on organizing lectures, balls and soirées, distributing information material in French, Arabic and Hebrew, assisting non-Egyptian *'olīm* (new immigrants), and collecting the *shekel* (membership fee) as well as contributions to the Jewish national funds. Returns were never as high as might have been expected from a community with so prosperous a middle and upper class as the Egyptian.[18] Enough *shekalim* were collected, though, to have the movement represented at various Zionist Conferences. In 1925, one hundred members of the Jewish community in Egypt attended the inauguration of the Hebrew University in Jerusalem, and with them came the Rector of the Cairo University, Aḥmad Luṭfī al-Sayyid.[19] At about the same time, a cultural center, *Bet ha-'Am*, was opened in Alexandria, and a group of young ladies from the very best families founded a section of the WIZO[20] [Women's International Zionist Organization]. All efforts launched to resuscitate the Zionist Federation, however, were doomed to failure.

When in the summer of 1929, news of the Western Wall incidents in Jerusalem reached Egypt, the leaders of the Cairo Community intervened with the authorities to stop Palestinian anti-Zionist and anti-Jewish propaganda, but simultaneously urged the local Zionists to suspend all overt activities. The latter obliged, and the Zionist Organizations, which had been preparing for "hibernation"[21] for a number of years, went to sleep completely not to wake for some time to come. In a letter to the *Keren Kayemet le-Yisrael*, representatives of the Cairo organization wrote in December 1929:[22]

> "Vous comprenez bien que le souci de conserver intacte l'amitié séculaire qui règne entre les éléments arabes et juifs d'Egypte a obligé nos chefs d'arrêter ici tout travail sioniste, toute allusion en public des événements malheureux de Palestine, toute fête au profit des fonds sionistes . . . "

Despite the total prohibition against the collection of money for Palestine passed by the Chief Rabbi of Egypt in February 1930, collections for the national funds were carried on in secret and under various guises.[23] But there were protests from within the communities against such activities

18 CZA KKL5/1416 Keren Kayemet to Saporta 20.9.1943 or *Aperçu* 20.

19 CZA KKL5/438 Organisation Sioniste du Caire 8.6.1925 and Z4/2051 Berger Dec. 1925.

20 *L'Aurore* 15.2.1925, and for the WIZO *Israël* 16.3.1934.

21 CZA Z4/32291 Grünhut Oct. 1927.

22 CZA KH4B/451 Kohn 19.12.1929. Also KKL5/472 Weissman, Cairo 29.1.1930 or KH4B/451 n.S., Cairo 17.2.1930.

23 Prohibition in CZA KH4B/451 Bension, Alexandria 21.2.1930. For collections see *ib.*, n.S., Cairo 17.2.1930 or KKL5/617 n.S., Alexandria 12.7.1932.

liable to compromise the Jews in their country of residence. A Zionist activist reported from Alexandria in March 1930:[24]

> "It is not only that people are frightened, but a decided animosity and antipathy to Zionist aims has sprung up. They look upon it as something that threatens their own peace and must be discouraged. The doors have been completely shut, with a solid determination not to allow anything to be done . . . "

Hitler's rise to power in Germany, in January 1933, definitely strengthened the concern for Jewish affairs in general and Palestine in particular among Egyptian Jews. In spring 1933, an Egyptian section of the *Ligue Internationale Contre l'Antisémitisme Allemand* (LICA) under the chairmanship of the lawyer Léon Castro, was created to fight Nazi propaganda in Egypt and the Middle East at large.[25] In May 1933, Jewish notables in Alexandria and Cairo formed, on a strictly humanitarian, non-Zionist basis, (separate) committees to help German emigrants to get settled in Palestine.[26] The Jewish press in Egypt covered events in Germany and Europe in great detail. But the Zionist movement proper did not profit much from this growing interest in Judaism and Palestine, even though quite an impressive number of Zionist clubs sprang up in Cairo and Alexandria. Most were cultural in orientation, but — for the first time — some were orientated towards pioneer work and *'aliya*, notably *Ha-'ivrī ha-tza'ir* (Cairo 1932) and *He-ḥalūtz* (Cairo June 1933, Alexandria July 1934).[27] All these movements remained small in scale — membership ranging between 15 and 30 — and, except for the pioneer groups, were short-lived. The Zionist Organization of Alexandria numbered 300 paying members in 1937, and its Cairo counterpart an estimated 100 to 120.[28]

One of the groups most active at the time was undoubtedly the revisionist movement led by the journalist Albert Staraselski. It was particularly influential among Italian Jews in Alexandria, some of whom were suspected of harboring Fascist sympathies.[29] According to a later activist, members were mostly Sephardim (i.e. Sephardi and oriental Jews) of

24 CZA KH4B/451 Bension, Alexandria to Hermann 5.3.1930. Very similar Z4/3229I Grünhut 2.7.1930.

25 AA Abteilung III P0-2, German Legation, Cairo 1933-35 *passim* and FO 141/699 f. 581 (1933) and 141/426 f. 106 (1934) *passim*.

26 CZA KH4B/450 Helfmann 28.5.1933.

27 CZA KKL5/949 Bassan, Cairo 11.9.1936 and *Israël* 20.12.1934 and 18.9.1935 (*Ha-'ivrī*), *ib.*, 25.8.1933 (*He-ḥalūtz*).

28 CZA S5/2213 Blumberg, Alexandria 2.5.1937 and *ib.*, Lauterbach 19.1.1937.

29 CZA KH4B/452 Erlich 1935 or *ib.*, Ben Ascher, Alexandria 11.2.1935. On Staraselski Ghunaim/Abū Kaff *op. cit.* 46 and 100 ff.

lower and lower-middle-class background (many workers, but no students), with a certain amount of support from the professional middle-class.[30] Between 1931 and 1934, Staraselski even edited his own paper, *La Voix Juive*.

In the late 1930's, events in Palestine began to cast their shadow on Egypt, too, which until the Arab revolt in 1936-39, had hardly been involved in the Palestine issue. In 1936, members of the non-parliamentary opposition such as Young Egypt, the Young Men's Muslim Association (YMMA) and the Muslim Brotherhood began to attack not only Zionists, but Egyptian Jews in general as Zionism's alleged "Fifth Column" in the country. In 1938, anti-Zionist and anti-Jewish agitation rose sharply.[31] The community leaders reacted in exactly the same way as they had done under less serious circumstances in 1929 and, as was their wont, in all situations involving a potential threat to Jewish security in Egypt. They intervened, on a private level, with the Egyptian authorities and leading politicians, enlisted the support of the British Residency and other foreign representatives, paid high sums of money to the local Arab press, and asked the Zionist leaders to stop all open activities. And, again, the Zionists concurred.[32] Funds destined for the Palestine *yishūv* continued to be collected secretly, and with improving results,[33] but of the many Zionist groups only *Ha-'ivrī ha-tza'īr* in Cairo and *He-ḥalūtz* in Alexandria were active in 1939. The Zionist Organizations of the two main cities were virtually non-existent at the outbreak of World War II.[34]

There are many reasons for the relative weakness of Zionism in Egypt throughout the inter-war period (and beyond). Among them the language problem, or rather the lack of material in the languages spoken locally — Arabic, French, Italian among the Sephardi and oriental majority, Yiddish among the Ashkenazi minority only — which had besetted Zionist propaganda from the very start, was relegated to second rank, even though Zionist information material in French and Arabic did remain scarce until the late 1940's.[35] The same applies to the lack of certificates, and the consequent, restricted possibilities of legal immigration into Palestine.

30 OH (61) 45 Tzvi Shesh 30.1.1971, also CZA S5/490 undated (early 1938).

31 James Jankowski: "Egyptian Responses to the Palestine Problem in the interwar Period", in: IJMES 12 (1980), 11-38. For the effect on the Jewish community, Gudrun Krämer: "Minderheit, Millet, Nation? Die Juden in Ägypten, 1914-1952." Wiesbaden 1982 (= *Studien zum Minderheitenproblem im Islam* N.S., vol 7), ch. IV.

32 CZA S5/490 Lichtheim, Cairo 8.12.1937, KKL5/1143 Subotnik, Cairo 11.11.1938 or *ib.*, James, Cairo 10.7.1939.

33 *ib.*, James (note 32) or AIU I.C.23 Avigdor, Cairo 6.12.1937 and CZA KKL5/1143 Subotnik, Alexandria 22.2.1939.

34 CZA S5/490 Subotnik April 1939 or *ib.*, Ben Ascher, Alex. 10.11.1940.

35 CZA Z4/2051 Landsberg 25.9.1924 or *Israël* 11.11.1935.

Certificates were allocated in preference to Jewish immigrants from areas of persecution, i.e. Europe, and mainly to those immigrants who were physically able and properly trained to do manual work. This regional and occupational bias went against Egyptian applicants, most of whom belonged to the commercial and white collar middle-class. The small number of certificates (never more than 15-20 per year) failed to meet the demand of the pioneering youth movements, and motivation to engage in Zionist activities consequently suffered.[36] However, as Zionist activists themselves stated, Egyptian Jews did not show any massive demand to go to Palestine in the period before 1948. According to the Israeli census of 1961, 890 Jews immigrated from Egypt and the Sudan in the period up to 1931; 1,145 followed between 1932 and 1939, and 1,985 between 1940 and 1947.[37] Many of these *'ōlīm* were oriental Jews from Yemen, Aden or Morocco, or Ashkenazi Jews from Eastern Europe, who had only stopped over in Egypt on their way to Palestine, whence they proceeded as soon as conditions permitted.[38]

Far more important than the lack of information material, certificates and forceful speakers were several internal "obstacles" to quick success among Egyptian Jewry. One factor always mentioned by both Zionist and non-Zionist observers was truly basic: the security and the material comfort enjoyed by the broad middle and upper classes of the community, and the absence of explicit anti-Jewish or anti-semitic feelings in the general Egyptian public (with the exception of groups like Young Egypt or the Muslim Brothers which, until the late 1930's, were dismissed as the radical fringe, not to be taken seriously so long as they were not backed by influential politicians or the government), and the resulting lack of that specific "sense of suffering" known to their Eastern European coreligionists. There was no "Jewish Question" in Egypt in the inter-war period, and Egyptian Jews consequently did not regard Zionism as an issue relevant to their own situation.[39] Aid and investment to build up the national home in Palestine were given primarily for humanitarian reasons, Palestine being seen as an indispensable refuge for persecuted coreligionists from other parts of the world, notably, of course, from Eastern and Western Europe.[40]

Most deplored by (Ashkenazi) Jewish visitors from Europe and Palestine, was the apparent lack of Jewish life — as they knew it; the pervading

36 CZA S6/2538, 1933 and 1934 *passim*, e.g. Weissman, Cairo 1.11.1933.

37 CZA S6/3840 Shaool, Cairo 20.7.1942 (no demand) and State of Israel. Central Bureau of Statistics. *Census of Population and Housing 1961. Demographic Characteristics of the Population.* Part IV. Publication no.22 (Jerusalem 1964), table 8 p.24.

38 CZA S5/490 unsigned, undated (1938) or Maurice Fargeon: *Les Juifs en Egypte depuis les origines jusqu'à ce jour.* Cairo 1938, 296 and 300.

39 e.g. CZA Z3/752 Wolkowizc, Cairo 21.2.1913 or AIU I.G.24 Benneys, Tanta 15.3.1928.

40 RS 1.5.1920 quoting L.Castro or CZA KKL5/472 Grünhut 2.7.1930 and S5/940 Tschernowitz 9.1.1939.

spirit of materialism; the absence of any superior cultural or spiritual interests in this "oriental non-intellectual (*ungeistig*) environment",[41] and the basic indifference of most Jews in Egypt to things specifically Jewish. Outwardly at least, they were "good" Jews most of whom kept the fundamental rules of the Jewish code, but who did so out of tradition rather than out of religious conviction. Emotional attachment to traditional Judaism in its various forms was best preserved among the poorest sections of the community, indigenous Egyptian, Ashkenazi and Yemeni Jews living together in special quarters in Cairo and also in Port Said. Among the Western-educated middle and upper classes, who sent their children to non-Jewish (preferably Christian missionary) schools, conversions occurred in sufficient numbers to alarm both the religious and the laic hierarchies.[42] In the 1930's and 40's, there were only five or six *yeshīvōt* (Jewish Halachic schools) in the whole of Egypt, and the rabbis all came from outside the country.

Efforts to revive Jewish life and traditions were intensified during the 1920's and 30's, and not necessarily in Zionist quarters alone. The Egyptian Jewish press informed its public about contemporary Jewish and world affairs, Jewish history, religion and contributions to the European and Middle Eastern cultures. The Chief Rabbis of Cairo and Alexandria made great efforts to encourage Jewish learning, opened *yeshīvōt* and clubs, edited papers and frequently gave lectures, nevertheless they failed to arouse the community and especially the youth, from its apathy.[43]

A considerable portion of Zionist work had consequently to be devoted to educational purposes with a strong emphasis on the cultural rather than the political aspects of Zionism. The statutes of the Alexandria Zionist Organization of 1937, for instance, declared the principles of Zionism to reside in Jewish tradition and Jewish determination to reconstruct Jerusalem as the ancient seat of Jewish culture. Its principal objective was to "develop within the community the sense (sentiment) of Jewish national consciousness", and its *programme d'action* to create a cultural center, to organize excursions to Palestine and to carry out "serious, intelligent and rational" propaganda for the Jewish national funds. No mention was made of *'aliya*.

What most Zionist observers seem to have failed to take sufficiently into account was that despite the lack of deep religiosity and Jewish solidarity

41 CZA S5/490 Lichtheim to Lauterbach 8.12.1937; very similar Rudolf Nassau: "Brief aus Cairo", in: *Die Welt* (Vienna) no. 13, 3 and no. 20, 7 (both 1904) or Mme. Benneys in 1928 (note 39). Also *L'Aurore* 24.7.1925 or *al-Shams* 2.1.1936, 14.1.1944 or 11.7.1947.

42 For conversions see e.g. MAE. Afrique-Asie. Egypte 34. Gaillard to Briand 29.11.1929 or *ib.*, Egypte 102, 1930 *passim*. Also CZA S25/5218 Ben Ascher, Alexandria 16.1.1939.

43 e.g. CZA KH4B/450 Berger 9.4.1928, *L'Aurore* 5.6.1925 or *Israël* 23.2.1929 and 14.3.1930. For failure *ib.*, 21.8.1935.

(as expressed in generous contributions to the Palestine *yishūv*), most Jews in Egypt were "traditional" enough to reject the explicitly secularist, if not openly anti-religious attitude of certain representatives of Eastern European socialist Zionism. In the inter-war period, socialism and communism were not yet as popular among educated Jewish youth as they were to be after World War II, and the older generation seems to have had as much difficulty keeping "Bolshevism", atheism and Zionism — all three represented by Ashkenazi immigrants from Europe and Palestine — apart as had the Egyptian authorities and the British Residency.[44] The stricter notions pertaining to family life and, most of all, to the conduct of girls and women no doubt made parents think with horror of the "promiscuity" reigning within the Zionist youth clubs in Egypt, not to mention the *kibbutzim* in Eretz Yisrael itself.[45]

An additional problem neared its head in the late 1920's, when representatives of the Sephardi minority in Palestine claimed that Sephardi and oriental Jews were being discriminated against by the predominantly Ashkenazi Zionist leadership. The Sephardi middle-class and elite of Egyptian Jewry were considerably disturbed by the "Sephardi question", which remained an issue throughout the 1930's and 40's.[46]

These misgivings regarding the Ashkenazi character of the Zionist movement were closely related to a fundamental problem: the socio-cultural barriers separating various groups of differing regional origins, religious affiliation, cultural orientation and social status within the Jewish community in Egypt. The indigenous and some oriental Jews, the Karaites and most of the Ashkenazim formed the Arabic (or, respectively, Yiddish)-speaking lower, and lower-middle classes (workers, artisans, pedlars, small shopkeepers and employees). Most of the Sephardim, a large section of the oriental Jews and only a minority of the Ashkenazim and Karaites belonged to the French, Italian or Arabic-speaking upper-middle-class (businessmen, executives, professionals). In its turn, the upper class and communal elite (bankers, businessmen, landowners) was made up almost exclusively of French-speaking Sephardim of long residence in the country.[47] None of the Zionist emissaries failed to comment on the snobbery and arrogance of the class-conscious Sephardi (viz. Sephardi and oriental) elite and middle-class vis-à-vis the Ashkenazi newcomers — the *Shlechtes* (bad

44 CZA KH4B/451 Bension, Cairo 17.1.1931, KH4B/452 Erlich 1935 or FO 372/2564 Kisch, Jerusalem 12.11.1928.

45 CZA S6/1982 Peron, Cairo undated (late 1946) or KKL5/1697 Saporta, Cairo 27.6.1947.

46 CZA KH4B/451 Confédération Universelle des Juifs Séphardim, Jerusalem to S.Abrabanel, Cairo 31.1.1929, KH4B/450 Pazi, Alexandria 12.2.1928, KH4B/452 Erlich 1935 or S6/1982 Peron (note 45).

47 Krämer *op. cit.* (note 31) ch. II.

ones), as they were frequently called[48] — even where the latter lacked neither money nor culture (which culture, however, was generally not French). The mutual distance seriously hampered cooperation between Ashkenazi, Sephardi and oriental supporters of the Zionist movement up to the mid-'40's.[49]

Before, as well as after, World War II, the rank and file of the Zionist organizations, the fund-raising committees and the various youth movements was made up of lower-middle-class employees and schoolteachers, most of them young, and many of them women. The early Ashkenazi activists were joined by more and more oriental and Sephardi sympathizers until the latter, in the 1940's, comprised the majority of the youth movements.[50] Hardly any members were recruited among the little-educated indigenous Jews in the Cairo Jewish quarter (*ḥāra*) and the provincial centers.[51] On the other hand, there was little to attract the Sephardi elite to this predominantly lower-middle-class movement of Ashkenazi origin. In the late 1930's, the Alexandria elite still looked upon Zionism as "très peu chic", the petty affair of "honest but infinitely insignificant people", as it was put by an upper-class supporter of Zionism.[52]

The logical conclusion for Zionist leaders in Egypt to draw was that in order to make a greater impact on the Sephardi and oriental majority in the country, they had to win over its elite.[53] This strategy to 'win the rich' met with a certain success in Alexandria, where internal divisions were less marked than in 'oriental' Cairo, and where the Chief Rabbis, David Prato and later Dr. Moise Ventura, supported the movement.[54] Generally speaking, however, the goal was not reached, for even though the Zionist organization did win a few members of the elite — Jack and Albert Mosseri, Felix and Jacques Elie de Menasce, Felix Green or Ralph Harari — they were usually too busy to devote sufficient time to Zionist ends, they were absent in Europe throughout the summer months, and they withdrew from active participation as soon as it seemed to involve personal risk. Interestingly enough, they were almost all married to women with strong, if loosely-defined Zionist sympathies. It was these high-class ladies who, apart from the employees and schoolteachers, contributed most to Zionist funds and enterprises (such as the WIZO). They acted in most cases on

48 Nassau *op. cit.* (note 41) no. 13, 4 (1904) or CZA Z4/3229I Grünhut 29.11.1927.

49 Grünhut *ib.*, or S25/2038 of 12.11.1926. Also KH4B/451 Kohn 10.12.1928.

50 *Aperçu* 19: CZA KKL5/438 Nemoi, Alexandria 3.5.1925; Grünhut 1927 (note 48) or S5/75 membership lists of *Ha-'ivrī* and *Ha-tza'īr* 12. and 26.10.1946.

51 CZA S5/490 Lichtheim to Lauterbach 8.12.1937 or S6/3841, 14.5.1947, similar S5/793 Alexander, Cairo 4.1.1944.

52 CZA KKL5/1143 n.S., Alexandria 9.2.1938 (peu chic) and KH4B/451 Kohn 10.12.1928 quoting R.Harari.

53 CZA Z3/753 Mosseri 5.6.1916 or L.Castro in F21/3 of 26.2.1920.

54 CZA Z4/2051 Berger Dec. 1925 or S5/490 Subotnik April 1939.

philanthropic rather than political grounds and frequently without any clear notions as to the exact implications of 'Zionism'.[55]

The only communal institution of influence to sympathize with Zionist aspirations, cultural but also political, were the lodges of the *Bnai Brith*. Founded from 1887 onwards among the Ashkenazi and Sephardi communities in Cairo, Alexandria and the provincial towns, they comprised large sections of the increasingly wealthy middle-class. They worked actively on behalf of communal reform, and in 1917/18 openly voiced support for the Balfour Declaration. In the 1930's and '40's, however, they avoided being associated with the Zionist movement, even though on an individual basis, many members continued to cooperate.[56]

There were no more demonstrations of widespread solidarity with the National Home in Palestine after the mid-1920's. By that time it had become quite clear that the King, Fu'ād I, though anything but anti-Jewish, was opposed to political Zionism as a movement aiming at the establishment of a Jewish National Home (let alone a state) on Arab soil in Palestine. It also seemed that the British Residency was developing a more reserved and cooler attitude.[57] The Cairo Community in particular took a clear anti-Zionist position. Its president, Joseph Aslan de Cattaoui Pasha (in office 1924-42), defined himself as an Egyptian of Jewish faith and on all occasions stressed his community's loyalty to King and country. The Chief Rabbi, Ḥaim Naḥum Efendi (in office 1925-61) adopted a less clear-cut stand, to avoid antagonizing both the authorities and the Zionists, and counselled caution and moderation.[58] Even in Alexandria, where conditions were generally more favorable to the Zionist side, the communal leaders succeeded in restricting the activities of their pro-Zionist rabbis, David Prato (in office 1927-36) and Dr. Moise Ventura (in office 1938-48), both of whom left their post after long and bitter quarrels with the lay council.[59] The councils were, of course, motivated by the fear of possible reactions of the Egyptian public against Zionists in particular and Egyptian Jews in general. Their response was to maintain as low a profile as possible in order not to draw undue attention to the existence of a Jewish minority in the country, let alone an active Zionist movement working in its midst.

The potential dangers of Zionist activity and propaganda in Egypt were not lost on those in charge of the movement, either. Their idea, however, was to exploit Egypt's pivotal position in the Arab world and the wide

55 CZA Z4/3229I Grünhut 29.11.1927, KH4B/450 Berger 9.4.1928 or OH (35)2 Iris Levy 18.6.1965.

56 RS 11.1.1918 or Ha-Menora 1923 and 1924*passim*; for the '30's CZA S25/1887 Bension, Alexandria 6.12.1930 or S5/2213 Harari 14.6.1937 and S5/490 Tschernowitz 9.1.1939.

57 Grünhut in CZA Z4/3229I of 22.3., 24.4. and 6.11.1927.

58 CZA KH4B/450 Berger 9.4.1928 or Z4/2797/99 Ben Ascher 22.10.1939.

59 CZA S5/490 Subotnik April 1939; on Prato e.g. Berger 1928 (note 58), on Ventura *al-Kalīm* (Karaite) and *al-Shams* 1.6.1948.

circulation of its press to influence public opinion, not only in Egypt itself, but in the Arab world at large. Certain themes, which had first been expressed in 1913 by a member of the Zionist Executive, Dr. Ya'akov Thon, ran through Jewish contributions to the Egyptian press, and were later taken up the local Jewish press: a strong emphasis on the oriental origins of the Jewish nation, on the close cultural and racial affinities between Jew and Arab, on the Jewish contribution to the common Middle Eastern civilization, and on the economic, cultural and political benefits to be derived from unrestricted Jewish immigration to Palestine and from close cooperation between Jews and Arabs in the area.[60] When it proved necessary to explain the undeniable conflicts between Jews and Arabs in Palestine, perfidious Albion, i.e. British imperialism as the source of all evil in the area, was brought into the play. Britain, it was said, thwarted all efforts to achieve cooperation in order to keep the Middle East under control.[61]

Attempts were also made throughout the inter-war period and World War II — involving among others Chaim Weizmann, Col. Kisch, Herbert Samuel, David Ben-Gurion, and later Moshe Shertok and Eliahu Sassoon — to use the excellent contacts of prominent local Jews in order to get in touch with leading Arab politicians. Local Jewish leaders, greatly alarmed at the evolving Arab-Jewish confrontation in Palestine and upset by the way the Zionist Executive was handling (or, in their eyes, rather mishandling) the Arab question, strongly endorsed all moves towards understanding and cooperation, but were evidently in no position to bridge the existing differences.[62]

When in September 1939, the Egyptian government introduced martial law and strict press censorship, anti-Zionist as well as Zionist activities came to a standstill. And yet the War was to bring Zionism in Egypt its first upsurge of lasting effect. The abolition of the 'Capitulations' in the Convention of Montreux signed in 1937, the rising tide of Islamic feeling and Arabo-Islamic nationalism in its several variants, the drive to Egyptianize business and administration in the country involving the dismissal of non-Egyptian nationals (who made up about 70-75% of the Jewish community[63]) coinciding with war-time scarcity and inflation and, later, with large-scale unemployment sharpened the latent sense of material and emotional insecurity among the non-Muslim, local 'foreign' minorities.

60 CZA Z3/115 Thon, Jaff to Zionistisches Zentralbüro, Berlin 9.3.1913. Also CZA F21/2 of 1.8. and 2.10.1919 or KH4B/451 Bassan, Cairo 15.1.1932. See e.g. RS 4.1.1918 or *al-Shams* 29.3.1935.

61 e.g. *al-Shams* 3.11.1944 and 11.10.1946.

62 CZA Z4/3229II Prato to Weizmann 7.5.1931, S25/1887 Bension, Alex. 10.2.1931 or Z4/17425 Cattaoui to Weizmann 2.11.1938.

63 Egypt. *Annuaire Statistique* 1917 (Cairo 1918), table XII p. 22 and *Annuaire Statistique* 1933-34 (Cairo 1936), table V p. 20.

The growing impact of the Palestine issue affected the Jewish minority in a more particular fashion. So did the advance of the German Africa Corps under Field Marshal Rommel in the spring and early summer of 1942, which was halted only by the British victory at al-'Alamayn in November 1942.[64]

In a striking parallel to World War I, these internal developments were accompanied by a large-scale influx of Jews from neighboring Palestine. From 1940 onwards, Allied armies swept the country, among them thousands of Jewish soldiers from Palestine. For these Jewish soldiers special clubs were opened by members of the pro-British Jewish elite, the *Bnai Brith* and the Zionist Organizations of Cairo and Alexandria. There they met members of the local communities and, by way of personal contact, reached individuals hitherto impervious to Zionist propaganda.[65] The servicemen, moreover, visited the schools and *yeshīvōt* to talk about Zionism and Palestine, to teach Hebrew and to form the first nuclei of the various youth movements affiliated to the Palestine branches of the Zionist movement.[66]

Organized work began in the summer of 1943 (i.e. after the German defeat at al-'Alamayn), when the first three emissaries from the Palestine *yishūv*, who had been selected and trained by the Jewish Agency and the *Mōssad* for *'Aliya Bet* (illegal immigration), arrived in Egypt under false names, wearing British uniforms.[67] The despatch of these emissaries (*shlīḥīm*) marked a turning point in the attitude of the Zionist leadership in Palestine towards Middle Eastern Jewry in general and Egyptian Jewry in particular. Whereas up to the outbreak of World War II, and since, all eyes had been turned to Europe and the destruction of the Jewish communities there, the focus now shifted to the Middle East, where under war-time conditions communications were relatively easy (particularly in the case of British-occupied Egypt), where urgently-needed funds could still be collected, and where, at the same time, anti-Jewish moves were (rightly or wrongly) considered probable in certain areas, such as Iraq.[68]

The *shlīḥīm* to Cairo, Alexandria, and Port Said were sent to build up pioneer movements among Jewish youth, whom they regarded as the only section of the local community amenable to Zionist ideals and, further-

64 CZA S25/2027 Aspects of the Situation in Egypt up to Wednesday July 1st, 1942 in the evening. n.S., Jerusalem 5.7.1942 or S6/3840 July 1942 *passim*.

65 JC 22.10.1942, CZA S5/490 Ben Ascher, Alex. 10.11.1940; Ben Ascher *ib.*, 7.5. and 13.5.1945 (clubs).

66 CZA S6/1982 Alexander 14.11.1943 and 17.2.1944.

67 Interviews with these *shlīḥīm* in OH (61)2 Akiva Eiger 28.3.1969, (61)25 Raphael Ricanati 26.8.1969 and (61)16 Gershon Ben Avi 30.4.1969. Also (61)6 Avraham Mattalon 18.2.1969.

68 L.Castro quoted in FO 371/45404 Jenkins to Smart 2.2.1945 and interview with Shlomo Hillel, Jerusalem 5.7.1980.

more, to practical work. Young people of both sexes, aged 10-26, many of whom attended the communal schools, were given theoretical and, to a lesser extent, also practical instruction and were then by various legal and illegal means taken to Palestine. The language used was mainly French (in the Cairo *ḥāra*, Arabic), one group alone, the "Bar Kokhba", being able to use Hebrew in its daily activities.[69]

By November 1943, about 500 young people had joined the various Zionist youth groups in Alexandria (the *Ha-'ivrī ha-tza'īr* excepted), of whom 300-400 remained in 1946/47. In Cairo, the combined membership of all groups (again, excepting *Ha-'ivrī*) numbered 500-600 members in 1944, and about 400 in November 1947. In Port Said, the *He-ḥalūtz ha-tza'īr* numbered about 60 in June 1944. Another 500-600 young people had joined the independent *Ha-'ivrī ha-tza'īr*. Overall membership would accordingly have reached about 1,500 between 1944 and 1948, but as a result of constant fluctuation may well have been somewhat lower.[70]

All efforts to create a unified youth movement for the whole of Egypt failed. By 1944, there were four major organizations working more or less independently of each other. (1) The "non-political" *He-ḥalūtz ha-tza'īr* affiliated to the worldwide *Ḥalūtz* (Zionist pioneering movement). The Cairo branch (400-500 members) formed part of the Jewish boy scout movement of *Makkabī*, which in 1938 had been integrated into the Egyptian boy scout movement and was officially registered with the Egyptian Ministry of Social Affairs. The Alexandria branch (250-400 members) was also registered as a scouting movement ("Les Eclaireurs Israélites"), but operated independently of the purely sportive, non-Zionist Alexandria *Makkabī*.[71] Around 1947, *He-ḥalūtz ha-tza'īr* in its turn split into two rival groups: *Ha-bōnīm*, which continued the previous line, and *Dror* which adopted the line of the leftist *Aḥdūt ha-'Avōda*.[72] (2) *Ha-'ivrī ha-tza'īr* (500-600 members), which was founded in Cairo in 1932, was reorganized by *shlīḥīm* as of 1942/43 onwards and affiliated to the leftist *Ha-shōmer ha-tza'īr*, refused to recognize the *shlīḥīm* of *He-ḥalūtz ha-tza'īr* as leaders of the local youth movement and cooperated on an informal basis only on those committees involved in the organization of clandestine *'aliya*. *Ha-'ivrī ha-tza'īr*, which was more overtly political than *He-ḥalūtz ha-tza'īr*, advocated a socialist, bi-national solution in Palestine and established good contacts with the leftist youth in the *Wafd* and the socialist groups in Egypt,

69 CZA S6/1982 Alexander 17.2.1944 and note 67.

70 CZA S6/1982 n.S. 20.11.1943, *ib.*, Alexander 17.2.1944, I.Levy 24.11.1947 and n.S., Cairo 25.1.1948; for Port Said S5/793 Alexander 21.6.1944; for *Ha-'ivrī* KKL5/1697 Eiger 26.10.1945 and *ib.*, *Ha-'ivrī ha-tza'īr*, Cairo 6.1.1947.

71 CZA S5/490 Subotnik April 1939, *ib.*, Ben Ascher 20.11.1940; S6/1982 Alexander 2.10.1942 and S25/5218 Peron, Cairo 20.5.1947. Also *al-Shams* 10.11.1938.

72 Interviews with O.Danon and S.Hillel, both Jerusalem 3.7.1980.

but does not seem to have put undue emphasis on the non-religious, socialist stand of its Palestinian counterpart (whose name it did not adopt) in order not to alienate potential members from among the local Jewish community.[73] (3) The small *Bnei 'Akīvā* group (120-150 members) affiliated to the religious *Mizraḥī* Zionists, which cooperated with the others on *'aliya.*[74]

There was no cooperation at all between these three organizations and the fourth, the Egyptian section of the revisionist "New Zionist Organization" led by Albert Staraselski (about 100 members in 1944).[75] The general Zionists strongly objected to the activities of *Irgūn* (Irgūn Tzeva'ī Le'umī) and *Leḥī* (Loḥamei Ḥerūt Israel) in Egypt, involving mostly arms smuggling. After the murder of Lord Moyne in November 1944, which forced all the *shlīḥīm* to leave Egypt temporarily, they began to supervise their operations more closely. Staraselski himself was arrested and subsequently expelled from the country in May 1945, and revisionism ceased to play a role among the local Jewish community.[76]

Although all these groups differed from each other in their political outlook and were in sharp competition, it seems that as a rule it was not so much political conviction which made young Egyptian Jews join any one of them, but rather non-political motives such as friendship ties or quite simply the wish to meet young people and to get away from home. These personal motives appear to have been particularly marked among the girls, who made up about 10-20% of the pioneering movements (but only 5-10% of the *ōlīm*),[77], and for whom this was the only way to escape close parental supervision.

Zionists in Egypt and Jerusalem were of the opinion that the work of these various youth groups for *'aliya* among the young was insufficient and that a new central organization was needed to control and coordinate activities. In January 1944, therefore, the Zionist Executive in Jerusalem appointed Léon Castro (b. 1884 in Smyrna), a lawyer and journalist, veteran member of both the Egyptian national and the Zionist movements and prominent member of *Bnai Brith*, as president of a *Comité Provisoire de la Fédération Sioniste d'Egypte* with full powers to reorganize and coordinate Zionist work in Egypt.[78] By November 1946, an estimated 1,000

73 CZA S6/1982 Ben Avi 8.2.1944, *ib.*, Alexander 17.2.1944; S5/76 Memorandum of *Ha-'ivrī ha-tza'īr*, Cairo 12.11.1946.

74 Alexander (note 73) and interviews with former members N.Safran, R.Dassa and Y.Marzuq, all Tel Aviv 30.6.1980.

75 MAE. Guerre 1939-1945. Alger 1313, 23.4. and Alger 1037, 14.7.1944.

76 CZA S5/793 Alexander 21.6.1944 or OH (61)5 Benjamin Sedbon 21.6.1969 and (61)14 Ye'ir Do'ar 21.3.1969. Ghunaym/Abū Kaff *op. cit.* 100 ff.

77 CZA S6/1982 Peron, Cairo undated (late 1946) and KKL5/1697 n.S., 9.5.1946. Also S5/793 n.S., Cairo 21.5.1945.

78 CZA S5/793 Shertok to Castro 11.1.1944. On Castro e.g. *Annuaire des Juifs d'Egypte et*

members had joined the Federation.[79] To the great confusion of the British and the Egyptian authorities it represented itself as being the Egyptian office of the Jewish Agency for Palestine in Cairo, and *He-ḥalūtz ha-tza'īr* in Alexandria. The *Comité Central* under Castro and the lawyer Emile Najar, and the *Grand Comité d'Action* under Jacob Weissman, a businessman from Palestine, were elected at the First Territorial Conference of Egyptian Zionism in Alexandria on January 7, 1945. It included among its forty members a considerable number of wealthy businessmen, some of them quite influential in the Cairo and Alexandria community councils.[80]

The Zionist Federation as well as the youth movements were able to work (if discreetly) legally and without any serious hindrance on the part of the Egyptian authorities, who considered them as much less of a threat to the socio-political order of the country than their communist rivals, at least until November 1947.[81] In 1944/45, the Egyptian Undersecretary of State, Ḥasan Rif'at Pasha, consulted the security officer at the British Residency, Jenkins, regarding Zionist activities in Egypt, which he wished to curtail without going so far as to close the offices of the Zionist Federation in Cairo and Alexandria. The Foreign Office, however, instructed its local representatives on March 14, 1945 to "if possible keep out of any Zionist-Egyptian squabbles",[82] and so no steps were taken. As long as the war was on, Zionist leaders from Palestine visited frequently to consult with local activists; delegates were sent to the Zionist World Conferences in 1946 and 1947, though open elections to the Zionist Federation were not held;[83] funds officially destined for various charitable institutions (amounting, according to Léon Castro, to £100,000 in 1943/44[84]) were secretly transferred to Palestine. In 1945, large-scale demonstrations were organized on November 2 (Balfour Day) by the Muslim Brotherhood and other Islamic and nationalist groups. Riots followed during which an unspecified 'mob' attacked the Jewish quarter in Cairo and destroyed Jewish- and other foreign-owned shops and burned the Ashkenazi synagogue. By way of response, Zionist youths formed self-defence (*hagana*) units. They were

du Proche Orient. Cairo: Société des Editions Historiques Juives d'Egypte 1942, or *al-Shams* 28.1.1944.

79 CZA S5/76 Fédération Sioniste, Cairo 7.11.1946.

80 *ib.*, and FO 371/45404 Jenkins to Rif'at 16.1.1945 and to Smart 2.2.1945, *ib.* Killearn to Eden 12.2.1945.

81 e.g. CZA S25/5218 Alexander: The Egyptian Jews on the Eve of the Great Decision 24. (31.) 10.1945 or S6/1982 Peron 1946 and *ib.*, Alexander 17.2.1944. *Ṣawt al-Umma* 22. and 25.4.1947.

82 FO 371/45404 Killearn to Eden 12.2.1945.

83 CZA S5/75 Najar 12. and 26.10.1946 and S5/76 Najar 13.10.1946.

84 Castro on 7.1.1945 quoted in FO 371/45404 Jenkins to Smart 2.2.1945. See also CZA S6/1782 Klueger 22.3.1943 or KKL5/1697 Do'ar, Alexandria 26.3.1947.

even provided with arms taken from British supplies, to defend Jewish dwelling areas and institutions against future attacks.[85]

Opposition to Zionist propaganda and work at that period came from two separate camps within the Jewish population: the communal leadership and the communist groups. The established leaders of the Jewish communities saw more occasion than ever to fear that Zionist activities carried on in a country which was getting more deeply involved in the Palestine issue, could hardly fail to compromise the entire Jewish population, Zionists and non-Zionists alike. The presidents of the Alexandria and Cairo communities, Robert J. Rolo (in office 1934-48) and René Cattaoui (in office 1943-46), were strongly opposed to the aims of political Zionism. In a memorandum to the American Jewish Conference in the summer of 1944, they suggested that a refuge outside the Arab world be found to absorb Jewish refugees and displaced persons.[86] In October 1944, René Cattaoui wrote a letter to Léon Castro calling upon him to close the (*hakhshara*) camps in which boys and girls were given practical training for *'aliya* and *kibbutz* life, as they were of a nature to harm the "sacred institution of the family" and to compromise the relations of the Jewish community with the Egyptian authorities. On January 1, 1945, he warned Castro that the council would regard itself as obligated to "solicit, in the public interest, the intervention of the Egyptian authorities", if his previous demand was not met.[87] It was not, and nothing happened. Cattaoui, who faced a strong Zionist faction within the community council, declared his resignation in October 1945, withdrew it shortly afterwards, but made it final in August 1946.[88] His Zionist opponents, on the other hand, could not prevent the Chief Rabbi from issuing an openly anti-Zionist statement on behalf of Egyptian Jewry after the incidents of November 1945.[89] In Alexandria, the pro-Zionist chief Rabbi, Dr. Moise Ventura, finally resigned, in January 1948, and left for Italy in May.[90].

Opposition to Zionism also came from the leftist camp, which during and after World War II, had gained support from a considerable portion of the Jewish youth, in particular among the middle and upper class students attending the French Lycées in Cairo and Alexandria, where the Zionist movement, based primarily on lower and lower-middle-class youth, found

85 CZA S25/5218 Incidents of 2 and 3 November 1945 in Cairo, Egypt. n.S., Cairo 21.11.1945; Z4/14620 M. to Mosche 10.11.1945 and FO 371/45394 Bowker to FO 2.-6.11.1945. For *hagana* units OH (61)44 David Basri 28.1.1971, (61)14 Do'ar, (61)2 Eiger.

86 CZA S25/5218, 21.11.1945 (note 85), App. III. Protest mentioned in S6/1982 n.S., 20.11.1943 or S5/793 n.S., Cairo 21.5.1945.

87 Included in FO 371/45404 Killearn to Eden 12.2.1945.

88 CZA S25/5218 Alexander 24.10.1945 (note 81), *al-Shams* 2.9.1946.

89 *ib.*, 21.11.1945 (note 85), App. II and Z4/14620 M. to Mosche 10.11.1945.

90 cf. note 59.

few adherents.[91] In 1947, Jewish members of *Iskra*, one of the largest communist groups in the country, who had also been active within the Cairo *Makkabī* club, founded a *Ligue Juive contre le Sionisme "Egypte"*, which was led by Ezra Harari, to fight Zionist influence within the community and to demonstrate that by no means were all Jews in Egypt Zionist. Manifestos denouncing Zionism as a tool of British imperialism and calling for the creation of a secular democratic state in Palestine issued in May and June of that year were seized by the police; the League was disbanded and its leaders arrested.[92] By December 1947, however, Ezra Harari had founded a new anti-Zionist Forum Group, which, according to the British Residency, had "a considerable following among the Jewish Colony in Cairo".[93]

Neither the communal leadership nor the Jewish Left achieved their object of restricting Zionist operations in Egypt. But when the UN decision in favor of partition sparked off anti-Zionist demonstrations and renewed attacks on foreign-owned stores, Jewish firms, institutions and residential areas in December 1947, the Zionist leaders, who were aware that they were kept under surveillance, began to consider going underground.[94] Early in 1948, *He-ḥalūtz ha-tza'īr* closed its office in Alexandria, and at the beginning of May the Jewish Agency for Palestine in Cairo followed suit.[95] By the time martial law was declared and the first local activists were interned, all *shlīḥīm* had returned to Palestine.[96] Zionism as an organized movement of cultural and political intent came to an end in May 1948. By contrast, large-scale operations to transfer those Jews wishing to emigrate to Israel, started only then and were to continue well into the 1950's.

Zionism, then, played an ambiguous rôle in the Egyptian context. At first sight one might be tempted to call it an imported solution to imported problems — Western-type nationalism, the Palestine conflict — were it not for the fact that some of the changes which affected Egyptian Jews adversely in the 1930's and 40's were indeed local products — Islamization first and foremost, and Egyptianization as practiced in the late 1940's. Yet it cannot be denied that up to 1948, political Zionism and the yearning for *'aliya* to the Promised Land remained alien to the large majority of Jews in Egypt. It was only after the Arab-Israeli war(s) that they left the country in great and ever-growing numbers. In the case of Egypt, the practical aim

91 e.g. OH (61)49 Ya'akov Benzakein 9.12.1971 or (35)6 Jacqueline Kahanoff *mémoirs* 11.6.1965; CZA S5/5218 n.S. 8.11.1945.

92 *ib.*, Peron, Cairo 20.5.1947 and unsigned report *ib.*, 1.7.1947. Rif'at al-Sa'īd: *al-Yasār al-Miṣrī wa'l-Qaḍiyya al-Filasṭīniyya*. Beirut 1974, 184-192 and 197-199. Also FO 371/61759 Campbell to Bevin 25.10.1947.

93 FO 371/69210 FO Research Dept. 30.12.1947.

94 FO 371/62994 Chancery, Cairo 4.-6.12.1947. CZA S6/1982 n.S., Cairo 25.1.1948.

95 OH (61)51 Raphael Dwek 21.5.1972 and (61)46 Willy Sachs 25.3.1971.

96 OH (61)43 Ari Schlossberg 30.1.1971.

(and outcome) of political Zionism — i.e. the establishment of a Jewish state in Palestine — formed a major factor in creating the very problem which, under different historical circumstances, it was meant to solve, that of anti-Jewish feeling and action undermining the coexistence of Jews and non-Jews in one country.

Abbreviations

AA	Auswärtiges Amt (Bonn)
AIU	Alliance Israélite Universelle (Paris), Egypte
BE	Bourse Egyptienne
CZA	Central Zionist Archives (Jerusalem)
EG	Egyptian Gazette
JC	Jewish Chronicle (London)
MAE	Ministère des Affaires Etrangères (Paris)
n.S.	no signature
OH	Oral History Department, Institute of Contemporary Jewry, Hebrew University (Jerusalem) (35) Interviews in French (61) Interviews in Hebrew
PRO	Public Record Office (London)
RS	Revue Sioniste (Cairo)

JACOB M. LANDAU

The Confused Image: Egypt as Perceived by Jewish Emigrants

Image research has acquired a fairly large number of adepts-practitioners and has played a prominent role in attitude and opinion research in general — particularly since the Second World War — utilizing questionnaire-based polls and surveys, interviews, tests and content analysis as its main tools. Although there has been great interest in such research, its emphasis upon quantification has minimized presentation of all-important nuances and shades of difference in the results; merely summarizing these would have the same effect as reducing Othello to a drama in which a jealous husband murders his wife — true, of course, but not very revealing.

Despite these possibly unavoidable limitations, image research has produced a corpus of published work, the bulk of which appears to have dealt with attitudes of individuals and groups. One characteristic example is a fairly large volume, published twenty-two years ago, entitled *As Others See Us: The United States Through Foreign Eyes,*[1] which incidentally includes papers about Israel, Egypt, Turkey and Iran as well. Its twenty authors contributed rather impressionistic essays, chiefly dealing with their own experiences and impressions and their resulting perceptions of the images of the United States and its people. The value of the work, with its markedly subjective and even antithetical approach, lies in its wealth of personal detail, while it suffers a disadvantage in comprising merely a collection of single cases, without any real attempt made at comparison. Another example of a much more integrated work is Harold R. Isaacs' *Images of Asia: American Views of China and India,*[2] which examined the image of those countries by interviewing Americans who had had experience with or at least some knowledge of them. A number of publications touching on image research, scholarly or otherwise, have dealt with the Middle East,

1 Edited by Franz M. Joseph, Princeton, 1959, 360 pp.

2 New York, 1962, 416 pp. This was published originally as *Scratching Our Minds* by M.I.T. Press in 1958.

too. These include analyses of the Arab-Israel conflict,[3] perceptions of Jews and Israel in the Arab world in general[4] or in certain sectors thereof (such as Muslim theologians[5]) or, convesely, Israeli perceptions of the Arabs.[6] This is a vast field, with many avenues of image research open. An exhaustive study would require many years of research and perhaps ought to be postponed pending the cooling off of tempers in this area. Nevertheless, image research may even benefit at present from studies of more restricted scope concerning various aspects, such as the perceptions of emigrants regarding their erstwhile homelands. While much has been written about the memoirs of the Arab refugees,[7] little to no studies published have analyzed the writings of Jewish emigrants from Arab lands.[8] This paper is a preliminary attempt to consider the writings of several Jews who emigrated from Egypt to Palestine (and later, to Israel), where they either settled or remained for a period of time, in which perceptions of their former homelands were expressed. Out tentative concluding remarks concerning the image of Egypt as reflected in those writings are not necessarily of a general purport; nevertheless, these observations may hopefully indicate more than merely isolated trends.

The brief scope of this paper does not allow for discussion of the rather numerous articles published by ex-Egyptian Jews, a large number of which concern the authors' native land. Hence one example must suffice: *Qehīl-lat Yehūdey Qahīr* (Hebrew: "The Jewish Community of Cairo"), an article published in 1967.[9] Its author, Shelomo Cohen-Tzidon,[10] an Egypttian Jew who emigrated to Israel and became a lawyer and politician, evokes the image of the Jewish community in which he grew up. Cohen-Tzidon expresses a great deal of sympathy for the period of Fu'ād's reign, which he greatly prefers to that of Fārūq and even more so to that of 'Abd

3 See, e.g., Y. Harkabi, *Arab Attitudes to Israel*, London, 1972, esp. pp. 115 ff., 353 ff.

4 For example, Gil Carl Alroy, ed., *Attitudes Toward Jewish Statehood in the Arab World*, New York, 1971, 187 pp.

5 *Arab Theologians on Jews and Israel*, Geneva, 1971, 80 pp. A French translation appeared in 1972.

6 E.g., Aharon Cohen, *Shekheneynū ha-'Aravīm* (Hebrew: *Our Arab Neighbors*), N.p., 1969, 200 pp. This is mostly a collection of texts.

7 Examples in Shimon Ballas, *Ha-Sifrūt ha-'Aravīt be-Tzel ha-Milḥama* (Hebrew: *Arabic Literature Under the Shadow of War*), Tel Aviv, 1978, *passim*.

8 What may be a first attempt is my review article "Bittersweet Nostalgia: Memoirs of Jewish Emigrants From the Arab Countries," *The Middle East Journal*, vol. 35, No. 2: Spring 1981, pp. 229-235 (a few paragraphs of which have been incorporated into the present paper).

9 Shelōmō Cōhen-Tzīdōn, "Qehīllat Yehūdey Qahīr," *Maḥanayim* (Israel Defence Forces' monthly), 114, Second Adar 5727 (1967) pp. 38-45.

10 The names of the authors have been transliterated, from Hebrew and Arabic, in the standard way, unless they themselves employed a Europeanized version of their own names.

al-Nāṣir, describing Fu'ād's reign as "the good old days", to be remembered affectionately.

Our primary concern, however, will be to deal with several books at hand, differing from one another rather substantially in character, which offer more relevant material for image research of Egypt at the time.

The first of these works, to be considered rather summarily, is a history of Egyptian Jews, entitled *Yehūdey Mitzrayim* (Hebrew: *The Jews of Egypt*),[11] written anonymously and signed Bat Ye'or (Hebrew: Daughter of the Nile), pseudonym of an Egyptian Jewish lady who emigrated to Western Europe and visits Israel quite regularly. Essentially, this book is a revised and considerably enlarged version of a pamphlet written by the same person under the pseudonym of 'Yahudiya Masriya' and entitled *Les Juifs en Egypte.*[12] This book is especially interesting in that it is not the work of a scholar, but rather of an involved participant. In the latter half of the book, the author interweaves her own impressions of Jewish and other affairs during the inter-war period, the Second World War and subsequently. These are expressed vehemently and even impetuously, with a ring of personal conviction.The general picture is one of political turmoil and internal strife in Egypt, accompanied by acts of terror — particularly since 1945 — directed against Egyptians as well as foreigners; in both cases, the Jews suffered physically, economically and morally. Official and private anti-Jewish propaganda and activities carried out during the Fārūq and 'Abd al-Nāṣir eras are the main concern of the writer, whose image of Egypt becomes rather one-dimensional — that of a country whose turbulent politics adversely influenced its minorities, particularly its Jews, driving them to emigrate to Palestine/Israel and elsewhere.

The memoirs of Rahel Maccabi, entitled *Mitzrayim Shellī* (Hebrew: *My Egypt*),[13] constitute a different sort of work. The writer, now a member of a *kibbutz*, vividly describes her childhood and youth in Alexandria, primarily referring to the 1920s and 1930s (she emigrated to Palestine in 1935 or 1936). The book reads like an authentic account, all the more convincing because of its minute details of daily behavior: social manners, dress, food, buildings, people, smells and sounds. Maccabi's work is a love story — love for Egypt, the beautiful Nile, the wonderful Alexandria seashore, the attractions of yesteryear, undamped by her newly-acquired love for Israel. Nevertheless her image of Egypt is one of a country which was largely alien to her, even when she lived there. Maccabi grew up in a middle-class family whose views were preponderantly Victorian (p. 38). Tutored by British and French governesses, the girl had hardly had any contacts with 'the Arabs' who seemed alien and even threatening to her (pp. 38-9). She was ignorant

11 N.p. [Tel Aviv], 1974; 192 pp.

12 Geneva, 1971, 74 pp.

13 Merhavya, 1968, 141 pp.

of Egypt's geography (she virtually knew only Alexandria and Cairo, having visited an Egyptian village only briefly, pp. 75-76), history (she had heard about Zaghlūl only casually, at second hand, p. 102) and culture (she was never exposed to modern Arabic literature and art, p. 104). Her father was the only one among her family members and friends who could read Arabic (p. 16), while her mother was always reading foreign magazines in English or French. The author's mother, although not religious-minded, "was very proud of her Jewishness and always claimed that there could be no comparison between Jews and gentiles; the only gentiles with whom she had associated at all were Scotsmen, essentially because they had been reared on the Bible" (p. 43). Indeed, when the girl did meet Egyptians, it was mostly accidental, since even the servants were non-Egyptians, as were the greater part of tradesmen and artisans in the vicinity, who were primarily Italians or Greeks. Her peer group consisted mostly of Jewish and Christian girls, usually of foreign nationality. According to her book, Maccabi's image was merely of a slim sector of Egyptian society, that of the foreign middle-class, oddly resembling the one which the average European tourist may well have taken home with him. Consequently, when Maccabi revisited Egypt, ten years after she had left it, she felt an outsider there, noting that "she does not belong" and that "everything has changed" (p. 122). Some things had changed, of course, especially the social circles in which she had moved.

Maurice Mizrahi's *L'Egypte et ses Juifs: le temps révolu*[14] is part history, part personal narrative. As such, it falls between the category of Bat Ye'or's history-writing and that of Maccabi's strictly personal memoirs. It differs, however, from both in that Mizrahi, by his own account, never doubted that he was an Egyptian through and through. Born in Egypt in 1905, he resided there until his exile in 1960; since then, he has resided mostly in Switzerland. He describes himself as having felt "comme Juif engagé et comme citoyen égyptien" (p. 9) during those first fifty-five years. Simultaneously an Egyptian patriot and a member of the Jewish people, the author left his homeland because of anti-Jewish propaganda and the authorities' suspecting him and other Jews of pro-Israel sympathies (pp. 126-143). Years later, he still smarts and grieves about his unjustified expulsion from a country he loved (p. 14). As he phrases it himself, "...c'est en Egypte que j'ai connu la joie de vivre, les luttes quotidiennes et le bonheur familial. C'est aussi en Egypte que j'ai ressenti, adolescent, la ferveur de la lutte patriotique" (p. 11). The greater part of Mizrahi's historical exposé and its appendices tend to indicate the considerable extent of the Egyptian Jewish community's integration. Only the final chapters discuss increasing tensions, which the author feels were essentially based upon a misunderstanding that he bitterly regrets and condemns. Maurice

14 Lausanne, 1977, 267 pp.

Mizrahi's image of his native country is one of a beloved homeland, where he lived happily and which he has been compelled to leave through what he considers an aberration of Egypt's rulers. The implication is that after the long-desired peace between Egyptians and Israelis is signed (p. 14), he might indeed wish to return to his homeland.

Jacqueline Kahanoff's *Mi-Mizraḥ Shemesh* (Hebrew: *From the East*)[15] is a collection of essays by one of Israel's most gifted freelance journalists. Born in Egypt to a Jewish family of Tunisian-Iraqi background, she left Egypt of her own free will — like Maccabi and unlike Mizrahi: "I loved Egypt, but could not bear myself living in it, although I did acknowledge the peculiar charm of our life" (p. 31). Thus she emigrated to the United States before the Second World War, spent the war years there and, after a stretch in liberated Paris, settled in Israel in the 1950s, where she died in 1979. Several of her essays reminisce candidly about the Egypt of Fu'ād and of the young Fārūq;[16] many are dominated by the author's long search for her own identity. This began when she was a child, unable to reply when asked what she was (p. 12). She knew that she was not British as she had come to hate cordially the foreign rulers of her land; however she could hardly consider herself an Arab, for "the Arabs were more numerous than other people and they were poor" (p. 11). Moreover, she was acquainted with very few Muslims in her age-group (p. 17). Although taught by Christians, she felt that she was not one of them, yet her Jewish awareness was rather shaky. While the older Jewish generation was pro-British, Kahanoff and her peers thought of themselves as patriotic Egyptians. However, she confesses, "they felt dissociated from the people and the country in which they were living" (p. 18). Much of this feeling of alienation resulted from the rich ethnic and socio-economic heterogeneousness of Egypt's population (p. 11), of which she was hardly aware; she could not belong to any of its groups. This feeling was very probably no less due to her perception of Levantinism, which she criticized as a dominant trait of Egyptian culture at that time: "We thought that the Muslims were imitating the most superficial phenomena of Europe, without striving to perceive the superiority upon which its rule was based. The very wealthy among them showed off with black Buick cars and blonde imported mistresses, while those who had to work for their livelihood dreamed of a 'diploma' which would enable them to chase flies in a government office — none of them attempting to become part of that elite needed to bring Egypt into the modern world. It is no accident that the small industry which existed in Egypt was set up by foreigners and minority members, not by Muslims — not even the rich ones. For the latter, European civilization meant merely a foreign veneer endowing one with class prestige" (p. 29). Considering these

15 Tel Aviv, 1978, 288 pp.
16 *Ibid.*, esp. pp. 11-67, 286-288.

premises, it is hardly surprising that Kahanoff opted for European culture as she and some other middle-class Jews in Egypt perceived it.

Itzhak Gormejano Goren, born in Egypt in 1941, left for Israel late in 1951, a few months before the end of Fārūq's reign. His *Qayitz Aleksandrōnī* (Hebrew: *Alexandrian Summer*),[17] essentially a novel, is closely based upon a boy's memories of his last summer in Egypt, which he and his family, habitually residing in Cairo, came to spend in Alexandria. The record of the boy's impressions, a quarter of a century later, constitutes a convincingly written 'period piece'. Robert (Goren himself) offers a deceptively simple account of several families spending time together in a large summer house; the story deals with love, flirting, dancing, gossip, horse racing and personality clashes, with details of daily life and *mores* in Alexandria. Virtually without exception, relations between Jews and non-Jews are on the business level or in master-servant situations. Nevertheless, antagonism between the communities pervades these fictionalized memoirs almost throughout. This is partially expressed in a constant apprehension of mixed marriages, but much more so in the main theme: the bitter rivalry between the Muslim and Jewish jockeys and their supporters, reaching its peak in an eruption of xenophobia. The dominant figure is Joseph, head of one of the families spending their Alexandrian summer together. He is actually a Muslim Turk who converted to Judaism, thirty years before the events of 1951, in order to marry his Jewish lady-love. More than any other character, Joseph in both his life and tragic death, symbolizes the great difficulty in bridging communities and religions. The emigration of the author and his family from Egypt soon after the events described serves to emphasize the apparent failure to find true accomodation before the Jewish minority and the Muslim majority.

An even more recent work is *al-Shaykh Shabtāy wa-Ḥikāyāt min Ḥārat al-Yahūd* (Arabic: *The Shaikh Shabtāy and* [*Other*] *Stories From the Jewish Quarter*),[18] a collection of ten short stories by Maurice Shammās (also known by his pseudonym Abū Farīd). The author, born in Cairo in 1930, emigrated to Israel in 1951 (like Goren) and has been employed since in the Arabic-language department of the Israel Broadcasting Authority, where he now serves as director of musical programs. This volume was intentionally published after the meetings and negotiations between Sādāt and Begin, to both of whom it is dedicated. The stories evoke — frequently in dramatic detail — memories of a childhood in the old Jewish Quarter, or *ḥāra*, of Cairo, mostly during the early 1940s. Although Shammās does not appear in person in these stories, they bear a markedly authentic flavor nonetheless. The life and characters in these stories differ considerably from the environment described in the works of Maccabi, Kahanoff and Goren.

17 Tel-Aviv, 1978, 198 pp.
18 Jerusalem, 1979, 133 pp.

The social life of the Jewish community is presented as less secluded; the participants are less highbrow and display fewer prejudices, mixing much more freely with one another. The characters evidently have Jewish names, although several of the stories could have applied, with equal realism, to a Muslim or Christian neighborhood, merely by changing these names accordingly. An entire gallery of successive portraits ensues, mostly describing the poor and needy Jews who were part and parcel of Egypt's population. Here, one notices a warm personal relationship not only among the residents themselves, but also between those Jews and the non-Jews. One example may be found in the story "Uncle Maḥmūd" (pp. 43-53), which focuses upon the amicable relations between a Muslim who, by his own choice, came to live and work in the Jewish *ḥāra*, whose residents accepted him warmly as one of their own. Despite this, however, the community feelings of the Cairene Jews about whom Shammās writes appear very strong, as reflected in a short story entitled "Café Lenciano" (pp. 73-82), an apt presentation of the vivid reactions of those Cairene Jews to reports about the rumored conversion to Islam of the female singer Laylā Murād. These stories give one the impression of a well-integrated Jewish community, mostly poor, religiously-minded and generally successful in its relations with non-Jews.

The last item to be considered is a volume of poems entitled *Me-ha-Pīramīdōt la-Karmel* (Hebrew: *From the Pyramids to the Carmel*),[19] by Ada Aharoni. The author was born in Cairo in 1933, and emigrated to Israel in 1950. She studied literature at the Hebrew University of Jerusalem and at the University of London and currently lectures in literature at the University of Haifa. Aharoni has been writing poetry since she was fifteen, first in English, then in Hebrew. Several of the poems collected here have been translated from English into Hebrew. Some are nostalgic, reminiscing over the Pyramids, the Sphinx, the Nile, hieroglyphics and members of her family, all of which are dear to her and indeed form a part of her ("The Serpent in Alexandria," pp. 16-17). At one point, however, while Aharoni was still in Egypt, alienation commenced its insidious work. In a poem entitled "From Haifa to the near-remote Cairo" (pp. 14-15), Aharoni writes to her childhood friend, a girl named Qadriyya, telling her how, despite her rapport for Egypt, "I was told that I was only a guest, although I had been born in the land of the Nile." She expands upon this theme in an open, frankly autobiographical letter appended to this volume, entitled "From Haifa to Cairo, with Love" (pp. 75-80).[20] Written in 1975 and addressed to the same Qadriyya, this letter is a moving document in which Aharoni reveals her ambivalent sentiments for her native homeland. Reminiscing over life at school, Ada Aharoni remembers how she and Qadriyya parted in 1949. Qadriyya asked her then, "Why are you leaving Egypt?

19 Tel-Aviv, 1978, 83 pp.

20 It was first published in the daily *Ha-Aretz* (Tel Aviv) on 20 June 1975.

After all, you were born here and this is your country?!" Years later, Ada Aharoni answers this query unequivocally, "Egypt was your country, but not mine." To explain this attitude to her friend — and, most probably, to herself — Aharoni describes, in vivid detail, a traumatic experience she underwent at the age of seven. From her secluded residence, she was taken by a maid-servant for a walk (unauthorized by the girl's parents) through Cairo's native quarters. She was deeply shocked by what she considered the uncouth manners of children and grownups there and, no less, by some xenophobic remarks she had heard. *Franjiyya* seemed to her a personal insult, particularly when the term was explained to her as follows, "You are not an Arab like us; your face is white, not brown like ours; you are a stranger, a foreigner." Later, Aharoni adds, she was accused not only of being a *Franjiyya*, but also a *Ṣahyūniyya*, which she interpreted at the time as an antisemitic slur. More and more confused about her true identity, she left for Israel where, at last, she "found herself" — although her Egyptian childhood did leave its indelible mark upon her.

Several tentative conclusions may be reached regarding the above-mentioned works. While many of the opinions expressed evoke echoes of *déjà entendu* — in conversations with emigrants from Egypt — the written materials appear less elusive and are easier to examine and categorize.

We have considered one article, two history works, a volume of memoirs, a collection of essays, a novel, a collection of short stories and a book of verse (in Hebrew, Arabic and French), all eight published within the span of a dozen years (between 1967 and 1979), with writers equally divided between men and women. Of the six who supply information about the dates they left Egypt, two left during the late 1930s (Maccabi and Kahanoff), three during the very early 1950s (Aharoni, Goren and Shammās) and one in 1960 (Mizrahi). All reminisce about Fu'ād's and Fārūq's Egypt only, with the exception of Mizrahi (who lived there during the early years of the Republic as well). The time which elapsed between an author's leaving Egypt and writing about it may have influenced the nostalgia expressed: it is not easy to analyze the impact of this factor, however. It does appear rather clear that nostalgia had conditioned the contents and style of writing for all eight. Otherwise, the books present rather varied images of Egypt, although, even within these parameters, several patterns may be observed.

A certain ambivalence conditioned the attitudes of most writers towards their native homeland. At times, a love-hate relationship is expressed — love for a beautiful and hospitable country, hatred for the web of circumstances which made their departure imperative. Love is preponderant throughout, tempered with a nostalgia which generally selects only pleasant experiences from the past. Images of Egypt evoked by such selective memory are obviously multi-dimensional; even so, however, the extent of the variety appears to follow two general models.

Firstly, there is the image of an Egypt somewhat alien to such Jewish emigrants as Maccabi, Kahanoff, Goren and Aharoni, whose writings evoke a secluded existence within a sheltered middle-class Jewish minority with some contacts with other minority groups and few, if any, meaningful ones with the large Muslim majority. As great admirers of the West — chiefly of France, Great Britain, or both — they were avowedly ignorant of native Egyptian life and of the renascent Arabic and Islamic culture, even when they shared sentiments of Egyptian patriotism (as in Kahanoff's case). Confused as to their identity, largely unaware of the life and aspirations of the masses surrounding them, these Jews have compiled a rather confused image of Egypt in their time.

Secondly, there is the image of another Egypt, that of the Muslim masses as known to Mizrahi and Shammās. The former carries memories of professional circles, whereas the latter recalls the poorer class in the Jewish quarter of Cairo. On both levels, this image differs from that held by middle-class Jews, as it evinces much more familiarity with Egypt as it really was at that time, a country vibrant with the pulsebeat of life and its pressing problems of survival. The problem of identity was different and only slightly less acute for these writers than it was for the middle-class Jews. They were, first and foremost, Jews, although ready and willing — at least, in Mizrahi's case — to regard themselves as patriotic Egyptians. Since Egypt's rulers and possibly a part of its population refused to acknowledge their patriotism, their own attitudes to the homeland became somewhat confused, too. For these people, as for middle-class Jews, emigration emerged as the obvious solution. However, nearly all left with mixed feelings and express in their writings an implicit or even explicit desire to return, at least for a soul-searching visit, to a land which has remained close to their hearts.

The perceptions we have considered briefly here, constituting an alloy of what Goethe once called *Wahrheit und Dichtung*, are very real and immediate to their exponents. Individual uniqueness notwithstanding, nearly all the images evoked are of Alexandria and Cairo alone, which continue to represent Egypt to these emigrants. Their images of Egypt are varied and sometimes confused, but almost always appealing and interesting. One may confidently expect further writing by Egyptian Jews about their native homeland; this preliminary report may hopefully at least indicate the initial status of this genre.

List of Contributors

Butrus Abu-Manneh, Haifa University
David Ayalon, Hebrew University of Jerusalem
Jere L. Bacharach, University of Washington, Seattle
Gabriel Baer, Hebrew University of Jerusalem
Amnon Cohen, Hebrew University of Jerusalem
Mark R. Cohen, Princeton University
Andrew S. Ehrenkreutz, University of Michigan, Ann Arbor
Joseph R. Hacker, Hebrew University of Jerusalem
Sylvia G. Haim, London, England
Miriam Hoexter, Hebrew University of Jerusalem
J. C. Hurewitz, Columbia University, New York
James Jankowski, University of Colorado, Boulder
Gudrun Krämer, Stiftung Wissenschaft und Politik, Ebenhausen
Uri M. Kupferschmidt, Haifa University
Jacob M. Landau, Hebrew University of Jerusalem
Donald P. Little, McGill University, Montreal
Thomas Mayer, Tel-Aviv University
Thomas Philipp, Harvard University, Cambridge, Mass.
Minna Rozen, Tel-Aviv University
Shimon Shamir, Tel-Aviv University
Boaz Shoshan, Ben-Gurion University of the Negev, Beersheba
Robert L. Tignor, Princeton University
Michael Winter, Tel-Aviv University

Index*

* Prepared by Shunit Degani.
For reasons of uniformity both *Ibn* and *ben* appear under *Ibn*.

Editors

Gabriel Baer (1919-1982) edited the quarterly *Asian and African Studies* since its foundation in 1965.

Among his books were:
Egyptian Guilds in Modern Times, 1964
Studies in the History of Modern Egypt, 1969
Fellah and Townsman in the Middle East, 1982

Amnon Cohen's recent publications:
Jewish Life under Islam, 1984
Political Parties in the West Bank under the Jordanian Regime (1949-1967), 1982
Population and Revenue in the Towns of Palestine in the Sixteenth Century (with Bernard Lewis), 1978